# Travel, Pilgrimage and Social Interaction from Antiquity to the Middle Ages

Mobility and travel have always been key characteristics of human societies, having various cultural, social and religious aims and purposes. Travels shaped religions and societies and were a way for people to understand themselves, this world and the transcendent. This book analyses travelling in its social context in ancient and medieval societies. Why did people travel, how did they travel and what kind of communal networks and negotiations were inherent in their travels? Travel was not only the privilege of the wealthy or the male, but people from all social groups, genders and physical abilities travelled. Their reasons to travel varied from profane to sacred, but often these two were intermingled in the reasons for travelling. The chapters cover a long chronology from Antiquity to the end of the Middle Ages, offering the reader insights into the developments and continuities of travel and pilgrimage as a phenomenon of vital importance.

**Jenni Kuuliala** is a university researcher at Tampere University, Finland. Her research interests include hagiography, pilgrimage and the social history of medicine in the Middle Ages and the early modern period.

**Jussi Rantala** is a postdoctoral researcher at Tampere University, Finland. His research concentrates on historiography, identity and power in Classical Antiquity, particularly in the Roman Empire.

# Studies in Medieval History and Culture

Recent titles include

**The Charisma of Distant Places**
Travel and Religion in the Early Middle Ages
*Courtney Luckhardt*

**The Death Penalty in Late Medieval Catalonia**
Evidence and Signification
*Flocel Sabaté*

**Church, Society and University**
The Paris Condemnation of 1241/4
*Deborah Grice*

**The Sense of Smell in the Middle Ages**
A Source of Certainty
*Katelynn Robinson*

**Travel, Pilgrimage and Social Interaction from Antiquity to the Middle Ages**
*Edited by Jenni Kuuliala and Jussi Rantala*

# Travel, Pilgrimage and Social Interaction from Antiquity to the Middle Ages

Edited by Jenni Kuuliala and
Jussi Rantala

LONDON AND NEW YORK

First published 2020
by Routledge
2 Park Square, Milton Park, Abingdon, Oxon OX14 4RN

and by Routledge
52 Vanderbilt Avenue, New York, NY 10017

*Routledge is an imprint of the Taylor & Francis Group, an informa business*

© 2020 selection and editorial matter, Jenni Kuuliala and Jussi Rantala;
individual chapters, the contributors

The right of Jenni Kuuliala and Jussi Rantala to be identified as the authors
of the editorial material, and of the authors for their individual chapters,
has been asserted in accordance with sections 77 and 78 of the Copyright,
Designs and Patents Act 1988.

All rights reserved. No part of this book may be reprinted or reproduced or
utilised in any form or by any electronic, mechanical, or other means, now
known or hereafter invented, including photocopying and recording, or in
any information storage or retrieval system, without permission in writing
from the publishers.

*Trademark notice*: Product or corporate names may be trademarks or
registered trademarks, and are used only for identification and explanation
without intent to infringe.

*British Library Cataloguing-in-Publication Data*
A catalogue record for this book is available from the British Library

*Library of Congress Cataloging-in-Publication Data*
A catalog record has been requested for this book

ISBN: 978-0-367-13756-4 (hbk)
ISBN: 978-0-429-02845-8 (ebk)

Typeset in Times New Roman
by Deanta Global Publishing Services, Chennai, India

# Contents

| | | |
|---|---|---|
| *List of figures* | | vii |
| *List of maps* | | viii |
| *Preface* | | ix |

**1 Introduction: travelling, religion, and society from Antiquity to the Middle Ages**    1
JENNI KUULIALA AND JUSSI RANTALA

**2 Pilgrimage, mobile behaviours and the creation of religious place in early Roman Latium**    15
EMMA-JAYNE GRAHAM

**3 The meaning of roads: a reinterpretation of the Roman Empire**    37
RAY LAURENCE

**4 The sacred travel of Valesius' family: children and the liminal stage**    64
KATARIINA MUSTAKALLIO

**5 When kings and gods meet: agency and experience in sacred travel from Alexander the Great to Caracalla**    78
JAAKKOJUHANI PELTONEN

**6 Roman Imperial family on the road: power and interaction in the Roman East during the Antonine Era**    100
SANNA JOSKA

**7 Pilgrimage in Pausanias**    122
JUSSI RANTALA AND VILLE VUOLANTO

vi *Contents*

8 **Pilgrim's devotion? Christian graffiti from Antiquity to the Middle Ages**  141
EVA-MARIA BUTZ AND ALFONS ZETTLER

9 **The rise of St. James' cult and the concept of pilgrimage**  165
KLAUS HERBERS

10 ***Pedes habent et non ambulabunt:* mobility impairment in Merovingian Gaul**  183
CHRISTIAN LAES

11 **Sacralizing the journey: liturgies of travel and pilgrimage before the Crusades**  205
M. CECILIA GAPOSCHKIN

12 **'Not all those who wander are lost': saintly travellers and their companions in medieval Scandinavia**  226
SARA ELLIS NILSSON

13 **'The wagon rests in winter, the sleigh in summer, the horse never': practices of interurban travelling on horseback from Antiquity to the Middle Ages**  248
FABIENNE MEIERS

14 **Entertaining and educating the audience at home: eye-witnessing in late medieval pilgrimage reports**  270
STEFAN SCHRÖDER

15 **An indigenous lord in the Spanish royal court: the transatlantic voyage of Don Pedro de Henao, Cacique of Ipiales**  295
LAURI UUSITALO

*Index*  313

# Figures

| | |
|---|---|
| 8.1 | Rome. Old Basilica of St. Peter in the Vatican, St. Peter's Memory, phase d: wall g · 143 |
| 8.2 | Rome. Old Basilica of St. Peter in the Vatican, St. Peter's Memory, graffiti on the plaster of wall g · 144 |
| 8.3 | Rome. Via Appia, S. Sebastiano, Memoria Apostolorum · 146 |
| 8.4 | Rome. Via Appia, S. Sebastiano, Memoria Apostolorum, graffiti · 147 |
| 8.5 | Trier. Early Christian churches · 148 |
| 8.6 | Trier. Early Christian church underneath the actual Liebfrauenkirche, graffiti II 35 and II 42 · 149 |
| 8.7 | Monte Sant'Angelo. S. Michele, groundplan · 150 |
| 8.8 | Monte Sant'Angelo. S. Michele, Gaidemari fecit · 151 |
| 8.9 | Monte Sant'Angelo. S. Michele, graffito of Leo de Bergamo · 151 |
| 8.10 | Monte Sant'Angelo. S. Michele, graffito of Turo peregrinus · 152 |
| 8.11 | Reichenau-Niederzell. St. Peter and Paul, mensa of the main altar (9th century), graffiti and 'dipinti' (in ink) · 153 |
| 8.12 | St. Gallen. Verbrüderungsbuch (Stiftsarchiv Ms. C3B55, p. 6), graffito of otger eps · 154 |
| 8.13 | St. Gallen. Verbrüderungsbuch (Stiftsarchiv Ms. C3B55, p. 46), graffito of pertuolt · 155 |
| 9.1 | Inventio; Historia Compostellana, Ms. Univ. Salamanca 2658, f. 14r · 167 |
| 9.2 | Beatus of Liébana, Commentary on the Apocalypse, Cathedral of Girona, Archive, Ms. 7 · 169 |
| 9.3 | Reliqiuary of Charlemagne, Aachen · 175 |
| 9.4 | Künig von Vach (15th century); Herbers, Klaus and Robert Plötz, ed. 2004 · 176 |

# Maps

1      The medieval routes of St. James to Santiago de Compostela;
Herbers, Klaus, ed. 1998      171
2      Route of Hieronymus Münzer (1494/95); ed. Klaus Herbers et al.:
*Hieronymus Münzer, Itinerarium*      177
3      The bishoprics of the three medieval Scandinavian ecclesiastical
provinces      228

# Preface

Most of the papers included in this volume were first presented at the conference *On the Road. Travels, Pilgrimages and Social Interaction: Passages from Antiquity to the Middle Ages VI* at the University of Tampere in 2015. Thus, the editors wish to thank all the participants of the occasion for inspiring presentations and discussions. The conference was made possible by support from The Federation of Finnish Learned Societies and the School of Social Sciences and Humanities at the University of Tampere, to which we also express our gratitude. Finally, we would like to thank all the other members of the organizing committee: Sari Katajala-Peltomaa, Christian Krötzl, Katariina Mustakallio, Miikka Tamminen, Lauri Uusitalo and Ville Vuolanto, as well as all the other people who efficiently took care of practical issues during the conference.

Jenni Kuuliala and Jussi Rantala

# 1 Introduction

## Travelling, religion, and society from Antiquity to the Middle Ages

*Jenni Kuuliala and Jussi Rantala*

Travel has always been inherent in all human societies, shaping and changing the lives of individuals and communities. The motives for travel could be economic, religious, political, personal, or all of these, yet they always had communal undertones. This volume focuses on social and cultural approaches to travelling, mobility, and pilgrimages from Classical Antiquity to early Christian centuries and the Late Middle Ages in Western Europe.[1] Although the interaction between society and space has been a key interest of scholars after the 'Spatial Turn', greater comparisons between eras and cultures are for the most part missing; this is the gap we seek to fill.[2]

The chapters in this volume concentrate on cultural and social interaction before, during, and after periods of travel. What motivations were there for ancient and medieval people to get on the road, and what negotiations and networks were intrinsic to travelling? How were these later reported and what cultural meanings were given to travels? As this volume has a *longue durée* perspective, the same topics are addressed within chapters focusing on different time periods and cultures. Encounters with the sacred and the role of religion in travel are analysed from both non-Christian and Christian perspectives. Similarly, attention is given to the different means and experiences of travel in varying contexts. The chapters therefore discuss the diversity of people travelling and the diversity in their experiences of travel. Pilgrimage and, generally, religious journeys in various forms is the central theme in most of the chapters. However, sacred travels are not addressed only as a medieval, Christian concept; their non-Christian roots and development are analysed as well. In order to trace continuity as well as change throughout this long time span, the chapters proceed chronologically, from mid-Republican Rome all the way to the Late Middle Ages.

Travel shaped the cultural and social landscape not just as an activity occurring at a moment in time, but also as the theme of stories later retold. The act of travelling, as well as narrations about travel, also shaped religious and cultural practices. The earliest records of travel during Antiquity were travel poems, the most famous and culturally influential one being Homer's *Odyssey*, which came to serve as the embodiment of the restlessness of travel.[3] This tradition continued into the Roman period, where we can find texts from poets such as Lucilius, Virgil, Ausonius, and Rutilius, to mention a few, describing travels of different

## 2  *Jenni Kuuliala and Jussi Rantala*

sorts.[4] During medieval times, the travels of Abraham, Adam, or Moses were central to the ideals of travel, as was Christ's journey to Emmaus and the apostles' travels that followed Christ's instructions.[5] Religious travel and the retelling of such travels were a way to engage in religious practice and create new ways of doing so, even as a means to shape one's sense of self; writing about religious travel cannot be entirely separated from its completion.[6] At the same time, the realities of travel – the practical challenges of setting out for a journey, as well as the dangers of the road – were not dependent on the incentive but rather on distance and geography, the traveller's social status and functional ability, and the political climate.[7] A premodern traveller had to negotiate these factors in varying ways, some of which were intertwined with the religious practices of travel while other approaches were much more practical. All of these aspects shaped personal experiences and the later retelling of travel events.

While the descriptions of religious travel are not abundant in chronicles of the pre-Christian world compared to later Christian narratives, we do have many traces of sacred travels recorded in Antiquity. Considering the Greek world, even if we lack individual testimonies, epigraphy and literature give us enough glimpses into the past to realize that the Greeks travelled to their sacred places for over a thousand years, at least from the sixth century BCE to the fourth century CE, and that sacred travellers were a common sight on Greek roads and landscapes in general. The most famous destinations of these journeys were various Panhellenic games, such as Olympian, or the most important oracles, particularly the one at Delphi, yet the significance of religious travel went well beyond these.[8] However, when dealing with sacred travel in the ancient world, pilgrimage journeys in the pre-Christian Roman Empire – particularly during the Roman Republican period – have proven to be a somewhat problematic subject. While Italian communities of the Republican era did possess a rich variety of sacred sites among them, we lack evidence of sacred travel similar to that of the Greek world or, later, the Christian Roman Empire. This has led many to the conclusion that pilgrimages did not matter in Roman religion as much as they did in Hellenistic Greece or the Christian Roman Empire.[9] Focusing on archaeological evidence from three sacred sites in Latium that were active during the Roman mid-Republic, Emma-Jayne Graham challenges this idea. As she argues in Chapter 2, instead of just seeking evidence analogous to the aforementioned two, better known periods of sacred travel, we should acknowledge the nature of pilgrimages in early Roman Italy as a set of behaviours closely related to 'ordinary' Roman religious practice; this would explain the apparent lack of direct evidence of pilgrimages during the period in question. Thus, as she mentions, the absence of evidence for the forms of pilgrimage with which we are familiar from other contexts need not indicate that pilgrimages did not exist, were infrequent, or were unimportant; they just did not need to be identified as a somewhat 'special' type of behaviour.[10]

As sacred spaces were numerous in the Roman Republic and later on in the Imperial era as well, it is obvious that people travelling by land encountered a large number of different kinds of sanctuaries, temples, herms, roadside shrines, and so on during their journeys.[11] Moreover, travellers often carried portable

*Introduction*   3

shrines with them for their personal religious purposes – whether for purification of the space after they arrived, for protection during their travel, or for something similar. As expressed by Steven Muir (2011), ancient travellers felt the presence of gods while on the road, and linked both home- and civic-based religion with it; this interaction with the divinities, both those celebrated in local shrines throughout the empire and those 'home gods' who travelled with them, maintained the identity of the travellers during the journey.[12] Thus, we may claim that the significance of roads went well beyond simple mobility and transportation. This becomes evident in Chapter 3 by Ray Laurence, who points out how roads also served as a 'tool' for the Roman state by bringing individuals into contact with its agency. As Laurence mentions, already in the Republican period, the roads had considerably shaped the settlement pattern of the Italian peninsula, and by the time of Augustus, their significance was widely recognized. With the passage of time, road building became something that characterized the Roman state, with the roads themselves even becoming a symbol of it. The restoration of roads represented imperial power over landscape, and roads not only connected various parts of the empire together, but also represented a connection between the Roman power and the public.

While very tangible constructions such as roads thus had immense value for Republican and Imperial Rome and the self-understanding of its people, more mythical journeys, featured in various narratives, were likewise an important part of Roman culture and identity. The most famous example is probably the *Aeneid* by Virgil, describing the travels of Aeneas from the burning city of Troy to the shores of Latium, fulfilling his destiny as the first true Roman hero.[13] As Virgil's epic poem indicates, the key to the success for a traveller such as Aeneas was to observe and obey the will of the gods; only by acting according to their instructions could he bring 'order to the chaos', that is, end his life as a refugee and find a permanent homeland which would provide a secure future for him and his descendants. Another example of a mythical journey is provided by Katariina Mustakallio in Chapter 4, where she relates the story of Valesius, a powerful Sabine man from the famous *gens* of Valerian, whose travel was motivated by an attempt to find a cure for his sick children. As Mustakallio demonstrates, the story, which describes various events and experiences during a journey, takes place in a mythical past and reveals the Roman religious mentality, emphasizing especially certain liminality, ambiguity, or disorientation. On the other hand, it is a reminder of how essential it was for Romans to take good care of their relations with gods by performing religious rituals, ceremonies, and sacrifices properly, and to take notice of the orders and advice given from the supernatural sphere. Only then would *pax deorum*, the peace of the gods, prevail.

While religious agency during journeys – whether real or mythical – had a significant place in Roman culture, it is, in particular, the destination of the travel, along with the actions occurring there, which usually stand at the heart of religious travel. This observation is, in fact, related to the major question surrounding ancient pilgrimage: what are the characteristics that make a pilgrim within ancient culture?[14] In Chapter 5, Jaakkojuhani Peltonen considers precisely the

# 4 *Jenni Kuuliala and Jussi Rantala*

ritualistic activities (sacrifices, prayers, divination or consultation with the priests, and so on) that occur at the site of a visit as the crucial factor that makes a journey 'sacred', emphasizing especially the arrival to a destination considered sacred.[15] This definition enables us to trace a significant tradition of pilgrimages in pre-Christian literature. Peltonen concentrates on stories which were, despite their often legendary nature, nevertheless based on historical cases, for example, narratives of sacred travel conducted by Alexander the Great, famous Roman warlords, and Roman emperors to visit tombs and oracular shrines. Examining these narratives from the viewpoint of agency and experience, Peltonen traces the recurrent themes in ancient literature, noting how descriptions of famous figures of the past, visiting various sacred spaces, created standards and expectations, as well as offered shared realities and imagination for their audience. Moreover, the stories legitimized even more the sanctity of the places they described. As Peltonen's chapter demonstrates, sacred travel indeed existed, not only as a concrete phenomenon, but also as a rich literary tradition in the Graeco-Roman culture, possibly even paving the way for later ideas of pilgrimage in Christianity and Islam.

Roman roads connected imperial power and its subjects in many symbolic ways, as noted earlier. However, the roads also provided the means for a very concrete interaction with rulers and their people. This was the case with imperial travels to provinces. In fact, journeys of the emperors and their families can also be considered as 'sacred' travels, from the point of view of the imperial cult. While Roman emperors never declared themselves as living gods, their status was indeed quite close to divine. As dead emperors were usually deified, their successors were, if not gods themselves, at least heirs of such. Moreover, people made offerings in behalf of the health of the living emperor, his *genius*, and in many cases the emperors were identified in their propaganda so closely to certain gods of the Roman pantheon that the separation between man and god was often more or less unclear. In addition, there was no such thing as a single Imperial cult, as practices changed very much throughout various parts of the empire; it was a vast collection of local customs, often very different from each other.[16] For example, it is possible that even the living emperor was worshipped in the eastern parts of the empire, where people still perhaps followed the tradition of Hellenistic ruler-cults.[17] Thus, the visits of emperors during their travels were, if somewhat rare, still an extremely important occasion for local people. Such travels shaped the relationship between the emperor and Romans living outside the capital in two ways: they provided an opportunity for local provincials to see the emperor in person and possibly enjoy imperial favours from him, and, conversely, the ruler received expressions of loyalty and support from his subjects. In Chapter 6, Sanna Joska takes a closer look at the emperor's travels with a focus on the imperial children of the Antonine dynasty, travelling with their parents, and their role in the interaction between rulers and their subjects during Imperial journeys. She shows that Imperial children had an important role in the interaction between the ruling family and local people honouring their visit. For the emperor, his children were a valuable tool when conducting public politics and reinforced his relationships with important provincial groups. On the other hand, local elites were, by

*Introduction*  5

honouring the visit of the Imperial family by various means, able to strengthen the status of their city and ensure the goodwill of the emperor towards it in the future.

In addition to Imperial sacred travel, the age of the Antonines in general is a rather famous period from the viewpoint of ancient pilgrimages. In particular, the literature of the era is very rich on the subject; Apuleius, Aristides, Lucian, and other famous writers described sacred travel in their accounts, providing interesting narratives from many points of view. Perhaps the most famous of them all is Pausanias. Writing the most comprehensive account of sacred travel among all pre-Christian authors, he has been an object of much debate about whether he himself can be considered a pilgrim or not.[18] In Chapter 7 by Jussi Rantala and Ville Vuolanto, a somewhat different approach is provided; they concentrate on ritual activities as part of sacred travel in the narrative of Pausanias. Tracing, analysing, and comparing these actions, the chapter looks for patterns of religion, and asks if those who practised such can be called pilgrims or not. The chapter thus provides a new view on ancient pilgrimage accounts, focusing above all on the observations of the writer instead of on the writer himself. Moreover, the article also contextualizes Pausanias' account with medieval pilgrim studies and looks for similar patterns of pilgrimage found in high medieval culture; this helps us to understand a certain continuity in observing the nature and categories of sacred travel through the centuries.

While Pausanias and many other pre-Christian authors indeed provided a number of accounts on sacred travel, it was the result of the rise of Christianity that pilgrimage as a religious and social concept became increasingly and frequently recorded.[19] There has been some discussion about the possible contradictory views about pilgrimages in Late Antiquity among Christian writers, some of whom allegedly considered it to be mainly a practice of the 'ignorant' laity. But as Brouria Bitton-Ashkelony has written, there is no evidence of any dichotomy between 'popular' and 'elite' religion in this sense, and in Late Antiquity, pilgrims journeying to holy spaces came from all social strata.[20] Considering this aspect, Chapter 8 by Eva-Maria Butz and Alfons Zettler gives an interesting point of view, concentrating on Christian graffiti – a written record of Antiquity and the Middle Ages of a very spontaneous nature. The chapter traces motives of those members of the Christian church whom we could easily consider as part of the 'lower' strata, people who scratched graffiti on architectural elements, liturgical objects, and so-called *libri vitae*. The chapter takes a closer view at these markings, examining them as an experience in certain religious and cultural contexts of Late Antiquity and the Early Middle Ages. Moreover, returning to the question of the nature of pilgrimages, the chapter evaluates the possibilities of examining graffiti as evidence of a pilgrimage, and the various problems related to it.

The development of the concept of pilgrimage, or *peregrinatio*, in the medieval period is discussed in Chapter 9 by Klaus Herbers, who analyses the developments of the destinations of sacred journeys, focusing particularly on the Santiago de Compostela and the cult of St. James. As Herbers points out, the Old Testament already largely consists of stories about migration; in late antique and early medieval terminology, many of these migrants were denoted as *peregrini*. Difficult

## 6  *Jenni Kuuliala and Jussi Rantala*

journeys for religious exile were central to the acts of late antique hermits as well as Irish and Anglo-Saxon eremitical monks, who lived true to the idea of life as a pilgrimage, or *vita est peregrinatio*, where life is seen only as a transition towards the real goal, God.[21] In this context, *peregrinatio* was a religious attitude or way of living.[22]

Pilgrimage to a sacred location, *ad loca sancta*, was another branch of the development of pilgrimages. First, visits to the graves of martyrs as well as to locations central to the events of Christ's life became common practice. During Late Antiquity, the concept of a saint began to include men and women who had lived a virtuous life, and by the end of the sixth century, the graves of saints had become the centres of religious life. Saints were believed to exist in two places at the same time: in their relics and in heaven. Unlike the graves of ordinary people, the graves of saints became public locations that were made accessible to all.[23] The reasons for travel to these locations were manifold; general veneration, the wish to obtain a miracle, penitence,[24] indulgences,[25] crusading,[26] or simply a wish to see the world[27] could all be among the incentives for people's decisions to set off on a journey.

Over the course of time, certain locations emerged as primary destinations of pilgrimages for the whole of Christendom. In addition to Jerusalem,[28] the graves of the apostles became such locations.[29] Together with Rome as the final resting place of Saints Peter and Paul,[30] the Santiago de Compostela was the most successful of these developments. As Herbers discusses in his chapter, the process of establishing such an important cult site was, however, not always straightforward. Instead, important pilgrimage sites played a significant role in the societal, political, and economic situation of a given area. This was also the case in Compostela, where there was conflict between various Christian groups in the eighth century.[31] The Santiago de Compostela's status was later enhanced with the writing of *Liber S. Jacobi*, a distinctive hagiographic work including a pilgrim's guide. Herbers shows how the text advanced the Santiago de Compostela from a European periphery to the centre, as one of the most important pilgrimages using the figure of Charlemagne to emphasize the site's religious and political importance, and by exceptionally highlighting the meaning of travel in miracle narratives.

In addition to major pilgrimage sites (from the twelfth century onwards also the relics of the Three Magi in Cologne and the shrine of St. Thomas Becket in Canterbury), people frequently travelled to nearby regional or local shrines. These could either be graves of local saints who had been active in the immediate area and whose cults are usually the best documented ones,[32] or Marian shrines, for example, which became increasingly popular from the fourteenth century onwards.[33] The best documented motivation for starting a pilgrimage to such locations was the wish to receive a miraculous grace, or the need to thank a saint who had performed a miracle.[34] Following biblical example, the vast majority of recorded miracles have always been healings,[35] and therefore, they provide an excellent source group for the social history of healing, disability, and illness, while showing one very practical reason for religious travel – the search for a

*Introduction* 7

cure.[36] Chapter 10 by Christian Laes discusses Merovingian miracle collections from the viewpoint of people with mobility impairments who later experienced a miraculous cure. Laes demonstrates the multitude of attitudes and concepts of conditions impairing mobility in this period and shows the vitality of pilgrimage for the religio-medical milieu of the time. At the same time, his examples show how most narratives about pilgrimages concluded with a miracle, and detailed descriptions of the journey itself were not necessary. The journey was inherent to a miracle narrative, which focused on the thaumaturgic deed of the saint and its effects on the petitioner's body.

Regardless of the motivation behind travelling, departing for a pilgrimage was a religious, ritual act in itself. Pilgrims held a specific status, of which their staff and scrip were physical signs. The rituals, which were built upon the blessing of the two objects, and their cultural meanings from their first appearance up to the crusading period, are discussed in Chapter 11 by M. Cecilia Gaposchkin, who shows how the religio-cultural ideals of sacred travel were preserved and remodelled with the continuously changing ideals of religious travel. The first liturgical rites for those setting off on a pilgrimage appeared in the eighth century. The primary theme in the rituals, which continued during the following centuries, was the pilgrims' safety. This shows how religious ideals intermingled with the vagaries of travel – these were also recognized in the laws of the time, many of which protected pilgrims. At the same time, the developments of pilgrimage, especially the growing popularity of penitential travel, influenced the forms the rituals took, with a growing emphasis on the destination and motivation of the travels. Gaposchkin also shows how from the turn of the twelfth century, the same rituals were adapted for those becoming crusaders, and how the first crusaders travelling to Jerusalem did so as pilgrims, with the same marks, similar rituals, and ideals that originated in liturgical rituals. The biblical ideals mentioned in the beginning of this chapter also played an important role in the mindset of crusading, as crusaders were seen as fulfilling the models and destinies of these characters.

Pilgrimage was performative by nature; this was built into the rituals and also into the motivations for travel.[37] In the words of Robert Maniura (2004, 90), pilgrimage offered the pilgrim a chance to "'…be good at being themselves" and, in a Christian society, "'…to be good at being Christian'". Maniura distinguishes this idea from the famous view of Edith and Victor Turner about pilgrimage as breaking the established structures of society, as the performed self was still socially constructed.[38] In the case of saints, whether officially canonized or considered holy at a more communal level, the performance of being an extremely good Christian could enhance their holy reputation, and narratives about saints' pilgrimages were used in a similar manner. At the same time, the travels of saints, starting from the early Irish monks, played an important role in the conversion of new regions. Chapter 12 by Sara Ellis Nilsson discusses the travels of Scandinavian saints in the twelfth and thirteenth centuries, when the area had just recently converted to Christianity. In this area, an abundance of local cults arose following the conversion, while the sources of these cults and travelling saints mostly reflect later

## 8 *Jenni Kuuliala and Jussi Rantala*

ideas about the conversion period. The holiness of these saints was largely constructed by their difficult missionary journeys and other travels, some of which were vision-like. Travelling was used to construct their, and the society's, transience, following the long tradition of the motif *vita est peregrinatio*.

In addition to the religious meanings given to travelling, the narratives about saints' voyages reflect the lived realities of travel. Ellis Nilsson shows that the hardships of the road were included in the narratives, and specific meanings were given to them, especially as highlighters of the saints' *patientia* when facing adversities. The means and difficulties of travel are further addressed in Chapter 13 by Fabienne Meiers, who discusses the use of horses in the *longue durée* from Antiquity to the Late Middle Ages. The changing political situations, as well as the social situation of the traveller, influenced the lived realities of travel.

Performing religious travels through later retellings can also be extended to travel narrations about pilgrimages, which became increasingly popular in the Middle Ages. *Mandeville's Travels* is often seen as the principal model for such works. The audiences of pilgrimage narratives were diverse, and so writers were communicating their experiences and views with a wide set of communities.[39] Focusing on fifteenth-century Dominican Felix Fabri's pilgrimage narration as life-writing, in Chapter 14 Stefan Schröder analyses the ways a pilgrim's experience was transferred into a written narrative, and what techniques were at the disposal of the author to deliver his message to entertain and educate. The abandoning of some of the established traditions of narrating travels to the Holy Land and with a focus on himself as an eyewitness, Fabri's account is an example of a more 'modern' strategy to give more weight to lived experiences. At the same time, he also followed many earlier conventions such as using old authorities and written evidence. Schröder further shows how travel writing could be for the purpose of influencing, for example, by emphasizing the superiority of the Christian religion and, at the same time, criticizing defects and grievances at home. Reporting pilgrimage could therefore serve several different religious and cultural purposes, which complemented each other.

At the end of the medieval period, the 'discovery' of the New World brought along new routes for travel. More and more people crossed the Atlantic, whether for political, economic, and/or religious purposes. Simultaneously, the Christian faith, the veneration of saints, and the cultural importance of shrines were disseminated by missionaries.[40] The new social groups of the Spanish Americas also frequently travelled to Europe. In the final chapter of the volume, by Lauri Uusitalo, the focus shifts to the sixteenth century. Uusitalo follows the travels of Don Pedro de Henao, a Pasto cacique, who travelled to Spain to visit the royal court. As a native lord who was, at the same time, a Hispanicized Christian, his journey manifests with many phenomena of the 'new' travelling between the Old and the New World. His multicultural background and understanding were crucial for his position and travels, but at the same time he was living in between the two cultures. As Uusitalo shows, in this particular case travelling was a key element in the negotiation process that developed the colonial society.

*Introduction*  9

All in all, travelling and pilgrimages affected people's lives in countless ways during Classical Antiquity and the Middle Ages. Thus, they are a significant factor when dealing with questions of both everyday life and the mentalities of the premodern world. As the chapters demonstrate, being 'on the road' was much more than simply moving from one place to another; before the journey, during it, and at the time of arrival, people acted in many ways and experienced many things that certainly affected their social lives, beliefs, and identities. Moreover, even when people did not experience travels personally, accounts of journeys and pilgrimages, as well as various legends attached to them, evoked cultural ideas at both the individual and collective levels. Stories about travelling passed on values and remained an important part of life from Antiquity to the Middle Ages, both before and after the arrival of Christianity.

## Notes

1 While this volume focuses on travel and religion in Western Europe, these concepts of course also had a remarkable social, political, and cultural value in the Byzantine Empire. For travel and pilgrimage in the Byzantine world, see e.g. Ariantzi and Eichner 2018; Kaldellis 2009; Macrides 2002.
2 Among recent studies, one of the few with a comparative perspective on transport systems and their cultural importance in the premodern world (although omitting European Middle Ages) is provided in Alcock, Bodel, and Talbert 2012.
3 See Keierstead 2019.
4 From Classical Antiquity, we can also trace a completely different tradition, a pastoral idea of a 'Golden Age', a period thought to have existed in the legendary past where things such as travel or commerce did not exist. While this image was of course far from the realities of life, it nevertheless provided a powerful cultural idea which lived for centuries – and partly still does; see Mackenthun, Nicolas, and Wodianka 2017, 9–10.
5 Coleman and Elsner 2003, 1–3. See also Klaus Herbers' and M. Cecilia Gaposchkin's chapters in this volume.
6 Petsalis-Diomidis 2003; Williams 2003. See also Katajala-Peltomaa and Toivo 2016 for lived religion and performing the self. Pilgrimage reports as life writing are discussed in Stefan Schröder's chapter in this volume.
7 One of the profound studies on the practicalities of travel in the Middle Ages is Newman 2011.
8 Dillon 1997, xvii–xviii; 81–82; 99–104.
9 See, e.g., introduction in Elsner and Rutherford 2005. Sacred travel in the Greek world (both pre-Roman and Roman Greece) as well as in the Eastern Mediterranean world of Late Antiquity are fairly well covered: see e.g. Dillon 1997; Elsner and Rutherford 2005; Harland 2011; Kristensen and Wiebke 2017. For ancient Roman sacred travelling, see e.g. Kiernan 2012 and various chapters in Kristensen and Wiebke 2017.
10 Thus, we might argue that pilgrimage was a normal aspect of so-called lived religion in pre-Christian Roman culture; for 'lived religion', see e.g. McGuire 2008.
11 On travelling in general in the Roman world, the first study was provided by Lionel Casson in 1974. More recent studies include, e.g., Adams and Laurence 2001; André and Baslez 1993; Guédon 2010; Heinz 2003; Laurence 1999.
12 Muir 2011, 36–39; 45. For lived religion in general, see also Rüpke 2016.
13 For the story of the travels of Aeneas and its significance for Roman thought, see, e.g., Fletcher 2014.

## 10 Jenni Kuuliala and Jussi Rantala

14 The problem is dealt with, e.g., in Bremmer 2017; Dillon 1997; Grünewald 2017; Stevens 2017. For discussion, see also the chapter by Rantala and Vuolanto in this volume.

15 Cf. the classic study of Casson (1974), where ancient visitors to the old cultic sites were considered simply as tourists; since then, the picture has become much more diverse. For tourism in ancient Rome in general, see, e.g., D'Arms 2003.

16 Rantala 2017, 77–78.

17 Chamoux 2003, 324–325.

18 See e.g. Elsner 1992; Hutton 2005. A different view is provided in, e.g., Arafat 1996, which denies pilgrimage to Pausanias. This claim is refuted in Rutherford 2001.

19 A classic study on the development of European pilgrimage is Sumption 2013 (first published 1975).

20 Bitton-Ashkelony 2005, 2–3. See also Frank 2000 for Late Antique pilgrimages.

21 For the Irish monks, their journeys, and spiritual eschatology, see Ritari 2016.

22 See Plötz 1992, 38.

23 Brown 2013, 3–9.

24 From the mid-thirteenth century onwards, secular and ecclesiastical authorities could order penitentiary pilgrimages for heretics and other wrongdoers. The motivation for these sentences was not just corrective, as they were also meant to keep the offender out of harm's way. Webb 2001, 53–54.

25 Indulgence meant the remission of the temporal punishment due to sin. The idea of plenary indulgences grew slowly from the high medieval period onwards. The first plenary indulgence was Urban II's declaration at the council of Clermont in 1095 which granted all crusaders an indulgence erasing the penance for their sins. From then on various churches received them, especially during the jubilee years, the first of which was in 1300 and which granted indulgences to those undertaking certain pilgrimage routes in Rome. Indulgences became an important phenomenon for the whole of Christendom. For indulgences and pilgrimage in the late Middle Ages, see Maniura 2004, 91–96; Webb 2000, 93–110.

26 See e.g. Gaposchkin 2013 for crusades as pilgrimages.

27 See Stefan Schröder's chapter in this volume for the pilgrims' curiosity and wish to explore.

28 See Chareyron 2005 for pilgrimages to Jerusalem.

29 Bartlett 2013, 429.

30 See Birch 2002 for pilgrimages to Rome. It is worth pointing out, however, that the wish to receive a miracle was not the main motivation for travelling to all pilgrimage sites. There is no evidence for pilgrims travelling to Rome in search of a miracle, for example. Their pilgrims' primary motive most likely was the absolution of their sins; see Birch 2002, 39–40.

31 The connection of power and the shrine was different in the areas of the Eastern Church. In the West, the power of the bishop and the shrine coerced, whereas the pilgrimage sites in the Eastern Mediterranean and the Near East, Jerusalem included, were not used to form a lasting power structure in the same manner. Brown 2013, 9–10.

32 See Vauchez 1988, 157–246 for the concept of 'local sainthood'.

33 See e.g. Boyarin 2010; Christian 1981; Heal 2007; Krötzl 2000; Signori 1996a, 1996b; Swanson 1995, 144–146.

34 The literature on pilgrimage and miracles in the Middle Ages is vast. See, e.g., Finucane 1995; Katajala-Peltomaa 2009, 2011; Krötzl 1994; Rawcliffe 2002; Sigal 1985; Signori 2003.

35 See Ward 1982, 20–24, for the biblical models of miracles.

36 See e.g. Farmer 2002; Kuuliala 2016; Laes 2011; Wilson 2010.

37 See e.g. Morrison 2004. For this idea from an anthropological perspective, see Dubisch 1995.

Introduction    11

38  Maniura 2004, 90; Turner and Turner 1978. See also M. Cecilia Gaposchkin's chapter in this volume for the idea of pilgrimage as a liminal state.
39  See Beebe 2014 for late medieval pilgrimage literature.
40  See e.g. Crumrine and Morinis 1991; Morgan 2002; Smoller 2014.


## Bibliography

Adams, Colin and Ray Laurence (eds.). 2001. *Travel and Geography in the Roman Empire*. London and New York: Routledge.

Alcock, Susan E., John Bodel, and Richard J. A. Talbert (eds.). 2012. *Highways, Byways, and Road Systems in the Pre-Modern World*. Chichester: Wiley-Blackwell.

André, Jean-Marie and Marie-Francoise Baslez. 1993. *Voyager dans l'antiquité*. Paris: Faynard.

Arafat, Karim W. 1996. *Pausanias' Greece. Ancient Artists and Roman Rulers*. Cambridge: Cambridge University Press.

Ariantzi, Despoina and Ina Eichner (eds.). 2018. *Für Seelenheil und Lebensglück: Das byzantinische Pilgerwesen und seine Wurzeln.* Byzanz zwischen Orient und Okzident 10. Regensburg: Verlag Schnell & Steine.

Bartlett, Robert. 2013. *Why Can the Dead Do Such Great Things?: Saints and Worshippers from the Martyrs to the Reformation.* Princeton: Princeton University Press.

Beebe, Kathryne. 2014. *Pilgrim and Preacher: The Audiences and Observant Spirituality of Friar Felix Fabri (1437/8–1502)*. Oxford: Oxford University Press.

Birch, Debra J. 2002. *Pilgrimage to Rome in the Middle Ages*. Woodbridge: Boydell & Brewer.

Bitton-Ashkelony, Brouria. 2005. *Encountering the Sacred: The Debate on Christian Pilgrimage in Late Antiquity*. Berkeley and Los Angeles: University of California Press.

Boyerin, Andrianne Williams. 2010. *Miracles of the Virgin in Medieval England: Law and Jewishness in Marian Legends*. Woodbridge: Boydell & Brewer.

Bremmer, Jan. 2017. "Pilgrimage Progress?" In *Excavating Pilgrimage: Archaeological Approaches to Sacred Travel and Movement in the Ancient World*, edited by Troels Myrup Kristensen and Wiebke Friese, 275–284. London and New York: Routledge.

Casson, Lionel. 1974. *Travel in the Ancient World*. London: Allen & Unwin.

Chamoux, Francois. 2003. *Hellenistic Civilization*. Oxford: Blackwell.

Chareyron, Nicole. 2005. *Pilgrims to Jerusalem in the Middle Ages*, translated by W. Donald Wilson. New York: Columbia University Press.

Christian, William A. 1981. *Apparitions in Late Medieval and Renaissance Spain*. Princeton, NJ: Princeton University Press.

Coleman, Simon and John Elsner. 2003. "Pilgrim Voices. Authoring Christian Pilgrimage." In *Pilgrim Voices: Narrative and Authorship in Christian Pilgrimage*, edited by Simon Coleman and John Elsner, 1–16. New York and Oxford: Berghahn Books.

Crumrine, N. Ross and E. Alan Morinis (eds.). 1991. *Pilgrimage in Latin America*. New York: Greenwood Publishing Group.

D'Arms, John. 2003. *Romans on the Bay of Naples and Other Essays on Roman Campania*. Bari: Edipuglia.

Dillon, Matthew. 1997. *Pilgrims and Pilgrimage in Ancient Greece*. Abingdon and New York: Routledge.

Dubisch, Jill. 1995. *In a Different Place: Pilgrimage, Gender and Politics at a Greek Island Shrine*. Princeton, NJ: Princeton University Press.

## 12  *Jenni Kuuliala and Jussi Rantala*

Elsner, Jas. 1992. "Pausanias: A Greek Pilgrim in the Roman World." *Past and Present* 135: 3–29.

Elsner, Jas and Ian Rutherford (eds.). 2005. *Pilgrimage in Graeco-Roman and Early Christian Antiquity: Seeing the Gods*. Oxford: Oxford University Press.

Farmer, Sharon. 2002. "Young, Male and Disabled." In *Le Petit Peuple Dans L'Occident Médiéval: Terminologies, Perceptions, Réalités*, edited by Pierre Boglioni, Robert Delort, and Claude Gauvard, 437–451. Paris: Publications de la Sorbonne.

Finucane, Ronald C. 1995. *Miracles and Pilgrims: Popular Beliefs in Medieval England*. New York: St. Martin's Press.

Fletcher, Kristopher. 2014. *Finding Italy: Travel, Colonization and Nation in Vergil's Aeneid*. Ann Arbor: The University of Michigan Press.

Frank, Georgia. 2000. *The Memory of the Eyes: Pilgrims to Living Saints in Christian Late Antiquity*. Los Angeles and Berkeley: The University of California Press.

Gaposchkin, M. Cecilia. 2013. "From Pilgrimage to Crusade: The Liturgy of Departure, 1095–1300." *Speculum* 88(1): 44–91.

Grünewald, Martin. 2017. "Roman Healing Pilgrimage North of the Alps." In *Excavating Pilgrimage. Archaeological Approaches to Sacred Travel and Movement in the Ancient World*, edited by Troels Myrup Kristensen and Wiebke Friese, 130–151. London and New York: Routledge.

Guédon, Stéphanie. 2010. *La voyage dans l'Afrique romaine*. Ausonius Éditions, Scripta Antiqua 25. Pessac: Ausonius.

Harland, Philip A. (ed.). 2011. *Travel and Religion in Antiquity*. Studies in Christianity and Judaism 21. Waterloo: Wilfrid Laurier University Press.

Heal, Bridget. 2007. *The Cult of the Virgin Mary in Early Modern Germany: Protestant and Catholic Early Modern Germany: Protestant and Catholic Piety, 1500–1648*. Cambridge: Cambridge University Press.

Heinz, Werner. 2003. *Reisewege der Antike: Unterwegs im Römischen Reich*. Stuttgart: Theiss.

Kaldellis, Anthony. 2009. *The Christian Parthenon: Classicism and Pilgrimage in Byzantine Athens*. Cambridge: Cambridge University Press.

Hutton, William. 2005. *Describing Greece. Landscape and Literature in the Periegesis of Pausanias*.

Katajala-Peltomaa, Sari. 2009. *Gender, Miracles and Daily Life: The Evidence of Fourteenth-Century Canonization Processes*. Turnhout: Brepols.

Katajala-Peltomaa, Sari. 2011. "Gender, Networks and Collaboration: Pilgrimages in Fourteenth-Century Canonization Processes." In *De Amicitia: Friendship and Social Networks in Antiquity and the Middle Ages*, edited by Katariina Mustakallio and Christian Krötzl, 231–243. Rome: Institutum Romanum Finlandiae.

Katajala-Peltomaa, Sari and Raisa Maria Toivo. 2016. "Religion as an Experience." In *Lived Religion and the Long Reformation in Northern Europe c. 1300–1700*, edited by Sari Katajala-Peltomaa and Raisa Maria Toivo, 1–19. Leiden: Brill.

Keirstead, Christopher M. 2019. "Travel and Poetry." In *The Cambridge History of Travel Writing*, edited by Nandini Das and Tim Young, 442–455. Cambridge: Cambridge University Press.

Kiernan, Philip. 2012. "Pagan Pilgrimage in Rome's Western Provinces." *HEROM* 1: 79–106.

Kristensen, Troels Myrup and Wiebke Friese (eds.). 2017. *Excavating Pilgrimage: Archaeological Approaches to Sacred Travel and Movement in the Ancient World*. London and New York: Routledge.

*Introduction* 13

Krötzl, Christian. 1994. *Pilger, Mirakel und Alltag: Formen des Verhaltens im skandinavischen Mittelalter. 12.-15. Jahrhundert.* Helsinki: SHS.

Krötzl, Christian. 2000. "Miracles au tombeau – miracles à distance. Approches Typologiques." In *Miracle et Karama. Hagiographies médiévales comparées*, edited by Denise Aigle, 557–576. Turnhout: Brepols.

Kuuliala, Jenni. 2016. *Childhood Disability and Social Integration in the Middle Ages: Constructions of Impairments in Thirteenth- and Fourteenth-Century Canonization Processes.* Turnhout: Brepols.

Laes, Christian. 2011. "Disabled Children in Gregory of Tours." In *The Dark Side of Childhood in Late Antiquity and the Middle Ages*, edited by Katariina Mustakallio and Christian Laes, 39–62. Oxford: Oxbow.

Laurence, Ray. 1999. *The Roads of Roman Italy: Mobility and Cultural Change.* Abingdon and New York: Routledge.

Mackenthun, Gesa, Andea Nicolas and Stephanie Wodianks (eds.). 2017. *Travel, Agency, and the Circulation of Knowledge.* Münster and New York.

Macrides, Ruth. 2002. *Travel in the Byzantine World: Papers from the Thirty-Fourth Spring Symposium of Byzantine Studies, Birmingham, April 2000.* Abingdon and New York: Routledge.

Maniura, Robert. 2004. *Pilgrimage to the Images in the Fifteenth Century: The Origins of the Cult of Our Lady of Częstochowa.* Woodbridge: The Boydell Press.

McGuire, Meredith B. 2008. *Lived Religion: Faith and Practice in Everyday Life.* Oxford: Oxford University Press.

Morgan, Ronald J. 2002. *Spanish American Saints and the Rhetoric of Identity, 1600–1810.* Tucson: University of Arizona Press.

Morrison, Susan S. 2004. *Women Pilgrims in Late Medieval England: Private Piety as Public Performance.* London and New York: Routledge.

Muir, Steven. 2011. "Religion on the Road in Ancient Greece and Rome." In *Travel and Religion in Antiquity.* Studies in Christianity and Judaism 21, edited by Philip A. Harland, 29–47. Waterloo: Wilfrid Laurier University Press.

Newman, Paul. 2011. *Travel and Trade in the Middle Ages.* Jefferson, NC: McFarland.

Petsalis-Diomidis, Alexia. 2003. "Narratives of Transformation: Pilgrimage Patterns and Authorical Self-Representation in Three Pilgrimage Texts." In *Pilgrim Voices: Narrative and Authorship in Christian Pilgrimage*, edited by Simon Coleman and John Elsner, 84–109. New York and Oxford: Berghahn Books.

Plötz, Robert. 1992. "Peregrinatio ad Limina Sancti Jacobi." In *The Codex Calixtinus and the Shrine of St. James*, edited by John Williams, 37–50. Tübingen: Gunter Narr Verlag.

Rantala, Jussi. 2017. *The Ludi Saeculares of Septimius Severus: The Ideologies of a New Roman Empire.* Abingdon and New York: Routledge.

Rawcliffe, Carole. 2002. "Curing Bodies and Healing Souls: Pilgrimage and the Sick in Medieval East Anglia." In *Pilgrimage: The English Experience from Becket to Bunyan*, edited by Colin Morris and Peter Roberts, 108–140. Cambridge: Cambridge University Press.

Ritari, Katja. 2016. *Pilgrimage to Heaven: Eschatology and Monastic Spirituality in Early Medieval Ireland.* Turnhout: Brepols.

Rüpke, Jörg. 2016. *On Roman Religion: Lived Religion and the Individual in Ancient Rome.* Ithaca, NY: Cornell University Press.

Sigal, Pierre-André. 1985. *L'homme et le miracle dans la France médiévale (XIe–XIIe siècle).* Paris: Les Éditions du Cerf.

## 14   Jenni Kuuliala and Jussi Rantala

Signori, Gabriela. 1996a. "La bienheureuse polysémie. Miracles et pèlerinages de la Vierge: modèles pastoraux et pouvoir thaumaturge (Xe–XIIIe siècle)." In *Marie. Le culte de la vierge dans la société médiévale*, edited by Dominique Iogna-Prat, Éric Palazzo, and Daniel Russo, 591–617. Paris: Beauchesne.

Signori, Gabriela. 1996b. "The Miracle Kitchen and Its Ingredients. A Methodical and Critical Approach to Marian Shrine Wonders." *Hagiographica* 3: 277–303.

Signori, Gabriela (ed.). 2003. *Heilige, Reliquien, Wallfahrt und Wunder im Mittelalter*. Bielefeld: Verlag für Regionalgeschichte.

Smoller, Laura Ackermann. 2014. *The Saint and the Chopped-Up Baby: The Cult of Vincent Ferrer in Medieval and Early Modern Europe*. Ithaca, NY and London: Cornell University Press.

Stevens, Saskia. 2017. "Visiting the Ancestors: Ritual Movement in Rome's Urban Borderland." In *Excavating Pilgrimage. Archaeological Approaches to Sacred Travel and Movement in the Ancient World*, edited by Troels Myrup Kristensen and Wiebke Friese, 152–165. London and New York: Routledge.

Sumption, Jonathan. 2013 [1975]. *The Age of Pilgrimage: The Medieval Journey to God*. Mahwah, NJ: Hidden Spring.

Swanson, Robert N. 1995. *Religion and Devotion in Europe, C.1215–C.1515*. Cambridge: Cambridge University Press.

Turner, Victor and Edith Turner. 1978. *Image and Pilgrimage in Christian Culture*. New York: Columbia University Press.

Vauchez, André. 1988 [1981]. La *sainteté en Occident aux derniers siècles du Moyen Âge. D'après les procès de canonisation et les documents hagiographiques*. Rome: École française de Rome.

Ward, Benedicta. 1982. *Miracles and the Medieval Mind: Theory, Record and Event 1000–1215*. London: Scholar Press.

Webb, Diana. 2000. *Pilgrimage in Medieval England*. Hambledon and London: Bloomsbury.

Webb, Diana. 2001. *Pilgrims and Pilgrimage in Medieval West*. London and New York: I. B. Tauris.

Williams, Wes. 2003. "The Diplomat, The *Trucheman*, and the The Mystagogue: Forms of Belonging in Early Modern Jerusalem." In *Pilgrim Voices: Narrative and Authorship in Christian Pilgrimage*, edited by Simon Coleman and John Elsner, 17–39. New York and Oxford: Berghahn Books.

Wilson, Louise E. 2010. "Hagiographical Interpretations of Disability in the Twelfth-Century Miracula of St Frideswide of Oxford." In *The Treatment of Disabled Persons in Medieval Europe: Examining Disability in the Historical, Legal, Literary, Medical, and Religious Discourses of the Middle Ages*, edited by Wendy J. Turner and Tory Vandeventer Pearman, 135–165. Lewiston: The Edwin Mellen Press.

# 2 Pilgrimage, mobile behaviours and the creation of religious place in early Roman Latium[1]

*Emma-Jayne Graham*

## Introduction

A little over a decade ago, it was claimed that pilgrimage 'seems to play a smaller part in Roman religion than in Greek' (Elsner and Rutherford 2005, 24). Since then, studies of ancient pilgrimage have continued to expand and develop in new directions, broadening our knowledge of particular instances of pilgrimage, the locations involved, the journeys undertaken by individuals and groups, and the types of evidence that can be used to identify and assess these.[2] Nevertheless, with very few exceptions, there remains one constant within these studies: the foregrounding of sources, contexts, sites, communities, activities, and experiences which relate primarily to the Greek world, the eastern Mediterranean or Late Antiquity.[3] This situation has (unintentionally) perpetuated the conclusion reached by Elsner and Rutherford that the absence of directly comparable evidence for pilgrimage activities by Roman individuals or communities, in Italy and the western Mediterranean, must therefore mean that this type of behaviour was simply a less important aspect of religious practice and identity. This state of affairs is made abundantly clear, for example, by an excellent recent volume focused on the archaeological evidence for pilgrimage across the ancient Mediterranean, which features eleven chapters dedicated to Near Eastern, Greek and Late Antique pilgrimage, but only two which examine western Roman contexts.[4]

The primary reasons behind the absence of sustained work on pilgrimage in Republican and Imperial period Italy and the western Roman world can be identified as equal parts methodological (concerning the way in which 'pilgrimage' is defined, typologised and subsequently identified), and evidential (a distinct lack of epigraphic and textual sources providing the same level of detailed information available for other periods and places).[5] This chapter seeks to address these problems by offering an alternative methodology for the study of pilgrimage in early Roman Italy. Rather than attempting to identify a new and coherent suite of textual or material sources, locations, or motives that can then be labelled as 'evidence for Roman pilgrimage', I begin instead by asking how an exploration of mobility – one of the typical behaviours that characterises pilgrimage – might offer a lens through which to re-evaluate what is already known about the religious practices of this period and region. Put another way, rather than attempting

16    *Emma-Jayne Graham*

to isolate pilgrimage as an activity that was special or otherwise separate from ordinary religious practices, what happens if we assume that essential pilgrimage behaviours were deeply embedded within traditional religious activities? How might this make it possible to better understand the complexities of Roman religious knowledge and experience? To achieve this, the chapter focuses particularly on questions concerning mobility and its relationship with the production, nature, and role of religious place, investigating the archaeological and textual evidence associated with two sacred sites in the Latium region of Italy: the well-known sanctuary dedicated to Diana Nemorensis near Aricia, and a much less well-known natural cave and spring at Pantanacci, Lanuvium. These examples demonstrate that foregrounding concepts of mobility and place, rather than seeking pilgrimage 'sites', can provide a means through which to address assumptions about the practice, prevalence, and significance of pilgrimage behaviours in early Roman Italy.

## Towards a definition of ancient pilgrimage

Any study of pilgrimage, past or present, faces the problem of how to define the activity which lies at its heart. Space constraints prevent a comprehensive overview of such a vast multidisciplinary field here but, broadly speaking, as a subject which crosses both the humanities and social sciences, definitions of pilgrimage are typically characterised by the concerns of the discipline that produces or uses them. Thus, geographers have tended to emphasise the spatial and mobility aspects of the journeys, locations and experiences involved in pilgrimage; anthropologists and sociologists have stressed the social aspects of community building and identity creation through the performance of ritual activities, as well as its connection with secular forms of travel and tourism, sometimes overlapping with theological and religious studies' approaches, which have drawn attention to the spiritual motivations or consequences of sacred journeys and sites.[6] The most influential, if now much critiqued, work on pilgrimage remains that of Victor Turner, who advocated the concepts of *communitas* and liminality, anti-structure, and the pitching together of people taken out of their normal social world, resulting in new collective bonds.[7] Even if it has largely been reduced to a critical backboard against which to bounce revised concepts, Turner's work continues to influence pilgrimage studies. Richard Scriven (2014, 258), for example, has noted that 'core ideas around liminality and the solidarity among participants still resonate' within geographical and mobilities scholarship. Consequently, although Turner's theories are concerned less with the implications of pilgrimage for understandings of the production and role of religious place than they are with understanding social dynamics more broadly, the idea that pilgrimage might produce a particular state of being or understanding of the world endures as an undercurrent to the discussion below.

Studies of ancient pilgrimage have tended to be guided primarily by the availability of suitable evidence, especially texts and inscriptions which describe activities and ascribe to them motivations and understandings that align with a flexible

*Pilgrimage, mobile behaviours and religious place*   17

definition of pilgrimage, such as that put forward by Ian Rutherford (2012, 5325): 'a journey of unusual length to a sacred place for a religious reason.' Indeed, as Jaś Elsner and Ian Rutherford pointed out, ancient pilgrimage is very difficult to define, and Philip Kiernan has bemoaned the extent to which the term is applied 'remarkably casually' to archaeological evidence.[8] This is a circumstance that is complicated further by the fact that individual pieces of scholarship on ancient pilgrimage are also disposed towards asking specific questions about community, identity, the nature of sacred sites, spiritual transformation and enlightenment that, by necessity, draw unevenly upon the wider multidisciplinary field of pilgrimage studies described above. The overarching 'pick and mix' picture that emerges of ancient pilgrimage limits the practical application of the term for explaining cross-cultural or cross-period phenomena in a meaningful way, resulting instead in the production of region- or period-specific accounts and typologies. Recent work has drawn critical attention to these methodological problems, and has to some extent side-stepped the difficulties of drawing together cross-disciplinary methods, theories and strands of research into a single coherent definition either by promoting a very loose understanding of the term or, as already noted, by continuing to develop context- or disciplinary-specific understandings that target a particular collection of material or speak to a particular set of concerns.[9] On the evidential front, Jaś Elsner (2017, 267–68) has suggested that it is in fact impossible to study pilgrimage without texts, highlighting the dangers of inferring 'ritual, let alone pilgrimage, from any given artefact or space,' and arguing that the narrative constructed and expressed in written form by participants is the only guaranteed way of avoiding what he calls 'speculative whimsy' and ensuring a secure identification of an act of pilgrimage. Whilst he does note that rejecting pilgrimage entirely as an interpretation for material culture would be reductive, he remains committed to the idea of pilgrimage as 'a *post-eventum* explanatory narrative' (Elsner 2017, 270). In contrast, this chapter demonstrates that archaeological evidence can have a significant role to play in discourses surrounding the role of pilgrimage behaviours within ancient religious practices and understandings, if pilgrimage is thought of as comprising particular forms of behaviour and not just post hoc rationalisation.

Amongst the other reasons supplied by Elsner and Rutherford for why scholars of antiquity have tended to shy away from investigating pilgrimage as a form of sacred travel is the term's overtly Christianizing overtones.[10] This problem is neatly demonstrated by a description of Roman-period pilgrimage given in a recent work:

> Like those of Christian pilgrims, the journeys were mostly made on foot, *covering twenty to thirty kilometres per day*. The pilgrims certainly carried part of their nourishment with them while a part *could have* been obtained from farmers or shops. Some nights were spent in *places of worship and hospices* that offered shelter, food and sometimes baths. Other nights were *probably* passed in relay stations, in inns or with local inhabitants, but *presumably* very few under the stars since there was a real fear of wild animals, outlaws and

18  *Emma-Jayne Graham*

> ghosts. We can *only speculate* about the different states and *ritual practices that may have punctuated these voyages*, but it is *probable* that by repeatedly stopping at *consecrated places* found along the way to *the large and important sanctuaries* served as a psychological preparation for the pilgrims.[11]

From the direct parallel made by its opening words, to its mention of hospices and large sanctuaries, as well as its extensive reliance on adverbs, this passage is replete with Christianizing and other assumptions, the many gaps in existing knowledge readily filled by comparison with later forms of pilgrimage. On the other hand, however, it also conveniently encapsulates quite how little is known about Roman practices and experiences of pilgrimage. Perhaps, then, if it is so difficult to identify and define, we should consider abandoning any attempt to use pilgrimage as a framework for investigations of Roman religious practice and performance. Doing so, however, brings its own problems: choosing *not* to explore Roman period religious activities and behaviours through the lens of pilgrimage would be tantamount to a tacit acknowledgement that this moment in time and space was, in one way or another, unusual for a marked *insignificance* of pilgrimage or pilgrimage-like activities, when evidence certainly indicates such an extreme conclusion to be false. Instead, there is an urgent need to adopt a new approach which makes it possible to assess the relative value of this form of behaviour to Roman individuals and communities.

Work already exists which can help with this. Instead of focusing purely on contexts – the legacy of what might be described as the 'who, what, when, where, and why' typology of around 20 types (and subtypes) of ancient pilgrimage set out by Elsner and Rutherford – Joy McCorriston has established five behavioural criteria for identifying ancient pilgrimage.[12] She describes pilgrimage as 'a constellation of characteristics including mobility, an affirmation of social identity and inscription of belonging, material and economic exchanges, punctuated rather than habitual participation, and dramatic rites' (McCorriston 2017, 11). Although under certain circumstances the attributes that she highlights might be seen to characterise *any* form of ancient religious behaviour, such as performing a sacrifice or making a votive dedication, McCorriston's model, which includes an emphasis on mobility and time, nevertheless provides a useful way of breaking down the fundamental elements of pilgrimage into a set of activities or outcomes that might vary in terms of their relevance or significance in different settings or on different occasions. As Richard Scriven (2014, 251) has similarly argued, 'the study of pilgrimage can be cultivated in considering how movements, beliefs and embodied practices function individually and together in the creation of pilgrims and pilgrimage places.' Rather than attempting to define, identify, and evaluate 'Roman pilgrimage' as a discrete activity, this chapter builds on Scriven's words and McCorriston's approach by using the features and behaviours commonly associated with pilgrimage – especially mobility – to prompt an investigation of what people were actually doing in the past, not what traditional models of pilgrimage suggest they ought to have been doing. From this perspective more

*Pilgrimage, mobile behaviours and religious place*   19

nuanced questions can be asked about the significance and consequences of those behaviours for understanding ancient religious practice as a lived experience.[13]

## Producing religious place in Republican Italy

Joy McCorriston (2017, 12–13) points out the significance of forms of mobility as a particular characteristic of pilgrimage when she states that 'Pilgrimage movement is distinct from other journeys because of its socially constituting aspects outside of daily practice – pilgrims may be habitually sedentary, mobile, or both, but their interaction is in-habitual.' She goes on to stress the importance of studying the 'localities where pilgrimage has left its mark,' or in other words, archaeological evidence that can attest to 'episodic gatherings' (McCorriston 2017, 13). The corollary of recognising mobility as a key characteristic of pilgrimage is, therefore, the need to identify and understand its relationship with place. But, as Alan Morinis (1992, 4) reminds us, the places implicated in acts of pilgrimage might be both tangible and intangible:

> At its most conventional, the end of the pilgrimage is an actual shrine located at some fixed geographical point. … One who journeys to a place of importance to himself alone may also be a pilgrim. The allegorical pilgrimage seeks out a place not located in the geographical sphere. Some sacred journeys are wanderings that have no fixed goal; the pilgrimage here is the search for an unknown or hidden goal.

Pilgrimage places in Roman Italy have usually been assumed to be highly tangible, even heavily monumental, fixed geographical points, as Elsner and Rutherford's (2005, 24) qualification of their comments about the reduced role of pilgrimage in Roman religion demonstrate:

> Many centres for pilgrimage are known: the official sanctuaries of the Alban Mount, locale for the *Feriae Latinae* and Lavinium; other Latin centres were Lake Nemi, where there was a yearly festival of Diana; Fregellae, on the border between Samnite and Latin territory where there was a cult of Neptune and Aesculapius; and the grove of Helernus (Alernus) near the mouth of the Tiber.

These 'centres for pilgrimage' (one of which is explored in more detail below) appear to have been identified primarily on the basis of their size or monumentality and the presence of epigraphy and references in written sources to large, periodic, sometimes political gatherings, thus aligning them with the Panhellenic sanctuaries that dominate the rest of their typology. However, once pilgrimage is defined as a set of behaviours rather than physical features, one need only observe the presence in the wider archaeological record of many other sites with sacred connotations to which people in Italy journeyed on a periodic basis, especially during the Republic. Vast quantities of votive offerings, for example, have been

## 20    *Emma-Jayne Graham*

recovered from 'ordinary' monumentalised and non-monumentalised urban, extra-urban, and rural sanctuaries across the landscape of central Italy, providing ample evidence for people travelling to locations near and far for the performance of particular personal and communal ritual activities and acts of exchange.[14] From the third to first century BCE, votive deposits at these sites are dominated by terracotta anatomical votives, commonly connected with requests for healing, well-being, fertility, good fortune, and other forms of divine protection.[15] These objects number into the tens, hundreds, sometimes thousands, even at the smallest rural sanctuaries, each one connected with an episodic individual request or gesture of thanksgiving. In addition, several sites in Republican Latium housed oracles, including the great terraced sanctuaries at Praeneste (Palestrina), Tarracina (modern-day Terracina) and Gabii.[16] Oracles such as these were surely consulted by visitors who travelled, in potentially impromptu ways, from both the local urban community and further afield. Indeed, despite Ian Rutherford's suggestion cited above that pilgrimage involved 'a journey of unusual length', there is no reason at all to assume that within early Roman Italy visiting any sacred site entailed or necessitated long-distance travel: the countryside was littered with shrines, sacred springs, caves, and groves, as well as larger monumentalised sanctuaries, which provided equal levels of access to the divine, and which served the needs of individual and community alike.[17] This type of sacred landscape, produced and sustained by largely localised forms of mobility, is known from other historical contexts which, whilst not directly comparable in terms of religious practice, are at least suggestive of its potential effects. In late medieval England, for example, 'for many pilgrims of the time, going on pilgrimage was less like launching on a journey to the ends of the earth and more like going to the local market. Shrines mapped the familiar as much as they were signposts to the other world' (Coleman and Eade 2004, 13 paraphrasing Duffy 2002, 165). This compels a rethink of the landscape of pilgrimage for Republican Italy, challenging the necessity of identifying evidence for 'major centres', and potentially long journeys, in order to securely attest to the practice of pilgrimage behaviour.

Not enough is known about most Republican sacred sites to establish how frequently or regularly visits were made to them, but they appear to have combined both habitual and more periodic events. A bronze tablet documenting the formal religious calendar of a grove dedicated to Ceres at Agnone near Pietrabbondante (Samnium) suggests that we should imagine visits to sanctuary sites taking a range of individual and communal forms throughout the year.[18] Listing fifteen annual ceremonies, the tablet establishes that although the local elite were responsible for the maintenance of the grove and the regular performance of appropriate rites, there were also special festival days that must have attracted 'changing groups of worshippers, not all of whom will necessarily have come from the strictly local remit' (Scopacasa 2014, 79). On certain occasions in the annual cycle, then, mobility was responsible for creating more or less substantial gatherings of transient worshippers, and bringing about a reconfiguration of the religious community at Agnone, perhaps also bringing with it an altered phenomenological experience of the activities performed there and of the grove itself or, that is, its associated

*Pilgrimage, mobile behaviours and religious place* 21

sense of place.[19] Indeed, although 'place' has traditionally been viewed as static, and as a location in which movement is effectively paused, this understanding has been challenged by scholarship in both the social sciences and archaeology, which argues that place is dynamic and 'constantly in the process of becoming'.[20] From this standpoint, rather than existing as a fixed point in space – i.e. a location, locale or site – place is better understood as an ephemeral experience that results from a dynamic combination of the material attributes of a location, the bodies which animate it and the moment in time at which they do so. In other words, the 'weaving together of moving bodies and their sensory engagement with the world at particular moments in time actively produces place that is temporally specific, which in turn contributes to the creation of certain kinds of personal knowledge and identities' (Graham 2018, p.3).[21] Indeed, for ancient cult contexts, Peter Biehl (2007, 178) has stressed how sacred places 'not only exist as material entities, they also happen. They are continuously being made and remade, and are always changing'. That places 'happen' is an important observation in the context of ancient pilgrimage, since it draws attention to the temporal aspects of place, a temporality that is brought about principally by human movement to and from a location. The people who come to be present at that location at any one time comprise a unique gathering of temporally specific bodies and minds experiencing the material nature of that location and engaging in ritual performances in highly personal sensory and embodied ways. The ultimate product of this 'sensuous interrelationship of body-mind-environment' (Howes 2005, 7), and the temporal and spatial experiences it involves, is a sense of place that belongs to that moment and to those participants only. Subsequent gatherings or events at the same location, however similar in form, will always produce further singular senses of place, either because the key agents (e.g. human bodies and minds in action, moment in time) are different, or have changed as a consequence of earlier experiences, or because they combine in subtly different ways.[22] Accordingly, place can be conceived of as an unrepeatable 'time-space event' and 'a gathering that brings together people and things in the here and now' (Moser and Feldman 2014, 6).[23] The potential connection between the production of religious place and the mobile behaviours central to pilgrimage could not be clearer.

These observations, together with the example of Agnone, suggest that the traditional starting point in the search for 'places of pilgrimage' in Republican Italy may, in fact, be fundamentally flawed. Instead of seeking distinctive sites characterised by a collection of similar buildings or monumental features, which were visited periodically by large numbers of people travelling long distances, or which display epigraphic evidence for communal dedications, our approach to Roman places of pilgrimage might profitably be transformed by an assessment of how pilgrimage behaviours and related activities, operating at a range of different scales, might in themselves produce less tangible, but no less significant, religious places. New questions thus begin to emerge about the significance of visits to the same location by different people not necessarily involving the same experience or understanding of place. An equality of experience cannot be assumed in cases such as Agnone, where festival days swelled the 'ordinary' community, or at sites such as Praeneste

## 22    Emma-Jayne Graham

where it is likely that both ad hoc oracular and votive activities took place alongside the more regular communal worship of the primary deity. Although these were not mutually exclusive categories of activity or groups of people, acknowledging their role in the active production of potentially dissimilar forms of religious place at one location makes it possible to better understand the consequences of pilgrimage as a kinetic activity, whilst also removing the need to seek major 'centres'. Instead, we might think about how this set of kinaesthetic behaviours may have contributed more widely to the production of distinctively Roman forms of religious knowledge. To explore this in practice, the rest of this chapter examines the evidence from two locations in early Roman Latium, both of which can be distinguished by at least two separate experiences of place brought about as a result of mobile behaviours. Together these suggest that visiting sacred locations involved producing, experiencing, and engaging with a different religious place each time, even if the geospatial location in which they occurred remained essentially the same.

## Celebrating the cult of Diana Nemorensis

The sanctuary dedicated to Diana Nemorensis was located in an isolated position on the shore of Lake Nemi (also referred to as *speculum Dianae*, Mirror of Diana), situated in a volcanic crater approximately 25 kilometres south-east of Rome. Probably under the jurisdiction of the nearby urban community of Aricia, the site originally comprised a *lucus* (a clearing in a *nemus*, sacred wood) that was dedicated to Diana, and also served as a meeting point for the confederation of communities known as the Latin League, until its defeat in 338 BCE.[24] The sanctuary is most well-known for its connection with the *rex Nemorensis*, an unusual priestly office held by an escaped slave who ritually murdered his predecessor, which was made (in)famous by James Frazer's pioneering anthropological study *The Golden Bough* (1890). The existence and role of the *rex* are not discussed here, in part because so little is certain about whether it continued in anything other than a symbolic form, but also because its uniqueness offers little of relevance to a study of the significance of mobile pilgrimage behaviours within the region more broadly. The site of the sanctuary was first investigated in the mid-seventeenth century, before being excavated in a piecemeal way in 1885 by Sir John Savile, who identified a rectangular structure, set to one side of an arcaded precinct and portico, as a temple building, as well as an imperial period theatre, baths, and granary complex.[25] More than 400 votive offerings and several sculptures were recovered during these excavations, the former having been cleared away during antiquity from their original place within the temple for deposition in a deep pit in the southern corner of the precinct, along with coins and burnt material assumed to originate from sacrificial fires.[26] These artefacts, many of which are now housed in Nottingham Castle Museum (UK), comprise bronze and terracotta votive figurines – including statuettes of Diana and other deities, as well as so-called Tanagra figures – and terracotta anatomical and miniature temple models, all dating primarily to the third or second century BCE.[27]

More recent excavations have clarified the building phases of the temple, which was constructed on a site that had been used for cult activities from at least

*Pilgrimage, mobile behaviours and religious place*   23

the Archaic period, with the first formalised temple structure – oriented towards the lake – constructed between the end of the fourth and the start of the third century BCE.[28] This underwent further monumentalisation during the second half of the second century BCE, when a small circular shrine was added and the orientation of the temple was altered in order to create a transverse cella, before further enlargement took place a century later.[29] Excavation also revealed a series of additional structures, dating between the late second century BCE and the second century CE, on the terrace above the temple precinct, including a late Republican nymphaeum.[30] The terrace also revealed evidence for a hoard of middle Bronze Age axes, to the east of which were found late Bronze Age ceramics and carbonised materials that appear to have demarcated an area intentionally left free of structures, which the excavators suggest was perhaps memorialised as the site of the original *lucus*.[31] Immediately to the south of the proposed *lucus* there once stood a small square structure which Giuseppina Ghini and Francesca Diosono propose might have protected the sacred tree, the removal of a branch from which gave a runaway slave the right to challenge the *rex Nemorensis*.[32] In architectural terms, these remains offer little to facilitate a secure reconstruction of the performance of ritual activities or movements around the sanctuary (the location of an altar, for example, remains unknown). However, when combined with written sources describing events associated with the celebration of the festival of Diana Nemorensis, it is possible to identify at least two types of periodic ritual activity that people might choose to travel to the site in order to participate in.

Sources from the Augustan period describe the performance of a custom established in a much earlier period: in order to celebrate the annual festival of Diana each August, worshippers made their way en masse along the Via Appia from Rome in what appears to have been a nocturnal torch-lit procession (this is probably the event which, combined with the sanctuary's role in the Latin League, led Elsner and Rutherford to include it in their list of 'centres of pilgrimage' in Roman-era Italy, see above). These descriptions are worth citing at length because they provide an evocative insight into both the nature of the procession, the landscape and atmosphere through which its participants moved, and the sensory aspects of the religious place which consequently emerged from this act of mobility:

> It is the season when the most scorching region of the heavens takes over the land and the keen dog-star Sirius, so often struck by Hyperion's sun, burns the gasping fields. Now is the day when Trivia's Arician grove, convenient for fugitive kings, grows smoky, and the lake, having guilty knowledge of Hippolytus, glitters with the reflection of a multitude of torches; Diana herself garlands the deserving hunting dogs and polishes the arrowheads and allows the wild animals to go in safety, and at virtuous hearths all Italy celebrates the Hecatean Ides.[33]

> I wish you would promenade here in all your leisure hours, Cynthia! But the world of men forbids me to trust you, when they see you hurrying with kindled torches to worship at the Arician grove and carrying lights for the goddess Trivia.[34]

## 24    *Emma-Jayne Graham*

In the Arician vale there is a lake begirt by shady woods and hallowed by religion from of old. Here Hippolytus lies hid, who by the reins of his steeds was rent in pieces: hence no horses enter that grove. The long fence is draped with hanging threads, and many a tablet there attests the merit of the goddess. Often doth a woman, whose prayer has been answered, carry from the City burning torches, while garlands wreathe her brows. The strong of hand and fleet of foot do there reign kings, and each is slain thereafter even as himself had slain. A pebbly brook flows down with fitful murmur; oft have I drunk of it, but in little sips.[35]

According to these sources, the participants who walked from Rome to Aricia in order to take part in the festival of Diana were predominantly women, and all three writers emphasise the dramatic use of torches and their impact on the experience, Statius specifically drawing attention to the way in which the grove 'grows smoky, and the lake ... glitters with the reflection of a multitude of torches'. There was only one route in and out of the crater, so after perhaps 3 or 4 hours of moderately paced walking, in order to reach the sanctuary itself this mobile group was compelled to leave the main road and follow another secondary basalt-paved route, moving over the southwestern edge of the crater and down towards the lake.[36] Here they made their way towards the main sanctuary structures, situated on a flat area of ground at the north-eastern end of the lake, moving around its forested edge, walking through the darkened trees with the natural scents and sounds of the woodland evoking the wilderness over which Diana exercised control. Like all visitors to the sanctuary, they therefore moved from a (partially) tamed world outside the crater to a largely wild one within, with the timing of the festival itself – taking place at the driest, warmest part of the year – perhaps contributing further to the production of a deeply sensory experience of a place distinct from that outside the crater, or in Rome itself.[37] Carin Green has suggested that the festival, which she assigns to the Ides of August, lasted 3 days, making it likely that participants stayed for several nights by the side of the lake, perhaps in temporary structures or tents.[38] Propertius (2.32.3–6) certainly complained about Cynthia going away from him for protracted periods on what appear to be comparable trips in order to participate in religious performances: 'Why, Cynthia, do you seek riddling oracles at Praeneste, why seek the walls of Aeaean Telegonus? Why so oft are you taken by your carriage to Herculean Tibur, why so oft by the Appian Way to Lanuvium?'

The sense of place produced and experienced by the gathering together of a large group of women, nocturnal celebrations, the garlanding of the grove and banishment of certain animals, and movement over varied terrain each time this celebration of Diana's annual festival occurred, was therefore generated by mobility. After all, it was mobility which actively brought together a discrete group of people, at a particular time, to perform religious rituals in relation to a specific location. Mobility was also responsible for sustaining that sense of place for a well-defined period only, since the subsequent departure of participants brought about both the scattering of its members and the dissolving of the temporary place their co-presence and actions had created. What can be identified here, then, is an example of the type of mobility behaviour commonly associated with pilgrimage – the periodic 'there and back again' movement of a discrete and changeable group of people – producing a distinct yet temporally specific sense of place that effectively dissipated along with the departure of the agents which sustained it. It suggests that the real significance of pilgrimage movement might lie in the fact that it could produce religious places that were largely ephemeral, temporary, and context-specific.

Being part of a mobile group that moved from one location to another was perhaps also significant for the way in which it shaped religious experiences and knowledge in other ways. Movement as part of a procession, for example, is something which, as Thierry Luginbühl (2015, 50) argues, could produce a sense of communal identity: 'the action of progressing together, as a coherent body, procures for the participants particular sensations and impressions, the sensation of being scrutinized or, more exactly, as being on display'. Moreover, Eftychia Stavrianopoulou (2015, 350) includes aspects of movement in her assessment of community building through participation in ritual performances when she writes:

> It is not the co-presence of participants and spectators that creates community, but rather the interplay between actors and spectators, between them and aesthetic elements (clothing, smell, music and song, group arrangement) or the particular space to be traversed that generate instances, which, in turn, evoke the creation or collapse of communities.

Moving as part of a procession, such as that from Rome to Lake Nemi, emphasized the role of the participants in creating the 'here and now-ness' not only of that community but, it can be argued, also of the place that they co-created and co-habited. Their shared experience produced a time-space event that was associated with *that* celebration of Diana only.

Nevertheless, people also travelled to Diana's sanctuary on the shores of Lake Nemi at other times and for other purposes, as attested by the large numbers of excavated votive offerings. These objects provide evidence for periodic visits by individuals with another specific goal in mind: making requests or gestures of thanksgiving connected with personal issues of healing, fertility, well-being, and good fortune. Some of these objects may have been dedicated by the women who participated in the August festival celebrations, but the likelihood of votive activities comprising a core component of the summer rites is rendered unlikely by the comparatively short-lived nature of this behaviour and the apparent end of the practice of making such offerings after the second century BCE, with no evidence for the substitution of terracotta objects with those of a different material form (e.g. inscriptions or dedicatory altars). The two activities therefore appear to have been largely separate. Votive dedicants were compelled to follow the same route from the Via Appia to the sanctuary as the women who were involved in the night-time procession, but they did so under different circumstances, perhaps alone or, in the case of those who sought help from the goddess for illness or

## 26 *Emma-Jayne Graham*

impairment, as part of a smaller group of family or friends, and most probably during daylight hours.[39] These visits occurred in a more informal or spontaneous manner at numerous points throughout the year. Aside from seasonal or temporal variations in the natural landscape through which they travelled, these visiting petitioners of the goddess experienced the same material setting for their activities, but their act of mobility, their bodies and motivations, and the activities they performed on arrival at the sanctuary (and perhaps also on departure) involved the production of place that was unlike that of the festival celebrants.[40] In part, this also resulted from the fact that, in contrast to the female-oriented torchlight procession and the rites associated with the festival of Diana, the votive offerings indicate that her assistance could be sought by both male and female petitioners. It might be expected that a cult of Diana (considered to provide protection in childbirth), especially one with such a specifically female-oriented festival, would attract many dedications of wombs, breasts, nursing figures, swaddled infants, and other items indicative of concerns related to female fertility, childbirth, motherhood, and infant health. This is not the case at Nemi, where although some offerings of this type are present, and large quantities of female figurines are known, no swaddled babies or breasts have been recorded and there are only two uteri in the Nottingham collection.[41] There is no evidence that the votive petitioners were exclusively women and instead they appear to have been drawn from a wider cross-section of society than the participants in the annual festival. It can therefore be suggested that there were at least two different types of 'religious community' making use of the sanctuary at Nemi, each producing a sense of place that embodied their own particular behaviours, activities, and understandings. It does not appear, however, that these different communities, discourses, or experiences of place were in active competition, as scholars of pilgrimage in modern contexts have claimed for other 'contested' locations at which different worldviews and agendas can be seen to conflict.[42]

In sum, focusing on mobility as a form of religious behaviour reveals that it was the temporality of the type of 'there and back again' movement traditionally associated with pilgrimage that was fundamental to the production of multiple senses of religious place at the sanctuary of Diana Nemorensis. Here, religious place was produced *by* pilgrimage behaviours, not for them. The geospatial location associated with the cult of Diana, off the beaten track of the main road system and not directly on the way to anywhere else, certainly contributed to this, meaning that undertaking some form of mobility was an essential part of the performance of any and all cult activities associated with it. But even more significantly, the varied experiences of mobility that this entailed resulted in the production of multiple, temporally specific senses of religious place. Worshippers of Diana undertook a host of personal and communal journeys with different companions and diverse goals, as well as engaging in a range of activities once they had reached her sanctuary. There were also differences in the composition of the two mobile communities described here, not to mention amongst the many other individual visitors who, although more difficult to identify, must have made their way to the site on other occasions and for other purposes. Their own activities

## Pilgrimage, mobile behaviours and religious place   27

and agency produced still more understandings of religious place associated with Diana Nemorensis.

## Into the woods at Pantanacci, Lanuvium

Exploring other sites in the region of Latium where evidence for the performance of parallel ritual activities can be detected makes it possible to confirm that the phenomenon outlined for Nemi was not unique. A useful point of comparison can be found only a short distance away: a cave in the forested area of Pantanacci, 1.5 kilometres outside the urban limits of the Latin city of Lanuvium (home to the more well-known temple of Juno Sospita) and approximately 33 kilometres southwest of Rome. Discovered in 2012, when the Guardia di Finanza successfully thwarted a clandestine excavation intended to supply the antiquities market, the cave is one of several natural cavities opening into a cliff edge.[43] Within the cave, spring water emerges spontaneously from fissures in the rock, running down the walls before being collected in a small pool (possibly intentionally, perhaps for therapeutic purposes), with large slabs of stone laid down in places to level the floor.[44] That the interior of the cave was used for votive activities is confirmed by the deposition of a series of ceramic items of different types, dating primarily to a period between the fourth and second centuries BCE, placed in small natural cavities and artificial niches or on flat stones and tiles set on the ground close to the walls.[45] No objects were found in the area filled by the pool. Evidence for burning was detected on the walls and on some tiles and stones, along with the remains of nuts, peas, shellfish, poultry and sheep, suggesting that foodstuffs were offered to the divine alongside the more durable objects.[46] Amongst the latter, 33% of the assemblage studied to date comprises impasto and black-glazed ware ceramic vessels, including small cups and miniature *skyphoi*, as well as a large quantity of terracotta anatomical votives.[47] Amongst the terracotta items, nearly all known types of anatomical model were represented, except for eyes, with a high proportion of uteri (8%), statuettes (7%) and male heads (5%), as well as an unusual set of oral cavities (4%).[48] Significantly, unlike most votive offerings, including those from Nemi, which were cleared away from their primary place of deposition (sometimes for reburial in pits called *favissae* or *stipes*), these objects remain in situ, making it possible to investigate the nature of the ritual activities in which they were implicated. In particular, the excavators noted a tendency for some items to be stacked together, something that was achieved by placing one inside the concave cavity of another before they were sealed with a fine clay.[49] This suggests either that worshippers returned to the cave on multiple occasions to make additional offerings, or that dedicants interacted directly with the dedications made by previous visitors. The latter may have served to create or formalise a sense of belonging to a wider transitory group, not only of worshippers of the same deity, but of people who had made a similar journey to the cave in order to engage in comparable activities. The range of anatomical votives is too broad to indicate whether the divinity (or divinities) with whom visitors to the cave communicated was associated with a particular aspect of well-being, health,

28   *Emma-Jayne Graham*

fertility, or the life-course. Indeed, the assemblage reflects a situation familiar from many others of mid and late Republican date: an unknown deity (or deities) petitioned and thanked for assistance, good fortune, and protection by a range of male, female, and perhaps young and old individuals of varied status and place of origin. As at Nemi, mobile behaviours are therefore attested at Pantanacci in a secondary form, through the objects that people left behind after a temporary visit to that location.

However, certain people travelled to the cave at Pantanacci for other reasons, too. Amongst the excavated artefacts are four large pieces of peperino stone (a type of granite) shaped into drums approximately 30 cm in diameter and carved with a scale-like pattern.[50] Dated tentatively to the third century BCE, and thus contemporary with the votive dedications, the blocks do not attach directly to one another, although it has been suggested that they were originally held together by a metallic band fixed into a spiral groove.[51] The stones have been interpreted as the fragmented remains of a cult statue depicting a 3–4 metre-long serpent.[52] This is not an insignificant find for a grotto-like cave in the vicinity of Lanuvium, which was a centre described in Roman texts as the location for ceremonies involving processions of young women taking bread offerings to a serpent who dwelt in cave in a sacred wood dedicated to Juno Sospita (note that Aelian confuses Lavinium with Lanuvium):

> Lanuvium has enjoyed from of old the protection of an ancient serpent (an hour spent here on so infrequent a visit is well worth while). Where the sacred slope is reft by a dark chasm, at that point the offering to the hungry serpent makes its way—maiden, beware of all such paths—when he demands his annual tribute and hurls hisses from the depths of the earth. He seizes the morsel held out to him by the virgin: the very basket trembles in the virgin's hands. Maidens sent down to such a rite turn pale when blindly entrusting their hand to the serpent's lips. If they have been chaste, they return to embrace their parents, and the farmers cry: 'It will be a fruitful year'.[53]

> It seems that one peculiarity of snakes is their faculty of divination. At any rate in the town of Lavinium [Lanuvium], which is in Latium—it is so named after Lavinia the daughter of Latinus at the time when he fought as an ally of Aeneas against the people called Rutulians and overcame them. And Aeneas of Troy, son of Anchises, founded the aforesaid town; and it might be, in a manner of speaking, the grandmother of Rome, because it was from Rome that Ascanius, the son of Aeneas and Creüsa the Trojan, set out to found Alba, and Rome was a colony of Alba.—Well, there is a sacred grove in Lavinium [Lanuvium] of wide area and thickly planted, and nearby is a shrine to Hera of Argolis. And in the grove there is a vast and deep cavern, and it is the lair of a Serpent. And on certain fixed days holy maidens enter the grove bearing a barley-cake in their hands and with their eyes bandaged. And divine inspiration leads them straight to the Serpent's resting-place, and they move forward without stumbling and at a gentle pace just as if they saw with their

*Pilgrimage, mobile behaviours and religious place* 29

eyes unveiled. And if they are virgins, the Serpent accepts the food as sacred and as fit for a creature beloved of god. Otherwise the food remains untasted, because the Serpent already knows and has divined their impurity. And ants crumble the cake of the deflowered maid into small pieces so that they can be carried easily, and transport them without the grove, cleansing the spot. And the inhabitants get to know what has occurred and the maidens who came in are examined, and the one who has shamed her virginity is punished in accordance with the law. This is the way in which I would demonstrate the faculty of divination in serpents.[54]

The eventual fate of the maidens in these passages might rest with different agents (either the serpent itself or the human community), but both recount a ritual connected with fertility. If the snake accepted the offering there would be future prosperity, but if the maiden making that offering was impure the serpent would reject it and a bad harvest would follow.[55] For centuries scholars have sought to identify the location of the cave described in these accounts, sometimes reluctantly assuming that the substructures of the urban temple of Juno Sospita must have acted as an artificial cave for the performance of these longstanding rites.[56] The discovery of the Pantanacci cave, with the remains of what appears to be the image of a giant serpent in an area which retains the toponym 'Dragonello' or 'Stragonello' (derived from *draco*), does not provide definitive proof that this was where these rites were performed but it seems very likely.[57]

As a result, the evidence from Pantanacci demonstrates a situation that is not dissimilar from that at Nemi, with at least two different groups of individuals making, in this case, relatively localised journeys in order to perform periodically discrete rituals. The physical location visited by both the dedicants of votive objects and the (ever-changing group of) young women involved in the annual fertility procession remained much the same, but the religious place produced by those participants and their actions at discrete moments in time was always context-specific and unique. For the former, place was produced through, and experienced in relation to, spontaneously periodic acts of mobility that were motivated by personal thanksgiving and embodied concerns about one's own well-being and fortunes, as well as the maintenance of an individual relationship with the supernatural world. On the other hand, more formal yet still episodic mobility was a central element of the appeasement of the serpent, and for the women involved in that procession must have produced a sense of religious place that embodied the concerns of the wider community of the city as well as affirming their own place within its society. We can only speculate about how a woman involved in both activities at discrete moments in her life-course steered a course through these alternative time-space experiences to produce yet another complex and multilayered understanding of the Pantanacci cave as a sacred place.

The successful completion of both sets of activities and the production of religious place for each depended upon behaviours that were profoundly mobile in nature. Even if, in both of the instances outlined here, the journey between city and cave was comparatively short and unlikely to have proved especially arduous,

30   *Emma-Jayne Graham*

as an experience this movement was crucial for producing a deeply embodied sense of place. Participants moved from an urban to an extra-urban setting, from a built environment to a natural one, with all the attendant sensory implications that come with moving through dense woodland, replete with its distinctive organic scents and sounds, the cool dappled light and shade of the trees and, eventually, the chill darkness of the cave and the moving reflection of flames on the water of its pool. As noted above for late medieval English contexts, mobile behaviours such as these could be important for the way in which they 'mapped the familiar', creating a layered local geography of sacred place that was produced through lived experiences of diverse types of movement between geospatially separate and architecturally distinct locations. In the case of the serpent ritual, for example, mobile behaviour could simultaneously communicate and embody, yet also repeatedly sustain and rework, the spatial relationship between religious place as experienced as a whole community at the urban monumentalised temple, and as a more select group, with an altered annual composition, at the extra-urban grotto. In other words, this was a relationship that became momentarily tangible only through the moving bodies of ritual participants and which itself remained in a constant process of 'becoming' or in need of perpetual, if periodic, affirmation.

## Conclusions

According to Richard Scriven (2014, 255), 'Through the combination of prioritising movement, connecting meanings and experiences, and recognising the mutual roles of the mobile and the fixed, we can enhance our insights into pilgrimage.' This chapter has sought to put this argument into practice, arguing that more nuanced understandings of the significance of ancient religious practice and place emerge when the dynamic behaviours that underpin pilgrimage activities are examined in new ways. When approached from a traditional perspective it might appear anachronistic to attempt to connect pilgrimage (ostensibly about movement) with the concept of place (customarily characterised by the absence of movement). However, as this chapter has shown, a more critical approach that advocates a move away from understandings of place that are based on definable sets of structures, towards understandings of place as the product of dynamic 'time-space events', makes it possible to recognise the powerful complexities of the locations at which religious activities were performed, such as the cave at Pantanacci and the lakeside sanctuary of Diana. What emerges as a result is the impression of geospatial locations that gained significance as religious place through a series of periodically repeated but always unique cumulative movements. The consequent prospect of a religious landscape comprised of overlapping, effectively intangible and short-lived places produced by pilgrimage behaviours, conjures a panorama of mobility that is difficult to map in traditional ways and which will never align with attempts to plot the location of 'great pilgrimage centres'. Perhaps this is why pilgrimage has proved to be so ungraspable for Roman Italy and thus has appeared to be less significant than in other cultural contexts.

*Pilgrimage, mobile behaviours and religious place* 31

Rather than seeking to define and then identify secure instances of pilgrimage to sites within Republican Latium, the discussion above has sought to demonstrate how the types of activities that pilgrimage involves, in particular, its dependence upon episodic acts of movement and the mobility of individuals and groups, could be integral to the production and experience of religious place during this period. From this perspective, rather than pilgrimage representing a special or discrete aspect of religious practice in early Roman Italy, it can thus be better understood as a set of behaviours that provided a sustaining foundation for many of the ordinary activities that were performed as part of Roman religious practice. In turn, this might also go some way to explaining why 'pilgrimage' does not stand out in the evidence for Roman religious practice in the way that it does for other ancient contexts and, moreover, why the Latin/Roman community of Italy felt no need to coin a particular term for it.[58] The absence of evidence for the forms of pilgrimage with which we are familiar from other contexts, both past and present, need not therefore indicate that it did not exist, did not occur very frequently, or that it was considered unimportant, but that it simply did not need to be identified as a type of behaviour that was in some way different, special or otherwise significant. Instead, the significance of 'pilgrimage' in this period and region lay in the behaviours at its heart and, as demonstrated here, at least in part, in the role it played in the production of religious place.

## Notes

1 Thank you to Christian Laes and to the editors of the volume for inviting me to write this chapter and for their patience whilst I worked on it. Earlier versions were presented as research seminars at the Universities of Kent and Exeter, and I am grateful for the feedback provided by both audiences.
2 For example, McCorriston 2011; Rutherford 2013; Kristensen and Friese 2017.
3 Exceptions include Kiernan 2012; Grünewald 2017; Stevens 2017.
4 Kristensen and Friese 2017.
5 For critiques see Kiernan 2012, 79–80; Friese and Kristensen 2017, 3.
6 For geographical approaches see Urry 2002; Slavin 2003; Scriven 2014. For anthropological, sociological and religious studies approaches see Eade and Sallnow 1991; Morinis 1992; Holloway 2003; Coleman and Eade 2004; Bowie 2006, 237-259; Rountree 2006.
7 Turner 1974; Bowie 2006, 240; Kinnard 2014.
8 Elsner and Rutherford 2005; Kiernan 2012, 79.
9 For example, Kiernan 2012; Friese and Kristensen 2017, 1-3; Bremmer 2017.
10 Elsner and Rutherford 2005, 2–4.
11 Luginbühl 2015, 54–55, emphasis added.
12 Elsner and Rutherford 2005, 12–30; McCorriston 2011; 2017.
13 On lived religion see McGuire 2008; Rüpke 2016.
14 Comella 1981; Graham 2017; forthcoming.
15 Recke 2013; Flemming 2016; Graham and Draycott 2017; Graham 2017; Hughes 2017
16 Coarelli 1987; Buchholz 2013.
17 Edlund 1987; Stek 2009.
18 Scopacasa 2014; Crawford 2011, 1203, no. Teruentum 34.
19 Graham forthcoming.
20 Rohl 2015, 6; see also Edensor 2000; Ingold 2004; Thrift 2004; Phillips 2005; Biehl 2007; Moser and Feldman 2014; Scriven 2014; Knott 2015.

## 32  *Emma-Jayne Graham*

21  See also Scriven 2014, 256–257.
22  For example, Kinnard 2004, xi–xiv.
23  Also Knott 2015, 29.
24  Cato *Orig.* 2; Blagg 1985; Green 2007.
25  Blagg 1985; Green 2007; Ghini and Diosono 2012a.
26  Blagg and MacCormick 1983, 22; Hughes 2016.
27  Blagg and MacCormick 1983, 46–53.
28  Ghini and Diosono 2012a, 271 and 274.
29  Ghini and Diosono 2012a, 272–273 and 275.
30  Diosono, Romagnoli and Batocchioni 2013.
31  Ghini and Diosono 2012b, 130.
32  Ghini and Diosono 2012b, 130; Servius *ad Aen.* 6.136.
33  Stat. *Silv.* 3.1.52-60, trans. D.R. Shackleton Bailey and C.A. Parrott.
34  Prop.2.32.7-10, trans. G.P. Goold.
35  Ov. *Fast.* 3.263–74, trans. J.G. Frazer and G.P. Goold.
36  Green 2007, 3; Ghini and Diosono 2012b, 121.
37  On the crater's microclimate: Green 2007, 6–7.
38  Green 2007, 62; this has also been suggested for pilgrimage sites in other parts of Roman Europe: Kiernan 2012; Grünewald 2017.
39  Graham 2017; forthcoming.
40  For the wider importance of nature in the production of place see Graham 2018.
41  Blagg 1986, 214.
42  For example, Eade and Sallnow 1991; Bowie 2006, 242.
43  Attenni 2013; Attenni et al. 2013; Attenni and Ghini 2014; 2017; Hermans 2016.
44  Attenni and Ghini 2014, 155–157.
45  Attenni 2013, 6.
46  Attenni 2013, 6.
47  Attenni and Ghini 2017, 63; Attenni 2017, 29 reports a total of at least 1500 terracotta votives, but only 1020 of all of the objects from the cave, including both ceramic vessels and terracotta votives, have been studied at the time of writing.
48  Attenni and Ghini 2014, 158, fig. 9.
49  Attenni and Ghini 2014, 156.
50  Attenni 2015; Attenni and Ghini 2017, 66–67.
51  Attenni and Ghini 2014, 157–158.
52  Attenni and Ghini 2014, 158; Attenni 2015, 36; Hermans 2016; Attenni and Ghini 2017, 66.
53  Prop. 4.8.3–14, trans. G.P. Goold.
54  Ael. *NA* 11.16, trans. A.F. Scholfield.
55  See Attenni 2015, 36.
56  Hermans 2016.
57  Attenni and Ghini 2017, 67.
58  See Bremmer 2017, 277–278.

## Bibliography

Attenni, Luca. 2013. "The Pantanacci Votive Deposit: New Archaeological Discoveries." *Etruscan News* 15: 1, 6.
Attenni, Luca. 2015. "New Finds From the Pantanacci Votive Deposit." *Etruscan News* 17: 36.
Attenni, Luca. 2017. "Sacra Nemora." In *Sacra Nemora: La Cultura del Sacro nei Contesti Santuariali in area Albana*, edited by Luca Attenni, 28–29. Mozzecane: Dielle Editore.

## Pilgrimage, mobile behaviours and religious place   33

Attenni, Luca and Giuseppina Ghini. 2014. "La Stipe Votiva in Località Pantanacci (Genzano di Roma-Lanuvio, Roma)." *Lazio e Sabina* 10: 153–161.

Attenni, Luca and Giuseppina Ghini. 2017. "La Stipe Votiva in Località Pantanacci." In *Sacra Nemora: La Cultura del Sacro nei Contesti Santuariali in area Albana*, edited by Luca Attenni, 59–71. Mozzecane: Dielle Editore.

Attenni, Luca, Elena Calandra, Giuseppina Ghini, and Massimo Rossi. 2013. "La stipe votiva di Pantanacci: Per Grazia Ricevuta." *Archeologia Viva* 159: 14–26.

Biehl, Peter F. 2007. "Enclosing Places: A Contextual Approach to Cult and Religion in Neolithic Central Europe." In *Cult in Context: Reconsidering Ritual in Archaeology*, edited by David A. Barrowclough and Caroline Malone, 173–182. Oxford: Oxbow.

Blagg, Thomas F.C. 1985. "Cult Practice and Its Social Context in the Religious Sanctuaries of Latium and Southern Etruria: The Sanctuary of Diana at Nemi." In *Papers in Italian Archaeology IV*, edited by Caroline Malone and Simon Stoddart, 33–50. Oxford: BAR International Series 246.

Blagg, Thomas F.C. 1986. "The Cult and Sanctuary of Diana Nemorensis." In *Pagan Gods and Shrines of the Roman Empire*, edited by Martin Henig and Anthony King, 211–220. Oxford: Oxford University Committee for Archaeology.

Blagg, Thomas F.C. and A.G. MacCormick. 1983. *Mysteries of Diana: The Antiquities from Nemi in Nottingham Museums*. Nottingham: Nottingham Castle Museum.

Bowie, Fiona. 2006. *The Anthropology of Religion*. Malden, MA and Oxford: Blackwell.

Bremmer, Jan N. 2017. "Pilgrimage Progress?" In *Excavating Pilgrimage. Archaeological Approaches to Sacred Travel and Movement in the Ancient World*, edited by Troels Myrup Kristensen and Wiebke Friese, 275–284. London and New York: Routledge.

Buchholz, Laura. 2013. "Identifying the Oracular 'Sortes' of Italy." In *Studies in Ancient Oracles and Divination*, edited by Mika Kajava, 111–144. Rome: Acta Instituti Romani Finlandiae 40.

Coarelli, Filippo. 1987. *I Santuari del Lazio in Età Repubblicana*. Rome: La Nuova Italia Scientifica.

Coleman, Simon and John Eade. 2004. "Introduction: Reframing Pilgrimage." In *Reframing Pilgrimage. Cultures in Motion*, edited by Simon Coleman and John Eade, 1–25. London and New York: Routledge.

Comella, Annamaria. 1981. "Tipologia e diffusione dei complessi votivi in Italia in epoca medio- e tardo-repubblicana." *Mélanges de l'École française de Rome, Antiquité* 93: 717–803.

Crawford, Michael H. 2011. *Imagines Italicae: A Corpus of Italic Inscriptions*. London: Bulletin of the Institute of Classical Studies Supplement 110.

Diosono, Francesca, Laura Romagnoli, and Guido Batocchioni. 2013. "Il ninfeo del santuario di Diana a Nemi. Una proposta di ricostruzione." *Lazio e Sabina* 9: 285–289.

Duffy, Eamon. 2002. "The Dynamics of Pilgrimage in Late Medieval England." In *Pilgrimage: The English Experience from Becket to Bunyan*, edited by Colin Morris and Peter Roberts, 164–177. Cambridge: Cambridge University Press.

Eade, John and Michael J. Sallnow, eds. 1991. *Contesting the Sacred: The Anthropology of Christian Pilgrimage*. London and New York: Routledge.

Edensor, Tim. 2000. "Walking in the British Countryside: Reflexivity, Embodied Practices and Ways to Escape." *Body and Society* 6 (3–4): 81–106.

Edlund, Ingrid E.M. 1987. *The Gods and the Place. Location and Function of Sanctuaries in the Countryside of Etruria and Magna Graecia (700-400 BC)*. Stockholm: Paul Åströms.

## 34 Emma-Jayne Graham

Elsner, Jaś. 2017. "Excavating Pilgrimage." In *Excavating Pilgrimage. Archaeological Approaches to Sacred Travel and Movement in the Ancient World*, edited by Troels Myrup Kristensen and Wiebke Friese, 265–274. London and New York: Routledge.

Elsner, Jaś and Ian Rutherford. 2005. "Introduction." In *Pilgrimage in Graeco-Roman and Early Christian Antiquity: Seeing the Gods*, edited by Jaś Elsner and Ian Rutherford, 1–38. Oxford: Oxford University Press.

Flemming, Rebecca. 2016. "Anatomical Votives: Popular Medicine in Republican Italy?" In *Popular Medicine in Graeco-Roman Antiquity: Explorations*, edited by William V. Harris, 105–125. Leiden and Boston: Brill.

Frazer, James G. 1890. *The Golden Bough: A Study in Comparative Religion*. London: Macmillan and Co.

Friese, Wiebke and Troels Myrup Kristensen. 2017. "Archaeologies of Pilgrimage." In *Excavating Pilgrimage. Archaeological Approaches to Sacred Travel and Movement in the Ancient World*, edited by Troels Myrup Kristensen and Wiebke Friese, 1–10. London and New York: Routledge.

Ghini, Giuseppina and Francesca Diosono. 2012a. "Il Tempio di Diana a Nemi: una rilettura alla luce dei recenti scavi." *Lazio e Sabina* 8: 269–276.

Ghini, Giuseppina and Francesca Diosono. 2012b. "Il santuario di Diana a Nemi: recenti acquisizioni dai nuovi scavi." *Ostraka: Rivista di Antichità, Volume Speciale* 2012: 119–137.

Graham, Emma-Jayne. 2017. "Mobility Impairment in the Sanctuaries of Early Roman Italy." In *Disability in Antiquity*, edited by Christian Laes, 248–266. London and New York: Routledge.

Graham, Emma-Jayne. 2018. "'There Buds the Laurel': Nature, Temporality and the Making of Place in the Cemeteries of Roman Italy." *Theoretical Roman Archaeology Journal* 1: 3.

Graham, Emma-Jayne. Forthcoming. "Mobility, Kinaesthesia, Imagined Movement and the Making of Place in the Sanctuaries of Ancient Italy." In *Archaeology of Ritual in the Ancient Mediterranean: Recent Finds and Interpretative Approaches*, edited by Erica Angliker and Michael A. Fowler. Paris: Éditions De Boccard.

Graham, Emma-Jayne and Jane Draycott. 2017. "Debating the Anatomical Votive." In *Bodies of Evidence: Ancient Anatomical Votives Past, Present and Future*, edited by Jane Draycott and Emma-Jayne Graham, 1–19. London and New York: Routledge.

Green, Carin M.C. 2007. *Roman Religion and the Cult of Diana at Aricia*. Cambridge: Cambridge University Press.

Grünewald, Martin. 2017. "Roman Healing Pilgrimage North of the Alps." In *Excavating Pilgrimage. Archaeological Approaches to Sacred Travel and Movement in the Ancient World*, edited by Troels Myrup Kristensen and Wiebke Friese, 130–151. London and New York: Routledge.

Hermans, Rianne. 2016. "Juno Sospita and the *draco*: Myth, Image, and Ritual in the Landscape of the Alban Hills." In *Valuing Landscape in Classical Antiquity: Natural Environment and Cultural Imagination*, edited by Jeremy McInerney and Ineke Sluiter, 196–227. Leiden: Brill.

Holloway, Julian. 2003. "Make-Believe: Spiritual Practice, Embodiment, and Sacred Space." *Environment and Planning A* 35 (4): 1961–1974.

Howes, David. 2005. "Introduction: Empires of the Senses." In *Empire of the Senses: The Sensual Cultural Reader*, edited by David Howes, 1–17. Oxford: Berg.

Hughes, Jessica. 2016. "Fractured Narratives: Writing the Biography of a Votive Offering." In *Ex Voto: Votive Giving Across Cultures*, edited by Ittai Weinryb, 23–48. Chicago: University of Chicago Press.

## Pilgrimage, mobile behaviours and religious place 35

Hughes, Jessica. 2017. *Votive Body Parts in Greek and Roman Religion*. Cambridge: Cambridge University Press.

Ingold, Tim. 2004. "Culture on the Ground: The World Perceived Through the Feet." *Journal of Material Culture* 9 (3): 315–340.

Kiernan, Philip. 2012. "Pagan Pilgrimage in Rome's Western Provinces." *HEROM* 1: 79–106.

Kinnard, Jacob N. 2014. *Places in Motion: The Fluid Identities of Temples, Images, and Pilgrims*. Oxford: Oxford University Press.

Knott, Kim. 2005. *The Location of Religion: A Spatial Analysis*. London and New York: Routledge.

Kristensen, Troels Myrup. 2012. "The Material Culture of Roman and Early Christian Pilgrimage: An Introduction." *HEROM* 1: 67–78.

Kristensen, Troels Myrup and Wiebke Friese, eds. 2017. *Excavating Pilgrimage. Archaeological Approaches to Sacred Travel and Movement in the Ancient World*. London and New York: Routledge.

Luginbühl, Thierry. 2015. "Ritual Activities, Processions and Pilgrimages." In *A Companion to the Archaeology of Religion in the Ancient World*, edited by Rubina Raja and Jörg Rüpke, 41–59. Malden, MA and Oxford: Wiley Blackwell.

McCorriston, Joy. 2011. *Pilgrimage and Household in the Ancient Near East*. Cambridge: Cambridge University Press.

McCorriston, Joy. 2017. "Inter-Cultural Pilgrimage, Identity, and the Axial Age in the Ancient Near East." In *Excavating Pilgrimage. Archaeological Approaches to Sacred Travel and Movement in the Ancient World*, edited by Troels Myrup Kristensen and Wiebke Friese, 11–27. London and New York: Routledge.

McGuire, Meredith B. 2008. *Lived Religion: Faith and Practice in Everyday Life*. Oxford: Oxford University Press.

Morinis, Alan. 1992. "Introduction: The Territory of the Anthropology of Pilgrimage." In *Sacred Journeys. The Anthropology of Pilgrimage*, edited by Alan Morinis, 1–28. Westport, CT and London: Greenwood Press.

Moser, Claudia and Cecelia Feldman. 2014. "Introduction." In *Locating the Sacred. Theoretical Approaches to the Emplacement of Religion*, edited by Claudia Moser and Cecelia Feldman, 1–12. Oxford: Oxbow.

Phillips, Andrea. 2005. "Cultural Geographies in Practice: Walking and Looking." *Cultural Geographies* 12: 507–513.

Propertius. 1990. *Elegies*, edited and translated by George Patrick Goold. Loeb Classical Library 18. Cambridge, MA: Harvard University Press.

Recke, Matthias. 2013. "Science as Art: Etruscan Anatomical Votives." In *The Etruscan World*, edited by Jean M. Turfa, 1068–1085. London and New York: Routledge.

Rohl, Darrell J. 2015. "Place Theory, Genealogy, and the Cultural Biography of Roman Monuments." In *TRAC 2014. Proceedings of the Twenty-Fourth Theoretical Roman Archaeology Conference, Reading 2014*, edited by Tom Brindle, Martyn Allen, Emma Durham, and Alex Smith, 1–16. Oxford: Oxbow.

Rountree, Kathryn. 2006. "Performing the Divine: Neo-Pagan Pilgrimages and Embodiment at Sacred Sites." *Body and Society* 12 (4): 95–115.

Rüpke, Jörg. 2016. *On Roman Religion: Lived Religion and the Individual in Ancient Rome*. Ithaca, NY: Cornell University Press.

Rutherford, Ian. 2012. "Pilgrimage." In *The Encyclopedia of Ancient History*, edited by Roger S. Bagnall, Kai Brodersen, Craige B. Champion, Andrew Erskine, and Sabine R. Huebner, 5325–5327. Malden, MA and Oxford: Wiley-Blackwell.

Rutherford, Ian. 2013. *State Pilgrims and Sacred Observers in Ancient Greece: A Study of Theōriā and Theōroi*. Cambridge: Cambridge University Press.

## 36 Emma-Jayne Graham

Scopacasa, Rafael. 2014. "Building Communities in Ancient Samnium: Cult, Ethnicity and Nested Identities." *Oxford Journal of Archaeology* 33 (1): 69–87.

Scriven, Richard. 2014. "Geographies of Pilgrimage: Meaningful Movements and Embodied Mobilities." *Geography Compass* 8 (4): 249–261.

Slavin, Sean. 2003. "Walking as Spiritual Practice: The Pilgrimage to Santiago de Compostela." *Body and Society* 9 (3): 1–18.

Stavrianopoulou, Eftychia. 2015. "The Archaeology of Processions." In *A Companion to the Archaeology of Religion in the Ancient World*, edited by Rubina Raja and Jörg Rüpke, 349–361. Malden, MA and Oxford: Wiley Blackwell.

Stek, Tesse D. 2009. *Cult Places and Cultural Change in Republican Italy*. Amsterdam: Amsterdam University Press.

Stevens, Saskia. 2017. "Visiting the Ancestors: Ritual Movement in Rome's Urban Borderland." In *Excavating Pilgrimage. Archaeological Approaches to Sacred Travel and Movement in the Ancient World*, edited by Troels Myrup Kristensen and Wiebke Friese, 152–165. London and New York: Routledge.

Thrift, Nigel. 2004. "Intensities of Feeling: Towards a Spatial Politics of Affect." *Geografiska Annaler* 86B (1): 57–78.

Turner, Victor. 1974. *Dramas, Fields and Metaphors*. Ithaca, NY: Cornell University Press.

Urry, John. 2002. "Mobility and Proximity." *Sociology* 36 (2): 255–274.

# 3 The meaning of roads

## A reinterpretation of the Roman Empire

*Ray Laurence*

## Introduction

Travel, the movement of goods over land, and the physical remains of Roman roads tend to be areas of research that sit by themselves; or are subject to a level of serial misinterpretation of the significance of land transport.[1] Helmuth Schneider locates the intersection between land transport and shipping, pointing to the observation made by Strabo that Rome's roads were constructed for the transport of entire shiploads by cart.[2] Another Greek commentator, Dionysius of Halicarnassus commented that the greatness of Rome's empire was encapsulated in the aqueducts, paved roads, and sewers – not least because of the magnitude of the cost of their creation.[3] This chapter is less concerned with economics and instead takes a different view focussed on travel as an experience that brought individuals into contact with the agency of the Roman state. This form of contact included the power of the state over travellers – as seen through the collection of customs dues.[4] I have dwelt on this topic before with reference to Roman Italy and argued that the establishment of roads created a new space-time geography that reshaped the physical geography of Italy.[5] This paper does not re-hash the arguments of more than twenty years ago, but seeks to move forward to draw on what has now become established as a series of spatial turns that focus on territory, place, networks and scale as key phenomena to be analysed. The case studies utilised in this chapter will allow us to explore how these four phenomena may help us to explain the structuration of space-time within the Roman Empire.

Territory may be considered to apply to area, specifically that of provinces and individual cities. In contrast, place appears on the[6] roads that formed a network criss-crossing the empire. Scale can refer to the differentiation between a territory of a city and that of a province and, finally, the territory of the empire. There is a similar differentiation in terms of scale between the largest city and the smallest *mansio* (inn) at which a traveller changed equids or stayed the night.[7] These four phenomena have been recently explored in connection with the analysis of mobility in the city of Rome and can be read in conjunction with this chapter to draw out the relationship between Rome's: *urbs* and its *orbis*.[8] This chapter seeks to avoid an abstract discussion of these terms and, instead, places the traveller at the centre of our attention by focussing on the representations of space that could be seen on

## 38   *Ray Laurence*

a journey: the milestones with their inscriptions and the images of travel found on coins; and spatial practices associated with the use of *mansiones*, the collection of tolls, and the crossing of rivers. Yet, the road's simplicity as a linear form, or as Pietro Janni describes it, as *spazio odologico*, brings it into contact with these other forms of space.[9] The road might be described as the spatial strategy of the Roman state that made sense of local territories, networked places, and existed at a larger scale than other geographical forms; whilst at the same time resisting the abstraction of space into the format of a map.[10] Indeed, maps, and, for that matter, textual representations of geography were composed of roads and coasts embedding the Roman state's spatial strategy in the creation of global visions.

Roads as a linear space would seem to have little in common with the study of place, yet, we will find that roads like places (*loci*) within the city were named as *celeberrimus*. In cities such places were defined by movement and it would seem to be the aspect of motion – alongside a sense of spatial aesthetics that was rectilinear and featured monuments and statues that pointed out the naming of places. Thus, also roads, often enhanced with inscriptions, created a more enduring memory. The consolidation of meaning with the implication that these spaces – roads and places – had greater longevity over time through the Roman period and into the Middle Ages.[11] Our focus will be on the provinces rather than Italy,[12] and will also assume knowledge of literary texts relating to travel.[13] Thus, I am seeking to extend the range of the evidence often used in the discussion of Roman roads and also the geographical range of discussion to include a wider *orbis* and to resist studies of single geographical territories (i.e. a single province such as Britannia or region such as Iberia). The chapter also has a focus on how the road, as a linear structure, connected the local to the global.[14] In so doing, I wish to allow Roman historians to view Roman roads as a key spatial strategy and at the same time allow historians of later periods to look in on the Roman Empire and to consider how the structure of mobility was adjusted to new political and social situations associated with the development of kingship and Christianity.

### Roads and Roman power: A geography of Empire

By 27 BCE, the roads of Italy were identified as *celeberrimus* (famous) and identified as such on the Arch of Augustus in Rimini.[15] These famous roads had existed for more than 300 years with most of the major routes being over 100 years old.[16] The roads provided Italy with a land-based geography and have shaped the peninsula's settlement pattern.[17] As Claude Nicolet has shown, these roads structured the pattern of Strabo's account of Italy's geography.[18] Certainly, the named roads found in the Antonine Itineraries or the Peutinger Table were defined in terms of their position with respect to the towns along their route that can also be traced to earlier sources, such as the so-called Elogium of Polla.[19] The roads were spatially defined structures with a fixed width of eight Roman feet with curved sections of sixteen feet from as early as the laws known as the Twelve Tables of c.450 BCE.[20]

However, Richard Talbert has recently cautioned against seeing this as an integrated system – due perhaps to a lack of standardisation or an ability to identify a road policy or branch of government in our sources.[21] This runs counter to recent uses of algorithms to analyse the network of towns featured in the Antonine Itineraries that demonstrate a clustered form of urban network present in that text.[22] These two very different perspectives, in all probability, reflect the fact that there is no literary text to tell us what the Romans did or considered their policy on roads to be. Such an argument from silence arises for the simple fact that the Roman Empire was not a centralised state in the manner of the modern Nation State, and instead distributed power to political, military, and geographical units: legions, provinces, cities, and, I would add also roads.[23]

The conception of the relation of roads to geography is underpinned by the mobility paradigm formulated by the late John Urry, in which he suggested that the nature of mobility is a cultural feature worthy of explanation and can be seen as a defining feature of any society.[24] Thus, my focus in this paper is with mobility and to examine how mobility or the facilitation of mobility may allow us to understand the Roman Empire as a state in a quite different way: to extend the observation of the intersection of power of Rome/its emperor and road building,[25] and to fill the spatial gap or simple omission of mobility from the discussion of the ancient state.[26]

## The state as a distributed network of power

Much has been written about the *cursus publicus*,[27] and we will not be here dwelling on the mechanics of that system, but instead seek to examine it as a means to understand the relationship between mobility and the state. At the outset, it is important to realise that there is a fracture between the system of *vehiculatio* established by Augustus to transport people and the *cursus publicus* that emerges in the third century to transport goods and people.[28] We will only be dealing with the *vehiculatio* in this chapter. Augustus, initially, established a relay system of men stationed at intervals along the roads that proved in some way unsatisfactory and was replaced by a network of roadside stations to make provisions for travellers.[29] The discovery of inscriptions referring to the regulation of abuses of the system provide us with an understanding of the role of the state in relation to the use of these minor roadside settlements.

The first text, published by Stephen Mitchell in 1976, is an edict of the governor of Galatia – Sex. Sotidius Strabo Libuscidianus – in the reign of the Tiberius. This edict regulates who might use the *mansio*: the legate and members of his staff, military personnel from other provinces, and slaves and freedmen of the emperor. Effectively, the *mansio* was for the use of those who held power or were agents of the state: the governor with his staff, the military, and imperial slaves and former slaves. The inscription also defines who might be provided with mules or donkeys and wagons at a fixed price: the imperial procurator and his son, military personnel with a diploma, senators, *equites* on imperial service, and centurions on military service. Every type of personnel mentioned were effectively agents of the state and, thus, needed to be mobile to enforce the will of the state. What the *mansio* provided was accommodation and transport for the state for what Mitchell suggests was for a distance of fifty-five kilometres from Sagalassos to Cormasa.[30]

40   *Ray Laurence*

The abuse of the system by soldiers is also found in an inscription recording an edict of Hadrian that reveals another aspect of the role of roads: no soldier had the right to a guide, because the soldiers did not need to leave the public road.[31] Thus, the road was seen as a known route-way and one that could have been followed with no difficulty (unless there was snow, when a guide was permitted). The inscription also alludes to what goods might be transported by these soldiers: money, prisoners, and wild beasts. It addresses a specific set of abuses, rather than setting out the full regulation of the use of *mansiones*. Hence, a public road was constituted by the road itself and the stopping places. Both the road and the *mansiones* were regulated by edicts of governors and emperors to ensure that transport was facilitated for agents of the state, without the exploitation of the locals providing the resources to enable their transport to carry out the state's will.[32]

The mobility of military personnel tends to be underplayed in favour of viewing the archaeology of forts as the places of the military.[33] However, as Hadrian made clear in his address to the legion at Lambaesis, soldiers were frequently assigned to *stationes* across the province of Africa.[34] Nelis-Clément suggests that the stationing of the military along the route-ways of Italy and the provinces from the time of Augustus formed 'micro-cells' or 'antennae of power' that mediated the power of the emperor at a local level.[35] The publication of the excavation of a *statio* at Obernburg am Main provided further information for our understanding of the use of these local military outposts. The building, as published by the excavators, was in the form of a Mediterranean style courtyard house (47 m by 27 m) located on a road leading to a major fort. To the rear of this structure, 160 altars were found, each one dedicated to the god/genius of the place in January or July, dating from 144–224 CE.[36] The density of inscriptions, although only partially published, suggests that the military personnel – *beneficiarii* – moved from *statio to statio* every six months. Another *statio* of the *beneficiarii* has been excavated at Sirmium, again associated with a series of dedicatory altars, dating from 157–231 CE.[37] The full corpus of evidence has been published, as far as is possible, by Nelis-Clément, and shows the ubiquity of the *beneficiarii* across all parts of the Roman Empire.[38] Placing these *stationes* into sharper focus, allows us to view the roads of the state as much more than functional infrastructure into a means by which state power was delivered at a local level, even stretching into the highest reaches of the Alps to between 2,200 and 2,400 metres above sea level.[39] Indeed, it has been shown recently that the *stationes* was a key feature of state power and we might expect all travellers on the roads to experience contact with the military.[40]

## Roads and territory

Milestones defined the route of a road and marked it as a written space that was linear in form, but subdivided into miles and marked by milestones.[41] The building of the Via Nova from the boundary of Syria to the Red Sea by Trajan resulted in the erection of numerous milestones that make clear the action as *redacta in formam provinciae Arabiae viam novam a finibus Syriae usque ad mare rubrum*

*The meaning of roads*   41

*aperuit et stravit.*[42] The road, in fact, followed the Nabatean King's Highway.[43] The milestones mark the road, not as a restoration but new and paved – even though it overlies or over-writes an existing caravan route.[44] They also make it very clear that the form of the province as a territory was connected to the building of the new road, and it is worth remembering that the milestones appear at the same time as the first Arabia coins are issued.[45] Effectively, Rome over-wrote the previous culture through issuing new coins and ensuring the main route/s through the province were clearly marked with milestones and new paving. This was not a new phenomenon, when Rome took over the Attalid kingdom, in the second century BCE, Manlius Aquillius over-wrote the existing road network with a series of bilingual Latin and Greek milestones that specifically referred to the restoration of the roads.[46]

The conception of territory in the definition of Arabia was *from* the boundary of Syria to the Red Sea; in other words, from a known point to a lesser-known point. Other milestones express the conception of boundaries differently with the boundary of a province as the destination. For example, the restoration of a road from Carthage in 237 CE was described as to the *Fines Numidiae.*[47] It was the road that took you from Carthage to the edge of the governor's jurisdiction – across the boundary lay a description of space on the milestones with reference to points within the province of Numidia. This format from the major city of Carthage to an edge of a territory should be seen as a hierarchical description of space, wherever you were on the road: the milestones informed you consistently that you were between Carthage – a city – and the edge of Numidia. The road was represented to take you right across the province – the cities or places along its route are simply not mentioned. There is, however, an ideological point being made in these inscriptions that also state that the road had *longa incuria corruptam adque dilapsam* suggesting that: the renewal of the road was an act of good government and fitted into the imperial theme of roads being of benefit to the people of the empire.[48] Travel had been made possible, whereas previously it had been difficult and arduous.

In the *Itinerarium Burdigalense*, the crossing into another province is noted by *inde incipiunt Alpes Cottiae, inde incipit Italiae* or by the crossing of mountains *inde ascenditur Gaura mons* or *inde surgunt Alpes Iuliae*, but also included *fines Italiae et Norci* and *fines Pannoniae et Misiae*, and *fines Daciae et Traciae* and *finis Apuliae et Campanae.*[49] Journeys across such boundaries were associated with the paying of customs duties. It is not our concern here to discuss the historical development of customs duties or the detailed record keeping at these places.[50] Instead, I wish to set out how the levying of customs duties created a series of places – *stationes* for that purpose and set out the relationship between road construction and the levying of customs duties. Within the Antonine Itineraries, the place name associated with a stopping point *Fines* or *Ad Fines* on the boundaries – sometimes specifically associated with a *mansio* or a *mutatio.*[51] The *fines* of a province were clearly boundaries at which customs could be exacted, according to the Customs' Law of Asia, and to be provisioned with a building for this purpose no more than thirty feet by thirty feet.[52] This text also points to the exaction

42    *Ray Laurence*

of customs at the port of a city and at the boundaries of a city.[53] Such a system of taxation can also be found elsewhere, the appearance of the Vicarello goblets that record a journey from Cadiz to Rome of a place name *Ad Fines* has been identified as the abbreviation for the *statio ad Fines Cottii* and the collection of the tax on goods known as the *Quadragesima Galliarum* at 2.5%.[54] Epigraphy associated with the *Quadragesima Galliarum* indicates the presence of a procurator and staff that included *tabularii*, a *vilicus* and *vernae* at individual *stationes*.[55] Just as the *stationes* of the *beneficarii* included the dedication of altars to Jupiter or to the genius of the *statio* as a place, we can identify at the *stationes* of the 'XXXX' (*Quadragesima*): altars dedicated to Jupiter Optimus Maximus.[56] What we see is an overall pattern of *stationes* of the *Quadragesima Galliarum* found in ports, on key mountain routes and also in Rome.[57] We might also assume a level of movement of the customs dues collected to the central *statio* in Rome. Peter Bang has set out the transaction costs of transporting goods in relation to the payment of customs duties and suggests that travellers could have been subjected to abuse at the *statio*, where they paid their dues.[58] To circumvent over-charging, at Zarai (Algeria), we find an inscription dated to 202 CE that sets out the charges for slaves, horses, mules, (a denarius and a quinarius each), donkeys, and oxen (a quinarius each), plus various charges for pigs, piglets, sheep, goats, and lambs.[59] There were also listed charges for items of clothing, shoes, sponge, amphorae containing wine and garum, figs, as well as various minerals such as alum.[60] Thus, connection between road-building to a boundary of another province reflects the governance of a territory (province), and the segmentation of travel by the boundaries of provinces that was a feature of travel and also enabled the collection of tax in the form of custom dues from travellers.

## Janus, coins, and bridges in the provinces

Bridges were an integral part of the construction of Roman roads, both for their utility and an aesthetic beauty of form. This is seen most clearly in Plutarch's discussion of Gaius Gracchus' road building in the second century BCE. The roads were straight and paved with quarried stone, but importantly ravines were bridged over 'and both sides of the roads were of equal and corresponding height, so that the work had everywhere an even and beautiful appearance'.[61] This created the bridges as a crucial element of road construction that is also found both in inscriptions associated with the road stating that both the road and the bridges were constructed, and also on Augustan coinage that should be seen in the context of the creation of new towns, provincial boundaries, and places associated with the terminus of a road. The coinage of Octavian/Augustus issued coins with the legend: *QUOD VIAE MUN SUNT*.[62] The imagery features either a bridge with a 'triumphal' arch at its centre or 'triumphal' arches at either end of the bridge. This coin issue is connected to the much earlier restoration by Augustus of the Via Flaminia from the Mulvian Bridge (Rome) to Rimini, where an arch commemorated this action, dating it to 27 BCE with archaeological evidence that the road was raised by c. 1.1 metres.[63] A similar legend to that found on the Spanish coinage minted by L. Vinicius, which is dated to 17–16 BCE, includes the image of an inscribed *cippus* with an inscription acknowledging Augustus' role in road construction: *S(enatus) P(opulus)q(ue) R(omanus) Imp(eratori) Cae(sari) quod v(iae) m(unitae) s(unt) ex ea p(ecunia) q(uam) is ad a(erarium) de(lata est).*[64] What is different about the Spanish examples is that they all show a bridge with an arch at its centre or with arches at either side. The coinage with the legend *QUOD VIAE MUN SUNT* should be viewed less in the context of the Augustan restoration of the Via Flaminia and much more in the context of the building of roads generally. The first coins with this legend were struck before the restoration of the road and issues continued through to 2 BCE. The imagery shifts from a 'triumphal' arch on the centre of the bridge with Octavian/Augustus in a chariot drawn by elephants to first, the same imagery with horses drawing the chariot to the final version that shows a bridge with a 'triumphal' arch on either side. The imagery was utilised by mints in Italy, Rome, Spain, and Lugdunum with a certain consistency and dating that makes it difficult to attribute to any particular episode of road building. Thus, this is the means to represent road building as an action undertaken on a grand scale by Augustus. The important features for our discussion are that the act of road building was represented by a bridge and a 'triumphal' arch.

The linkage between the combination of an arch and a bridge on the coins and roads needs further investigation. Robert Etienne draws attention to milestones in Spain that include the mention of an arch marking the end of the Via Augusta at the Baetis River that focusses attention on the river and a Janus Augustus as a terminus for the Via Augusta built in 2 BCE.[65] Later milestones of Domitian refer to this point as having an arch and being at the beginning of Baetica.[66] Etienne connects this arch to the coinage of Mérida featuring a gateway that would have faced the surviving bridge that crosses the Guidana River, utilising sixty-two arches with a length of 755 metres.[67] The coin image has much in common with the arch constructed in front of the gate of Rimini to commemorate Augustus' restoration of that road in 27 BCE.[68] The images on these coins are featured above the representation of the arch, a crescent-shaped structure that has parallels with the representation of bridges on coins.[69] It is worth noting that the coinage issued by the new colony of Mérida, founded in 25 BCE, shows a direct connection to a spitting river goddess.[70]

The use of the words Janus Augustus needs some further commentary in relation to the *Tabula Siarensis* that included the establishment of a Janus to honour Germanicus in the Circus Flaminius and two others: one on the banks of the Rhine and another in the grove of Mount Amanus in Syria – on the border with Cilicia.[71] These arches recognised his achievements, but also included (or perhaps better contained) images of the peoples conquered by him.[72] Their placement at boundaries, particularly on the Rhine, next to the tomb of Drusus, was a place of veneration for the Gallic provincials. The arches marked both the creation of boundaries and the organisation of the territory within the provinces by Germanicus, whilst also containing representations of the people conquered (or protected) by Rome.[73] It is worth remembering that it was Janus in Ovid's *Fasti*, a work re-dedicated

44    *Ray Laurence*

to Germanicus, who announced the year as auspicious to commanders to ensure earth and sea enjoy peace and freedom.[74]

This information may allow us to view the Janus Augustus on the border of Baetica in a similar light: it was a point of transition similar to the arch of Augustus at Rimini that included images of both land and sea gods (Jupiter, Neptune, Apollo, and Minerva) located at the entrance to a city, the end of a road, as well as close to the boundary of the Rubicon.[75] Rivers gave shape to the Roman Empire and the conception of space. Indeed, Evan Haley has suggested that the Janus of Augustus on the Baetis River should be connected to L. Domitius Ahenobarbus' erection of an altar in the same year (2 BCE) on the banks of the Elbe, that also coincides with the year in which Augustus completed the work on Agrippa's map in the Porticus Vipsania.[76] These two examples show the intersection between rivers and roads, but also an intersection between territory (represented as an area) and the dominant mode of spatial representation based around an itinerary through space. Richard Talbert has suggested that this was a conception of space developed in the Augustan period and was characterised by the definition of provinces and 'a web of mainland routes'.[77] Later such boundaries, as they appear in the *Itinerarium Burdigalense,* subdivided a listing of unfamiliar stopping places.[78] One of these boundaries between provinces was associated with bridges in the *Itinerarium Burdigalense* (for example at 561.5 *transis pontem, intras Pannoniam*) and utilised not the third person but the second person to provide a more immediate conception of the journey: you cross the bridge, you enter Pannonia.[79] The mention of the bridge as well as the boundary is unique in this text, but we do find numerous places mentioned for changing equids on the route associated with bridges: *mutatio Ponte Aureoli*; *mutatio Ponte Ucasi*; *mutatio Ponte Campano* and *mutatio Ponte Secies*.[80] These stopping points associated with bridges marked by the action of crossing a river were included within a new Christian form of travel or pilgrimage. The crossing of rivers, the start of journeys or stages of journeys and the marking of boundaries were all associated with the god Janus – as seen in our discussion above of the establishment of an arch or Janus at the boundary of Baetica.[81] The dropping or throwing of coins and/or artefacts into rivers from bridges would seem to have been a feature of their existence.[82] It is worth adding here that roads were constructed from a river and/or to a river: *viam Aemiliam ab Arimino ad flumen Trebiam*;[83] *viam Julia Augusta a flumine Trebia*;[84] *viam Claudiam novam a Forulis ad confluentis Atternum et Tirinum*;[85] *viam ad Bathinum flumen*;[86] *ab Atrante ad flumen Savum*;[87] *ab Aquileia ad Titium flumen*;[88] *ab Altino ad flumen Danuvium*;[89] and *viam Claudiam Augustan...munit a flumine Pado ad flumen Danuvium*.[90] Presumably, the named river marked the end of the road, because there was not a recognised town at that point or the river was seen as a stopping point with its own deity. At Lugdunum, an altar and a temple to Rome set up *ad confluentes Araris et Rhodoni*.[91] Perhaps, it is also worth remembering that travellers paid customs dues at bridges to cross rivers. As we find in a Jewish critique of Rome from the second century CE, bridges became places to levy tolls: 'Everything they have made they have made for themselves: market-places – for whores; baths – to wallow in; bridges – to levy tolls'.[92]

The place name found in (552.9) between Arles and Nimes was listed as *mutatio Ponte Aerarium* (stopping place of the bridge of the treasury). Other places were listed as just *Ad Pontes/Pontem* or *Pontibus* in the Antonine Itineraries.[93] Other names are more elaborate and reveal the development of settlements associated with a bridge, such as *Ponte Zita municipium* and we find others such as *Ponte Aufidi, Ponte Aeni, Ponte Mansuetiana, Ponte Longo, Ponte Sarvix, Pontes Caldis and Ponte Neviae*.[94] All of these suggest travel and the presence of a bridge created a name for a settlement or at the least a place at which to stay or change equids. The ability to travel through a geography shaped by rivers was enabled by the construction of bridges, which involved the assertion of imperial power over the personification of a river.[95]

## The Viae Domitiana and Traiana: Roads, bridges and arches in Italy

The examples of bridges, roads, and arches discussed so far have been derived from coins and inscriptions resulting in a discussion at a macro-level. It is now necessary to turn to Italy and consider rather more detailed information about the configuration of an arch, a road and a bridge, or bridges. Statius, in his road-building poem, has the Volturnus River speak of Domitian's new road with its bridge that included the definition of the banks and confines of the river.[96] The entry point to this new road was an *arcus* in marble commemorating Domitian's victories.[97] Statius (*Silv.*4.3) identifies the arch as being located at the *Ianua* (doorway) and at the *limen* (sacred threshold) of the road – thus, utilising the language associated with the Roman house.[98] If we were to see this *arcus* through the lens of the earlier language as a *Ianus*, drawing on Jason Banta's linkage between Janus and agriculture, we might regard the arch as marking the start, both in time and space, of not just the road but the bringing of agriculture to the region – including the river valley of Volturnus.[99] This broadens the landscape of travel – the road – to include its geographical area as well; exemplified earlier in the marking of the end of the Via Augusta with an *Ianus* at the boundary of Baetica and Lusitania. That *Ianus* marked the start of a new provincial landscape that had been reconquered by Augustus and resulted in the closing of the doors of the temple of Janus in Rome in 25 BCE and the foundation of the colony at Mérida.[100] The local *Ianus* also stood before a bridge that tamed a spitting river goddess found on the coins of the local colony at Mérida.[101] It is also worth contemplating the imagery of ploughing the *pomerium* found on these local coins that connects Mérida in 25 BCE to both the foundation of Rome and also to the worship of Janus in the Roman calendar of Ovid's *Fasti*, which includes a presence for Janus at the ploughing of Rome's *pomerium* by Romulus/Quirinus.[102]

The interconnection of these features is also found on the Arch of Benevento marking the beginning of the Via Traiana (set-up between 109 and 114 CE) and includes the military achievements of Trajan in ensuring peace through warfare.[103] The scenes on the arch include a plough and children – a clear reference to town foundation and the rearing of children to become future soldiers.[104] Often the

46   *Ray Laurence*

images on the arch have been divided as facing the town of Benevento and facing the countryside; however, Michael Spiedel suggests what is represented is the life course of the military – if read together – from childhood through to recruitment and, then, to discharge and old age.[105] The arch marked an entry/exit point onto the landscape of the new Via Traiana – in the same way as the arch at the beginning of Statius' Via Domitiana. The landscape of the traveller was marked by new milestones and new bridges to create an engineered space similar to that represented by Plutarch (*CG* 7) with the milestones informing the traveller Trajan had built the road *VIAM A BENEVENTO BRUNDISIUM,* and inscriptions on bridges *VIAM ET PONTES A BENEVENTO BRUNDISIUM.*[106] A traveller covering the twenty-one Roman miles from Beneventum to the first stopping point in the Antonine Itineraries (Equum Tuticum) would have crossed nine bridges,[107] whilst being able to read off each mile that they travelled.[108] This created the road as a written space that was made by Trajan from which travellers could measure off the stages of their journey – as represented in the Antonine Itineraries – with each stopping place being represented by its own local epigraphic culture.[109] The Via Traiana provides us with the closest physical manifestation of the landscape of a road depicted by Statius in the *Silvae.*

Trajanic coinage has references as Augustus' did to road building. The issue of coinage with the legend *VIA TRAIANA* with the representation of a reclining goddess holding a wheel and a whip was an innovation by the mint in Rome that sits alongside others, such as that related to the *ALIMENTA* and to the *ANNONA* in relation to the themes of the restoration of Italy.[110] The mint also issued a coin depicting Trajan as a priest ploughing a *pomerium* that reminds us of the Augustan coinage of Mérida.[111] It is more difficult to locate an *Ianus* or triumphal arch to match that of the arch at Beneventum. The issue that shows an arch or *Ianus* was clearly labelled *FORUM TRAIAN* that includes a single doorway at its centre, a *quadriga,* and triumphal imagery.[112] This is clearly an entrance to and from the Forum of Trajan in Rome, but may have much in common with the *Ianus* set up in the Circus Flaminius on Germanicus' death. There is also an issue from 100 CE that represents a much clearer triumphal arch,[113] and we even find the representation of a covered bridge.[114] The imagery is there, but is much less explicit than the Augustan examples from Spain and is somewhat submerged by other imagery of the *ANNONA, ALIMENTA* and so on. The Trajanic Arch at Beneventum, though, provides the clearest example of the placement of an arch at the start of a new road (i.e. the point from which distance would have been measured and recorded on the milestones), which displayed images of the emperor's victories, his help for his people, and relations with the gods.[115]

To look beyond Italy to another Trajanic example of an arch marking the beginning/end of a journey or section of a journey, travellers to Britain, landing at Richborough, were greeted by a monumental arch, dated by coins to the late Flavian period, but completed under Trajan.[116] A road paved in tufa was built to enable the construction to take place.[117] The result was a *quadrifons* arch clad in Luni marble with bronze statuary. The foundations of this structure were about nine metres in depth with the *quadrifons* gateway or *Ianus* rising to twenty-six metres in height.[118] It was inscribed and had bronze letters incorporated into some of the inscriptions with the bronze sculptural fragments suggesting that the subject matter was the emperor Trajan.[119] For Strong, this was a classic territorial arch similar to others on the Macedonian-Illyricum border at Ossigi and Bara or in Cilicia, but was also similar to the arch of Trajan at his newly constructed harbour at Ancona.[120] From Richborough, the Antonine Itineraries pointed the traveller in the direction of London along Watling Street that has been found in places to have been paved in polygonally cut Kentish Ragstone.[121] This monument at Richborough expressed a conception of geography that can be found elsewhere in the empire – even across the Ocean – a *Ianus* could have marked the beginning of a journey and a concept of mobility that was familiar: marked by milestones, associated with bridges; in other words, a mobility that was similar to everywhere else in the empire.[122] As we have seen already, above, end points of roads could be the Ocean (as in Cadiz) or might be the Red Sea (as in Arabia) and Richborough fits this pattern as a place on the Ocean. It is worth suggesting though that the setting up of an arch (or an *Ianus*) would have been connected to the ability of Trajan to organise or re-organise the provincial space of Britain.[123] For those leaving Britain, the arch marked their arrival at the Ocean and at the end of their journey by road.

Our discussion has returned us to Janus and we need to understand the relationship of the traveller to a *Janus* (or an *arcus*), which still needs to be connected to the action of travel. Robert Turcan has presented the evidence for the addition under Augustus to Janus of the cognomen Quirinus.[124] Ovid's Janus at the beginning of the *Fasti* is one that opens a year, but also holds in his hands the well-being of senators and the *populus* – thus all Romans whether located in Rome or with Ovid in exile.[125] As the god of doors, not surprisingly he carried a key, but he also carried a rod to represent his role as the *rector viarum*,[126] which could be understood as a protector or guide of travellers. The construction of an *Ianus* to mark the start of the road through which a traveller entered on a journey defined a transition into the care of the god Janus. Thus, placing an arch or *Ianus* at the start of a road through which travellers passed across a *limen* may allow us to identify further examples of the Roman combination of arch and road that are not so readily identified. It was part of the structure of these new roads that created a journey and a landscape of certainty with distances measured and nature subjected to Rome's power.

## Roads, communities and the state

The conception of roads being an intrinsic part of what made up a *civitas* (city or community) was articulated by Cicero in *De Officiis* and was linked to his discussion of a *civitas* as having a series of shared features in *De Republica* including its temples.[127] Those shared things included meeting places – *forum* and *fana* (shrines) and places of movement or circulation – *porticus* and *viae*.[128] In consequence, a *civitas* was the provider of roads and movement was defined as a vital aspect of a city, alongside laws, justice, elections, and the worship of the gods.

48   *Ray Laurence*

The view of Cicero is confirmed by town charters. The Lex Tarentina (39–42) makes it clear that local magistrates were responsible for the construction, the alteration, the building, and the paving of roads within the boundaries of the city's territory (*municipium*). Rome was an exception with the aediles only responsible for the roads within the city and to a mile from the limit of 'continuous habitation' – after that point, repair was undertaken by others.[129] Perhaps it should not come as a surprise that it was the local communities of the empire that provided for their upkeep, even though a road as a thing belonging to the Roman state was defined as a continuous space over hundreds of miles, crossing numerous boundaries between communities. The intersection between the boundaries of the territory of communities (area) with long-distance roads (linear space) elucidates the relationship between state and local power structures within the geographical conception of space in the Roman Empire.

There is evidence ranging from the first century BCE through to the later empire that the provincials were forced to work on or pay for the upkeep of roads.[130] The responsibility of upkeep also fell on landowners with property adjoining the road from as early as the second century BCE;[131] a process of repair also found in works such as those associated with land surveying with the additional provision for repair by communities.[132] The latter is also referred to by the *Lex Irnitania,* dating to 91 CE.[133] The aediles held the right and power to manage the roads (along with corn supply, sacred buildings, sacred and holy places, the town, the districts [*vicos*], the drains, the baths, and the market, checking weights and measures ch.19); whereas the duumviri had the right to create or alter roads, ways, ditches, and drains, but only within the boundaries (*fines*) of the *municipium* (ch.82). The eighty-eight territorial disputes, identified by Burton, cause us to realise that the definition of a city's territory could be questioned and raised with governors, procurators, or even the emperor.[134] Thus, the road – a linear space – crossed the lands of communities defined as a space with boundaries and containing a population, whose duties to the community included that of the repair of the road.[135] Intriguingly, some of these disputes, discussed by Kissel, were connected to the action of the repair and responsibility of repair of a road.[136] Inscriptions from the Via Egnatia would suggest that the maintenance of each individual mile of the road was attributed to a specific community.[137] This leads to the possibility that it was the governor (or at least within his reach in an archive), who held knowledge of which communities were responsible for the upkeep of sections of the road.[138]

The building of the Alcantara Bridge or Pons Alcantarensis under Trajan with its inscription from 105/106 CE provide a further indication of how the involvement of communities in major projects was to be celebrated.[139] Of the fourteen municipia from Lusitania, who are named as constructors of the bridge, not one of these is within the locality: Igaeditani, Lancienses, Oppidani, Talori, Interannienses, Colarni, Lancienses, Transcudani, Aravi, Meidubrigenses, Arabrigenses, Banienses, and Paesubres. The intersection of members of these communities with others at the site of the bridge resulted in a dedication of a shrine to Trajan by a member of the Igaeditani, who are listed first in the inscription on the bridge itself.[140] The involvement of these distant communities in the construction of the bridge is further evidence of how their involvement needed to be commemorated and acknowledged, but also created a temple on the banks of the river Tagus next to the bridge. The inscription explicitly sees the bridge as lasting forever and to be a thing that will be famous in its own right and was a part of the landscape to be recalled by travellers. Although we can understand the involvement of communities as a *munus*, it is worth seeing these actions as a contribution to the future of the state and a means of communities to be directly involved in the creation of infrastructure that was to last long into the future.

## Roads and time – *Vetustate*

With a dating system (*ab urbe condita*) that pointed out the time-depth of their culture, Romans can be seen by the second century CE to have been producing more robust approaches to building – sometimes called 'the concrete revolution' that might be seen to have also addressed more immediate threats to the built environment such as fire. This architecture was designed to create a resilience to the onslaught of ageing that can be found in literary texts, not least Lucretius, perhaps most ably put by Plautus in relating the collapse of a house to a man's ageing.[141] Only renewal or restoration might prevent the onslaught of *vetustas* that was a manifestation of the power of time over the brevity of human existence.[142] This accounts also for the link between human memory and the need to keep records of events in the past, via the *Annales,* that lay beyond the memory of the fathers or grandfathers of a community, who might at ages of more than eighty know what few others could have known.[143] The ageing of poorly made buildings was seen in connection to depreciation at a rate of one eightieth per annum until after eighty years, it would be worth nothing.[144] The repair of aged shrines of the Lares Augusti provides another means to calibrate *vetustate,* because the inscriptions include the year after the establishment of this new cult in 7 BCE and we find restorations after 61, 107, and 121 years.[145] Even, well-built structures, such as the Aquae Anio and Appia, would decay over time – in this case 127 years.[146] This pattern of time taking its toll was extended to the whole community of the Roman people: 'From the time of Caesar Augustus down to our own age there has been a period of not much less than two hundred years, during which, owing to the inactivity of the emperors, the Roman people, as it were, grew old and lost its potency, save that under the rule of Trajan it again stirred its arms and, contrary to general expectation, again renewed its vigour with youth as it were restored'.[147] Thomas and Witschel in a study of building inscriptions have identified numerous examples, where the reason given for a restoration proved to be false. Notably, old age – *vetustate* – was picked out as a reason for restoration, when in fact more immediate causes were found for a restoration. They suggest that these examples illustrated how the emperor could negate the effects of time and this is the main reason for the deployment of the word *vetustate.*[148] This shifts the epigraphic record of reconstruction of ageing buildings from the action of reconstruction into the realm of the representation of the power of the emperor and, as these scholars suggest, the reality of the claim need not have been fulfilled. Their concern was

50   *Ray Laurence*

with the evidential basis for specific buildings in cities, whereas – here I wish to point to a cultural expectation and observation of the ageing of the empire through the decay and renewal (real-and/or-imagined) of the man-made infrastructure of the empire.

Roads are described as old in more than 200 inscriptions from across the Roman Empire, sometimes these inscriptions specify that it was the road and the bridges that had become old. We should also recognise that roads were subject to damage from earthquakes, landslides, and floods.[149] There is sense in which a restoration is explained by the collapse or ageing of infrastructure. This can be seen as an aspect of the ideological impact of road building, clearly articulated both by Statius and Dio Chrysostom with reference to Domitian and Trajan as good rulers.[150] It is even felt by Galen, who could identify Trajan with the laying of stone causeways across marshes, hacking through scrubland, bridging danger-ous rivers, shortening the route or making it easier with the result that the lonely roads infested with wild beasts became broad highways.[151] The victory arches placed on such roads marked Rome's triumph over nature, as much as Rome's triumph over barbarians.[152] Galen compares his own achievement in medicine with that of the emperor in road building: Hippocrates discovered and planned the road, but it was Galen – like Trajan – 'who swept aside the tangled confusion, repairing and realigning the old ways of Hippocrates; and his implicit claim was that the Galenic system of medicine would be as impressive and enduring as the road system of Trajan'.[153] This sense of Trajanic landscape transformation also made itself felt in Plutarch's biography of Gaius Gracchus (7) with straight paved roads, ravines bridged, marked by milestones and an object of beauty, which are seen by some scholars to reflect the road-making of the Plutarch's own time – rather than being a report of the actions of a tribune in the second century BCE.[154] Even, the measurement of space by a simple milestone was subject to a choice over materials with clear evidence for a gradual preference, in Italy at least, for the use of imported marble emerging under Constantine as the material for milestones commemorating the emperor's actions.[155]

## Experience, agency and interaction

The argument that the Roman state was characterised by road building and this action defined the nature of the state has been presented above. The magisterial path of the Roman elite also featured the action of road building. The earliest offices held by those moving into the senate, the vignitivirate, included four indi-viduals – *quattuorviri viarum curandarum* – an experience, we may assume, that stayed with them and may have been essential for a higher office than that of the aediles, which brought with it responsibility for the cleaning and maintenance of Rome's streets. At the highest levels, the governors and legates in the provinces included within their remit the maintenance of roads, and beyond this office lay the *curatores viarum* in Italy. Thus, it is essential to see the involvement of the senatorial elite in road building and maintenance, as much as in the military or in dispensing justice. Even Cicero could discuss the maintenance of roads and the quality of road surfaces with his brother, drawing on his experience of measuring the road over 150 paces himself.[156] This comes in a letter reporting on a range of improvements to Quintus' properties across Italy. The elite maintained not just public roads, but also private roads to and from their properties at a distance from Rome. In order to maintain and run their properties, they needed to travel to them – this experience informed them of standard practices and expectations of a road –as Cicero informs his brother: *viam perspexi; quae mihi ita placuit ut opus publicum videretur esse* (I examined the road, which I thought good enough to be a public highway). It is worth noting that state roads were of the highest quality and provided the measure for private works. This example shows us how the elite had experience and knowledge of road building, which could be applied in other contexts – for example, the maintenance and building of public roads. In the latter, they became the agents of the state – who could require others to undertake the actual construction, which the elite would return to check that it was of the right quality.

The senate under Tiberius, in 21 CE, discussed the appalling condition of the roads due to the neglect of the relevant magistrates, the *curatores viarum*, and the dishonesty of the contractors, *mancipes*.[157] Domitius Corbulo undertook to prosecute these men, whose property was sold. Later, Corbulo assisted Caligula in 39 CE to prosecute current and former *curatores viarum* and contractors on the pretence that they had actually spent no money on the roads.[158] The money raised from these fines was returned by 43 CE.[159] The series of incidents demonstrates how individuals were capable of assessing whether a contract to repair a road had been fulfilled or neglected. Caligula's false accusations were seen as exactly that; whereas, Dio could also describe Corbulo as a nuisance in harassing the *curatores viarum* and becoming a nuisance in the senate. The details are less important than the process. It was the senate that held the magistrates and contractors to account as the executive body of the state and it was seen by Tacitus as intended to benefit the public to bring these prosecutions to ensure that the roads were maintained.[160]

Having looked at how roads could become symbolic of all the things that were going wrong with the state, it is worth remembering that when roads were built it reflected on their creator or the person in charge. Plutarch presents Gaius Gracchus as an excellent project manager, who was at ease when dealing with contractors and artisans with every courtesy with the result that the roads that were built were of both utility and beauty.[161] The relationship between Gaius Gracchus as their curator and the road created, for Plutarch, was compelling evidence of the energy with which he pursued these projects with bridges, straight roads, and milestones measuring off the distances. For Plutarch, this tangible outcome was a vehicle to explain the character of Gaius Gracchus – he was a man who was a skilful popular leader due to his ability not in rhetoric and speeches from the *rostra,* but in his private dealings with men and his business transactions.[162] This was a different form of power from that found in the forum at Rome, and was only curtailed when Livius Drusus made similar bids for projects on a grander scale. Thus, through road building, the power of Gaius Gracchus was demonstrated to travellers through actions rather than words.[163]

52  *Ray Laurence*

The phenomenon of power expressed through road building and road maintenance lasted into the future. By the time of Augustus, as we have seen, the roads of Italy were famous – even if in need of restoration. The latter allowed emperors to assert their authority over the landscape and to advertise their actions on milestones to travellers. Tertullian,[164] as a Christian writer, saw the paved roads connecting up places that otherwise would have been remote. This connectivity based upon the creation of public roads as things belonging to the state caused Rome's material culture to change and for Pliny, brought in all the luxuries and vices to his society.[165] Underpinning the maintenance of this system of roads were a series of interactions between the emperor, his *curatores viarum* and/or governors of provinces, the contractors working for the public, and those landholders (*possessores*) who contributed money or labour.[166] The interface between the road, defined as public land, and the farms adjoining it gave rise to considerable legal thinking on how the public road could be damaged by its neighbours.[167] An absence of road maintenance prevented the public from using the road, encapsulated the concept of poor government for the reason that the road belonged to everyone and, thus, can be seen to have symbolised the health or otherwise of the state, or the way in which the emperor had cared for the public.[168] The latter is a conception of government found in Pliny's *Panegyricus*, but we might also see it manifested in the presence of milestones explaining the emperor's actions in restoring a road.[169] Taken from the point of view of a traveller, the condition of a public road was not simply about practical convenience – it was also symbolic of the relationship between the peoples resident beside the road and the emperor, as well as the reach of the emperor to care for the road as a public thing owned by all citizens in the state. Thus, the road really did symbolise the Roman state, as well as connecting its many parts together to create a geographical entity or even a *res publica.*

## Notes

 1  E.g. Finley 1973, 126–28; Saller 2002, 254; Morley 2007, 571; Bang 2008, 133–36.
 2  Schneider 2007, 163–645; Strabo 5.1.8, 5.1.12; Plin. *NH* 14.132.
 3  Dion. Hal. 3.67.5.
 4  Mattingly 1997 for discussion on *power over.*
 5  Laurence 1999.
 6  Jessop et al 2008.
 7  Corsi 2000, 23–28 for ancient sources.
 8  Laurence 2015.
 9  Janni 1984.
10  See Newsome 2013, 67–8 on spatial strategy/tactics in Rome developed from de Certeau 1984.
11  Newsome 2011, 20–26; Trifilò 2008, 115–17; Gros 2005, 191–92; Stewart 2003, 136–40; Trifilò 2013, 169–70.
12  For roads in Italy, see Laurence 1999.
13  van Tilburg 2007 for collation of texts.
14  Laurence and Trifilò 2015 and papers in Pitts and Versluys 2015a.
15  *CIL* 11.365; Manusuelli 1960; for Augustus and the roads of Italy: Suet.*Aug.*30; Dio 53.22; *CIL* 10.6895, 6897, 6899–6901; Tibul.1.7.57–60.
16  Laurence 1999, 39–57, 2004, 45–47.

17 Discussed in Laurence 1999.
18 Nicolet 1990.
19 *CIL* 10.6950; Salway 2001, 2007, 2011; Talbert 2007, 2011, 177–90; Laurence 1999, 78–94, 2001.
20 *Dig*.8.3.8; Varro *LL* 7.15; Festus 508L; Hyg.*Const*.134bh.
21 Talbert 2012, discussed in Laurence 2016.
22 Maas and Ruths 2012; Grahame 2006.
23 Laurence 2016.
24 Urry 2007, 17.
25 E.g. Plut.*CG* 7; discussed by Ando 2000, 323–24.
26 E.g. in Bang and Scheidel 2013.
27 Kolb 2000; Di Paola 1999; Corsi 2000; Black 1995.
28 Lemke 2016.
29 Suet.*Aug*.49.3, Lemke 2016, 19.
30 Mitchell 1976, 117–8.
31 Hauken and Malay 2009 provide text, translation and discussion, compare Whittaker 2002, 81–82 on Caesar's need for a guide in Suet.*Caes*.31.
32 For other examples of the abuse of locals, see Mitchell 1976, 114–15.
33 E.g. Farnum 2005.
34 *CIL* 8.2532; Tert. *Apol*.2.8.
35 Nelis-Clément 2006; for origins of this system of distributed power: Suet.*Aug*.32.1, *Tib*.37.1.
36 Steidl 2005.
37 Popović 1989; Mirković 1994; Nelis-Clément 2000, 141–48.
38 Nelis-Clément 2000.
39 France and Nelis-Clément 2014b; Leveau 2014.
40 See papers in France and Nelis-Clément 2014a.
41 Compare papers on written space in Sears et al. 2013.
42 E.g. *AE* 1897. 65; Humbert & Desreumaux 1998; Graf 1995; Talbert 2000, 29–30.
43 Bowersock 1983, 91–2.
44 Graf 1995.
45 Bowersock 1983, 83–4; *BMC* Roman Empire III, p.185, no.877.
46 French 2012, 7.
47 *CIL* 8 22020, 22056, 22073, 22123.
48 *CIL* 8 22020, 22056, 22073, 22123, see Nutton 1978.
49 Talbert 2005; Elsner 2000, 186–90.
50 On historical development, see De Laet 1949; on record keeping e.g. Sijpesteijn 1989; Gallazzi and Sijpesteijn 1989.
51 Calzolari 1996, 416–17; for text see Cuntz 1929, 232.2, 238.1, 274.6, 285.3, 341.2, 343.4, 356.13, 364.4, 379.7, 387.2, 398.5, 460.1, 461.6, 462.1, 555.5, 559.2, 574.4.
52 ll.32–36, Mitchell 2008, 173, 183–88.
53 ll. 103–104, *portorium importationis exportationisque terra marique intra fines portusque*.
54 *CIL* 11. 3284; Heurgon 1952, 47; France 2001, 81–90; Scuderi 2001; De Laet 1949, 125–74.
55 *CIL* 10.6668, *AE* 1915: 58; *CIL* 13.1817; *AE* 1945: 99.
56 *CIL* 5.7209 and 7214; Pellizzari 2007.
57 *CIL* 6.8592.
58 Bang 2008, 202–38.
59 *CIL* 8.4508.
60 Trousset 2005 for discussion.
61 Plut. *CG* 7.
62 Wiegels 2016, 115–51; *RIC* 315–317; *RIC*² 140–144; Mattingly 1965, 75, nos 432–35; Giard 1976 nos 1252, 1254, 1257–63.

## 54   Ray Laurence

63 Fell 1951, 80; Cass. Dio 53.22; *RG* 20.5; Cooley 2009, 195–97; Mansuelli 1960; on raising of road level see Mansuelli 1941, 78.
64 *RIC* [2] 360–62; Giard 1976, nos 352–61.
65 Étienne 1992, 362; compare Frothingham 1915, 160–61, for inscriptions see Sillières 1990 nos 26, 28, 42, 45, 48, 49, 53; on arches Haley 2003, 34–5. The formula *a Baete et Iano August(o) ad Oceanum* was maintained to the reign of Vespasian.
66 Sillières 1990, nos 35, 36, 41 for milestones with the formula: *ab arcu unde incipit Baetica viam Augustam militarem vetustate corruptam restituit.*
67 For coinage: Burnett et al 1992, nos 10, 12, 20–27, 30–33, 38, 41–45; for the bridge: Leather 2006, 84–91.
68 Mansuelli 1960, fig. 3a for reconstruction.
69 Compare Hill 1989, 105–7.
70 Burnett et al 1992, 69; Dio 53.25 for foundation date.
71 *Tabula Siarensis* frag 1. *AE* 1984, 138; González 1999, 125–6, 2000, 116–27.
72 Tac. *Ann.*2.83 refers to these monuments as *arcus;* Wallace-Hadrill 1990, 142–44.
73 Millar 1988, 16–17.
74 Ov. *Fast.* 1.63–70; Herbert-Brown 1994, 185–89.
75 Mansuelli 1960.
76 Haley 2003, 34–5; Dio 55.10a.2; Tac. *Ann.*4.44.3; Plin. *NH* 3.17; Wells 1972, 70, and 158–59.
77 Talbert 2005, supported by amongst other references: Cass. Dio 53.12.4–9; Strabo 17.3.25; also Plin. *NH* 3–6.
78 Talbert 2005, 27.
79 Elsner 2000, 195.
80 Cuntz 1929, 558.4, 567.10, 611.5, 616.10
81 Frothingham 1915; Holland 1961.
82 Brookes 1974.
83 *CIL* 11.8103.
84 *CIL* 5.8102, 8103, 8106.
85 *CIL* 9.5959; Gardner 1913.
86 *CIL* 3.3198b.
87 *CIL* 3.3705.
88 *AE* 1999, 684.
89 *CIL* 5.8002.
90 *CIL* 5.8002, 8003.
91 *CIL* 13. 1672, 1674, 1702.
92 Translation from in De Lange 1978, 268.
93 Cuntz 1929, 257.5, 363.1, 409.2, 477.7, 478.4.
94 Cuntz 1929, 60.2, 121.1, 236.2, 257.2, 258.8, 259.7, 267.6, 314.5, 372.1, 376.8, 430.10.
95 Ptolemy *Geography* for their prominence or Strabo on the Baetis 3.2.1–3, 3.4.12; for construction of bridge supports in rivers - Brandon 2014
96 *Silv.*4.3.67–94, Newlands 2012, 52–61 Statius' focus on fluid boundaries.
97 *Silv.*4.3.95–100, on text see: Håkanson 1969, 117–18; Coleman 1988, 126–29 Liberman 2010, 338; Kleiner 1991.
98 Lauritsen 2014, but see for *limen* e.g. Mart.*Ep.*8.44; Sen. *De Brev.Vit.*14.
99 Banta 2007; Kleiner 1991; Smolenaars 2006.
100 Dio 53.26; Oros. 6.21.1; Syme 1991; Syme 1979.
101 Green 2000 on Janus and containment.
102 Ov. *Fast.* 1.198–202; for coins Burnett et al 1992, nos 5/6, 6, 7, 11, 13.
103 Hassel 1966, Rotili 1972 for description and images.
104 Hölscher 2002, 143.
105 Spiedel 2005/6, 202–205.

The meaning of roads 55

106 Ceraudo 2008; Silvestrini 1983; Mertens 1994; Ashby and Gardner 1916; Ceraudo 2012; Chelotti et al 1985, nos 246–80.
107 Ceraudo 2012 fig.1.
108 One third of all the milestones survived into the modern age and have been documented from this road, Ceraudo 2008, 108.
109 See Silvestrini 1999; Chelotti et al 1985.
110 Hill 1989, 96; Mattingly 1936, ci–cv, nos 484–91, 986–89, 998–99, 1012.
111 Mattingly 1936, no. 829.
112 Mattingly 1936, nos 509, 665, Packer 1997, 247–83 for reconstruction of the Forum of Trajan.
113 Hill 1989, 50; Robertson 1971 no. 228l; compare Mattingly 1936 no. 842 issued later in the reign.
114 Robertson 1971 nos 320–24; Mattingly 1936 nos 847–52.
115 Hamberg 1945, 63–75; Pietrangeli 1945; Hassel 1966.
116 Bushe-Fox 1926, 6; 1928, 10–13; 1932, 17–20; Strong 1968; compare examples from Egypt in Talbert 2004, 30–31.
117 Cunliffe 1968, 5.
118 Bushe-Fox 1949, 38–48.
119 Strong 1968, 69–70.
120 Strong 1968, 72–73.
121 Payne 1898; and Payne 1895.
122 Laurence 2001.
123 Millett and Wilmott 2003; Wilmott et al 2007 for nature of urbanism at Richborough.
124 *RG* 13; Turcan 1981, 376–80.
125 King 2006, 66–102; Green 2004, 60.
126 Macr. *Sat.* 1.9.7.
127 Cic. *Off.* 1.53–4, Dyck 1996, 169–72; and Cic. *Rep.* 1.39–41; Zetzel 1995, 126–29 on temples.
128 Rémy 1930, discussed by Dyck 1996, 172.
129 *Tabula Heracleensis* 20–45; Crawford 1996, 363–64, 373–74, 380–81.
130 Cic. *Font.*8.17; Tac. *Agr.*31; *Dig.*49.18, 50.4.1; *Cod. Theod.*11.16.10, 15, 18; Kissel 2002 for further evidence and discussion.
131 Cato *Agr.*2.4.
132 Siculus Flaccus 145.11L, Campbell 2000, 112–13, compare *Dig.*43.8.2.21–22.
133 González 1986 for text, translation and commentary.
134 Burton 2000.
135 Burton 2000, 197–8.
136 Kissel 2002, 140; Frend 1956.
137 Mottas 1989.
138 Kissel 2004, 141.
139 *CIL* 2.759–60.
140 *CIL* 2.761.
141 Segal 1990, 94–114; Plaut. *Mostell.* 146–48; Thomas and Witschel 1992, 143.
142 Lucr.1.225, 5.306–17; Thomas and Witschel 1992, 143; Berns 1976.
143 Liv. 27.8; 3.71.
144 Vitr.2.8.8; Rihll 2013.
145 *AE* 1960: 61; *CIL* 6.451, 452, see Lott 2004.
146 Frontin. *Aq.*7.
147 Flor. 1.8, compare Seneca preserved in Lactant. *Inst. Div.*7.15.4, also *CIL* 6. 40520.
148 Thomas and Witschel 1992, 147.
149 As detailed by Kissel 2002, 132
150 Stat. *Silv.*4.3; Dio Chry. 3.127.
151 Galen 10.632–33; see Nutton 1978, 218–19 for discussion.

56  *Ray Laurence*

152  Kleiner 1991.
153  Nutton 1978, 219.
154  Plut.*C.G.*7; Nutton 1978, 218–19; Laurence 1999, 40–41; for relations between Plutarch and Trajan, see Stadter 2014, 17–20.
155  Grossi 2006.
156  Cic. *QF* 3.1.4.
157  Tac. *Ann.*3.31.5, Woodman and Martin 1996, 282–83; Eck 1992, 243–44.
158  Cass. Dio 59.15.3–4.
159  Cass. Dio 60.17.
160  Tac. *Ann.* 3.31.5.
161  Plut.*C.G.*6.3–7, compare App. *B.C.*1.23.
162  Plut.*C.G.*6.4.
163  Compare Laurence 1999, 15–18 on power of Appius Claudius and his descendants.
164  Tert. *De anima* 30.3.
165  Plin. *N.H.* 36.1–8.
166  Siculus Flaccus 146L.
167  *Dig.*43.8.21–45.
168  *Dig.*43.7.1.
169  Roche 2011 on *Panegyricus.*


## Bibliography

Ando, Clifford. 2000. *Imperial Ideology and Provincial Loyalty in the Roman Empire.* Berkeley: University of California Press.

Ashby, Thomas and Robert Gardner. 1916. "The Via Traiana." *Papers of the British School at Rome* 8: 104–171.

Bang, Peter F. 2008. *The Roman Bazaar. A Comparative Study of Trade and Markets in a Tributary Empire.* Cambridge: Cambridge University Press.

Bang, Peter F. and Walter Scheidel. 2013. *The Oxford Handbook of the State in the Ancient Near East and Mediterranean.* Oxford: Oxford University Press.

Banta, Jason. 2007. "The Gates of Janus: Bakhtin and Plutarch's Roman *meta-chronotope.*" In *The Sites of Rome: Time, Space and Memory,* edited by David H.J. Larmour and Diana Spencer, 8–70. Oxford: Oxford University Press.

Berns, Gisela. 1976. "Time and Nature in Lucretius *De Rerum Natura.*" *Hermes* 104: 477–492.

Black, Ernest W. 1995. *Cursus Publicus: the Infrastructure of Government in Roman Britain.* Oxford: BAR British Series 241.

Bowersock, Glen W. 1983. *Roman Arabia.* Cambridge: Harvard University Press.

Brandon, Cristopher. 2014. "Roman Formwork used for Underwater Concrete Construction." *Building for Eternity: The History and Technology of Roman Concrete Engineering in the Sea,* edited by John P. Oleson, 189–222. Oxford: Oxford University Press.

Brookes, Alan C. 1974. "Minturnae: The Via Appia Bridge." *American Journal of Archaeology* 78: 41–48.

Burnett, Andrew, Michael Amandry, and Pere Pau Ripollès. 1992. *Roman Provincial Coinage Volume I: From the death of Caesar to the death of Vitellius (44 BC–AD 69).* London: British Museum Press.

Bushe-Fox, Joscelyn P. 1926. *First Report on the Excavation of the Roman Fort at Richborough, Kent.* London: Society of Antiquaries.

Bushe-Fox, Joscelyn P. 1928. *Second Report on the Excavation of the Roman Fort at Richborough, Kent.* London: Society of Antiquaries.

The meaning of roads 57

Bushe-Fox, Joscelyn P. 1932. *Third Report on the Excavation of the Roman Fort at Richborough, Kent*. London: Society of Antiquaries.

Bushe-Fox, Joscelyn P. 1949. *Fourth Report on the Excavation of the Roman Fort at Richborough, Kent*. London: Society of Antiquaries.

Calzolari, Mauro. 1996. *Introduzione allo studio della rete stradale dell'Italia romana: L'Itinerarium Antonini*. Rome: Academia Nazionale dei Lincei.

Campbell, Brian. 2000. *The Writings of the Roman Land Surveyors*. London: Society for the Promotion of Roman Studies.

Carvalho, Pedro C. 2009. "O Forum *Igaeditani* os Primeiros Tempos da *Civitas Igaeditanorum* (Idanha-a-Velha, Portugal)." *Archivo Español de Arqueología* 82: 115–131.

Ceraudo, Giuseppe. 2008. *Sulle trace della via Traiana. Indagini aerotopografiche da Aecae a Herdonia*. Foggia: Grenzi.

Ceraudo, Giuseppe. 2009. "Un nuovo miliario della Via Traiana dal territorio di Aequum Tuticum." *Epigrafica* 71: 107–118.

Ceraudo, Giuseppe. 2012. "Due nuove lastre iscritte dei ponti della Via Traiana." *Zeitschrift für Papyrologie und Epigraphik* 183: 255–258.

Chelotti, Marcella, Rosanna Gaeta, Vincenza Morizio, and Marina Silvestrini. 1985. *Le epigrafi romane di Canosa*. Bari: Edipuglia.

Coleman, Kathleen. 1988. *Statius Silvae IV*. Oxford: Clarendon.

Cooley, Alison. 2009. *Res Gestae Divi Augusti. Text, Translation, and Commentary*. Cambridge: Cambridge University Press.

Corsi, Cristina. 2000. "Stazioni stradali <<*cursus publicus*>>: note di tipologia dell'insediamento lungo la viabilitá romana." *Orrizonti* 1: 245–252.

Crawford, Michael. 1996. *Roman Statutes*. London: Bulletin of the Institute of Classical Studies.

Cunliffe, Barry W. (ed.). 1968. *Fifth Report on the Excavation of the Roman Fort at Richborough, Kent*. London: Society of Antiquaries.

Cuntz, Otto. 1929. *Itineraria Romana I: Itineraria Antonini Augusti et Burdigalense*. Leipzig: Teubner.

De Certeau, Michel. 1984. *The Practice of Everyday Life*. Berkeley: University of California Press.

De Laet, Siegfried J. 1949. *Portorium. Étude sur l'organisation douanière chez les romains*. Brugge: De Tempel.

De Lange Nicholas R. M. 1978. "Jewish Attitudes to the Roman Empire." In *Imperialism in the Ancient World*, edited by Peter D.A. Garnsey and C.R. Whittaker, 255–282. Cambridge: Cambridge University Press.

Di Paola, Lucietta. 1999. *Viaggi, trasporti e istituzioni. Studi dul cursus publicus*. Messina: Dipartimento di scienze dell'Antichità dell'università degli studi di Messina.

Dyck, Andrew R. 1996. *A Commentary on Cicero, De Officiis*. Ann Arbor: University of Michigan Press.

Eck, Werner. 1992. "*Cura viarum* und *cura operum publicorum* als kollegiale Ämter im frühen Prinzipat." *Klio* 74: 237–245.

Elsner, Jaś. 2000. "The *Itinerarium Burdigalense*: Politics and Salvation in the Geography of Constantine's Empire." *JRS* 90: 181–195.

Étienne, Robert. 1992. "L'horloge de la *Civitas Igaeditanorum* et la creation de la province de Lusitanie." *Revue des Études Anciennes* 94: 355–362.

Farnum, Jerome H. 2005. *The Positioning of the Roman Imperial Legions*. Oxford: BAR Int. Ser. 1458.

## 58   Ray Laurence

Finley, Moses I. 1973. *The Ancient Economy*. Berkeley: University of California Press.

France, Jérôme. 2001. "Quadragesima Galliarum." *L'organisation douanière des provinces Alpestres, Gauloises, et Germaniques de l'empire romain*. Rome: École française de Rome.

France, Jérôme and Jocelyne Nelis-Clément. 2014. "La *statio*. Archéologie d'un lieu de pouvoir dans l'empire romain." In *La statio. Archéologie d'un lieu de pouvoir dans l'empire romain*, edited by Jérôme France and Jocelyne Nelis-Clément, 11–17. Bordeaux: Ausonius.

French, David H. 2012. *Roman Roads and Milestones of Asia Minor Volume 3: Milestones*. London: British Institute at Ankara.

Frend, W.H.C. 1956. "A Third Century Inscription Relating to *Angareia* in Phrygia." *Journal of Roman Studies* 56: 46–56.

Frothingham, Arthur L. 1915. "The Roman Territorial Arch." *American Journal of Archaeology* 19: 155–174.

Gallazzi, Claudio and Pieter J. Sijpesteijn. 1989. "Receipts Issued to an Overseer of a Customs Station." *Zeitschrift fur Papyrologie und Epigraphik* 78: 119–122.

Gardner, Robert. 1913. "The Via Claudia Nova." *Journal of Roman Studies* 3: 205–232.

Giard, Jean-Baptíste. 1976. *Bibliothèque Nationale Catalogue des Monnaies de l'Empire Romain I: Auguste*. Paris: Bibliothèque Nationale.

González, Julián. 1986. "The Lex Irnitania: A New Copy of the Flavian Municipal Law." *Journal of Roman Studies* 76: 147–243.

González, Julián. 1999. "Tacitus, Germanicus, Piso and the *Tabula Siarensis*." *American Journal of Philology* 120: 122–142.

González, Julián. 2000. "*Tab. Siar*. Frag. I: Problemas de Restitucion." In *La Commemorazione di Germanico nella Documentazione Epigrafica*, edited by Augusto Fraschetti, 95–130. Rome: Bretschneider.

Graf, David F. 1995. "The *Via Nova Traiana* in Arabia Petraea." In *The Roman and Byzantine Army in the East*, edited by Edward Dabrowa, 141–167. Portsmouth RI: JRA Suppl. 14.

Graham, Shawn. 2006. "Networks, Agent-based Models and the Antonine Itineraries: Implications for Roman Archaeology." *Journal of Mediterranean Archaeology* 19: 45–64.

Green, Steven. 2004. *Ovid, Fasti 1: A Commentary*. Leiden: Brill.

Green, Steven J. 2000. "Multiple Interpretation of the Opening and Closing of the Temple of Janus: A Misunderstanding of Ovid *Fasti* 1.281." *Mnemosyne* 53: 302–309.

Gros, Pierre. 2005. "Le role du people de Rome dans la definition, l'organisation et le déplacement des lieux de la convergence sous l'empire." In *Popolo e Potere nel Mondo Antico*, edited by Gianpaolo Urso, 191–214. Pisa: ETS.

Grossi, Piergiovanna. 2007. "Pietre Miliari della VIII Regio: Analisi litologiche, provienza dei materiali e loro distribuzione." *Epigraphica* 69: 181–207.

Håkanson, Lennart. 1969. *Statius' Silvae. Critical and exegetical remarks with some notes on the Thebaid*. Lund: Gleerup.

Haley, Evan W. 2003. *Baetica Felix: People and Prosperity in Southern Spain from Caesar to Septimus Severus*. Austin: University of Texas Press.

Hamberg, Per Gustaf. 1945. *Studies in Roman Imperial Art*. Stockholm: Almqvist & Wiksells.

Hassel, Franz Josef. 1966. *Der Trajansbogen in Benevent. Ein Bauwerk des römischen Senates*. Mainz: Zabern.

Hauken, Tor and Hasan Malay. 2009. "A New Edict of Hadrian from the Province of Asia Setting Out Regulations for Requisitioned Transport." In *Selbstdarstellung und*

*Kommunikation: Die Veröffentlichung staatlicher Urkunden auf Stein und Bronze in der römischen Welt*, edited by Rudolf Haensch, 327–348. Munich: Beck.

Herbert- Brown, Geraldine. 1994. *Ovid and the Fasti: An Historical Study*. Oxford: Clarendon.

Heurgon, Jacques. 1952. "La date des Gobelets de Vicarello." *Revue des Études Anciennes* 54: 39–50.

Hill, Philip V. 1989. *The Monuments of Ancient Rome as Coin Types*. London: B.A. Seaby.

Holland, Louise Adams. 1961. *Janus and the Bridge*. Rome: American Academy in Rome.

Hölscher, Tonio. 2002. "Bilder der Macht und Herrschaft." In *Traian: ein Kaiser der Superlative am beginn einer Umbruchzeit?*, edited by Annette Nünnerich-Asmus, 127–144. Mainz: P. von Zabern.

Humbert, Jean-Baptiste and Alain Desreumaux. 1998. *Fouilles de Khirbet Es-Samra en Jordanie I: La Voie Romaine, Le Cemetière, Les Documents Épigraphiques*. Turnhout: Brepols.

Isaac, Benjamin. 1992. *The Limits of Empire. The Roman Army in the East*, revised edition. Oxford: Oxford University Press.

Janni, Pietro. 1984. *La Mappa e il Periplo. Cartografia antica e spazio odologico*. Rome: Bretschneider.

Jessop, Bob, Neil Brenner and Martin Jones. 2008. "Theorizing Sociospatial Relations." *Environment and Planning D: Society and Space* 26: 389–401.

King, Richard J. 2006. *Desiring Rome. Male Subjectivity and Reading Ovid's Fasti*. Columbus: Ohio State University Press.

Kissel, Theodor. 2002. "Road-Building as a *Munus Publicum*." In *The Roman Army and the Economy*, edited by Paul Erdkamp, 127–160. Amsterdam: J.C. Gieben.

Kleiner, Fred S. 1991. "The Trophy on the Bridge and the Roman Triumph over Nature." *L'Antiquité Classique* 60: 182–192.

Kolb, Anne. 2000. *Transport und Nahrichtentransfer im Römischen Reich*. Berlin: Akademie Verlag.

Laurence, Ray. 1999. *The Roads of Roman Italy: Mobility and Cultural Change*. London: Routledge.

Laurence, Ray. 2001. "The Creation of Geography: An Interpretation of Roman Britain." In *Travel and Geography in the Roman Empire*, edited by Colin Adams and Ray Laurence, 67–94. London: Routledge.

Laurence, Ray. 2004. "Milestones, Communications and Political Stability." In *Travel, Communication and Geography in Late Antiquity: Sacred and Profane*, edited by Linda Ellis and Frank L. Kidner, 41–60. Aldershot: Ashgate.

Laurence, Ray. 2015. "Towards a History of Mobility in Ancient Rome (300 BCE to 100 CE)." In *The Moving City: Processions, Passages and Promenades in Ancient Rome*, edited by Ida Östenberg, Simon Malmberg, and Jonas Bjørnebye, 175–186 and 302–307. London: Bloomsbury.

Laurence, Ray. 2016. "Connectivity, Roads and Transport: Essays on Roman Roads to Speak to Other Disciplines?" *Journal of Roman Archaeology* 29: 692–695.

Laurence, Ray and Francesco Trifilò. 2015. "The Global and the Local in the Roman Empire." In *Globalisation and the Roman Empire*, edited by Martin Pitts and Miguel John Versluys, 99–122. Cambridge: Cambridge University Press.

Lauritsen, Michael Taylor. 2014. *Ante Ostium Contextualizing Boundaries in the Houses of Pompeii and Herculaneum*. PhD thesis, University of Edinburgh.

## 60  Ray Laurence

Lemke, Lukas. 2016. *Imperial Transportation and Communication from the Third to the Late Fourth Century: The Golden Age of the Cursus Publicus*. Cambridge: Cambridge University Press.

Leveau, Philippe. 2014. "Stations routières et *stationes viarum*. Une contribution à l'archéologie de la station en Gaule Narbonnaise et dans les provinces alpines voisines." In *La statio. Archéologie d'un lieu de pouvoir dans l'empire romain*, edited by Jérôme France and Jocelyne Nelis-Clément, 17–56. Bordeaux: Ausonius.

Liberman, Gauthier. 2010. *Stace Silves*. Paris: Calepinas.

Lott, J. Bert. 2004. *The Neighbourhoods of Augustan Rome*. Cambridge: Cambridge University Press.

Maas, Michael and Derek Ruths. 2012. "Road Connectivity and the Structure of Ancient Empires: A Case Study from Late Antiquity." In *Highways, Byways, and Road Systems in the Pre-Modern World*, edited by Susan E. Alcock, John Bodel and Richard J.A. Talbert, 255–264. Chichester: Wiley-Blackwell.

Mansuelli, Guido A. 1941. *Ariminum (Rimini)*. Rome: Istituto di Studi Romani.

Mansuelli, Guido A. 1960. *Il monument augusteo del 27 a.c. Nuove ricerche sull'Arco di Rimini*. Bologna: s.n.

Mattingly, David J. 1997. *Dialogues in Roman Imperialism*. Portsmouth RI: *Journal of Roman Archaeology* (Suppl. 23).

Mattingly, Harold. 1965. *Coins of the Roman Empire in the British Museum Volume I: Augustus to Vitellius*. London: British Museum.

Mennella, Giovanni. 1992. "La *Quadragesima Galliarum* nelle Alpes Maritimae." *Mélanges de l'École française de Rome* 104: 209–232.

Mertens, Jozef. 1994. "Les ponts de la Via Traiana dans la traversé du Tavoliere de Foggia." In *Strade Romane: Percorsi e Infrastrutture*, edited by L. Quilici and S. Quilici Gigli, 7–18. Rome: Bretschneider.

Millar, Fergus. 1988. "Imperial Ideology in the *Tabula Siarensis*." In *Estudios sobre La Tabula Siarensis*, edited by Julián González and Javier Arce, 1–20. Madrid: Centro de Estudios Históricos.

Millett, M. and T. Wilmott. 2003. "Rethinking Richborough." In *The Archaeology of Roman Towns*, edited by Pete Wilson, 184–194. Oxford: Oxbow.

Mirković, Miroslava. 1994. *"Beneficiarii consularis* in Sirmium." *Chiron* 24: 345–404.

Mitchell, S. 1976. "Requisitioned Transport in the Roman Empire: A New Inscription from Pisidia." *Journal of Roman Studies* 66: 106–138.

Mitchell, S. 2008. "Geography, Politics, and Imperialism in the Asian Customs Law." In *The Customs Law of Asia*, edited by M. Cottier, M. Crawford, C.V. Crowther, J.-L. Ferrary, B.M. Levick, O. Salomies, and M. Wörrle, 165–201. Oxford: Oxford University Press.

Morley, Neville. 2007. "The Early Roman Empire: Distribution." In *The Cambridge Economic History of the Greco-Roman World*, edited by Walter Scheidel, Ian Morris, and Richard P. Saller, 570–591. Cambridge: Cambridge University Press.

Mottas, François. 1989. "Les voies de communication antiques de la Thrace égéenne." *Historia Einzelschriften* 60: 82–104.

Nelis-Clément, Jocelyne. 2000. *Les Beneficiarii: Militaires et Administrateurs au Service de L'Empire*. Bordeaux: Ausonius.

Nelis-Clément, Jocelyne. 2006. "Les stations comme espace et transmission du pouvoir." In *Herrschaftsstrukturen und Herschaftsprxis*, edited by Anne Kolb, 269–298. Berlin: Akademie Verlag.

Newlands, Carole E. 2012. *Statius, Poet between Rome and Naples*. Cambridge: Cambridge University Press.

The meaning of roads 61

Newsome, David. 2011. "Introduction: Making Movement Meaningful." In *Rome, Ostia, Pompeii: Movement and Space*, edited by Ray Laurence and David Newsome, 1–56, Oxford: Oxford University Press.

Newsome, David. 2013. "Movement, Rhythmns, and the (Re)production of Written Space." In *Written Space in the Latin West, 200 BC to AD 300*, edited by Gareth, Peter Keegan and Ray Laurence, 64–81. London: Bloomsbury.

Nicolet, Claude. 1990. "Strabon. Les routes d'Italie et les document géographiques du temps d'Auguste." *Archeologia Laziale* 10: 13–20.

Nutton, Vivian. 1978. "The Beneficial Ideology." In *Imperialism in the Ancient World*, edited by Peter D.A. Garnsey and C.R. Whittaker, 209–221. Cambridge: Cambridge University Press.

Packer, James E. 1997. *The Forum of Trajan in Rome*. Berkeley: University of California Press.

Payne, George. 1895. "Roman Rochester." *Archaeologia Cantiana* 21: 1–16.

Payne, George. 1898. "Roman Discoveries." *Archaeologia Cantiana* 23: 1–23.

Pellizzari, Andrea. 2007. "Viabilità e insediamenti nell'area subalpine della Regio XI: *ad Fines* e il suo territorio." In *Geografi et viaggi nell' antichità*, edited by Stefano Conti, Barbara Scardigli and Maria Cristina Torchio, 185–195. Ancona: Affinità Elettive Edizioni.

Pietrangeli, Carlo. 1945. *L'Arco di Traiano a Benevento*. Novara: Istituto Geografico di Agostini.

Pitts, Martin and Miguel John Versluys (eds.). 2015. *Globalisation and the Roman Empire*. Cambridge: Cambridge University Press.

Popović, V. 1989. "Une station de bénéficiares à Sirmium." *Comptes rendus des séances de l'Académie* 1989: 116–122.

Rémy, E. 1930. "Du groupement des peoples en états d'après le De officiis de Cicéron I, 53." In *Mélanges Paul Thomas*, 583–593. Bruges: Impremerie Sainte Catherine.

Rihll, Tracey. 2013. "Depreciation in Vitruvius." *Classical Quarterly* 63: 893–897.

Robertson, Anne. 1971. *Roman Imperial Coins in the Hunter Coin Cabinet, University of Glasgow, II: Trajan to Commodus*. Oxford: Clarendon.

Roche, Paul. 2011. "The *Panegyricus* and the Monuments of Rome." In *Pliny's Praise. The Panegyricus in the Roman World*, edited by Paul Roche, 45–66. Cambridge: Cambridge University Press.

Rotili, Mario. 1972. *L'Arco di Traiano a Benevento*. Rome: Istituto Poligrafico dello Stato.

Saller, Richard. 2002. "Framing the Debate Over Growth in the Ancient Economy." In *The Ancient Economy*, edited by Walter Scheidel and Sitta von Reden, 251–269. Edinburgh: Edinburgh University Press.

Salway, Benet. 2001. "Travel, *Itineraria* and *Tabellaria*." In *Travel and Geography in the Roman Empire*, edited by Colin Adams and Ray Laurence, 22–66. London: Routledge.

Salway, Benet. 2007. "The Perception and Description of Space in Roman Itineraries." In *Wahrnehmung und Erfassung geograohischer Räume in der Antike*, edited by Michael Rathmann, 181–209. Mainz: Philipp von Zabern.

Salway, Benet. 2011. "Putting the World in Order: Mapping in Roman Texts." In *Ancient Perspectives: Maps and Their Place in Mesopotamia, Egypt, Greece and Rome*, edited by Richard J.A. Talbert, 193–234. Chicago: Chicago University Press.

Schneider, Helmuth. 2007. "Technology." In *The Cambridge Economic History of the Greco-Roman World*, edited by Walter Scheidel, Ian Morris, and Richard Saller, 144–171. Cambridge: Cambridge University Press.

Scuderi, Rita. 2001. "Confine amministrativo e confine douganale nelle Alpi occidental durante l'alto impero." In *Les Anciens et La Montagne*, edited by Silvia Giorcelli

## 62  Ray Laurence

Bersani, 167–184. Torino: CELID. Sears, Gareth, Peter Keegan, and Ray Laurence (eds.). 2013. *Written Space in the Latin West, 200 BC to AD 300*. London: Bloomsbury.

Segal, Charles. 1990. *Lucretius on Death and Anxiety*. Princeton: Princeton University Press.

Sijpesteijn, Pieter J. 1989. "A Money Account of Customs Duties?" *Zeitschrift für Papyrologie und Epigraphik* 78: 100–102.

Sillières, Pierre. 1990. *Les voies de communication de l'Hispaniae méridionale*. Paris: De Boccard.

Silvestrini, Marina. 1983. "Miliari della via Traiana." In *Epigrafia e territorio: politica e società I*, 79–136. Bari: Edipuglia.

Silvestrini, Marina. 1999. *Un itinerario epigrafico lungo la via Traiana. Aecae, Herdonia, Canusium*. Bari: Edipuglia.

Smolenaars, Johannes J.L. 2006. "Ideology and Poetics along the Via Domitiana: Statius *Silvae* 4.3." In *Flavian Poetry*, edited by Ruud R. Nauta, Johannes J.L. Smolenaars, and Harm-Jam van Dam, 223–244. Leiden: Brill.

Speidel, Michael. 2005/2006. "Trajan's Column and the Arch of Benevento." *Römische Mitteilungen* 112: 189–206.

Stadter, Philip A. 2014. "Plutarch and Rome." In *A Companion to Plutarch*, edited by Mark Beck, 13–31. Chichester: Wiley-Blackwell.

Steidl, Bernd. 2005. "Die station der beneficiarii consularis in Obernburg am Main." *Germania* 83: 67–94.

Stewart, Peter. 2003. *Statues in Roman Society: Representation and Response*. Oxford: Oxford University Press.

Strong, D.E. 1968. "The monument." In *Fifth Report on the Excavation of the Roman Fort at Richborough, Kent*, edited by Barry W. Cunliffe, 40–73. London: Society of Antiquaries.

Syme, Ronald. 1979. "Problems about Janus." *American Journal of Philology* 100: 188–212.

Syme, Ronald. 1991. "Janus and Parthia in Horace." In *Roman Papers VI*, edited by Anthony Birley, 441–450. Oxford: Clarendon.

Talbert, Richard J.A. 2003. "Rome's Provinces as a Framework for World-View." In *Roman Rule and Civic Life: Local and Regional Perspectives*, edited by Luuk de Ligt, Emily Hemelrijk and H.W. Singor, 21–37. Amsterdam: J.C. Gieben.

Talbert, Richard J.A. 2005. "*Ubique Fines*: Boundaries within the Roman Empire." *Caesardonum* 39: 93–101.

Talbert, Richard J.A. 2007. "Peutinger's Roman Map: The Physical Landscape Framework." *Wahrnehmung und Erfassung geograohischer Räume in der Antike*, edited by Michael Rathmann, 220–230. Mainz: von Zabern.

Talbert, Richard J.A. 2011. "*Urbs Roma* to *Orbis Romanus*: Roman Mapping on the Grand Scale." In *Ancient Perspectives: Maps and Their Place in Mesopotamia, Egypt, Greece and Rome*, edited by Richard J.A. Talbert, 163–191. Chicago: University of Chicago Press.

Talbert, Richard J.A. 2012. "Roads not Featured: A Roman Failure to Communicate?" In *Highways, Byways, and Road Systems in the Pre-Modern World*, edited by Susan E. Alcock, John Bodel, and Richard J.A., 235–254. Chichester: Wiley-Blackwell.

Thomas, Edmund and Christian Witschel. 1992. "Constructing Reconstruction: Claim and Reality of Roman Rebuilding Inscriptions from the Latin West." *Papers of the British School at Rome* 60: 135–178.

Trifilò, Francesco. 2008. "Power, Architecture, and Community in the Distribution of Honorary Statues in Roman Public Space." In *TRAC 2007. Proceedings of the Seventeenth Annual Theoretical Roman Archaeology Conference*, edited by Corisande Fenwick, Meredith Wiggins, and Dave Wythe, 109–120. Oxford: Oxbow.

Trifilò, Francesco. 2013. "Text, Space and the Urban Community: A Study of *Platea* as Written Space." In *Written Space in the Latin West, 200 BC to AD 300*, edited by Gareth Sears, Peter Keegan, and Ray Laurence, 169–183. London: Bloomsbury.

Trousset, Pol. 2005. "Tarif de Zaraï: Essai sur les circuits commerciaux dans la zone présaharienne." *Antiquités Africaines* 38–39: 355–373.

Turcan, Robert. 1981. "Janus à l'Empire Impèriale." *Aufstieg und Niedergang der römischen Welt II* 17(1): 374–402.

Urry, John. 2007. *Mobilities*. Cambridge: Polity.

Van Tilburg, Cornelis. 2007. *Traffic and Congestion in the Roman Empire*. London: Routledge.

Wallace-Hadrill, Andrew. 1990. "Roman Arches and Greek Honours: The Language of Power at Rome." *Proceedings of the Cambridge Philological Society* 36: 143–181.

Wells, Colin M. 1972. *The German Policy of Augustus*. Oxford.

Whittaker, C.R. 2002. "Mental Maps: Seeing Like a Roman." In *Thinking Like a Lawyer. Essays on Legal History and General History for John Crook on His Eightieth Birthday*, edited by Paul McKechnie, 81–112. Leiden: Brill.

Wiegels, Rainer. 2016. *Kleine Schriften zur Germanienpolitik in der römischen Kaiserzeit*. Stuttgart: Steiner.

Wilmott, Tony, Neil Linford and Louise Martin. 2007. "A Roman Amphitheatre at Richborough (Rutupiae)," Kent: Non-Invasive Research.

# 4 The sacred travel of Valesius' family
## Children and the liminal stage

*Katariina Mustakallio*

### Introduction

Origin myths of ancient cults open an interesting perspective onto the assumptions concerning relationships between human beings and divine forces. According to classical authors, the Romans were a people with a close connection with their gods. The greatness of Rome depended – according to this thinking – on proper relations with the gods, and the *pax deorum*, the peace of the gods. Therefore, it was necessary for the Romans to take good care of their relations with the supernatural sphere by performing religious rituals, ceremonies and sacrifices carefully.[1]

The story connected to the Valesius and his family is a mythical narrative of a sacred nature, connected with a certain ritual. In studies of mythical narratives, myths – often defined as tales believed to be true and sacred – are set in the distant past or legendary times or places. Such tales, described as origin myths, function to provide order to the world. As such, mythical narratives help to establish important values and to maintain order of the universe essential to the community.[2] These kinds of narratives are fundamental for the associated faith system as well as for the social order and continuity of the community.[3]

The interest in this paper lies in the story of a powerful Sabine man, Valesius/ Volesus, from whom the prominent Valerian family of Rome was later descended. The main narrative motive in the story is a travel of a father, Valesius, with his children from their hometown, Eretum, towards Ostia, and the reason for the travel is a search for a cure for his sick children. This is an aetiological story of the *Ludi Tarentini/Ludi Tauri*, later known as *Ludi Saeculares*, the Roman Secular Games. During historical times, the *Ludi Saeculares* festival was a magnificent manifestation of the beginning of a new era, 'a remarkable occasion, a magnificent and extremely rare religious ritual, which was only supposed to be officially celebrated once in 100 (or 110) years', as Jussi Rantala has pointed out.[4]

The narratives connected to the journey by Valesius reflect many different historical layers, but the main plot was largely written by the authors of the Augustan era and the Early Empire. In this chapter, I will concentrate on the role of the father and his children described in these narratives and especially on the interaction and the agency of each actor during the journey. In this story, the participants

The sacred travel of Valesius' family 65

come across many strange and even frightening occurrences, which lead them into uncertain situations. The ways and the methods in which Valesius finds help for his sick children are of central interest here, as well as the information the story gives about the relations between the family members and the gods. In this context, I will also analyse some other comparable cases from Roman legendary history especially connected to the Valerian family. Firstly, I will introduce the sources and the plot of the story, and then I will concentrate on the central components of the narratives, and finally turn to the messages or motives of the story.[5]

## Authors and their approaches

Valerius Maximus, who wrote in the reign of Tiberius, compiled a collection of 'memorable deeds and sayings', arranged in nine books and subdivided into chapters according to topics, such as moral quality, religious observance, omens, etc. We do not have much information about the writer himself, but the dedication of the work tells about his closeness to the emperor.[6] Valerius Maximus was interested in the stories that related his own family history. His story of Valesius agrees in the main with Zosimus, and they appear to have derived from the same annalist, Valerius Antias. The story of the Tarentine Games belongs to the section in which Valerius concentrates on the games and spectacles and their origins.[7]

Zosimus was a Greek historian who lived in Constantinople during the reign of the Eastern Roman emperor Anastasius I (491–518). He was a highly esteemed *comes* and held the office of advocate of the imperial treasury. The story of the *Ludi saeculares* at the beginning of his second book is strongly reminiscent of the version of Valerius Maximus and tells the same story. He also gave an exact description of the ceremonies connected to the *Ludi Tarentini*.[8] The reason for his interest has much to do with his critical attitude to his own time. According to Rantala, Zosimus promoted the idea that the Roman Empire was secure as long as the traditional pagan religious obligations were fulfilled, but when the *Ludi saeculares* were neglected, as during his own age, Rome fell into decay.[9]

The author who adds some interesting details to our story is Festus, who lived in Rome in the third century CE. In his epitome, *De verborum significatione*, he mentions briefly two terms related to our story: *Terentum* and *Seculares ludi*, the Secular Games. According to him, Terentum was a part of the Campus Martius, Field of Mars in Rome, and there was a subterranean altar dedicated to Dis Pater, a Roman god of the Underworld.[10] Furthermore, archaeological excavations made in the Field of Mars at the beginning of the last century give interesting information about the memory of the place.[11]

The scarcity of the information about the journey of Valesius and the time gap between when it originally happened (if it happened), and the time when the story was written down – several hundred years later – raise questions and demand explanations.[12] If our interest lay in the authenticity of the story, the challenges would be huge. However, my aim here is not to argue about the historicity of the details of the story, but to approach it from the wider social and cultural context, as a legend that includes information and reconstructs social values, cultural

## 66 *Katariina Mustakallio*

assumptions, and attitudes, mostly connected to the first centuries of the Imperial era. My interest here focuses on the social roles and agency of the participants, father and children, in a very unusual and frightening situation.

In historical research, there has been a great tendency of seeing children as passive objects in the social life of the adults. Nevertheless, as Ville Vuolanto has put it, 'children have an active role in their growing and learning processes, transforming and renewing the cultural as well as religious heritage they were born into'. The recent scholarly discussion over the socialization and the formation of agency in a community encourage us to approach more closely the composition of the legend, the roles of the participants, and especially the agency of the children in cultic context.[13]

Discussions over the *rites de passage* and the concept of *liminality* are also relevant for our unusual story. Behind these concepts lie great scholars of folklore and cultural anthropology such as Arnold van Gennep and Victor Turner.[14] In his classic work, *Rites of Passage*, van Gennep identifies three phases associated with a rite of passage: separation, transition, and incorporation. During these phases, the ritual subject stays in a *liminal stage*, characterized as the quality of ambiguity or disorientation.[15] The concept of liminality is central to a story of Valesius and its explanation.

## The story of Valesius

Next, we move on to the plot of the story. Near the house of Valesius was a grove of beautiful trees, which were burnt by lightning. At the same time, his children were suffering from the plague, which devastated the whole city and the neighborhood. In this terrifying situation, Valesius asked first for help from his household gods, and begged them to divert to himself and his wife the danger that threatened his children. The gods advised him to go on a journey with his children and to fetch some holy water to heal the children from the altar of Dis Pater and Proserpina, the gods of the Underworld, following the course of the Tiber as far as Tarentum. Valesius was astonished, because Tarentum, a famous site in southern Italy, was far away from Tiber River. Anyway, he obeyed the voice and put his three sick children (two boys and one girl, according to Valerius Maximus) into the boat. They stopped sailing near the Field of Mars in Rome because his children were very thirsty, and the father went to seek water. Then he carried the water to a spot where the soil was smoking, heated it and gave it to his children to drink. Here comes the turning point of the story: the children fell asleep, and during their dream they were healed. In their dreams, a god was sponging their bodies (a detail we owe to Valerius Maximus), and gave them orders for the sacrifices. They were ordered to sacrifice to Dis and Proserpina some black victims on the altar from where the water had been brought, then to celebrate *lectisternia*, a rite of setting a meal out before images of the gods, and to arrange nocturnal games for three nights, according to the number of children – as mentioned by Valerius Maximus. Then the father returned to the place and tried to build an altar

## The sacred travel of Valesius' family 67

for the deities, but he found one already there, dedicated precisely to the same two Underworld deities.[16]

After performing the prescribed sacrifices and the rites of the *ludi*, the children got well. The family of *Valerii* moved to Rome with King Titus Tatius and became one of the leading families there.

## Omens and portents

In our story, sacred powers manifest their existence by means of omens or portents.[17] When historical writers of Early Rome, like Livy or Dionysius of Halicarnassus, tell about the dangerous situations in the city, such as wars and illnesses, they often mention frightening portents. Valesius' story consists of several interesting details and incidents connected to the sacred sphere. We notice some terrifying things happening: there is a fire in the woods; illness sent by the gods; then supernatural voices, signs of divine anger. From the beginning, the audience is aware that the possible failure in the decisions of the main actor, the father, could cause a sad end for the children and the whole family, and perhaps even for the whole community. Initially, the situation is desperate, because the father is not aware of which deity is angry and whom he must placate.[18]

In the Roman legendary history, especially in connection with the Early and Republican period, we come across thunder and lightning as a sign of a divine anger, often caused by a religious ritual that is performed incorrectly. For example, when the legendary King Tullus Hostilius (672–640 BCE) was struck by a thunderbolt and his house was reduced to ashes, this was interpreted as a defect in sacrifices performed in honor of Jupiter Elicius.[19] Thunder and lightning were clear signals and direct manifestations of the anger of the gods, and warnings of the coming vengeance. In Roman historical tradition, there are several stories of these kinds of bad omens. In 114 BCE, the virgin daughter of a Roman *eques* was struck dead by a lightning bolt. The omen was interpreted to mean that the sacred rituals were contaminated because the priestesses of Vesta had broken their vows of virginity. In consequence, the Vestals Aemilia, Licinia, and Marcia were condemned to death, together with several men of the equestrian class.[20] The meaning of the divine sign of thunder and lightning was central in Roman thinking: Even later, during the Imperial period, the structures or trees where the lightning hit were regarded as ill-omened and sacred.[21] Lightning was a clear warning connected to the divine forces, especially when related to the Tarentine Games, as Gary Forsythe has pointed out.[22]

The next and even more drastic sign was the illness of the people, and especially of Valesius' offspring. Illness connected to pregnant women, or to children in general, was a serious matter. Valesius, without knowing which divinity was involved, turned to the nearest divine powers and asked help and advice from his household gods. According to Zosimus, the first god named here is Vesta, goddess of the domestic hearth. In Valerius Maximus the gods were Lares, the protectors of the household. Both usually took care of the family and its continuity.[23]

## 68    *Katariina Mustakallio*

In this context, we come across a very peculiar situation: to placate the angry gods, Valesius was ready to offer his own and his wife's lives in place of the children. In the Roman legendary history, we find some devoted couples offering their lives on behalf of another, but parents offering their lives on behalf of their own children very seldom. The idea of a possible human sacrifice is not a common feature either. This was employed only in situations of the utmost crisis, for example, when a general in war sacrificed himself on behalf of his army.[24]

In historical legends related to the Valerian family, we have another example connected to human sacrifices. According to Pseudo-Plutarch, Valeria Luperca, a young girl living in Falerii, was chosen to be sacrificed to Juno, because of the *pestilentia,* a serious disease, which was devastating the city. However, she was able to placate the goddess without sacrificing herself, and finally she even cured the entire population of Falerii from the illness.[25] This story was very popular during the Republican period, and the *gens Valeria* kept the memory of Valeria Luperca alive by using the image of the heroine on several coins.[26]

After telling the story of Valesius, Zosimus goes on to recount other examples of illnesses as signs of the anger of the gods. According to him, Valerius Publicola, one of the first Roman consuls (504 BCE), also celebrated the Tarentine Games to placate Pluto and Proserpina and to cure the whole city of Rome from the plague. He sacrificed a black bull and a black heifer to Pluto and Proserpina.[27] In Roman historical tradition, the *gens Valeria* was connected for generations to the cult of Dis and Proserpina, the gods of the Underworld.[28]

### Travel through Tiber to Tarentum

The story tells about divine voices that commanded Valesius to travel by boat to Tarentum with his children, and to sacrifice to the powers of death there, in order to cure the sick children. Supernatural voices occur in many accounts of the Roman legendary history. The above-mentioned Valerius Publicola, for example, fought with the help of his colleague Brutus against the Etruscans in the Battle of *Silva Arsia,* when they heard a loud voice connected to the god Silvanus informing them about the coming victory of the Roman people.[29]

Furthermore, there is also a story, this time about a heroine of the family, Valeria, the leader of the women's group protecting their patria, Rome, in the story of Coriolanus, a famous general who betrayed his fellow Romans in 488 BCE. Valeria was one of the women who heard the goddess Fortuna speaking and giving orders to the group of women. In these cases, the voices of the gods were helping human beings.[30] Another story related to a young girl of the *gens Valeria* and the river Tiber is connected to the battles against the Etruscan kings during the first years of the Republic. King Porsenna of Clusium took hostages from the youngsters of Rome, boys and girls of the leading families, during these wars. There was, however, one girl named Valeria (or Cloelia) who had the courage to lead the hostages, the younger generation of Rome, back home across the dangerous Tiber.[31]

The River Tiber, and especially its water, plays the main role in our story. The story of Valesius deals with the liminality in many ways: like crossing over Tiber as well as crossing over the boundaries of life and death. As van Gennep and Turner have argued, during the *rites de passage* the ritual subject stays in a liminal stage. The first phase is separation, which clearly demarcates sacred space and time from profane or secular space and time; spatial passage involves moving, such as crossing waters, frontiers, or pilgrimage.[32] This type of liminality is a very specific one, and typical of the initiation rites of passage.[33]

In our story, the children are very sick, almost on the point of death. Their unawareness of the real purpose of their travel shows the unusual character of this journey. These travelling people are in a liminal stage. The role of the Tiber is relevant here: Only the water of the Tiber has the curative properties to save the children after it is heated at the right sacred place.

The contradictory orders of the gods are a part of the disorientation and liminality of the story. The father understands their destiny only when he realizes that Tarentum is located in Rome.[34] The field where Tarentum situated was a very peculiar, peripheral, and liminal place, outside the centre of Rome: It was a vast area dedicated to Mars, a chthonic god of agriculture and warfare, with whose cult the family had connections.[35] Near the river where the ground was smoldering, they found an underground sacred altar, almost like a *mundus*, where the contact with the chthonic deities, Dis and Proserpina, was possible.[36] In this context, the journey starts to remind a *katabasis*, the epic convention of the hero's trip into the Underworld.[37] The difference with the heroic stories of *katabasis* is that only the children are in contact with the gods of the Underworld, not the father.

## The cult place at Terentum

A birth of a cult takes place spiritually or mentally, in people's minds and in stories telling about them, while a cult place, an altar or a temple, constitutes a clear and concrete boundary with certain physical implications. Cult objects are often flexible; they can travel from one place to another.[38] Sometimes, instead, a sacred spot or an altar already exists in a certain holy place, and people travel there as pilgrims.[39]

In the case of the Terentum/Tarentum in the Campus Martius, some archeological evidence was discovered during excavations. According to our legend, Valesius tried to construct an altar to the gods there, but instead found one in the earth twenty feet below the ground. This altar was already dedicated, according to the inscription, to Dis and Proserpina. The altar connected to the cult and dated to the Roman Imperial period, was discovered in the excavations of 1886–1887, behind the Palazzo Cesarini, about five metres below the level of the modern Corso Vittorio Emanuele. Nearby, there were also found large portions of the marble slabs containing the inscriptions that mentions the celebrations of the *ludi saeculares* by Augustus in 17 BCE and by Severus in CE 204.[40]

According to Filippo Coarelli, the Tarentine rites were initially observed by the members of the Valerian family until they were taken over by the Roman state

70   *Katariina Mustakallio*

as early as 249 BCE. It was quite usual for the old Roman families to take care of certain cults on behalf of the community. For example, the *Pinarii* and *Potitii* took care of the rites of Hercules at the *Ara Maxima* in the Roman *Forum Boarium*. This gentilician cult later became a public Roman cult.[41] Nevertheless, the memory of the cult of the Valerian family was kept in mind even later. According to Zosimus, Valesius was later called Manius Valerius Tarentinus. Zosimus gave the explanation of the name as: 'For the Romans call the infernal gods Manes, and *Valere* signifies to be in good health; and the Tarentinus derived from Tarentum where he sacrificed'.[42] The close connection between the powers of life and death and Tarentum was recognized here.

## The role of the children

Interestingly, the genders and the number of the children – two sons and one daughter – are specified in the account by Valerius Maximus (2.4.5). The roles of children become central when they start to act as mediators of the divine orders. Valesius' children received the messages in a dream: they were told to sacrifice black victims on the altar to Dis/Pluto and Proserpina, and to celebrate *lectisternia*, and nocturnal games for three nights – according to the number of the children – with singing and dancing. These orders were given to them by a huge godlike man who advised them to perform these rituals in the Campus Martius. In this situation, children who were recovering their health became important mediators of the divine will, and this time they played the main role.

Dreams as mediators between the gods and human beings frequently are referred to in classical literature. This time, the divine powers are the terrifying divinities of death, Proserpina and Dis Pater, who show their anger by means of various *prodigia*. They were able to burn groves as well as the city walls. They brought pestilence to the people when they were unsatisfied. In our case, nevertheless, after showing their fury, they took care of the children. The children were sick, polluted by the pestilence, but they became pure by drinking the water heated in a sacred altar, and by an act of a godlike figure who washed their bodies in an incubation dream.[43]

This raises the broader question of children's place and role as mediators in cultic connections. Children were often present and helped the adults in various sacrificial rituals and other religious practices in the Greco-Roman world. There were also some cults where they acted in a main role. In the cult of *Fortuna Primigenia* of Praenestae, they mediated prophesies by drawing lots, giving the answers to questions that were asked. We find this kind of phenomenon also in the Ostian cult of Hercules.[44]

In Roman religious ceremonies, the question of the purity was fundamental. The capacity to be in contact with the divine forces demanded certain preconditions. Children, in general, were considered to possess proper qualities in several religious rituals, as Mantle and Vuolanto have shown.[45] In the present case, we are in close connection with the powers of death, in a very specific and frightening situation. In particular, the line between the pure and the polluted is fundamental

*The sacred travel of Valesius' family* 71

here. The children of Valesius are brought back to life from the domain of sickness and death only by the good will of the gods of the Underworld.

Returning to the theory of *rites de Passage* and *liminality*, in our story we may see that the phase of separation started with the journey, and the children went through the phase of transition while they were sleeping. As Turner has pointed out, during the passage, participators of rituals acquire a special kind of freedom and a sacred power. 'They are, in fact, temporarily undefined, beyond the normative social structure'. This is evident in our case, too, when the children are in sleep and meet a godlike figure who gives them sacred knowledge. Turner continues, 'It places them too in a close connection with powers of life and death, where the social order may seem to have been turned upside down'. In our story, we see the same progress, when the children start to give orders to their father, and not *vice versa* (which would be the normal case). And finally, through the rituals performed in honor of the gods, they are incorporated anew into the community.[46] As representatives of the continuity of family line and the hope for future, the role of children is of central importance here.

According to Vuolanto, children appeared in three different contexts in Roman religious rituals. They were active in rituals of their own life, then in rituals connected to family or community, representing a group of young ones, and thirdly, in religious practices where children were thought to possess oracular capacities or divine insight. Besides this, children were seen as channels for divine contact through dreams and visions.[47] In the case of Valesius' children, they had the capacity to receive divine instructions in a dream, but this happened only after they were purified and washed by the gods, and after they had been transformed from their contaminated state of illness to a pure and healthy state. They were cured by drinking the water from the Tiber, and in a dream, they got divine help and a message. The important role of the children and young people, girls and boys, was central also in the later celebrations of the *Ludi Saeculares*. The continuity of the family line and fertility were the main concern of the Secular Games even during the Imperial times.[48]

## The legend and its implications: Interaction, experience, and agency

A story of a father who travelled with his sick children searching for help and found a sacred place where his children were cured is astonishing and rare in the Roman literary tradition. The story has many interesting details, but as a whole, it reveals some specific insights into the religious mentality. If one is to survive in a world, the advice of the gods is badly needed. The observance of the sacred things, omens and portents and the interaction between the humans and the gods, must continue uninterruptedly.

When we look at the role of the *gens Valeria* in the Roman historical memory, the function of the story becomes clearer. The story is a founding legend of the *gens Valeria* and, as such, it emphasises the divine will and *Fatum*: Valesius had to obey the advice of his gods, Lares or Vesta, and the advice given in a dream, for

## 72 *Katariina Mustakallio*

the story of the Valerian family had to be continued. It became a story of Rome, because the *Valerii,* with some other important Roman families, were needed to build and strengthen the Roman power – according to the Roman historical tradition.[49] They were many times in central role and their agency clearly left its remarks to the history.

The Valerian family had certain privileges. When they moved to Rome, they built their house in the central place of the Forum, in Velia. Perhaps because of their close relationship with the forces of death, they even were allowed to bury their dead in Velia, inside the city walls. This was exceptional, for the Roman Law and custom decreed that tombs were to be placed outside the city walls, in accordance with religious regulations, to keep the city pure from the pollution of death.[50]

This emphasizes the liminal character of the sacred travel of Valesius via the Tiber to the unknown holy place at Campus Martius. Liminality, in general, is characterized as the quality of ambiguity or disorientation. Several phases in the story are connected with the liminality: a dangerous journey towards an unknown destiny, which is the place in the periphery of the field of Mars; the age and the sickness of the young participants; the dream with a divine message; the character of the cult and sacrifices to the powerful deities of Hades, Dis Pater, and Proserpina. The power, *valetudo,* of the Valerian family is in the forefront. They are characterized as a family with a strong connection to the frightful divine powers. In the mentality of the early Imperial era, when the antiquarian interest was strong, and the colorful stories connected to the legendary origins of the cults and families were popular, the story of the *Valerii* accorded especially well with the agenda of Valerius Maximus. At the same time, the introduction of Dis and Proserpina to Rome fits the pattern seen in the introduction of other new cults, like Aesculapius and Magna Mater, revealing the openness of the Roman state to the new cults, if they benefited Rome.

The origin myth connected to the *Ludi Saeculares,* brings the message to the new era, with the renaissance of the Secular Games during the reign of Augustus. These kinds of origin myths connected to the certain noble families like *Valerii* were very valuable, especially for the cultural and social capacity of the family in the public life during the conservative and traditionalist period of Augustus when many of the old families had ceased to exist during the civil wars.

## Notes

1 For the *pax deorum,* see e.g. Cic. *Har. Resp.* 19, *Nat. Deor.* 2.8; 3.5; See Liebeschuetz 1996, 1 and 58 and Rosenstein 1990, 89. The attitude of the Romans accords well with Turner's analysis of sacred and profane work: public services to the gods are the sacred part of work, which promotes success in the profane part of work, for example in the wellbeing of the community or the greatness of Rome. Turner 1974, 63–64.

2 Pascom 1954, 333–349 and 1965, 3–20; Leeming 1990, 3, 13.

3 See e.g. Magoulic 2015. Narratives are not only fundamental for human communication and cognition but for comprehension of the world and the constitution of identity in any levels, see e.g. Spencer 2016, 1–3, *Introduction.*

The sacred travel of Valesius' family   73

4   Rantala 2017, 41.
5   The main literary sources are Val. Max. 2.4.5; Zos. 2.3-4; Fest. 328, 350; Censorinus, *De Die Nat.* c17.
6   Val. Max. 1 praef: *Te igitur huic coepto, penes quem hominum deorumque consensus maris ac terrae regimen esse voluit, certissima salus patriae, Caesar, invoco...*
7   Val. Max. 2.4.5.
8   Zos. 2.4. For the analysis of the ceremonies and rites connected to the Terentine Games, see e.g. Scheid 2011, 81.
9   Rantala 2017, 19; Zos. 2.7.
10  *Terentum: locus in campo Martio dictus, quod ex loco ara Ditis patris terra occultaretur.*
11  Coarelli 1997, 260.
12  I.e. before the Valerian family moved to Rome at the beginning of the Republican era.
13  For the theory of socialization and agency, see Vuolanto, 2017, 11–13 and 2013, 47–74. See also Barker 2005, 448.
14  For liminality and 'communitas', see Turner 2008 (foreword by Roger D. Abrahams). The concept of liminality was first developed in the early twentieth century by the folklorist Arnold van Gennep, (*Rite de Passage*,1909) and was later taken up by Turner, who extends Van Gennep's notion of the liminal phase of rites of passage to a more general level. For rites of passages in Ancient Greece, see also Padilla 1999 and Dodd and Faraone 2003.
15  Turner 1974, 56–58.
16  Val. Max. 2.4.5; Zos. 2.4.
17  Festus, the third-century scholar, names four types of omens in his *De Verborum Significatione* in Fest. 140 (98): *monstrum, prodigium, portentum, ostentum.* See Beerden 2013, 110. See also MacBain 1982.
18  For gods and the fear connected to them, especially because of *prodigia*, see Liv. 43.13; 45.16; Diod. 22.12.2; 42.19.2. Liebeschuetz 1996, 56-57
19  Liv. 1.31.8.
20  Bauman 2002 (1992), 53
21  Festus links specific sacred cakes offered in cases of trees being struck by lightning (376L and 377L). Plin. *Nat.* 16.24; 14.119; *religio fulgurum* 17.124. See Hunt 2016, 155.
22  Forsythe 2012, 61. Varro has written about the situation in *De Scaenicis Originibus* 1.22, 905–10. 'When many portents occurred, and the wall and tower between the Colline and Esquiline Gates were touched from heaven, and when the *decemviri* therefore approached the Sibylline Books, they reported that the Tarentine Games to Father Dis and Proserpina in the Campus Martius should be performed for three nights, that black victims should be sacrificed, and that the games should be performed every 110 years' (Cardauns Appendix ad librum Xa), see also Herbert-Brown 2002, 95.
23  For the household gods, see Bettini 2013, 25; Mustakallio 2013, 52 and 80.
24  For *devotio* and evocation, see Mustakallio 2013, 43; on human sacrifices, see Mustakallio 2013, 44.
25  Pseudo Plut. *Par. Min.* (35). See also Forsythe 2012, 52. Falerii, a modern Civita Castellana.
26  On coins, Valeria Luperca is depicted riding a heifer and holding a veil above her head, see e.g. Crawford 474/1b (45 BCE).
27  See Zos. 1, 2. Val. Max. 2.4.5-6 and Plut. *Publ.* 21, also mentions Valerius Publicola. Scheid 2011, 83. For the role of Proserpina and Dis Pater later in Roman history, see Beard, North, and Price 1999, 71. Sacrifices of 249 BCE: Varro in *Censorinus* 17.8 (black victims sacrificed at Terentum).
28  For the relation of the Valerian family to the cult, see Forsythe 2012, 52 (citing Coarelli).
29  Liv. 2.7. and Zos. 1. 2.

## 74  *Katariina Mustakallio*

30  Mustakallio 1990, 128-130. We have also Valeria, daughter of Publicola, who had the courage to oppose even the King Porsenna; see Plut. *Publ.* 19.3-4.

31  Plin. *Nat.* 34.29; Plut. *Publ.*19.5; Liv. 2.13.6-11. According to Pliny and Plutarch, Valeria got an equestrian statue at the *summa sacra via* in the *Forum Romanum*. According to Livy, she was the first woman whose statue was set up in a public place in Rome. See, Mustakallio 2012, 165–174, esp. 169–171; Coarelli 1983, 82–83.

32  Turner 1974, 56–58.

33  The ritual contexts of water and travelling with a ship, see Faranda 2009, 47–66 and Gallini 1963.

34  Festus: 478 L; 479 L (Paul.) 440 L. Cfr. Zos. 2. 4. For *Tarentum*: Forsythe 2012, 52, refers to Kurt Latte in his note 36. Without positing a direct connection between the *ludi Tarentini* and the city of Tarentum, according to Forsythe, it is clear that the cult, which was of importance in Magna Graecia and in Tarentum itself, found a new home in Rome in the middle of the third century BCE.

35  For the Campus Martius, see Patterson 2000, 85–103.There is an archaic inscription, found in 1977 during excavations by C.M. Stibbe from the ruins of Satricum, a village of Southern Latium. The inscription, dated to the late sixth or early fifth centuries BCE, mentions a member of this family: *(?)IEI STETERAI POPLIOSIO VALESIOSIO/ SVODALES MAMARTEI* ("The (?) dedicated this, as companions of Poplios Valesios, to Mars"). *CIL* I2, 2832a. For the analysis of the text, see Balbi 1999, 166.

36  For *Mundus* at the Forum Romanum, as a center of universe, see Coarelli 1997, 80. For the vulcanic ground of the Campus Martius, and fire on the Tarentum, see Pascal 1979, 532–537. For Mars as a chthonic deity, see e.g. Mustakallio 2013, 20, 25, 34. Censorinus ascribes the first celebration to the consul Valerius Poplicola. This account admits that the worship of Dis and Proserpina had existed long before, but states that the games and sacrifices were now performed for the first time to avert a plague, and in that part of the Campus Martius which had belonged to the last king, Tarquinius, from whom the place derived its name Tarentum; cf. also Serv. *ad. Aen.* 2. 140; Varro *ap. Censorin.*

37  For *katabasis*, see e.g. Edmonds 2004.

38  As in the stories concerning the cults of Aesculapius and Magna Mater in Republican Rome. The cult of Aesculapius, with a sacred snake, came to Rome in 292 BCE (Beard et al.1998, 69), as did the cult object of Cybele, or Magna Mater, a black stone that arrived by boat at 204 BCE (Beard et al 1998, 80), both by the decision of the Roman Senate after consultation of the Sibylline books and the oracles.

39  For the problematic connection between pilgrimage and sacred places in antiquity, see Rantala and Vuolanto in this volume.

40  The altar itself is no longer visible; see Orlin 2010.

41  Coarelli 1997, 260. Val. Max. 2.4.5. Valerius Publicola (consul with Brutus in 509 BCE) was said to have been the first to stage *Ludi Tarentini* to the benefit of the Roman people.

42  Zos. 1.2.

43  For dreams as a medicine in the cult of Persephone, see Dimou 2001, 75–92. For incubation, see Ogden 2001, 75–92.

44  Champeaux 1981, 3–147, (section I). For the Ostian cult of Hercules, a relief found near the Temple of Hercules at Ostia, see Pavolini 2006, 119. In the scene on the right appears to show a statue of Hercules. In the central scene, Hercules hands a tablet with an oracle to a boy.

45  Mantle 2002, 85–106; Vuolanto 2010, 147.

46  Turner 1974, 58–60.

47  Vuolanto 2010, 147–48.

48  Rantala 2017, 122 and 142–144.

The sacred travel of Valesius' family   75

49 The power of the old families and especially of the the *gens Valerii* has been exaggerated, but their role in the historical drama of the Roman people, as remembered by Livy, Dionysius of Halicarnassus and Plutarch, is nevertheless central. For the critical point of view, see e.g. Salmon 1967, 197.
50 Dion. Hal. 5.48.3; Plut. *quaest. Rom.* 79, *Popl.* 23, See Coarelli 1983, 80. For the pollution caused by dead people, see Cic. *Leg.* 2.23.58; also, Toynbee 1971, 48 and Mustakallio 1994, 28.

## Bibliography

Balbi, Philip. 1999. "Observations of Two Latin Inscriptions." In *The Emergence of the Modern Language Sciences: In Honour of E. F. K. Koerner, II Methodological Perspectives and Applications*, edited by Sheila M. Embleton, John Earl Joseph, and Hans-Josef Niederehe, 165–174. Amsterdam: John Benjamins Publishing Co.

Barker, Chris. 2005. *Cultural Studies: Theory and Practice*. London: Sage.

Bauman, Rickhard. 2002. *Women in Politics in Ancient Rome*. London and New York: Routledge.

Beard, Mary, John North, and Simon Price. 1998. *Religions of Rome*, vol. 1. Cambridge: Cambridge University Press.

Beerden, Kim. 2013. *Worlds Full of Signs: Ancient Greek Divination in Context*. Leiden: Brill.

Bettini, Maurizio. 2013. "The Lar Familiaris of the Romans, a Simple God." In *Religious Participation in Ancient and Medieval Societies. Rituals, Interaction and Identity* (Acta IRF 41), edited by Sari Katajala-Peltomaa and Ville Vuolanto, 25–38. Rome: Institutum Romanum Finlandiae.

Champeaux, Jacqueline. 1982. *Fortuna. Recherche sur le culte de la Fortune à Rome et dans le monde romain, des origins à la mort de César*, vol. I. Rome: Collection de École française 64.

Coarelli, Filippo. 1983. *Il foro romano. Periodo arcaico*. Roma: Edizione Quasar.

Coarelli, Filippo. 1997. *Roma, Guide archeologiche di Mondadori*. Roma: Mondadori.

Crawson, Michael Hewson. 1985. *Coinage and Money under the Roman Republic: Italy and the Mediterranean Economy*. Berkeley: University of California Press.

Dimou, Alexandra. 2016. *La déesse Korè-Perséphone: mythe, culte et magie en Attique* (Recherches sur les rhétoriques religieuses 18). Turnhout: Brepols.

Dodd, David B. and Cristopher A. Faraone (eds.). 2003. *Initiation in Ancient Greek Rituals and Narratives. New Critical Perspectives*. London and New York: Routledge.

Edmonds III, Radcliffe G. 2004. *Myths of the Underworld Journey: Plato, Aristophanes, and the 'Orphic' Gold Tablets*. Cambridge: Cambridge University Press.

Faranda, Laura. 2009. *Viaggi di ritorno: itinerari antropologici nella Grecia antica*. Roma: Armando Editore.

Forsythe, Gary. 2012. *Time in Roman Religion: One Thousand Years of Religious History. Routledge Studies in Ancient History*. London and New York: Routledge.

Gallini, Clara. 1963. "Katapontismos." *Studi e Materiali di Storia delle Religioni* XXXIV: 61–90.

Herbert-Brown, Geraldine (ed.). 2002. *Ovid's Fasti: Historical Readings at Its Bimillennium*. Oxford: Oxford University Press.

Hunt, Ailsa. 2016. *Reviving Roman Religion. Sacred Trees in the Roman World*. Cambridge: Cambridge University Press.

76  *Katariina Mustakallio*

Leeming, David E. 1990. *The World of Myth: An Anthology*. Oxford: Oxford University Press.

Liebeschuetz, John. 1996. *Continuity and Change in Roman Religion*. Oxford: Clarendon Press.

MacBain, Bruce. 1982. *Prodigy and Expiation: A Study in Religion and Politics in Republican Rome*. Brussels: Collection Latomus 177.

Magoulic, Mary. 2015. "What Is Myth." https://mfjrinc.wordpress.com/2014/01/30/mary-magoulick-what-is-myth/.

Mantle, Inga C. 2002. "The Roles of Children in Roman Religion." *Greece and Rome* 49.1: 85–106.

Mustakallio, Katariina. 1990. "Some Aspects of the Story of Coriolanus and the Women behind the Cult of Fortuna Muliebris." In *Roman Eastern Policy and Other Studies in Roman History*, edited by Heikki Solin and Mika Kajava, 125–131. Helsinki: Finnish Society of Sciences and Letters.

Mustakallio, Katariina. 1994. *Death and Disgrace. Capital Penalties with Post Mortem Sanctions in Early Roman Historiography*. Helsinki: Academia Scientiarum Fennica.

Mustakallio, Katariina. 2012. "Women Outside Their Homes, the Female Voice in Early Republican Memory." *Index* 40: 165–174.

Mustakallio, Katariina. 2013. *Sive deus sive dea. La presenza della religion nello sviluppo della società romana*. Pisa: Edizione ETS.

Ogden, Daniel. 2001. *Greek and Roman Necromancy*. Princeton and Oxford: Princeton University Press.

Orlin, Erich. 2010. *Foreign Cults in Rome. Creating Roman Empire*. Oxford: Oxford University Press.

Padilla, Mark W. (ed.). 1999. *Rites of Passage in Ancient Greece: Literature, Religion, Society*. Lewisburg: Bucknell University Press.

Pascal, C. Bennett. 1979. "Fire on the Tarentum." *The American Journal of Philology* 100.4: 532–537.

Pascom, William R. 1954. "Four Functions of Folklore." *The Journal of American Folklore* 67: 333–349.

Pascom, William R. 1965. "The Forms of Folklore: Prose Narratives." *The Journal of American Folklore* 78: 3–20.

Patterson, John R. 2000. "On the Margins of Rome." In *Death and Diseases in the Ancient City*, edited by Valerie M. Hope and Eireann Marshall, 85–103. London and New York: Routledge.

Pavolini, Carlo. 2006. *Ostia. Guide Archeologiche Laterza*. Roma-Bari: Laterza.

Rantala, Jussi. 2017. *The Ludi Saeculares of Septimius Severus. The Ideologies of a New Roman Empire*. London and New York: Routledge.

Rosenstein, Nathan S. 1990. *Imperatores Victi: Military Defeat and Aristocratic Competition in the Aristocratic Competition in the Middle and Late Republic*. Berkeley: University of California Press.

Salmon, Edward T. 1967. *Samnium and the Samnites*. Cambridge: Cambridge University Press.

Scheid, John. 2011. *Quando fare è credere. I riti sacrificiali dei Romani*. Roma: Laterza.

Spencer, Alexander. 2016. *Romantic Narratives in International Politics: Pirates, Rebels and Mercenaries*. Manchester: Manchester University Press.

Toynbee, Jocelyn M. C. 1971. *Death and Burial in the Roman World*. London: Thames and Hudson.

Turner, Victor. 1974. "Liminal to Liminoid, in Play, Flow, and Ritual: An Essay in Comparative Symbology." *Rice Institute Pamphlet - Rice University Studies* 60.3: 53–92.

Turner, Victor. 2008. *The Ritual Process: Structure and Anti-Structure*. New Brunswick: Aldine Transaction Press.

Van Gennep, Arnold. 1909. *Les rites de passage*. Paris: Nourry.

Vuolanto, Ville. 2010. "Faith and Religion." In *A Cultural History of Childhood and Family in Antiquity*, edited by Mary Harlow and Ray Laurence, 133–151. London and New York: Bloomsbury.

Vuolanto, Ville. 2013. "Family Relations and the Socialization of Children in the Autobiographical Narratives of Late Antiquity." In *Approaches to the Byzantine Family*, edited by L. Brubaker and S. Tougher, 47–74. Farnham: Ashgate.

Vuolanto, Ville. 2017. "Experience, Agency, and the Children in the Past. The Case of Roman Childhood." In *Children and Everyday Life in the Roman and Late Antique World*, edited by Christian Laes and Ville Vuolanto, 11–13. London and New York: Routledge.

# 5 When kings and gods meet

## Agency and experience in sacred travel from Alexander the Great to Caracalla

*Jaakkojuhani Peltonen*

### Introduction

A monarch visiting a sacred site is a popular topic in classical historiography. In Greco-Roman culture – as in many religious systems – gods, demigods, and deceased ancestors were worshipped in temples, tombs, and oracular shrines. These places became objects of sacred travel where people venerated and made contact with divine forces. One of the most famous sacred travelers of antiquity was Alexander the Great (356–323 BCE). Narratives of his journeys spread far and wide and were mythologized soon after his successful Persian and Indian campaigns and sudden death. His undisputed legacy of conquest and greatness motivated Roman rulers and emperors to imitate his heroic persona and practices.[1] One way of doing this was to visit sacred places.

In this article, I examine sacred travel narratives of antiquity from the perspective of agency and experience. The material under consideration comprises stories of Alexander and famous Roman warlords and emperors visiting tombs and oracular shrines. In this chapter, my study gives an interesting angle on the way sacred travel is depicted in ancient narratives portraying visits alleged to be historical. In the context of a study of ancient narratives of sacred travel it will be productive to examine the literary images of agency and experience, as literature is one of our best sources of the meanings that were given to sacred travel and the thematic concerns of classical people. Stories of the sacred travel by famous monarchs undoubtedly made an impact on the ways people saw visits to famed sacred places. In addition, their reported visits made an impact on the way narratives of late antiquity and the Middle Ages portrayed kings carrying out such activities.

In this study, I approach the sources from an intertextual angle, examining sacred travel narratives as a literary genre. My intent is to explore the intertextual literary themes that exist in sacred-travel writing, so the historical reality, 'what really happened', remains a side issue here. The main questions this paper explores are: What motivations were given for the sacred travels in the narratives, and how did these narratives portray agency and experience during the sacred travels? What functions and thematic concerns do these narratives contain? The aim of this study is to distinguish whether there are literary conventions in and intertextuality between different texts.

*When kings and gods meet*   79

In classical literature, we find passages of sacred travel in epic poetry, histories, and first-person travel depictions like those written by Pausanias.[2] Here, I concentrate on texts composed by writers other than the visitors themselves, but they belong to a tradition describing the deeds of notable individuals. Diodorus, Curtius, Plutarch, Arrian, and Justin composed narratives of Alexander the Great's sacred travels some 300 or 400 years after the alleged historical events and they drew on the literary tradition created by the early Hellenistic writers.[3] The same can be said of passages by Strabo and Josephus, and from the *Alexander Romance,* all of which I use as my source material. Suetonius, Tacitus, Appian, Cassius Dio, Herodian, Aurelius Victor, and the *Historia Augusta* portray Roman emperors visiting sacred sites and link their accounts to the memory of Alexander. Their works were written by both contemporaries (cf. Cassius Dio on Caracalla) and non-contemporaries (cf. Suetonius on Augustus) of the events they describe.

Sacred travel/pilgrimage in antiquity has received growing interest from classical scholars. Their recent research has often concentrated on sacred travel carried out by the ordinary people, studied by using archeological and epigraphical evidence.[4] The famous visits made by monarchs to oracular sites or tombs have been treated as history of sometimes doubtful veracity. For example, the religiosity of the 'historical' Alexander, his divination, and the role of gods and oracles during the Persian expedition have received attention in previous scholarship.[5] When it comes to the visits of notable Romans to the tomb of Alexander the Great, scholars have concentrated on the tomb itself and have long been obsessed with finding it.[6] Since the historical reality is often difficult to reconstruct from the classical literature, it is rewarding and useful to explore the ways these narratives present sacred travel.[7]

This article elaborates the connection between the sacred travels of Alexander the Great and those of Roman emperors. In previous scholarship, this connection has been noted by Henrichs (1968), who highlighted the common features in the oracular visit of Alexander in Egypt and Vespasian's visit to the Serapeion in Alexandria.[8] Instead of concentrating on one episode, I take the whole tradition of Alexander's visits and those of the Roman emperors together.

In existing scholarship, it has been debated whether the term pilgrimage should be applied to Greco-Roman antiquity or restricted only to the medieval era.[9] In my study, I prefer to use the term sacred travel. Besides sacred travel, one might consider my source material evidence for sightseeing and tourism in antiquity. However, since in my source material ancient writers refer to ritualistic activities such as sacrifices, prayers or divination/consultation with the priests taking place at the site, I consider the term sacred travel, or alternatively sacred tourism,[10] more appropriate than merely sightseeing or tourism.[11]

Classical historiography focuses on the actions of great individuals, so it is not surprising that its accounts and epics of sacred travel are stories of notable persons paying a visit to a sacred site. In the literary genre of writing history, the actual journey to the sacred space is depicted in detail only rarely.[12] In most of the cases, the religious site is visited during a sojourn in the city or when passing through the area.[13] On the other hand, Alexander's journey to the oracle of

80    *Jaakkojuhani Peltonen*

Ammon at Siwah, which required a six-week, 1100 km detour from the king's expected route, was made solely in order to visit an oracular shrine of religious or cultural significance.[14]

In the first part of this chapter, I focus on the given motives for the sacred activity of a monarch who visits Troy and the tombs of Homeric heroes and the Persian king Cyrus. Next, I examine stories of notable Romans visiting the tombs of Alexander and Pompey from the angle of agency and experience. Afterwards I turn to sacred travel narratives depicting oracular visits like that of Alexander to Siwah, Gordium, and Jerusalem and Vespasian and Titus to various oracles. How do stories of oracular visits portray agency, motivation, and experience? In the last part of the chapter, I explore the experience of oracular consultation as a means to praise the power of the gods and the way that authors construct negative character development with their portraits of sacred travel.

## Agency and visiting the tombs of Trojan heroes and Cyrus the Great

Visiting sacred sites was a tradition before Alexander the Great. The Greek historian Herodotus wrote in 440 BCE that before entering Greece with his enormous army in 480 BCE, Xerxes visited old Troy: 'After viewing the site, and inquiring into its particulars and past, he [Xerxes] sacrificed 1,000 head of cattle to Athena of Ilium, and the Magi poured libations to the heroes'.[15] In the passage, Xerxes does not take the lead in rituals but leaves it to his holy men, the Magi. Classical and Persian texts do not portray the Magi strictly as priests but as ritual experts who accompanied the Persian king wherever he went.[16] Recent research has regarded these actions of Xerxes as a strategy to win over the Greeks of Asia Minor by using Greek myths and to present the Persian kings as successors of the Trojan kings avenging the sack of their city.[17] Herodotus, on the other hand, may have included this passage because he was presenting the Trojan War as a predecessor of the Persian wars, so the visit suited his literary theme.[18]

Herodotus' account was widely read among the Greeks, and 140 years later Alexander intended to present his war against Persia as a new Trojan war justified as revenge for the Persian Wars.[19] Alexander's court-historian Callisthenes wrote about the king as a new Achilles and Agamemnon, commanding Greek armies on a massive expedition against the Persian Darius III.[20] In this literary tradition – best preserved in Arrian's *Anabasis*, composed in the second century CE – Alexander is presented as an agent in the rituals and taking an active role by paying visits to sacred sites. In contrast to the Persian king, whose Magi take the lead in the rituals in Herodotus' narrative, it is Alexander himself who carries out the rituals.[21]

Before Alexander reaches Troy, he marches with his Macedonians to Elaeus where he sacrifices at the tomb of Protesilaus.[22] Arrian writes that Alexander was praying to Protesilaus at Elaeus in the hope of avoiding Protesilaus' fate, as he was believed to be the first victim of the Trojan War. Next, the king travels to ancient Ilium (Troy) to visit the temple of Athene Ilias.[23] During his stay in Troy,

Alexander is said to have sacrificed to Priam at the altar of Zeus of the Enclosures and prayed that he could avoid the wrath of Priam since he himself belonged to the race of Neoptolemus.[24] From there he heads for Sigeum (Troy Menoetius) where Achilleus' tomb was located. At the site, Alexander puts a wreath on the tomb of Achilles and his friend Hephaestion places one on Patroclus' tomb, and they oil their bodies and contest as athletes.[25]

The actions before the tombs of the Trojan heroes are portrayed in Arrian as motivated by the king's personal religious thoughts. The king visits religious sites to gain divine power and protection in the war against Persia. In addition to the pan-Hellenistic war propaganda, these actions must be seen in the context of the hero cult which was an essential part of Greek religion.[26] As we know, the hero was a divine being, who had lived on earth and had suffered death, which was the main distinction between a god and hero.[27] Their supposed tombs may have been the focus of a cult. By rituals commemorating deceased heroes – who had often suffered a premature death by violence and therefore had been wronged and were perhaps embittered by their fate – the person who carried them out hoped to assuage their anger and hoped that the heroes would become their defenders and protectors.[28]

A sacred journey involves travelers not only in enacting rituals but also inter-acting with holy objects. As a part of the Greek hero cult, the supposed pos-sessions of heroes were displayed as relics in sanctuaries, revered objects such as shields, spears, weaponry, clothing or chariots.[29] During the visit, the Ilians showed Alexander the arms used in the Trojan War. According to Arrian, Alexander dedicated his full panoply of arms and weapons ($\pi\alpha\nu o\pi\lambda\acute{\iota}\alpha$, denoting shield, helmet, breastplate, greaves, sword, and spear) to Athene, the guardian goddess of the Greeks in the Trojan War, as a votive gift.[30] The king also took from the temple some of the dedicated arms remaining from the Trojan War. Diodorus writes that after giving away his armor, the king took the finest armor that had been deposited in the temple and formerly used in the Trojan War and put it on.[31] Diodorus says that the king used these weapons in the Battle of Granicus, while Arrian says the royal bodyguard Peucestas carried the sacred shield carried by Achilleus and taken from the temple of Athena in the battle against the Malli.[32] These passages stress the importance of religious objects, symbolizing the visit to the sacred site and the relationship between the visitor and divine forces, and also the image of the visitor who desperately wants to acquire the sacred power linked to the holy sites and its items.

According to Arrian and Plutarch, when the king visited the tomb of Achilleus he blessed the hero for having a poet such as Homer to proclaim his deeds for later generations.[33] Plutarch adds that at this moment Alexander also proclaimed that Achilleus was lucky to have such a faithful friend (referring to Patroclus). Achilleus as Alexander's favorite hero was commonplace in the literary tradi-tion.[34] The representation of the event in these narratives gives the impression that the visit and his participation in the rituals had a personal significance for Alexander, who thus becomes closer to his hero. In addition, the king's reaction and his eagerness to participate in cultic rituals reflect the fear of being not com-memorated by posterity.[35]

## 82  *Jaakkojuhani Peltonen*

In antiquity, the fear that future generations would forget a person's deeds and neglect their tomb was a common theme in Classical literature and surviving epitaphs.[36] The desire to be memorialized in a suitable manner is reflected in the stories of Alexander visiting the tomb of the Persian monarch Cyrus at Pasargadae in 324 BCE and paying honor to him. Curtius, Strabo, Arrian, and Plutarch all write about the visit and Alexander's reaction when he sees that the tomb has been robbed and desecrated.[37] In Curtius the king orders that the tomb of Cyrus be opened and wishes to make offerings for the dead king (*dare volebat inferias*).[38] Persian sources support the idea that the tomb cult of Cyrus at Pasargadae was historical and not a literary 'invention' of the Classical authors.[39] Curtius uses the Latin term *inferiae* to refer to sacrifices in honor of the dead. In the narrative, the king expects the tomb to be filled with gold and silver, but he finds that most of the precious items have been stolen. He sets the golden crown on the sarcophagus and drapes it with his own cloak. Alexander is amazed that so illustrious a king has been buried like a common person.[40] Arrian explains that the desecration of the tomb distressed Alexander and he ordered his engineer Aristobulos to restore the tomb and reproduce the lost items and place them in it.[41]

Alexander is portrayed as a pious monarch who not only honored but fought for the memorialization of his predecessor. Plutarch's, the shortest account of the visit, lacks religious agency: when Alexander sees the tomb of Cyrus in ruins, he reads the inscription on the tomb and orders it to be translated into Greek letters.[42] Plutarch writes that Alexander was emotionally affected by the visit and reminded of the uncertainty and mutability of life. Alexander's desire to imitate Cyrus is an oft-appearing topic in the accounts of the Alexander historians.[43] In addition, the king's portrayed reaction when visiting the house of the dead reflects the Classical value-system, where valuing the memory of the deceased was of great importance.

### The 'Roman Alexanders' encounter their divine heroes

After his death, Alexander was worshipped as the founder of the city of Alexandria and as a god of a state-cult created by the Ptolemaic dynasty.[44] According to the tradition, after the king had died in Babylon, for several days his dead body remained uncorrupted as if 'the breath of life was still in him' and the king was still alive.[45] This mythical belief might have given a certain flavor of holiness to the body of Alexander and credibility to the stories that the body of the Macedonian conqueror was seen as a relic. Like those of the Greek heroes, who were worshipped as demi-gods and whose weapons were sacred and carried in battle, the belongings of Alexander became symbols of his fortune and power and they were used as talismans.[46] Caligula is said to have taken the breastplate of Alexander from the tomb and used it on some occasions.[47] Against this background, Alexander's tomb and sarcophagus in the city of Alexandria became a focus of tourism and sacred travel by famous Romans in the Classical tradition.[48]

Julius Caesar, himself an admirer and imitator of Alexander, is the first famous Roman recorded as visiting the tomb.[49] In Lucan's epic *Civil War,* Caesar was

*When kings and gods meet* 83

keener to visit the tomb of his hero than to see the great buildings and architecture of Alexandria.[50] Lucan's passage does not describe in detail what Caesar does during his visit, but he presents a summary of Alexander's fame and conquests. He concludes with the somewhat cynical observation that the result of the once great king's endeavors is that he now lies dead in the sarcophagus. The visit presented by Lucan highlights Alexander as the hero to whom the famous Romans pay homage.

Octavian's visit to the tomb, described by Suetonius and Cassius Dio, took place in 30 BCE after his victory over the forces of Cleopatra and Antony at Actium. In contrast to Lucan's treatment, Suetonius creates a more dynamic scene, stressing the agency of the visitor:

> About this time he [Octavian] had the sarcophagus and body of Alexander the Great brought forth from its shrine, and after gazing on it, showed his respect by placing upon it a golden crown and strewing it with flowers; and being then asked whether he wished to see the tomb of the Ptolemies as well, he replied, 'My wish was to see a king, not corpses.'[51]

Octavian visits the tomb of the most respected monarch and places a golden crown on the sarcophagus in a scene resembling Alexander's visit to the tomb of Cyrus.[52] In antiquity, flowers were laid upon the tomb and they were part of the funeral ceremonies.[53] Octavian does not merely take a quick glance at the corpse of the king, but he takes time to show his respect to the embalmed corpse. In Cassius Dio's narrative, Augustus not only views the body but even touches the mummy of Alexander. Dio writes that this careless gesture was said to have broken off a piece of Alexander's nose.[54]

Undoubtedly the visit had political motives: Octavian's purpose was to show that as the new ruler of Egypt, he accepted Alexander as his predecessor, if not the Ptolemaic dynasty. The narrative itself stresses the agency of the emperor during the visit and thus creates the impression that divine charisma was transferred to Octavian from Alexander. It is possible that the emperor decided to build his dynastic mausoleum in 28 BCE in imitation of the tomb of Alexander.[55]

In the early third century, Cassius Dio continues the literary tradition portraying Roman emperors' visits to sacred places linked to the memory of Alexander. In Dio's presentation, Emperor Trajan visits the ruins of Babylon during his Parthian War (115–117 CE) and offers sacrifices to Alexander in the room where the king had died.[56] Cassius Dio uses the verb ἐνᾰγίζω, meaning 'offering sacrifice to the dead' which clearly refers to a tomb cult and/or hero-cult. Contemporaries reading Cassius Dio's presentation of Trajan's campaign against the eastern enemy Parthia (seen as successor or even a revival of Persia) might have drawn parallels between Trajan's expedition and Alexander's conquest of the East, even though Trajan did not defeat the Parthians in a decisive battle.[57]

Among the Roman emperors, the most famous admirer and imitator of Alexander was Caracalla, whose actions have been seen as 'Alexander-mania'.[58] We are told that Caracalla visited both Troy and the tomb of Alexander at Alexandria.

84   *Jaakkojuhani Peltonen*

Herodian's story of Caracalla's visit has connotations of the visit of Alexander to Troy, even though imitation of Alexander is not mentioned explicitly:

> He [Caracalla] visited all the ruins of that city, coming last to the tomb of Achilles; he adorned this tomb lavishly with garlands of flowers, and immediately he became Achilles. Casting about for a Patroclus, he found one ready to hand in Festus, his favorite freedman.[59]

This passage has striking similarities with the stories of Alexander's visit. Alexander (as Caracalla in Herodian) goes to the tomb as the last act of his visit to Troy, adorns the tomb with garlands and identifies himself with Achilles and his friend Hephaestion with Patroclus.[60] Herodian's passage may indicate that Caracalla had read about Alexander's visit and imitated it, or it may be a deliberate imitation by the author of passages of Plutarch's and Arrian describing Alexander's visit, intended to illustrate the desire of Caracalla to emulate the king.

In Herodian's account, when Caracalla visited the tomb of Alexander in Alexandria, the emperor removed the purple cloak he was wearing and his belts and finger rings of precious stones and anything valuable he was carrying and put them upon the tomb.[61] The narrative gives the impression of a feeling of very close affinity to Alexander. The public gestures follow the same literary pattern as the visits of Alexander to the tomb of Cyrus, or that of Octavian in Alexandria described by earlier historians. Similarly, as admiration and imitation are implied as the motives for Alexander's visits to the tombs of Achilleus and Cyrus, the famous Romans are visiting sites linked with Alexander because of their admiration and identification with him, the Macedonian world-conqueror.[62]

Alexander was not the only deceased hero whose tomb was visited by Roman emperors. Hadrian's visit to the tomb of Pompey and his religious veneration for the famous triumvir, consul and general who had met his end tragically in Egypt after the Battle of Pharsalus in 48 BCE is well-known. In the tradition, during his trip to Egypt, near Pelusium, Mons Cassius, Hadrian offered a sacrifice to Pompey's spirit (*manes*). In addition, he is said to have composed a poem at the tomb and renovated it as it was in ruins and covered by sand. He also found and restored the many statues of Pompey. The story has similarities with Alexander's visit to the tomb of Cyrus and his decision to renovate the tomb.[63] Like Alexander, Hadrian is appalled by the state of the tomb and the dishonor shown to Pompey's memory and spirit, and shows he cares about the duties of the living to the dead. After Hadrian's renovation, Septimius Severus is said to have visited the tomb when he was entering Egypt. Cassius Dio writes that Severus sacrificed at the tomb of Pompey.[64]

The stories about Xerxes, Alexander, and Roman emperors visiting Troy and famous tombs can be regarded as both symbolical sacred travel and sacred tourism. Paying honors to the deceased when visiting the tombs of Homeric heroes, Cyrus, Alexander, and Pompey created an image of a world where history and its great individuals encountered the present. When the Roman writers composed narratives of Roman rulers visiting sacred sites related to Alexander's memory, they followed

*When kings and gods meet* 85

the literary tradition of Alexander created by the Alexander historians, thus presenting Alexander as a model for Caesar, Octavian, Trajan, or Caracalla. Altogether, these anecdotes – whether involving Alexander or the Roman emperors – create an image of rulers seeking to make contact with the divine powers and acquire the religious and mythical value of the sacred space. The things that he does: viewing the site,[65] laying a wreath on the tomb, renovating the shrine, identifying himself with the hero, these are all stressing the piety of the ruler and his relationship with the deceased. Ancient authors' accounts reflect a world where the dead, especially those who were famous, could only be kept content by funeral rituals; nor could assistance or acquisition of their power be expected otherwise. These texts also emphasize the fear of not being remembered by posterity.

## Agency and given motivations for oracular visits

Consulting oracles was an important motive for a sacred journey in classical antiquity. It was a common belief that the gods spoke to people through oracles. The oracle was a remarkable institution that had a lot of power and prestige in the ancient world.[66] Even though couriers could consult oracles without the enquirer's physical presence, there are a few stories of monarchs and future emperors personally visiting oracular shrines. In the historiographical tradition, monarchs and future emperors consulted oracles as private individuals, not as representatives of the empire, kingdom or city-state. The tradition of Alexander and Roman future emperors seeking oracular consultation highlights the notable visitor's agency and personal interests.[67]

The most famous oracular visitor, Alexander the Great, leans on the authority of the oracles and wants to heed their counsel and fulfil the prophecies given by them. The initiative to visit oracular sites comes from the king himself. The Alexander historians use a term 'yearning' (πόθος and its Latin equivalent *ingens cupido*) to describe his strong desire to visit an oracle.[68] The phrase explaining the sacred journey creates an image of a king whose emotional and religious experience is so strong that he is forced to visit places which would not have been included in his expedition for non-sacred reasons (e.g. political, military, curiosity, etc.).[69] Another explanation for the oracular visits is Alexander's admiration for, imitation of and vying with heroes like Heracles and Perseus.[70]

Alexander's visit to the oracle of Ammon Zeus at Siwa takes place before encountering the armies of Darius in the decisive battle of Gaugamela. As a literary tradition, consulting an oracle before a conclusive clash between two empires had already appeared in Herodotus' history over 100 years prior to Alexander's time. Herodotus wrote that the Lydian king Croesus sent an embassy to ask the oracle of Apollo at Delphi whether he should wage a war against the Persians.[71] In the journey to the oracle of Ammon, Alexander's will and strength encourages others to continue even though there are hardships during the trip, like a sandstorm lasting several days and lack of water.[72] When they miraculously finally arrive at their destination, the shrine, it is Alexander who enters the sanctuary and has the conversation with the priests.

## 86  *Jaakkojuhani Peltonen*

In the works of Diodorus, Curtius, Plutarch, and Justin/Trogus, the oracular discussion between Alexander and the priests has the same pattern. Arrian's differs from all other accounts by leaving what the king asks of the god open, whereas in Strabo's short account of the visit the narratives are condemned as mere flattery.[73] In Diodorus' account, Alexander asks: 'Tell me if you give me the rule of the whole world', and the priest, after consulting the image of the god, replies that the god responded affirmatively.[74] In Plutarch, Alexander asks whether he will become the lord of all men.[75] In Curtius, the king asks whether he will become the ruler of whole world (*totius orbis imperium*).[76] Furthermore, the king asks whether he has punished all the murderers of his father, to which the priest gives a positive answer.[77] In summary, the king seeks for hidden information and knowledge of the future from a god who is supposed to possess knowledge beyond that available to humans.

The question of world dominion and the king's personal desire to know what will happen in the future also appears in Alexander's other oracular consultations, taking place before the above-mentioned visit to Siwah. In these other passages, Alexander is portrayed as a monarch in constant interaction with the gods, and this contact is part of his image of victorious world-conqueror as a man fulfilling his destiny as the victor of battles and world conqueror. According to Plutarch, before starting the expedition in Asia, Alexander wished to consult the oracle of Apollo at Delphi.[78] Diodorus goes on to say that the oracular responses Alexander received from the Pythia in Delphi and later from Ammon in Siwa motivated and inspired Alexander's self-perception as invincible conqueror and thus gave him confidence on the battlefield.[79] Later, in Gordium, Alexander, driven by desire ($\pi \acute{o} \theta o \varsigma$), wants to fulfil the prophecy that the first person who unties the famous knot will become king of Asia.[80] Curtius adds that as soon as Alexander heard of the prophecy, the desire (*cupido*) entered his mind.[81] We encounter the tradition also in the story of the first-century Jewish historian Josephus. He writes of Alexander visiting the temple of Jerusalem, where the king is told that God had promised that he would become the master of Asia. In addition, Alexander is pleased to hear the prophecy of his world dominion foretold by the Jewish prophet Daniel.[82]

In the historiographical tradition of the oracular visits performed by notable Roman rulers, world dominion and personal power-interests remain central themes. As in Alexander's case, the future Roman emperors themselves are the main agents in the stories. The most important questions are presented in a private oracular consultation. In CE 69, Vespasian consults the oracle of Serapis during his stay in Egypt, when the civil war against Vitellius, the then occupant of the imperial throne, was about to end. In the narratives of Tacitus and Suetonius, when Vespasian visits the shrine of Serapeion, the future emperor dismisses all his attendants and enters the sanctuary alone, like Alexander in Siwah. In Tacitus, Vespasian wants to consult about the affairs of the empire know about the stability of his empire, while Suetonius points out that he wanted to know the duration of his power. Both Tacitus and Suetonius describe him as seeing a vision while performing religious rituals.[83]

*When kings and gods meet* 87

In another tale of Tacitus and Suetonius, the son of Vespasian, Titus, visits the Paphian oracle of Aphrodite to ask the oracle about his sea voyage. The answer was that the sea would be favorable.[84] In the longer account of Tacitus, Titus asks about himself, and the priest, who was called Sostratus, gives at first a brief and general reply, but then invites the Roman for a private consultation. Tacitus writes that it was during the private consultation that the oracle revealed the future of Titus. In Suetonius's shorter account, the oracle encourages Titus to strive for imperial power.[85]

Besides quoting the discussions between the Roman rulers and the priests, the authors present these future emperors performing the rituals demanded according to the protocols of the oracle they visit. In Suetonius, Tiberius visits the oracle of Geryon near Patavium. The oracle suggests that he go to the fount of Aponus. There, Tiberius performs a ritual and throws sacred golden dice, as the oracle recommends.[86] In the passage Suetonius does not tell us what questions Tiberius asked of the oracle, but the visit takes place before his accession as the successor of Octavian Augustus. The theme of world power and oracular consultation of an 'emperor-candidate', so to speak, appears also in *Historia Augusta,* where Hadrian consults the oracles of Apollo at Cumae and Jupiter at Nicephorium about his future and future position, and receives favorable predictions.[87]

In the Tacitean tradition, the famous Romans following in the footsteps of Alexander have the same motivation – personal desire (*cupido* Latin equivalent to πόθος). Tacitus writes that Vespasian had a strong yearning to consult the oracle and Titus had a desire (*cupido*) to visit and examine the temple of Paphian Venus.[88] We encounter the same expression when we read about Germanicus' desire to give honor to the fallen Roman soldiers and their leader who had died in the Battle of Teutoburg when he traversed the area.[89] Here Tacitus, whether on purpose or not, uses the same term, *cupido,* as Curtius had done in his *History of Alexander.*[90] However, we must remember that it was not only Curtius who portrays the visit to the oracle of Siwah as motivated by *cupido,* as all Alexander historians use similar phraseology repeatedly in the context of sacred travel. More likely, we may regard it as an oft-appearing topos where the sacred travel of the monarch is portrayed as taking place because of personal intent and religious piety.

When classical authors portray a monarch visiting oracular sites for personal or religious reasons, the motives for the visit do not differ from those of ordinary persons. Similarly, the stories of monarchs visiting tombs or oracles stress the agency of the king or emperor, who wholeheartedly participates in the demanded rituals. In antiquity, people went to oracular sites for religious purposes and to seek advice and information from the best sources available.[91] The monarch willing to perform every religious obligation is depicted as operating like ordinary people in a world governed by divine powers. The oracular visits often take place before the king or emperor gains absolute power: Alexander before his victory over Darius; Tiberius prior to his accession; Vespasian before his victory over Vitellius; Titus and Hadrian when they are not yet sure of their succession. In each case, the oracular response corresponds to what subsequently happened. It is

## 88  *Jaakkojuhani Peltonen*

almost as if the authors explain the course of history by the oracular consultations. What they did do, of course, was emphasize the divine acceptance of the regime that ensued.

### Experiencing blessed oracular visits and the power of the gods

A decisive factor for a successful sacred journey is a revelation of the divine; a religious experience which is a proof for the visitor that the gods look with favor on the journey or performed rituals. The literary tradition stresses both the divine status of the visitor and the power of the god whose sanctuary is visited. This is clearly seen in the stories of Alexander visiting Gordium, the oracle of Zeus/Ammon at Siwah, and the temple of Jerusalem.

Alexander's visit to the sanctuary of Gordium proved to be a great success and gained the favor of Zeus. According to Arrian, signs from heaven appeared showing that Alexander had fulfilled the prophecy by undoing the knot. The thunder and lightning in the night sky was a sign of Zeus' acceptance, and therefore, the very next day Alexander offered sacrifice to show respect to the gods who had helped him to undo the knot.[92]

Diodorus, Arrian, and Plutarch construct an idealistic presentation of Alexander's sacred journey to meet the oracle of Siwah. The journey to the shrine is depicted as dangerous and full of hardships, but every obstacle is overcome with divine help. According to Plutarch, during the journey it was the 'assistance rendered him by heaven' which made the king trust the oracle's words even more.[93] Among the miracles, they had plenty of rain while marching through a waterless land, and when they got lost, ravens appeared and showed them the way ahead. These birds flew in front of them and even waited for Alexander and his men while they travelled. Arrian expresses his trust in the truthfulness of the tradition of the divine help, stating that it was confirmed and reported by several different authors.[94] Diodorus writes that Alexander took those incidents as an omen showing that the visit pleased the god, so he pushed on with speed.[95] In Diodorus and Plutarch, Alexander was delighted with the answers received, and honored the god and his priests with rich gifts.[96] Arrian writes: 'Alexander surveyed the site with wonder, and made his enquiry of the god; he received the answer his heart desired, as he said, and turned back for Egypt'.[97]

This divine aspect of the visit is even more explicit in the Alexander Romance, where the king learns of the might of Ammon during his visit to Siwah.[98] The king leaves his army to wait on the island of Proteus and goes by himself to make a sacrifice to Ammon. Alexander prays for a sign to confirm his mother's claim that he is a son of god. He receives a vision of Ammon embracing his mother. In the narrative, Alexander repairs the sanctuary and has the wooden image of the god covered with/painted gold.[99] All these above-mentioned texts propagate a genuine religious experience performed with pure motives, when the physical world and the spiritual world intertwine in *loca sancta*. Implicitly, these texts recommend sacred journeys to their audience and promote the power of the god and the reputation of his/her oracles or sacred sites.

*When kings and gods meet* 89

Alexander's visit to the temple of Jerusalem has the same pattern of personal experience, and a theme of the Hebrew god's ability to reveal a future unknown to the monarch himself.[100] In Josephus' account, the encounter of Alexander and the Jewish high priest as God's representative becomes a positive turning point. At first, the angry king is ready to destroy the Jewish people, who had denied him military supplies. Then, after an emotional religious experience and having understood the might of the true God, he enters the city of Jerusalem in peace along with the high priest.[101] Under the instruction of the high priest, the king sacrifices to God in the temple and during the visit the king is shown the Book of Daniel, where the prophet foretold that it would be a Greek ruler who would destroy the Persian Empire.[102] Alexander realizes that the prophet had foretold his victory. Here, the purpose of the passage is highlighting the ability of the Jewish God to foretell the future. In this sense, the passage has similarities with the accounts of Alexander's visit to Siwah. All mentioned narratives construct the feeling of expectation which is rewarded after arriving at the site. In all cases, the king gives lavish gifts to the local priests and the shrine.[103] Narratives of sacred travel emphasize the power of the god whose sanctuary the king visits. In Alexander's case, the power of the god is verified by the king's eventual destruction of the Persian armies and success in becoming the ruler of the whole inhabited world.

Like the above-mentioned sacred journeys of Alexander, the oracular visits made by Roman emperors stress the might of the gods and the oracles. Moreover, the divine revelations are presented as an important motivating factor for the visiting monarchs. In Suetonius, after Vespasian sees the divine vision in the Serapeion and understands that he will gain the imperial throne, he receives the message that Vitellius has lost the decisive battle.[104] In another aftermath of oracular consultation, Titus is greatly encouraged, and sails to see his father, bringing great confidence to his troops who were in a state of uncertainty.[105] Tiberius on the route to Illyria consults the oracle of Geryon at Patavium (Padua) by the ritual of casting the holy dice and the response was favorable for him.[106] The visit and references to other omens appear before Tiberius finally becomes the successor to Augustus.

In ancient literary tradition, the gods interfere in the politics and warfare of men. Therefore, it is no wonder that the above-mentioned narratives of sacred travel make high claims for the powers of gods: they share a topos that was already common to Herodotus' histories and Greek tragedies, neither of which criticized the authority of the gods or the oracles serving as mediators between men and gods.[107] In the classical tradition, it is within the power of the gods to decide whether they should pass on knowledge of future changes in political power. Sometimes the response of the oracle was not positive for the ruler. In the case of Germanicus, who visits the oracle of Apollo at Claros, the oracle foretells that Germanicus would die within a year.[108] In a similar way, even though Caracalla visits the sacred sites by himself to seek a cure from Serapis and Asclepius and a Celtic deity Apollo Grannus, the gods do not heal him.[109] However, another common feature of the tradition was that the gods themselves were not to be blamed or accused, even if Caracalla or anyone else did not get what they hoped and asked for. Gods are always correct in their predictions in classical historiography, even

## 90 *Jaakkojuhani Peltonen*

if the humans do not understand the messages that oracles give to the people, or in case the content of the answer turns out to be injurious for the visitor. The effect of the sacred travel accounts was therefore to reinforce the contemporary belief system.

### The visitor's experience and negative character development

In the historiographical tradition, visits could also be presented as an initiator of incorrect self-perception. In Curtius Quintus Rufus and Justin's epitome of Pompeius Trogus, the visitor's self-presentation changes radically after an oracular visit, which thus highlights the false self-perception and low moral conduct of the visitor.[110] Here their narratives are a critique of Alexander and the interaction between him and the priests of Ammon. Curtius makes critical remarks about the motivation of Alexander: 'Alexander had an overwhelming desire to visit the temple of Jupiter (Ammon-Zeus) since he was dissatisfied with his mortal status. He either considered, or wanted others to believe, that Jupiter was his ancestor'.[111]

Whether or not Alexander received divine help during the journey is left open by Curtius, who writes that the miraculous rain took place either by the gift of gods (*deorum manus*) or by pure chance (*casus*).[112] In Justin's shorter narrative, Alexander even sends men ahead to bribe the priests to give the desired responses.[113] When the king finally reaches the oracle, the interaction and the following experience turns out to be disastrous. Alexander, forgetting his mortal state (*humanae sortis*), accepts that the eldest of the priests calls him 'son', *filium*, the name Jupiter had given him.[114] Curtius writes that the priest, who was as ready as anyone else to flatter Alexander, answered that the king was going to rule over all the earth.[115] Curtius thinks Alexander should have taken a critical attitude to these vague (*vana*) responses of the oracle and responded with sound and honest argument.[116] In Curtius' interpretation, the visit to the oracle is a step on the road towards the wrong kind of autocracy, which ultimately alienated the Macedonians from their king.[117]

Justin writes that the oracle ordered the king's companions to venerate Alexander as a god rather than a king. This swelled the king's pride (*animo increvit*), eliminating the geniality he had acquired from Greek literature and upbringing.[118] In other words, both writers describe the sacred journey as having a negative result. In the Roman world travel for sacred purposes was not as common as among the Greeks.[119] Curtius' narrative may reflect Roman senatorial attitudes towards divination and absolute monarchy. Curtius writes about divination elsewhere in his work as harmful *superstitio*, even though he does not reject the possibility of divination and he subscribes to predestination.[120] The divinations of the oracle are sheer deceit, which serves to feed the overweening ambition of the monarch and leads to a breakdown in his relationship with his fellow Macedonians.

Curtius also criticizes other reported sacred travel, for instance, the visit to Mount Merus in Nysa, which Father Liber/Dionysius was said to have visited during his mythical journey. In Arrian there is no similar moralistic critique. Curtius writes that on the mountain Alexander some of his elite troops spent 10 days in the worship of Father Liber as bacchants:[121]

> Personally I do not believe it was a result of divine inspiration but simply to amuse themselves that the soldiers began to pick ivy and vine fronds here and there, and wandered the length of the wood wearing leaf-garlands like bacchants.[122]

Curtius denies that there was any piety or communing with the gods in the action: it was just drunken revelry. The soldiers invoked the god by their shouts that Curtius calls *licentia*, which denotes to dissoluteness.[123] He mentions that Alexander was not averse to this opportunity for revelry and furnished everything needed for feasting.[124] Here Curtius presents the visit as a negative experience that involved indecent actions. That the king did not try to stop the ecstatic behavior is a sign of his degeneration.

In the literary tradition about the Roman nobles, Caracalla's megalomaniac character and almost obsessive desire to imitate Alexander was due to his harmful visit to the tomb of Alexander. The Roman historian Aurelius Victor writes that after Caracalla viewed the embalmed body of Alexander of Macedon, he ordered that he be called 'the Great' and 'Alexander'. The moment when the emperor saw the body of the king lying in the sarcophagus is the crisis point. In addition, Aurelius Victor writes that there were several flatterers who encouraged the emperor to believe that he looked like the Macedonian king. Caracalla was motivated to imitate Alexander, convincing himself that he was very much like him. The emperor tried to imitate Alexander's facial gestures, such as his fierce expression and the head turned toward the left shoulder.[125]

When a sacred journey is presented in a negative tone, the author's purpose is to give a moralistic lesson, to point out negative and weak traits in the character of the traveler. A visit made with the wrong motives is injurious because the visitor himself has a moral weakness. In addition, the visit feeds *hybris*: the monarch starts to think of himself as more than a man; he is yearning for a divine or a heroic status because of his overblown self-importance. To an extent the moralistic tone of such passages could be regarded as a critique of religious practices; stupid and morally inferior acts can be done in the name of religion. However, once again, the gods are not to blame if men use religious practices to violate the norm of proper action and thinking. Aurelius Victor does not condemn paying homage to a deceased hero, but he does condemn the act if the attitudes and motives of the visitor were wrong.

## Conclusions

There is a degree of intertextuality between passages portraying sacred travel by monarchs in the Classical tradition. As far as we know, the literary tradition started with Herodotus. His account of Xerxes in Troy undoubtedly had an impact on the way the actions of Alexander were later portrayed. The stories of Alexander, in

## 92 *Jaakkojuhani Peltonen*

turn, had an influence on the tradition of Caracalla visiting Troy in the third century CE. Furthermore, Alexander's visits to the tombs of Achilleus and Cyrus were evidently in the minds of the ancient authors who wrote about the Roman monarchs visiting the tombs of Alexander and Pompey. Either Alexander and the later Roman emperors were aware of the previous narratives of sacred travel and wanted to present a similar self-image, or the authors were just following a common literary topos. In either case, the portrait of agency and experience during the visit has similarities in the literary tradition.

The passages of sacred travel created standards and expectations for the visits to the sacred places. They offered shared realities and imagination for their audience. Stories of famous visitors ascending to certain sacred sites enhanced the legacy of these places. For example, the legendary stories of Alexander's divination at Siwah caused the site and its oracle to increase in popularity among the classical audience who heard or read about the journey.

The power of the classical belief systems and authority of religious sites and oracular institutions are emphasized in the sacred travel narratives. The culmination of the stories of sacred travel is arrival at a sacrally charged space associated with a deity. Alexander and the emperors are portrayed doing what is demanded of them in a religious context. Mostly the writers are conservatively supporting the institutions as oracles or veneration shown to heroes. In the narratives, the motivation for sacred travel is personal and authors do not criticize the rituals themselves. The experience following the visit stresses the character development of the king as good and bad.

The stories referred to above reflected a society where sacred travel was part of the religious life. When Christianity and Islam replaced Greek and Roman polytheistic religions, pilgrimage was transferred as an important part of the religious life in monotheistic culture. In Christian lands, the tomb of Alexander as a famous place to visit was replaced by the tombs of Christ and tombs and shrines of famous Christian saints, which became the sacred sites to visit from the fourth century CE onwards. Even though Christianity silenced the ancient oracles, the classical stories of sacred travel had already left their mark on the later saints' legends. Classical literature continued to be read widely and undoubtedly the narratives of sacred travel carried by the famous monarchs made an impact on the way Christians and Muslims wrote about pilgrimage. In addition, these classical stories promoted the divinity connected with the site and the sacred site itself, just as the later Christian miracle stories promoted the reputation of saints and their shrines or tombs and the God who acted through them.

## Notes

1 For the *imitatio Alexandri* in Roman politics, see also Hannestad 1992; Isager 1992; Spencer 2002, 15–31; Spencer 2009, 253–267.
2 Cf. Virgil, *Aen.* 3.70-120. describing Troians visiting the oracle at Delos. For the first-person narratives, Cf. Paus.1.34.2; Ath. 13.574f.
3 For the Hellenistic Alexander historians, see Pearson (1960); Zambrini (2007).
4 Cf. Ousterhout (1990); Dillon (1997); Elsner (2007).

## When kings and gods meet 93

5 Cf. Edmunds (1971); Fredricksmeyer (2003); Dreyer (2009). For example, the historical reconstruction of Alexander's visit to the oracle of Ammon/Zeus in Siwah and its relationship to his divinity has received enormous interest and scholarly discussion. Cf. Tarn 1948, 347–359. Badian 1981, 27–71. Brunt, Arrian 1 in the Loeb edition, 467–480, Bosworth 1977, 51–75, Fredricksmeyer 2003, 270–273, Cartledge 2004, 221–222, 266–270. Bowden (2017) recently represents a different approach, as he explores the attitudes of the Alexander historians to divination.

6 Even though Erskine (2002), Saunders (2006) and Chugg (2007) write about visits to the tomb of Alexander, their focus is on exploring the history of the tomb and its location.

7 Cf. Kindt 2016, 5–6, 10. In her study, Kindt does not approach the sources on the oracle of Delphi from the angle 'what really happened' but from the angle of storytelling.

8 Henrichs 1968, 55–60 sees that accounts of Vespasian's visit to the Serapeion borrow highlights of the story of Alexander's visit to the Ammonium.

9 For the debate, and arguments for applying the concept 'pilgrimage' to classical antiquity and its limitations, see Elsner 2007, 1–9. In ancient Greek, there is no word corresponding to our word 'pilgrimage,' but the description is literal: the person went to the shrine etc. Dillon 1997, xiv.

10 Sacred tourism refers to motivation to see oneself the sanctuary or statue of god. Cf. Elsner 2007, 21–22.

11 Cf. Tac. *Ann.* 2.61 where Tacitus describes Germanicus as sightseeing in Egypt. This kind of visit does not have religious connotations, even if the site had some religious meaning. In Tac. *Ann.* 2.53, 54, 60. The visits to the tomb of Alexander, for example, can be seen as both tourism and sacred travel where the visitor participates in the tomb cult or shows veneration that can be regarded as religious. Leemreize (2014) 61–68, analyzes the sightseeing trip of Germanicus in Egypt from the context of how the Egyptian past was used in praise of the Roman present in Tacitus.

12 Alexander's and his companions' journey to the oracle of Zeus Ammon at Siwah (situated in Libyan desert) is probably the longest account, which may have impacted on the later stories of emperors visiting oracular sites. Cf. Elsner 2007, 25.

13 For example, the illustrious Roman visits the tomb of Alexander when he arrives in the city of Alexandria after an important battle or settling the political order in Egypt.

14 From the military point of view, it might be seen as counterproductive, since it gave Darius time to prepare his army for the coming campaign further east. Cf. Cartledge 2004, 221.

15 Hdt. 7.43.2 (transl. Robert B. Strassler).

16 Briant 2002, 245–246.

17 Erskine 2001, 85; 145. In Rose 2013, 144 the real motive for sacrificing 1,000 head of cattle is presented as securing meat for the Persian army.

18 Hdt. 1.3.1-1.5.1.

19 For a discussion of the panhellenistic propaganda of freedom and revenge in Alexander's expedition, see Flower 2000. Heckel 2008. Squillace 2010. Kremmydas 2013.

20 Squillace 2010, 78–79. For the work of Callisthenes, see Pearson 1960, 22–49; Cartledge 2004, 247–249.

21 Cf. Hdt.7.37; 7.43; 7.113; 7.191.

22 Arr. *An.* 1.11.5.

23 Arr.*An.* 1.11.7. Diod. Sic. 17.17.6-7-18.1.1. Plut. *Alex.* 15.4-5.

24 Arr.*An.* 1.11.8.

25 Plut. *Alex.* 15.4. Arr. *An.* 1.12.1; Phil. *Her.* 5.3.16. Just. *Epit.* 11.5.12 states briefly that Alexander conducted sacrifices at Troy before the tombs of the heroes who had died in the war.
   For the tomb of Achilleus, see Burgess 2009, 112.

26 Not only heroes were worshipped but also dead ancestors. The cult of the dead had similarities to the hero-cults.

94   *Jaakkojuhani Peltonen*

27 Ekroth 2004, 100–101.
28 Ekroth 2004, 104–105.
29 Ekroth 2004, 111.
30 Arr. *An.* 1.11.7-8.
31 Diod. Sic. 17.18.1.
32 Arr. *An.* 6.9.3. 6.10.2. Diod. Sic. 17.18.1. 17.21.2.
33 Arr. *An.* 1.12.1. Plut. Alex. 15.4.
34 Cf. Arr. *An.* 17.14.4. Edmunds 1971, 371–375.
35 In addition, in classical literature the anecdote stresses the need for high-quality writers who will write about the past. Cf. Cic. *Arch.* 24.1-5. SHA *Prob.*1.1-2. Jer. *Vita. Hil.* pref. 9-11. For a detailed discussion on this topic, see Peltonen 2019, 150–155.
36 Erasmo 2012, 109. Cf. Plin. *Ep.* 6.10.
37 Strab. 15.3.7. Curt. 10.1.30–35; Arr. *An.* 6.29.4–10; Plut. *Alex.* 69.1–3. Strabo writes that Alexander visited the tomb twice, also when the king first arrived in Pasargadae. Bosworth 1988, 46-55, discusses the literary tradition of Alexander's visit to Cyrus' tomb and the historical reconstruction of the visit.
38 Curt. 10.1.30. Atkinson 2009, 98–99 sees Curtius' account as most likely unhistorical.
39 Wiesehöfer 2017, 60.
40 Curt.10.1.31-32.
41 Arr. *An.* 6.29.11. Alexander arrested and tortured the Magi who had guarded the tomb to learn who had desecrated it. Plutarch says that Alexander executed the Macedonian Poulamakhos for the crime. Plut. *Alex.* 69.3-4.
42 Plut. *Alex.* 69.1-3.
43 Curt. 7.6.20. Cf. Arr. *An.* 3.27.5.
44 Erskine 2002, 175–176.
45 Curt. 10.10.9-13. Ael. *VH* 12.64.
46 Perdiccas is said to have worn the king's armor, diadem and royal scepter and Mithradates the cloak of Alexander. Appian. Mithridatic Wars. 24.117. Appian 23.117. Cf. Mayor 2010, 38–39. Octavian used a signet ring once used by Alexander. Suet. *Aug.* 50. Plin. *NH* 37.10. The Roman Macriani family used rings and bracelets with talismanic images of Alexander. SHA, *Tyranni Triginta,* 14. 2–6.
47 Suet. *Calig.* 52. Cf. Cass. Dio. 59.17.3.
48 Cf. Curt.10.10.20. Saunders 2006, 79–95.
49 Green 1978.
50 Luc. 10.10-45.
51 Suet. *Aug.* 18.1; transl. J. C. Rolfe.
52 Atkinson 2009, 98–99.
53 Erasmo 2012, 69.
54 Cass. Dio. 51.16.5.
55 Pollini 2012, 172.
56 Cass. Dio. 68.30.1
57 Carlsen 2016, 322–323.
58 Baharal 1994, 524–567. Carlsen 2016, 316, 324–328. Dahmen 2007, 142–143. Caracalla is said to have used belongings of Alexander. He drank his wine from goblets supposedly used by the king and ordered statues and paintings of his hero. Cass. Dio. 78.7.4-78.8.4; Hdn. 4.8.1.
59 Hdn. 4.8.4. (transl. Edward C. Echols). Cass. Dio. 78.16.7. gives a similar account of Caracalla's visit to Troy.
60 Plut. *Alex.* 15.4. Arr. *An.* 1.12.1.
61 Hdn. 4.8.9.
62 Cassius Dio writes that Caracalla was 'so enthusiastic about Alexander' (78.7.1.) and says his reason for using elephants was imitating Alexander or even Dionysius (78.7.4). In another instance Dio calls Caracalla a 'great admirer of Alexander' (78.9.1.). Herodian mentions Alexander as Caracalla's 'hero'. The anonymous

*When kings and gods meet* 95

author of *Historia Augusta* says that Caracalla thought he must imitate Alexander (SHA *M. Ant.* 2.1).

63 Appian gives a longer account of Hadrian's visit. See, App. *B. Civ.* 2.86. Cass. Dio. 69.11.1.

64 Cass. Dio 76.13.1.

65 Cf. Plut. *Alex.* 15.5.

66 For studies on classical oracles, see Vandenberg (1982); Curnow (2004); Bowden (2005); Stoneman (2011). In his study, Curnow lists all ancient oracular sites and their modern locations. There were several oracles to visit, including both major shrines and more local ones.

67 It seems to be a topos that, when the historian writes about the visit, he provides an account of the history of the oracle, a portrait of the landscape, the sanctuary, and the methods of consultation. The digression appears when Alexander historians portray the oracle of Ammon, see Arr. *An.* 3.4.1-2. Diod. 17.50.1-6. Curt. 4.7.16-24. Cf. Tacitus' accounts of Aphrodite's sanctuary in Paphos and oracle of Serapis at Alexandria: Tac. *Hist.* 2.3. 4.83-84.

68 The phrase occurs in Arrian 10 times; cf. Arr. *An.* 1.3.5; 3.3.1. For the list of the occurrences, see Stewart 1994, 84 (note 47). For yearning as an explanation, see also Blits 2011, 46–48. Bosworth 1980, 62, sees the formula as Herodotean and a phrase not copied from Nearchus or Ptolemy.

69 We encounter this explanation when the king wants to see the Gordian knot and fulfill the prophecy, see Ar.*An.* 3.1.5. Curt. 4.7.8. and when visiting the oracle of Ammon at Siwah, see Ar. *An.* 3.3.1. Curt. 4.7.8 and the holy mountain of Dionysius in India, see Ar. *An.* 5.2.5.

70 Ar. an. 3.3.1-2. Strab. 17.43.

71 Stoneman 2011, 40–43. Hdt. 1.53.2-1.54.1-2.

72 Cf. Plut. *Alex.* 26.6.

73 Arr. *An.* 3.4.5. Strab. 17.43.

74 Diod. Sic. 17.51.1-3.

75 Plut. *Alex.* 27. 3-4.

76 Curt. 4.7.26-27.

77 Plut. *Alex.* 27.4. Diod. Sic. 17.51.2. Curt. 4.7.27. Just. *Epit.* 11.11.9.

78 Plut. *Alex.* 14.4. In the story, Alexander arrives at the oracular site on a day when it was not lawful to deliver oracles. First Alexander asks for a private consultation, and when the oracle refuses to meet him, the king goes to see him personally and tries to drag the Pythia to the temple. She famously exclaims 'You are invincible my son', and Alexander says he needs no other prophecy.

79 Diod. Sic. 17.93.4.

80 Arr.*An.* 2.2.3. The whole story of the visit, see Arr. *An.* 2.2.3-8; Curt. 3.1.14-18; Plut. *Alex.*18.1-2; Justin 11.7.3-16.

81 Curt. 3.1.16-17.

82 Joseph. *AJ* 11.331-338.

83 Tac. *Hist.* 4.81-84. Suet. *Vesp.* 7.1-2. Cf. Strab. 17.43.

84 Tac. *Hist.* 2.4. Suet. *Titus* 5.1.

85 Suet. *Vesp.* 5.1.

86 Suet. *Tib.* 14.3.

87 SHA *Hadr.* 2.8-9.

88 Tac. *Hist.* 4.82.1. *Altior inde Vespasioano cupido adeundi sacram sedem.* Tac. *Hist.* 2.2.

89 Tac. *Ann.* 1.61.1. In Thracia Germanicus was struck by a desire to visit ancient and famed regions (*veteres et fama celebratos*).

90 Cf. Henrichs 1968, 56. note 18. Trevor 2010, 81–82 accepts Henrich's view that Tacitus' account of Vespasian's visit to the Serapeion may derive from the tradition of Alexander's visit to the oracle of Ammon at Siwah.

96 *Jaakkojuhani Peltonen*

91 Cf. Curnow 2004, 3–5. Stoneman 2011, 14–15.
92 Arr. *An.* 2.3.8.
93 Plut. *Alex.* 27.1.
94 Arr. *An.* 3.3.6.
95 Diod. Sic. 17.49.6.
96 Diod. Sic. 17.51.4. Plut. *Alex.* 27.4.
97 Arr *An.* 3.4.5 (transl. P. E. Brunt).
98 The earliest datable Greek version of the Romance comes from the third or fourth century CE. For different versions of the Alexander Romance, see Stoneman 1991, 28–32. Stoneman 2008, 231–245.
99 *Alex. Rom.* I. 30.
100 The visit and these themes appear also in the Jewish version of the *Alexander Romance*, see *Alex. Rom.* 2.24.
101 Cf. Joseph. *AJ* 11.318-319.
102 Joseph. *AJ* 11.336-337.
103 In Joseph. *AJ* 11.337-339 Alexander, for example, tells them to ask for any gifts the Jews might desire.
104 Suet. *Vesp.* 7.1. Tac. Hist. 4.82.
105 Tac. *Hist.* 2.4.
106 Suet. *Tib.* 14.3.
107 Stoneman 2011, 11–13 writes that traditionally stories of oracles promote the view that the gods are always right. For example, when Croesus seeks wisdom from the Pythia, Apollo gives the right answer, but Croesus interprets it wrongly. Oracles in stories always come true. Stoneman 2011, 41–43.
108 Tac. *Ann.* 2.54.
109 Cass. Dio 77.15.6.
110 Curt. 4.7. Just. 11.11.12.
111 Curt. 4.7.8 (transl. John Yardley).
112 Curt. 4.7.13. Baynham 1998, 162.
113 Just. *Epit.*11.11.6.
114 Curt.4.7.25.
115 Curt. 4.7.26.
116 Ibid. 4.7.29-31.
117 Curt. 4.7.8-9, 25-26, 29-31. Cf. Baynham 1998, 162–164.
118 Just. *Epit.* 11.11.12.
119 Elsner 2007, 24.
120 Bowden 2017, 152–153.
121 Arr. *An.* 5.2.5-7.
122 Curt. 8.10.15 (transl. John C. Rolfe).
123 Curt. 8.10.16.
124 Curt. 8.10.17.
125 Aur.Vic 21.4.

## Bibliography

Atkinson, John. 2009. *Curtius Rufus' Histories of Alexander the Great Book 10*. Oxford: Oxford University Press.

Badian, Ernst. 1981. "The Deification of Alexander the Great." In *Ancient Macedonian Studies in Honour of Charles F. Edson*, edited by H.J. Dell, 27–71. Thessaloniki: Institute for Balkan Studies.

Baharal, Drora. 1994. "Caracalla and Alexander the Great: A Reappraisal." *Latomus* 227: 524–567.

Baynham, Elizabeth. 1998. *Alexander the Great. The Unique History of Quintus Curtius.* Ann Arbor: University of Michigan Press.

Bosworth, Albert Brian. 1977. "Alexander and Ammon." In *Greece and Eastern Mediterranean in Ancient History and Prehistory: Studies Presented to Fritz Schachermeyr on the Occasion of His Eightieth Birthday,* edited by K. Kinzl, 51–75. Berlin: W. de Gruyter.

Bosworth, Albert Brian. 1980. *A Historical Commentary on Arrian's History of Alexander. Vol. 1, Commentary on Books I–III.* Oxford: Clarendon Press.

Bosworth, Albert Brian. 1988. *From Arrian to Alexander.* Oxford: Clarendon Press.

Bowden, Hugh. 2005. *Classical Athens and the Delphic Oracle: Divination and Democracy.* Cambridge: Cambridge University Press.

Bowden, Hugh. 2017. "The Eagle Has Landed: Divination in the Alexander Historians." In *Ancient Historiography on War and Empire,* edited by Timothy Howe, Sabine Muller, and Richard Stoneman, 149–169. Oxford: Oxbow Books.

Briant, Pierre. 2002. *From Cyrus to Alexander – A History of the Persian Empire.* Pennsylvania: Eisenbrauns.

Burgess, Jonathan. 2009. *The Death and Afterlife of Achilles.* Baltimore: John Hopkins University Press.

Carlsen, Jesper. 2016. "Alexander the Great in Cassius Dio." In *Cassius Dio – Greek Intellectual and Roman Politician,* edited by Carsten Hjort Lange, and Jesper Majbom Madsen, 316–333. Leiden: Brill.

Cartledge, Paul. 2004. *Alexander the Great. The Hunt for a New Past.* London: Macmillan.

Chugg, Andrew Michael. 2007. *The Quest for the Tomb of Alexander the Great.* AMC Publications.

Coleman, Simon and John Elsner. 1995. *Pilgrimage: Past and Present in the World Religions.* Cambridge, MA: Harvard University Press.

Curnow, Trevor. 2004. *The Oracles of the Ancient World.* London: Duckworth.

Dahm, Karsten. 2007. *The Legend of Alexander the Great on Greek and Roman Coins.* London: Routledge.

Dillon, Matthew. 1997. *Pilgrims and Pilgrimage in Ancient Greece.* London: Routledge.

Dreyer, Boris. 2009. "Heroes, Cults, and Divinity." In *Alexander the Great. A New History,* edited by Waldemar Heckel and A. Lawrence, 218–235. Chichester: Tritle Wiley-Blackwell.

Edmunds, Lowell. 1971. "Alexander's Religiosity." *Greek, Roman and Byzantine Studies* 12: 363–391.

Elsner, Jas and Ian Rutherford (eds.). 2007. *Pilgrimage in Graeco-Roman and Early Christian Antiquity: Seeing the Gods.* Oxford: Oxford University Press.

Erasmo, Mario. 2012. *Death Antiquity and Its Legacy.* London: I. B Tauris.

Erskine, Andrew. 2001. *Troy between Greece and Rome – Local Tradition and Imperial Power.* Oxford: Oxford University Press.

Erskine, Andrew. 2002. "Life after Death: Alexandria and the Body of Alexander." *Greece & Rome* 49.2: 163–179.

Flower, Michael. 2000. "Alexander the Great and Panhellenism." In *Alexander the Great in Fact and Fiction,* edited by Brian Bosworth and Elizabeth Baynham, 50–96. Oxford: Oxford University Press.

Fredricksmeyer, Ernst. 2003. "Alexander's Religion and Divinity." In *Brill's Companion to Alexander the Great,* edited by Joseph Roisman, 253–278. Leiden: Brill.

Green, Peter. 1978. "Caesar and Alexander: Aemulatio, Imitatio, Comparatio." *Journal of Ancient History* 3: 1–26.

98    *Jaakkojuhani Peltonen*

Heckel, Waldemar. 2008. *The Conquests of Alexander the Great*. Cambridge: Cambridge University Press.

Henrichs, Albert. 1968. "Vespasian's Visit to Alexandria." *Zeitschrift für Papyrologie und Epigraphik* 3: 51–80.

Isager, Jacob. 1993. "Alexander the Great in Roman Literature from Pompey to Vespasian." In *Alexander the Great: Reality and Myth*, edited by Jesper Carlsen (Analecta Romana Instituti Danici, Supplementum 20), 75–85. Rome: Bretschneider.

Kindt, Julia. 2016. *Revisiting Delphi: Religion and Storytelling in Ancient Greece*. Cambridge: Cambridge University Press.

Kremmydas, Christos. 2013. "Alexander the Great, Athens, and the Rhetoric of the Persian Wars." In *Marathon – 2,500 Years Proceedings of the Marathon Conference*, edited by Carey Christopher and Michael Edwards, 199–213. London: The Institute of Classical Studies – University of London.

Leemreize, Maaike. 2014. "The Egyptian Past in the Roman Present." In *Valuing the Past in the Greco-Roman World. Proceedings from the Penn-Leiden Colloquia on Ancient Values 7*, edited by James Ker and Christoph Pieper, 52–82. Leiden: Brill.

Luke, Trevor. 2010. "A Healing Touch for the Empire: Vespasian's Wonders in Domitianic Rome." *Greece and Rome* 57.1: 77–106.

Mayor, Adrienne. 2010. *The Poison King – The Life and Legend of Mithradates, Rome's Deadliest Enemy*. Princeton: Princeton University Press.

Ousterhout, Robert. 1990. *The Blessings of Pilgrimage*. Urbana: University of Illinois Press.

Pearson, Lionel. 1960. *The Lost Histories of Alexander the Great*. New York: American Philological Association.

Peltonen, Jaakkojuhani. 2019. *Alexander the Great in the Roman Empire, 150 BC to AD 600*. London: Routledge.

Pollini, John. 2012. *From Republic to Empire: Rhetoric, Religion, and Power in the Visual Culture of Ancient Rome*. Norman: University of Oklahoma Press.

Rose, Charles Brian. 2013. *The Archaeology of Greek and Roman Troy*. Cambridge: Cambridge University Press.

Saunders, Nicholas J. 2006. *Alexander's Tomb: The Two Thousand Year Obsession to Find the Lost Conqueror*. New York: Basic Books.

Spencer, Diana. 2002. *The Roman Alexander. Reading a Cultural Myth*. Exeter: University of Exeter Press.

Spencer, Diana. 2009. "Roman Alexanders: Epistemology and Identity." In *Alexander the Great. A New History*, edited by Waldemar Heckel and A. Lawrence Tritle, 251–274. Chichester: Blackwell.

Squillace, Giuseppe. 2010. "Consensus Strategies under Philip and Alexander – The Revenge Theme." In *Philip II and Alexander the Great: Father and Son, Lives and Afterlives*, edited by Elizabeth Carney and Daniel Ogden, 69–80. Oxford: Oxford University Press.

Stewart, Andrew. 1994. *Faces of Power: Alexander's Image and Hellenistic Politics*. Berkeley: University of California Press.

Stoneman, Richard. 2011. *The Ancient Oracles: Making the Gods Speak*. London: Yale University Press.

Vandenberg, Philip. 1982. *Mysteries of the Oracles: The Last Secrets of Antiquity*. London: Tauris Parke.

Wiesehöfer, Josef. 2017. "Cyrus the Great and the Sacrifices for a Dead King." In *Ancient Historiography on War and Empire*, edited by Timothy Howe, Sabine Muller and Richard Stoneman, 55–62. Oxford: Oxbow Books.

Zambrini, Andrea. 2007. "The Historians of Alexander the Great." In *A Companion to Greek and Roman Historiography*, edited by John Marincola, 210–221. Oxford: Blackwell.

# 6 Roman Imperial family on the road

## Power and interaction in the Roman East during the Antonine Era

*Sanna Joska*

### Introduction

Imperial travels to the provinces of the wide Roman Empire were one of the central means for gaining interaction between the Roman emperor and his subjects. The visits of emperors gave provincial populations chances to see their distant ruler in person and also possibilities to enjoy his targeted patronage while offering these communities and individuals chances to present their wealth and show loyalty to the ruler. Essentially, the travels of Roman emperors offered personal chances of interaction between ruler and subject and thus new and unique opportunities to express both the emperor's and his subjects' power and status and (re)define both as needed or useful.

The travels of a Roman emperor were always an occasion. The rulers were accompanied by their family members, officials, generals, and other *comites* as well as key staff.[1] An emperor's party might grow to be substantial in size, which in turn could produce practical challenges for those cities that hosted the emperor during his journey.[2] Nevertheless, imperial visits and the presence of an emperor in person were rare, but still very valued occasions. The imperial party's arrival in a city was prepared for in advance and the citizens celebrated the emperor by organizing ceremonies, entertainment and public audiences where the citizens could actually see the ruler.[3] Larger cities, such as provincial capitals, could naturally expect more visits from emperors. Smaller towns in the area where visits took place had the opportunity to send an embassy to meet and interact with the imperial party. Contacts with the imperial family were actively sought by citizens, who in practice were usually represented by the decision-making elites. The more personal an emperor's visit was, the more honour and prestige that visit bought to the city.[4]

Empresses and other members of the imperial family could accompany the emperors of Rome to the provinces. This study pays special attention to certain members of the imperial family – the children. Literal, epigraphic, and numismatic evidence is traced to answer questions on the roles of the imperial children during their imperial travels and how their presence functioned as a point of political and cultural interaction. Through an analysis of those passages' speaking of the presence of children on these journeys, this article presents new aspects of

*Roman Imperial family on the road* 101

imperial travel. Travel is in modern studies usually seen as a matter that concerns only the emperors.

The focus of this study is on one of the imperial families who had small children, the Antonines in the second century CE. The dynasty of the Antonines was built in part by Hadrian, who adopted Antoninus Pius as his heir in CE 138 and made Pius in turn adopt two boys, Marcus Aurelius and Lucius Verus as his own future heirs. Pius married his daughter, Faustina the Younger, to his Caesar Marcus in CE 145 as soon as Faustina was of marriageable age. Their first child was born two years later in CE 147, and Faustina was given the honorary title of Augusta while Marcus gained his share of imperial power in the form of *tribunicia potestas* and *imperium*.[5] Marcus followed Pius as emperor, together with his adoptive brother, Lucius, in CE 161. Both Marcus and Lucius spent long periods of their reign in the provinces. Dynasty building continued, as one of the daughters of Marcus and Faustina, Lucilla, was married to Lucius Verus, and one of their sons, Commodus, followed his father, Marcus, as emperor in CE 180. Commodus's rise to the throne ended the era of the Adoptive Emperors.[6] The Antonine era is considered a time of relative peace, especially under the reign of Antoninus Pius. Pius, however, did not travel, but rather stayed in Italy for his entire reign. He reigned between two travelling emperors, Hadrian and Marcus, who were forced to travel because of the growing unrest on the borders of the empire toward the end of the second century CE.

By looking at the role of Antonine imperial children, this study offers new perspectives on the study of imperial power relations. It pays more attention to children and childhood and to the roles given to them both by the emperor and his subjects and traces the agency of those provincials connected to those roles. The children were a point of interaction between the subjects and the Roman emperor, and their presence on imperial travels offers a chance to study this relationship more specifically. Attention will also be paid to the role of imperial women as often these children travelled with their mothers.

In order to trace the presence of imperial children and the interaction that travel created between the ruler and the ruled, several different source types are utilized, including ancient literacy, honorific monuments, and coin types. Ancient literacy presents, especially when discussing the second century CE, the views of writers who lived considerably later than the era about which they wrote. This fact inevitably affects the value that these passages have for tracing the historical events connected to the children.[7] Coinage and honorific monuments (researchable usually as honorific inscriptions) present contemporary source material created as the outcome of decisions made by an emperor or local actors in the provinces.[8]

The fundamental work on these discourses, the politics, and the practicalities of imperial travel became Helmut Halfmann's *Itinera principum* (1986). This study discusses imperial travel from various perspectives, ranging from the motivation of the travel to its ideological side. It presents the travel routes of individual emperors from Augustus to Diocletian and Theodosius. Halfmann discusses the family members who travelled along very briefly.[9] Forms of interaction born from imperial travel have also been studied in articles by Jakob Munk Højte

102   *Sanna Joska*

(2000, 2009) and Haim Gitler (1990–1991). Højte's studies discuss imperial travels from the viewpoint of the honorific statue, while Gitler uses numismatic evidence to trace the route of Marcus Aurelius in the East. Of all the emperors, the widely travelled Hadrian has been the focus of many studies that discussed the importance of imperial travel using his case.[10] Imperial travels and the presence of children have been discussed as a side note in the biographies of emperors, empresses, and other notable members of the ruling family. The biographies of Agrippina the Elder by Anthony A. Barrett (1999), Julia Augusti, the daughter of Augustus by Elaine Fantham (2006), Antonia Augusta by Nikos Kokkinos (1992) and the two Faustinae by Barbara Levick (2014) and Julia Domna also by Levick (2007) each discuss the presence of these women in the provinces of the empire with their husbands and children.

The Antonines are known for their politics that focused on the themes of fertility, children, and childhood. These concepts were represented on imperial coinage by Antoninus Pius and Marcus Aurelius through the women and children of the imperial family.[11] In the following discussion, this imperial policy and the responses to it are discussed by examining three themes – the interaction between the emperor and provincial cities, individuals and the army – that are connected to the presence of imperial children in the provinces.

## An imperial wedding at Ephesus

The first case discusses a journey that took a daughter of the imperial family from girl to adult and involves an imperial marriage that quite exceptionally took place in a provincial city instead of in Rome. In the year 164, Lucilla, the eldest surviving daughter of Marcus and Faustina, attained the age of fourteen. She was to marry the co-emperor of her father, Lucius Verus, who at that time was 33, more than double her age. They had been betrothed since the year 161 when Marcus and Lucius became emperors. In honour of the betrothal, Marcus set up new orders and through them gave distributions from imperial funds to boys and girls.[12] The marriage between Lucilla and Lucius served dynastic purposes, as it strengthened the bond between the two Emperors, who were adoptive brothers because of the arrangements made by Hadrian some three decades earlier. Lucius had waited long to marry. The plan of Emperor Hadrian had been to wed Lucius to Faustina the Younger and Marcus to a sister of Lucius, but Antoninus Pius cancelled the plans of his adoptive father and decided to marry his daughter to Marcus instead.[13]

In CE 164, Lucilla was finally of marriageable age.[14] Her status was still that of a child, although she had been betrothed to Lucius for some years.[15] When his fiancée reached an age suitable for marriage, Lucius, however, was in Syria commanding the Roman army against the rebellious Parthians. He had been sent to the East already in CE 162 when trouble had emerged and had spent quite some time reaching his destination. Lucius enjoyed his slow travel through the Mediterranean, spending time hunting and celebrating in various cities on the way.[16] He took on a mistress named Panthea who was admired by the satirist, Lucian, for her beauty, intelligence, and the power she had over Lucius.[17]

## Roman Imperial family on the road   103

It was decided that for the marriage to take place, both Lucilla and Lucius would travel to Ephesus, the capital of the province of Asia. Ephesus, the 'metropolis of Asia', was located on the western coast of Asia Minor, now modern Turkey. Its importance to the empire was prominent, the city being one of the largest cities in the Roman East and the home of the cult of Ephesian Artemis.[18] The relationship of the Antonine emperors and Ephesus had already begun before the rule of Antoninus Pius. Per the order of Hadrian, Pius was stationed in Ephesus for one year from CE 134 and 135 as the proconsul of Asia. It is likely that his wife, Faustina the Elder, accompanied him there.[19] The Republican tradition was to leave wives and other family behind when governors or commanders left for the provinces. The practice changed during the late Republic.[20] Faustina the Younger would have been about of four or five at the time of Pius's proconsulate, and perhaps she stayed abroad with her parents.[21] Antoninus Pius did not visit Ephesus after becoming emperor, but the city prospered under his rule. The close relationship between the Emperor and Ephesus is reflected in many public honours, such as dedications that titled Pius as the saviour and founder of the city.[22]

Lucilla, a girl of fourteen, began her long journey to Ephesus accompanied by her father. Marcus escorted Lucilla to the harbour city of Brundisium in southern Italy. From there, Lucilla continued her journey in the company of an uncle and sister of Lucius Verus.[23] Not even her mother, Faustina, was present, perhaps because of pregnancy or because she had small children to take care of.[24] The absence of Lucilla's parents on the journey and from the wedding celebrations, as well as the reckless behaviour of Lucius and his charming mistress set a certain tone for the event, making the marriage seem less official and less celebratory. This view is reflected in the *Historia Augusta* where the writer says that before Lucilla's journey, Marcus wrote to the proconsul stationed in Ephesus and asked him not to meet the girl on her journey.[25]

Even though the literal evidence of the marriage and Lucilla's journey create a gloomy picture of the event, for the city of Ephesus the celebration of an imperial wedding must have been an occasion. Unfortunately, nothing is known of the celebrations themselves, and when taking into account the dynastic importance of this occasion, the lack of material evidence speaking of the wedding is rather surprising. There are no inscriptions to prove there were any honorary monuments or coinage issued in Ephesus that would directly celebrate the marriage. This is surprising because we have a large amount of other evidence depicting and honouring the Antonine family in Ephesus. Unless the wedding was celebrated on a very low profile, one would expect that the city set up at least some public monuments to honour Lucius and Lucilla, but that these have not been preserved for us to see today.

The wedding, however, was celebrated by Marcus Aurelius. From her marriage, Lucilla gained the honorary title of Augusta, which her mother Faustina had been granted only after giving birth to her first child.[26] Lucilla was now a Roman *matrona* and, moreover, an empress. A coin type with the portraits of Lucius and Lucilla was issued as *sestertii* after the wedding, and the marriage was also celebrated on imperial medallions.[27] Medallions were given by emperors as personal

104    *Sanna Joska*

gifts to members of the senatorial elite and other important allies.[28] The medallion of Lucilla and Lucius celebrates *concordia felix*, the happy harmony between the married couple, and it pictures the couple in the gesture of *dextrarum iunctio*.[29] This gesture symbolised the *concordia* presented in the inscription.[30] Since the actual wedding took place in Ephesus, Marcus used the medallions and coinage to enhance the political value of the marriage. After they were married, Lucilla and Lucius headed back to Syria. Lucilla may have stayed in Syria until CE 166 when Lucius returned to Rome to celebrate a triumph. The couple had three children, and at least their first child was born in Syria.[31]

The marriage appears to be just one step in the long relationship of the city of Ephesus and the ruler. The Antonines were honoured with several public monuments in Ephesus, set up in the name of the community and by private citizens. The most well-known monument is the so-called Parthian monument, which is in existence now only as relief panels. This monument, which is perhaps better called the Antonine monument, has been the focus of various studies, but relatively little is known of it other than the preserved panels. The reliefs picture members of the Antonine dynasty, various deities and their personifications, battle scenes, and an apotheosis of an emperor.[32] The original location and date of the monument are not known for certain, as it is not even the original form of the monument. Two theories on the date of the monument do prevail. It has been dated either to CE 138 when Hadrian adopted Pius or to CE 169 and the death of Lucius Verus.[33] The original location of the monument may have been near the Arkadiane, the main street leading to the harbour. The monument is most often reconstructed as an altar in the fashion of the *Ara Pacis*.[34]

The Adoption relief of the monument depicts five figures, two elder men, one youth, one child, and a further, more idealized character in the background. These represent the Emperors Hadrian and Antoninus Pius and the two adoptive sons of the latter. Marcus Caesar is represented as a youth and Lucius as a child, protected by Pius's hand. The fifth character might be a genius, perhaps Populus Romanus, the dead father of Lucius, or the city of Ephesus. It might even represent Faustina the Elder, the wife of Pius.[35] The Adoption series consists of at least five other panels that depict various men, women, and children and also sacrificial scenes. Among the people depicted are the Empresses Sabina and Faustina the Elder and likely also Faustina the Younger.[36]

It is probable, however, that the series is not a depiction of the actual event of adoption. Instead it should be read, as stated by Barbara Levick, as a 'state of play, showing the dynasty as it was when Pius took over with Hadrian as benevolent founder'.[37] This interpretation would date the relief to the first years of Pius's reign. The monument does represent an important point of interaction between the Emperor and Roman citizens in the provinces. It is of course a symbol of imperial power, but above all, it is an effort made by (presumably) the citizens of Ephesus. For Ephesians, the building of the monument itself was a massive effort and an effective message to the Roman government about their devotion to Pius's rule. Pius and his family members were honoured by several other monuments too, and during the reign of Marcus at least three other honorary monuments were set up.[38]

*Roman Imperial family on the road* 105

One monument was set up at the turn of the 140's by a local aristocrat and senator, P. Vedius Antoninus, in the city's council building that he had refurbished with his wife.[39] Vedius Antoninus[40] was a member of the family of Vedii, one of the wealthiest and most influential families in Ephesus, and a personal friend of Pius. The two men probably became acquainted during Pius's proconsulate and their relationship continued through Pius's reign.[41] Vedius's relationship to the imperial family also continued under Marcus and Lucius. He met Lucius Verus during the Emperor's stay at Ephesus on his way to Syria in 162/3. An inscription speaks of the involvement of Vedius (or his father) in the festivities that were arranged in honour of the visiting emperor.[42] Returning to the wedding of Lucilla and Lucius, I suggest it is very likely that Vedius Antoninus was also present at the wedding a year later.[43] The case of the Vedii family presents the interaction between the ruler and the ruled on a personal level. The Vedii benefitted greatly from their long ties with the emperors, as Vedius Antoninus became a senator, the first of his family and the first among the Ephesians. The relationship of the Vedii and the emperors must have continued with Vedius's son, Vedius IV, also a senator.[44] In addition to their importance on a communal level imperial visits, such as the wedding, appear as a matter for strengthening and defining the relationship between members of the provincial elite and the ruling family, indeed as a space for personal interaction.

## Children at military camps

The second case discusses the presence of imperial children at military camps. Wars took emperors regularly to the provinces and a great majority of imperial travel took place for military reasons.[45] Marcus and Lucius had triumphed in their victory over the Parthians in CE 166, but this victory did not mean an end to the fighting. Unrest grew now on the northeastern border, as the Marcomanni and other peoples of the area took action against Roman power. Lucius Verus died in CE 169, and Marcus was forced to take on the role of commander alone. He ended up spending a great deal of the rest of his reign touring the provinces and war fronts.[46] Members of Marcus's family sometimes travelled with him. A dedication on behalf of the safe return and victory over the Marcomanni for Marcus also mentions his children, *liberorumque eius*, which implies that some of them travelled with their father between the years 169 and 172.[47] More precise evidence tells of the presence of Faustina the Younger, the son Commodus, and a young daughter at the military camps.

The presence of the children of the imperial family at war camps was not unheard of prior to the Antonines. Germanicus, the adopted heir of Emperor Tiberius, had his wife, Agrippina the Elder, and their small children with him on military campaigns.[48] We especially hear of the future emperor, Caligula, who accompanied Germanicus on his campaigns in Germany at the age of only two or three. The historian, Suetonius, notes that the troops grew very fond of the young boy and that his childhood spent among them secured him the support of the army when he became the emperor in CE 37. Agrippina and the children followed

106   *Sanna Joska*

Germanicus also to Syria where he died in CE 19. His grief-stricken wife and her children returned to Rome, bearing the ashes of the beloved Germanicus.[49]

In the Antonine era, it is the son and appointed heir of Marcus Aurelius, Commodus, who is especially connected to the military. The young prince travelled with his father to meet Roman troops on several occasions. Commodus was appointed as Caesar in the year 166 at the age of five. In 172, the boy undertook his first official travel with his father. The pair travelled to headquarters in Carnuntum in Pannonia.[50] There Commodus, now age eleven, was introduced to the soldiers. During their stay at the headquarters Marcus Aurelius was awarded the victory title of Germanicus for his victories over the Marcomanni. The title was conferred also on the young Commodus.[51] Lucilla and her new husband, Pompeianus, who was Marcus's general-in-chief for the Marcomannic war, may also have been present.[52] Commodus's presence at the military camp was memorialized on the reverse of coinage issued by Marcus. The Emperor and his Caesar were pictured standing on a platform, addressing the soldiers.[53] The types were issued as bronze coins, which was the denomination most used in daily transactions, and thus it assured that the message reached a wide audience.[54]

The travel to Carnuntum and Commodus's introduction to the army took place before the boy had officially entered adulthood and began his public career. After visiting the headquarters, Commodus returned to Italy, but he was summoned to meet his father again in the year 175. It was now time for Commodus to take his *toga virilis* at the age of fourteen. Commodus left Rome in May and travelled two to three weeks to Pannonia where Marcus was still situated. His headquarters was now at Sirmium. Commodus' ceremony took place on July 7.[55] Taking the toga of manhood and leaving behind the *toga praetexta* worn by boys was the first step that a Roman youngster belonging to the upper classes took on his way to legal adulthood.[56]

It is significant that Marcus decided that the event should take place in front of the army at the war front. The timing and place of Commodus's rite of adulthood are partially explained by the current political situation. The age, fourteen, at which he assumed the *toga virilis* was customary.[57] The venue, however, was dictated by the ongoing war as well as new trouble that had emerged in the East. Avidius Cassius, the governor of Syria, had proclaimed himself emperor after hearing rumours of Marcus's death and gained extensive support as well in Egypt and Palestina.[58] Marcus was forced to take action, but before he headed to the East, he called Commodus to his side and secured for the young prince the support of the Roman army.[59] The importance of the army is evident here in a situation of crisis when Marcus's authority was challenged by Avidius Cassius and Commodus's position as Marcus's heir had to be legitimized. These cases show that travel and personal interaction with the troops were essential tools for acquiring the support of the army.

Before continuing to discuss the travel of the Emperor and his family to the East to solve the problem presented by Cassius's rebellion, one additional case about the presence of children at military contexts needs to be discussed here. This case presents a young daughter at Sirmium, which is the same city in Pannonia to

*Roman Imperial family on the road* 107

which Commodus was summoned. A year before Commodus, in CE 174, Marcus Aurelius was at Sirmium to attend the trial of Herodes Atticus. Herodes Atticus, the famous, wealthy sophist and senator and a teacher of Marcus Aurelius's, had fallen into conflict with two Athenians.[60] The sophist, Philostratus, wrote about the trial some fifty years later in his *Lives of the Sophists* which he noted the presence of a young daughter of Marcus Aurelius who attempted to influence the decision of her father on the issue:

> Not only was he himself [Marcus the Emperor] convinced that he ought to treat them with this benevolence, but also, he was induced to do so by his wife and by his little daughter who could not yet speak plainly; for she above all used to fall at her father's knees with many blandishments and implore him to save the Athenians for her.[61]

Philostratus also offers the reaction of Herodes to the actions of the child. Herodes, clearly filled with emotion, replied to the Emperor: 'These are the grounds on which you judge men, and you sacrifice me to the whim of a woman and a three-year-old child!'[62] The daughter in question could be the last child of Marcus and Faustina, named Vibia Aurelia Sabina. She was born likely before CE 170, which would make her a few years older than what Herodes mentions the child as being. The child in question could, however, also be another daughter who is otherwise unknown.[63] The passage shows that Faustina the Younger and her youngest child had travelled with Marcus on his journey. The young girl travelled with her mother, perhaps due to her young age. Sirmium functioned as the headquarters for Marcus, and it is likely that his family might have stayed even if Marcus was obliged to occasionally move from there. No preserved evidence in Sirmium, such as inscriptions or coinage, however, further confirms the presence of Faustina and Sabina, or other children, for that matter.

Other children may have been present, but as the case of Commodus shows, older children could also stay in Rome in the care of other family members.[64] Sabina might have been the last child of the imperial couple, but before her, two sons had been born, Annius Verus in CE 162 and after him, Hadrianus who did not live long.[65] Annius Verus died the same year as Lucius Verus, and after his death, there were no small children in the family before the birth of Sabina. Besides Commodus, there were four daughters who were either already married, like Lucilla was, or soon would be a marriageable age.[66] The situation was quite different than back in CE 164 when Faustina could not travel to Ephesus for the wedding of Lucilla.

It is not known when Faustina and the child followed Marcus to Pannonia, as Marcus had not been in Rome since the year 169 and the funeral of Lucius Verus. It could even be possible that Faustina travelled to meet Marcus when she was pregnant and gave birth to her daughter somewhere in Pannonia. Julia, the daughter of Emperor Augustus, had followed her husband, Marcus Agrippa, on his journeys and gave birth to several of their children during these travels. Her presence is reflected in some of the honorary statues set up for her and the family in Greece

108 *Sanna Joska*

and Asia. Few dedications honour Julia as Kalliteknos, the bearer of beautiful children.[67] As has been mentioned, Agrippina the Elder, Julia's daughter, followed her husband, Germanicus, along with their two infant children to Gaul and to the East and gave birth to their additional children there.[68] Also, Antonia the Younger, the wife of the military commander, Drusus, gave birth to some of her children outside of Rome. The future emperor, Claudius was born in the city of Lugdunum in Gaul.[69]

It is very evident that Faustina, too, was not afraid of travelling for some weeks from Rome to Pannonia to meet her husband either while pregnant or with a small child. Elaine Fantham uses pregnancy and infant children as deterrents for any unnecessary travel for Julia.[70] This might be true to a certain point, but Julia's example more than hundred years prior to the time of the Antonines also proves that long distances could be travelled then both when pregnant and/or with small children. This factor alone is important to fully attest to when assessing the lived experience of ancient travel and the possibilities or limits of the travel by women and children.[71] The next chapter moves on further to discuss in more detail the presence of the women and children of the imperial family in the provinces.

## An imperial family on tour in the East

In July of 175 Marcus Aurelius continued eastward from the Danube, accompanied with at least Faustina and their two children, Commodus and a young girl, perhaps Sabina. The family headed toward Syria in the aftermath of the rebellious Avidius Cassius. Cassius had been killed shortly before Marcus even started his journey, but the Emperor saw it necessary to visit in person those areas that had supported Cassius. Their route through the Eastern empire took them from the Danube through Central Anatolia to Syria and Palestine and onwards to Egypt to stabilize the situation in these provinces. The family returned to Rome at the end of year 176.[72]

The travels of Marcus Agrippa and Julia in the East between 17 and 12 BCE had resulted in several honorific statues of the general and his wife.[73] Honorific statues by the cities that the imperial entourage visited are now seen as points of interaction between representatives of the Roman rule and the ruled and, essentially, a form of interaction that can be reached by modern researchers. It must be kept in mind, however, that a direct line cannot be drawn between honorific dedication and the presence of a member of the imperial family in a specific city.[74] For example, Agrippa and Julia were honoured in Thespiae by statues. The statue group gave honours also to Livia, wife of Augustus, and the three children of Agrippa and Julia.[75] Livia, however, was not with them on the journey, and thus, the presence of the children remains questionable.[76]

Julia travelled with her husband whom Augustus had assigned to the East to deal with imperial business. Elaine Fantham presents an interesting reason for the presence of Julia on these travels. Her role was to legitimize the position of Agrippa based on her status as the daughter of the highest authority, Augustus.[77] Julia presented a direct link to her father, and her presence ensured that Agrippa

*Roman Imperial family on the road* 109

was acting under the authority of the Emperor. This was also the state of her marriage, as she was the binding link between Augustus and Agrippa. A similar role was also held by Faustina the Younger. Her marriage to Marcus Aurelius, the primary heir of Antoninus Pius, further strengthened the unity of the imperial family.[78]

The presence of Faustina on some of the journeys of Marcus Aurelius can also be seen against this same background, although Marcus's rule needed very little assuring. Faustina, however, played a role in the affirmation of Commodus's position as Marcus's chosen heir. As discussed in this chapter earlier, Commodus had to step forward in year 175 after rumours of the death of Marcus Aurelius had caused Avidius Cassius to take action. Marcus then hurried to affirm the status of Commodus as his heir by introducing the boy to the army and to the coinage. One coin type issued in CE 177 portrays both Commodus and his mother, Faustina, on the reverse side of Marcus's coin. Commodus is introduced as Caesar and *Augusti filius* and Faustina's status as the daughter of the Emperor Antoninus Pius is emphasized in the coin inscription by calling her *Pii Augusti filia*.[79] The coin type builds a picture of three generations of imperial power by reminding the people of the biological ties on which the dynasty was built.

Another aspect of Faustina's presence on Marcus's travels is the honorary title of *mater castrorum*, which she received in year 174. This was a title that had never before been given to any Roman empress.[80] The title presented quite a change in Faustina's public image that had previously concentrated on her fertility. The maternal aspect of the Empress's image remained, but it was now transferred from the sphere of family to that of the military. Faustina became the 'mother of the camps', and the title was introduced to Faustina's coinage.[81] Maternal aspects and the army were thus united. The title is clearly connected to the relationship of the Emperor and the army that was growing in its importance and presented a way in which Marcus attempted to secure the support of the troops. It can also be connected to the upcoming dynastic events in which Commodus's position as the legitimate heir was confirmed by holding his *toga virilis* ceremony in front of the troops.[82]

Faustina did not enjoy her new title for long. When the imperial party was travelling through Anatolia to reach Syria, Faustina died in the village of Halala in Cappadocia.[83] Marcus took the necessary commemorative actions, but the journey still continued.[84] Faustina's death sparked a reaction in Ephesus where a large honorary group was set up for the imperial family. The group was set up by the council and the citizens of Ephesus and can be dated between CE 175 and CE 180. It includes honours expressed towards Marcus Aurelius, *thea* Faustina, and six of their children.[85] These were all the children who were alive at the time of the monument's dedication. The presence of Marcus and his family in Ephesus during their tour in the East is not certain, but on the way back to Rome, they did visit at least Smyrna, a close neighbour of Ephesus.[86]

The statuary group was set up in Artemision, the temple of the Ephesian Artemis, a prominent and prestigious public place in the city. Connected to the Artemision was a separate building for the imperial cult, Sebasteion.[87] The cult

110 *Sanna Joska*

was one of the key features used to define the relationship between the imperial house and the citizens of the provinces. Ephesus could title itself *neokoros*, a temple warden of the cult of the emperors. It was considered a great privilege and a matter of civic pride for a city to gain from an emperor the right to build a temple for the imperial cult.[88] The cult was connected similarly to the status of private citizens since holding a priesthood in the cult was a matter of personal and family pride. For instance, the high priesthood of the imperial cult in the province of Asia was held by the family of Flavia Papiane, wife of the above-mentioned Vedius Antoninus III. Flavia Papiane thus became the *archiereia* of Asia.[89] There are no descriptions of actual ritual activities in connection with the imperial cult, and it cannot be determined how an emperor's children or grandchildren were included.[90] During Antoninus Pius's reign, Ephesians celebrated the Emperor's birthday each year for five days, and public money was distributed to the citizens, so they could make sacrifices on behalf of the Emperor.[91]

Before the dedication of the statues in Sebasteion, the Ephesians had already set up one monument in honour of Marcus Aurelius's family. This monument included statues of at least four of Marcus's children and most likely also of the Emperor and Empress.[92] This action continues the practice begun under the reign of Antoninus Pius when Ephesians had already dedicated several monuments in honour of the ruling family. These new honorary monuments presented yet another sign of the continuing relationship between the Antonines and Ephesus and the willingness of the Ephesians to highlight that relationship.

In Syria, we have another honorific monument that might have been motivated by the presence of the imperial family. In Heliopolis (Baalbek), the citizens set up honorary inscriptions to the Emperor Marcus Aurelius and his daughter, Sabina.[93] The dedications can be dated somewhere between the birth of Sabina before CE 170 and the death of Marcus in CE 180. If the monument was inspired by an imperial visit to the city, then it could be expected that other members of the family were also originally honoured in addition to Marcus and his daughter, Sabina. It is, however, not known what cities the entourage visited in Syria, except for their visit to Antioch on their return journey.[94]

The city of Heliopolis was an important cultic centre in the Roman Syria area. It hosted the grand temple of Jupiter-Baal and other temples were constructed under Roman rule. The sanctuary of the Heliopolitan Jupiter served as a place of pilgrimage and had an oracle that was consulted at least by the Emperor Trajan.[95] Antoninus Pius was involved in the building of the court of the temple of Jupiter and finishing the building of the temple of Bacchus.[96] Even if the city did not gain imperial visitors, the citizens of Heliopolis may have sent an embassy to another town to meet the Emperor to tell him of these honours or ask his personal permission to set them up. It was not necessary to gain direct permission from the Emperor to erect honorific monuments to him, but the act of asking for one could be used as a strategy to make a city more prestigious in the eyes of the ruler.[97] The dedications to Marcus and Sabina were made in Latin, which in Roman Syria was the language of public dedications, as well as the inscriptions used on coinage.

The use of Latin instead of Aramaic highlighted the fact of the eastern province belonging to the Roman Empire.[98]

Haim Gitler suggests that a coin type issued by the city of Aelia Capitolina (formerly Jerusalem, but renamed by Hadrian after the Bar Kokhba revolt) may have been a response to the presence of the imperial family in the area, or even in the city itself.[99] The city's officials issued two coin types with portraits of Marcus Aurelius and Commodus. The other type presented Commodus on horseback, raising his hand. The reverse inscriptions name the prince as Caesar and Germanicus, dating these types after CE 172 and likely also after 175.[100] CE 175 is the date when Marcus began issuing coinage with Commodus's portrait, so it can be expected that provincial mints followed the imperial example.[101] If not direct evidence of the visit of the imperial family to the city, the coin types can at least be read as indirect influence that the presence of the imperial family had in the provinces.[102] Minting coinage with the portrait of the designated heir of the emperor sent a strong message of loyalty to the ruling dynasty.

From Syria and Palestina, the imperial entourage continued to Egypt where they spent the winter of CE 175–176 in the city of Alexandria.[103] As with Palestina, it is reasonable to ask whether the visit to Egypt was reflected in the coinage issued in that area. The provincial mint in Alexandria started issuing coinage with Commodus's portrait from CE 175/176 – precisely the time of the imperial visit – onwards.[104] Here, however, the tie between the visit and the beginning of minting remains rather dim, I do argue. The mint in Alexandria was a provincial mint that acted under the authority of the emperors to a greater degree than did the city mints in the East.[105] Because provincial mints followed the policies set by the ruler to a larger extent, it would have, in the fashion of typical imperial coinage, started issuing coin types for Commodus Caesar had he visited the city in person or had he not.

In connection with the visit of the imperial party to Alexandria, the writer of *Historia Augusta* offers an intriguing comment about Marcus's action: 'And although the citizens of Alexandria had been outspoken in wishing Cassius success, he forgave everything and left his daughter among them'.[106] Who was this daughter? This passage might, of course, be the invention of the biographer. The part of the text aims at showing the righteous and even lenient nature of Marcus and his reaction to the rebellion by Avidius Cassius.[107] The comment seems strange if it is purely imaginary, as it does not seem to be connected to any other issue in this passage. However, this might imply that there is at least some truth behind it. On the other hand, there is no further evidence concerning a daughter of Marcus being in Alexandria.

The passage has also been surpassed as simply a side note by modern researchers. Levick suggests the daughter in question was 'presumably the wife of the general Pompeianus', Lucilla, but it does not give any motivation for this argument.[108] Lucilla was at that moment married to T. Claudius Pompeianus, a trusted man of Marcus and the commander in chief of his army in Pannonia.[109] If the daughter who was left in Alexandria was Lucilla, this would mean that she had travelled with Marcus to the East, even if her husband, Pompeianus, had not.[110]

112   *Sanna Joska*

The presence of Lucilla and Pompeianus on this journey cannot be confirmed either way, but I am prone to think that Marcus would not have left Lucilla, married to one of his closest officers, in Alexandria, because Lucilla's role was now to be the wife of Pompeianus and a mother to at least one child sired by him.[111] Lucilla would thus have most likely followed Pompeianus and stayed where he stayed.

The presence of Marcus and Faustina's other daughters, Faustina, Fadilla, and Cornificia, on the journey is likewise uncertain. Faustina was married before the journey took place and Fadilla and Cornificia were in their mid-teens. Their marriages might have taken place after Marcus returned from the journey to the East.[112] Because they either were already married or about to be married, it is unlikely that any one of these daughters would have been left behind in Alexandria, if they even had travelled along. The only option then would be the young daughter who we know travelled along, namely, either Sabina or the otherwise unknown daughter.

There is, however, the further option that the comment concerns a daughter of Avidius Cassius, instead. Avidius Cassius had children whose faith Marcus had to solve after Cassius's death and one of them was a daughter named Avidia Alexandria.[113] She and her husband had the right to move freely, but they were entrusted to the protection of an older male relative.[114] Could she be the daughter left in Alexandria instead of one of the daughters of Marcus? This matter is complicated, and it would certainly be interesting to know whether one of the children of the imperial family was used as a tool to solve a political situation, but as the evidence is limited, this issue must remain only speculation.

From Egypt, whether leaving a daughter behind or not, the imperial party started their way back to Rome. Marcus had now personally visited the areas that had supported the rebellious Avidius Cassius, and by this visit had again ensured his own position in power. The Emperor had, at the same time, effectively introduced his son and heir, Commodus, to the provincials.[115] Their route took them through Asia and Greece where they visited Antioch, Smyrna, and Athens at least.[116] In Athens, Marcus Aurelius and Commodus were initiated into the mysteries of Eleusis, as Hadrian and Lucius Verus had been before them.[117]

The imperial family was finally back in Rome in the autumn of CE 176. Marcus had not been in the capital since CE 169 and the funeral of Lucius Verus, and Commodus's absence had lasted more than a year. The return of the heir was celebrated by *adventus* coins, issued as *aurei*, and show Commodus on horseback.[118] *Adventus* was the ceremony of return of emperors to Rome and included celebrations and processions.[119] We do not know whether an actual ceremony was celebrated or whether the return of the Emperor and his Caesar was just chosen as a motive for the coinage. Marcus did celebrate a triumph in December 176 for his victories against the Marcomanni. This triumph also served as a dynastic event, as Marcus had recently named Commodus as *Imperator*, a step in the path to making Commodus his co-ruler.[120] Travel in the eastern part of the empire had played a major role in the legitimization of Commodus's role, as he was now, after touring the provinces and securing the support of the troops, ready to take his position in power.

## Conclusion

This chapter discusses travel in the Roman world from the viewpoint of the inter-action between the ruler and the ruled through a special group, the children of the imperial family. The discussion takes as its initial premises the fact that impe-rial travel and the personal presence of the Roman emperor in the provinces was a greatly valued part of conducting and maintaining the relationship between the ruler and his subjects. The study follows the routes in the eastern part of the empire taken by the imperial family of Emperor Marcus Aurelius during the CE 160s and 170s. This interaction is traced by examining literal passages, hon-orary monuments, and civic coinage that speak on behalf of the presence of the children in provincial cities and of the reactions that this presence sparked in the provincial citizens of the Roman empire. The analysis shows that due to the nature of the evidence, the agency of the provincials could only be understood on a general level. Nevertheless, it can be stated that the presence of imperial children was indeed noticed and may have been a motivation for the provincials to include them on the honorific monuments and when issuing coin types. For an emperor, the presence of his children functioned as a tool of his public politics and also as a way of reinforcing his relationships with certain important groups in that society.

The discussion also touches on the subject of lived realities the children had on long journeys. The cases that are discussed show that imperial children travelled the Roman empire widely. They could travel with their parents no matter how young they were, and many might even have been born in the provinces while their mother was accompanying her husband on his travels. Lucilla, when about to marry in Ephesus, and Commodus, when joining his father at the war front in CE 175, travelled long distances without their parents. Both also experienced travel as part of their rite of passage from childhood to adulthood. It was a reality for these children to travel thousands of kilometres and visit several cities. Among the highest class in society, travel was clearly not a question of age.

In terms of the level of political interaction, the fact that imperial children travelled widely along with their parents presents one way of delivering public, political visibility for the imperial children, indeed a matter that has not been the focus of systematic study before now. As the children arrived in cities around the empire with their father and mother, they too became the focus of celebra-tions that the hosting cities arranged in honour of the imperial visitors. When an emperor received greetings from members of the public, his children were likely present and they were likely included in the celebrations of the provincial imperial cult. From the viewpoint of an emperor, these travelling imperial children could be viewed as one of the political messages that the ruler created to manifest his power. During the Antonine era, the children's presence was essentially used as a complementing factor in the pictures created on the Antonine coinage and other media.

The recipients of these messages were all subjects of imperial rule, but certain groups stand out from among the gathered evidence. In this study, these groups are especially the army, one of the most central groups for the power of the

114  *Sanna Joska*

emperors, and local city elites, the local power holders. The army's role appears central for the continuity of dynastic rule, as is clearly evident from the fact that young Commodus was actually introduced to the troops on several occasions. Also, other children as well as their mother, Faustina the Younger, stayed with Marcus Aurelius at the headquarters. The importance of the army is also clear when viewing the travels of previous imperial families, such as Julia Augusti or Agrippina the Elder and their children.

The local elites, on the other hand, were those members of the society who were in charge of erecting monuments and minting city coinage and organizing actual celebrations if an emperor should honour their city with his presence. The men and women belonging to these city councils were those responsible for the use of public money and space and for maintaining the relationship of their city with the ruling power – and of course, also maintaining their personal relationship with an emperor, if possible. The agency of the local elites is evident in the public monuments that honoured children of the imperial family and in the coinage that was minted in their honour. Paying attention to these children was done to act out their loyalty to the imperial house, but essentially, it can also be seen in light of securing future benefaction and visualizing the connections and status of the cities of that time in history. These children were the future emperors and empresses who would continue their father's favours in the future.

## Notes

1  Halfmann 1986, 90–110.
2  Sijpesteijn 1969, 109–110 on the costs of imperial visits to cities and 116–118 on a letter noting the preparations for Hadrian's visit to Egypt.
3  Halfmann 1986, 118–124. See also Hdn. 1.7.2 on Commodus's reception (transl. by C. R. Whittaker): 'Everywhere as he passed through the cities on his journey he was given a royal reception. Making his appearance to the festive crowds, he was hailed as the darling of the people when they saw him.'
4  Lendon 1997, 136–137 on imperial favour increasing a town's honour.
5  Recorded in the *Fasti Ostienses*: Vidman, *FO* 51; SHA *Marc*. 6.6; Birley 1987, 103, 114.
6  For the era of the Antonines see e.g. Birley 1987 on Marcus Aurelius, Grant 1994 on the Antonine emperors, Hekster 2002 on Commodus and Levick 2014 on the Faustinas.
7  The analysis includes writings from the collection of imperial biographies known as the *Historia Augusta*, Cassius Dio, Herodian, Philostratus, Galen, Lucian and Aelius Aristides. Besides the *Historia Augusta,* these represent the writings of late second- and third- century writers. For the reliability of the *Historia Augusta*, written during the fourth century, concerning the biographies of the Antonine emperors, see Birley 2012a, 18–26.
8  Coinage and honorific monuments are discussed as forms of communication that transferred messages of power. For coinage as communication, see Noreña 2011a and Heuchert 2005 and for honorific monuments, see Miles 2000, 29–36.
9  See Halfmann 1986, 90–92.
10 Birley (2003) on Hadrian's travels and the evidence concerning them; Boatwright (2000) on Hadrian's munificence and personal attention to the provincial cities; Syme (1988) also traces Hadrian's journeys using ancient evidence.

## Roman Imperial family on the road 115

11 Especially the coinage of Faustina the Younger was filled with these themes, see Levick 2014, 110–111 on Faustina's role as mother. On imperial ideology and the role of children during the Antonine era, see esp. Rawson 2003, 64–66 and Rawson 2001. Joska 2018 discusses in detail the legitimization of imperial and local power through imperial children in the Antonine era.

12 SHA *Marc.* 7.8.

13 SHA *Marc.* 6.2.

14 She was born c. CE 150, see Levick 2014, 116 with further references.

15 For a Roman girl, childhood ended with marriage, see Rawson 2003, 145.

16 SHA *Verus* 6.7–7.10; Birley 1987, 125–126.

17 Luc. *Im.* and *Pr.Im.* praise Panthea.

18 Hanson 2011, 252–257.

19 Levick 2014, 49.

20 Brennan 2012, 359; Fantham 2006, 57–58.

21 Antoninus Pius and Faustina the Elder had also three other children, but the older daughter, Aurelia Fadilla, died before Pius's proconsulate, and their two sons were dead by the time Pius became the emperor, see SHA *Ant. Pius* 1.7, 3.6. Their epitaphs: *CIL* VI 988–990.

22 *I.Ephesos* 1504, 2050.

23 SHA *Marc.* 9.4. The uncle was M. Vettulenus Civica Barbarus. The *Historia Augusta* mentions Marcus's sister as accompanying Lucilla, but his sister was dead by that time. Instead, Ceionia Fabia, one of the sisters of Lucius Verus, must have been meant. Ceionia Fabia is mentioned in an inscription set up in Ephesus (*AE* 1939, 127 = *I.Ephesos* 704). The honour in question is made to her son, who is mentioned as the son of Ceionia and the nephew of *theos* Verus. The mention does not confirm Ceionia's presence in the city at the time of the wedding, but if she visited Ephesus, that could explain the willingness to use her name in the honour.

24 Birley 1987, 131.

25 SHA *Marc.* 9.6.

26 Levick 2014, 71.

27 *BMCRE* IV (Marcus Aurelius) 1228.

28 On medallions see Toynbee 1986.

29 Gnecchi 1912, 50 no 2.

30 *Dextrarum iunctio* was used also on funerary reliefs to mark marital harmony, see Hersch 2010, 205–211. The gesture symbolised political concord, see e.g. the coinage of Marcus and Lucius: *RIC* III (Marcus Aurelius) 7–10.

31 Birley 1987, 145–146; Fittschen 1982, 72–75.

32 Oberleitner 2009, 223–266.

33 See Levick 2014, 53 n. 66 for a review on the discussion of the dating of the monument, which has especially raised much discussion. An early Antonine dating is suggested in Taeuber 2006.

34 Oberleitner 2009, 393–406, 429.

35 Levick 2014, 53–54; Oberleitner 2009, 216. Liverani 1996/1997 emphasizes that Antoninus Pius, not Lucius Verus, is the central person on the monument. Fittschen 2006 comments on the portraits of the relief.

36 Oberleitner 2009, 215–218.

37 Levick 2014, 54.

38 *I.Ephesos* 284d; *I.Ephesos* 287.1–9; *I.Ephesos* 288.1–5; *I.Ephesos* 290.1–2 and *SEG* XXXIV 1090.1–2; *I.Ephesos* 2049.

39 *SEG* IV 402–408.

40 See Halfmann 1979, 168–169, Halfmann 2001, 77–80 and Keil 1955, 563 on Vedius Antoninus III and the family of the Vedii. The Vedius Antoninus in question and his father, Vedius Antoninus II, were adopted into the family after CE 128. Their adoptive

## 116 *Sanna Joska*

father, Vedius I, was acquainted with Hadrian, see Kalinowski 2002, 119. Vedius III's career: *I.Ephesos* 4110 and Kalinowski 2002, 117–121. Chausson 2006, 38 notes that a relationship might have existed between the family of the Vedii and the family of the Arrii, the family of Antoninus Pius's mother.

41 See Kalinowski 2002, 110–117 on Pius's involvement in the dispute between Vedius Antoninus and the Ephesians.

42 *I.Ephesos* 728. Kalinowski 2002, 130 suggests the object of honour was Vedius II, the father of Vedius III, because the inscription does not mention Vedius III's office as a quaestor designate. Vedius II would have been very elderly at the time.

43 See also Birley 1987, 145.

44 Kalinowski 2002, 138.

45 Birley 2003, 425. Hadrian was an exception to this rule.

46 For the Marcomannic wars see Birley 2012b, 222–230.

47 *AE* 1964, 181, set up in Lilybaeum, Sicily.

48 Suet. *Calig.* 8 mentions that Agrippina gave birth to several of their children on these travels.

49 Suet. *Calig.* 9, 10.1, 13.

50 *AE* 1982, 778 has by some researchers been interpreted as proof of the presence of Commodus in Carnuntum. The dedication is in a very fractured state, however, and could alternatively honour Antoninus Pius and Marcus Aurelius as Caesar, see Birley 1987, 174; Hekster 2002, 33.

51 SHA *Comm.* 11.14; Birley 1987, 174.

52 Birley 1987, 174–175.

53 *RIC* III (Marcus Aurelius) 1046; *BMCRE* IV (Marcus Aurelius) 1425–1426.

54 See Hekster 2003 on audience targeting through different denominations.

55 SHA *Comm.* 2.2; Halfmann 1986, 213.

56 Harlow and Laurence 2002, 67.

57 Laes and Strubbe 2014, 55–58 on the rituals of adulthood. The age at which a boy assumed the toga of an adult man was decided by his father.

58 Birley 1987, 184–189 and Grant 1994, 49–52 on Cassius's rebellion.

59 Hekster 2002, 35–36.

60 On the conflict, see Birley 1987, 180.

61 Philostr. *VS* 2.560 (transl. by W. C. Wright).

62 Philostr. *VS* 2.561.

63 Levick 2014, 117–118. Birley 1987, 248 suggests there was an unknown daughter. Sabina's birth was dated to be 166 by Fittschen 1982, 31–32.

64 The accounts of the physicist, Galen, speak of Commodus in the care of a tutor named Pitholaus and Annia Faustina, 'a very close relative', see Gal. *Praen.* 9.7–8, 10.22, 12.1–12 and Hekster 2002, 33–34.

65 The son, Hadrianus, was born some time between CE 161 and 175 and is known only from two inscriptions: *CIG* 2968b and *I.Ephesos* 288.4.

66 These daughters were Lucilla, Annia Faustina, Fadilla, and Cornificia. See Levick 2014, 116–117.

67 Fantham 2006, 61–67; Habicht 1996; Kajava 2008. Julia's travelling life continued with Tiberius, her third husband; Julia gave birth to at least one of their children at Aquileia, see Fantham 2006, 83.

68 Fantham 2006, 117.

69 Kokkinos 1992, 13.

70 Fantham 2006, 66. See also Carucci 2016, 184–186 on the risks of travelling for pregnant women and mothers with small children.

71 See the recent study by Bruun in 2016 on travel, especially migration and mobility, of women and children in the Roman world.

72 Birley 1987, 189–195.

Roman Imperial family on the road 117

73 See list in Fantham 2006, 135.
74 Højte 2000, 211–235. Højte argues, on the basis of evidence on the Emperors Trajan, Hadrian and Antoninus Pius, that imperial visits generally did not motivate the provincials to set up statues for emperors; rather the statues were erected instead for multiple reasons. See also Højte 2009, 108: 'as a general rule no connections can be established between imperial travels and the dedication of honorary statues. There are however exceptions to this rule.'
75 *BCH* 50 (1926), 448, 89 = *AE* 1928, 49–50.
76 Fantham 2006, 61–62; Rose 1997, 109.
77 Fantham 2006, 61.
78 Levick 2014, 61–63.
79 *BMCRE* IV (Marcus Aurelius) 1226.
80 Boatwright 2003, 250; Levick 2014, 78. Ancient sources on the title: Cass. Dio. 72.10; SHA *Marc.* 26.8.
81 *RIC* III (Marcus Aurelius) 751–754, 1659–1662, 1711–1714. See also Boatwright 2003, 259–265 on women and the military and the presence of imperial women among the Roman troops. Especially Agrippina the Elder was said to have had great influence over soldiers, who also respected her in return, see Tac. *Ann.* 1.69; Fantham 2006, 119.
82 Boatwright 2003, 266.
83 Halfmann 1986, 213 dates Faustina's death to the return journey, like the *Historia Augusta* (SHA *Marc.* 26.4), but see Levick 2014, 87 on the likelihood that she had already died in CE 175, based on Marcus's letter to the senate.
84 Faustina was deified by the senate, received a temple, and Marcus also issued commemorative coinage for her. He renamed the village where Faustina died Faustinopolis. See Levick 2014, 135–137.
85 *I.Ephesos* 287.1–9. The children were Commodus, Fadilla, Lucilla, Faustina, Cornificia, and Sabina.
86 Philostr. *VS* 2.582–583. At Smyrna, the imperial party met the orator, Aelius Aristides, who mentions the imperial daughters being present with their father: Aristid. *Or.* 42.13 (Keil), also Halfmann 1986, 92.
87 Price 1984, 254.
88 Burrell 2004, 59–85. Ephesus gained its first neocorate under Nero and the second under Hadrian with further ones under the Severans and Valerian and Gallienus. See Price 1984, 254–256 on the buildings that were connected to the imperial cult in Ephesus.
89 Flavia's priesthood: *I.Ephesos* 729; Kalinowski 2002, 109–117.
90 Friesen 1993, 142.
91 Knibbe 1980, 787; Price 1984, 112.
92 *I.Ephesos* 288.1–5.
93 *CIL* III 14387b = *IGLS* VI 2764; *IGLS* VI 2763. The original place of either statue base is not known. *CIL* III 14387b was reused later as building material for the walls of a temple dedicated to Sol.
94 Marcus at first refused to visit Antioch because Avidius Cassius had lived there, see Halfmann 1986, 213; Birley 1987, 192–193.
95 Butcher 2003, 115–116, 365–367; Macrob. *Sat.* 1.23.13–16 on Trajan at the oracle at Heliopolis. It must be noted, however, that Macrobius wrote his *Saturnalia* during the early fifth century.
96 Hajjar 1990, 2496.
97 Højte 2005, 155–156; Noreña 2011b, 267–268; Rose 1997, 8–9 on the known letters sent to emperors asking for permissions; Fejfer 2008, 420–421 on letters and permissions as politics.
98 Eck 2009, 26–39.

118   *Sanna Joska*

  99   Gitler 1990–1991, 41.

100   *RPC* IV (online) 6419, 6420.

101   Commodus's first coins: *RIC* III (Marcus Aurelius) 335, 336, 597–603, 1153, 1513–1522. In *RIC,* the types have been dated to 172–175 on the basis of a lack of the title, Sarmaticus, but they are more likely datable to CE 175 because the reverse designs refer to the events of CE 175 when Commodus took his *toga virilis.* See also *BMCRE* IV pp. 476–477 where the same coin types have been dated to CE 175. See Howgego 2005, 14–16 on the relationship of Roman and local images on provincial coinage.

102   Gitler 1990–1991, 42–44 lists coin types that were minted shortly after the visit.

103   Halfmann 1986, 213.

104   *RPC* IV (online) 16032, 16428.

105   For provincial mints, see Heuchert 2005, 30.

106   SHA *Marc.* 26.3: *et cum multa Alexandrini in Cassium dixissent fausta, tamen omnibus ignovit et filiam suam apud eos reliquit.*

107   Adams 2014, 119.

108   Birley 1987, 193; Levick 2014, 87.

109   Birley 1987, 161–162.

110   Birley 1987, 191 assumes Pompeianus might have stayed in Pannonia.

111   A son, Aurelius Pompeianus, born after CE 170, see Pflaum 1961, 33. It is mentioned, however, in the *Historia Augusta*, that Lucilla disliked her new husband at least at the beginning of their marriage, SHA *Marc.* 20.6–7.

112   See Levick 2014, 76–77 on the marriages of these three daughters.

113   *PFOS* 129.

114   SHA *Marc.* 26.10–12; SHA *Avid. Cass.* 9.2–4; Birley 1987, 192. In addition to Alexandria, there were two sons, one of whom was killed soon after his father; the other was banished.

115   Emphasized also by Hekster 2002, 37–38.

116   Birley 1987, 193–194; Halfmann 1986, 213. For Hadrian's initiation, see Clinton 1989, 56–57.

117   Cass Dio 72.31.3; SHA *Marc.* 27.1; Philostr. *V S* 2.562–563.

118   *RIC* III (Marcus Aurelius) 604.

119   See MacCormack 1972, 723 on these ceremonies.

120   Birley 1987, 195–197.

## Bibliography

Adams, Geoff W. 2014. *Marcus Aurelius in the Historia Augusta and Beyond.* Lanham: Lexington Books.

Barrett, Anthony A. 1999. *Agrippina: Sex, Power and Politics in the Early Empire.* London: Routledge.

Birley, Anthony R. 1987 (2000). *Marcus Aurelius: A Biography.* Routledge: London.

Birley, Anthony R. 2003. "Hadrian's Travels." In *The Representation and Perception of Roman Imperial Power,* edited by Lukas de Blois et al., 425–441. Amsterdam: J. C. Gieben.

Birley, Anthony R. 2012a. "Cassius Dio and the *Historia Augusta.*" In *A Companion to Marcus Aurelius,* edited by Marcel van Ackeren, 13–28. Blackwell Companions to the Ancient World. Malden: Wiley-Blackwell.

Birley, Anthony R. 2012b. "The Wars and Revolts." In *A Companion to Marcus Aurelius,* edited by Marcel van Ackeren, 217–233. Blackwell Companions to the Ancient World. Malden: Wiley-Blackwell.

Boatwright, Mary T. 2000. *Hadrian and the Cities of the Roman Empire.* Princeton: Princeton University Press.

Roman Imperial family on the road 119

Boatwright, Mary T. 2003. "Faustina the Younger, 'mater castrorvm.'" In *Les femmes antiques entre sphère privée et sphère publique*, edited by Regula Frei-Stolba, Anne Bielman and Olivier Bianchi, 249–268. Bern: P. Lang.

Brennan, T. Corey. 2012. "Perceptions of Women's Power in the Late Republic: Terentia, Fulvia, and the Generation of 63 BCE." In *A Companion to Women in the Ancient World*, edited by Sharon L. James and Sheila Dillon, 354–366. Blackwell Companions to the Ancient World. Malden: Wiley-Blackwell.

Bruun, Christer. 2016. "Tracing Familial Mobility: Female and Child Migrants in the Roman West." In *Migration and Mobility in the Early Roman Empire*, edited by Luuk de Ligt and Laurens E. Tacoma, 176–204. Leiden: Brill.

Burrell, Barbara. 2004. *Neokoroi: Greek Cities and Roman Emperors*. Leiden: Brill.

Butcher, Kevin. 2003. *Roman Syria and the Near East*. London: British Museum.

Carucci, Margherita. 2016. "The Dangers of Female Mobility in Roman Imperial Times." In *Impact of Mobility and Migration in the Roman Empire: Proceedings of the Twelfth Workshop of the International Network Impact of Empire* (Rome, June 17–19, 2015), edited by Elio Lo Cascio and Laurens E. Tacoma, 173–190. Leiden: Brill.

Chausson, François. 2006. "Antonin le Pieux, Éphèse et les Parthes." In *Das Partherdenkmal von Ephesos. Akten des Kolloquiums Wien 27. – 28. April 2003* (Schriften des Kunsthistorischen Museums 10), edited by Wilfried Seipel, 33–69. Wien: Kunsthistorisches Museum Wien.

Clinton, Kevin. 1989. "Hadrian's Contribution to the Renaissance of Eleusis." In *The Greek Renaissance in the Roman Empire* (BICS Supplement 55), edited by Susan Walker and Cameron Averil, 56–68. London: Institute of Classical Studies.

Eck, Werner. 2009. "The Presence, Role and Significance of Latin in the Epigraphy and Culture of the Roman Near East." In *From Hellenism to Islam: Cultural and Linguistic Change in the Roman Near East*, edited by Hannah M. Cotton et al., 15–42. Cambridge: Cambridge University Press.

Fantham, Elaine. 2006. *Julia Augusti: The Emperor's Daughter*. London: Routledge.

Fejfer, Jane. 2008. *Roman Portraits in Context*. Berlin: De Gruyter.

Fittschen, Klaus. 1982. *Die Bildnistypen der Faustina minor und die Fecunditas Augustae*. Göttingen: Vandenhoeck & Ruprecht.

Fittschen, Klaus. 2006. "Die Porträts am sogenannten Parthermonument. Vorbilder und Datierung." In *Das Partherdenkmal von Ephesos. Akten des Kolloquiums Wien 27. – 28. April 2003* (Schriften des Kunsthistorischen Museums 10), edited by Wilfried Seipel, 71–87. Wien: Kunsthistorisches Museum Wien.

Friesen, Steven J. 1993. *Twice Neokoros: Ephesus, Asia, and the Cult of the Flavian Imperial Family* (Religions in the Graeco-Roman World 116). Leiden: Brill.

Gitler, Haim. 1990–1991. "Numismatic Evidence on the Visit of Marcus Aurelius to the East." *Israel Numismatic Journal* 11: 36–52.

Gnecchi, Francesco. 1912. *I medaglioni romani vol. II: Gran moduli*. Milano: U. Hoepli.

Grant, Michael. 1994. *The Antonines: The Roman Empire in Transition*. London: Routledge.

Habicht, Christian. 1996. "Iulia Kalliteknos." *Museum Helveticum* 53: 156–159.

Hajjar, Youssef. 1990. "Baalbek, grand centre religieux sous l'Empire." *Aufstieg und Niedergang der römischen Welt II* 18(4): 2458–2508.

Halfmann, Helmut. 1979. *Die Senatoren aus dem östlichen Teil des Imperium Romanum bis zum Ende des 2.Jh. n. Chr* (Hypomnemata 58). Göttingen: Vandenhoeck & Ruprecht.

Halfmann, Helmut. 1986. *Itinera principum: Geschichte und Typologie der Kaiserreisen im Römischen Reich* (Heidelberger Althistorische Beiträge und Epigraphische Studien 2). Stuttgart: Franz Steiner.

120    *Sanna Joska*

Halfmann, Helmut. 2001. *Städtebau und Bauherren im römischen Kleinasien: Ein Vergleich zwischen Pergamon und Ephesos* (Istanbuler Mitteilungen, Beiheft 43). Tübingen: Ernst Wasmuth.

Hanson, J. W. 2011. "The Urban System of Roman Asia Minor and Wider Urban Connectivity." In *Settlement, Urbanization, and Population* (Oxford Studies on the Roman Economy 2), edited by Alan K. Bowman and Andrew Wilson, 229–275. Oxford: Oxford University Press.

Harlow, Mary and Ray Laurence. 2002. *Growing Up and Growing Old in Ancient Rome: A Life Course Approach.* London: Routledge.

Hekster, Olivier. 2002. *Commodus: An Emperor at the Crossroads.* Amsterdam: Gieben.

Hekster, Olivier. 2003. "Coins and Messages: Audience Targeting on Coins of Different Denominations?" In *The Representation and Perception of Roman Imperial Power*, edited by Lukas de Blois et al., 20–35. Amsterdam: J. C. Gieben.

Hersch, Karen K. 2010. *The Roman Wedding: Ritual and Meaning in Antiquity.* Cambridge: Cambridge University Press.

Heuchert, Volker. 2005. "The Chronological Development of Roman Provincial Coin Iconography." In *Coinage and Identity in the Roman Provinces*, edited by Christopher Howgego, Volker Heuchert and Andrew Burnett, 29–56. Oxford: Oxford University Press.

Højte, Jakob Munk. 2000. "Imperial Visits as Occasion for the Erection of Portrait Statues?" *Zeitschrift für Papyrologie und Epigraphik* 133: 211–235.

Howgego, Christopher. 2005. "Coinage and Identity in the Roman Provinces." In *Coinage and Identity in the Roman Provinces*, edited by Christopher Howgego, Volker Heuchert and Andrew Burnett, 1–17. Oxford: Oxford University Press.

Højte, Jakob Munk. 2005. *Roman Imperial Statue Bases from Augustus to Commodus.* Aarhus: Aarhus University Press.

Højte, Jakob Munk. 2009. "Roman Imperial Portrait Statues and the Emperor on the Move: The Epigraphical Evidence." In *Les Entrées royales et impériales. Histoire, représentation et diffusion d'une cérémonie publique, de l'Orient ancien à Byzance*, edited by Agnès Bérenger and Éric Perrin-Samindayar, 101–110. Paris: De Boccard.

Joska, Sanna. 2018. *Augusti filii et filiae: The Role of Antonine Offspring in Negotiations of Roman Imperial and Local Power.* Tampere: University of Tampere (Unpublished PhD dissertation).

Kajava, Mika. 2008. "Julia Kalliteknos and Gaius Caesar at Euromus." *Arctos* 42: 69–76.

Kalinowski, Angela. 2002. "The Vedii Antonini: Aspects of Patronage and Benefaction in Second-Century Ephesus." *Phoenix* 56: 109–149.

Keil, J. 1955. "Vedii Antonini." *Realencyclopädie der classischen Altertumswissenschaft* VIII A(1): 563–570.

Knibbe, Dieter. 1980. "Ephesos vom Beginn der römischen Herrschaft in Kleinasien bis zum Ende der Principatszeit." *Aufstieg und Niedergang der römischen Welt II* 7(2): 748–830.

Kokkinos, Nikos. 1992. *Antonia Augusta: Portrait of a Great Roman Lady.* London: Routledge.

Laes, Christian and Johan Strubbe. 2014. *Youth in the Roman Empire: The Young and the Restless Years?* Cambridge: Cambridge University Press.

Lendon, J. E. 1997. *Empire of Honour: The Art of Government in the Roman World.* Oxford: Oxford University Press.

Levick, Barbara. 2007. *Julia Domna: Syrian Empress.* London: Routledge.

Levick, Barbara. 2014. *Faustina I and II: Imperial Women of the Golden Age*. Oxford: Oxford University Press.

Liverani, Paolo. 1996–1997. "Il monumento antonino di Efeso." *Rivista dell'Istituto Nazionale di Archeologia e Storia dell'Arte* 19–20: 153–174.

MacCormack, Sabine. 1972. "Change and Continuity in Late Antiquity: The Ceremony of *Adventus.*" *Historia* 21: 721–752.

Miles, Richard. 2000. "Communicating Culture, Identity and Power." In *Experiencing Rome: Culture, Identity and Power in the Roman Empire*, edited by Janet Huskinson, 29–62. London: Routledge.

Noreña, Carlos F. 2011a. "Coins and Communication." In *The Oxford Handbook of Social Relations in the Roman World*, edited by Michael Peachin, 248–268. Oxford: Oxford University Press.

Noreña, Carlos F. 2011b. *Imperial Ideals in the Roman West: Representation, Circulation, Power*. Cambridge: Cambridge University Press.

Oberleitner, Wolfgang. 2009. *Das Partherdenkmal von Ephesos: ein Siegesmonument für Lucius Verus und Marcus Aurelius* (Schriften des Kunsthistorischen Museums 11). Wien: Kunsthistorisches Museum Wien.

Pflaum, Hans-Georg. 1961. "Les gendres de Marc-Aurèle." *Journal des Savants* 1: 28–41.

Price, Simon. 1984. *Rituals and Power: The Roman Imperial Cult in Asia Minor*. Cambridge: Cambridge University Press.

Rawson, Beryl. 2001. "Children as Cultural Symbols: Imperial Ideology in the Second Century." In *Childhood, Class and Kin in the Roman World*, edited by Suzanne Dixon, 21–42. London: Routledge.

Rawson, Beryl. 2003. *Children and Childhood in Roman Italy*. Oxford: Oxford University Press.

Rose, Charles Brian. 1997. *Dynastic Commemoration and Imperial Portraiture in the Julio-Claudian Period*. Cambridge: Cambridge University Press.

Sijpesteijn, P.J. 1969. "A New Document Concerning Hadrian's Visit to Egypt." *Historia* 18: 109–118.

Syme, Ronald. 1988. "Journeys of Hadrian." *Zeitschrift für Papyrologie und Epigraphik* 73: 159–170.

Taeuber, Hans. 2006. "Das 'Parthermonument' – historische Grundlagen." In *Das Partherdenkmal von Ephesos. Akten des Kolloquiums Wien 27. – 28. April 2003* (Schriften des Kunsthistorischen Museums 10), edited by Wilfried Seipel, 25–31. Wien: Kunsthistorisches Museum Wien.

Toynbee, Jocelyn M.C. 1986. *Roman Medallions*. New York: American Numismatic Society.

Vidman, Ladislav. 1982. *Fasti Ostienses*. Pragae: Academia.

# 7 Pilgrimage in Pausanias

*Jussi Rantala and Ville Vuolanto*

## Introduction

The Antonine era is generally considered to have been a heyday of the so called Second Sophistic in Roman Empire, and literature dealing with sacred travelling was an important part of the movement. Texts from authors such as Apuleius, Lucian, Plutarch, and Aristides, with some later works such as those of Philostratus, provide valuable information about pre-Christian pilgrimage in the Roman world.[1] Moreover, we also possess descriptions by many historians and biographers about Roman emperors taking sacred journeys during the first three centuries CE.[2] Indeed, because of the large number of literature dedicated on sacred travelling, the Antonine period has even been described as a 'golden age of pilgrimage'.[3]

Pausanias (c. 115–180 CE) is one of the most well-known figures belonging to this tradition. Probably a native of Magnesia on Sipylos, a city in western Asia Minor (and Roman province of Asia),[4] Pausanias' account on Greece, known as *Hellados Periegesis* (Description of Greece), is geographically the most comprehensive account related to sacred travelling among all ancient, pre-Christian authors dealing with the subject.[5] However, while Pausanias' work was very much part of this general trend, it did not concentrate solely on sacred travelling, but instead included many digressions to subjects such as myths, religion and history of Greece. The completeness of his work makes Pausanias unique among other writers. He describes a continuous tour around the mainland of Greece, instead of individual journeys, observing not just one particular sanctuary but many different sacred sites. Other differences can be found as well; for example, while some other writers would mention things such as instructions given by gods or physical and mental hardships during travels, Pausanias keeps silent with those kinds of issues. Likewise, for example, Aristides provides an 'emic' view focusing on individual trips and personal religious experiences, while Pausanias' work is an 'etic' description of a grand tour, including cults, sacred places, and practices scattered in the landscape of Roman Greece.[6]

As a prolific writer, Pausanias has obviously received a lot of attention from modern scholars. While the issue of sacred travel has indeed been one of the issues at stage, most of the studies have been concentrating on the question if

Pausanias himself can be considered a pilgrim.[7] The present chapter, however, has a different approach. We concentrate on the neglected side of Pausanias' work: our aim is to trace, compare and analyse religious practices and actions which Pausanias himself connects with the sacred travelling. Moreover, we have limited our systematic study on the practices Pausanias describes as contemporary to his own experiences – his remarks on the sacred travelling before his age is dealt with only in contexts where it illuminates Pausanias choices and experiences of the situation of his own age, the mid-second century CE.[8]

Our task can be divided into two: first, we are interested in the forms of lived religion, asking in which sense the practitioners in cults in question can be considered pilgrims (or not). Second, we will be pondering Pausanias' own interests and intentions: why he describes certain local practices and travellers but passes over some others – this is a question not previously pondered by the scholarship. Our aim is also to contextualize Pausanias' description of the contemporary patterns of sacred travel with modern pilgrim studies more generally. Can there be found traceable patterns of pilgrimage similar with, for example, high medieval culture? This analysis, in turn, would help us to contextualize Pausanias' own position as a sacred traveller in the early Roman Empire, a theme indeed much discussed in former studies, and a question we will return at the very end of our chapter.

## Leaving and arriving – travel or not?

Before entering discussion on Pausanias and the actual religious travellers in 'his' landscape, it is necessary to point out that the major part of Pausanias' narrative dedicated to religious participation is seldom connected with any travelling.[9] Most often Pausanias simply chooses to present people worshipping their gods in the very place they live in. This is often casually to be inferred from the references of local people carrying on their religious activities within their settlements and towns, like when he explains how the Megarian women re-enact the story of Demeter and Persefone 'on the rock near Prytaneion' in Megara, that is, at the very centre of the community.[10]

Moreover, often Pausanias' references to the cultic activity are very vague, leaving the actual identity and origin of the worshippers quite open. Pausanias is noting, for example, that at Gerenia there is a sanctuary for Asclepius' son Machaon, where people ask him to cure their diseases. Likewise, there is a reference to the sanctuary of Nymphs at Herakleia some ten kilometres from Olympia, where, 'if you wash in the spring, you can be cured of all kinds of aches and pains'.[11] Thus, there surely were active healing cults, but Pausanias is not interested (or does not know) if they would have involved any sacred travelling beyond such occasional travellers as himself. Thus, as Pausanias is not sharing our interest in the sacred travel *per se*, a reference for such an activity is not appearing in many contexts where there actually could well have been such participants involved.[12] Instead, Pausanias concentrated on living (and already dead) cultic activities scattered in the landscape and along his own travel routes.

124   *Jussi Rantala and Ville Vuolanto*

## Local practices and local travel

For the following discussion, we have categorized the contexts for Pausanias' depictions of religious travelling roughly into three: local, regional, and Panhellenic. Of these, the most frequently mentioned are the local travels, or merely moving around in local surroundings. Even if Pausanias seems seldom to have been interested in the origins of people participating in the ritual activities as such (except when they would come from very far away), it is significant how often he refers to short-range sacred travel, with a distance from less than one kilometre to some ten kilometres from any larger community. In many of these occasions Pausanias clearly presumes – and occasionally even explicitly claims – that the people taking part in the rituals would come from the local (urban) settlements; regularly he connects certain rituals and festivals with particular nearby towns and with their inhabitants. These distances were such that they could have been covered by foot in a less than a day, if necessary, back and forth, and frequently the length of the trip between the settlement and the shrine in question was minimal. For example, at Kynaitha, Pausanias gives the distance of a half a kilometre from the town to a spring, the water of which is used to heal any wound or other problem caused by a dog.[13] Similarly, just outside of the 'Marsh gates' of Megalopolis, there was a sacred precinct of the North-east Wind, in which the people from the city sacrificed regularly every year.[14] However, these distances are not to be understood as the length of the actual trip taken by the single devotees, who would regularly be gathering from a wider area, but they show the minimum need for travel in an individual case.

Many sanctuaries would have located quite near the urban centres, but still in a remote place, like on a peninsula, at the top of a mountain, in a grotto, or across a river. There was, for example, on the way down from the town of Boura a grotto by the river, where 'a small Heracles' was giving oracle responses with a board and dice.[15] At the sanctuary of the Mistress (*Despoina*) in Arcadia, some nine kilometres from Megalopolis, a big area with various statues, altars, and other sights, the Arkadians would offer every kind of fruits (except pomegranates) in the temple proper, and perform sacrifices and mysteries in the adjacent hall.[16] In the nearby altar of Lykaian Zeus, used to offer secret sacrifices to Zeus was, in turn, on the highest peak of the Mount Lykaion. On the other side of the same mountain, there was also a sanctuary of Parrasian Apollo, with an annual festival: the festival begins with a sacrifice at the marketplace (of which town is not specified), with the sacrificed boar taken to the sanctuary in a procession.[17]

According to Pausanias, the communities would often have organized annual festivals in sanctuaries near their administrative centres. For example, the sanctuary of Eurynome was each year opened by the people from the nearby (some two kilometres) Phigalia. This happened at the same time every year for both public and private sacrifices. Pausanias was sad to remark that he was not able to be present at the time of this festival.[18] A little further away, six kilometres from Phigalia, there was a cave of Black Demeter, with an oracle and an also otherwise active cultic life:

*Pilgrimage in Pausanias*  125

Private individuals and once a year the whole Phigalian community should take the fruit of cultivated trees, particularly the grape and the honeycomb, and greasy unspun wool, and lay them on the altar constructed in front of the cave with oil poured over them ...[19]

Mantineans, in turn, would have held a festival every year in the sanctuary of Demeter, some four to five kilometres from the city 'in a plain called Waste', beyond ruins of the village of Nestane.[20] Also, another annual festival refers to Mantineia: Pausanias explains that there is a sanctuary of Artemis Hymnia, shared by Mantineians and Orchomenoans. The common festival took place at the sanctuary, and it seems to have involved people from both communities. A priestess and a priest lived there in perfect purity and separated from the rest of humanity, not allowed, for example, ever to enter a private house.[21] Occasionally, the festivities might have taken place also in longer intervals, as for example in Kelei, which was situated about one kilometre from the city of Sikyon, where the mysteries of Demeter were celebrated once in every fourth year, with, for example, a new priest elected every time.[22] Also in several other towns, the local community would have celebrated festivals away from the actual inhabited area.[23]

For some cults, Pausanias is vaguer of the actual intervals and ways of ritual action. At Pheneos, for example, there is a temple of Demeter of Right some three kilometres from the city, where, as Pausanias writes, they 'still' are celebrating the mysteries. Likewise, when leaving Pheneos, after about three kilometres there are the ruins of a temple of Pythian Apollo, the altar of which was still used, according to Pausanias, to offer sacrifices to Apollo and Artemis.[24] Somewhat different is the anecdote Pausanias tells from the island of Samos: there, people fallen in love had the habit of praying at the tomb of Radine and Leontichos, which was located along the sacred road between the city of Samos and Heraion some six kilometres away from the first mentioned.[25]

Thus, the cultic activities would in many cases have taken place clearly outside of the community's area, even if the distance to be covered was not necessarily a long one, and often these shrines were seen as intimately linked with the actual inhabited area. These cultic locations were connected with the community centres with rituals and processions, and with local individuals regularly travelling between the sanctuaries and their homes.

Should we consider the people involved in above-mentioned practices 'pilgrims'? The distance does not seem to be the defining factor in Greek pre-Christian thought dealing with sacred travel. For Pausanias, there was no need, and therefore not either any special concepts, to make a difference between the very short distance travellers and those coming from the other part of the local territory. Also, more generally, the Greek authors simply refer to pilgrims with expressions such as 'those who travel to sacred places' or 'those who attend to festivals'.[26] Pausanias was not interested in what actually happened during those short journeys, nor was he systematically paying attention to the identity and origin of people taking part in the religious rituals. Still, he often explicitly mentions

126 *Jussi Rantala and Ville Vuolanto*

that travelling indeed took place, acknowledging the action itself even for short distances.

Moreover, in terms of sacred travel, no clear-cut difference can be made between cult places inside of the communities proper and those shrines which were located a little outside of the communities. The visiting of both would have required at least a temporary rejection of everyday duties. Even a sanctuary at the very heart of the community would require transition and even modest travelling, especially for those community members living at the outskirts of the urbanized area or the area governed by the *polis* more widely. After all, any *polis* was a religious centre for its area, and in many ways the identity and even existence of the community were dependent on the *polis* ability to serve as a centre for cultic activity.[27]

We should not underestimate the significance of even very small-scale mobility, which, in any case, would have needed preparations before the departure and leaving of the everyday responsibilities temporarily behind. This would indeed include 'paying a visit to a sacred site outside the boundaries of one's own physical environment' for a specifically religious purpose (as far as we can assess this!), which Matthew Dillon considers essential features in defining pilgrimage in the context of the ancient world. However, his third requirement, that of staying overnight at the religious centre, was probably not fulfilled in many of these smallest scale religious travels. For us, this last requirement, which we see as somewhat arbitrary, would not constitute a *sine qua non* in understanding a sacred traveller as a pilgrim.[28] Instead, what we consider here essential is the religious motivation, the interruption of the everyday tasks and movement in space (that is, departures and arrivals from both home and the shrine), and a performative aspect, like a certain diet, temporary sexual abstinence, or taking part in some sort of ritual action.[29] Indeed, any definition requiring the travel to be of a certain length is problematic, and we prefer a more flexible definition based on the living environment of an individual – pilgrimage would require something out-of-the-ordinary also in this sense, but no absolute distances can be given. Indeed, sometimes even short distance journeys might have been challenging – at least for those people troubled by sickness and travelling to healing sanctuaries. For example, we might take a clue from Aristides who provides many stories of how he was almost too sick to rise from his bed, but still conducted pilgrimages despite physical hardships and discomfort of the journey.[30]

## Intraregional and interregional shrines

In some occasions, religious festivals were linked to the more widely recognized cultic practices. A good example is the festival of Daidala. According to Pausanias, the little Daidala was celebrated by the Plataians with the interval every few years.[31] On these occasions, the Palataians would go to an oak near the ancient town of Alalkomenai with servings, omen watching and for making a wooden cultic figure, a *daidalon*. However, for the festival of the great Daidala, celebrated once in 59 years, all Boiotia joined in.[32] Not only this meant that

Pilgrimage in Pausanias   127

people would have travelled to the spot from all corners of Boiotia, but also that there would have taken place a procession through the landscape, with fourteen Boiotian towns, each having one wooden *daidalon* figure.

> They take the statue to the Asopos and set it up on a wagon with a woman to be a bridesmaid. Then they decide the order of procession by taking lots again, and drive the wagons up from the river to the peak of Kithairon. On the crest of the mountain they have ready an altar.[33]

Each town slaughters a cow and burns it with their *daidalon* to give an offering on the altar. There would also be private sacrifices, according to Pausanias, both by rich and poor.

These kinds of festivals are examples of cultic activities which, although local, still had a more widespread fame and, as a result, could have included 'foreign' visitors taking part in the rituals. For another example, Eleans held a feast called Thyia some one-and-a-half kilometres from their city, in which the empty basins in sealed rooms would be filled with wine during the night. Pausanias asserts that the most distinguished men in Elis and foreigners alike had been testifying this miracle to take place, even if he could not be there at the time of the festival.[34] Also the sacred grove of Asclepius at Epidauros was mentioned to have been visited also by foreigners, but Pausanias gives no further details if this would have been common on his days.[35] Similarly, a shrine of Asclepios, some 14 kilometres from Tithorea, is mentioned by Pausanias the have been honoured not only by Tithoreans but also everyone else in Phocis. Moreover, some eight kilometres away from the sanctuary of Asclepios, there was a precinct consecrated to Isis – the tradition degreed that no one should live there, and only those who had been summoned by Isis in their sleep were allowed to visit the sanctuary. Still, there was a three-day festival taking place twice a year there, with a procession from a place less than a half kilometre away.[36] Apart from festivals, some local sanctuaries were also famous for the relics they possessed. For example, Pausanias mentions spear of Achilles in the sanctuary of Athene in Phaselis, and Memnon's sword in the temple of Asklepios at Nikomedia. These probably drew visitors and were thus objects of intraregional travelling. Although Pausanias does not explicitly mention this, he occasionally refers to local guides and their stories related to the relics and, after all, he was himself able to see some of these.[37]

For Pausanias himself, the rituals in Lebedeia certainly seem to have been of special interest, even of personal importance. The exact location of the central cult place itself, the cave of Trophonios, is not known to us, but it seems to have situated some distance outside of the city of Lebadeia, on the other side of the river Herkyna. The place clearly was a widely recognized sanctuary still at the time of Pausanias, who himself had consulted the oracle there. He gives much detail, and implies a constant flow of consultants, but does not mention any other contemporary 'foreign' visitors there.[38] Visitors would stay there a number of days to purify themselves with baths in the river and meat diet (from sacrifices), with a final offering of a ram to Trophonius, his children, and to the gods. If the omens

128   *Jussi Rantala and Ville Vuolanto*

read from the entrails were favourable, the visitor would have been led at night to the river to be anointed and washed again. After having drunk the water of Lethe and the water of Mnemosyne, the visitor would have prayed by a statue and then approach the oracle itself, through an opening in the earth, from where the visitor was suddenly dragged into a cave, and was given an oracle.[39]

A prime example of interregional cultic activity is presented by the Athenian women, who would have visited every year Parnassos to perform mysteries for Dionysos with the women of Delphi. Pausanias gives the impression that these mysteries were indeed still performed at this time, even if there were no longer the dances on the road from Athens, which were 'traditionally performed' by women called the Thyiades.[40] Somewhat surprisingly this detail is, in fact, the only reference Pausanias provides in connection to Delphi of any contemporary cultic activity beyond the local people living there. All the other Pausanias' stories about Delphi are situated in the past. This is not necessarily to say Delphi would not have served as destination of interregional cultic activities and religious travel in Pausanias' times, but for him the significance of these places was elsewhere.

## The great past of Pausanias: the Panhellenic rituals

Delphi is a prime example of a location having obtained a distinctive Panhellenic, or even more cosmopolitan, status in Greco-Roman religious landscape during the centuries. There were also others of the kind, among which two main groups can be separated: the great oracles and the sacred games. Due to the certain uniqueness of their character and their significance as (potential) destinations for pilgrims from a very long distance – all over the Mediterranean world – Pausanias' records of them are naturally of interest when evaluating his attitudes on sacred travelling and the contemporary practices.

In Pausanias work, Delphi is discussed in many stories and contexts. It is described as a site which had drawn visitors, both private and those travelling with the businesses of their home cities, from all around the Greek world. However, the accounts of Pausanias on Delphi deal with historical and mythical anecdotes, not with contemporary activities. Pausanias describes, for example, how Greeks during their fighting against Persians dedicated a bronze Apollo at Delphi from the naval spoils of Artemision and Salamis, and how Themistocles brought Persian spoils to Apollo at Delphi.[41] Delphi's significance for Pausanias was not restricted to these most well-known struggles of Greek history: for example, Pausanias mentions the much older conflict, the second Messenian war (in seventh century BCE); according to him, Lacedaemonians, after they had suffered great losses during the war, went to Delphi for consultation on many different occasions. Pausanias also points out that in the past, Delphi has been recognised as a place fit for dedications by many Greek cities, such as Corfu, Tegea, and Sparta.[42]

The significance of Delphi as a former religious centre of the Greek world is obviously the reason why Pausanias gives a lot of attention to it. For hundreds of years religious travellers from all over the Greek world visited Delphi.[43] Clearly, for Pausanias, the contemporary Delphi had, however, lost its fame and position as an 'international' centre of religious (and political) travel. Other sources of the first and second century CE appear to confirm this. Strabo does describe the oracle of Delphi as the one that had been 'the most truthful of all',[44] but his account appears to refer to somewhat legendary, not so much to a contemporary, state of affairs. Moreover, the story of Plutarch about guides working at the oracle with fixed itineraries, but with limited knowledge about their subject, makes one wonder if the shrine was more like a museum than a religious centre during the first century CE, when Plutarch wrote his text.[45] Indeed, Plutarch also mentions quite directly that Delphi during his lifetime received fewer visitors than in the past:

> But when Greece, since God so willed, had grown strong in cities and the place was full of people, they used to employ two prophetic priestesses who were sent down in turn; and a third was appointed to be held in reserve. But today there is one priestess and we do not complain, for she meets every need.[46]

Delphi was not the only place to receive this kind of treatment from Pausanias. He mentions, for example, how there used to be an infallible oracle on the Sanctuary of Ptoan Apollo (about three kilometres from the city of Akraiphnion), who gave an oracle to an emissary of Mardonios, a certain Mys from Euromos. After he had asked a question in an oriental language, he got a reply in Carian. According to Pausanias, this would had happened before the invasion of Alexander of Macedon and the extermination of Thebes – in 335 BCE.[47] Pausanias, in general, was keen to connect the places he visited and described to their mythical and historical contexts, and in this way to highlight their historical importance. Thus, for him it was essential to tell, for example, that Thebeans of his day still would have told stories about how they sent questions to various oracles, including the god at Lebadeia.[48]

Together four games – Pythian, Isthmian, Nemean, and Olympian – were traditionally recognised all over the Greek world.[49] They were occasions which had drawn people all over the Mediterranean area as they were both regular and 'intraregional' festivals. While these games were contests for athletes, musicians, and equestrians, they were religious celebrations by their very nature: the competitions taking place would honour the gods or heroes to whom the ceremonies were dedicated.[50] Thus, people travelling to these festivals can be considered pilgrims, as watching contests was very much one way of participating in the ritual.[51] Out of these four games, the ones dedicated to Zeus at Olympia were the most significant. This is also expressed by Pausanias, as he gives a lavish description about the history of Olympic games and records the sanctuaries and statues at the place of the games with great detail.[52] As he puts it himself, 'there are a lot of truly wonderful things you can see and hear about in Greece, but there is a unique divinity of disposition about the mysteries at Eleusis and the games at Olympia'.[53] However, from the viewpoint of pilgrimage, he does not record travels or other actions of people coming to witness the games. Instead, he limits his account mostly to those individuals from different city-states who had gained success as competitors at Olympia,[54] or gives general remarks about athletes who had participated in the

130   *Jussi Rantala and Ville Vuolanto*

games.[55] In addition, he does record a few cases in the past which would underline the Panhellenic character of Olympia as a sanctuary. For example, he writes how some Syracusans were travelling to Olympia with a sacrifice from Dionysios, the tyrant of Syracuse.[56] He also mentions an inscription at Olympia on the dedications given by Choiros from Tegea in order to cure his son, witnessing in turn the significance of Olympia as a destination for intra-regional sacred travellers from the whole Greek world.[57]

Other major games as recorded by Pausanias have even more limited value if we evaluate them from the perspective of sacred travelling. On Nemean games Pausanias has only a few sentences, mostly about their institution and mentioning, for example, how the Argives offer a sacrifice to Zeus, elect a priest of the god and offer a price for the winter competitions of the games.[58] Pythian games receive a bit more attention. Pausanias not only deals with the history of the contest,[59] but also mentions a few cases about the origins of some of the contestants, again demonstrating the interregional character of the games.[60] Similarly, Pausanius gives a description of the origins and history of the Isthmian games, but not much else.[61]

Overall, Pausanias clearly considers the games, especially those of Olympia, as historically important events. Pausanias shows great interest in the history and development of the games, as well as the sites where the games are held. For him, the games represent from their own part the great history of Greece, but as a contemporary religious centre, he has not much to say. Pausanias clearly recognises and even highlights their past interregional and identity-forming character by citing by name and origin contestants from all over the Greek world who had taken part in games.[62] Pausanias seems to have made here a distinction between travel destinations: those places, whose renown depends on their great past and the visible remains still *in situ*, and those places which have had enough contemporary religious significance and relevance to be noted by him.

## Conclusions I: Pausanias the observer

It seems that any rigid categorization of Pausanius' view of religious travel cannot make full justice to his thinking, as he simply is not interested on the travels associated with religious participation *per se*. By no means does he pay any special attention to this aspect of the rituals. For Pausanias, the sites themselves are interesting as destinations for travellers and as 'monuments' representing Greece, its history, myths, and identity, while sacred sites as destinations for sacred travel appear to him as uninteresting in most cases. Through the narrative of Pausanias, we are not able to grasp what was included in a 'typical' sacred travel in Roman Greece of the second century CE. Instead, we are looking the activities through the eyes of Pausanias – what he saw as culturally significant within the context he is active and making his remarks. It is clear that for Pausanias, travel as a form of religious participation is part of the ordinary, and not worth any further discussion.[63]

Therefore, methodologically it is not possible to infer from his text any negative conclusions of the importance of a particular place based on missing information on visitors. In Pausanias' text, Delphi is a prime example of a place the importance of which was based no longer on its contemporary cultic life or on its visitors across the Mediterranean, but on its spectacular history – and of the visible remains of this past. For Pausanias the consultations of the Delphic oracle during the sixth to fourth century BCE would appear frequent and colourful in comparison to the boring and uninteresting contemporary situation at Delphi. Clearly, the importance of Delphi for sacred travellers had diminished, but its actual religious significance for the contemporary Greco-Roman world of the second century CE cannot be deciphered from the notes of Pausanias. This is shown also in Pausanias' description of the mysteries at Eleusis, traditionally a prestigious destination for religious travel even from outside of Greece.[64] While Pausanias does indeed hint that he had some knowledge about the rites, he mentions them mostly in context of the history of the cult.[65] Considering the secret nature of the mysteries, this is to be expected – in fact, Pausanias bluntly mentions how:

> My dream forbade the description of the things within the wall of the sanctuary, and the uninitiated are of course not permitted to learn that which they are prevented from seeing.[66]

In all, Pausanias does not describe the contemporary intra-regional character of the cult in Eleusis in much detail either, although he indicates its significance for Greeks in general, for example, by mentioning how the rituals have been 'copied' in other parts of Greece.[67]

However, in highlighting the importance of particular places as worth seeing or visiting, Pausanias would present the importance of the place and the power of its deity as an argument for a detour – and in this, a place's ability to bring in people from further distances would yield an argument worth presenting in these contexts. Indeed, Pausanias presents a fair number of modest shrines and temples which draw visitors from the neighbouring villages and cities, and occasionally even from further away. Mostly these are the shrines of the healing gods, especially Asclepios – a feature probably reflecting also their actual importance as destinations for pilgrimage in the Roman Empire.[68] He presents many shrines as locations of continuous visits of the local people; most often this comes out in the connection of mentioning festivals which are held in regular intervals (often yearly). In these occasions, the religious travel involved is, if viewed by its length, not an overtly visible aspect of the religious participation, even if it still involves departures and arrivals to and from the household, that is, mobility outside of the boundaries of ordinary environment and interruption of the everyday routines. Moreover, in Pausanias' account it comes forcibly out, that he sees this kind of religious observance as a natural part of any community's functioning: cult and lived religion brings people together. This is also – at least partly – behind Pausanias' descriptions of the mythic past of these rituals: he sees them as reflecting a common Greek heritage and a particular civic identity.[69]

Thus, we return to the question if the concept of 'pilgrimage' would be fitting in analysing this kind of varied and quite short journeys, often of less than a day back and forth from the homes. Jan Bremmer or Martin Grünewald would

## 132   *Jussi Rantala and Ville Vuolanto*

answer to this negatively, David Frankfurter and Saskia Stevens positively.[70] We approach the theme pragmatically – concepts are tools for the scholars. For us, seeking to understand the phenomenon of sacred travelling in the context of cross-cultural comparison, and using the concept of pilgrimage for these kinds of visits to sacred sites, outside the boundaries of one's own normal physical environment, and including performative elements connected to religious life and strengthening of the social identities, is simply – useful.

Interestingly for us, if we analyse Pausanias' account on sacred travelling, we notice that there appears a pattern quite similar with the classification of pilgrimage more generally, and especially in the Medieval West. In Pausanias' work we can trace some Panhellenic or even 'international' pilgrimage destinations (even if, interestingly, the number and importance of these shrines was diminishing in Roman Greece); a few shrines which are more local, but still arouse interest and draw visitors across the regional borders, and thus serve as goals for middle range pilgrimage; and, finally, numerous local shrines and temples, some quite a distance from the villages, which are destinations for the local pilgrimage, either continuously, or as locations for annual festivals. Similarly, in medieval times, categorization of pilgrimage was a well-known practice, and the separation of three types of pilgrimage, according to the distance to be covered by a pilgrim ('minor', 'major', 'oversees') was officially defined by the medieval courts, who ordered people found guilty in various crimes to take a journey as penitential pilgrim. While the practice was started by the French inquisition (which defined journeys to Jerusalem as 'oversees', to Canterbury, Santiago, Cologne, and Rome as 'major' and to local French shrines as 'minor' pilgrimages), it spread first to civil courts in France, and later to elsewhere in Europe.[71] In modern scholarship, in turn, Robert Stoddard categorizes pilgrimage in three classes: 'regional', 'national' and 'international'.[72] While ancient sacred travelling perhaps does not fall to exact similar categories (after all, modern concepts such as 'national' and 'international' are not something we can adapt to ancient societies in a straight-forward manner), descriptions of local, intra-regional and international/Panhellenic sacred travelling can be found in Pausanias' accounts, as we have seen.

However, when comparing the pre-Christian and Christian pilgrimage in Europe, one should keep in mind a difference in cultural contexts. In Christianity pilgrimage can be seen as a metaphor for the Christian life: personal journey to the sacred site represents personal life with all its suffering and even physical death, while reaching the target refers to the salvation from death. Therefore, discomfort and penance during the journey are an essential part of the Christian pilgrimage. On the other hand, in pre-Christian culture the nature of the pilgrimages as social occasions of joy and celebration was stressed.[73] Thus, while the length of journey and its discomforts probably were on many occasions even an essential part of Christian pilgrimage, this was a rather irrelevant aspect for pre-Christian sacred travelling and lived religion. This neutral attitude may explain why Pausanias only occasionally pays attention to pilgrimages and travel in his narration of shrines and religious participation.

## Conclusions II: Pausanias the nostalgic pilgrim

As Pausanias does not concentrate very much on actions of any individual (even of himself) at the sanctuaries or during 'his'[74] journeys, one may wonder if he can be considered as a pilgrim. In this respect he is clearly dissimilar to figures such as Aristides, Lucian, or Philostratus, who stressed the personal religious experience during the sacred journeys. On the other hand, these differences should not be exaggerated either. While the other writers perhaps describe the actions of pilgrims more often than Pausanias, one of their tasks is nevertheless to 'bring' their readers to the site they describe – in other words, to present the sacred geography of the Greek world (and beyond) to their audience.[75] For Pausanias, the task is similar, even if his method is different in the sense that he uses a much less personal approach. Thus, the general lack of religious action in Pausanias' account does not need to make him less of a pilgrim *per se* – especially if Pausanius the traveller is to be separated from Pausanias the narrator.

Were Pausanias' travels religiously motivated, then? Naturally, we cannot know for sure – we have little means to make any absolute distinctions between touristic, social, and religious motivations even among present day travellers, and, as Vinciane Pirenne-Delfolge points out, making the separation between 'secular' tourism and 'religious' pilgrimage would have even less relevance in the context of Pausanius or of any ancient traveller or travelogue: going on a pilgrimage would have been quite compatible with the cultural ideas for a place or ritual being worth seeing and of being preserved in (cultural) memory.[76] If we still enter into evaluating Pausanias as a sacred traveller himself, we do well not to seek any unifying definition for what Pausanias was, or what he did. Apparently, he conducted many trips around Greece, and, in total, his travels took a long time. Would it be, then, quite natural to think that in such framework a traveller may take many roles in different times and places? For example, Pausanias takes much care to describe and even try to lead the reader to experience with him the mysteries of Trophonios near Lebedeia – whereas his description of places of such fame as Olympia is very much concentrated on describing the site and its sights. He has a lot to say about its religious and mythological past, but not much about any religious rituals taking place during his own time. Pausanias reminds here the hypothetical religiously motivated traveller in modern southern Bourgogne, who would indeed visit Cluny with the great ruins of the medieval abbey, describing the buildings and the museum, with some half-mythical tales about the founding of the monastery complex and its subsequent fate, but not paying attention to the present-day religious activities of some five thousand modern inhabitants of the community. From Cluny the modern traveller would then continue to Taize, some ten kilometres away, and report from here, in turn, the contemporary religious life and rituals of the ecumenical Christian community while taking part in these as a pilgrim. Would the detour to Cluny make her less a pilgrim?[77]

Thus, it seems that Pausanias was motivated to travel and describe, if not all or even many, but at least some sacred spaces and their contemporary rituals because of his personal religious interest. In other words, Pausanias seems to approach

## 134   *Jussi Rantala and Ville Vuolanto*

certain sanctuaries as a pilgrim himself, while many others he examines with a more general and historical manner. Moreover, everywhere there seems to prevail a nostalgic and even patriotic attitude to the role these places would have played in Greek myths and history. This nostalgia would not make Pausanias less a pilgrim, but rather, a nostalgic pilgrim.

## Notes

1  While it appears that pilgrimage had a somewhat smaller role in traditional Roman religion, if compared to Greek and earlier Hellenistic practices, centres of pilgrimages are known from early Italy as well. Moreover, Delphic oracle was visited from Rome already during the Republican era, and contacts between Romans and other Greek sanctuaries begun in the late third century BCE at latest. Elsner and Rutherford 2005, 24–25.

2  For example, Vespasian visiting the sanctuary of Serapis in Alexandria (Suet. *Vesp.* 7.1; Tac. *Hist.* 4.82); Hadrian being initiated into the Eleusinian mysteries in Greece (Cass. Dio 66.11; *HA Hadr.* 13.1.); Septimius Severus visiting 'practically all' sanctuaries of Egypt (Cass. Dio 76[75].13); and Caracalla making a journey to the temple of the moon-god Selene at Carrhae in Mesopotamia (during which he was murdered; Herod. 4.13.3).

3  Rutherford 2001, 50.

4  Pausanias provides very little information about his personal life, only a few lines in his work hints towards his place of origin; see Pretzler 2007, 22–23.

5  Pausanias' aim was indeed to write a description of whole country, as it was understood in the second century CE. Some parts of Greece are missing in his work, probably due the fact that the tenth book is incomplete. See Habicht 1985, 4–7.

6  Rutherford 2001, 51–52. For religion in Pausanias' *Periegesis* in general, see particularly Pirenne-Delforge 2008.

7  Pausanias as a pilgrim: see Elsner 1992 and Hutton 2005b. Different view is provided, for example, in Arafat 1996 denying pilgrimage to Pausanias – his thesis convincingly refuted in Rutherford 2001. For the discussion, see also Pirenne-Delfolge 2008, 98–102. For the concept of pilgrimage, and on the research on sacred travel in Greco-Roman world, see now Bremmer 2017 (on Pausanias, see esp. p. 275). For studies on religious travelling in general, see Harland 2011 (on Pausanias, see p. 6).

8  Even if there is some discussion going on, whether we can call Pausanias a pilgrim or not, it seems nevertheless clear that his *Periegesis* is part of the tradition of pilgrimage literature; as explained by Hutton (2005a, 292–296), Pausanias' work was both based on the author's own travels and, on the other hand, his travels were (at least partly) motivated by religious sensibilities.

9  This is somewhat in line with his descriptions of himself as a traveller: Pausanias does only rarely mention about his own experiences that is, the actions he made during his actual journeys from one place to another, even if travel is constantly 'present' in his account. See Akujärvi 2005, 131–162.

10  Paus. 1.43.2. Not surprisingly, considering the centrality of the sacrifice for Greek religion, Pausanias' descriptions of sacrifices are particularly rich; however, as mentioned, they very rarely include any explicit remarks of travelling or pilgrimage, but simply explain the ritual. The role of sacrifice in Pausanias' work is dealt in Pirenne-Delforge 2008, 177–241.

11  Paus. 3.26.9; 6.22.7. See also e.g. Paus. 4.31.4: at the springs of the Pamisos, on the way to Arkadia from Thouria, little children are cured. No distances are given, but Pausanias gives an impression that there are no nearby settlements (Of the Hellenistic temple there, see Luraghi 2008, 120–121). Paus. 3.22.9: about two kilometres from the

city of Asopos there is a sanctuary of Asklepios 'the People's friend', where enormous human bones were worshipped (Pausanias gives an impression that still in his times).

12 Likewise, it is hard to know if, for example, the people taking part in the seven-day festival of Demeter in Mysaion are from the neighbourhood of the sanctuary, or rather from Pellene, some 11 kilometres away – which is the closest town Pausanias mentions here. Near the Mysaion Demeter was also a place called Kyros, a sanctuary of Asclepios with healing springs and a statue of the god. Paus. 7.27.4-5 (9-11). Similarly, Pausanias mentions for example how at the very centre of Olympia, at the peak of the Kronion hill, Kronos is offered a sacrifice at spring equinox; how in a nearby sanctuary a local demonic spirit is worshipped; and how in Hippodameion 'women go in once a year to perform ceremonies in honour of Hippodameia' (Paus. 6.20.1-3; 6.20.7). Thus, there are no references of where the worshippers came from, and if they would have included any persons travelling from further away.

13 Paus. 8.19.2-3.

14 Paus. 8.36.6. Between the precinct mentioned and the city gates there is also a sanctuary of Athene mentioned, but Pausanias does not connect any cultic activity in it; from the narrative, one is able to infer that the distance between the gates and the precinct was less than some 800 meters.

15 Paus. 7.25.6: 'To consult the god you pray in front of the statue, and then take dice ... and throw four on the table. For every throw of dice there is an interpretation written on the board'.

16 Paus. 8.37.1, 7-8.

17 Paus. 8.38.7-8. See also Paus. 5.5.11: there was a cave on the other side of the river from the city of Samikos. 'The traditional law is that anyone who enters it with any kind of leprosy first prays to the nymphs and promises whatever sacrifice it may be, and then wipes the diseased parts of his body, and when he swims across the river he leaves his disgrace in its waters, and comes out healthy and clear-skinned' (transl. William Jones).

18 Paus. 8.41.4-6.

19 Paus. 8.42.1; 8.42.22 (transl. Peter Levi).

20 Paus. 8.8.1, with Paus.7.1.4 and 8.7.1 on the location.

21 Paus. 13.1.

22 Paus. 2.14.1. Pausanias records that Phlisians admitted they had copied rituals from Eleuis.

23 See e.g. Paus. 2.25.4: At Lyrkeia, midway between Argos and Orneia (some 11 kilometres from both), in the middle of ancient ruins, the Argives had an annual beacon festival; Paus. 2.11.3: Four kilometres from Sikyon towards Titane there was a shrine of the Kindly Ones. Each year the Sikyons held a one-day festival for them, slaughtering pregnant ewes; Paus. 3.24.9: Near the town of Hypsoi (on the territory of the city of Las), a festival is held every year in a temple of Artemis Diktynna on a peninsula; Paus. 8.23.4: Townspeople of Kaphyai hold an annual mystery to Artemis on Mount Knakalos.

24 Paus. 8.15.4-5, with 8.15.1-3 on the Eleusinian Demeter at Phenos itself. See also Paus. 8.29.1. Pausanias is approaching Megalopolis and mentions the biannual mysteries of the Great Goddesses held in a place called Bathos ('Depth'). According to Pausanias, all the nearby settlements (Brenthe, Trapezous) are in ruins.

25 Paus. 7.5.5 (13).

26 Dillon 1997, xv–xvi.

27 For the link between the group identity, local communities, and the religious practices, see Katajala-Peltomaa and Vuolanto 2013, 15–17, with further studies.

28 See Dillon 1997, xviii.

29 See also Kristensen and Friese, 2017, 2–3.

30 See, Aristid. Or. 2.19.-23; 5.1-3; 5.49. On the other hand, David Frankfurter's view (1998, 18) that even going 'down an alley' could be considered a pilgrimage is maybe

136 *Jussi Rantala and Ville Vuolanto*

not that helpful – not because of the short distance at play, but rather because of the probable lack of the 'arrival and departure' aspect of the sacred journey.

31 Pausanias writes (9.3.3) that the local guide claims this to happen once in seven years, but he claims this actually happened more often; it is unclear where Pausanias had this information, perhaps by counting from the intervals of the greater Daidala – but this question is outside of the scope of present study. Clark (1998, 20) gives the interval as four years.

32 Paus. 9.3.3-4. For the rituals, see Clark 1998, 20–23. Pausanias was not present during the great Daidala, so we cannot be certain if the festival was still practiced; however, Pausanias writes as it indeed was.

33 Paus. 9.3.7 (transl. William Jones).

34 Paus. 6.26.1-2.

35 Paus 2.27.1. Inside the enclosure 'no men die, and no women bear children: the ritual law is the same as on the island of Delos. Everyone, Epidaurian or foreigner, consumes his sacrifice inside the boundaries' (transl. William Jones).

36 Paus.10.32.8-9. On the temple and festival, see Bommas 2011, 85–91.

37 Paus. 3.3.8. Other relics in sanctuaries: e.g. Paus. 3.3.6-7; 3.16.1; 3.22.9; 4.16.7. Significance of relics in Greek religious and political life is studied in Osborne 2010.

38 Even if he refers to case taking place about two hundred years before his own time: king Demetrios' bodyguard had died when consulting an oracle.

39 Paus. 9.39.3-4. For rituals in Lebedeia, see Bonnechere 2003.

40 Paus. 10.4.2. See also Plutarch (*De Is. et Os.* 35), who lived at Chaironeia and was a priest in Delphi: 'That Osiris is identical with Dionysus who could more fittingly know than yourself, Clea? For you are at the head of the inspired maidens of Delphi, and have been consecrated by your father and mother in the holy rites of Osiris' (transl. William Jones).

41 Paus. 10.14.5.

42 Paus. 4.12.1; 4.12.3; 4.15.6; 4.16.7; Corfu (10.9.2), Tegea (10.9.3), and Sparta (10.14.3). For other stories about visitors in Delphi, see Paus. 4.32.5; 5.26.10; 6.11.7.

43 Dillon 1997, 81–82.

44 Strabo 9.3.6.

45 Plut. *De Pyth. or.* 394e-400f. Pausanias hints to the same direction regarding guides (10.28.7), although it should be noticed that descriptions of guides with somewhat lacking knowledge are not limited to Delphi – see Paus. 2.9.7 (Sicyon) and 9.3.3 (Plataea).

46 Plut. *De def. or.* 414b-c (transl. Bernadotte Perrin). For a detailed study on Delphi's lost position as 'international' religious centre of activity, see McInerney 2004; for Delphi's decline as a political centre, see Arnush 2005 (claiming that the decline begun already in the fourth century BCE).

47 Paus. 9.23.3. Other consultation was mentioned to have taken place in 371 BCE, when the battle of Leuktra was about to be fought.

48 Paus. 4.32.5.

49 Mikalson 2005, 111–113.

50 Dillon 1997, 99–104.

51 Rutherford 2001, 43.

52 Especially Paus. 5.7.6-.9.6; 5.21.2-18.

53 Paus. 5.10.1 (transl. William Jones).

54 E.g. Paus. 3.8.1; 6.4.2; 6.6.3; 6.8.1.

55 E.g. Paus. 5.21.2; 5.24.9.

56 Paus. 6.2.6; this taking place in early fourth century BCE.

57 Paus. 5.26.5. See also e.g. Paus. 5.26.7 with the Herakleans (on Black Sea) brought the statues of Herakles' labours to Olympia after a victory over the barbarous Mariandynians.

58 Paus. 10.25.7; Paus. 2.15.3.

59 Paus. 2.32.2; 10.7.2-8; 10.33.8.

60 Paus. 6.7.4 (Thurii); 6.14.9 (Thesprotia); 8.18.8 (Lousoi, of which nothing remained during Pausanias' own time).

Pilgrimage in Pausanias   137

61  E.g. Paus. 1.44.8; 2.1.3; 2.2.2; Paus. 3.10.1; 5.2.1-5.
62  For Pausanias' interest on local and Greek history, see also Akujärvi 2005, 200–205; for the identity formation and religious patriotism in Pausanias, see Pirenne-Delfolge 2008, esp. 349–350.
63  As mentioned by Scullion (2005, 118–119) there was no need to problematize ritual action or work it out in a systematic way, as it was seen as something very natural. Pausanias' attitude seems to be in accordance with this idea.
64  Clinton 1998 and 1989 on Eleusis as a site for religiously motivated travellers during the second century CE. See also Nielsen 2017, 29–35; for significance of Eleusinian mysteries particularly in Roman context, see Camia 2017.
65  E.g. Paus. 1.38.3; 1.37.4.; 10.31.11.
66  Paus. 1.38.7 (transl. William Jones).
67  Paus. 2.14.1; 8.15.1. Pausanias also mentions (10.31.11) how the earlier Greeks held mysteries of Eleusis in a higher regard compared to other cults 'as gods are higher than heroes'. He also mentions the sacred road between Eleusis and Athens, a route taken by a procession celebrating the Eleusinian mysteries, describing its tombs, statues and sanctuaries (Paus. 1.36.3-38.5). About the possible ritual significance of these sacred spaces *en route* to people travelling to Eleusis he does not explicitly mention, though.
68  For pilgrimage and votive donations in healing sanctuaries in the Roman world, see e.g. Kiernan 2012 and Grünewald 2017 with further references.
69  For further (theoretical) discussion on lived religion, identity and belonging in the pre-modern world, see Katajala-Peltomaa and Vuolanto 2013, 15–18 with references.
70  Bremmer 2017; Grünewald 2017, 130; Stevens 2017, esp. 160–161; Frankfurter 1998, 18–24.
71  Bell and Dale 2011, 621–622; Sumption 2003, 145–146.
72  Stoddard 1997, esp. 50–51.
73  Rutherford 2001, 40–41.
74  On Pausanias' 'I' (as a narrator and as a traveller) see Akujärvi 2005, 162–163, 173–175.
75  For similarities between (Pseudo-) Lucian and Pausanias, see Elsner 2006, 129–130. For Philostratus' literary motives, see Elsner 1997, esp. 22–25.
76  Pirenne-Delfolge 2008, 100–102.
77  For the 'afterlife' of the Abbey of Cluny, see Marquardt 2007. For Taizé as a modern centre for pilgrimage, see Vilaça 2010, esp. 149–151. For other examples of such on-off pilgrims in Roman world, see also Myrup Kristensen snd Friese 2017, 3.

## Bibliography

Akujärvi, Johanna. 2005. *Researcher, Traveller, Narrator. Studies in Pausanias' Periegesis* (Studia Graeca et Latina Ludensia 12). Stockholm: Almqvist and Wiksell International.

Arafat, Karim W. 1996. *Pausanias' Greece. Ancient Artists and Roman Rulers*. Cambridge: Cambridge University Press.

Arnush, Michael. 2005. "Pilgrimage to the Oracle of Apollo at Delphi: Patterns of Public and Private Consultation." In *Pilgrimage in Graeco-Roman & Early Christian Antiquity: Seeing the Gods*, edited by Jas Elsner and Ian Rutherford, 97–110. Oxford: Oxford University Press.

Bell, Adrian and Richard Dale. 2011. "The Medieval Pilgrimage Business." *Enterprise & Society* 12.3: 601–627.

Bommas, Martin. 2011. "Pausanias' Egypt." In *Cultural Memory and Identity in Ancient Societies* (Cultural Memory and History in Antiquity 1), edited by Martin Bommas, 79–108. London: Continuum.

Bonnechere, Pierre. 2003. *Trophonios de Lébadée. Cultes et mythes d'une cité béotienne au miroir de la mentalité antique*. Leiden: Brill.

## 138  *Jussi Rantala and Ville Vuolanto*

Bremmer, Jan. 2017. "Pilgrimage Progress?" In *Excavating Pilgrimage. Archaeological Approaches to Sacred Travel and Movement in the Ancient World*, edited by Troels Myrup Kristensen and Wiebke Friese, 275–285. London and New York: Routledge.

Camia, Francesco. 2017. "Cultic and Social Dynamics in the Eleusinian Sanctuary under the Empire." In *Empire and Religion: Religious Change in Greek Cities under Roman Rule*, edited by Elena Grijalvo, Juan Copete, and Lozano Gomez, 45–66. Leiden: Brill.

Clark, Isabelle. 1998. "The *gamos* of Hera: Myth and Ritual." In *The Sacred and the Feminine in Ancient Greece*, edited by Sue Blundell and Margaret Williamson, 13–26. London: Routledge.

Clinton, Kevin. 1989. "The Eleusinian Mysteries. Roman Initiates and Benefactors, Second Century B. C. to A.D. 267." *Aufstieg und Niedergang der römischen Welt, II* 18.2: 1499–1539.

Clinton, Kevin. 1998. "Eleusis and the Romans: Late Republic to Marcus Aurelius." In *The Romanization of Athens: Proceedings of an International Conference Held at Lincoln, Nebraska (April 1996)*, edited by Michael C. Hoff and Susan Rotroff, 161–182. Oxford: Oxbow Books.

Dillon, Matthew. 1997. *Pilgrims and Pilgrimage in Ancient Greece*. London: Routledge.

Elsner, Jas. 1992. "Pausanias: A Greek Pilgrim in the Roman World." *Past and Present* 135: 3–29.

Elsner, Jas. 1997. "Hagiographic Geography: Travel and Allegory in the Life of Apollonius of Tyana." *The Journal of Hellenic Studies* 117: 22–37.

Elsner, Jas. 2006. "Describing Self in the Language of Other: Pseudo (?) Lucian at the Temple of Hierapolis." In *Being Greek Under Rome: Cultural Identity, the Second Sophistic and the Development of Empire*, edited by Simon Goldhill, 123–153. Cambridge: Cambridge University Press.

Elsner, Jas and Ian Rutherford. 2005. "Introduction." In *Pilgrimage in Graeco-Roman & Early Christian Antiquity: Seeing the Gods*, edited by Jas Elsner and Ian Rutherford, 1–38. Oxford: Oxford University Press.

Frankfurter, David. 1998. "Introduction: Approaches to Coptic Pilgrimage." In *Pilgrimage and Holy Space in Late Antique Egypt*, edited by David Frankfurter, 3–48. Leiden: Brill.

Grünewald, Martin. 2017. "Roman Healing Pilgrimage North of the Alps." In *Excavating Pilgrimage. Archaeological Approaches to Sacred Travel and Movement in the Ancient World*, edited by Troels Myrup Kristensen and Wiebke Friese, 130–151. London and New York: Routledge.

Habicht, Christian. 1985. *Pausanias' Guide to Ancient Greece*. Berkeley: University of California Press.

Harland, Philip A. 2011. "Pausing at the Intersection of Religion and Travel." In *Travel and Religion in Antiquity* (Studies in Christianity and Judaism 21), edited by Philip A. Harland, 1–26. Waterloo: Wilfrid Laurier University Press.

Hutton, William. 2005a. "The Construction of Religious Space in Pausanias." In *Pilgrimage in Graeco-Roman & Early Christian Antiquity: Seeing the Gods*, edited by Jas Elsner and Ian Rutherford, 291–317. Oxford: Oxford University Press.

Hutton, William. 2005b. *Describing Greece. Landscape and Literature in the Periegesis of Pausanias*. Cambridge: Cambridge University Press.

Katajala-Peltomaa, Sari and Ville Vuolanto. 2013. "Religious Practices and Social Interaction in the Ancient and Medieval World." In *Religious Participation in Ancient* and Medieval Societies. Rituals, Interaction, and Identity, edited by Sari Katajala-Pelromaa and Ville Vuolanto, 11–24. Rome: Institutum Romanum Finlandiae.

Kiernan, Philip. 2012. "Pagan Pilgrimage in Rome's Western Provinces." *HEROM. Journal on Hellenistic and Roman Material Culture* 1.1: 79–105.

Kristensen, Troels Myrup and Wiebke Friese. 2017. "Introduction: Archaeologies of Pilgrimage." In *Archaeological Approaches to Sacred Travel and Movement in the Ancient World*, edited by Troels Myrup Kristersen and Wiebke Friese, 1–10. London and New York: Routledge.

Luraghi, Nino. 2008. *The Ancient Messenians: Constructions of Ethnicity and Memory*. Cambridge: Cambridge University Press.

Marquardt, Janet. 2007. *From Martyr to Monument: The Abbey of Cluny as Cultural Patrimony*. Newcastle upon Tyne: Cambridge Scholars Publishing.

McInerney, Jeremy. 2004. "Do You See What I See? Plutarch and Pausanias at Delphi." In *The Statesman in Plutarch's Works, Volume I. Proceedings of the Sixth International Conference of the International Plutarch Society, Nijmegen/Castle Hernen, May 1–5, 2002*, edited by Lukas De Blois, Jeroen Bons, Ton Kessels, and Dirk M. Schenkeveld, 43–55. Leiden: Brill.

Mikalson, Jon D. 2005. *Ancient Greek Religion*. Oxford: Blackwell.

Muir, Steven. 2011. "Religion on the Road in Ancient Greece and Rome." In *Travel and Religion in Antiquity* (Studies in Christianity and Judaism 21), edited by Philip A. Harland, 29–47. Waterloo: Wilfrid Laurier University Press.

Nielsen, Inge. 2017. "Collective Mysteries and Greek Pilgrimage. The Cases of Eleusis, Thebes and Andania." In *Excavating Pilgrimage. Archaeological Approaches to Sacred Travel and Movement in the Ancient World*, edited by Troels Myrup Kristensen and Wiebke Friese, 28–46. London and New York: Routledge.

Osborne, Robin. 2010. "Relics and Remains in an Ancient Greek World Full of Anthropomorphic Gods." *Past and Present* 206, suppl. 5: 56–72.

Pirenne-Delforge, Vinciane. 2008. *Retour à la source. Pausanias et la religion grecque*. Liege: Centre International d'Étude de la Religion Grecque Antique.

Pretzler, Maria. 2007. *Pausanias. Travel Writing in Ancient Greece*. London: Duckworth.

Rutherford, Ian. 1998. "Islands of the Extremity: Space, Language and Power in the Pilgrimage Traditions of Philae." In *Pilgrimage and Holy Space in Late Antique Egypt* (Religions in the Graeco-Roman World 134), edited by David Frankfurter, 227–256. Leiden: Brill.

Rutherford, Ian. 2001. "Tourism and the Sacred: Pausanias and the Tradition of Greek Pilgrimage." In *Pausanias. Travel and Memory in Roman Greece*, edited by Susan E. Alcock, John F. Cherry, and Jas Elsner, 40–52. Oxford: Oxford University Press.

Scullion, Scott. 2005. "'Pilgrimage' and Greek Religion: Sacred and Secular in the Pagan Polis." In *Pilgrimage in Graeco-Roman & Early Christian Antiquity: Seeing the Gods*, edited by Jas Elsner and Ian Rutherford, 111–130. Oxford: Oxford University Press.

Stephens, John. 2013. *The Dreams and Visions of Aelius Aristides. A Case-Study in the History of Religions* (Perspective on Philosophy and Religious Thought 10). Piscataway, NJ: Gorgias Press.

Stevens, Saskia. 2017. "Visiting the Ancestors. Ritual Movement in Rome's Urban Borderland." In *Excavating Pilgrimage. Archaeological Approaches to Sacred Travel and Movement in the Ancient World*, edited by Troels Myrup Kristensen and Wiebke Friese, 152–165. London and New York: Routledge.

Stoddard, Robert H. 1997. "Defining and Classifying Pilgrimages." In *Sacred Places, Sacred Spaces: The Geography of Pilgrimages* (Geoscience and Man 34), edited by Robert H. Stoddard and Alan Morinis, 41–60. Baton Rouge: Louisiana State University.

Sumption, Jonathan. 2003. *The Age of Pilgrimage: The Medieval Journey to God.* Mahwah: Paulist Press.

Vilaça, Helena. 2010. "Pilgrims and Pilgrimages: Fatima, Santiago de Compostela and Taize." *Nordic Journal of Religion and Society* 23.2: 137–155.

# 8   Pilgrim's devotion?

## Christian graffiti from Antiquity to the Middle Ages

*Eva-Maria Butz and Alfons Zettler*

## Introduction

In our world, the term 'graffiti' denotes a widespread and popular form of artistic expression called Street Art, or in other terms Urban Art, Guerrilla Art, even Post-Graffiti and Neo-Graffiti. Street Art is, in a sense, a new branch of the Fine Arts, and the term includes: painting in public, spray-paintings, or other sorts of painting and scribbling walls or the surface of roads and squares.[1] It is visual art created in public locations, usually unsanctioned artwork executed outside of the context of traditional art venues.[2] Hence they also speak of 'Schmierereien' in the German language, and the authors of modern graffiti remain anonymous, as a rule.[3] Modern 'graffiti' include traditional spray-painted artwork like the work of the well-known Zurich Sprayer, for example, as well as Stencil Graffiti, like those of the famous artist Banksy whose identity remains unknown to this very day.[4]

'Graffiti' is an Italian word originally and traditionally denoting 'markings scratched onto a surface, whether of text or pictures'.[5] Graffiti might get scratched on, or carved into the surface of building blocks, for example, of wall plaster, of wall paintings, of metal, of all sorts of objects, and even of parchment. As they are made spontaneously, graffiti appear on surfaces which had not been made for such purpose. In archaeology and prehistory, the term 'graffiti' is also used for a certain way of decorating pottery. Markings scratched on surfaces are known from all periods in the history of mankind. As Antiquity was an age and a culture of inscriptions it seems only natural that antique Greece and Rome passed down lots of graffiti.[6] We just mention the well-known inventories of dipinti and graffiti in the cities of Pompeji, Stabiae, and Herculaneum,[7] and in the Coliseum of Rome. Whereas epigraphs and professional inscriptions have been a main field of research since the rediscovery of the culture of Antiquity in the age of the Renaissance, ancient graffiti are being regarded as testimonies to everyday life rather than important historical sources[8] – except from the urban Roman catacombs where epigraphs and graffiti often tend to coalesce and converge, and where even graffiti have long been respected as valuable testimonies to the history of Christendom and the early Urban Christian community. And clearly graffiti are coming to be regarded more and more important sources to the history of travelling and pilgrimage in Antiquity[9] and in the middle ages.[10]

## 142   Eva-Maria Butz and Alfons Zettler

Graffiti, as a more or less spontaneous sort of written records, have lately been examined under various aspects. Ann Marie Yasin, for example, discusses some early Christian graffiti collections both from the East and the West in their cultural and spatial context. She also tries to determine those graffiti in respect to their audience and remarks on graffiti's power to materialize the presence and prayers of their authors. Putting the stress on the materiality of 'devotional graffiti',[11] and on the production of early Christian sacred space,[12] Yasin points out their value as material artefacts of devotional and social behaviour. On the other hand, she subordinates both the problem of the identity and the origin of the individuals involved and the most important question of the graffiti's liturgical and memorial function and context.[13] In this chapter, selected collections of Christian graffiti from Antiquity to the central middle ages will be discussed focusing on the above-mentioned problems and on a *longue durée* perspective. We have selected six inventories: the Memory of St. Peter's under the Vatican basilica (3rd and early 4th centuries), the so-called *Memoria Apostolorum* at San Sebastiano (*Basilica Apostolorum*) on Via Appia (mid-3rd to mid-4th centuries), the early Christian church on the site of the actual Liebfrauenkirche at Trier (4th century), the Sanctuary of S. Michele, Monte Gargano (7th to 9th centuries), the altar mensa of Reichenau-Niederzell (9th to 11th centuries), and the *Liber Memorialis* of St. Gallen (9th century). On the one hand, the individual persons attested to by the graffiti of these collections need further examination. Had these graffiti been created by pilgrims, by travellers, or rather by members of the local and regional Christian communities? On the other hand, the *longe durée* perspective chosen here, crossing traditional boundaries of time periods and disciplines, will allow us to follow essential aspects of these graffiti's liturgical and memorial quality. We must not forget though that the archaeology of each individual site presents its specific window onto graffiti activity either in a relatively concentrated time frame, or over a longer period.[14]

## Vatican City, St. Peter's Memory (Italy)

The so-called Grey Wall, or Graffiti Wall, which was part of the first Memory of St. Peter's regarded as a cult centre underneath the Constantinian Vatican Basilica,[15] is counted among the earliest monuments of Christian graffiti.[16] Before the Basilica had been built in CE 318–328, there was a small and unpretentious Christian cult centre at the place within a cemetery mainly composed of lavish mausolea.[17] A small plot of this area was closed off on one side by a wall, the so-called Red Wall, arching over one of the graves – this grave apparently being believed to be St. Peter's grave.[18] Known to the Christian community as 'Trophy' of St. Peter's, as a sign of his victory over death by c. 200 CE,[19] this monument of martyr's shrine obviously attracted, in the course of the 3rd and early 4th centuries, a large number of graffiti. It is on the so-called Grey Wall, or Wall g, in the context of those complex structures underneath the high altar of St. Peter's Basilica where the graffiti have been preserved on a patch of plaster on just one side of the 'Grey Wall' (Figure 8.1).

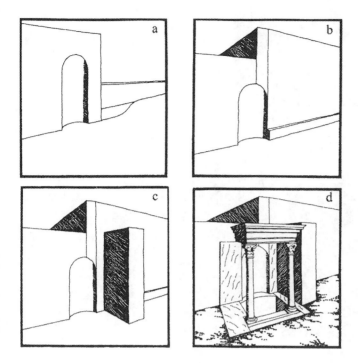

*Figure 8.1* Rome. Old Basilica of St. Peter in the Vatican, St. Peter's Memory, phase d: wall g ('Grey Wall') (Thümmel 1999, fig 45).

Margherita Guarducci who published the pre-Constantinian graffiti of the Vatican counted one hundred and two items.[20] But as the plaster has been scribbled on in a very close-packed way – there are two or three superimposed layers, in places – we cannot be sure of the original number of items. And it must be added that the patch of plaster on the Grey Wall is just a small fragment. Thus, the surviving graffiti seem to represent just a tiny fraction of the erstwhile inventory. Guarducci undertook the Sisyphean task of deciphering the whole set of surviving Vatican graffiti, but recent work makes it clear that they need re-reading, and also re-examining.[21] There are 102 graffiti, more or less legible, which have been preserved. They consist, for the most part, of personal names and short set phrases or acclamations like VICTOR [et] GAVDENTIA VIVATE IN XP[o], to cite a typical entry. But there are just a few well preserved and rather complete examples. With more than 70 of 102 items (*c.* 70%) where the names are now missing (Figure 8.2).

About 20 entries have the formula 'vivas/vivite' (*c.* 20%), and there is a similar number of chi-rho symbols like in the graffito of Victor and Gaudentia cited above. Thus, we may conclude that the graffiti underneath the Vatican Basilica once matched up, for the most part, with the entry of VICTOR [et] GAVDENTIA

*Figure 8.2* Rome. Old Basilica of St. Peter in the Vatican, St. Peter's Memory, graffiti on the plaster of wall g ('Grey Wall') (Guarducci 1958, t.3: pl. 7).

VIVATE IN XP[o], and that they had been composed to this or a similar pattern: 'Ille vivas in Christo', or 'in Deo'. In this respect they are composed very similar to the slightly later graffiti from the early Christian church underneath the Cathedral/ Liebfrauenkirche of Trier in Germany. Toynbee and Ward Perkins hold that the Vatican graffiti must not be regarded as invocations of Saint Peter. They speak of 'names and simple prayers of pilgrims for the spiritual well-being of their relatives or friends, living or dead'.[22] Another interpretation was suggested by Andrea Binsfeld. She concluded that the visitors at the grave of St. Peter wanted to place their names and acclamations next to the Apostle's Memory to gain his assistance to their pursuit of future life in heaven. Binsfeld does not explicitly speak of pilgrims, and as the formula 'Ille vivas in Christo', or 'in Deo' etc., also appears in many Early Christian epitaphs, Binsfeld leaves it an open and unresolved question whether the individual persons mentioned were dead or alive at the time their names got scribbled on the wall, respectively, whether these graffiti comprised the names of dead and living persons at the same time.[23] Furthermore, this comparatively small number of names surviving does not allow for any conclusion if the individuals mentioned are to be regarded as local visitors or long-distance pilgrims.[24] It has already been mentioned that the pre-Constantinian Christian

*Pilgrim's devotion?* 145

community of Rome regarded the monument erected on top of the alleged grave of the Apostle as 'Trophy' of St. Peter's, as a token of his true martyrdom and his victory over death. In this context, St. Peter's Memory underneath the Vatican Basilica might be regarded as a Christian cult centre particularly dedicated to the cult of St. Peter as a martyr, the Vatican graffiti might be interpreted as material substrate of popular devotion to, and veneration of, the Apostle and martyr. In this case, the Vatican graffiti would reflect the desire of pre-Constantinian Christians to visit and touch Peter's grave and relics, and their striving to remain 'present' at 'his place' by scribbling their names onto the wall.[25]

## Rome, Via Appia, San Sebastiano (Italy)

The small early Christian cult centre now covered by San Sebastiano (*Basilica Apostolorum*)[26] on the Via Appia with its cluster of graffiti may be regarded as another key monument in our context. Reaching back to the pre-Constantinian period too, the Memory of Saints Peter and Paul, or *Memoria Apostolorum*, at the church and grave of the Christian martyr Sebastian was laid out equally unpretentious as St. Peter's Memory in the Vatican.[27] And the *Memoria Apostolorum* (*c.* CE 258) on Via Appia seems to have been connected very closely to St. Peter's Trophy in the Vatican because this place known as *Ad catacumbas* obviously served, in the same period, as a cult centre for the veneration of the Princes of the Apostles whose feasts (or even relics) are supposed to have been moved to this catacomb cemetery[28] situated underneath the actual basilica of San Sebastiano.[29]

The Memory of the Apostles at San Sebastiano was set in a small courtyard terminated by a niche and bounded to the north by a line of Columbaria, i.e. small mausolea for cremation burials whereas the west and south sides were enclosed by walls. The north-eastern corner of the place consisted of a large shed or room, the so-called *triclia* (literally: 'dining room', or 'drinking-place'), equipped with a masonry bench along the wall decorated with rustic wall-paintings, and a kitchen. Flanked on the north and west by covered porticos the triclia overlooked, but does not seem to have communicated directly with, the paved courtyard.[30] A long flight of steps descended to a deep spring underneath the shed or peristyle. Thus, if it had not been for the graffiti, this early Christian cult centre would have appeared as Richard Krautheimer put it, like any tavern on the green (Figure 8.3).[31] When consulting the graffiti, it does not import that the origin of the cult of the Apostles by the Via Appia outside of Rome remains an unsolved problem. Scholars agree – and this is important in our context and for the aspects taken in this chapter – that the cult centre *Ad catacumbas* must have been established around the year CE 258 as a consequence of the Valerianic persecution of the Christians. It remained in use until the *Basilica Apostolorum* and church of San Sebastiano were built (mid-4th century).[32]

Even if the origin of the cult of the Apostles by the Via Appia – where later on, in the middle of the fourth century, the Basilica of San Sebastiano was built – has not been clarified, the graffiti are of major interest in the context of this chapter. It was the painted rear wall of the so-called triclia above the masonry

146  *Eva-Maria Butz and Alfons Zettler*

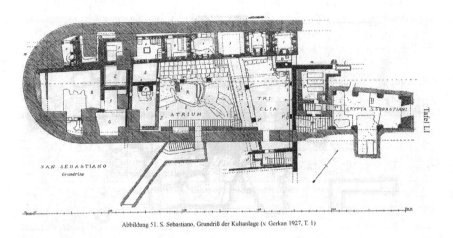

*Figure 8.3* Rome. Via Appia, S. Sebastiano, Memoria Apostolorum (Thümmel 1999, fig 51).

bench that was awash with hundreds of graffiti of pious visitors[33] (one graffito dated CE 260[34]). They attest to more than 400 individuals whose names had been inscribed in the period between the mid-3rd century and the construction of the *Basilica Apostolorum* in the early 4th century. Some 30 of these graffiti have been preserved in their original site on the wall plaster, and fragments of more than 170 items have been collected from the rubble during excavations in 1915.[35] According to Richard Krautheimer, the graffiti are 'obviously mostly those of participants in funerary banquets in honour of the Apostles'.[36] Toynbee and Ward Perkins hold that they are to be regarded rather 'simple prayers invoking the aid of the Apostles'.[37] In fact, there are just a few scribblings mentioning *refrigeria* explicitly, or even funeral banquets. Those roughly two hundred items which have been preserved more or less complete and legible, consist for the most part of personal names and short set phrases or acclamations and prayers almost exclusively appealing to Saints Peter and Paul, e.g. *PAVLE ET PETRE PETITE PRO VICTORE* ('Paul and Peter, pray for Victor!'),[38] and *PETRE ET PAVLE SVBVENITE PRIMO PECCATORI* ('Peter and Paul, help Primus, a sinner!').[39] Both graffiti may be regarded as typical entries (Figure 8.4).

Again, there is no way to establish the number of graffiti that once had covered the walls of the site *Ad catacumbas*. We examined 100 well-preserved items and found *c.* 35% of female names (37) as opposed to *c.* 65% names of male individuals (73). In this whole lot of 100 items we counted three times the *vivas*-formula and just one chi-rho symbol. Ninety-eight percent of the entries examined here have the acclamation 'PAVLE ET PETRE' (98). The most common prayer at the *Memoria Apostolorum* appealed to the apostles Peter and Paul to 'remember so-and-so' ('in mente habete'), documented at least 60 times. The prayers adopt the grammatical form of a direct address to the Apostles (using imperatives and vocatives). The result is an extremely densely packed field of graffiti, as if the

*Figure 8.4* Rome. Via Appia, S. Sebastiano, Memoria Apostolorum, graffiti (Thümmel 1999, fig 64).

walls themselves would speak on behalf of or in the voice of the texts' authors to call out to the Apostles by name.[40] As to the question of the origin of all those faithful who scratched their names, Toynbee and Ward Perkins suggested they were all pilgrims[41] whereas Binsfeld thinks of local and regional participants at the *refrigeria*. It is true there is one graffito mentioning a person from Benevent,[42] but there is no explicit reference to pilgrims whatsoever. Other scholars suppose that the veneration of the Apostles at the *Memoria Apostolorum* by the Via Appia had been connected to a particular culture of *vota* and *refrigeria*[43] held by both local visitors and pilgrims.[44]

The area of San Sebastiano was called *Ad catacumbas* in Antiquity as mentioned earlier, and was, as such, eponymous to the catacombs which functioned as centres of early Christian cult and memory of the dead during the pre-Constantinian period. Large urban catacombs are situated close to the *Basilica Apostolorum* (San Sebastiano) on Via Appia.[45] Thus the *Memoria Apostolorum* may also be cited, in this chapter, as an example for the vast number of early Christian graffiti in the context of urban catacombs in general. Graffiti can be found in most Roman catacombs, in particular close to the graves of martyrs and saints, and these graffiti seem to be directly connected to the cult of the martyrs and the phenomenon of Christian pilgrimage.[46] More than forty thousand inscriptions have been counted in the Roman catacombs, and many graffiti among them mostly regarded as scribblings and carvings of visitors and pilgrims.[47]

## Trier, Liebfrauenkirche (Germany)

We have already mentioned the inventory of graffiti preserved in the context of the early Christian churches excavated on the site of the cathedral precinct of Trier. These graffiti had been scratched on the plaster covering walls used as a choir screen ('Schranke I, II') in the mid-4th-century church (Figure 8.5).[48] The church underneath the actual Liebfrauenkirche was discovered in the course of archaeological excavations in 1949. As the screen walls of the choir had been demolished in a later phase of building just a small fraction of the graffiti scribbled onto the plaster were collected from the rubble, and these items are surviving in small fragments only.[49] As many as 133 items have been puzzled out from those fragments of plaster,[50] and the examples we selected reveal the main pattern to which the best part of those graffiti would have been composed: 'ille vivas in Christo...', 'ille vivas in Deo semper' etc.[51] The *vivas*-formula has been counted up to the number of 34 among all of the fragments collected there,[52] and there are 56 chi-rho symbols.[53] Thus, we may suppose the graffiti of Trier had mostly been composed to the above-mentioned pattern, or similar patterns (Figure 8.6). The proportion of sexes in 34 legible names is *c.* 80% of male individuals (27) as opposed to *c.* 20% of females (7); one single person was introduced as *peccator*.[54]

Even though the early Christian graffiti of Trier have been examined carefully and thoroughly, their very sense and function remain unclear. The elementary problems inherent, like the status of the individuals mentioned, and whether these persons had been alive or dead at the moment their names got carved into the plaster, eventually remain unresolved. Andrea Binsfeld concluded as a result of her research into the comparatively small collection of graffiti transmitted at Trier, that some evidence might point to the veneration of martyrs or the cult of saints as one of the motives to carve those personal names and blessings into the plaster of the choir screen. She would not like to speak of pilgrims in general as other

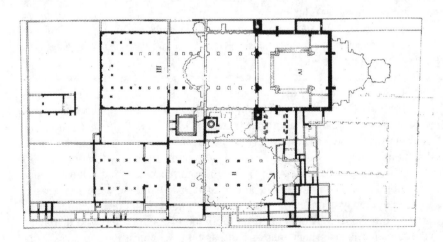

*Figure 8.5* Trier. Early Christian churches (Binsfeld 2006, 16 fig 1).

*Figure 8.6* Trier. Early Christian church underneath the actual Liebfrauenkirche, graffiti II 35 and II 42: MARTI VIVAS IN DEO XP SEM[…]; […]NIO VIVAS IN DEO XP SEM[…] (Binsfeld 2006, 200 pl. 9a).

scholars do.[55] Mark Handley, on the other hand, lists 'the 28 graffiti' from Trier in his chapter on 'Pilgrim Graffiti', and he is convinced 'the pilgrims to Trier's cathedral *could* have been attracted to relics of its early bishops such as Eucharius, Paulinus, or Maximinus'.[56]

## Monte Sant'Angelo (Monte Gargano), San Michele (Italy)

With our next example, we leave Christian Antiquity and proceed to the middle ages. It is a grotto in the Gargano Mountains where, according to the legend, Saint Michael the Archangel appeared in CE 490, 492, and 493.[57] Since then, this grotto has been housing the most famous sanctuary of Saint Michael attracting pilgrims from all parts of Europe.[58] The church within and in front of the grotto was first built in late Antiquity and has since been the aim of many famous pilgrimages that often started out from Mont Saint-Michel in Normandy/France.[59] Some of the oldest parts of this sanctuary have been uncovered by excavations in 1949 (Figure 8.7).[60] The buildings excavated underneath the present Church include a gallery forty meters long which is leading to a vestibule with two staircases. Both the gallery, with its façade, and the staircases attracted *c.* 165 graffiti, mostly scratched or carved on the surface of building blocks and other architectural elements.[61] All of those thirteen pillars in the cave have graffiti, and some of these graffiti deserve to be called inscriptions because they had been carved

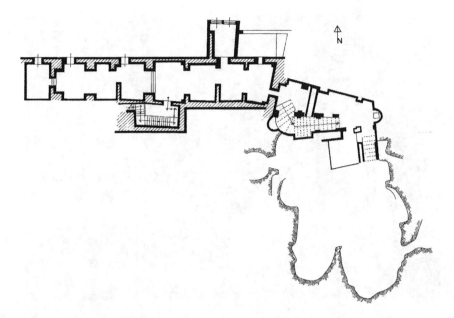

*Figure 8.7* Monte Sant'Angelo. S. Michele, groundplan (Carletti and Otranto 1980, pl. I–II).

and produced by a professional chiseller who even put his name under his work: 'Gaidemari fecit'. The text has it that 'Duke Romuald acting with pious zeal, ordered offerings to be made and donated to God and the holy Archangel'.[62] Duke Romuald I ruled Benevento from CE 671 to 687, and we may conclude from further historical evidence that all of these 165 graffiti may be dated to the period from the reign of King Grimoald I in the mid-7th century up to the destruction of the sanctuary by the Saracens in 869 (Figure 8.8).[63]

There are 160 males among those 175 individual persons whose names have been deciphered, and 15 women. Nearly 50% of the names are preceded by the *signum crucis* indicating personal presence or even the fact that these individuals would have carved their names by their own hands. The formula 'ille vivat...' in all its varieties, almost omnipresent among the Vatican graffiti and at Trier, occurs in no more than 20 items in the Gargano sanctuary (*c*. 13%), and the same is true for the chi-rho symbol.[64] The graffito of 'Rumildi biba in deo'[65] may be regarded as an example for the use of the above mentioned formula, whereas '+Leo de Bergamo' is not only introduced and preceded by the *signum crucis* but we might also think of an explicit geographical indication concerning the origin of Leo's (Figure 8.9).[66] Thus, Leo 'de Bergamo' might be regarded as an early example for a traveller or pilgrim reaching Mount Gargano, which later on came to be one of the most famous shrine and pilgrim centres in Europe.[67] Moreover, one 'EADRHID SAXSO vir honestus', a man from the British Isles or Continental

   + d[e]donis d(e)i et[s(an)]c(t)i a[rcha]n
   + geli fiere iusse et don[avit
3 + Romouald dux age[r]e pietate
   + Gaidemari fecit

Figure 8.8 Monte Sant'Angelo. S. Michele, Gaidemari fecit (Carletti and Otranto 1980, 90 no. 82).

+ Leo de
Bergamo

Figure 8.9 Monte Sant'Angelo. S. Michele, graffito of Leo de Bergamo (Carletti and Otranto 1980, 145 no. 163).

*Turo pele[gri]nus*
*viva[s i]n d(e)o [se]mpr[e*
*tu[q]ui l[eg]is ora*
*pro me*

*Figure 8.10* Monte Sant'Angelo. S. Michele, graffito of Turo peregrinus (Carletti and Otranto 1980, 86 no. 79).

Saxony, obviously, and no doubt a traveller or pilgrim, left his signature in the sanctuary of Monte Sant'Angelo.[68] There are in fact a few inscriptions in runes, or runic graffiti,[69] on the Gargano indicating that the sanctuary was visited by Scandinavians or persons of Anglo-Saxon origin.[70] Our last example from the Gargano is the signature of a man called Turo.[71] Turo refers to himself as *pelegrinus*, he might stand for three other pilgrims explicitly attested as such among the early visitors of Mount Gargano (Figure 8.10).[72]

## Reichenau-Niederzell, Church of Saints Peter and Paul, Altar Stone (Germany)

We would like to complete this panorama of early Christian graffiti by touching on two remarkable medieval examples. One is the mensa of the high altar of the Carolingian church of Niederzell, the other one is in the *Liber Memorialis* of St. Gallen in Switzerland. It was in 1976 when, in the course of building works, the mensa stone of an early medieval altar was discovered in the Church of Saints Peter and Paul in Reichenau-Niederzell. Made of a regional variety of sandstone, the rectangular slab measures 1.6 × 1.1 m and was once part of the high altar of the first church in Niederzell founded by Bishop Egino of Verona. Egino left his bishop's see in order to resile in Reichenau where he had a church built on the western-most head of the monastery island.[73] Three years before he died he dedicated his church to the

Apostle Peter (CE 799).[74] The graffiti stone once covered the main altar of Egino's church, its surface had been open to carving and writing till the mid-11th century when the Carolingian building complex was dismantled and replaced by the actual basilica.[75] At this time the antique altar slab awash with hundreds of graffiti and 'dipinti', was carefully removed and put upside down on top of the high altar of the Romanesque basilica – in order to conserve the inscriptions and graffiti on the slab, obviously, respecting the intentions, the memory, and the devotion of their authors.[76]

There are 341 names and fragments legible on the comparatively smooth surface of the altar mensa including both graffiti (60%) according to the current definition, and 'dipinti', i.e. entries written in ink mostly by skilled scriptors (40%) – as if the stone was a piece of parchment or manuscript.[77] More than 80% of the names are those of males whereas 11% denote women.[78] Some of the individuals mentioned were explicitly defined as clerics, abbots, monks, and noblemen, one male person is called *peccator* (10%) whereas pilgrims are completely lacking.[79] Comparing the inventory of the names recorded on the slab to other written records makes it clear that the inscriptions are mostly those of residents of the Lake Constance area and region from the 10th and 11th centuries (Figure 8.11).[80]

The altar of Reichenau-Niederzell with its names written in ink on sandstone (!) seems to have been a unique specimen in the world of ancient Christian graffiti. There are other medieval altars, of course, which have attracted inscriptions.[81]

*Figure 8.11* Reichenau-Niederzell. St. Peter and Paul, mensa of the main altar (9th century), graffiti and 'dipinti' (in ink) (Geuenich, Neumüllers-Klauser, and Schmid 1983, pl. 41).

## 154   Eva-Maria Butz and Alfons Zettler

We might refer to the most famous altar mensa of Minerve (France) with 93 names carved into the marble stone.[82] But none of these other early medieval altar stones have been scribbled on by means of plume and ink![83]

### Sankt Gallen, *Liber Memorialis* (Switzerland)

Most consequently, the last item of our selection is a liturgical book, the Carolingian *Liber Memorialis* of St. Gallen. The first *Liber Memorialis* of the Abbey of St. Gallen was produced during the ultimate years of the reign of Charlemagne (*d.* 814) in the monastery's *scriptorium*.[84] In our context, this manuscript transmitted as a fragment[85] seems to play a minor role. Nevertheless, it is worthwhile mentioning this sample here because it makes clear that even in a liturgical book like that, we are likely to detect a few graffiti, i. e. names scratched on the parchment by means of a pointed instrument like, for example, a stylus. Such scribblings would not be expected in a book used on the altar for celebrating mass, made of parchment and due to get filled with names written in ink.[86] Some ten names scratched and carved into the parchment have been detected a couple of years ago when the book was re-examined in the course of its restoration.[87] Our examples are on the 3rd and on the 23rd folios, the first one written on two lines, *otger ep*[*iscopu*]*s*, and the other one in between two scratched lines: *pertuolt* (Figur 8.12 and 8.13).[88]

*Figure 8.12* St. Gallen. Verbrüderungsbuch (Stiftsarchiv Ms. C3B55, p. 6), graffito of otger eps. (Erhart 2010, 50 fig 19).

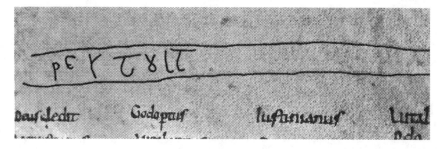

*Figure 8.13* St. Gallen. Verbrüderungsbuch (Stiftsarchiv Ms. C3B55, p. 46), graffito of pertuolt (Erhart 2010, 50 fig 20).

## Conclusion

Once the graffiti in the Vatican on the Via Appia and in Trier had been uncovered in the course of the last century, most scholars were convinced – as Toynbee and Ward Perkins put it – that those graffiti had been 'scratched [...] by visiting pilgrims, who were obviously humble and sometimes illiterate persons'.[89] More cautiously recent research has suggested that most of the early Christian graffiti were those of 'church members and the faithful', writs and scribblings directly 'connected to the cult of the martyrs and the phenomenon of pilgrimages'.[90] Assessing our choice of collections of ancient and medieval Christian graffiti, some clear and unmistakable facts should be noted as follows.

First, there are very few graffiti among the material analyzed here which would bear explicit testimony to pilgrims. Exactly four pilgrims are attested as such among nearly 200 individuals mentioned by the graffiti of the Gargano sanctuary – which is the only pronounced pilgrimage place among the sites and examples we examined.[91]

Secondly, at all places men and women are documented not at even rates. There are always more males than females mentioned – similar to what we find in the early medieval *libri memoriales*. The proportion of sexes is, in other words, neither well-balanced nor completely disproportioned. Roughly speaking we normally find one third of female and two thirds of male individuals. It is only the collection of San Michele on Mount Gargano, as a major place of pilgrimage in the Middle Ages, that does not match the other inventories. In San Michele, we get starkly disproportional numbers, 15 female names and 160 males, i.e. short 10% of women. Such proportions would perfectly correspond to recent estimations that at most 10% among late antique and medieval pilgrims would have been females.[92]

Thirdly, two very early graffiti sites and collections have been reconsidered here, St. Peter's Memory in the Vatican and the *Memoria Apostolorum* of San Sebastiano on Via Appia. Both sites date from the pre-Constantinian period, and hence from the period of the persecution of the Christians. The period of the

156    *Eva-Maria Butz and Alfons Zettler*

persecutions was the age of martyrdom and not a period of pilgrimage. And nearly all of the phrases and formulas frequently used in antique and medieval Christian graffiti appear in the context of these pre-Constantinian inventories of both St. Peter's Memory in the Vatican and the *Memoria Apostolorum* of San Sebastiano.

Thus, we may conclude that we must not classify late antique and early medieval Christian graffiti as pilgrims' carvings in general. For every single site the portion and percentage of pilgrims must be individually and separately defined. Assessing six sample sites in this chapter, our impression is that the share of (far) pilgrims is very low, except among the graffiti of San Michele on Mount Gargano. The sanctuary of San Michele, a place that functioned both as a cult centre for the Langobardic Duchy or State of Benevento, to put it this way, and later on as a major place of pilgrimage. At this point, we leave aside the subject matter suggested by the title of this paper, i.e. the field of pilgrimage and pilgrims. In order to understand ancient and medieval Christian graffiti, we need further studies. First of all: writing down one's name in a sacred place or shrine or book! Why would people do that? Studies of Christian diptychs including the names of those who were to be commemorated in prayer,[93] and of the mosaic floors of early Christian churches,[94] have found that the names written down in places like that used to be recited in the course of the liturgy of the holy mass. This is in the context of the prayer *Memento Domine* before the transubstantiation, and this specific act of commemoration of persons by reciting their names is meant to effect the actual 'presence' of the respective individuals at mass and hence before God – even if these persons would not be present bodily.[95] And what is more, the early medieval *libri memoriales* had been filled with thousands of names because they were regarded as *libri vitae*,[96] earthly copies of the Book of Life mentioned in the Bible.[97] The Book of Life is a heavenly book, of course, God's book, containing the names of the elect. As a consequence, it was believed that the names written down in those books kept on the altar would also be inscribed in God's heavenly Book of Life.[98]

The text of the *Visio cuiusdam pauperculae mulieris* (*c.* 830) allows us to catch another glimpse of the perception and function of writing down personal names in sacred places. The historical context of the *Visio* is the rebellion of King Bernard of Italy in 817.[99] As a consequence, Bernard had been deposed and blinded by command of his uncle Louis the Pious, and the emperor was blamed for Bernard's subsequent death. The text describes the dream of a poor woman recognizing on the wall of Paradise where the names of the elect are inscribed, the name of King Bernard in shining letters of gold, while the name of Emperor Louis on the same wall of Paradise only cast a feeble light and was nearly effaced: 'What does it mean, the poor woman said, that this name is so obliterated? Before the emperor committed homicide against Bernard, the Angel said, no one's name was clearer. The death of the one was the obliteration of the other'.[100] Indeed, it should be stressed that putting down names in sacred places, holy shrines, or liturgical books is a phenomenon that needs further studies, as we have mentioned. Graffiti are the most spontaneous form of this habit. Furthermore, all formulas and phrases that go with the names in the context of Christian graffiti will deserve

*Pilgrim's devotion?* 157

thorough research and need to be compared with early Christian mosaic inscriptions, epitaphs and – last but not least – with liturgical diptychs and *libri vitae*. It is only when we understand the motives of the faithful and the members of the Church scratching graffiti on architectural elements and altars of churches, holy shrines, liturgical books, *et cetera*, that we will be able to interpret and evaluate these documents as historical evidence.

## Notes

1 Cf. Deitch, Gastman, and Rose 2011; Yasin 2015, 36–60, esp. 38–39.
2 Stewart 1987, 161–180.
3 Cf. Smith 1986, 100–105.
4 Banksy 2006, 133; cf. Bull 2010, BR2 ('Window Lovers').
5 Baird and Taylor 2011, 3.
6 Cf. Meyer 1973, 77–82; Schmidt 2015, 73–82; Baird and Taylor 2011, 1–17, esp. 16.
7 Zangemeister and Schoene 1871; Gigante 1979; Benefiel and Keegan 2016.
8 Cf. Bagnall 2011, 1–5; Baird and Taylor 2011, 11–16.
9 Eck 1995, 206–222.
10 Koch 1999, 442–445 (the *Lexikon* lacks the headword 'graffiti'!); cf. Kraack and Lingens 2001; Tedeschi 2014, 363–381.
11 'For the pious visitor, carving a graffito was one of a range of devotional gestures that could have accompanied a visit to a holy place. But unlike bowing in supplication, intoning a prayer, lighting a candle or partaking of the Eucharist, inscribing a graffito offered a tangible interaction with the very substance of the site'; Yasin 2015, 54.
12 Yasin 2015, 48–54.
13 Yasin 2015, 54.
14 Yasin 2015, 39.
15 Brandenburg 2013, 96–106.
16 Krautheimer 1980, 19–20; Thümmel 1999, 15–72; Liverani 1999, 39–42, 139–144; Liverani and Spinola 2010, 40–55; Heid 2011, 283–308; Brandenburg 2011, 351–382; Weber 2016, 257–263.
17 Fiocchi Nicolai 2001, 7–13, esp. 12–13.
18 Thümmel 1999, 45–49.
19 Wehr 1996, 357–387; Liverani 1999, 142–144; Liverani and Spinola 2010, 47, 54–55.
20 Guarducci 1953; Guarducci 1958; Guarducci 1989; Krautheimer 1980, 19–20; Thümmel 1999, 60–62.
21 Ferrua 1959, 231–235; Binsfeld 2006, 43–54.
22 Toynbee and Ward Perkins [1956], 165.
23 Binsfeld 2006, 54.
24 Cf. Binsfeld 2006, 46–47; Eck 1995, 206–222, esp. 222.
25 Cf. Binsfeld 2006, 54; Gnilka, Heid, and Riesner 2010, esp. 157–163.
26 Brandenburg 2013, 64–70; Weber 2016, 257–263.
27 Cf. Fiocchi Nicolai 2001, 7–13, 34–36.
28 Cf. e.g. Pergola 2000, 67–72; Hertling and Kirschbaum 1960, 106–120; Fink and Asamer 1997, esp. 16–27, 33; Fiocchi Nicolai, Bisconti, and Mazzoleni[2] 2000.
29 Toynbee and Ward Perkins [1956], 170–182; cf. Wehr 1996, 357–387; Thümmel 1999, 73–95; Jäggi 2005, 306–322, esp. 315.
30 Toynbee and Ward Perkins [1956], 170–171; cf. Pergola 2000, 68–69.
31 Krautheimer 1980, 19.
32 Toynbee and Ward Perkins [1956], 181; cf. Thümmel 1999, 93–95.
33 Styger 1935, t.1: 15–36; Tolotti 1953; Krautheimer and Corbett 1970, t.4: 99–147, esp. 114–118; Silvagni, Ferrua, Mazzoleni, and Carletti 1922–1992, t.5: 12907–13096;

## 158    Eva-Maria Butz and Alfons Zettler

Ferrua 1965, 428–437; Toynbee and Ward Perkins [1956], 170–172; Krautheimer 1980, 19; Ferrua 1990; Thümmel 1999, 78–82.

34  Thümmel 1999, esp. 79, 82.
35  Cf. Toynbee and Ward Perkins [1956], 170.
36  Krautheimer 1980, 19.
37  Toynbee and Ward Perkins [1956], 171.
38  Binsfeld 2006, 58; Hertling and Kirschbaum 1960, 111; Thümmel 1999, 82.
39  Binsfeld 2006, 58; cf. Toynbee and Ward Perkins [1956], 171.
40  Yasin 2015, 44.
41  '...graffiti, scratched on the plaster by visiting pilgrims, who were obviously humble and sometimes illiterate persons'; Toynbee and Ward Perkins [1956], 171.
42  'Nicht nur Römer, auch Ortsfremde haben hier ihre Bitten hinterlassen'; Binsfeld 2006, 66–67.
43  'Der Kult [...] war ja doch vom antiken Totenmahl geprägt'; Thümmel 1999, 95.
44  'Zuweilen handelt es sich um Pilger oder Reisende, die sich mit der Inschrift gleichsam von Rom verabschieden, in anderen Fällen muss man mit einem zweimaligen Besuch der Stätte rechnen'; Gnilka, Heid, and Riesner 2010, 163–173.
45  Hertling and Kirschbaum 1960, 177–195, cf. 113–114; Fink and Asamer 1997, 16–27.
46  Cf. e. g. Carletti 1995, 197–225; Carletti 2002, 323–360; Binsfeld 2006, 70–85.
47  Cf. Fiocchi Nicolai 2001, 126–127; Fiocchi Nicolai, Bisconti, and Mazzoleni[2] 2000, 180–185; Yasin 2015, 39–40.
48  Binsfeld 2006, 15–22; cf. Weber 2004, 225–234, esp. 229–231.
49  Binsfeld 2006, 20–22; cf. Ristow 2007, 193–203.
50  Binsfeld 2006, 24–26; cf. Binsfeld 2004, 235–252; Handley 2001, 187–200.
51  Binsfeld 2006, 22–23, 171–190; cf. Handley 2001, 193–194.
52  Binsfeld 2006, 35–38.
53  Binsfeld 2006, 39–41.
54  Binsfeld 2006, 38–39.
55  Binsfeld 2004, 251–252.
56  Handley, 2003, 163–164; cf. Handley 2001.
57  Cf. Campione 2007, 7–16.
58  Cf. Bertelli 2009, 421–440.
59  Juhel and Vincent 2007, 183–207.
60  Carletti and Otranto 1980.
61  Edited by Carletti and Otranto 1980, 9–159.
62  On the so-called Rulers' Pillar; cf. Derolez and Schwab 1983, 95–130, 100–105.
63  Carletti and Otranto 1980, 11–18.
64  Cf. Derolez and Schwab 1983, 99.
65  Carletti and Otranto 1980, 38 no. 7.
66  Carletti and Otranto 1980, 145 no. 163.
67  Cf. Campione 2007, 7–16; Bertelli 2009, 421–440.
68  Carletti and Otranto 1980, 72 no. 56; cf. Derolez and Schwab 1983, 105.
69  Mastrelli 1980, 319–322; Arcamone 1981, 157–171; Derolez and Schwab 1983, 95–130; Arcamone 1994, 185–189.
70  Cf. Waßenhoven 2006, 75–76.
71  Carletti and Otranto 1980, 86 no. 79.
72  Carletti and Otranto 1980, no. 9, 75, 160.
73  Berschin and Zettler 1999, 7–14, 58–68; Zettler 2009, 363–385.
74  Berschin and Zettler 1999, 63–65.
75  Zettler 2005, 357–376, esp. 364–367.
76  Geuenich, Neumüllers-Klauser, and Schmid 1983, 11 and 40–41.
77  Geuenich, Neumüllers-Klauser, and Schmid 1983, 11–15, 20, 47–49.
78  Geuenich, Neumüllers-Klauser, and Schmid 1983, 20, 47–49.

*Pilgrim's devotion?* 159

79 Geuenich, Neumüllers-Klauser, and Schmid 1983, 21, 47–49.
80 Geuenich, Neumüllers-Klauser, and Schmid 1983, 22–27.
81 Geuenich, Neumüllers-Klauser, and Schmid 1983, 17–19; cf. Miglio and Tedeschi 2012, t.2: 605–628, esp. 611.
82 Le Blant 1856, 428–454; for other collections of graffiti on altar slabs see Leclercq 1907, t.6: 1453–1542, esp. 1501–1534.
83 Geuenich, Neumüllers-Klauser, and Schmid 1983, 15.
84 Cf. Ludwig 2015, 175–201.
85 The so-called Verbrüderungsbuch of St. Gallen consists of the fragments of two early medieval manuscripts, see Schmid 1986a, 15–38; Schmid 1986b, 81–283; cf. Schmenk 2003, 35–51.
86 There are some other *libri memoriales* containing graffiti; cf. Bischoff 1966, 88–92.
87 Erhart 2010, 47–50.
88 Erhart 2010, 50 Fig. 19.
89 Toynbee and Ward Perkins [1956], 171; cf. Fiocchi Nicolai, Bisconti, and Mazzoleni[2] 2000, 180.
90 Fiocchi Nicolai, Bisconti, and Mazzoleni[2] 2000, 180.
91 Cf. Bertelli 2009, 421–440; Bouet, Otranto, and Vauchez 2007.
92 Rottloff 2007, 9–10.
93 Cf. Jakobi 1986, 186–212; Taft 1991, esp. 1–33.
94 Cf. Zettler 2001, 145–164.
95 Cf. Oexle 1985, 74–104. For the term of 'messaggi unidirezionali' see Carletti 2002, 333; Carletti 1995, 73; sceptical Yasin 2015, 54: 'What is more, although some scholars have argued that Christian graffiti were not meant for a human audience, that the inscribed prayers were rather fully about communicating with the divine, the form and placement of the inscriptions suggest otherwise'.
96 Geuenich and Ludwig 2015.
97 Koep 1952, 31–33, 46–89, 100–109; Kohlenberger 1999, t.2: 813–814; Angenendt 1984, 79–199, esp. 188–195; Berndt 2014, 13–19.
98 Cf. McKitterick 2004; Hugener 2014, 30–32, 51–54; Butz and Zettler 2013, 173–186, esp. 173–176.
99 Jarnut 2002, 329–340. For the reign of Louis the Pious see De Jong 2009.
100 Houben 1976, 31–42; cf. Neiske 1986, 137–185, esp. 154–156; Dutton 1994; Butz 2016, 145–159, esp. 153–155.

## Bibliography

Angenendt, Arnold. 1984. "Theologie und Liturgie der mittelalterlichen Toten-Memoria." In *Memoria. Der geschichtliche Zeugniswert des liturgischen Gedenkens im Mittelalter*, edited by Karl Schmid and Joachim Wollasch, 79–199. München: Verlag Wilhelm Fink.

Arcamone, Maria Giovanna. 1981. "Le iscrizioni runiche di Monte Sant'Angelo sul Gargano." *Vetera Christianorum* 18: 157–171.

Arcamone, Maria Giovanna. 1994. "Una nuova iscrizione runica da Monte Sant'Angelo." In *Culto ed insediamenti micaelici nell'Italia meridionale fra tarda antichità e medioevo*, edited by Carlo Carletti and Giorgio Otranto, 185–189. Bari: Edipuglia.

Bagnall, Roger S. 2011. *Everyday Writing in the Graeco-Roman East*. Berkeley and London: University of California Press.

Baird, Jennifer A. and Claire Taylor (eds.). 2011. *Ancient Graffiti in Context*. New York and London: Routledge.

Banksy. 2006. *Wall and Piece*. London: Random House.

160    *Eva-Maria Butz and Alfons Zettler*

Benefiel, R. and P. Keegan (eds.). 2016. *Inscriptions in the Private Sphere in the Greco-Roman World*. Leiden and Boston: Brill.

Berndt, Rainer. 2014. "'Freut Euch, daß Eure Namen im Buch des Lebens geschrieben sind' (Lc 10 20). Textgeschichtliche Spuren eines altlateinischen Bibelverses bis ins Mittelalter." In *'Eure Namen sind im Buch des Lebens geschrieben'. Antike und mittelalterliche Quellen als Grundlage moderner prosopographischer Forschung*, edited by Rainer Berndt, 13–19. Münster: Aschendorff.

Berndt, Rainer (ed.). 2014. *'Eure Namen sind im Buch des Lebens geschrieben'. Antike und mittelalterliche Quellen als Grundlage moderner prosopographischer Forschung*. Münster: Aschendorff.

Berschin, Walter and Alfons Zettler. 1999. *Egino von Verona – Gründer von Reichenau-Niederzell, 799*. Sigmaringen: Thorbecke.

Bertelli, Gioia. 2009. "Percorsi di eta medieval per la grotta di San Michele arcangelo sul Gargano. L'itinerario Ergitium-Monte Sant'Angelo e alcuni tracciati meridionali." In *Pellegrinaggi e santuari di San Michele nell'Occidente medievale – Pèlerinages et sanctuaires de Saint-Michel dans l'Occident médiéval*, edited by Giampietro Casiraghi and Giuseppe Sergi, 421–440. Bari: Edipuglia.

Binsfeld, Andrea. 2004. "Die Graffiti der frühchristlichen Kirchenanlage in Trier." In *Neue Forschungen zu den Anfängen des Christentums im Rheinland*, edited by Sebastian Ristow, 235–252. Münster: Aschendorff.

Binsfeld, Andrea. 2006. *Vivas in deo. Die Graffiti der frühchristlichen Kirchenanlagen in Trier*. Trier: Museum am Dom Trier.

Bischoff, Bernhard. 1966. "Über Einritzungen in Handschriften des frühen Mittelalters." *Mittelalterliche Studien. Ausgewählte Aufsätze zur Schriftkunde und Literaturgeschichte*, t.1: 88–92.

Bouet, Pierre, Giorgio Otranto and André Vauchez (eds.). 2007. *Culto e santuari di San Michele nell'Europa medievale – Culte et sanctuaires de saint Michel dans l'Europe médiévale*. Bari: Edipuglia.

Brandenburg, Hugo. 2011. "Die Aussagen der Schriftquellen und der archäologischen Zeugnisse zum Kult der Apostelfürsten in Rom". In *Petrus und Paulus in Rom. Eine interdisziplinäre Debatte*, edited by Stefan Heid, 351–382. Freiburg: Verlag Herder.

Brandenburg, Hugo. 2013. *Die frühchristlichen Kirchen in Rom*. Regensburg: Schnell & Steiner.

Bull, Martin. 2010. *Banksy Locations (& A Tour) – Vol. 2: A Collection of Graffiti Locations & Photographs in Britain*. London: PM Press.

Butz, Eva-Maria. 2016. "Die Memoria Ludwigs des Frommen in St. Gallen und auf der Reichenau. Herrschergedenken zwischen Krise und Konsens." In *817 – Die urkundliche Ersterwähnung von Villingen und Schwenningen. Alemannien und das Reich in der Zeit Kaiser Ludwigs des Frommen*, edited by Jürgen Dendorfer, Heinrich Maulhardt, R. Johanna Regnath, and Thomas Zotz, 145–159. Ostfildern: Jan Thorbecke Verlag.

Butz, Eva-Maria and Alfons Zettler. 2013. "From Collective to Individual Commemoration of the Dead: Case Studies in Early Medieval Religious Practice." In *Religious Participation in Ancient and Medieval Societies. Rituals, Interaction and Identity*, edited by Sari Katajala-Peltomaa and Ville Vuolanto, 173–186. Rome: Institutum Romanum Finlandiae.

Campione, Ada. 2007. *Il culto di san Michele in Campania, Antonino e Catello*. Bari: Edipuglia.

Carletti, Carlo. 1995. "Viatores ad martyres: Testimonianze scritte altomedievali nelle catacombe romane." In *Epigrafia medievale greca e latina: ideologia e funzione. Atti*

*del Seminario di Erice, 12–18 settembre 1991*, edited by Guglielmo Cavallo and Cyril A. Mango, 197–225. Spoleto: Centro italiano di studi sull'Alto medioevo.
Carletti, Carlo. 2002. "Scrivere i santi": epigrafia del pellegrinaggio a Roma nei secoli VII–IX." In *Roma fra Oriente e Occidente, 19–24 aprile 2001*, 323–360. Spoleto: Centro italiano di studi sull'alto Medioevo.
Carletti, Carlo and Giorgio Otranto (eds.). 1980. *Il santuario di S. Michele sul Gargano dal VI al IX secolo. Contributo alla storia della Langobardia meridionale. Atti del convegno tenuto a Monte Sant'Angelo il 9–10 dicembre 1978*. Bari: Edipuglia.
Casiraghi, Giampietro and Giuseppe Sergi (eds.). 2009. *Pellegrinaggi e santuari di San Michele nell'Occidente medievale – Pèlerinages et sanctuaires de Saint-Michel dans LOccident médiéval*. Bari: Edipuglia.
Deitch, Jeffery, Roger Gastman and Aaron Rose (eds.). 2011. *Art in the Streets*. New York: Skira Rizzoli.
De Jong, Mayke. 2009. *The Penitential State. Authority and Atonement in the Age of Louis the Pious, 814–840*. Cambridge: Cambridge University Press.
Derolez, René and Ute Schwab. 1983. "The Runic Inscriptions of Monte S. Angelo (Gargano)." *Academiae Analecta* 1983: 95–130.
Dutton, Paul E. 1994. *The Politics of Dreaming in the Carolingian Empire*. Lincoln: University of Nebraska Press.
Eck, Werner. 1995. "Graffiti an Pilgerorten im spätrömischen Reich." In *Akten des XII. Internationalen Kongresses für Christliche Archäologie, Bonn, 22.–28. September 1991*, edited by Ernst Dassmann, t. 1, 206–222. Münster: Aschendorffsche Verlagsbuchhandlung.
Erhart, Peter. 2010. "Die St. Galler Verbrüderungsbücher im Restaurierungsatelier." In *Bücher des Lebens – Lebendige Bücher*, edited by Peter Erhart and Jakob Kuratli Hüeblin, 47–50. St. Gallen: Stiftsarchiv St. Gallen.
Ferrua, Antonio. 1959. "La criptografia mistica ed i graffiti Vaticani." *Rivista di Archeologia Cristiana* 35: 231–235.
Ferrua, Antonio. 1965. "Rileggendo i graffiti di S. Sebastiano." *La civiltà cattolica* 116: 428–437.
Ferrua, Antonio. 1990. *La basilica e la cattacomba di S. Sebastiano* (second edition). Vatican City: Pontificia Commissione di Archeologia Sacra.
Fink, Josef. and Beatrix Asamer. 1997. *Die römischen Katakomben*. Mainz am Rhein: Zabern Philipp von GmbH.
Fiocchi Nicolai, Vincenzo. 2001. *Strutture funerarie ed edifici di culto paleocristiani di roma dal IV al VI secolo*. Città del Vaticano: Istituto grafico editoriale romano.
Fiocchi Nicolai, Vincenzo, Fabrizio Bisconti and Danilo Mazzoleni. 2000. *Roms christliche Katakomben* (2. Auflage). Regensburg: Wissenschaftliche Buchgesellschaft.
Geuenich, Dieter and Uwe Ludwig (eds.). 2015. *Libri vitae. Gebetsgedenken in der Gesellschaft des Frühen Mittelalters*. Köln, Weimar and Wien: Böhlau.
Geuenich, Dieter, Renate Neumüllers-Klauser and Karl Schmid (eds.). 1983. *Die Altarplatte von Reichenau-Niederzell*. Hannover: Hahnsche Buchhandlung.
Gigante, Marcello. 1979. *Civiltà delle forme letterarie nell'antica Pompei*. Napoli: Bibliopolis.
Gnilka, Christian, Stefan Heid, and Rainer Riesner. 2010. *Blutzeuge. Tod und Grab des Petrus in Rom*. Regensburg: Schnell & Steiner.
Guarducci, Margherita. 1953. *Ein vorkonstantinisches Denkmal Christi und Petri in der vatikanischen Nekropole*. Rome: Istituto Poligrafico dello Stato.
Guarducci, Margherita. 1958. *I graffiti sotto la confessione di San Pietro in Vaticano*. Città del Vaticano: Libreria editrice Vaticana.

162  *Eva-Maria Butz and Alfons Zettler*

Guarducci, Margherita. 1989. *La tomba di San Pietro. Una straordinaria vicenda*. Milano: Rusconi.

Handley, Mark A. 2001. "Beyond Hagiography: Epigraphic Commemoration and the Cult of Saints in Late Antique Trier." In *Society and Culture in Late Antique Gaul: Revisiting the Sources*, edited by Ralph W. Mathisen and Danuta Shanzer, 187–200. London: Routledge.

Handley, Mark A. 2003. *Death, Society and Culture: Inscriptions and Epitaphs in Gaul and Spain, AD 300–750*. Oxford: British Archaeological Reports.

Heid, Stefan. 2011. "Die Anfänge der Verehrung der apostolischen Gräber in Rom." In *Petrus und Paulus in Rom. Eine interdisziplinäre Debatte*, edited by Stefan Heid, 283–308. Freiburg, Basel and Wien: Verlag Herder.

Hertling, Ludwig, and Engelbert Kirschbaum. 1960. *The Roman Catacombs And Their Martyr* (revised edition). London: Darton, Longman & Todd.

Houben, Hubert. 1976. "Visio cuiusdam pauperculae mulieris. Überlieferung und Herkunft eines frühmittelalterlichen Visionstextes (mit Neuedition)." *Zeitschrift für die Geschichte des Oberrheins* 124: 31–42.

Hugener, Rainer. 2014. *Buchführung für die Ewigkeit. Totengedenken, Verschriftlichung und Traditionsbildung im Spätmittelalter*. Zürich: Chronos.

Jäggi, Carola. 2005. "Archäologische Zeugnisse für die Anfänge der Paulus-Verehrung." In *Biographie und Persönlichkeit des Paulus*, edited by Eve-Marie Becker, and Peter Pilhofer, 306–322. Tübingen: Mohr Siebeck.

Jakobi, Franz-Josef. 1986. "Diptychen als frühe Form der Gedenk-Aufzeichnungen. Zum ‚Herrscher-Diptychon' im Liber Memorialis von Remiremont."*Frühmittelalterliche Studien* 20: 186–212.

Jarnut, Jörg. 2002. "Kaiser Ludwig der Fromme und König Bernhard von Italien. Der Versuch einer Rehabilitierung." In *Herrschaft und Ethnogenese im Frühmittelalter. Gesammelte Aufsätze von Jörg Jarnut. Festgabe zum 60. Geburtstag*, edited by Matthias Becher, Stefanie Dick and Nicola Karthaus, 329–340. Münster: Scriptorium.

Juhel, Vincent, and Catherine Vincent. 2007. "Culte et sanctuaires de saint Michel en France." In *Culto e santuari di San Michele nell'Europa medievale – Culte et sanctuaires de saint Michel dans l'Europe médiévale*, edited by Pierre Bouet, Giorgio Otranto, and André Vauchez, 183–207. Bari: Edipuglia.

Koch, Walter. 1999. "Inschriften." In *Lexikon des Mittelalters. Studienausgabe*, t.5: 442–445.

Koep, Leo. 1952. *Das himmlische Buch in Antike und Christentum. Eine religionsgeschichtliche Untersuchung zur altchristlichen Bildersprache*. Bonn: P. Hanstein.

Kohlenberger, Helmut. 1999. "Buch des Lebens." In *Lexikon des Mittelalters. Studienausgabe*, t.2: 813–814.

Kraack, Detlev, and Peter Lingens. 2001. *Bibliographie zu historischen Graffiti zwischen Antike und Moderne*. Krems: Medium Aevum Quotidianum.

Krautheimer, Richard. 1980. *Rome. Profile of a City*, 312–1308. Princeton, NJ: Princeton University Press.

Krautheimer, Richard, and Spencer Corbett. 1970. "S. Sebastiano." In *Corpus Basilicarum Christianarum Romae. The Early Christian Basilicas of Rome (IV–IX Cent.)*, t.4: 99–147. Vatican City: Pontificio istituto di archeologia cristiana.

Le Blant, E. 1856. *Inscriptions chrétiennes de la Gaule antérieures au VIIIe siècle: Provinces gallicanes*, t.1. Paris: Imprimerie Impériale.

Leclercq, Henri. 1907. "Graffiti." *Dictionnaire d'archéologie chrétienne et de liturgie*, t.6: 1453–1542.
Liverani, Paolo. 1999. *La topografia antica del Vaticano*. Città del Vaticano: Edizioni Musei Vaticani.
Liverani, Paolo, and Giandomenico Spinola. 2010. *The Vatican Necropoles: Rome's City of The Dead*. Milano, Città del Vaticano: Isd.
Ludwig, Uwe. 2015. "Die beiden St. Galler Libri vitae aus dem 9. Jahrhundert." In *Libri vitae. Gebetsgedenken in der Gesellschaft des Frühen Mittelalters*, edited by Dieter Geuenich and Uwe Ludwig, 175–201. Köln, Weimar and Wien: Böhlau.
Mastrelli, Carlo A. 1980. "Le iscrizioni runiche." In *Il santuario di S. Michele sul Gargano dal VI al IX secolo. Contributo alla storia della Langobardia meridionale. Atti del convegno tenuto a Monte Sant'Angelo il 9–10 dicembre 1978*, edited by Carlo Carletti and Giorgio Otranto, 319–322. Bari: Edipuglia.
McKitterick, Rosamond. 2004. *History and Memory in The Carolingian World*. Cambridge: Cambridge University Press.
Meyer, Ernst. 1973. *Einführung in die lateinische Epigraphik*. Darmstadt: Wissenschaftliche Buchegesellschaft.
Miglio, Luisa and Carlo Tedeschi. 2012. "Per lo studio dei graffiti medievali. Caratteri, categorie, esempi." In *Storie di cultura scritta. Studi per Francesco Magistrale*, edited by Paolo Fioretti, t.2, 605–628. Spoleto: Fondazione CISAM.
Neiske, Franz. 1986. "Vision und Totengedenken." *Frühmittelalterliche Studien* 20: 137–185.
Oexle, Otto G. 1985. "Die Gegenwart der Lebenden und Toten. Gedanken über Memoria." In *Gedächtnis, das Gemeinschaft stiftet*, edited by Karl Schmid, 74–104. Freiburg: Schnell & Steiner.
Pergola, Philippe. 2000. *Christian Rome. Early Christian Rome, Catacombs and Basilicas*. Padova: Getty Publications.
Ristow, Sebastian. 2007. *Frühes Christentum im Rheinland. Die Zeugnisse der archäologischen und historischen Quellen an Rhein, Maas und Mosel*. Aschendorff: Köln.
Rottloff, A. 2007. *Stärker als Männer und tapferer als Ritter. Pilgerinnen in Spätantike und Mittelalter*. Mainz am Rhein: Rheinischer Verein.
Schmenk, Holger. 2003. *Die frühmittelalterlichen Gedenkbücher des Bodenseeraums*. Marburg: Tectum Verlag.
Schmid, Karl. 1986a. "Das ältere und das neuentdeckte jüngere St. Galler Verbrüderungsbuch." In *Subsidia Sangallensia 1: Materialien und Untersuchungen zu den Verbrüderungsbüchern und zu den älteren Urkunden des Stiftsarchivs St. Gallen*, edited by Michael Borgolte, Dieter Geuenich, and Karl Schmid, 15–38. St. Gallen: Staatsarchiv St. Gallen.
Schmid, Karl. 1986b. "Versuch einer Rekonstruktion der St. Galler Verbrüderungsbücher." In *Subsidia Sangallensia 1: Materialien und Untersuchungen zu den Verbrüderungsbüchern und zu den älteren Urkunden des Stiftsarchivs St. Gallen*, edited by Michael Borgolte, Dieter Geuenich, and Karl Schmid, 81–283. St. Gallen: Staatsarchiv St. Gallen.
Schmid, Karl and Joachim Wollasch (eds.). 1984. *Memoria. Der geschichtliche Zeugniswert des liturgischen Gedenkens im Mittelalter*. München: Verlag Wilhelm Fink.
Schmidt, Manfred G. 2015. *Lateinische Epigraphik. Eine Einführung* (3. Auflage). Darmstadt: WBG.

## 164   *Eva-Maria Butz and Alfons Zettler*

Silvagni, Angelo, Antonio Ferrua, Danilo Mazzoleni, and Carlo Carletti, eds. 1922–1992. *Inscriptiones christianae urbis Romae septimo saeculo antiquiores NS.* Rome and Vatican City: Officina Libraria Doct. Befani.

Smith, Monica. 1986. "Walls Have Ears: A Contextual Approach to Graffiti." *International Folklore Review* 4: 100–105.

Stewart, Susan. 1987. "Ceci Tuera Cela: Graffiti as Crime and Art." In *Life after Postmodernism: Essays on Value and Culture*, edited by John Fekete, 161–180. New York: Palgrave.

Styger, Paul. 1935. *Römische Märtyrergrüfte.* Berlin: Verl. für Kunstwissenschaft.

Taft, Robert F. 1991. *A History of The Liturgy of St. John Chrysostom*, t.4: The Diptychs. Rome: Pontificium Institutum Studiorum Orientalium.

Tedeschi, Carlo. 2014. "I graffiti, una fonte scritta trascurata." In *Storia della scrittura ed altre storie*, edited by Daniele Bianconi, 363–381. Rome: Accademia Nazionale dei Lincei.

Thümmel, Hans G. 1999. *Die Memorien für Petrus und Paulus in Rom. Die archäologischen Denkmäler und die literarische Tradition.* Berlin and New York: W. de Gruyter.

Tolotti, Francesco. 1953. *Memorie degli Apostoli in Catacumbas.* Vatican City: Società "Amici delle Catacombe", Pontificio Istituto di Archeologia cristiana.

Toynbee, Jocelyn and John Ward Perkins. 1956. *The Shrine of St. Peter and the Vatican Excavations.* London, New York and Toronto: Longmans, Green.

Waßenhoven, Dominik. 2006. *Skandinavier unterwegs in Europa (1000–1250). Untersuchungen zu Mobilität und Kulturtransfer auf prosopographischer Grundlage.* Berlin: Akademie Verlag.

Weber, Winfried. 2004. "Neue Forschungen zur Trierer Domgrabung. Die archäologischen Ausgrabungen im Garten der Kurie von der Leyen." In *Neue Forschungen zu den Anfängen des Christentums im Rheinland*, edited by Sebastian Ristow, 225–234. Münster: Aschendorff.

Weber, Winfried. 2016. " Die Verehrung der Apostel Petrus und Paulus und die Stätten ihrer Memoria in Rom." In *Nero – Kaiser, Künstler und Tyrann*, edited by Rheinisches Landesmuseum Trier, 257–263. Darmstadt: Rheinischen Landesmuseums Trier.

Wehr, Lothar. 1996. *Petrus und Paulus – Kontrahenten und Partner.* Münster: Aschendorff Verlag.

Yasin, Ann Marie. 2015. "Prayers on Site: The Materiality of Devotional Graffiti and the Production of Early Christian Sacred Space." In *Viewing Inscriptions in the Late Antique And Medieval World*, edited by Antony Eastmond, 36–60. New York: Cambridge University Press.

Zangemeister, Karl, and Richard Schoene (eds.). 1871.

# 9 The rise of St. James' cult and the concept of pilgrimage

*Klaus Herbers*

## Introduction

*Qui multum peregrinantur raro sanctificantur.* Those who often go on a pilgrimage are seldom sanctified. This critical comment on pilgrimages goes back to Thomas a Kempis in the later Middle Ages,[1] and it judges a practice which had a long development throughout the Middle Ages. Hagiographic texts were commenting the opposite. The pilgrim's guide to Compostela describes the cathedral of St. James as a place where miracles take place and sins are forgiven:

> This church, furthermore, from the moment it was started until today, has shined by the refulgence of the miracles of the Blessed James: in fact, the sick have been restored to health in it, the blind have been rendered their eyesight, the tongue of the dumb has been untied, the ear of the deaf unplugged, movement has been restored to the lame, the possessed has been delivered and, what is more, the prayers of the faithful have been fulfilled, their wishes granted and their sins were forgiven.[2]

This is a very clear definition about how pilgrimage centers could work. But was this the unique concept of pilgrimage? What about the competition concurrence or about the development of other concepts? Did theory and practice differ at least in some cases? Did the evolution tend to emphasize certain aspects? Anyway, we have to ask ourselves why pilgrimages were so strongly criticized in the times of Humanism and Reformation and at the same time persisted with great success. The cult of St. James may serve as an example.

In this chapter, I will present the development of different concepts of pilgrimages in the Late Antiquity and Early Middle Ages (II), then I will focus on the rise of St. James's cult and the different contexts (III) taking into consideration the model furnished by this cult in its central period (IV), the means of divulgation and dissemination combined with the final question if there was a transformation of concepts (V).

## *Peregrinus* and *peregrinatio*. Concepts in the Late Antiquity and Early Middle Ages

The Latin word *peregrinatio* (pilgrimage) may originate from the sequence *per agrum* (across the fields). Thus, this word indicates a difficult way.

166   *Klaus Herbers*

Correspondingly, the word *peregrinus* means in classic Latin, the stranger, a person who is no member of the common social community to which the speaker belongs. The movement of these people was not further specified; it is left open if a classical *peregrinus* walked to a well-defined destination.

What about the Christian evolution of this concept? In the Antiquity and throughout the Early Middle Ages a spiritual conception of this movement dominated. According to several biblical quotations, the Old Testament told at the same time a history of migration. To look at men like Adam, Abraham, or Moses does also mean to look at moving people. Thus, those who left their land in order to start a new life in exile were denominated in the late Antiquity and in Latin terminology as *peregrini.*

To leave the familiar context and go into exile following the example of Jesus Christ was not only the goal of the first hermits in Egypt, but also of the Irish and Anglo-Saxon *monachi peregrini* who preached the Gospel on the Continent from the sixth century onwards. This *peregrinatio pro Christo* was a Christian model which established the *peregrines,* according to the classical meaning of the word, as a stranger[3]. Furthermore, at the same time, the Christian doctrine conceived the life of every Christian as a pilgrimage to the final destination (*vita est peregrinatio*).

Nevertheless, there existed pilgrimages to a fixed destination in former times. As the centre of Christianity moved from east to west, some voices claimed that one would understand the Bible easier and better if one knows the places where Christ had lived, acted, and suffered. In terms of this, Jerusalem and the places later designed as the Holy Land were the earliest destinations of pilgrims. We have some records like that of Egeria, who travelled to those places, and even the practice of liturgy in Jerusalem at the end of the fourth century is described in her account.[4]

In spite of that, the principal conception of the pilgrimage as a journey to precise places was strongly influenced and widespread by the cult of relics.[5] I do not like to deepen the roots of this cult. It should only be mentioned that from the sixth century onwards many people increasingly believed that a bridge between heaven and earth was established at the tombs of holy men and women. Above all, the tombs of martyrs were frequently visited, as according to a quotation of the Apocalypse (6:9) martyrs were placed directly next to the heavenly altar. Although the division of the *corpora* was not permitted, one can observe the repartition of relics from the eighth century onwards in Rome and other Western places. The holiness was conceived to be present even in the smallest parts of the bones or even in objects that had been put in contact with the relics.

The most evident proof of the virtues of these relics were the miracles happening at the saints' tombs. And as many of the relics caused miracles, the concept to go on a pilgrimage to precise places became more and more frequent from the Carolingian times onwards. The *peregrinatio ad loca sancta* was established: *peregrini*, strangers, made their spiritual journey to a precise destination.

This conception, to travel to the tombs of saints, arose simultaneously with the beginning of the Muslim conquests, which reminds us that also the pilgrimage to Mecca[6] leads to a fixed place. Within this context, it is needless to emphasize that pilgrimages to sacred places are not only a concept of Christianity, but also of other religions.

## The rising of St. James's cult

### Re-writing hagiographic traditions

The pilgrimage to St. James' tomb is a good example of a pilgrimage *ad loca sancta*. How did this cult rise? At the beginning of the ninth century a hermit, Pelayo, is said to have detected the Tomb of St. James the Elder in the northwest of Spain. The news soon spread all over Europe. Learned people in the archives and libraries of the monasteries were well informed about the events back then. Martyrologies of the second half of the ninth century, like the one of Ado of Vienne, noted the feast day of St. James, the 25th of July, and added the finding of his tomb near Compostela to it.[7] (Figure 9.1)

But it is not beyond interest that only a charter of the 17th of August, 1077, gives more details about the circumstances of the finding (*inventio*) in its *Narratio*.

*Figure 9.1* Inventio; Historia Compostellana, Ms. Univ. Salamanca 2658, f. 14r. (about 1140; cf. Herbers, Klaus: *Jakobus – der Heilige Europas, Geschichte und Kultur der Pilgerfahrten nach Santiago de Compostela*, Düsseldorf 2007, p. 45)

It states that in the time of Alfonso II of Asturias (791–842) an angel had revealed the tomb of an apostle to the hermit Pelayo who told his vision to the bishop Theodemiro from the near Iria Flavia. After fasting three days long, the tomb was found in the presence of many devotees. It was decorated with marble and the king, who was informed, is said to have ordered the erection of a church building. It is striking that these and other details about the discovery were apparently written down in Compostela not before two centuries afterwards. Meanwhile, Compostela became an important centre of pilgrimage. Thus, one might argue that curiosity increased to know in detail how the discovery had taken place. Obviously, the *Narratio* of the charter of 1077 tells the story of the discovery like other stories of *inventiones* in the Middle Ages of Europe. Actual questions and influences of the eleventh century thus determined the answers given in this text.[8]

The stories of the discovery of James' tomb contradict the biblical testimonials in a certain way: The Acts of the Apostles describe accurately that James had been killed by the sword near Jerusalem (Acts, 12:2). So, normally the tomb would have been supposed to be located in that region. Therefore, if the news from the finding near Compostela was right, it was necessary to explain how the body came from Palestine to northwestern Spain. The cited document of 1077 gives two hints: On the one hand, it claims the burial place had been unknown and hidden for a long time. On the other hand, it refers to a letter of a Pope Leon telling more about a miraculous journey by boat carrying the body of St. James from Joppe (Jaffa) to Galicia.

I cannot enter into detail on these different stories about a *translatio*, however, I made a comparison elsewhere.[9] But leaving the variety apart, the texts concerning the *translatio* of the apostolic body had one general aim: to harmonize the finding of the tomb in Galicia and the biblically documented place of death. In another respect, the translation could be joined with another element of the hagiographic traditions of St. James: his preaching during his lifetime in Spain. This fact could explain why St. James was transported to Spain after his death and not to another place. The missionary tradition could make it clear that James, having preached the gospel in Spain, should find his final rest in Spain. Thus, *Praedicatio, Passio, Translatio*, and *Inventio* could enter into close relation. However, it is significant that the preaching of James is not mentioned in every report of the *Translatio*.

Although this hagiographic structure seems to consist of a clear coherence, there existed other competing traditions of which we do not have any clear testimonies, only very short references or indications. Nevertheless, the different variants of the *Translatio* show clearly that hagiographic traditions had a lively structure and, according to actual necessities, the story of a saint, parts of his life or the circumstances of his translation could be written in a new perspective. 'La réécriture hagiographique', the re-writing of hagiographies, described and analyzed on different hagiographic material by Monique Goullet, Martin Heinzelmann, and others,[10] is evident not only for the *Translatio* and enables us to give historical-based answers on the development of the cult of St. James.

## Help for identity of northern Spain?

However, there is a lack: The texts concerning the *inventio* and *translatio* do not explain explicitly, why the discovery took place in Galicia and why the bones of St. James were found precisely at the beginning of the ninth century. Was it a response to the Arab Muslim conquest of great parts of the Iberian Peninsula from 711 onwards, as some scholars argue? Only in northern Spain some Christian kingdoms arose, the most important being Asturias. Nevertheless, the Christian faith continued also in the Arab-Muslim Emirate of Córdoba with its most important centre, Toledo. The popes, for example Hadrian I, kept in contact with these Christians of Toledo.[11] At the end of the eighth century, a great Christological debate arose about 'Adoptionism'.[12] I do not like to enter in detail into this dispute, only so far that archbishop Elipand of Toledo and abbot Beatus of Liébana in the north of Spain took different positions in the debate. The Carolingians were involved and the classical position was confirmed at the council of Frankfort, which corresponded to the position of Beatus of Liébana.

In dogmatic questions, Asturias and the North had gained the victory and it is striking that just after this decision the news of the discovery of St. James' tomb arose. Apparently, the dispute about Adoptionism was necessary to open the way for Asturias to establish a proper identity with the important traditions of an apostle. Thus, the finding depended on the Arab-Muslim conquest, but above all, it opposed a new northern tradition to the Christians in Toledo and the Emirate. Asturias was prepared. The same Beatus of Liébana composed a commentary on the Apocalypse based on Greek catalogues.[13] He described also the missionary areas of the apostles, Peter and Paul in Rome, Thomas in India, and so on. For St. James he reserved Spain and the regions of the occident (Figure 9.2).

If this commentary was correct, the Asturian abbot knew already before the discovery of the tomb that James had preached in Spain. Could the fact of knowing this tradition incite to reveal a tomb which was later on identified with the one of the apostle James? Apparently, Asturias prepared the finding and maybe even

*Figure 9.2* Beatus of Liébana, Commentary on the Apocalypse, Cathedral of Girona, Archive, Ms. 7 (about 975).

the hymn 'O Dei verbum' dedicated to king Mauregato (†788) might fit within this context. St. James appears as a protector against heresies and is even designed as chief, protector, and patron of Spain.[14]

Thus, after 711 not a Christian-Muslim confrontation, but rather the conflicts between different Christian groups living under different conditions in Spain in their struggle for influence incited the discovery of the tomb. The hagiographic texts which explain this difficult situation were the traditions of the *Praedicatio*, the *Passio* in Jerusalem, the *Translatio*, and the *Inventio* of the tomb.

## The pilgrimage to St. James in its central period: forms and models

The pilgrimage to St. James was, according to the sources, basically limited to local importance from the ninth to the eleventh centuries, although we have some notes of the tenth century about some pilgrims from north of the Pyrenees.[15] In the second half of the eleventh century, notes about pilgrims of other European countries became more frequent. The making of St. James' tomb as a European centre of pilgrimage is based on several aspects situated within a wider context concerning the history of Spain. Many authors characterize the transformation of northern Spain from the middle of the eleventh century onward as a process of 'Europeanisation'.[16] Strong influences from other parts of Europe, above all from France and Rome, determined the adaption of the Carolingian script, the Roman liturgy and forms of the Roman and canonical law as it was developed in the rest of Europe. The collapse of the caliphate and the small Muslim kingdoms in Spain (Taifas) enabled successful military actions of the so-called Reconquista, including the participation of foreigners. Churchmen from France occupied several important bishoprics in Spain and a new organization of the hierarchy was coming up.

Saint James of Compostela was involved in this development, but I cannot discuss the important steps of Diego Gelmírez (†1140) in detail, who pushed above all the change from a bishopric to an archbishopric (1120/1124), basically at the same time.[17] In the middle of the twelfth century, a compilation called *Liber Sancti Jacobi* reached its final form. It is also called *Codex Calixtinus*, because Pope Calixtus II (1119–1124), the great friend and endower of Santiago de Compostela, is supposed to be its author. Its compilation is most interesting for the development of the pilgrimage to St. James. The actual scholarship argues that the final act of compilation took place at Compostela in the middle of the twelfth century, but parts of the book might have been composed in other places at an earlier stage.[18]

Although the *Liber Sancti Jacobi* is partly hagiography, it is definitely different from other hagiographic *Libelli*. It is composed in five parts. Only the *passio* in the first book, the *Translatio* in the third – telling the journey of James' body from Palestine to Spain – and the collection of miracles in the second book would belong *strictu sensu* to a classical hagiographic dossier. But other parts are more extensive and represent other forms of text or literature: e.g. the first book including sermons and liturgical texts to ensure the correct worship of the saints' feast days, or the *Historia Turpini* conceiving Charlemagne as a fighter against Muslims and at the same time as the first pilgrim to St. James' shrine (book IV).

The last part, book V, is one of the first pilgrim's guides to Compostela. Book IV and V are important for models of pilgrimage, although some sermons in the first book are also conceiving forms of pilgrimage. Nevertheless, the fifth book, the pilgrim's guide was not intended to be a practical help for pilgrims as its form, content, and the transmission of the text suppose the opposite. Basically, the guide tries to give hints for a good pilgrimage and is more prescriptive than descriptive.

## Fixed ways to Santiago?

There are four roads which, leading to Santiago, coverage to form a single road at Puente la Reina, in Spanish territory. One crosses Saint-Gilles, Montpellier, Toulouse, and the pass of Somport; another goes through Notre-Dame of Le Puy, traverses Sainte-Marie-Madeleine of Vézelay, Saint-Léonard in the Limousin as well as the city of Périgueux; still another cuts through Saint-Martin of Tours, Saint-Hilaire of Poitiers, Saint-Jean-d'Angély, Saint-Eutrope of Saintes and the city of Bordeaux.

The road traverses Sainte-Foy, the one that proceeds through Saint-Léonard, and the one that does so through Saint-Martin meet at Ostabat and, having gained the pass of Cize, join at Puente la Reina the road that comes from Somport; thence a single road leads as far as Santiago.[19] (Map 1)

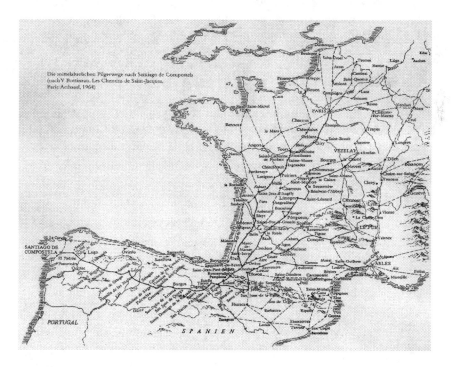

*Map 1* The medieval routes of St. James to Santiago de Compostela; Herbers, Klaus, ed. 1998. *Der Jakobsweg. Mit einem mittelalterlichen Pilgerführer unterwegs nach Santiago de Compostela.* Tübingen: G. Narr.

The fifth book of the *Liber Sancti Jacobi* starts with this enumeration. The text claims the existence of four different ways, as you can see on the map. All of them start in France: St. Gilles, Le Puy, Vézelay, and Tours. These utterances seem to have fixed the ways to St. James tomb and they sacralised and canonized them. But did they correspond to reality? Maybe they did so partially. Although these ways and corresponding maps are never missing in academic literature about pilgrim's ways, it has been shown that the very difficult routes from Vézélay or Le Puy were hardly frequented throughout the Middle Ages. Otherwise, the route from Arles or Paris/Tours followed, like the Camino in Spain's Roman roads. Therefore, the author of our guide might have invented some of his pilgrim's ways, which will be pointed out by the following remarks.

In the following chapters of the guide dealing with stages, possibilities to get water, crossings of rivers, or the different people living along the route, as well as the sanctuaries which the pilgrims have to visit (*visitanda sunt*), we can frequently detect a prescriptive character of the author's writing. Whilst enumerating the holy places in France and Spain, which the pilgrim should venerate, he subordinated very important centres of France to the final destination, Santiago de Compostela. In the eighth chapter, important shrines like St. Martin in Tours, Ste-Foy in Conques, St. Leonard in Limousin, or St. Sernin in Toulouse are enlisted as stations on the long way to the final destination, although the author skips their importance as independent pilgrim centres. Thus, the way to St. James evolved to be more important than the routes to other pilgrim centres, and the long-distanced Compostela on the periphery of Europe was ideally transferred into the centre. Santiago seemed to be closer than it was in reality. The tomb was in the centre of the world although it was geographically at its end (*finis terrae*).

This aspect was emphasized by the description of some miracles in the second book of the compilation. St. James helps on the way, enables sick pilgrims to arrive at his tomb within one night and so on. At the same time, he is defended at the same time as the most effective helper for pilgrims. In one of the miracles, he is even stronger than the classical Merovingian and Carolingian helper St. Martin of Tours. The third miracle even intends a comparison of these two men:

> This is new, and never heard of before, that a dead person raised someone from the dead. Blessed Martinus and our Lord raised – when they were still alive – three persons from the dead. But blessed James raised someone from the dead when he was dead himself. However, somebody might say against this: If our Lord and blessed Martinus, as can be read, did not raise anybody after their own deaths, but resurrected three persons each before they died, thus, not a dead person, but only a living person can raise someone from the dead. Saying this, it must be concluded: If a dead person cannot raise somebody from the dead, but only a living one, thus blessed James is, as God, truly alive and raised someone from the dead [...].[20]

The ninth chapter of the guide containing a description of Santiago de Compostela is still fascinating today as the text depicts monuments, which no longer exist or exist in a different way nowadays. The author might have been inspired by the descriptions of Rome in texts like the *Mirabilia Urbis Romae*. The visit of the apostolic basilica recalls the visit of the celestial Jerusalem. A complete harmony of the building has evolved and the author ends his description of the measures with the following words:

> In this church, in truth, one cannot find a single crack or defect: it is admirably built, large, spacious, luminous, of becoming dimensions, well-proportioned in width, length and height, of incredibly marvelous workmanship and even built on two levels as a royal palace. He who walks through the aisles of the triforium above, if he ascended in a sad mood, having seen the superior beauty of this temple, will leave happy and contented.[21]

Other chapters and some passages of the first book of the *Liber Sancti Jacobi* show the conception of the centre of the cult at that time. The author takes a strong position against collecting unjustified toll fees of pilgrims, he cautions the pilgrims about the ferrymen who let their boat overturn in order to get the pilgrims' possessions. Furthermore, he preaches against the malicious hosts who are only after their guests' money and goods. Obviously, he does not like Navarre and the Bask land as most of his quoted negative examples are attached to these regions. Otherwise, he is full of praise for those who had contributed to the arrangement of the road or had built bridges to secure the route. In the last chapter, he recalls to the inhabitants along the road to Compostela once again the words of the Gospel 'He who welcomes you, welcomes me' (Matthew 10:40). Three miracles underline the consequences for those who do not welcome the pilgrims of St. James. It is thus significant that the pilgrim's guide uses the hagiographic discourse within this context. The last chapter underlines the importance of miracles to enable a certain model of pilgrimage: It does not work without charity! The second book, the collection of miracles, also provides examples for a good practice of pilgrimage and the problems on the way. Quite many of the 22 miracles deal with the long way and the practical problems of pilgrimage. One of the stories tells us how the apostle carried an already or nearly dead pilgrim on his horseback during the night to Santiago de Compostela.

## St. James and Charlemagne

The first chapter of the pilgrim's guide proposes two possible ways to cross the Pyrenees: the Somport and Roncesvalles. We know that the Somport was also an important way for the economic traffic of different goods. The guide enumerates both passages and praises Somport furthermore in the fourth chapter. From the second half of the twelfth century on, Roncesvalles became more and more important. In the eighth chapter dealing with holy bodies on the way, Roncesvalles dominates clearly. This is above all due to an ideological argument: Charlemagne crossed the Pyrenees at this place.

> In the Basque country there is on the road of St. James a very high mountain, which is called Port-de-Cize, either because that is the gate of Spain,

or because it is by that mountain that the necessary goods are transported from one country to the other. Its ascent is eight miles long, and its descent, equally eight. In fact, its height is such that it seems to touch the sky: to him who climbs it, it seems as if he was able to touch the sky with his hand. From its summit one can see the sea of Bretagne and that of the west, as well as the boundaries of three regions, that is to say, Castilla, Aragón, and France. On the summit of this mountain there is a place called the Cross of Charles, because it was here that Charles, setting out with his armies for Spain, opened up once a passageway with axes, hatchets, pickaxes and other implements, and that he first erected the sign of the cross of the Lord and, falling on his knees and turning towards Galicia, addressed a prayer to God and St. James. Wherefore the pilgrims, falling on their knees and turning towards the land of St. James, use to offer there a prayer while each planted his own cross of the Lord like a standard. Indeed, one can find there up to a thousand crosses; and that is why that place is the first station of prayer of St. James.

On that mountain, before Christianity had spread out on Spanish lands, the impious Navarrese and the Basques used not merely to rob the pilgrims going to St. James, but also to ride them as if they were asses and before long to slay them. Near this mountain, to be sure, towards the north, there is a valley called Valcarlos where Charles himself encamped together with his armies after his warriors had been slain at Roncesvalles. Many pilgrims proceeding to Santiago who do not want to climb the mountain go that way. Afterwards, in descending from the summit, one finds the hospice and the church with the rock that Roland, the formidable hero, split with his sword in the middle, from top to bottom, in a triple stroke. Next, one comes to Roncesvalles, the site where, to be sure, once took place the big battle in which King Marsile, Roland, Olivier as well as forty thousand Christian and Saracen soldiers were slain. After this valley lies in the land of the Navarrese which abounds in bread, wine, milk, and livestock.[22]

This quotation summarizes the Spanish journey of Charlemagne, which is far longer exposed in the fourth book of the *Liber Sancti Jacobi* (*Historia Turpini*). This new European-Carolingian tradition about the Emperor as a pilgrim and fighter against the Moors lead to new aspects of the conception of pilgrimage, or better: it puts it into a European context. This perspective focused on Roncesvalles as a *lieu de mémoire*. The place, where King Charles de facto suffered a great defeat in 778, was now highlighted and became an important place for pilgrims. In any case, also later guides, for example in the fifteenth century Hermann Künig von Vach, describe Roncesvalles as the place to cross the Pyrenees.[23]

In the *Historia Turpini*, which is said to be composed by Charlemagne's contemporary archbishop Turpin of Reims, the beginnings of the cult of St. James are told differently and partly in opposition to the traditions of Compostela that

*Figure 9.3* Reliqiuary of Charlemagne, Aachen (12th century, finished 1215).

I presented in the first part of this chapter. The *Historia* tells about the individual battles of Charlemagne in Spain and does not mention the finding of the tomb by Pelayo. It is Charlemagne who is supposed to have visited the tomb of the apostle, which had been forgotten and unattended for a long time. The fight against the Moors and the exaltation of the pilgrim's goal concentrate in one person: the well-known European Emperor. This transferred Compostela more than other traditions into a European pilgrimage destination. The story was successful and became increasingly popular, especially since Charlemagne was declared a saint by the efforts of the chapter of Aquisgran and Frederik Barbarossa in 1165. The *Vita Karoli*, which relies in great parts on the *Historia Turpini*, was composed to prove his sainthood.[24] The reliefs of the shrine of Charlemagne, finished over 800 years ago in 1215, depict various scenes of him in Spain as a fighter and a devotee of St. James. In one of the reliefs, St. James appears to the Carolingian king in a dream similar to the first chapter of the *Historia Turpini* (and a picture in the manuscript) and encourages him to fight against the Muslims and to visit his tomb so many pilgrims might follow his example. (Figure 9.3)

## Conclusion: Forms of dissemination and transformation in the late Middle Ages

Let me add only a few final remarks about the dissemination and transformation of this model. From a classical hagiographic dossier formed from the ninth to the eleventh century, the cult was disseminated into a European context by stressing the importance of the way by the subordination of other important spiritual centers.

But there was more: The person of Charlemagne transferred the cult into a European setting. For this interpretation it is revealing that a shorter version of the *Liber Sancti Jacobi* was copied all over Europe. It usually contained the *Historia Turpini*, the miracles, and some other pieces. This *Libellus Sancti Jacobi* and more than 300 Latin and vernacular copies of the *Historia Turpini* assured the diffusion of this version of the cult.[25] Furthermore, over 50% of the miracles of the *Liber Sancti Jacobi* were included in the great legendaries of the thirteenth century onwards, like the one by Jacobus of Voragine.[26] Thus, a very precise model of pilgrimage took shape by means of miracles and the *Historia Turpini* which made Compostela comparable to Jerusalem and Rome.

Quite a lot of the miracles focus on the importance of the way itself, however, St. James appears also very often as a helper dealing with persons between life and death. St. James as a companion on the ways, in life and death, refers to the issue *Vita est peregrinatio*, the conception of human life as a pilgrimage mentioned at the beginning of this article, which appears as a certain subtext in the miracles of St. James. There was another development in the late Middle Ages: the pilgrimage to Compostela was also aspired by the pious zeal for an indulgence, although perhaps less than Rome. Nevertheless, the tradition of Holy Years from the fifteenth century onwards shows a certain development. The cited Hermann Künig von Vach writes in his German guide, printed probably in 1495, that one can gain 'römische gnad und ablaß'.[27] With regard to this, there was a certain transformation of the presented model of pilgrimage (Figure 9.4).

*Figures 9.4* Künig von Vach (15th century); Herbers, Klaus and Robert Plötz, ed. 2004. *Die Strass zu Sankt Jakob. Der älteste deutsche Pilgerführer nach Compostela.* Ostfildern: Jan Thorbecke.

Critics and partisans of a stronger personal piety without travelling to holy shrines can be found in the late Middle Ages, for example, Thomas a Kempis with his 'Qui multum peregrinantur raro sanctificantur', cited at the beginning of this chapter. Humanists like Hieronymus Münzer were even in 1494 still sceptic about the question if the body of James was really in Santiago de Compostela. Nevertheless, he is a good example to demonstrate the changes and at the same time the importance and the longevity of the classical and specific model of the Jacobean pilgrimage depicted in this chapter. The way of his journey and the visit to Compostela showed that travelers could start with various motivations as the map of his itinerary underlines (Map 2).

Münzer stayed nearly a week in Compostela. For what reason? He wanted to get a copy from a scribe of the *Historia Turpini*. Thus, even humanists were attracted by the combination of St. James and Charlemagne. Perhaps the fact that the healing of body and soul by miracles and the great narrative of Charlemagne as a fighter and pilgrim at the same time contributed in its combination to the long success of St. James and his shrine in Compostela, which could integrate even different concepts of pilgrimage.

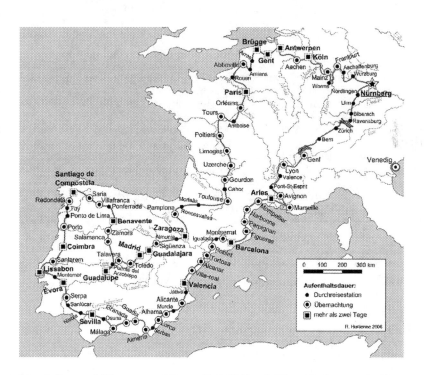

*Map 2* Route of Hieronymus Münzer (1494/95); ed. Klaus Herbers et al.: *Hieronymus Münzer, Itinerarium* (MGH Quellen zur Geistesgeschichte 31), Wiesbaden 2019.

## Notes

1 Lupo 1982, Liber I cap. 23, 4: *Pauci ex infirmitate emendantur; sic et qui multum peregrinantur, raro sanctificantur.* The following text follows the form of my paper at the Tampere-Conference in August 2015, adding above all notes concerning the cited sources. Thanks to Katharina Götz (Erlangen) for revising the English version of my paper and Benedict Rebohl (Erlangen) for his help.
2 Herbers and Santos Noya 1998, 256: 'Que etiam ecclesia a tempore quo fuit incepta usque in hodiernum diem, fulgore miraculorum beati Iacobi vernatur, egris enim in ea salus prestatur, cecis visus refunditur, mutorum lingua solvitur, surdis auditus panditur, claudis sana ambulacio datur, demoniacis liberacio conceditur, et quod maius est populorum fidelium preces exaudiuntur, vota suscipiuntur, delictorum vincula resolvuntur, pulsantibus celum aperitur, mestis consolacio datur, omnesque barbare gentes omnium mundi climatum catervatim ibi occurrunt, munera laudis Domino deferentes.' I am following the English translation of Melczer 1993, 130–131, but not in every detail.
3 Angenendt 1972; Angenendt 1982, 52–79; Wood 2001.
4 Röwekamp 1995. Recently also concerning holy places in and around Jerusalem: Verstegen 2015; Verstegen 2016, 31–54.
5 See e.g. Legler 1989; Angenendt 1997; Deuffic 2006; Bozóky 2006; Berthod 2014.
6 See e.g. Hawting 2014.
7 The origins of the cult of St. James have been treated in various studies: Plötz 1982; Herwaarden 1980; revised version in: Herwaarden 2003, 311–354 (cf. the other contributions in this volume); Díaz y Díaz 1988, 5–22; López Alsina 1988, 99–126; Herbers 1994, 177-275; Márquez Villanueva 2004, 31–163; Rucquoi 2014, 224–240; Rucquoi 2016, 119–140. Many new aspects recently in several articles; see Arlotta 2016. For a concise general view concerning the principal lines of this chapter, I refer to Herbers 2011b, esp. 10–32.
8 Cf. Freire Camaniel 1999; Freire Camaniel 2000; cf. Herwaarden 2003, 336. Perhaps this example illustrates the invention of a tradition, cf. Hobsbawm and Ranger 1992.
9 Cf. Herbers 2011b, 10–15; Herbers 2007, 16–33.
10 Goullet and Heinzelmann 2003; Goullet and Heinzelmann 2006; cf. Herbers and Bauer 2000.
11 Cf. Hadrian's letters Jaffé 2017: no. 4517, 4572 and 4496; Gundlach 1892, n. 95, 96, 97, 636–648; see concerning the dates (Gundlach 1892, 785–791); see also Hack 2006, 1079.
12 See a recent interpretation of Rucquoi 2015.
13 Romero Pose 1985, 191–192. For Apocryphal traditions of the Apostles, see Rose 2014, esp. 59–60 with further bibliography.
14 For the manuscript tradition, see the edition and interpretation: Herwaarden 1980, revised version Herwaarden 2003, 320–335.
15 Herbers 1991, 255–264; French version Herbers 1993; German version: Herbers 2011a, 341–349. About Godeschalcus from Le Puy and his presence in Compostela 950/51 cf. among others recently Rucquoi 2014, 18 and 116; Jacomet 2009, 9–44. It is not possible to quote the numerous contributions to the phenomena of pilgrimage. For a comparison with Scandinavian traditions cf. the fundamental study: Krötzl 1994.
16 About this concept cf. Herbers 2002, 11–31.
17 Cf. the instructive contributions in: López Alsina, Monteagudo, Villares, and Yzquierdo Perrín 2013.
18 Herbers and Santos Noya 1998. There is an abundant research on this Book; cf. among others: Díaz y Díaz 1988; Stones 1998; Herwaarden 1988, 355–378; Herbers 2010 (also in English and French). Cf. López Alsina 2013.
19 Latin text: Herbers and Santos Noya 1998, 235; my English version above follows Melczer 1993, 85.
20 Latin text: Herbers and Santos Noya 1998, 163.
21 Latin text: Herbers and Santos Noya 1998, 252; English version: Melczer 1993, 121.

22  Latin text: Herbers and Santos Noya 1998, 239–240; English version: Melczer 1993, 93–94.
23  Herbers and Plötz 2004, 70–71.
24  Cf. for these aspects the contributions in the two volumes: Herbers 2003a and Herbers 2003b.
25  Cf. previous note and Hämel 1950; Hämel 1953; cf. also de Mandach 1961/1963.
26  Cf. concerning the early diffusion of the miracles: Herbers 1992, 11–35; German version Herbers 2011c.
27  Herbers and Plötz 2004, 36-37.

## Bibliography

### Printed Sources

Gundlach, Wilhelm, ed. 1892. *Codex Carolinus*, Monumenta Germaniae Historica Epistolae III. Berlin: Weidmann.

Herbers, Klaus and Manuel Santos Noya, ed. 1998. *Liber Sancti Jacobi, Codex Calixtinus*. Santiago de Compostela: Xunta de Galicia.

Herbers, Klaus and Robert Plötz, ed. 2004. *Die Strass zu Sankt Jakob. Der älteste deutsche Pilgerführer nach Compostela*. Ostfildern: Jan Thorbecke.

Lupo, Tiburzio, ed. 1982. *Thomas a Kempis, De imitatione Christi libri quatuor*. Vatican City: Libreria Editrice Vaticana.

Melczer, William, ed. 1993. *The Pilgrim's Guide to Santiago de Compostela*. New York: Lightning Source Incorporated.

Romero Pose, Eugenio, ed. 1985. *Sancti Beati a Liebana Commentarius in Apocalypsin, vol. duo. Scriptores Graeci et Latini Consilio Academiae Lynceorum Editi*. Rome: Typis Officinae Polygraphicae.

Röwekamp, Georg, ed. 1995. *Egeria - Itinerarium – Reisebericht*, Fontes christiani 20. Freiburg: Herder.

Stones, Alison, ed. 1998. *The Pilgrim's Guide: A Critical Edition, I The Manuscripts: Their Creation, Production and Reception*, with Jeanne Krochalis, II, *The Text: Annotated English Translation*, with Paula Gerson and Annie Shaver-Crandell. London: Harvey Miller.

### Literature

Angenendt, Arnold. 1972. *Monachi peregrini. Studien zu Pirmin und den monastischen Vorstellungen des frühen Mittelalters*. Munich: Fink.

Angenendt, Arnold. 1982. "Die irische Peregrinatio und ihre Auswirkungen auf dem Kontinent vor dem Jahr 800." In *Die Iren und Europa im früheren Mittelalter*, vol. 1, edited by Heinz Löwe, 52–79. Stuttgart: Klett-Cotta.

Angenendt, Arnold. 1997. *Heilige und Reliquien. Die Geschichte ihres Kultes vom frühen Christentum bis zur Gegenwart*. Munich: C.H. Beck.

Arlotta, Guiseppe, ed. 2016. *De peregrinatione. Studi in onore di Paolo Caucci von Saucken*. Perugia: Edizioni Compostellane.

Berthod, Bernard. 2014. *Reliques et Reliquaires, l'émotion du sacré*. Paris: CLD.

Bozóky, Edina. 2006. *La politique des reliques de Constantin à Saint Louis. Protection collective et légitimation du pouvoir*. Paris: Editions Beauchesne.

de Mandach, André. 1961/1963. *Naissance et développement de la Chanson de Geste en Europe*, 2 vols. Genève: Droz.

Deuffic, Jean-Luc, ed. 2006. *Reliques et sainteté dans l'espace médiéval*. St. Denis: Pecia.
Díaz y Díaz, Manuel C. 1988. *El Códice Calixtino de la catedral de Santiago. Estudio codicológico y de contenido*, in collaboration with Ma Araceli García Piñeiro and Pilar del Oro Trigo. Santiago de Compostela: Centro de Estudios Jacobeos.
Freire Camaniel, José. 1999. "Los primeros documentos relativos a las Iglesias de Antealtares y Santiago I." *Compostellanum. Revista de la Archidiócesis de Santiago de Compostela* 44: 335–392.
Freire Camaniel, José. 2000. "Los primeros documentos relativos a las Iglesias de Antealtares y Santiago II." *Compostellanum. Revista de la Archidiócesis de Santiago de Compostela* 45: 725–755.
Goullet, Monique and Martin Heinzelmann, ed. 2003. *La Réécriture hagiographique dans l'occident médiéval*. Ostfildern: Jan Thorbecke.
Goullet, Monique and Martin Heinzelmann, ed. 2006. *Miracles, vies et réécritures dans l'occident médiéval*. Ostfildern: Jan Thorbecke.
Hack, Achim Thomas. 2006. *Codex Carolinus. Päpstliche Epistolographie im 8. Jahrhundert*. Stuttgart: A. Hiersemann.
Hämel, Adalbert. 1950. *Überlieferung und Bedeutung des Liber Sancti Jacobi und des Pseudo-Turpin*, Sitzungsberichte der Bayerischen Akademie der Wissenschaften, phil.-hist. Klasse 1950, 2. Munich: Verlag der Bayerischen Akademie der Wissenschaften.
Hämel, Adalbert. 1953. "Los manuscritos latinos del falso Turpino." *Estudios dedicados a Menéndez Pidal* 4: 67–85.
Hawting, Gerald. 2014. "Pilgrimage to Mecca: Humans Responses to a Divine Command." In *Unterwegs im Namen der Religion. Pilgern als Form von Kontingenzbewältigung und Zukunftssicherung in den Weltreligionen*, edited by Klaus Herbers and Hans-Christian Lehner, 73–84. Stuttgart: Franz Steiner.
Herbers, Klaus. 1991. "El primer peregrino ultrapirenaico a Compostela a comienzos del siglo X y las relaciones de la monarquía asturiana con Alemania del Sur." *Compostellanum. Revista de la Archidiócesis de Santiago de Compostela* 36: 255–264.
Herbers, Klaus. 1992. "The Miracles of St. James." In *The Codex Calixtinus and the Shrine of St. James*, edited by John Williams and Alison Stones, 11–35. Tübingen: G. Narr.
Herbers, Klaus. 1993. "Le premier pèlerin d'Outre-Pyrénées à Compostelle au début du Xe siècle et les relations entre la monarchie asturienne et le Sud de l'Allemagne." *Ultreia* 12: 46–55.
Herbers, Klaus. 1994. "Politik und Heiligenverehrung auf der Iberischen Halbinsel. Die Entwicklung des 'politischen Jakobus'." In *Politik und Heiligenverehrung im Hochmittelalter*, edited by Jürgen Petersohn, 177–275. Sigmaringen: Jan Thorbecke.
Herbers, Klaus. 2002. "'Europäisierung' und 'Afrikanisierung' – Zum Problem zweier wissenschaftlicher Konzepte und zu Fragen kulturellen Transfers." In *España y el 'Sacro Imperio'. Procesos de cambios, influencias y acciones recíprocas en la época de la 'Europeización' (siglos XI-XIII)*, edited by Karl Rudolf, Klaus Herbers, and Julio Valdeon, 11–31. Valladolid: Universidad de Valladolid.
Herbers, Klaus, ed. 2003a. *El Pseudo-Turpin. Lazo entre el culto Jacobeo y el culto de Carlomagno. Actas del VI Congreso Internacional de Estudios Jacobeos*. Santiago de Compostela: Xerencia de Promoción do Camiño de Santiago.
Herbers, Klaus, ed. 2003b. *Jakobus und Karl der Große. Von Einhards Karlsvita zum Pseudo-Turpin*. Tübingen: G. Narr.
Herbers, Klaus. 2007. *Jakobus – der Heilige Europas. Geschichte und Kultur der Pilgerfahrten nach Santiago de Compostela*. Düsseldorf: Patmos.

Herbers, Klaus. 2010. "El Códice Calixtino. El libro da la iglesia compostelana. In *Compostela y Europa. La historia de Diego Gelmírez*, edited by Manuel Castiñeiras, 122–141. Milano: Skira. [Also in English and French].
Herbers, Klaus. 2011a. "Die ersten mitteleuropäischen Jakobspilger zu Beginn des 10. Jahrhunderts und die Beziehungen der asturischen Monarchie zu Süddeutschland." In *Pilger, Päpste, Heilige. Ausgewählte Aufsätze zur europäischen Geschichte des Mittelalters*, edited by Gordon Blennemann, Wiebke Deimann, Matthias Maser, and Christofer Zwanzig, 341–349. Tübingen: G. Narr.
Herbers, Klaus. 2011b [2006]. *Jakobsweg. Geschichte und Kultur einer Pilgerfahrt*. Munich: C.H. Beck.
Herbers, Klaus. 2011c. "Die Mirakel des heiligen Jakobus." In *Pilger, Päpste, Heilige. Ausgewählte Aufsätze zur europäischen Geschichte des Mittelalters*, edited by Gordon Blennemann, Wiebke Deimann, Matthias Maser, and Christofer Zwanzig, 351–377. Tübingen: G. Narr.
Herbers, Klaus and Dieter Bauer, eds. 2000. *Hagiographie im Kontext. Wirkungsweisen und Möglichkeiten historischer Auswertung*. Stuttgart: Franz Steiner.
van Herwaarden, Jan. 1980. "The Origins of the Cult of St. James of Compostela." *Journal of Medieval History* 6: 1–35.
van Herwaarden, Jan, ed. 2003. *Between Saint James and Erasmus*. Leiden: Brill.
Hobsbawm, Eric and Terence O. Ranger, eds. 1992. *The Invention of Tradition*. Cambridge: Cambridge University Press.
Jacomet, Humbert. 2009. "Gotescalc, évêque de Sainte-Marie d'Anis, pèlerin de Saint Jacques (950-951)." *Compostelle. Cahiers du Centre d'études de recherche et d'histoire compostellanes* 12: 9–44.
Jaffé, Philipp. 2017. *Regesta Pontificum Romanorum, Tomvs II (ab a. 604 - ad a. 844)*, third edition, edited by Klaus Herbers, Waldemar Könighaus, and Thorsten Schlauwitz, with the support of Cornelia Scherer, and Markus Schütz. Göttingen: Vandenhoeck & Ruprecht.
Krötzl, Christian. 1994. *Pilger, Mirakel und Alltag. Formen des Verhaltens im skandinavischen Mittelalter*, 12–15. Jh. Helsinki: SHS.
Legler, Anton, ed. 1989. *Reliquien. Verehrung und Verklärung, Skizzen und Noten zur Thematik und Katalog zur Ausstellung der Kölner Sammlung Louis Peters im Schnütgen-Museum*. Cologne: Schnütgen-Museum.
López Alsina, Fernando. 1988. *La ciudad de Santiago de Compostela en la alta edad media*. Santiago de Compostela: Universidade de Santiago de Compostela.
López Alsina, Fernando. 2013. "Diego Gelmírez, las raíces del Liber Sancti Jacobi y el Códice Calixtino." In *O século de Xelmírez*, edited by Fernando López Alsina, Henrique Monteagudo, Ramón Villares, and Ramón Yzquierdo, 301–386. Santiago de Compostela: Consello da Cultura Galeg.
López Alsina, Fernando, Henrique Monteagudo, Ramón Villares, and Ramón Yzquierdo Perrín, eds. 2013. *O século de Xelmírez*. Santiago de Compostela: Consello da Cultura Galeg.
Márquez Villanueva, Francisco. 2004. *Santiago: Trayectoria de un mito*. Barcelona: Bellaterra.
Plötz, Robert. 1982. "Der Apostel Jacobus in Spanien bis zum 9. Jahrhundert." *Spanische Forschungen der Görresgesellschaft, Reihe 1: Gesammelte Aufsätze zur Kulturgeschichte Spaniens* 30: 19–145.
Rose, Els. 2014. "The Cult of the Apostles in the Early Medieval West: From Eyewitnesses to Blood Witnesses." In *Vom Blutzeugen zum Glaubenszeugen? Formen und*

*Vorstellungen des christlichen Martyriums im Wandel*, edited by Gordon Blennemann and Klaus Herbers, 57–70. Stuttgart: Franz Steiner.

Rucquoi, Adeline. 2014. *Mille fois à Compostelle. Pèlerins du Moyen Age*. Paris: Les Belles Lettres.

Rucquoi, Adeline. 2015. "Elipand et l'adoptianisme. Quelques hypothèses." *Bulletin de la Société Nationale des Antiquaires de France* 2008: 292–309.

Rucquoi, Adeline. 2016. "Littérature compostellane IXe – XIIe siècles. Textes et contexts." In *Unterwegs im Namen der Religion II/On the Road in the Name of Religion II. Wege und Ziele in vergleichender Perspektive – das mittelalterliche Europa und Asien/Ways and Destination in Comparativ Perspective – Medieval Europe and Asia*, edited by Klaus Herbers and Hans-Christian Lehner, 119–140. Stuttgart: Franz Steiner.

Verstegen, Ute. 2015. "Die architektonische Inszenierung der christlichen Erinnerungsorte im Heiligen Land. Architektursemantische Betrachtungen zu einem konstantinischen Innovationskonzept." *INSITU: Zeitschrift für Architekturgeschichte* 7(2): 151–171.

Verstegen, Ute. 2016. "Im Kontakt mit dem Allerheiligsten. Zur frühchristlichen Inszenierung der Heilsorte in der Jerusalemer Grabeskirche." In *Orte der Imagination. Räume des Affekts*, edited by Elke Koch and Heike Schliel, 31–54. Paderborn: Wilhelm Fink.

Wood, Ian. 2001. *The Missionary Life. Saints and the Evangelisation of Europe*. Harlow: Taylor & Francis.

# 10 *Pedes habent et non ambulabunt*
## Mobility impairment in Merovingian Gaul

*Christian Laes*

> *Une periode de l'Europe qui est à la fois bien plus documentée qu'on ne le croirait et bien moins connue qu'elle ne le devrait.*[1]

**Introduction: Continuity, change and ... disabilities**

In a volume which deals with travels and mobility, this chapter focuses on those who struggled with moving around, even in basic conditions of everyday life. The period and region under study will be one of passages. Indeed, for many reasons, Merovingian Gaul in the period of ca. 450 to ca. 800 CE is a subject that immediately comes to the mind in a volume which deals with transitions in times of continuity and change.

These were indeed times of profound political and military changes. While the Germanic Franks initially struggled with the Visigoths (as their king Euric had founded his own independent state in the west of Gaul about the year 476) and with the Burgundians (who had settled in the southeast part), it was eventually Childeric's ambitious son Clovis who expelled the Goths from Gaul in 507. He founded the Merovingian dynasty, which would last for more than 250 years. By 520, Clovis' sons got rid of the remains of the Burgundian kingdom in Gaul. In these conflicts and struggles, Rome and its army were remarkably absent. After the dismissal of the Germanic leader Odoacer, the Ostrogothic king Theoderic resided in the *Urbs Aeterna* and went to great efforts to secure at least the appearance of the continuation of the Roman Empire, affirming his loyalty and obedience to the emperor who by now governed from Constantinople. Roman writers from the fifth and sixth century now and then testify of the abruptly changed living conditions, and the sense that a part of their old world and security was irredeemably lost.[2]

These were also times of social and cultural changes and interaction.[3] The Germanic newcomers for a great part assimilated into the strong and vigorous Gallo-Roman culture, and the Roman elites adapted in many ways to the new situation of Merovingian rule and government. New court practices arose, for example, and specific legislation such as the *Pactus Legis Salica*e developed.

Christianity gradually became the dominant faith, though the process was by no means as fast and effective as the rather spectacular baptism of Clovis by bishop Remigius suggests. For centuries, remnants of the pagan religion intermingled in a slow transition with liturgy, ceremonies, and practices of the new Christian religion. Other spheres of life also continued much in the same way. Almost 90% of the population lived in the countryside and these lives presumably changed little. Not that there were no cities and centres of commercial importance: Tours, Arles, and Paris are examples. But all in all, agricultural activities became more and more self-sufficient.[4]

We should be careful not to overgeneralise from political and economic history. Some scholars – and in their wake popular opinion – have characterised the Merovingian period as marked by hard labour, constant food insufficiency, and harsh living conditions.[5] Self-sufficiency and the collapse of large trade, however, can have quite the opposite effect for farmers who were not dependent on anyone and who had enough from what the land gave them. As such, a large part of the agricultural population in Merovingian Gaul might have been reasonably well off, although there was always the impending danger of famine and shortage. After all, it was the periods of economic growth in the booming cities in the twelfth and thirteenth century or the epoch of industrialisation in the eighteenth century which caused urban inhabitants to suffer from malnutrition.[6]

As for the history of disabilities, the topic of this chapter, Merovingian Gaul has been studied to a certain extent. Some people with continuous bad health conditions (*debiles*) were named social outcasts, but others were perceived as people who were, on the contrary, part and parcel of everyday life, without suffering from significant degradation. The difference was partly explained by the socio-economic milieu, with 'lame or crippled' aristocrats being significantly better off than those who were poor and destitute.[7] Paralysis, mobility impairment, and eye problems have been the topic of separate studies.[8] Other studies have looked at a large collection of Merovingian miracle stories, thus taking into account such vital socio-cultural topics as age and gender, agency of the impaired, the role of the family and the social environment, and the issue of disability viewed as sin in the case of people being punished for a transgression.[9]

## Mobility impairment: What to study and how to study it?

### *What is mobility impairment?*

Compared to eye problems, skin diseases, deafness, or speech impairment, mobility impairment is a vague concept, especially in times when moving around freely wherever one wanted was never the ideal as it is cherished today. Even the Facts Sheets concerning Health Topics as developed by the World Health Organisation do not include mobility impairment as a separate item.[10] It is safe to say, though, that broken limbs and the consequences of partial recovery belong under this heading. The same goes for those who were perpetually or temporarily paralysed by accidents or the consequences of a stroke. Other cases are less clear. The leprous were often afflicted in their hands or legs. Severe fever could immobilise people. Mad people were sometimes considered a danger to themselves and their environment and were consequently bound. In such cases, mobility impairment seems to have been communally defined and decided, and not always caused by a clearly definable pathological condition. Generally, historians of disabilities opt for a practical solution when studying mobility impairment. They take into consideration all problems related to the limbs, along with the very basic primary delineator of walking difficulties (legs) and problems with eating and drinking, another vital and essential function.[11] Quite unsurprisingly, the Latin language as it appears in Merovingian writers, has an ample vocabulary to denote such conditions. Since many miracle stories were modelled on the Gospels, the words *paralyticus* (alternatively spelled *paraliticus*) and *claudus/clodus* have the most common occurrence.[12] Other word groups include *contractus, debilis, digitis/manibus/pedibus destitutus, infirmus, mancus,* or *truncus*.[13]

## Osteological and archaeological material

Earlier research had a tendency to offer a pessimistic view of the general physical condition for much of the pre-industrial population. According to some estimates, before the French Revolution, about 20% of the French population was unable to work full days, due to malnutrition.[14] There is, however, debate about these issues, and the historic truth probably lies somewhere between the extremes. For the Roman world, Kristina Killgrove has offered a more balanced view and warned against the methodological shortcomings that distort some outcomes of earlier research.[15] Still, the circumstances rendering at least part of the male adult population unfit for work would have had unmistakable implications for the involvement of Roman women and children in the labour process.[16] For the vast majority of the population, it was necessary to involve everyone as much as possible, even those whose physical and/or mental conditions made such involvement more difficult. Standing on the sidelines was simply not an option, as Lynn Rose explained with the 'community concept' which she introduced into the study of disability history.[17]

Conditions surely would not have been different for Merovingian Gaul. When archaeologists find bones of people which reveal traces of hard work and at the same times conditions which must have led to mobility impairment, such finds mostly confirm a general picture which is already well known. For Merovingian Gaul, such osteological research is sparse.[18] Some examples are revealing though an adult man aged between 35 and 45 years, buried around the year 700 in Altdorf (Bavaria), had a strong curve of the spinal column, due to tuberculosis of the bones. During and after his illness, he must have required considerable care. A skeleton of a 20-year-old woman in Pleidelsheim, Baden-Württemberg from the years 530–555 was found without feet. The presence of ceramic shoes and metal clips to fasten them to clothes indicates that she had walked around with prostheses. Queen Arnegund, wife to the Frankish king Clotaire I (515/20–565/70), whose grave was discovered in the church of Saint Denis in Paris, had a deformation of the right ankle and consequent shortening of the right leg, resulting from polio during childhood or youth. Though this must have caused visible limping, it did not prevent her from entering royal marriage and also being a mother. Tellingly, the malformation is never mentioned in the literary sources.[19] Another interesting instance for the dossier of mobility impairment is an adult aged between 30 and 40 years from Pleidelsheim, Baden-Württemberg, from the late fifth century. He wore a spatha. Due to a fracture of the femur, he must have faced mobility impairment for a large part of his life. He also suffered from a shortening of the right leg, and continuous osteomyelitis. Because of a painful swelling of the knee, he was in need of a stick or a crutch.[20] In Griesheim (Deisburg), an aristocrat had used a prosthesis made out of wood which replaced his lower leg.[21] Unfortunately, there are no Merovingian sanctuaries with *ex-votos* or depictions on the wall, which point to people searching for healing from walking difficulties.[22]

## *Literary texts*

Literary texts of the Merovingian period surely have a greater potential for the topic of mobility impairment, but again the nature of the texts needs to be considered. The so-called barbaric laws mention amputation as a punishment, as do Roman laws from Late Antiquity. They also mention cases of punishment in which a person was made *debilis* or *infirmus*. In such cases, a fine had to be paid. It is never explicitly said whether the damage done was permanent or temporary, and not much information on actual mobility impairment can be secured.[23]

Monastic rules refer occasionally to impairment – a situation to which Jerome hints when he complains about parents dedicating their 'deformed and crippled daughters' (*deformes et aliquo membro debiles filias*) to the life of virginity in a monastery (*Ep*. 130.6). When the monastic system developed, work and worship became the most institutionalised characteristics of the new lifestyle. Manual labour was vital for providing for the monastery. It also served an important spiritual purpose. Manual work and worship overlap in the rules, especially when the treatment of the *infirmi* is discussed. The question of the work of the *infirmi* intermingles with their attending the *lectio divina* and, though not explicitly stated, presumably also with the liturgy of the hours. On the whole, the rules are nearly unanimous in the big picture of regulating the care of the *infirmi*. Such members of the community were not necessarily stigmatised. The biggest difference among the rules is whether or not the topic of *infirmitas* ended up being regulated at all, and if so, which aspects. For Merovingian Gaul, the rules concerning female monastics by Donatus of Besançon (d. 660) might come to mind. Here, the issue of female monastics' manual labour and infirmity is not regulated at all, since female monasteries' subsistence was organised in such a way that they did not rely much on their own manual work.[24]

Historiographical work such as the chronicles is another possible source. Here also, the information on disabilities is limited to some anecdotal references concerning accidents or violent events leading to impairment.[25] This leaves us with the ample collection of miracle stories in saints' lives which, for the Merovingian period, have been collected in seven extensive volumes of the *Monumenta Germaniae Historica. Scriptores Rerum Merovingicarum* (MGH SRM). This collection contains the authors who in the *Vitae* dealt with saints from the Merovingian era, and who wrote before the year 800 (though some belong to a slightly later period). Obviously, such miracle stories are heavily modelled on the Gospel stories (see note 12). They were often written by clergymen. The promotion of a particular cult and the legitimisation of Christian customs against surviving pagan practices were among the main aims of such writings, next to normative functions such as reassuring and comforting believers. Quite repetitive in composition and structure, such stories were meant to be read aloud during sermons or on special occasions such as the saint's name day. This explains their simple language (most of the intended audience was illiterate), and their vivid details. As such, they partly belong to the oral tradition.[26]

## *Mobility impairment in the Merovingian Vitae. Some statistics*

After extensive reading of the six volumes of the MGH SRM, I collected 105 miracle stories on mobility impairment, as it is defined in section 2.1.[27] For a study like this, counting instances is always hazardous. Indeed, the presence of a *Vita* of a saint who was, say, specialised in eye diseases would be enough to skew the evidence towards one category of disabilities. Preferences of one author, region, cult, or even specific time period might influence factors of gender, age, or social class of the people mentioned.

In large samples, mobility problems and paralysis comprise about 25–30% of the total number of instances in the evidence. In these samples, they appear as the first or the second most frequent symptoms.[28] An admittedly rough sketch of the distribution of age and sex in the 105 mobility impairment healing stories offers the following results.[29]

|  | *Children*[30] | *Adults* |
| --- | --- | --- |
| Male | 8 | 58 |
| Female | 14 | 30 |
| More people involved[31] | 0 | 1 |
| **TOTAL** | **22** | **99** |

These numbers bear similarities to the distribution in Gregory of Tours. While with Gregory of Tours, the percentage of children amounts to 20% of the total of cases, the total of children in our sample is 21%. In both samples, there is a rather marked prevalence of adult males over adult females. In contrast with this, girls seem to receive more attention than boys in our sample.[32] A similar sample for visual impairment revealed similar results: 19% of children, more male adults than females, and markedly more girls than boys had visual impairments.[33]

188  *Christian Laes*

Even greater care is needed when quantifying the social network of people who appear to be helping or accompanying people with mobility problems. Miracle stories often focus only on the episode of healing, and therefore leave many things unsaid. As such, we are almost never told whether the disabled had recourse to doctors before they attended shrines for divine help. This reticence does not mean that people never visited doctors; it is just that this is not the concern of the writers of miracle stories.[34] Only in rare cases, the art of medicine is mentioned alongside miraculous healing. When Ursio broke his leg in a hunting accident, falling from his horse, the aid of doctors was sought in vain. Incantations, too, proved useless. After talking to his wife, the couple decided to seek the help of the Holy Oil in the candles at the Saint Praeiectus church. In the end, only this Holy Oil turned out to be helpful.[35]

In the same context, we are usually not told who accompanied those with mobility impairments to the shrines. It often appears as if they got there by themselves. Again, this is a matter of writers, and does not imply that such people were left without the help of parents, relatives, or friends. The following table only hints at possible scenarios, and the small numbers of instances make clear that in the majority of the 105 miracle stories, no help by a third party is mentioned at all.

| *Relation* | *Number of cases* |
|---|---|
| Father–daughter | 3 |
| Father–son | 2 |
| Parents–son | 1 |
| Parents–daughter | 4 |
| Husband–wife | 2 |
| Other relatives | 1 |
| Master–slave | 1 |
| Help by 'others' | 17 |

It appears that in only 29% of the miracle stories concerning mobility impairment explicit attention is paid to who accompanied the patients on their trip to the sanctuary. The biggest segment includes those who are not explicitly acknowledged as family or relatives ('others'); though again, the use of a passive as *portatur* may imply that the carriers were in fact relatives or friends – it is just not specified.[36] Quite unsurprisingly, the Merovingian sources seem to have some preference for the Latin verb *baiulare*, since this word resonates with the Germanic root that we find in the English 'to bear' or the German 'Bahre'. *Baiulare* often denotes the dependency of a younger mobility-impaired child, being carried by one of its parents.[37]

When one separates the cases attesting to family relations, one notices a dominance of parent-children relations. This pattern has already been found by Isabelle Réal in a much larger sample including a wide variety of healing miracles.[38] In all, it emphasises the social nature of care in the context of mobility impairment.

## The *Vita Boniti*: Donning the cap of literary and philological analysis

As I will argue in the next section of this chapter, the greatest value of studying these miracle stories lies in their richness of detail. Such wealth helps greatly to sketch a broader picture concerning the daily lives and possible socialisation of people facing mobility problems, as well as to understand how they were treated and viewed by their contemporaries.

To this, philologists versed in literary criticism might object that such a picture is only created by taking the texts out of their literary context. Indeed, it may be a worthy effort to analyse the function of mobility impairment within one specific *Vita*, thereby pointing to recurring motives, metaphors, or intertextual allusions. As such, each single *Vita* could be subjected to a similar approach. In order to point to the possibilities of such study, I have selected the *Vita Boniti* for analysis. Mobility impairment is an important theme in this story, since no less than five out of twelve miracle stories focus entirely on it. Saint Bonitus (623–709) was a former chancellor of the court of Sigibert III of Austrasia. He was a prominent member of the Merovingian court, who acted as prefect of Marseille and Provence on behalf of Theoderic III, and later as a bishop of Clermont in Auvergne, since 689 when his brother Avitus II had recommended him as his successor. Soon after his ordination as a bishop, he retired to live the life of an eremite, and afterwards to enter the abbey of Manlieu. His life was written around 720, by a monk of the same abbey of Manlieu.

In the most elaborated story about lameness of the *Vita Boniti*, we encounter a woman who originated from France, but actually lived in Britain, 'on the island on the other part of the ocean'. She bears the Celtic name Blada, quite ironically referring to being quick, fast, and agile.[39] She had lost her eyesight long ago time as well as the use of her hands and feet. Travellers from her native country came to pay her a visit. She apparently lived alone: there is no mention, at any rate, of other people in the house who looked after the visitors. Despite the considerable difficulties, which surely did not go unnoticed by her visitors, Blada managed to receive her guests hospitably. At this point, the guests mentioned their patron Bonitus of Auvergne, who, as a bishop, might well be able to release her from her hardships, if she would implore his help through prayers to God. At this point, Blada asked to be brought to a remote place, where she could pray at a quiet spot. Regrettably, the use of the passive *duci* does not make clear whether she asked the visitors to carry her, or if she was helped by people who lived with her. In any case, the prayers had an immediate effect: she regained her eyesight and all her limbs functioned well again. She then decided to leave her country with her parents and her relatives. (Does this mean that she was actually co-habitating with them? The story does not tell us). In other words, she became a pilgrim traveller herself. Just before she reached the town of Auvergne, she incidentally came across the holy man Bonitus, who was about to visit the monastery of Royat. She revealed herself as a pilgrim who had come to the country only to see him. At this point, Bonitus realised that she was in fact indigenous, and asked for further details.[40] Blada told him that she had come to thank him as the benefactor of her wellbeing. Bonitus admired her faith and gratitude and handed her over to the nuns' monastery he was about to visit. In fact, Blada now became a pilgrim, giving up her belongings and home to serve the Lord. Only after the death of Bonitus did she return to her house in Britain.[41]

This story from the *Vita Bonitii* confronts us with recurring themes about mobility impairment. Such impairment causes people to creep to the holy man. The act of creeping is even compared to the movement of snake and reptiles – devilish creatures. The healed are thus restored to their former state, which makes them upright in more than one sense.[42] Those who are healed give themselves to the service of the holy man.[43] During his life, Saint Bonitus is not always aware of his healing powers, which obviously come from God.[44] Even after his death, the mere presence of his holy body is enough to heal the lame.[45]

## Aetiology and symptoms of mobility impairment

Throughout the miracle stories, one finds glimpses of the causes people attributed to mobility impairment. It is immediately clear from the table that in the majority of the cases, the aetiology of the impairment was not of great importance to the hagiographers. What mattered more was the description of the difficult conditions the impaired were facing, and the consequent relief by the divine miracle.[46]

| Cause | Number of instances (percentage) |
|---|---|
| Accident | 2 (2%) |
| Congenital | 7 (7%) |
| Divine punishment | 19 (18%) |
| Illness | 3 (3%) |
| Nerves (dry, contracted) | 9 (8%) |

Despite Jesus' explicit claims of the opposite, the causal correlation between impairment and sin was also made by Christians.[47] For mobility problems, suffering in the hands or feet is explained as a punishment, mostly for working on Sundays. The sin pertains both to men and women.[48] With a total of 18%, the theme of divine punishment is much stronger for mobility impairment than for eye problems.[49] Again, it is social interaction and the community that gave meaning to the impairment. Given the strong intertextual connections between miracle stories and the Gospels, one should not be surprised by this link between mobility impairment and sin. In fact, Jesus himself in two healings of the paralysed referred to their sinful lives.[50] Still, one should be careful with making a general conclusion, claiming that medieval disabilities were often connected with sin and guilt. The theme of disability as a punishment seems to be a typical pre-occupation of certain authors, not the least Gregory of Tours. In the case of parents and children, both Jenni Kuuliala and Irina Metzler have demonstrated that the idea of (parental) sin causing disability is quite rare in the medieval sources.[51]

Medieval hagiographers linked paralysis with dryness of the nerves. In the same way that plants languish and slowly die without sufficient water, so people became immobilised because of problems with the 'humours'.[52] Though such a view of immobility in our eyes belongs to the medical realm, the distinction between religious and physiological aetiology was not always that sharp. In the case of a man from Rome who from early infancy could move only his tongue and his head and was carried around in a coffin, we read that the devil had caused the contraction of the nerves.[53] In the same *Vita*, a girl named Sinclisia was healed of her congenital mobility impairment, caused by a worm in her body and by a (further unspecified) sin, by contact with a saint's grave.[54] 'Contraction of the nerves' (*contractio nervorum*) and/or some form of 'dried nerves' indeed turns up in some descriptions of paralysis, though the total of 9 out of 105 stories only counts for 8%.[55] Other sources mention illnesses as the cause of immobility: dropsy,[56] gout,[57] and 'an unknown illness'.[58] A hunting accident and the consequent breaking of an arm and other limbs,[59] and a fall[60] are the only other instances of cases in which causes are mentioned.

In the description of symptoms, the most plastic descriptions of the contracted hand stand out.[61] Some stories focus on the duration of the paralysing infirmity,[62] sometimes with emphasising the congenital nature of the disorder.[63] In one case, the illness is explicitly mentioned as incurable.[64] When only symptoms are mentioned, scholars (and the general audience) are sometimes tempted by retrospective diagnosis, using the information in the ancient texts to figure out what was 'really' (i.e. medically) going on. Many studies, however, have warned against such interpretations.[65] It thus makes little sense to search for an explanation like Parkinson's disease in the case of heavily trembling hands, though the possibility cannot be ruled out entirely.[66] In the same way, nothing definite can be said about a medical condition like dwarfism in the case of 'a little man' who faced considerable problems in walking.[67] Swelling due to the presence of humidity is also mentioned in the sources. Again, one might associate this with a certain medical condition, though no further diagnosis is certain.[68] Some sources also indicate a paralysis of the tongue, causing muteness or at least difficult speech as an additional impairment.[69]

## Social realities, attitudes and reactions

Just as there is relative silence on who accompanied the mobility impaired, the majority of the stories do not focus on the social origin of those who sought for healing.

Some, surely, belonged to the more privileged social classes or were at least secured by their social environment.[70] We read about consecrated virgins in a nuns' monastery.[71] As a young man, Lupus was the favourite of his abbot Odo.[72] Some could resort to the aid and assistance of the most noble in society. In the year 782, a little girl who suffered from severe contraction of the knees was brought to Queen Hildegard to ask for help and alms. The queen took the girl to the monastery of Saint Gertrude in Nivelles. In the monastery, where the girl grew up, the nuns even provided a *peregrina*, who gave the girl her primary education. Saint Gertrude appeared many times to her in visions, and eventually she was healed. After her recovery, the family came to visit her in the monastery.[73] Some of the mobility impaired in our sources were married.[74] A *matrona* from Marseilles was carried around by her slaves. Being content with just touching the clothes of Saint Caesarius when he passed by – an obvious allusion to Luke 8:44 – she was forever grateful for the healing and the blessing she received.[75] Other stories also refer to the healing of married women of status.[76] Not a single source, however, mentions a mobility impairment before contracting the marriage.[77]

The condition of severe mobility impairment was sometimes associated with a life of begging.[78] In Bourges, a contracted poor man named Beroadus was found in rags under the gutter of a house. The noble consecrated Lady Bertoara had him carried to the church of Saint Austregisilus by her servants. He had longed to visit for a long time, but nobody had ever wanted to take him there. Eventually, he was healed after bathing in the sanctuary.[79] The paralysed are depicted as 'lying on the street',[80] in the entrance of a public building or just inside public space.[81] In such cases, we may presume a life of begging. In one instance, this is stated explicitly. We read about a lame person and a blind person who were begging for alms. When the saint says he is able to give neither gold nor silver, the beggars resort to violence. In the end, their belief and the signing by the cross causes their recovery.[82] We rarely learn anything about the living conditions of beggars who were, but in the case of an anonymous woman from the Alpine region who was cured by Eucherius (after Caesarius persuaded him to do so), we read that she, at least, had a little home to return to.[83] In this case, the inability to perform any other work and the necessity of providing an income for her family might have led the woman to beg. In this way, she was still communally integrated, as she made a living by the only work she could perform.[84]

Some stories point to the paralysed making use of specific instruments to make their way. These include walking sticks, crutches, or low footstools.[85] In extreme cases, they made their way by crawling.[86] Rarely, the use of a donkey or a horse is mentioned,[87] while only the most wealthy were carried around in a cart of their own.[88] The stories, and surely the side remarks one finds in them, offer us glimpses of common attitudes towards the mobility impaired. The most striking to modern sensitivities is the comparison of the paralysed person with a corpse, and recurring terms or descriptions as *cadaver*; *quasi mortuus*, or *quasi funus*. While the metaphor was mainly used to plastically describe the condition of immobility of the person concerned, one remains struck by the somewhat crude undertone.[89] Again, a nuanced approach is necessary. Such testimonies act as powerful rhetorical means to highlight the saint's power in restoring the patient back to full social life, much more than to stress the socially liminal position of those afflicted by mobility impairment.[90] One would indeed do injustice to the sources by stressing their negative undertone. Indeed, throughout the 105 miracle stories studied in this collection, there is little or no trace of derision or mockery of those with mobility impairments. For sure, derision was sometimes a social reality, but even in the detailed late medieval canonisation processes it appeared in very few individual cases. In the same way as the connotation with guilt and sin (see note

47), derisive remarks were preoccupations of specific writers.[91] Again, the sometimes very elaborate descriptions of miserable physical conditions and the consequences for the person concerned serve as a means to emphasise the greatness of the miracle performed by the saints or their relics.

Moreover, the paralysed, whether male or female, are sometimes depicted as strong agents, who took great care and initiative to rid themselves of conditions which severely hindered their lives. Thus, a *paralyticus* from Tours, who had been lying at the portico of a monastery, was persuaded by a vision to go to Vézelay to visit the holy man Pardulfus in order to be healed. He managed to persuade a monk to bring the case to the abbot, who eventually gave the poor man a donkey and two servants in order to make the arduous journey.[92] In the same way, a woman named Sigrada saw Saint Anstrudis in a vision, in which the saint healed her by anointing her arms and whole body with Holy Oil. Sigrada awoke and asked to be brought to the cathedral of Saint John the Baptist in Laon, where she prayed to Anstrudis and recovered fully, released of any pain.[93] A young man from Italy was so severely contracted in his limbs that he was not able to use any of them. Besides this, the nerves of his eyes, ears, and tongue were functioning so badly that he had been blind, deaf, and mute for almost three years. Despite all these impairments, he was admonished in a dream to travel to Paris, a journey he performed with the aid of a servant and a horse. Even in Paris, his belief and endurance were severely tested, and his first nights in the church of Saint Peter did not bring him any cure. Finally, the monks who were chanting the dominical matins were faced with a man who joyfully and loudly testified of his full recovery.[94] One can only marvel at the strength and courage of Aldefredus, who was born 'blind and crippled'. At age 80, he visited Saint Peter's tomb in Rome, where he was told to go to Saint Martin in Tours to get rid of his mobility impairment, and then to return to his native Antrim in Ireland to regain his eyesight.[95] Sometimes, patients themselves take the initiative, with holy men not being aware of their own powers of healing (see note 41). A paralysed woman with a hunchback, who had asked her neighbours to bring her to church, dared to address the holy man Austregisilus when he was saying mass. What followed was a touching dialogue, in which the saint eventually persuaded the woman that it is God who heals, and that after her healing she should never return to her sinful life.[96]

All in all, one has to keep in mind that in everyday life, many debilitating conditions must have gone by unnoticed. Despite their condition, most people just worked and made the best of it.[97] Their impairment did not significantly change their societal life. Such was the case with a 'senior and crippled' labourer (*senior et claudus*) who was travelling with a group of labourers. Saint Germanus helped him to cross a torrential river, by carrying his heavy axe and taking the man himself on his shoulders.[98]

## Conclusions

Tackling the issue of mobility impairment in the Merovingian miracle stories inevitably means facing the specific nature of the literary genre with which one is dealing. Compared to the information on impairment found in the thirteenth- or fourteenth-century canonisation processes, the Merovingian information is much more succinct. Indeed, the canonisation documents show laypeople from different social groups, describing in exceptionally rich testimonies conditions of impairment and events of miraculous cures. They offer us many details on various items about physical limitations and pain, inability to work, emotions and fear about the future, reactions in the family and the wider community, folk medicine and healing practices, and lived experiences of the impaired (the assumed origin of the impairment, social sphere and interaction, experienced bodily difference, self-image, and inclusion or exclusion).[99] Taking a closer look at the Merovingian miracle stories, however, shows that there is no reason to 'envy' the richer material other medievalists have at their disposal. Though written from the standpoint of literate hagiographers, the Merovingian *miracula* do actually reveal information about most of the issues mentioned above, albeit often in side remarks or through powerful rhetoric, in which the emphasis on physical conditions of pain, or familial and communal distress were meant to highlight the powers and virtues of the healing saints. As such, reading through the sources offers a richness of detail, not only about the daily lives of people with mobility impairment, but also on thoughts and attitudes regarding their experiences.

In the context of the present book volume, this brings us to the question of if there was anything as specific as a Merovingian mobility impairment. As for all questions regarding continuity and change, the issue needs to be approached with due methodological care, taking into account the level on which the presumed change took place and to which extent the sources under study allow us to claim such change.

Certainly, there were differences between this and the Roman, non-Christian period. The Merovingian discourse focused more on dryness and the *contractio nervorum* as a physiological explanation for paralysis. The vocabulary of mobility impairment in miracle stories was very much the terminology of paralysis in the Gospels. At least in these stories, the doctor's role was taken over by the saint and the miracle worker. For people who were searching for help, often as a last resort, monasteries, shrines, and churches replaced the role of pagan sanctuaries as institutions for care, support, and possibly miraculous relief. On the level of popular mentalities, personal sin and divine punishment were explanatory factors for mobility impairment, though this chapter again showed that it would be rash to see sin and moralistic explanations as the overarching Merovingian approach towards mobility impairment. The Merovingian miracle stories do not allow any claims about the evolution from original towards individual sin or a higher awareness of the themes of sin and death,[100] nor do they allow the use of symbols in literature, in which via the interplay between written and oral culture, the miracle healer took over the role of the physician.[101]

In fact, the stories treated in this chapter enabled us to encounter 'lived realities', memories and attitudes towards mobility impairment. They do so in a much more elaborate way than any other source from Antiquity. While we are mostly faced with the viewpoint of the external audience, careful reading also offers us glimpses of personal experiences. Surely, there was not a 'single' experience of mobility impairment. The miracles confront us with a wide range of explanations, solutions, possibilities, emotions, and attitudes. What stands out is the effort taken to include the infirm as much as possible into the community. In a society where mobility was not nearly the issue it is today, those who moved around with difficulty were part and parcel of the communal environment. Even making a living by begging could be an option to provide for the necessary family income. For sure, this communal concept does not allow for generalising or optimistic interpretations. No doubt, physical conditions were often painful, and working was the only option, despite the pain. As the story about Blada shows, pilgrimage and seeking for healing could also be part of this 'lived reality', though most of our sources are silent about those who took the effort to do so.

In the future, historians of disabilities will use detailed archaeological records and assess them with modern approaches as kinaesthetics. As such, (difficult) movement and mobility can be used to understand the way people experienced (religious) space.[102] Meanwhile, this careful reading of a large collection of sources not only contributes to the history of late ancient and early medieval disabilities, but also to the understanding of (im)mobility in a period of transition.

## Notes

1 Banniard 1989, 13. For language revision of this article I am most grateful to Lynn Rose (American University of Iraq, Sulaimani). Most of this chapter was written during a Senior Research Fellowship (2014–2016) at the Institute for Advanced Social Research at the University of Tampere. Due to the nature of the evidence, this article contains a lot of references to the texts of the *Monumenta Germania Historica. Scriptores Rerum Merovingicarum* (MGH SRM) now conveniently consultable on http://www.dmgh.de. To facilitate the reading of this article, I have included Latin quotations from the texts whenever needed. However, in order not to this chapter overload with copious quotation, I often only quote key words, understandable by themselves, without citing entire phrases. Between brackets, I always indicate the volume and the page number of the MGH SRM, so that readers may easily trace down the passage concerned.
2 Laes and Vuolanto 2017, 258–282 follows five generations of such writers, starting from the late fourth century. The most radical stress on change and a civilisation lost is undoubtedly by Ward-Perkins 2005.
3 For essential studies on the subject, see Wood 2008; Wickham 2009, 111–129.
4 Wickham 2005, 12 (cities, agriculture and economy). Self-sufficient: Devroey 2001, 97–129.
5 Böhme 2007, 211–226.
6 Wickham 2009, 111–129 and 575–577 sketches a nuanced picture of socio-economic conditions in Merovingian Gaul. See also Effros 2002.
7 Böhme 2007 has stressed the aristocratic side of the matter, while Goetz 2009, 21–55 points to *debiles* as social outcasts.
8 Sigal 1971, 193–211; De Mol 2015; Van den Abeele 2016.
9 See the most valuable study by Réal 2001. See also Laes 2011.
10 http://whoint/topics.
11 Thus Laes 2014, 166–168; Baroin 2018 [forthcoming]; Kuuliala 2016, 32–33. Baroin offers the most extensive account of terminology of mobility impairment in classical Latin. Current terms as *titubare* or *vacillare* do not entirely disappear in the

Merovingian sources, but they hardly ever are used in the context of mobility impairment. Note that also Baroin includes problems with the hands.

12 The miracle stories include: Mt. 9:1–8; Mc. 2:1–12; Lc. 5:17–26 (the lame man from Kafarnäum); Joh. 5:1–18 (lame at the Betzeta bath house); Acts 3:1–10 (lame from birth at the Speciosa Gate); Lc. 13:10–17 (benched woman); Mt. 8:5–13; Lc. 7:1–10; Joh. 5:46–52 (servant of the centurio; or son of the official); Acts 9:32–35 (Peter healing Eneas, eight years in bed).

13 See Kuuliala 2016, 33 for terms in later medieval sources. Contrary to Kuuliala, I have not included the terms *impotens* or *morbus* in my search, since they do not specifically point to immobility. On p. 34, Kuuliala offers a rich vocabulary of terms connoting medical conditions of mobility impairments. These rather technical words seem specific for accounts in canonisation processes, as they do not appear in the Merovingian miracle stories (e.g. *inflatura, mengassa, scrofula*).

14 See Saller 2012, 71–86, spec. 72 for a summary of this research and the example of the French population.

15 Killgrove 2010. See Killgrove 2019 and Kron 2019 for a recent status quaestionis on this controversy.

16 Saller 2012, 72.

17 Rose 2003.

18 When there exists such research, it often concerns a later period, as the tenth to sixteenth century. See http://www.vlaamsewerkgroepmedievistiek.org/wp-content/uploads/2015/06/Programma-colloquium-2015-Abdijmuseum-Ten-Duinen.pdf. There are very few references to the Merovigians in Roberts and Manchester 1995 (see p. 177 about a cemetery in South-Germany, from the years 500 to 700). The research by William Southwell-Wright rather focuses on Roman and early medieval Britain. See e.g. Southwell-Wright 2014, 111–131. For a rare study on Merovingian burial, see Effros 2000, 232–239. Interesting insights on osteology, disability history and everyday life in Ulrich-Boschler 2009.

19 Hähn 2017, 367–369 on these three case stories, with further references to archaeological and osteological specialised literature.

20 Böhme 2007, 214–215.

21 Böhme 2007, 217. See Laes 2011, 46 for instances of protheses in Antiquity and with Gregory of Tours. For the Middle Ages, see Kahlow 2009, 201–223.

22 In seventh century Nubia, a painting in a church shows a man who carries a cane and seems to have unsure footing. See Richardson 2012, 40. For early Roman Italy, Graham 2017 has extensively made use of the evidence of ex-voto's.

23 For extensive accounts, see Nehlsen 1972; von Olberg 1991. Only the punishment of blinding lends itself to more detailed studies for the history of disability. See Büttner 2009, 47–72.

24 See Kuuliala 2017, 343–346.

25 Laes 2011, 56 lists the (meagre) evidence for Gregory of Tours' *Historia Francorum*.

26 Réal 2001, 13–44 offers an introduction to the *Vitae* and their audience, as well as bibliographical details on quite some separate Vitae (46–58). An excellent introduction is Van Dam 1993.

27 Laes 2011 deals with the first volume of the MGH SRM, namely the writings by Gregory of Tours. See particularly p. 46–47 on paralysis and mobility impairment.

28 Laes 2011, 42–43 mentions 31% in the case of children and 25% in the case of adults for the *Octo Libri Miraculorum* by Gregory of Tours, where they appear as the most frequent symptom. De Mol 2015, 13, mentions 23% (second symptom after mental disorders).

29 When a miracle records two persons, I have counted them as two persons in the list. However, in order not to distort the evidence by singles instances as the healing of, say, ten *paralytici*, all cases in which more than two persons are involved have been

catalogued under 'more people involved'. When it is not explicitly stated that a child is involved, a case is always recorded in the category of adults. Particular problems come to the fore in the case of *filius/filia* being mentioned. Since all these sons or daughters are mentioned in the context of being cared for by their parents, I have included them in the category of children, though this cannot be ascertained beyond doubt. Even more difficult are the numerous instances of *pueri/puellae*, who can also be servants. When it is clear from the story that servants were meant, I have catalogued them under the heading 'adults', otherwise they are recorded as child.

30 Sometimes, the use of age terminology is ambivalent and problematic. In *Vita Rigoberti episcopi Remensis* 21 (7.60) we are entitled to think that the *iuvenis scolaris* was a boy attending school. However, other instances of *iuvenis* rather point to a young man, in his vigorous years, and not a child. See e.g. *Vita Faronis episcopi Meldensis* 118 (5.198) or *Vita Austrigisili episcopi Biturgi* 15 (4.199).

31 The instances where it is only generally recorded that 'the lame walked again', without referring to particular miracles, are not included in this table (see e.g. *Vita Nicetii episcopi Lugdunensis* 15 (3.524): *dum iugiter atque indesinenter populo teste clodis gressum, caecis visum, demoniacis remedium (...) confert*).

32 Laes 2011, 42 for Gregory of Tours.

33 Van den Abeele 2016, 7. The proportion girls:boys is 15–2.

34 See *Vita Germani episcopi Parisiaci auctore Venantio Fortunato* 27 (7.388–389) on a woman who first resorted to medicine (*postulans medicinam*). It may not be coincidental that she is called a *mulier barbara*. Canonisation processes on the contrary do explain former attempts as seeing a doctor or folk medicine and healing practices. See Kuuliala 2016, 198–220 (doctors) and 220–228 (folk medicine).

35 *Passio Praeecti episcopi et martyris Arverni* 38 (5.247). See also *Vita Germani episcopi Parisiaci auctore Venantio Fortunato* 38 (7.395) on Holy Oil being better than any art of doctors (*omnem artem medicorum*).

36 Typical cases which stress the dependency on others include: *Vita Ermenlandi abbatis Antrensis auctore Donato* 27 (5.708) (*bonorum devectus hominum iuvamine*); *Vita Ermenlandi abbatis Antrensis auctore Donato* 28 (5.709) (*a deferentibus ... aliorum iuvamine*); *Vita Anstrudis abbatissae Laudunensis* 32 (6.76) (*portare se fecit*).

37 *Vita Ermenlandi abbatis Antrensis auctore Donato* 25 (5.707) (*puer*, carried by his father); *Vita Trudonis* 26 (6.295) (*puer*, carried by his father) *Vita Trudonis* 30 (6.297) (adult woman); *Vita Germani episcopi Parisiaci auctore Venantio Fortunato* 38 (7.395) (on a *puer admodum parvulus*); *Translatio Germani episcopi Parisiaci* 2 (7.424–426) (adult man carried to church by a monk).

38 Réal 2011, 442 (table).

39 Holder 1961–1962, 443; De Mol 2015, 20.

40 Here, the editor understands *indigena* as *indigens* ('in need, poor'), but I believe it makes more sense to understand it as 'native', given the information that in Britain Blada was visited by fellow countrymen from Auvergne (*gentis suae peregrini*).

41 *Vita Boniti* 14 (6.126–127): 'Per iddem tempus, cum fama beati pontificis celeberrima haberetur, ut non solum in vicinis urbibus set aetiam oceanis partibus citra maris littora insulam, quam Britanorum gens sita aeccor continens vallat, pervenerit: nam in eadem provincia mulier quedam erat nomine *Blada*, qui *dudum* lumen oculorum amiserat necnon *manuum hac pedum officio destituta* manebat. Quadam namque die, cum gentis suae *peregrini in domo eius hospitalitatis gratia* declinassent et eam ita corporis difficultate laborantem cernerent, aiunt ad eam: "O mulier, si adsercioni nostrae accomodaris fidem, ut beati Boniti Arvernae urbis episcopi intervencionem apud Deum comendares, nos credimus, nec dubium est, quia vir sanctus potest apud Dominum tuum hunc allevare *laborem*". At illa hoc audito gavisa sermone, *foras se in remociorem locum duci praecepit*, statimque ut ex oracione e terra surrexit, lumen oculorum ac membrorum recepit sanitatem. Vidensque erga se ob viri Dei meritum

Domini tantae pietatis inesse virtutem, *relicto proprio solo parentibusque suisque omnibus*, ad beatum virum Arvernorum glebotenus pervenit. Cumque propter urbem pene iam *peregrina* gradaretur, vir Domini inopinatus ei obviam factus est. Ipse autem Rubiacensem cenobium, quod hinc indeque montibus septus, ab oriente panditur aditum et aut procul eminet urbi, visendi gratia consulendique adire properabat. Mulier in ipso initere humili eum atque supplici voce conpellens, se *peregrinam et ob eius famam advenisse* praedixit. Cumque ille, ut ei moris erat, eam *indigenam* cognovisset, paululum substitit, et quid vellet requisivit. At illa adventus sui causam per ordinem pandit eumque suae salutis apud omnipotentem Dominum auctorem declamat. Ille eius fidem atque devotionem miratus, eam secum ad monasterium ire praecepit atque matri ipsius monasterii tradens suaeque nepti *in coetu virginum conmendavit*. Ubi aliquamdiu degens, *post discessum beati viri ad proprium repedans solum, id est ad Britanicum rus regressa est.*'

42  *Vita Boniti* 12 (6.125): '*quidam in eodem itinere claudus postergum eum quo poterat conamine sequens*'; *Vita Boniti* 37 (6.137): *Nam quaedam puella Deo Dicata ad sepulcrum beati viri paralitica reptando, cunctis videntibus, venit*. See De Mol 2015, 23.

43  *Vita Boniti* 37 (6.137): the *puella Deo dicata* is admonished in a dream to remove the bars around the corpse of the saint and to give part of the relics back to Bonitus' home town; 41 (6.138–19): a *claudus* named Waldinus remains in the church as a ward after he got healed by the passing by of the corpse of Saint Bonitus.

44  *Vita Boniti* 12 (6.125): about a lame man approaching him (*Vir quoque Domini protinus eius infirmitatis misertus, paululum substitit, ignarus, quid posceret homo*). Saint Bonitus jocularly replies that the imposing of his hand might be compared to that of the contact with the feet of a cow. The man gets healed since Bonitus was a worker on the yards of God, in much the same way as a cow or an ox are ploughing the fields.

45  *Vita Boniti* 31 (6.134); 37 (6.137); 41 (6.138–139).

46  Contrary to canonisation processes, where people under interrogation went into details on the causes of the illness or infirmity. See Kuuliala 2016, 34 and 82–105.

47  For Late Antiquity, this way of thinking is particularly stressed by Kelley 2009, 199–216; Kelley 2011, 205–222.

48  *Vita Sancti Arnulfi* 19 (2.440) (woman, working on Sunday; *utraque manu contracta*); *Vita Sancti Arnulfi* 28 (2.445) (woman, working on Sunday; *manu contracta*); *Vita et virtutes Eparchii reclusi Ecolismensis* 15–16 (3.557–558) (man, being a recluse without clerical ordination; *digita palmis adfixa*); *Vita Austrigisili episcopi Biturgi* 9 (4.197) (woman who led a sinful life; *aridis membris, nervis contractis, incurvata*); *Vita Austrigisili episcopi Biturigi* 13 (4.198–199) (miller, working on Sunday; *manus adhaesit manubrio ferri illius*); *Vita Desiderii Cadurcae urbis episcopi* 39 (4.594) (cleric, punished for foul language, no healing; *officium manus dexterae amittere, a pedis gressu impediri, linguae usu denudari*); *Vita Desiderii Cadurcae urbis episcopi* 40 (4.594) (woman, divine punishment; *nervorum contractio*); *Vita Menelei abbatis Menatensis* 1.16–20 (5.144–146) (male, tried to murder the saint; blindness and *flexibiles digiti*); *Vita Dagobertis regis Francorum* 16 (5.522) (woman, weaving on the feast of the saint; *contrahuntur digiti ut ungulae*); *Miracula Audomari* 2 (5.776) (young boy, punishment for stealing grapes; *debilis*); *Vita Trudonis* 24 (6.293) (man, as a punishment for marrying; *claudicatio*); *Vita Trudonis* 26 (6.295) (boy, punishment for murdering a slave; *debilis, contractus*); *Vita Hugberti episcopi Traiectensis* 4 (6.485) (man, baking bread on Sunday; *digiti adflicti in palma, ungulae transpunctae ligati*); *Vita Corbiniani* 36 (6.588) (girl as a punishment for foul language; *claudicare*); *Vita Germani episcopi Parisiensis* 13 (7.382–383) (man, working on Sunday; *digitis contrahi*); *Vita Germani episcopi Parisiensis* 16 (7.383; girl/ slave, weaving on Sunday; *stupentes digiti*); *Vita Germani episcopi Parisiensis* 35 (7.394) (man, working as a sandal maker on Sunday; *debilitas manuum vel pedum*); *Vita Germani*

*episcopi Parisiensis* 49 (7.403) (man, working on Sunday; *digitis intumescere* and putrification of the arm); *Vita Germani episcopi Parisiensis* 57 (7.407) (man, working on Sunday; *manu contracta*).

49 Van den Abeele 2016, 32 only counts 6.5% (6 cases out of 91 stories).
50 Mt 9:2–5: *Et videns Iesus fidem illorum, dixit paralytico: "Confide, fili; remittuntur peccata tua". Et ecce quidam de scribis dixerunt intra se: "Hic blasphemat". Et cum vidisset Iesus cogitationes eorum, dixit: "Ut quid cogitatis mala in cordibus vestris? Quid enim est facilius, dicere: "Dimittuntur peccata tua", aut dicere: "Surge et ambula"?*; Joh. 5:14: *Postea invenit eum Iesus in templo et dixit illi: "Ecce sanus factus es; iam noli peccare, ne deterius tibi aliquid contingat.* See Kelley, cit. (n. 46) 209 and A. Allély, "Les enfants handicapés, infirmes et malformés à Rome en dans l'Empire romain pendant l'Antiquité tardive", *Pallas* 102 (2018) [forthcoming] on this connection, and the way patristic authors dealt with it.
51 Van Dam 1993, 87–88; Laes 2011, 51 on Gregory of Tours' preoccupation with the theme. Nuanced approaches, avoiding generalisations on disabilities and sin with Metzler 2006, 67 and 142; Kuuliala 2016, 82–105.
52 On this particular hagiographical concept of the link between dryness and being lame, opposed to physiological explanations by e.g. Galen, see Sigal 1971, 197–200.
53 *Vita Desiderii episcopi Vienensis* 2.10 (3.641–642): *Quidam homo pauperculus Romana origine natus, iam per multa loca iactatus (...) intercedente peccato, imminente diabolo universa loca nervorum suorum fuerant nimietate adtracta ut solo tanto capud et lingua a gestantibus agitaret* (Du Cange= *prima ab infantia*). He is carried around in a coffin: *coffino quo gerebatur*. He begs to be at the place of the martyr, and finally he gets healed. See also the marked detail: *veluti ut truncum se precatus est proiciendum*.
54 *Vita Desiderii episcopi Vienensis* 2.11 (3.642): daughter Sinclisia: *Et cum exigente causa peccati, a nativitate verme adherente crudele absque aliqua salute dampnata claudicaretur assidue et paene diffideret se nulla posse sanandi invenire fortuna*.
55 *Vita Sanctae Genovefae virginis Parisiensis* 33 (3.229); *Vita Sulpicii episcopi Biturigi* 9 (4.378–379); *Vita Wilifridi episcopi Eboracensis* 65 (6.261); *Vita Germani episcopi Autissiodorensis auctore Constantio* 26–27 (7.270–271); *Vita Germani episcopi Autissiodorensis auctore Constantio* 30 (7.273–274); *Vita Germani episcopi Parisiaci auctore Venantio Fortunato* 27 (7.388–389); *Vita Germani episcopi Parisiaci auctore Venantio Fortunato* 45 (7.400). Elaborate technical descriptions of the *contractio nervorum* occur in *Vita Germani episcopi Autissiodorensis auctore Constantio* 30 (7.273–274); *Translatio Germani episcopi Parisiaci* 2 (7.424–426).
56 *Vita Anstrudis abbatissae Laudunensis* 31 (6.76) (*hydropica*).
57 *Vita Germani episcopi Parisiensis auctore Venantio Fortunato* 47 (7.401–402) (*podagrae vulnere*).
58 *Vita Trudonis confessoris Hansbaniensis auctore Donato* 31 (6.297–298) (*nescio qua egritudine*).
59 *Passio Praeecti episcopi et martyris Arverni* 38 (5.247).
60 *Vita Caesarii episcopi Arelatensis* 2.25 (3.493) (*casu pede luxavit*).
61 See e.g. *Vita Hugberti episcopi Traiectensis* 4 (6.485): *digiti adflicti in palma, ungulae transpunctae ligati*; *Vita Dagobertis regis Francorum* 16 (5.522): *contrahuntur digiti ut ungulae*; *Vita Germani episcopi Autissiodorensis auctore Constantio* 30 (7.273–274): *crescentibus introrsum nimie unguentibus, cedente carnis teneritudine, tot inciperent esse vulnera quam digiti*. The two former cases deal with punishments for sins.
62 *Vita Lupi episcopi Trecensis* 9 (7.300) (ten months); *Vita Sanctae Genovefae virginis Parisiensis* 33 (3.229); (two years); *Vita Sanctae Genovefae virginis Parisiensis* 36 (3.230) (four years); *Vita Austrigisili episcopi Biturigi* 15 (4.199) (long time); *Miracula Austrigisili episcopi Biturigi* 18 (4.208) (many years); *Vita Sulpicii episcopi Biturigi*

9 (4.378–379) (long time); *Vita Anstrudis abbatissae Laudunensis* 32 (6.76) (eight years); *Vita Trudonis* 30 (6.297) (many years); *Vita Eligii episcopi Noviomagensis* 1.27 (4.685–686) (many years); *Vita Gamalberti presbyteri Michaelsbuchensis* 10 (nine years) (7.191).

63 *Virtutum Sanctae Geretrudis continuatio* 4 (2.473–474) (*a primevo aetatis suae*); *Vita Fridolini confessoris* 30 (3.368) (*a primis infantiae annis*); *Vita Desiderii episcopi Vienensis* 2.10 (3.641–642); *Vita Ermenlandi Abbatis Antrensis auctore Donato* 25 (5.707); *Vita Ermenlandi Abbatis Antrensis auctore Donato* 27 (5.708) (on an 80-year-old who was blind and lame from birth); *Vita Pardulfi abbatis Waractensis* 10 (7.30–31) *(ab utero matris suae)*; *Vita Germani episcopi Autissiodorensis auctore Constantio* 30 (7.273–274).

64 *Vita Fridolini confessoris* 30 (3.368) (*inremediabili miserabiliter debilitatus paralysi*).

65 See, among many others: Graumann 2000; Karenberg and Moog 2004.

66 *Vita Caesarii episcopi Arelatensis* 2.16 (3.490): *mulier ... quae tam horribilem infirmitatem incurrerat ut die noctuque incessanter manus eius ita inter se colliderentur, quasi aliquid volventes*. Constant trembling of hands and head also occur in *Vita Winnoci* 28 (5.775).

67 *Vita Sancti Arnulfi* 29 (2.445): *homuncio ... nequiter pedibus contractus*.

68 On humid and swelling, see e.g. *Vita Maximi episcopi Treverensis* 16 (3.80): *tibiam atque pedem humor noxius arefecerat*.

69 *Vita Fridolini confessoris* 30 (3.368) (stresses complete muteness); *Vita Desiderii Cadurcae urbis episcopi* 39 (4.594); *Vita Germani episcopi Parisiaci auctore Venantio Fortunato* 38 (7.395) (*nec lingua sonans volubili*); *Vita Winnoci* 28 (5.775); *Vita Germani episcopi Parisiaci auctore Venantio Fortunato* 45 (7.400–401) (*muta, cloda vel manca*); *Translatio Germani episcopi Parisiaci* 2 (7.424–426). See also *Vita Germani episcopi Parisiaci auctore Venantio Fortunato* 47 (7.401–402) for a family healing in which, next to the father being healed from gout, also his daughter is healed. The girl was blind, deaf and mute.

70 *Vita Sanctae Genovefae virginis Parisiensis* 33 (3.229) (*puella de ministerio*, referring to a servant girl, serving a large household).

71 *Vita Anstrudis abbatissae Laudunensis* 24 (6.75) (*quaedam Deo sacrata*); *Vita Boniti* 37 (6.137) (*puella Deo dicata*); *Vita Wilfridi I. episcopi Eboracensis auctore Stephano* 65 (6.260–261) (*paupercula sancta monialis*)

72 *Vita Faronis episcopi Meldensis* 118 (5.197–198).

73 *Virtutum Sanctae Gertrudis continuatio* 4 (4.473–474).

74 *Vita Trudonis* 24 (6.293) (married man); *Vita Germani episcopi Parisiaci auctore Venantio Fortunato* 47 (7.401–402) (married man).

75 *Vita Caesarii episcopi Arelatensis* 2.25 (3.493–494).

76 *Passio Acaunensium martyrum* 18 (3.89) (*materfamilias Quinti egregii atque honorati viri*); *Vita Lupi episcopi Trecensis* 9 (7.300) (*clarissima matrisfamilias*).

77 Also Kuuliala 2016, 116–118 mentions that the sources are mainly silent about people with physical impairments entering marriage. Surely facial deformity seems to have been an impediment. See p. 117 for an adult woman who had been limping from birth who had a son.

78 *Vita Galli auctore Walafrido* 1.31 (4.309) (*quidam mendicus*). See also *Vita Eligii episcopi Noviomagensis* 1.27 (4.685–686) (begging for alms).

79 *Vita Austrigisili episcopi Biturigi* 10 (4.197–198).

80 *Virtutes Fursei abbatis Latiniacensis* 18 (4.446) (*iacebat in via*); *Passio Leudegardi* 2.30 (5.353) (*in via iacens*).

81 *Vita Eligii episcopi Noviomagensis* 1.27 (4.685–686) (*pro foribus iacentem*); *Passio Leudegardi* 2.31 (5.355) (*iacebat in atrio*); *Vita Boniti* 41 (6.139) (*in foribus iacens*); *Vita Lupi episcopi Trecensis* 6 (7.299): *prostrata corpore in aggere publico*; *Vita Pardulfi* 14 (7.32) (five years *in porticu*).

## Pedes habent et non ambulabunt 201

82 *Vita Vedastris episcopi Atrebatensis* 5 (3.409): *clodus et caecus; alimonium postulantes (...) illi attentius pulsant ac de industria pecuniam quam haberet extorquere vim nitebantur.*
83 *Vita Caesarii* 1.47 (3.475): *in media strata infelix et infirma mulier (...) manibus pedibusque contractis, per terram reptabat.* After the healing: *pedibus suis atque omnibus membris recuperatis, ad hospitiolum suum incolumis ambulavit.*
84 On begging and disability, see also Laes 2011, 46–47; Metzler 2006, 165–167; Kuuliala 2016, 63–71.
85 *Vita Sancti Arnulfi* 29 (2.445) (*baculis; crociis*: the latter word referring to crutches as in the German word Krücke); *Vita Sulpicii episcopi Biturigi* 9 (4.378–379) (*sustentatione baculi*); *Vita Ermenlandi abbatis Antrensis auctore Donato* 28 (5.709) (*baculo*); *Vita Corbiniani* 36 (6.588) (*binis baculis*); *Vita Pardulfi abbatis Waractensis* 10 (7.30–31) (*cum scabello gradiebatur*); *Vita Rigoberti* 20 (7.74) (*bacilli* and *scabella* are mentioned as reminders of the illness); *Miracula Austrigisili episcopi Biturigi* 18 (4.208) (*baculo*); *Vita Richarii confessoris Centulensis auctore Alcuino* 15 (4.399) (*sustentacula infirmitatis* as reminders in the sanctuary).
86 *Vita Caesarii* 1.47 (3.475) (*reptabat*); *Vita Boniti* 37 (6.137) (*reptando*); *Vita Trudonis* 30 (6.297) (*aut niteretur manibus*); *Vita Gamalberti presbyteri Michaelbuchensis* 10 (7.191) (*reptaret*). In the latter case, note the addition that the man was creeping as a four-footed animal (*quasi quadrupes*). For the symbolic meaning of creeping, see supra note 41.
87 *Vita Pardulfi* 14 (7.32) (monks sends two servants and a donkey); *Translatio Germani episcopi Parisiaci* 2 (7.424–426) (horse and servant).
88 *Vita Desiderii episcopi Vienensis* 2.10 (3.641–642) (*coffino*); *Vita Caesarii episcopi Arelatensis* 2.25 (3.494) (*manibus sustentata servulorum suorum*). Note however that in generalising descriptions, crippled who were brought *en masse* in carts are mentioned: *Vita Eligii episcopi Noviomagensis* 2.80 (4.739) (*clodi carrucis advecti*). In *Vita Amandi* 1.25 (5.448) a paralysed monk is brought in a boat to Amandus by his fellow monks.
89 *Vita Desiderii episcopi Vienensis* 2.10 (3.641–642) (*veluti truncum*); *Vita Austrigisili episcopi Biturigi* 10 (4.197–198) (*quasi funus examine*); *Vita Austrigisili episcopi Biturigi* 13 (4.198–199); *Vita Ansberti episcopi Rotomagensis* 29 (5.637–638); *Vita Ermenlandi abbatis Antrensis auctore Donato* 28 (5.709); *Vita Germani episcopi Parisiaci auctore Venantio Fortunato* 45 (7.400–401).
90 See the nuanced remarks by Kuuliala 2016, 192–198, partly nuancing Metzler 2006, 155–156.
91 See Laes 2011, 44–45 and 50–51 on Gregory of Tours. On mockery of the disabled, see Metzler 2006, 162–163 (miracle stories) and Kuuliala 2016, 116 and 178–184.
92 *Vita Pardulfi* 14 (7.32).
93 *Vita Anstrudis abbatissae Laudunensis* 32 (6.76) (*portare se fecit*).
94 *Translatio Germani episcopi Parisiaci* 2 (7.424–426).
95 *Vita Ermenlandi abbatis Antrensis auctore Donato* 27 (5.708–709).
96 *Vita Austrigisili episcopi Biturgi* 9 (4.197).
97 See the community concept, a central theme in the work by Rose 2003.
98 *Vita Germani episcopi Autissiodorensis auctore Constantio* 31 (7.274).
99 See the headings of the rich study by Kuuliala 2016 who deals with these various items.
100 See the exhaustive and most careful book by Bradley 2008 based on the study of Carolingian miniatures.
101 de Nie 2003 for a collection of essays which are very much connected to the history of ideas and spirituality in the Merovingian Gaul and Gregory of Tours.
102 The most promising study by Graham 2017 may serve as a starting point for such studies. See also Laurence in this volume for the experience of traveling.

## Bibliography

### Primary sources

*Monumenta Germania Historica. Scriptores Rerum Merovingicarum*
*Vita Boniti*
*Vita Rigoberti episcopi Remensis*
*Vita Ermenlandi abbatis Antrensis auctore Donato*
*Vita Faronis episcopi Meldensis*
*Vita Austrigisili episcopi Biturgi*
*Vita Germani episcopi Parisiaci auctore Venantio Fortunato*
*Vita Sancti Arnulfi*

### Literature

Banniard, Michel. 1989. *Genèse culturelle de l'Europe (Ve-VIIIe siècle)*. Paris: Éditions du Seuil.
Baroin, Catherine. 2018. "Boiterie et boiteux dans le monde romain à l'époque classique." *Pallas* 106: 257–274.
Bradley, Jill. 2008. *"You Shall Surely Not Die": The Concepts of Sin and Death as Expressed in the Manuscript Art of Northwestern Europe*, c.800–c.1200. Leiden: Brill.
Böhme, H.W. 2007. "Krankheit, Heilung und früher Tod zu Beginn des Mittelalters." In *Gesund und krank im Mittelalter*, edited by Andreas Meyer and Jürgen Schulz-Grobert. Leipzig: Eudora-Verlag.
Büttner, Jan Ulrich. 2009. "Die Strafe der Blendung und das Leben blinder Menschen." *Medizin, Gesellschaft und Geschichte* 28: 47–72.
De Mol, Willem. 2015. "Immobiel in de middeleeuwen. Mobiliteitshandicaps in Merovingische mirakelverhalen." MA Thesis, University of Antwerp.
de Nie, Giselle. 2003. *Word, Image and Experience. Dynamics of Miracle and Self-Perception in Sixth-Century Gaul*. Aldershot: Ashgate.
Devroey, Jean-Pierre. 2001. "The Economy." In *The Early Middle Ages*, edited by Rosamund McKitterick, 97–129. Oxford: Oxford University Press.
Effros, Bonnie. 2000. "Skeletal Sex and Gender in Merovingian Mortuary Archaeology." *Antiquity*, 74: 232–239.
Effros, Bonnie. 2002. *Creating Community with Food and Drink in Merovingian Gaul*. New York: Palgrave Macmillan.
Goetz, Hans-Werner. 2009. "'Debilis'. Vorstellungen von menschlicher Gebrechlichkeit im frühen Mittelalter." In *Homo Debilis: Behinderte – Kranke – Versehrte in der Gesellschaft des Mittelalters*, edited by Cordula Nolte, 21–55. Korb: Didymos.
Graham, Emma-Jayne. 2017. "Mobility Impairment in the Sanctuaries of Early Roman Italy." In *Disability in Antiquity*, edited by Christian Laes, 248–266. London and New York: Routledge.
Graumann, Lutz Alexander. 2000. *Die Krankengeschichten der Epidemienbücher des Corpus Hippocraticum. Medizinhistorische Bedeutung und Möglichkeit der retrospektiven Diagnose*. Aachen: Shaker Verlag.
Holder, Alfred. 1961–1962. *Alt-celtischer Sprachschatz*, 3 vols. Leipzig: Teubner.
Hähn, Cathrin. 2017. "Frühmittelalterliche Grabfunde: das Zusammenspiel von Status, Körpermerkmalen und *Gender*." In *Dis/ability History der Vormoderne. Ein Handbuch. Premodern Dis/ability History. A Companion*, edited by Cordula Nolte, Bianca Frohne, Ute Halle, Sonja Kerth, 139–142. Affalterbach: Didymos.

Kahlow, Simone. 2009. "Prothesen im Mittelalter – ein Überblick aus archäologischer Sicht." In *Homo Debilis: Behinderte – Kranke – Versehrte in der Gesellschaft des Mittelalters*, edited by Cordula Nolte, 201–223. Korb: Didymos.

Karenberg, Axel and Ferdinand Peter Moog. 2004. "Next Emperor Please! No End to Retrospective Diagnostics." *Journal of the History of Neurosciences* 13: 143–149.

Kelley, Nicole. 2009. "The Deformed Child in Ancient Christianity." In *Children in Late Ancient Christianity*, edited by Cornelia B. Horn and Robert P. Phenix, 199–216. Tübingen: Mohr Siebeck.

Kelley, Nicole. 2011. "'The Punishment of the Devil was Apparent in the Torment of the Human Body': Epilepsy in Ancient Christianity." In *Disability Studies and Biblical Literature*, edited by Candida A. Moss and Jeremy Schipper, 205–222. New York: Palgrave Macmillan.

Killgrove, Kristina. 2010. "Migration and Mobility in Imperial Rome." PhD Diss., University of North Carolina.

Killgrove, Kristina. 2019. "Using Skeletal Remains as a Proxy for Roman Lifestyles: The Potential and Problems with Osteological Reconstructions of Health, Diet, and Stature in Imperial Rome." In *The Routledge Handbook of Diet and Nutrition in the Roman World*, edited by Paul Erdkamp and Claire Holleran, 245–258. London and New York: Routledge.

Kron, Geoffrey. 2019. "Comparative Perspectives on Nutrition and Social Inequality in the Roman World." In *The Routledge Handbook of Diet and Nutrition in the Roman World*, edited by Paul Erdkamp and Claire Holleran, 259–272. London and Hew York: Routledge.

Kuuliala, Jenni. 2016. *Childhood Disability and Social Integration in the Middle Ages. Constructions of Impairments in Thirteenth- and Fourteenth-Century Canonization Processes*. Turnhout: Brepols.

Kuuliala, Jenni. 2017. "*Infirmitas* in Monastic Rules." in *Disability in Antiquity*, edited by Christian Laes, 342–356. London and New York: Routledge.

Laes, Christian. 2011. "Disabled Children in Gregory of Tours." In *The Dark Side of Childhood in Late Antiquity and the Middle Ages*, edited by Katariina Mustakallio and Christian Laes, 39–62. Oxford: Oxbow Books.

Laes, Christian. 2014. *Beperkt? Gehandicapten in het Romeinse Rijk*. Leuven: Davidfonds Uitgeverij.

Laes, Christian and Ville Vuolanto. 2017. "Household and Family Dynamics in Late Antique Southern Gaul." In *Mediterranean Families in Antiquity. Households, Extended Families and Domestic Space*, edited by Sabine Huebner and Geoffrey Nathan, 258–282. Oxford: Wiley Blackwell.

Metzler, Irina. 2006. *Disability in Medieval Europe. Thinking about Physical Impairment during the High Middle Ages, c. 1100–1400*. London and New York: Routledge.

Murray, Alexander C. 2008. *From Roman to Merovingian Gaul. A Reader*. Toronto: Broadview Press.

Nehlsen, Hermann. 1972. *Sklavenrecht zwischen Antike und Mittelalter. Germanisches und Römisches Recht in den germanischen Rechtsaufzeichnungen. I. Ostgoten, Westgoten, Franken, Langobarden*. Göttingen: Musterscmidt.

Réal, Isabelle. 2001. *Vies des saints, vie de famille. Représentation du système de la parenté dans le Royaume mérovingien (481–751) d'après les sources hagiographiques*. Turnhout: Brepols.

Roberts, Charlotte and Keith Manchester. 1995. *The Archaeology of Disease*. New York: Cornell University Press.

Rose, Martha Lynn. 2003. *The Staff of Oedipus: Transforming Disability in Ancient Greece*. Ann Arbor: University of Michigan Press.

Richardson, Kristina L. 2012. *Difference and Disability in the Medieval Islamic World. Blighted Bodies*. Edinburgh: Edinburgh University Press.

Saller, R. 2012. "Human Capital and Growth." In *The Cambridge Companion to the Roman Economy*, edited by Walter Scheidel. Cambridge: Cambridge University Press.

Sigal, Pierre-André. 1971. "Comment on concevait et on traitait la paralysie en Occident dans le Haut Moyen Age (Ve-XIIe siècles)." *Revue d'Histoire des Sciences*, 24(3): 193–211.

Southwell-Wright, William. 2014. "Perceptions of Infant Disability in Roman Britain." In *Infant Health and Death in Roman Italy and Beyond*, edited by Maureen Carroll and Emma-Jayne Graham. *Journal of Archaeology Supplementary Series* 96: 111–131.

Ulrich-Boschler, Susi. 2009. "Kranke, Behinderte und Gebrechliche im Spiegel der Skelettreste aus mittelalterlichen Dörfern, Kirchen und Klöstern (Bern/Schweiz). Aussagemöglichkeiten zum individuellen Alltag." In *Homo Debilis: Behinderte – Kranke – Versehrte in der Gesellschaft des Mittelalters*, edited by Cordula Nolte, 184–202. Affalterbach: Didymos.

Van Dam, Raymond. 1993. *Saints and Their Miracles in Late Antique Gaul*. Princeton: Princeton University Press.

Van den Abeele, Frederik. 2016. "Een lichtpunt in de duisternis. Ondersteuning van visueel beperkten in de Merovingische periode." MA Thesis, University of Antwerp.

von Olberg, Gabriele. 1991. *Die Bezeichnung für Soziale Stände, Schichten und Gruppen in den Leges Barbarorum*. Berlin and New York: Walter De Gruyter.

Ward-Perkins, Bryan. 2005. *The Fall of Rome and the End of Civilization*. Oxford: Oxford University Press.

Wickham, Chris. 2005. *Framing the Early Middle Ages: Europe and the Mediterranean, 400–800*. Oxford: Oxford University Press.

Wickham, Chris. 2009. *The Inheritance of Rome. A History of Europe from 400 to 1000*. London: Viking.

Wood, Ian. 1994. *The Merovingian Kingdoms*. London and New York: Routledge.

# 11 Sacralizing the journey
## Liturgies of travel and pilgrimage before the Crusades

*M. Cecilia Gaposchkin*

**Introduction**

On 24 October 1094, Saint Anselm of Canterbury went on pilgrimage to Rome. Before leaving, Anselm preached a sermon to his monks, in which he explained why he was undertaking the journey and commended them to their vocation as men who follow God. According to his biographer Eadmer, Anselm told his flock, 'I go willingly, trusting in God's mercy that my journey will do something for the liberty of the Church'.[1] Then he explained that

> Through difficulties and adversities [the man who follows God] follows the way of His commandments; he warms his heart with an undying fire of love in the hope of the reward in store for him; and thus, strong in patience, he rejoices in all things, and says with the Psalmist: 'Great is the glory of the Lord' [Ps. 137.5]. This glory, even in this earthly pilgrimage, he has a taste of.

Anselm added that 'he is supported by the hope of attaining it, and consoled by it in the midst of all earthly dangers'. At the end of his sermon, Anselm arose, kissed each of the monks, and

> Went into the church [...] and in the presence of the monks, clerks and a large concourse of people, he took the scrip (*peram*) and staff (*baculum*) of the pilgrim before the altar; then he commended them all to Christ and setting forth with weeping and lamentation, he left.[2]

The story illustrates two interrelated ideals of medieval religious culture that this chapter seeks to explore: (1) the relationship between the journey through physical space and the moral or religious journey through life and towards God, both of which are referred to as *peregrinationes* and (2) the ritual and liturgical articulation of these ideals. Medieval liturgical books included rites for departing travelers, and somewhat later, departing pilgrims, that formally sacralized a traveler's upcoming journey. The liturgical ritual marked the beginning (and sometimes the end) of a period of travel, entry into new lands, interaction with new people, and introduction to new places. These rites took the form of simple blessings (*benedictiones*), prayers (*orationes*), or votive masses (*missae*). Such ceremonies constituted, pace Victor Turner, obvious rites of passage, marking a traveler's transition from the everyday into a special, liminal status, both physically and metaphysically separated from his (or her) regular community.[3] Victor and Edith Turner themselves used medieval pilgrimage practices as an example of liminality *par excellence*.[4] The *content* of these rites – the images and textures and appeals of these prayers – reveal core ideals: how the medieval world conceived of the salvific value of travel, the development of these ideals over time, as pilgrimage grew in popularity, and the way in which crusading, having grown out of pilgrimage, appropriated these ideals. The language used to bless these journeys offers a rich view of the aspirations, anxieties, and metaphorical interpretation of travel and its implications. In so doing, they point to how social and geographical movement was inflected with religious meaning in ways that reveal the lived experience of much travel in the Middle Ages and how the broader community embraced and sanctioned this form of pilgrimage. The purpose of this essay is to outline the development of the images and ideas embedded in these rites, starting with their earliest appearance in the eighth century, up through the height of the crusading movement in the thirteenth century.

In brief, special liturgical rites for departing travelers can be found in liturgical sources beginning in the eighth century.[5] Early examples introduced a series of important themes that would be carried forward in the tradition. In the earliest instances, the prayers asked principally for security and protection in the uncertainty and danger of the open world. The destination was not the issue, nor was the specific moral purpose of the journey. Rather, it was safety. In the tenth century, prayers begin to evoke a comparison between the physical journey through space and the moral Christian journey through life, adopting an Augustinian aura. The rise and popularity of penitential pilgrimage around the millennium led to the incorporation of pilgrimage-specific rites, which were sometimes introduced to manuscripts separately, and sometimes simply added onto existing travel rites. Across Europe, blessings of the scrip and staff, the two emblems of the pilgrim, were added, constituting thus rites specifically for pilgrimage. These formularies often incorporated elements of the earlier travel liturgies, but now the focus was also on the sacred destination (*locus sanctus*) and increasingly on the moral and penitential aspects of the journey. With the advent of the crusades following Urban II's famous call in 1095, these pilgrimage rites were in turn adapted to crusading by adding a cross blessing to the standard rites for departing pilgrims. As articulated in the liturgy's ongoing conversation with God, the challenges of travel shifted from physical dangers to moral dangers as the function of travel became increasingly associated with salvific activity (pilgrimage and crusade).

## Rites for travelers

Many of the earliest surviving sacramentaries included instructions for some kind of ad hoc benedictions or votive mass for travelers. The texts for these different rites are heavily interrelated. Our earliest surviving compilation, representing materials dating from around 600, the Verona Sacramentary,[6] included nothing for travelers, but most early collections attended to the spiritual needs of people setting out on a trip. The Gelasian Sacramentary (copied around 750, but apparently representing a seventh-century compilation) included a set of prayers for people leaving on a trip (*Orationes ad proficiscendum in itinere, Item orationes ad iter agentibus*), which introduced a series of mass prayers that would endure throughout the Middle Ages.[7] The prayers asked God to stay close so that the traveler might be protected from the vagaries of travel, that God should 'direct his way', 'deem it worthy to accompany [the traveler]', and that God should direct the traveler 'in Your will', so he might offer no offense.[8] Another asked that God should allow 'no difficulty to get in the way'.[9] The supplicant asked that God send an angel to guide the traveler, as he had done with Tobias (we will return to this).[10] And the final two prayers asked specifically for physical safety.

> [*Deus infinitae misericordiae*] Oh God, of infinite mercy, and of immense majesty, whom neither the breadth of space or length of time separates from those whom you watch over; aid Your servants who everywhere have faith in You, and throughout the entire journey which they will be walking, may You deign to be present as leader and companion [*or* as duke and count to them]. Let nothing of adversity harm these [travelers], nothing of difficulty stand in their way; let all health [be given] to them, all prosperity to them, and under the might of Your right [hand], each will beg with just desire [that] they might achieve the result.[11]

> [*Deus qui ad vitam*] God, you who lead [us] to and allow life, you watch over in your paternal protection; we beg that You grant an angelic companion to Your servant, present here, who is about to take leave from us, and that, protected by [the angel's] help, no terror might threaten him, no anxiety about adversity might press upon him; the pressures of no enemy attacks might threaten him; but, rather, that completing with fortunate steps the journey through the necessary space and returned happily to his home, he might discover all safe, and be free from debts thanks to Your name.[12]

These texts are emblematic. The prayers – especially *Deus infinitae misericordia* – are well attested in later volumes.[13] Copied repeatedly into books of the tenth and eleventh centuries – 'a grim period of war and hardship for western Europe'[14] – the overwhelming concern is for protection and security from the threats and dangers of the travel.

Several of these prayers are found in the Gregorian tradition, which in the Carolingian period would exert so much influence over the dissemination of liturgical practices. The Gregorian Sacramentary included a mass *pro iter agentibus* and several benedictions, two *Pro fratribus in via dirigendis* and one *Pro redeuntibus de itinere* (presumably both for monks).[15] Both sets of rites emphasize God's direction of and involvement in a safe journey. The Benedictions for travelers reflected the same sentiments, asking that God 'direct the journey of his servant in Your will so that he be protected by You, led by You, and that he will walk along the footpath of God without hindrance', that 'he be defended from all adversities by Your help everywhere', and finally that God grant that he return unharmed and healthy. The Gregorian Sacramentary also included rites for men and women traveling by sea, the 'mass for those who are sailing'.[16] It evoked the time God had led his people across the Red Sea, and asked him to watch over men now 'in this boat', hoping that they arrived at the desired harbor (*portu* = port, harbor, or refuge). The Aniane supplement, which dates to the second decade of the ninth century, also included a poetic preface (a special prayer to be read before the canon of the mass) for those about to journey by sail. It evoked Abraham, Isaac, and Jacob as models for travelers, protected by God's grace, and asked God to guide (*dirigere*) the journey (*iter*) in prosperity, and to guard the traveler 'through the vagaries of journey and life' (*inter viae et vitae huius varietates digneris custodire*).[17] Here, then, the liturgy was making explicit the relationship between the physical travel and the life journey.

These were immensely influential and longstanding themes. Many of these texts were also transmitted in the Gallican tradition, the family of manuscripts that represented the liturgical tradition in Frankish lands at the end of the eighth century.[18] These included a votive mass and several benedictions or orations for travelers that included several themes that were to be influential in the liturgies for pilgrimage – God's protection and accompaniment on the journey, the difficulties of the journey, and the angelic companion. The mass for those about to set off on a journey (*missa ad proficiscendum in itinere*) asked God to direct the journey of his servant as guide and companion so that he might 'walk through the path of justice without accident',[19] that 'no adversity or no difficulty should get in their way', 'that they be healthy and prosperous', that God guide the traveler and that no dangers should happen through 'chains of mountains, the narrowness of valleys, the fords of rivers, the poisons of serpents, the attacks of wild animals',[20] that God protect the traveler from dangers, and that God always 'stay near' to the travelers.[21] The supplicant hopes to be worthy to gain God's protection during the journey, and asks for 'favorable' travel and 'safe' return. The benedictions (found in a different part of the book) asked for God to ensure (*faciet*) a successful journey; that he should lead (*perducat*) the travelers through 'the heights of mountains, the slopes of valley, the flats of field, the fords of rivers, and the hidden places of the forests'; that the 'salvific shadow of the Lord surround' the traveler; and that the right hand of God should guide the traveler.[22] The prayers request not only protection during the unknown lengths and spaces of the journey, but also divine guidance, and thus takes on a moral hue. Also included is a prayer for the traveler's safe return under God's protection.[23] The sense of the whole is the physical safety of journey in an uncertain age.

The request that God provide an angelic companion and guide on the journey goes back to the earliest witnesses.[24] Sometimes this was simply the 'angel of peace' or the 'angel of divine peace'.[25] Usually the supplicant asked explicitly that God grant the angel Raphael as a companion. In Gallican sacramentaries, the mass for travelers appeals to angelic company at several junctures. It refers to Tobias, God's servant, whom God sent 'Your angel, as a leader to lead the way'.[26] God is asked to accept the oblation from the servant entrusting his journey to God and to have mercy on him 'to whom You, O Lord, might deign to send the angel of peace, Your saintly angel, just as you sent to Your servant Tobias the angel Raphael, who led him safe and unharmed all the way to the desired location'.[27] Later, God, 'who [is] leader of the saints and who direct[s] the angel of peace to us who may lead us to the desired location. May he happily be a companion to us so that no enemy may rip our life away from us'.[28] The reference to the Archangel Raphael and Tobias is apposite. In the book of Tobit, the angel Raphael, unbeknownst to Tobias, is sent by God in answer to the prayer of Tobias' mother, to accompany and protect her son on a long journey into Media on an errand for his father and to obtain his bride. Tobias asks Raphael if he knows the region, and 'the Angel replied, "I know it, and I have often walked through all the ways thereof"' [Tobt 5.8]; Raphael says to Tobit: 'I will conduct him there, and then bring him back to you' [Tob 5.15] and then again 'I will lead your son safely, and bring him to back to you again safely' [Tob 5.20]; and then Tobit to his wife, 'Weep not, our son will get there safely and will return to us safely, and your eyes will see him. For I believe that the good angel of God accompanies him and will arrange all things well that are done around him so that he will return to us with joy' [Tob 5.26–27]. The language of the entire mass appealed to the same themes and language from the book of Tobit, and the angelic companion was destined to endure.

The angelic companion was central in the Mozarabic rite, the liturgy practiced in Spain up through the end of the eleventh century. Owing to common ancestry and shared tradition, the Mozarabic rite had texts common with the Gallican and Roman rites practiced in France and Italy, although it had evolved between the seventh and tenth century with local accretions. The rites for travel echoed the Gregorian and Gelasian traditions, adopting certain items and including proper texts that essentially expanded on the same themes: the desire for a safe journey, the request to be directed by God, the request for the angelic companion. The rite for travelers, though, was far longer. It used the Gelasian texts that ask that travelers be protected, defended from all opposition through the help of God's right hand.[29] But a text proper to the Mozarbic tradition appealed specifically to 'Jesus Christ Our Lord', to direct the journey of the travelers and keep them strong in both body and soul.[30] It also drew on a host of scriptural passages appropriate to the themes of travel (for example: Exod 23.22–23: I send to you my angel, who precedes you and will guard you on the road'; Ps. 16.5: Perfect thou my goings in thy paths; that my footsteps be not moved'[31]). It adopted and expanded elements from the Gelasian tradition and evoked Raphael and Tobias,[32] repeatedly requesting the angelic guide for safe travel. And it asked God to bless the traveler and keep him safe on his journey and return. Twice, the Mozarabic rite spoke of the Lord as the *via, veritas et vita*.[33] The allusion came from John 14.6 – 'Jesus said to him: I am the way, and the truth, and the life' [*sum via et veritas et vita*], which had long been a foundation of a kind of *imitatio Christi*, in that Christ himself became the model for a true life of salvation.[34] It too was destined to long endure in rites of pilgrimage and then crusading.

In tenth-century England, the continental texts were influential and their essential meaning was adopted, but the texts themselves were altered and idea of the 'journey' (*iter*) was increasingly moralized. Both the Egbert Pontifical (BNF Lat. 10575) and the Benedictional of Robert of Jumieges (Rouen BM ms. 369), both written in England, include almost identical *benedictio pro iter agentibus* that asked God to clemently direct the journey of his servant, that God, the disposer of all things, direct his route, that God guide the pilgrim's journey to the desired location unharmed, that the traveler should have the companionship of the company of angels, that Raphael guide them, and finally that Christ should also accompany them.[35] Raphael is invoked not merely by comparison ('a guide like the one you gave Tobias[...]') but he is requested specifically. 'May great Raphael, the guardian and guide of Tobias, be with you so that you might avoid both human and diabolic trickery, and that you might merit having Christ himself, of the way, the truth, and the life, as a companion' (again, John 14.5–6). Here, moral themes are underscored; the dangers of the journey are not merely the physical dangers of travel but the moral temptations of the devil. The journey is not merely space traveled, but life lived. The final prayer asks that Christ's 'invincible shield be with you in your travel there and your return, by which you might overcome the misfortunes to body and soul, and that you might quickly obtain the things that you desire'.[36] Christ himself is associated with the travel in these texts, and he is evoked as a companion with the traveler on the trip. More than the Gelasian and Gregorian sources, a concern with human failure and diabolical deceits evokes a concern for the moral journey, not just the physical challenges of the journey.

In sum, whether simple benedictions or a full mass, the rites for travel in the central medieval period laid out basic themes that would be carried forth into the traditions for pilgrimage and then crusading. God was understood to be the principal guide and director of the journey. In the tenth century Christ emerged too as the source of divine protection. The rites asked to be protected, initially from physical dangers, but increasingly from moral dangers; the snares and dangers were initially understood as the secular dangers of journeys and became increasingly conceived in moral terms as the traps of the devil. A common theme was that God might send an angel – as He had sent Raphael to Tobias – as a companion and guide to keep the traveler safe and direct him appropriately to the desired destination. All rites entreated a safe and healthy return. By the eve of the great age of pilgrimage, the rites asked that travelers be kept safe and healthy, both in body and in soul.

## Rites for pilgrims

Many of these texts would be the basis of, or get incorporated into, a new form of rite for departing pilgrims. The eleventh century witnessed an efflorescence in pilgrimage. All evidence suggests increasing participation in the devotional practice both to local holy sites and to the great international pilgrimage destinations:

Jerusalem, Santiago, and Rome.[37] Contemporaries distinguished between two different types of pilgrimages – the *pereginatio religiosa,* the simple devotional pilgrimage (often for the purposes of a health miracles), and the penitential pilgrimage, a form of judicial exile, which was generally centered on the city of Rome.[38] The terms *peregrinus* and *peregrinatio* at this stage probably still referred to any kind of traveler or wanderer, and did not in itself convey the idea of sacred travel that it would in the course of the (consequential) eleventh century.[39] And yet, the pilgrim was different from the (mere) traveler in that he was setting out not only on a journey, but to a sacred destination, a *locus sanctus,* which gave the enterprise religious, salvific import.

The liturgical rite for departing pilgrims, which involved the special benediction of the scrip and staff, developed in this context. Pilgrimage was a special, and protected, category of travel, and the pilgrim, since at least the eighth century, had been afforded certain rights and protections by the church for the length of their journey.[40] As a visible sign of this legal, and quasi-sacral status, the pilgrim bore the emblems of pilgrimage, which were the scrip (wallet, or purse) and walking staff.[41] As with Saint Anselm in 1094 as he left for Rome, these were often granted to the pilgrim upon his departure by his priest or bishop in a liturgical rite from the altar. The pilgrim's departure, pace Turner, thus marked him as a kind of temporary monk.

Rites for blessing scrip and staff survive in a number of manuscripts from throughout Western Europe. Honorius Augustodunensis (d. ca. 1151) claimed that the rite for blessing the scrip and staff was, along with celebrating mass, dispensing the Eucharist, preaching, and a host of other ritual actions, the duty [*officium*] of all priests.[42] Although the rites themselves survive largely in pontificals (that is, rituals for bishops), they can also be found in sacramentaries, rituals, and ceremonials intended for priests and abbots. The rites themselves spoke of *peregrinatio,* though the rubrics to the rites in the liturgical manuscripts spoke usually of the blessing of the scrip and staff.[43] Certain themes established in the travel rites were particularly influential – most clearly in the evocation of Tobias and the angelic companion, Raphael, and the request for God's protection along the journey.

Despite the mass of local variety (discussed below), the rites for pilgrims were *always* built upon the blessings of the scrip and staff, often simply combining these blessings with older travel masses or prayers. The uniformity of this fact is curious, given the great regional variety of actual prayers that were composed to bless the scrip and staff, as if various liturgists spontaneously followed the same strategy. The scrip and staff themselves obviously had practical aspects, but their significance as identifiers was probably also related to scripture. David was said to have taken a scrip and staff as he set off to fight Goliath (I Kings 17.40). But, more likely, if oddly in its inversion, was Jesus' instructions to the Apostles to evangelize. Luke 9.2–3 reported that: 'he sent them to preach the kingdom of God, and to heal the sick. And he said to them: take nothing for your journey; neither staff, not scrip nor bread, nor money'.[44] Mark 6.8 reports of Jesus allowed them the staff, but not the scrip: 'And he commanded [the apostles] that they should take nothing for the journey; only a staff; no scrip, no bread, no money in their purse'.[45] However pilgrimage itself worked in relationship to this apostolic model, the scrip and staff were the long-held signifiers of the wandering traveler.

These rites were primarily intended for the 'great' international pilgrimages. The manuscripts from Germany and England tended to assume as its destination Rome (the *limina apostorum*[46]), not Jerusalem or Santiago. An eleventh-century addition to the great Romano-Germanic Pontifical (hereafter: RGP) indicated those who were seeking the limits and suffrages of the holy apostles.[47] Some exemplars were flexible enough to accommodate 'other places where one might have cause to go and pray' (*vel alia causa orandi dirigendis*).[48] Spanish exemplars assumed Rome *or* Santiago. A missal from the Cathedral of Vich (near Barcelona) that dates to 1038 includes a mass for monks leaving for pilgrimage to Rome ('*ad limina beatorum apostolorum Petri et Pauli*') or other holy sites ('*vel ad aliorum sanctorum*').[49] An eleventh-century pontifical for the bishop of Roda and Lerida (also in Catalonia) includes an 'Ordo for those who are leaving for the threshold of the apostles or who desire to seek out any other region for the intercession of the apostles or other saints for the love of God',[50] and a ritual from Burgos from the following century took the blessing for the scrip and staff known from the RGP and added Santiago to 'the threshold of the apostles' as a potential destination.[51]

The rites varied regionally, but expressed the same complement of themes. The tradition on the Iberian Peninsula was indebted to the rites for travel from the Gelasian traditions for travel, and constituted a scrip and staff blessing added to the travel liturgy. The rubric from the famous Vich Missal of 1038, '*Missa pro fratribus in via dirigendis*', reveals its debts to earlier traditions of travel blessings. This expansive rite added a new secret, an altered prayer for the *post-fractionem* (the prayer between the breaking of the host and the Agnus Dei) and a series of new prayers. The themes of the secret and the *post-fractionem* were familiar, asking God to direct our steps,[52] and to protect us continually on the journey from all mortal sins. The *post-fractionem* amplified the request for divine and angelic guidance, saying that God was the leader and companion for Abraham, Isaac, and Jacob, and provided Tobias with the (unnamed) angel as a guide.

The Vich formulary introduces the figure of Abraham as a model pilgrim, emphasizing pilgrimage (over merely journey) for the first time.

> O God, who watched over Abraham, your son, led from Ur of the Chaldeans, through all the paths of his pilgrimage [cf: Gen 11.28, 31, 15.7]; deign to watch over these, your male and female servants, striving with free will towards foreign lands for the love of your name, with the fortifications of your defenses.[53]

In Genesis 11–13, God commanded Abraham to leave the land of Ur of the Chaledeans and go into the land Canaan: 'Go from your country and your kindred and your father's house to the land that I will show you'. [Gen 12.1] The Vich prayer continues, employing mostly travel metaphors, calling the Lord the 'defense in battle, the harbor in shipwreck, the hostel on the road, the shelter in the storm, the light in the shadows, the walking staff (*baculum*) in the hazardous areas, security in adversity, care in prosperity', and then asks that God should bring the pilgrim back to him back, unharmed.[54] The emphasis is still primarily on the physical dangers of travel within the natural world. The next prayer addresses Jesus Christ, and then the bishop, 'with the desire for eternal salvation, places upon the pilgrim the habit of those setting out to foreign places', and asks again that the Lord send the holy angel to guard them awake and asleep, to guide them in their journey.[55] Finally, the prayer asks that Jesus might send them the Paraclete, and, reviving them with continual consolation, might direct their pilgrimage so that they 'might merit to be absolved from all sins, by their carnal debt, might merit to become eternal citizens of the heavenly Jerusalem'.[56] Here, finally, we have a reference to the remission of sins. The reference to Jerusalem, is not the earthly city in the Levant as a pilgrimage destination, but rather the usual metaphor for heaven and salvation.[57] The reference here to sin demonstrates how the prayers have shifted planes, from earthly to salvific journey.

The core benedictions for scrip and staff found in the Vich rite were, in some form, a principal element in all pilgrimage rites. The rubric in the Vich formulary indicates that as the pilgrim gets up from the ground, the bishop is to hand over the scrip and staff, asking God to allow the pilgrim, *castigatus, salvatus,* and *emendatus,* to arrive safely at the threshold of the Apostles Peter and Paul, and to return safely. In the Vich missal, the prayer followed with the bishop enjoining the pilgrim to 'Take this staff, the sustenance of your journey and the labor on the way of your pilgrimage so that you will be able to overcome all treachery of the enemy and arrive safely at the threshold of the blessed apostles Peter and Paul and the others whom you wish to go do, and, the course of this obedience having been finished, return to us in Joy'.[58] The danger has become, now, the devil proper. The version of this prayer added to the back of the famed Gellone Sacramentary added 'and his snares' (*et insidias eius*).[59] These same prayers were then added to the Gellone Sacramentary (BNF Lat 12048),[60] and other volumes on England and throughout the continent.[61] Ultimately, these prayers would make their way into Roman Pontifical of the Thirteenth Century (hereafter: RP13) and the Pontifical of William Durandus (ca. 1300), ensuring longevity throughout the Middle Ages.[62]

Like in Spain, in Germany a rite for scrips and staves (here *capsellas* and *fustes*) appeared sometime in the first half of the eleventh century. An eleventh century recension of the great Romano-Germanic Pontifical (The Pontifical of Saint Alban's, Mainz; Vienna pal. 701) indicates that it was intended for those going to Rome (*Benedictio super capsellas et fustes et super eos qui cum his limina ac suffragia sanctorum apostolorum petituri sunt*).[63] The texts appeared in a number of early German volumes. In a Pontifical from Freiburg, Clm 6427, the rubric of the essentially identical rite indicates that it ought be used for 'brothers' going to Rome or other places in order to pray.[64] The RGP adopted the entreaty that God send his angel (*tuum angelum*) as companion to Tobias, but now not simply as a guide, but rather to protect and defend him along the journey against the snares of enemies, visible and invisible. The visible enemies were the physical earthly enemies listed in the earliest travel prayers. Invisible enemies were the devil and his minions, that had now joined the passel of obstacles. Around this, the RGP added both prayers and psalmody that would become the standard on the continent. The Psalmody (Psalms 90, 118, and 143) emphasized themes of travel, obedience, and the merciful protection of God. Psalm 90.2: 'He shall abide under the protection of the God of Jacob; He shall say to the Lord "Thou art my protector, and my refuge [...] for he hath delivered me from the snares of hunters"'. Psalm 90 speaks of how God has given angels charge over him (90.11). Psalm 118 begins 'Blessed are those undefiled in the way, who walk in the law of the Lord'.

The rite from the RGP evokes both New Testament and Old Testament models.[65] The priest or bishop would asks that the Lord Christ, who ordered that his apostles take up the staff (*virgas*, cf. Mark 6.8) and go out and preach, bless the script and staffs that are received as the sign of pilgrimage (*signum peregrinationis*) and the forbearance of their bodies (*suorum corporum sustentationem*), so that in them, the defense of God's blessing might be secured and, 'in this way, the rod of Aaron sprouted in the temple of the Lord was justly separated from the rebellious Jews; thus, may you absolve from all sins those of us so adorned with the sign of Saint Peter, by which, on the day of judgment those who will be crowned will be separated from the impious'.[66] The reference to the Apostles came from Mark 6.8, discussed above. The pilgrim's walking staff is associated thus with the Apostles' staves (*virga*) as well as the rod of Aaron (*virga* again, Numbers 17.5–10). The staff is the *signum Petri*, associated with not only salvation but absolution of all sins. The priest then hands over both the scrip and the staff, and begs that the pilgrim should merit 'in this world, to receive the remission of all sins and the future company of all saints'.[67] Finally, this rite too invokes Abraham who went from the land of his birth to the land of promise, which God had promised to him, and the many portents God had done for the Israelites in the desert. Then, 'we beseech that You [God] remove these [people], who are going to the threshold of blessed Peter and Paul to worship you, from all dangers and free them from the debts of sin', and finally that they are protected by His aid from the perturbations of the world.

Separate traditions for pilgrims developed in England around the same time that demonstrate further variety.[68] Our earliest evidence of a pilgrimage liturgy is *sui generis*, found in two manuscripts from the later half of the eleventh century. A manuscript preserved in the British library from the ca. 1070, Cotton Vitellius E XII (fols. 156v-159r), includes the (fragmentary) pontifical used by the Archbishop of York, Aeldred, who crowned William the Conqueror, and includes an Episcopal benediction for scrips (*perae*) and staffs (*baculi*) quite possibly composed by Aeldred himself.[69] The bulk of the pontifical is a copy of the RGP written in Germany, probably acquired in 1054 on a visit to Cologne, but also includes a single quire in which were added what were probably Aeldred's own liturgical materials. The pilgrim's blessing belongs to this quire and Michael Lapidge has suggested a relationship between the pilgrim's rite here and Aeldred's own pilgrimage to Rome in 1058; it was then copied exactly into another mid-eleventh century Pontifical, Cambridge Corpus Christi College 163, perhaps made at Worcester and closely related to Cotton Vitellius E XII in a number of ways.[70] It consists of five prayers, interspersed with short blessings of the pilgrims attributes and is built around ideas drawn from key scriptural phrases that gave interpretive meaning to the idea of sacred travel.[71] It opens with surprisingly militant themes, actually adopted from the blessings for weapons [*Benedictio Armorum*] found in the tenth-century Egbert Pontifical; 'these arms, swords, indeed, and lances, or shield or helmets and standards' was replaced 'this scrip and this staff'. God is the militant 'Adonai' and 'Domine Sabaoth' of the Old Testament.[72] As with the travel rites, God is beseeched for security and health. 'Grant to him, Oh Lord, right faith, firm hope, the trustworthiness of heart, fortitude of body, and good health for all his limbs'.[73] Yet the themes are overwhelmingly penitential, asking for 'indulgence, remission, pity, [and] compassion' for the pilgrim's sins [*delicta*], and asking that he be given the 'grace from your sanctuary' now by the 'new bath of penitence and pilgrimage'. Adapting the old themes of physical wellbeing, the prayer then begs that the pilgrim might 'without any weakness or misfortune, merit to arrive, by the intercession of Saint Peter no less than all the apostles, according to his own wishes, safe in the Lord body and soul'.[74]

Although elements of Eadred's blessings survive in later English books,[75] Eadred's rite was mostly idiosyncratic.[76] More representative are the prayers found in two manuscripts dating from around the year 1100 – one from northern France (Reims) and one from England (Worcester) – that preserve a liturgical rite comprised of a long prayer embellished with two short benedictions said at the moment of handing over the scrip and staff.[77] It was adopted routinely in a series of French and English manuscripts, ultimately made its way into the Roman (papal) rite (but only in the thirteenth century), and would become one of the most widespread formularies of the Late Middle Ages.[78] It begins with a prayer (*Domine Iesu Christe qui tua ineffabili miseratione*) by acknowledging the ineffable power and mercy of God. The bishop is to implore God that

> 'he might deign to bless this scrip and staff so that those who, for love of Your name, might desire to fasten (*applicare*) [the scrip] to his (or her) side like humble arms, and to hang around his (or her) neck or bear by his (or her) hands, and so may desire to seek intercession by making pilgrimage, accompanied by humble devotions, so that they might merit to arrive, protected by the defense of your right hand, to the joy of the eternal home'.[79]

The final prayer is direct heir to the travel rites, asking God, 'who is the way, the truth, and the life', (John 14.6 again, *sum via et veritas et vita*), to send Raphael as a guardian to lead the pilgrim there and back; and then it beseeches Mary, apostles, angels, and saints as intercessors in order that the pilgrim might gain a remission of sins and acquire eternal life.

Indeed, the remission of sin was crucial to all of these rites. The English rite BL Cotton Vitellius E.XII and Cambridge Corpus Christi College 163 speaks broadly of God's clemency, power, indulgence, remission, pity, and compassion [*tuam clementiam, potentiam, indulgentiam, remissionem, miserationem, compassionem*], which the pilgrim leaving on the 'journey of penitence' [*iter penitudinis*], hopes will be granted for his 'crimes' [*facinoribus*]. He asks for 'prosperity, the remissions of sins, and eternal life', since he hopes to be 'improved through the new bath of penitence and pilgrimage', [*nunc novo lavacro penitentie peregrinationisque*]. In Spain, the Vich missal speaks of the pilgrim returning, joyful in the remission of sins [*letetur remissione peccatorum*].[80] The pontifical for the bishop of Roda and Lerida specifies that the supplicant must first confess to God and to his own bishop or another priest all his sins and crimes, and then, once his required penance is done, he must prostrate himself before the bishop on the floor before the altar, and at this point the seven penitential psalms are sung over him. The ceremony concludes with the rites for the departing pilgrim, including the mass *pro iter agentibus* and the giving of the scrip and staff.[81] In France, the Reims Pontifical of about 1100, asks God to grant an 'indulgence and remission of all of your sins', immediately before the blessing given at the moment when the bishop handed over the script.[82] More forcefully the eleventh-century recension of the RPG promised that through the intercession of Mary, the apostles, and the saints, the pilgrim 'might merit in this world to accept the remission of all sins and, in the future, to be in the company of all the blessed'.[83] The rite followed by asking that God 'absolve [the pilgrim] from all sins' so that he might be crowned on the day of judgment when sinners and separated from the just.[84] The rubrics in an early twelfth-century Beneventan Pontifical specified that confession be given after the bishop or abbot handed over the staff and before the final prayers.[85]

The devotional values embedded in the rite indicate that these were intended for pilgrims going not on local pilgrimages but rather, generally, to Rome. Given how often pilgrimages – particularly local pilgrimages – were undertaken in the hopes of a health cure or miracle (itself not necessarily unrelated to spiritual merit in the medieval world) it is worth noting that there is absolutely no hint that such a purpose was ever blessed or sanctified in these rites. What they emphasized instead was the different – greater – miracle of the remission of sin. Within the context of a penitential pilgrimage this is sensible, since the pilgrimage imposed as a form of judicial exile or an explicitly penitential exile necessarily carried with it the notion of a penitent's payment for sin, and in this sense, the penitential themes are embedded into the explicit purpose of the pilgrimage. The notion that pilgrimage itself would enjoin a remission from all sins would become commonplace in the pilgrim liturgies of the twelfth and thirteenth centuries, and from there were ultimately integrated in the rite for taking the cross that grew out of them. This is in line with the motivation for going on the greater pilgrimages, especially to Rome, since there – the home of Saint Peter, the holder of the keys – one might hope to obtain the absolution of sins.[86]

## Epilogue: Crusade as travel and pilgrimage

Going into the period of the crusade, the liturgy sacralized travel and pilgrimage through ritual, with a series of ideas and images, many rooted in scripture. Travel was increasingly moralized. The journey through space, and towards a holy place, became one with the journey through life, towards God. In the Old Testament, the model was above all Abraham, who appeared in a variety of traditions in different texts, but always represented the devout man chosen by God who undertook a sacred journey. In the New Testament, the model was the apostles, setting out on Christ's instructions (without their scrips (*peras*) and walking sticks (*virgas*)!). All rites asked for protection and safety. Over time, the dangers from which the supplicants asked God to protect them were increasingly the moral dangers of sin and the soul, more than the external dangers of beasts and brigands. The danger the serpent posed initially was merely his venom (*venena serpentium*), alongside the fords of rivers and the attack of beasts.[87] Later, it was the venomous incitement of the ancient serpent (*venenosis impulsionibus serpentis antique*), indicating how completely travel had become imbued with spiritual and religious meaning.[88] Supplicants asked for God, and increasingly Christ, to protect them; they asked God, and increasingly Christ, to join them in their journey as companion and guide. An angel of God was often requested; mostly, it was the Archangel Raphael, who had led Tobias safely on his journey in the Old Testament, who was requested to keep the pilgrim safe.

When, in 1095, Urban II preached the First Crusade, he preached it as a pilgrimage. And when the crusaders departed for Jerusalem, they went as pilgrims. Many appear to have participated in the liturgical ritual of departure, in which they took their scrip and stave as the emblems of their status.[89] These rites were soon adapted to Jerusalem travel. A pontifical from Bari, dating to the end of the twelfth century, was titled 'the rite for those who go to Jerusalem'.[90] Early crusading thus adopted the core ideals and religious meaning of travel and pilgrimage that had been seeded in part by these liturgical practices. Not least among these ideas was that to be a crusader was to fulfill the story of Abraham, to imitate the Apostles, and to follow in the footsteps of Christ, follow in his *via, veritas, et vita*. In the Crusade period, the model of Abraham as pilgrim was then tied to the Abrahamic covenant, which associated Abraham's pilgrimage with the promise of the Canaan, the Holy Land.[91] The prayer in the eleventh-century recension of the RGP which compared the pilgrim's journey to the threshold of the Apostles Peter and Paul (i.e., Rome) and directly to Abraham's journey from the land of his birth 'to the Promised land, which You [God] had promised him',[92] took on new meaning. Jerusalem itself came into increasing focus in the pilgrimage rites of the Crusade period.[93] Above all, early crusading also appropriated the idea that the journey was penitential, that the pilgrim was accompanied by angels, or by Christ himself, that the journey was itself salvific, and that ultimately, it could, when done with a contrite heart, involve the remission of sin.[94]

In time, the single element crucial to the religious practice of crusade – the cross – absent from the language and ideals around travel and pilgrimage – was also incorporated into the rite. Starting at the end of the twelfth century, blessings of the cross that the crusader wore upon his garb was added to the liturgical formulary, and thus to the religious ideals of being a crusader.[95] At the end of the thirteenth century, the great liturgist William Durandus composed a new rite for the departing pilgrim and crusader, which would become in some senses the standard rite of the fourteenth and fifteenth centuries.[96] His beautiful, elegant liturgy included all the principal imagery and ideals garnered from earlier travel and pilgrimage rites. In this way, in 1450, crusading still imbibed the ideals of salvific travel that had been established in the early travel rites of the eighth and ninth centuries, while yet having become something altogether different.

## Notes

1 Eadmer 1962, 93–94. Anselm was in fact leaving in exile, after a dispute with the king, William Rufus. See also Southern 1963.
2 Eadmer, *The Life of St. Anselm*, 97.
3 Turner 1969.
4 Turner and Turner 1978.
5 Earlier treatments of travel liturgies include Franz 1909 [reprint 2006], 2:271–289. Rivard 2009, 134–155.
6 Mohlberg et al. 1956.
7 *Liber sancramentorum romane aeclesiae*, 191–193. For these early traditions, see Chupungco 1997, 1:245–254 and Palazzo 1998, 21–61.
8 Mohlberg 1960, 191. *Adesto domine*.
9 Mohlberg 1960, 191–192. *Propitiare domine*
10 Mohlberg 1960, 192. *Hanc igitur oblationem...*
11 Mohlberg 1960, 192: 'Deus infinitae misericordiae et maiestatis inmensae, quem nec spatia locorum nec intervalla temporum ab his quos tueris abiungunt, adesto famulis tuis in te ubique fidentibus et per omnem quam acturi sunt viam dux eis et comis esse dignare; nihil illius adversitatis noceat, nihil difficultatis obsistat, cuncta eis salubria, cuncta sint prospera; ut sub ope dexterae tuae, quidquid iusto expetierunt desiderio, caeleri consequantur effectu'.
12 Mohlberg 1960, 192: 'Deus, qui ad vitam ducis et confitentes in te paterna protectione custodis, quaesumus, ut praesenti famulo tuo a nobis egrediente angelicum tribuas comitatu, et eius auxilio protectus nulla mali concuciatur formidine, nullo conpraematur adversistatis angore, nullus inruentis inimici molestetur insidiis, sed spacii<s> necessarii itineris prospero gressu peractus propriisque locis feliciter restitutus universos reperiat sospites ac debitas exsolvat tuo nomine gratis'.
13 Moeller and Clément 1992-, 2:185, 223.
14 Bynum 1987, 122.
15 Deshusses 1988–1992, 1:437–439.
16 Deshusses 1988–1992, 1:439; Warren 1968, 16.
17 Deshusses 1988–1992, 1:571.
18 For the 'Old Gelasian' Sacramentary, see Mohlberg 1960; Vogel 1986, 64–65.
19 Dumas 1981, 438, no. 2791. 'direge viam famuli tui *illi* in voluntate [m] <tua>, ut te protectore[m] et preduce per iustitie semitis sine offensione gradiamur'.
20 Dumas 1981, 438, rub. 2793: 'nullum periculum per spatia terre aut per iuga montium, angusta vallium, vadaque fuminum, venena serpentium, vel impetum bestiarum incurrant, sed sub tuo nomine ab omnibus malis defensi[s], ad locum destinatum perveniant'. Heiming 1984, 222; Coebergh and de Puniet 1977; Moeller 1980–1981, 365.
21 Dumas 1981, 438–440, rubs : 2790–2804.
22 Dumas 1981, 199: 'Prosperum iter faciet uobis deus salutarium nostrorum pateant que in vias directas arduam montium, convexa valeum, plena camporum, unda flumina, secreta siluarum [...] vos salutaris domini umbra circumtegat [...] deducat uos mirabiliter dextera dei'.

23 Dumas 1981, 440, rub: 2804.
24 Mohlberg 1960, 192, no. 1317.
25 Warren 1968, 10. Dumas 1981, 299, rub. 2098; Amiet 1974, 100. The Angelic companion is discussed by Rivard 2009, 143–144.
26 Dumas 1981, 438: 'Necnon et tobi famulo tuo angelum tuum ducem previum prestetisti'. Heiming 1984; Coebergh and de Puniet 1977.
27 Dumas 1981, 439, rub. 2794: 'Cui tu domine angelum pacis mittere digneris, angelum tuum sanctum, sicut misisti famulo tuo Tubie Rafahel angelum, qui eum saluum adque incolumen perducat usque ad loca destinanta, <et> iterato tempore oportuno omnibus rede perfectis, reduci eum faciat in tua sancta ecclesia, <et> letus tibi et nomine tuo gratias referat'.
28 Dumas 1981, 439, rubr. 2799: 'Domine sancte pater omnipotens eterne deus qui es ductur sanctorum et diregis itinera iustorum, direge angelum pacis nobiscum qui nos ad loca distinata perducat'.
29 Moeller 1971-, 2:554, no. 1234
30 Férotin 1996, 348: 'Ihesum Christum Dominum nostrum qui directa iternatium via et meantium salus est indefessa, Fratres karissimi, prece flagitemus continua: ut hos famulos suos in hac qua agrediuntur via et corporali salute pollentes et spiritualibus consiliis efficiantur fortiores'.
31 Férotin 1996, 347.
32 Franz 2006, 2:264, no. 3.
33 Férotin 1996, 94, 350.
34 Tinsley 1960, 61–72.
35 Banting 1989, 105; Wilson 1903, 55.
36 Banting 1989, 105–106: 'Sit ejus vobis inexpugnabilis clypeus eundo et redeundo, quo mentis et corporis incommoditate eruamini, habere et quicquid desideratis affectu celeri consequamini'.
37 The classic studies are: Sumption 1976; Birch 1998; Webb 1999.
38 Vogel 1963, 76–82.
39 Birch 1998, 2–5.
40 Garrisson 1965, 1168; Brundage 1969, 14–17.
41 Plötz 1986, 339–376.
42 Franz 2006, vol. 2, 272–274. The passage is found in the *Gemma animae*, Migne 1844–1891, 172:599.
43 So, for instance, in Munich CLM 6427: 'Benedictio super capsellas et fustes et super homines' (Franz vol. 2, 275); Vienna ÖNB ms. 701, 134r: 'Benediccio super capsellas et fustes et super eos qui cum his limina ac suffragia sanctorum apostolorum petituri sunt' (Vogel and Elze 1963, 362, CCXII); London BL Cotton Vitellius E.12: 'Benedictio pere et baculi'; Cambridge Corpus Christi ms. 146, 'Benedictio pere et baculi'; But, as discussed above, note the indebtedness to travel rites in Vich Biblioteca Capitular codice XLVIII (moderna ms. 66).
44 See also Luke 10.4, Matthew 10.10.
45 Mk 6.8.: Et precepit eis ne quid tollerent in via nisi virgatantum non peram non panem neque in zona aes. See also and Luke 9.3, 10.4.
46 For explanation of the phrase 'limina apostolorum', see: Birch 1998, 6–7.
47 Vogel and Elze 1963, 362: 'limina ac suffragia sanctorum apostolum petituri sunt'. See now also: Parkes 2015.
48 Franz 2006, 2:275.
49 Vich Cathedral Library Codex XLVIII (new sig. ms. 66), fols 56–58: 'Missa pro fratribus in via dirigendis'. The text is published in Olivar 1953, 215–216. And a translation is found in Webb 1999, 46–47.
50 Guidiol 1927: 111: 'Ordo de his qui peregre proficiscuntur ad limina apostolorum vel in aliqua regione suffragia apostolorum vel aliorum sanctorum pro Dei amore apetere cupiunt'.

51 Burgos Cath. Ms. 24, fols 86r-v: 'In nomine domini nostri Ihu Xpi accipiter hac [has] sportam [sportas] et hunc baculum habitum peregrinationis tue [vestre], ut bene castigatus [castigati] et bene savus [salvi] atque emendatus pervenire merearis [merearmini] ad limina iacobi apostoli [apostolorum petri & pauli] vel ad aliorum sanctorum quo pergere cupis [cupitis] & peracto itinere tuo [vestro] ad nos incolumis [incolumes] ren[*folio corner cut off*] *[86v]* merearis. Per'. Items in brackets are written above the line. Cf: Vogel and Elze 1963, 2:362.
52 Olivar 1953, 56.
53 Olivar 1953, 147: 'Deus qui Abraham puerum tuum de Hur Caldeorum eductum per omnes sue peregrinationis vias custodisti, custodire dignare hos famulos tuos vel famulas illas munimine tue deffensionis pro tui nominis amore sponte peregrina petentes'. Abraham was listed with Isaac and Jacob as travelers in the mass *pro fratribus in via dirigendis*.
54 Olivar 1953, 147: 'Esto eis, domine, in procinctu deffensio, in naufragio portus, in itinere diversorium, in estu umbraculum, in tenebris lux, in lubrico baculus, in merore gaudium, in tristicia consolacio, in aduersitate securitas, in properitate cautela'.
55 Olivar 1953, 147: 'quibusque desiderio salutis eterne peregrine proficiscentes abitum peregrinantis imponimus, tribue eis quesumus, domine, gratiam tuam deputans eis angelum tuum sanctum qui eos vigilantes et dormientes custodiat et viam eorum dirigat'.
56 Olivar 1953, 147. 'ab omnibus peccatorum vinculis absoluti deposito carnis honore Iherusalem celestis eterni cives effici mereantur'.
57 Bradshaw 1999.
58 Olivar 1953, 147: 'Accipe et hunc bacculum sustentationem itineris ac laboris viam peregrinationis tue ut devincere valeas omnes katervas inimici et pervenire securus ad limina beatorum apostolorum Petri et Pauli et aliorum quo pergere cupis et peracto obedientie cursu ad nos revertaris in gaudio'.
59 Dumas 1981, 519.
60 I admit to being suspicious of this early date. There is no evidence of other pilgrimage rites that I know of until the eleventh century in any other manuscript. Dumas 1981, 518–519.
61 'Accipe hanc peram, habitum peregrinationis tue' and 'Accipe et hunc baculum sustenationem itineris ac laboris in via peregrinationis tue'. These were among the most common blessings. Planas 1975; Franz 1904, 114; Henderson 1875, Appendix 209*, 210*; Burgos ms. 24, 85r-v; and many others. Budapest Orzagos Szechenyi Konyvtar ms lat. Med. Aev. 330, 155r; Burgos ms. 24. 85r-v; Montepellier Bibliothèque Universitaire, section medicine, ms. 314, 142R-143R; Andrieu 1940a, 419; Troyes BM 2140, 23v; Macerata, Biblioteca Comunale 'Mozzi-Borgetti' 378, edited in: Macerata, Biblioteca Comunale 'Mozzi-Borgetti' 378; Avignon 143; Archives of the Crown of Aragon, San Cugat, ms. 73; Cambridge University Library, ms Mm. 3.21, i94v-196v. The set ultimately makes it into the Sarum tradition.
62 Andrieu 1940a; Andrieu 1940b.
63 Vogel and Elze 1963, 2:362. On this tradition, see now Parkes 2015, 950–1050. The texts appeared in a number of early German volumes.
64 Clm 6427, fol 133–134; ed. in Franz vol. 2, 275–277: 'Pro fratribus in viam, id est ad limina apostolorum vel alias causa orandi dirigendis'.
65 Franz 2006, 2:287–288.
66 Franz 2006, 2:275–276: 'ut, quemadmodum virga Aaron in templo domini florens ab rebellium Iudenorum numero ipsius stirpem rite seiunxit, ita et hos signaculo sancti Petri adornandos ab omnibus peccatis absolvas, quo in die iudicii ab impiis segregate in dextera sint parte coronandi'.
67 Franz 2006, 2:276: 'Quando dabuntur capselle [bag, wallet] et fustes, dicatur hominbus: Accipite has capsellas et hos fustes et peragite ad limina apostolorum in nomine patris et filii et spiritus sancti, ut per intercessionem beate dei genetricis Marie et omnium

apostolorum atque omnium sanctorum mereamini in hoc seculo accipere remissionem omnium peccatorum et in future consortium omnium bonorum'.
68 Most of these are usefully collected in Henderson 1875, Appendix, 207*–210*. See also Brundage 1966.
69 Lapidge 1983, particularly at 19–20. The rite is printed in Henderson 1875, Appendix 207*.
70 Henderson 1875, 207*–208*. Lapidge 1983; Lapidge 1981; Gullick 1996.
71 Curiously, two of these were at least partly based on various blessings of weapons known from the tenth-century Egbert Pontifical.
72 Banting 1989, 138.
73 London BL Cotton Vitellius E.XII, fol. 156v: 'Presta ei, Domine, fidem rectam spem firmam, cordis fiduciam, corporis fortitudinem, omnium memborum valitudinem'.
74 London BL Cotton Vitellius E.XII: 156v-157r: 'clementiam, potentiam, indulgentiam, remissionem, miserationem, compassionem'; 'nunc novo lavacro penitentie peregrinationisque'; 'sine ullo languore et contrarietate mereatur sancti Petri omniumque Apostolorum necnon sanctorum pervenire intercessione, animo, corpore, secundum quod optat ad propria in Domino tutus'.
75 Henderson 1875, 208*.
76 'Domine, Deus omnipotens' is largely adopted. The opening clauses of 'Confortator et corroborator' are incorporated into later texts. Cf: the York manual (14th century), printed in Henderson 1875, p 103. Oxford Magdalen College ms 226 is edited in Wilson 1910; Kay 2007, 610.
77 The Worcester Pontifical is Cambridge Corpus Christi College ms. 146. The Reims Pontifical is Reims BM ms. 341. These are discussed and edited in Gaposchkin 2011: 280–281 (for Worcester), 281–284 (for Reims).
78 On the question of the development of the Papal pilgrimage rite, see Gaposchkin 2011, 261–286.
79 Andrieu 1938, 265, XLVII: 'te humiliter imploramus, quatinus sanctificando bene[+] dicere digneris hanc peram et hunc baculum, ut quicunque eam in tui nominis amore ad instar humilis armaturae lateri suo applicare atque collo suo suspendere sive in manibus suis gestare cupierint sicque peregrinando suffragia humili comitante devotione studuerint quaerere, dexterae tuae protecti munimine pervenire mereantur ad gaudia mansionis aeternae'.
80 Olivar 1953, 170; Vázquez de Parga et al. 1948–1949, vol. 3, 145.
81 Guidiol 1927, 111.
82 Reims BM 341, fol. 2r: 'Indulgentiam & remissionem omnium peccatorum vestrorum [tuorum] tribuat vobis [tibi] omnipotens dominus'.
83 Vogel and Elze 1963, 362: 'Accipite has capsellas et hos fustes et pergite ad limina apostolorum in nomine patris et filii et spiritus sancti, ut per intercessionem beatae Dei genetricis Mariae et omnium apostolorum atque omnium sanctorum mereamini in hoc seclo accipere remissionem omnium peccatorum et in futuro consorcium omnium beatorum'. Franz 1909, 3:277.
84 Vogel and Elze 1963, 362: 'ab omnibus peccatis absolvas'.
85 Gyug 1989, 402.
86 Ward 1987, 115–126.
87 Dumas 1981, 438–439. 'nullum periculum per spatia terre aut per iuga montium, angusta vallium, vadaque fluminum, venera serpentium, vel impetum bestiarum incurrant'.
88 Reims BM 341, 4v: 'resistere valeas venenosis impulsionibus serpentis antique'. The prayer is printed in: Andrieu, 1938, XLVII.3, p.265. I have argued elsewhere that this prayer is an interpolation into the RP12 tradition. See: Gaposchkin 2011.
89 Riley-Smith 1997, 81–85; Gaposchkin 2013a.
90 Graz Univ. ms. 239, 143v, edited in Pennington 1974, 431.

91 Gaposchkin 2013a, 70–71.
92 Vogel and Elze 1963, 362.
93 Gaposchkin 2013b.
94 On the larger spiritual ideals of early crusading, see Purkis 2008. On the specific adaptation of these rites for crusading, see Gaposchkin 2013a.
95 Gaposchkin 2013a, 44–91; Gaposchkin 2017, 65–92.
96 Gaposchkin 2013a, 74–77.

## Bibliography

### Manuscripts

Arxiu de la Corona d'Aragó, San Cugat, ms. 73
Avignon Bibliothèque Municipal ems. 143
Budapest Orzagos Szechenyi Konyvtar, ms lat. Med. Aev. 330
Burgos Archivo Histórico de la Catedral, ms. 24
Cambridge, Cambridge Corpus Christi Library ms. 146
Cambridge, Cambridge University Library, ms Mm. 3.21
London, British Library, Cotton Vitellius ms. E.XII
Macerata, Biblioteca Comunale "Mozzi-Borgetti" 378
Montepellier, Bibliothèque Universitaire, section medicine, ms. 314
Munich Bayerische StaatsBibliothek, codices latini monacenses (clm) ms 6427
Reims Bibliothèque Municipalems. 341
Troyes Bibliothèque Municipal ms. 2140
Vich, Biblioteca Capitular, códice XLVIII (moderna ms. 66)
Vienna Österreichische Nationalbibliothek ms. 701

### Printed Sources

Amiet, Robert. 1974. *The Benedictionals of Freising: Munich, Bayerische Staatsbibliothek, Cod. Lat: 6430*. Maidstone: British Legion Press.
Andrieu, Michel ed. 1938. *Le Pontifical Romain au Moyen-Age: Tome I: Le Pontitifical Roman du XII$^e$ siècle*. Vatican City: Bibliotheca apostolica vaticana.
Andrieu, Michel ed. 1940a. *Le Pontifical de la Curie Romaine au XIII$^e$ siècle*. Vatican City: Biblioteca apostolica vaticana.
Andrieu, Michel ed. 1940b. *Le Pontifical de Guillaume Durand*. Vatican City: Biblioteca apostolica vaticana.
Banting, H. M. J. ed. 1989. *Two Anglo-Saxon Pontificals (the Egbert and Signey Sussex Pontificals)*. London: Henry Bradshaw Society.
Coebergh C. and Pierre de Puniet. 1977. "Liber sacramentorum Romanae ecclesiae ordine exscarpsus." In *Corpus Christianorum Continuatio Mediaevalis*, vol. 47. Turnhout: Brepols.
Deshusses, Jean. 1988–1992. *Le Sacramentaire Grégorien: ses principales formes d'après les plus anciens manuscrits*, 2 ed., 3 vols. Spicilegium Friburgense 16 (3rd ed.), 24 (2nd ed.), 28 (2nd ed.). Fribourg: Éditions Universitaires.
Dumas, Antoine ed. 1981. *Liber Sacramentorum Gellonensis, 2 vols., Corpus Christianorum. Series Latina*, 159–159A. Turnhout: Brepols.
Eadmer. 1962. *The Life of St. Anselm, Archbishop of Canterbury*, edited with introduction, notes and translations by R. W. Southern. Oxford: Clarendon Press.

Férotin, Marius. 1996 [1904]. *Le liber ordinum: en usage dans l'église wisigothique et mozarabe d'Espagne du cinquième au onzième siècle*, Monumenta Ecclesiae liturgica 5. Paris: Firmin-Didot.
Franz, Adolph. 1904. *Das rituale von St. Florian aus dem zwölften jahrhundert*. Freiburg: Herder.
Franz, Adolph. 2006 [1909]. *Die kirchlichen Benediktionen im Mittelalter*, 2 vols. Bonn: Verlag nova & vetera.
Guidiol, Joseph. 1927. "Els peregrins i peregriatges religiosos catalans." *Analecta sacra Tarroconensia* 3: 93–119.
Heiming, O.S.B. ed. 1984. *Liber Sacramentorum Augustodunensis*, Corpus Christianorum Series Latina 49B. Turnhout: Brepols.
Henderson, W.G. ed. 1875. *Manuale et Processionale*, The Publications of the Surtees Society 63. Durham: Andrews and co.
*Liber sacramentorum romane aeclesiae*. 1960. Rome: Herder.
Migne, J.-P. ed. 1844–1891. *Patrologia cursus completus*. Series latina. Paris: J.-P. Migne..
Moeller, Edmond Eugène. 1980–1981. *Corpus praefationum*, 5 vols. Series Latina 161, 161 A-D. Turnhout: Brepols.
Moeller, Edmond Eugène ed. 1971. *Corpus benedictionum pontificalium*. Turnhout: Brepols.
Moeller, Edmond Eugene and Jean-Marie Clément eds. 1992–. *Corpus Orationum*, 14 vols. Corpus Christianorum Series Latina 160. Turnhout: Brepols.
Mohlberg, Leo Cunibert et al. eds. 1956. *Sacramentarium Veronense*, Rerum ecclesiasticarum documenta. Series maior. Fontes 1. Rome: Herder.
Mohlberg, Leo Cunibert ed. 1960. *Liber Sacramentorum Romanae Aeclesiae Ordinis anni circuli (Cod. Vat. Reg. lat 316/Paris Bibl. Nat. 7193, 41/65 (Sacramentarium Gelasianum)*, Rerum ecclesiasticarum documenta, Fontes IV. Rome: Herder.
Olivar, Alejandro ed. 1953. *El Sacramentario de Vich*, Monumenta Hispaniae Sacra, Serie liturgica 4. Barcelona: Consejo Superior de Investigaciones Científicas, Instituto P. Enrique Flórez.
Vogel, Cyrille and Reinhard Elze eds. 1963. *Le Pontifical romano-germanique*, 2 vols. Studi e testi 226–227. Vatican City: Biblioteca apostolica vaticana.
Warren, F.E. ed. 1883. *The Leofric Missal*. Oxford: Clarendon Press (reprint of original edition: Farnborough: Gregg, 1968).
Wilson, Henry A. ed. 1903. *The Benedictional of Archbishop Robert*. London: Henry Bradshaw Society.
Wilson, Henry A. 1910. *The Pontifical of Magdalen College: With an Appendix of Extracts from Other English MSS. of the Twelfth Century*. London: Henry Bradshaw Society.

## Literature

Birch, Debra. 1998. *Pilgrimage to Rome in the Middle Ages: Continuity and Change*. Woodbridge, Suffolk: Boydell Press.
Bradshaw, Paul. 1999. "The Influence of Jerusalem on Christian liturgy." In *Jerusalem: Its Sanctity and Centrality to Judaism, Christianity, and Islam*, edited by Lee I. Levine, 251–259. New York: Continuum.
Brundage, James A. 1966. "'Cruce Signari': the Rite for Taking the Cross in England." *Traditio* 22: 289–310.
Chupungco, Anscar J. ed. 1997. *Handbook for Liturgical Studies: Introduction to the liturgy*, 5 vols, vol. 1. Collegeville, MN: Liturgical Press.

Bynum, Caroline Walker. 1987. "Religious women in the later Middle Ages." In *Christian Spirituality: High Middle Ages and Reformation*, edited by Jill Raitt. New York: Crossroad Books.

Franz, Adolph. 1909. *Die kirchlichen Benediktionen im Mittelalter*, 2 vols. Freiburg: Herder.

Gaposchkin, M. Cecilia. 2011. "Origins and Development of the Pilgrimage and Cross Blessings in the Roman Pontificals of the Twelfth and Thirteenth Centuries (RP12 and RP13)." *Mediaeval Studies* 73: 261–286.

Gaposchkin, M. Cecilia. 2013a. "From Pilgrimage to Crusade: The Liturgy of Departure, 1095–1300." *Speculum* 88(1): 47–50.

Gaposchkin, M. Cecilia. 2013b. "The Role of Jerusalem in Western Crusading Rites of Departure (1095–1300)." *Catholic Historical Review* 99: 1–28.

Gaposchkin, M. Cecilia. 2017. *Invisible Weapons: Liturgy and the Making of Crusade Ideology*. Ithaca, NY: Cornell University Press.

Garrisson, Francis. 1965. "A propos des pèlerins et de leur condition juridique." In *Etudes d'histoire du droit canonique dediées à Gabriel Le Bras*, vol. 2, 1165–1181. Paris: Sirey.

Gullick, M. 1996. "The Origin and Date of Cambridge, Corpus Christi College MS 163." *Transactions of the Cambridge Bibliographical Society* 11: 89–91.

Gyug, Richard. 1989. "A Pontifical of Benevento (Macerata, Biblioteca Comunale 'Mozzi-Borgetti' 378." *Mediaeval Studies* 51: 355–423.

Kay, R. 2007. *Pontificalia: A repertory of Latin manuscript Pontificals and Benedictionals*. Lawrence, KS: University of Kansas. https://kuscholarworks.ku.edu/bitstream/handle/1808/4406/PONTIFICALIA.pdf;sequence=3

Lapidge, M. 1981. "The origin of CCCC 163." *Transactions of the Cambridge Bibliographical Society* 8: 18–28.

Lapidge, M. 1983. "Eadred of York and MS. Cotton Vitellius E.XII." *Yorkshire Archaeological Journal* 55: 11–25.

Palazzo, Eric. 1998. *A History of Liturgical Books from the Beginning to the Thirteenth Century*. Collegeville, MN: Liturgical Press.

Parkes, Henry. 2015. *The Making of Liturgy in the Ottonian Church: Books, Music and Ritual in Mainz, 950–1050*. Cambridge: Cambridge University Press.

Pennington, Kenneth. 1974. "The Rite for Taking the Cross in the Twelfth Century." *Traditio* 30: 429–435.

Planas, J.R. Barriga. 1975. *El sacramentari, ritual i pontifical de Roda: cod. 16 de l'arxiu de la catedral de Lleida, c. 1000*. Barcelona: Fundació Salvador Vives Casajuana.

Plötz, Robert. 1986. "'Benedictio perarum et baculorum' und 'coronatio peregrinorum': Beiträge zu der Ikonographie des Hl. Jacobus im deutschen Sparachgebiet." In *Volkskultur und Heimat. Festschrift für Josef Dünninger zum 80 Geburtstag*, edited by Dieter Harmening and Erich Wimmer, 339–376. Würzburg: Königshausen + Neumann.

Purkis, William J. 2008. *Crusading Spirituality in the Holy Land and Iberia, c. 1095–1187*. Woodbridge, ON: The Boydell Press.

Riley-Smith, Jonathan. 1997. *The First Crusaders, 1095–1131*. New York: Cambridge University Press.

Rivard, Derek A. 2009. *Blessing the World: Ritual and Lay Piety in Medieval Religion*. Washington, DC: Catholic University of America Press.

Southern, Richard. 1963. *Saint Anselm and his Biographer: A Study of Monastic Life and Thought, 1059-c. 1130*. Cambridge: Cambridge University Press.

Sumption, Jonathan. 1976. *Pilgrimage: An Image of Mediaeval Religion*. Totowa, NJ: Rowman and Littlefield.
Tinsley, Ernest John. 1960. *The Imitation of God in Christ: An Essay on the Biblical Basis of Christian Spirituality*. Philadelphia, PA: Westminster Press.
Turner, Victor. 1969. *The Ritual Process: Structure and Anti-structure*. Ithaca, NY: Cornell University Press.
Turner, Victor and Edith Turner. 1978. *Image and Pilgrimage in Christian Culture: Anthropological Perspectives*, Lectures of the History of Religions, ns 11. New York: Columbia University Press.
Vázquez de Parga, Luis, et al. 1948–1949. *Las peregrinaciones a Santiago de Compostela*, 3 vols. Madrid: Consejo Superior de Investigaciones Cient'ificas, Escuela de Estudios Medievales.
Vogel, Cyrille. 1963. "Le pèlerinage pénitential." In *Pellegrinaggi e culto dei Santi in Europa fino alla 1A Crociata*, 37–94. Todi: Convegni del Centro di Studi sulla Spiritualità Medievale.
Vogel, Cyrille. 1986. *Medieval Liturgy: An Introduction to the Sources*, trans. William G Storey. Washington, DC: Pastoral Press.
Ward, Benedicta. 1987 [1982]. *Miracles and the Medieval Mind*. Philadelphia, PA: University of Pennsylvania Press.
Webb, Diana. 1999. *Pilgrims and Pilgrimage in the Medieval West*. London: I.B.Tauris.

# 12 'Not all those who wander are lost'[1]
## Saintly travellers and their companions in medieval Scandinavia

*Sara Ellis Nilsson*

## Introduction

Travelling was not a foreign concept in the early medieval period, even in the peripheries of western Christendom. Many stories of travel activated the recipients' geographical imagination. The sixth-century Irish monastic saint Brendan of Clonfert provides a prime example. Brendan was famous for his seven-year voyage as part of his quest to find the Blessed Isles. His voyage and its description can also be alleged to have served other purposes than the devotional. It can be interpreted as a navigational story, i.e. a mnemonic device, used to assist in conveying navigational information to future generations. In this case, the objective of Brendan's voyage was to find a holy place, perhaps of later use to monks seeking solitude. Brendan's interactions with his travelling companions – fellow monks – also provide a model for future representations of voyages and especially pilgrimages.[2]

The geographical focus of this chapter is slightly to the east and north: Scandinavia. Its aim is to explore perceptions of travel in the past and its association with holiness by studying accounts of travel in the hagiographical texts that were composed for a selection of Danish and Swedish saints. Although not all were as well-travelled as the sixth-century St. Brendan, many early medieval Scandinavian saints were reported to have travelled over long distances for various purposes including pilgrimage. For instance, the concept of *vita est peregrinatio* – that life is a pilgrimage, a transitional stage on the journey to God – is clear in the lives of the early saints. This form of pilgrimage did not require a specific destination as with *peregrinatio loca sancta* ('pilgrimage to a holy place').[3] With regards to actual contemporary travel with which audiences would have been familiar, the later medieval miracle stories bear witness to journeys (that is, pilgrimages to holy places) undertaken in the hopes of saintly intercession or to carry out a vow after a miracle.[4] Often these voyages were undertaken together with at least one companion – named or unnamed – with the ensuing interaction being instrumental to the saint's life.

This article explores an approach presented in Courtney Luckhardt's dissertation (*Connecting Saints: Travel and Hagiography in the Northwestern Atlantic, 500-800*), wherein travel is argued to have played an integral part in the narratives found in early medieval (6th–9th century) hagiographies in, for instance, Francia, Ireland, and Northumbria. In Luckhardt's view, a saint's knowledge of geography demonstrated knowledge of the divine plan. In fact, she argues, a saint's reputation for being a traveller was as important as their reputation for being miracle workers (or ascetics).[5] Therefore, the chapter explores perceptions of historical saintly travel and discusses whether travelling was to convey a precise ideology or to provide an interpretation of a historical situation, highlighting social and communal aspects of travel. As part of this exploration of perceptions of travel, it addresses routes and destinations, who the saints' companions were, and the hagiographical use of social interaction reflected in these texts.

The sources include hagiographical texts from the medieval ecclesiastical provinces of Lund, i.e. medieval Denmark, and Uppsala, approximately medieval Sweden (Map 1).[6] These texts were all produced for the cults of local saints, whose shrines played an important role in later pilgrimage activity and the creation of holy places for the new religion (Christianity) throughout Scandinavia. In most cases, these texts were written sometime after the saint's death, and thus, it is likely that they reflect contemporary attitudes or perceptions of travel at the time of writing. For the purposes of this article, it is the type of travel and its association with a saint in the imagined religious past that are in focus.[7]

The missionaries and bishop-saints considered were all thought to have lived in the eleventh century: St Theodgarus, St Eskil, and St Sigfrid. However, the earliest hagiographical texts were composed in the late-twelfth or early thirteenth century. The laity are represented by the late-eleventh- and twelfth-century saints: St Botvid and St Elin, respectively.[8] Similarly to the missionary saints, their hagiographical texts were composed sometime after their deaths. Although Botvid's feast day is found on calendar fragments, the earliest extant lessons are from the thirteenth century. Elin's Office was completed by the end of the thirteenth century (although there appears to have been an earlier version). While Botvid and Elin were not the only lay saints in the early period, these two have been chosen as there are early local hagiographical traditions associated with them, and notably, they were not members of the royalty or nobility, whereas the majority of Scandinavian lay saints were. The hagiographical sources are, thus, relatively late; however, it is unusual – based on the extant sources – for non-royal saints in Scandinavia to have had *vitae* or liturgies written for them before the late-twelfth or early thirteenth century (Map 3).

## The sources and a historical perspective

The local saints in the north fulfilled various roles in their local communities as church-builders, formal and informal missionaries, and *exempla*. In addition, pilgrimage destinations were created in their honour, necessary for the devotional lives of the local people. After the papal decree of 1234, the canonization process became more bureaucratic – increasing the sources for the cults of saints; however, in the early period there were several other types of sources which provide

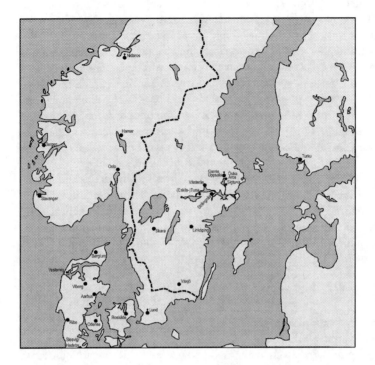

*Map 3* The bishoprics of the three medieval Scandinavian ecclesiastical provinces (Iceland, Greenland, the Atlantic Islands, and Rügen are not shown; Ellis Nilsson 2015, 3).

glimpses into the journeys and social interactions that saints in the north purportedly engaged in together with their travel companions.

Studying sources written for the cults of early local saints in Scandinavia can provide insights into previously neglected aspects of medieval history in the area.[9] Taking into consideration the mentalities – that is, the worldview or attitudes – expressed in hagiographical literature is also of importance in a holistic approach to the study of medieval society. As will be seen in this article, taking one specific aspect of daily life – travelling – and examining how the activity was approached in descriptions of the lives of saints provides a glimpse into behaviours expected of holy people, as well as a reflection of actual, contemporary expectations regarding, for instance, travel – even in a historical perspective.

The hagiographical sources used in this analysis were not, of course, written as travel guides. Their original purpose was primarily to emphasize the sanctity of the individual in question. Therefore, this aspect has had an influence on the portrayal and perception of travel found in these texts. In addition, it influenced the historical perception of saintly travels in that it enhanced their saintly reputation.[10]

In the Middle Ages, any hagiographical texts, whether they were late medieval canonization processes, legends, or liturgical texts, were primarily written by and for the clergy; however, they were also used as *exempla* for many different groups, especially in the case of sermons, and were intended for the laity as well. Moreover, stories of saints would have been shared and enjoyed among the laity for entertainment and elucidation. This implies that they were intended as ideological tools for religious didactical purposes – of both the clergy and the laity.[11]

It is possible, however, that – in addition to being used for *exempla* – their composition was historiographical in nature, as Felice Lifshitz suggests.[12] That is, no clear distinction was made between recording the history of a saint and that of a political figure.[13] The importance of studying hagiographical texts in terms of their role in creating mythopoetic moments has also been raised.[14] That is, the contents of hagiographical texts can reveal how contemporaries viewed their own local or regional history – in this case, in light of the area's place in Christian history. On the other hand, historiography could also lean towards the hagiographical. In principle, on some level, all history-writing was undertaken in order to reflect upon, elucidate, and convey the divine plan: the history of Christianity.

The twelfth- and thirteenth-century hagiographical texts discussed in this chapter – i.e. the *lectio* from the *proprium de sanctis* on the feast day of the saint in question – are all, arguably, clearly hagiographical in nature as they all focus on preserving the histories of saints. However, they would have, in the medieval period, also been considered historiographical as they tell the stories of important characters in the history of Christendom. Therefore, this implicates that information about travelling can be considered as reliable in hagiographical texts as that found in secular histories, at least with regards to actual or perceived journeys undertaken by the historical individuals in question. The information that can be gleaned from these texts is considerable.

In this chapter, the legends associated with the saints mentioned have been considered, in particular those elements found in the lessons (*lectio*) for the Daily Office (*officium*) found in the liturgy for a particular saint's feast day. These sources are the earliest extant versions of these particular saints' stories; however, as mentioned and will be discussed below in connection with each saint, most of the texts were written or compiled around a hundred years after the saints' lifetimes. The lessons from the reconstructed, early Offices of these local saints are based on the liturgical fragment material (where available) as well as interpretations of the development of the later breviaries. Each Office will be discussed in further detail below and will provide a glimpse into beliefs about the past that existed in the late twelfth and thirteenth centuries.

## Destinations and purpose of travel

In the following, an attempt will be made to contextualize the travels of these saints as portrayed in their legends. Exploring the routes and means of transportation will enhance the study of perceptions of mobility in this period.[15] In some cases, the actual destinations are specifically named in the texts, while the distance and possible routes to these locations can be inferred. These provide the audience with a context, spatialization, and geographical points of reference.

With regards to possible symbolic readings or interpretation(s) of the texts, it is important to consider the fact that the journeys of several of these saints contain a key motif of liminality.[16] The voyage itself can be seen as providing a liminal space on the way towards sainthood – similar to a pilgrimage. The journey is undertaken before the person becomes or is recognized as a saint and provides the saint with the motif of *transience*.[17] For instance, Sari Katajala-Peltomaa discusses how pilgrimage can be both *liminal* – social status needs to be suppressed in acts of humility and for some individuals it is a form of identity creation – as well as *not liminal* – social status continues to exist and in some cases is even reinforced throughout the pilgrimage.[18] As will be seen, this aspect is reflected in the way the saints are all represented as having travelled.[19] The voyage offers the saint the means of journeying from one form of being into another – enhancing his/her spiritual standing.[20] In some cases, these voyages are related to their first visits to the area, and the narrative follows their footsteps to the establishment of permanent ecclesiastical institutions as with the missionary saints Theodgarus, Eskil, and Sigfrid, or to a sanctified martyrdom, in the case of the lay saints Botvid and Elin.[21]

The first category or examples that will be discussed are missionary saints, who could also be described as itinerant bishops. How were their travels portrayed? How were they meant to be understood by the contemporary audience of the texts? Missionaries or itinerant bishops were, of course, expected to travel. The name provides clear associations with travelling and the stories can be interpreted as reflecting a realistic historical situation.

In the second category can be placed the two saintly members of the laity, who were under no such obligation to travel, although they could choose to do so. However, the descriptions of the journeys reflect later perceptions of the early medieval (conversion) period. In addition, when travel was undertaken in the local area and is described with a certain level of detail, it reflects local knowledge or perceptions of journeys in the neighbouring area.

## *Missionary saints*

With regards to the bishops and missionaries, according to their legends, St Eskil and St Sigfrid were eleventh-century itinerant bishops/missionaries who preached in what became the Ecclesiastical Province of Uppsala. Both reportedly came from England. In some later versions of his legend, Sigfrid is even reported to have been Archbishop of York. After having arrived in Tuna from his native England, Eskil's missionary work and travels were local to his new diocese of Tuna. He would travel by foot to preach and administer to his new converts. Eskil had travelling companions, his unnamed priests, and the first lesson of his thirteenth-century Office shows that he was also associated with St Sigfrid (although this connection is missing from Sigfrid's legend).[22]

According to his legend, eventually Eskil's itinerant missionary behaviour lead to his martyrdom, in or near Strängnäs. Lesson 5 relates that Bishop Eskil resided in Fors Church (across the river from Tuna) and makes his way to the place of those 'worshipers of idols'; this was presumably Strängnäs as is related in the previous lesson.[23] It is clear from the short description that it was deemed possible at the time of writing for Eskil to have travelled between Fors or Tuna and Strängnäs on foot. An understanding of travel could thus also be applied to a historical figure. The focus in Eskil's legend is on his holiness and martyrdom at the hands of pagans, however, rather than on describing his journeys in detail. As stated, these were not travel guides, although potential places of pilgrimage might have been discernible. Instead, the journeys provide a framework, founded in everyday experiences, and a setting upon which to construct the establishment of Eskil's holiness.

As for Sigfrid, the use of travelling is used throughout his legend and is an important motif in developing Sigfrid as a saint, connecting him to the various communities throughout what later became the ecclesiastical province. The use of travel as a narrative device is also important in Sigfrid's case. A few examples from his early thirteenth-century legend will be explored in the following.

Sigfrid's journey from England to Sweden is described as difficult and treacherous. This description emphasizes Sigfrid's holiness and dedication, two of the many aspects that would prove he was a saint.[24] In fact, a description of the preparations for the journey is included in his later *officium* in Lesson 2. It mentions the activity surrounding his departure – such as bidding the group farewell, accepting prayers, and acquiring the provisions needed for the ship. The lesson continues by indicating that the ship landed first in Denmark, where they were welcomed by the king and with whom they spent some time. The journey required permission from the king in order to continue his travels to Sweden. The roads are described as treacherous, crossing over steep mountains/cliffs and through thick woods.[25] In this passage, it appears important to emphasize the saint's endurance and determination in evangelizing to the inhabitants in order to enhance the audience's perception of his sanctity. At this point, the group arrives in Växjö which proves to be the final destination for some of them. This last point is especially important as Växjö laid claim to Sigfrid's early presence in the town as being the founding moment of the diocese.

As will be discussed below, Sigfrid did not travel alone on these arduous journeys; however, his companions (his nephews) were killed while Sigfrid had travelled north to preach to a King *Olauus* – probably in the eastern part of Västergötland which is quite a trek from Växjö in the province of Värend.[26] However, neither the journey there nor the one back to Växjö is described in detail; the text simply states that Sigfrid hurried back. Instead, the story of his nephews' martyrdom is the most important element required for the audience at this point, rather than the actual, physical journey that Sigfrid made.[27] There was no need to dwell on the length of this journey presuming the audience was familiar with the route.

Turning now to the third example of a missionary saint, St Theodgarus of Vestervig, who was born Thüringen, was an eleventh-century missionary to the Norwegians and the Danes after having travelled to England.[28] He settled in Vestervig on northeastern Jutland and built a church, which he served as priest until his death sometime in the early eleventh century. According to Theodgarus' legend, King Svend Estridsen (ca. 1019–1074), a well-known eleventh-century Danish king, was instrumental in establishing his cult, but Adam of Bremen, an eleventh-century monk and chronicler from Bremen, is silent on the matter in his *Gesta Hammaburgensis ecclesiae pontificum*.[29]

As mentioned, Theodgarus was described as travelling to England, Norway, and throughout Denmark before finally settling down and building a church in the northern part of Jutland. The purpose of his journey to England is unclear, but he was ordained a priest in Norway and the legend claims that he was made the chaplain of a King Olav.[30] After which, Theodgarus was active as a missionary and after Olav's death, he travelled to Denmark for missionary purposes.[31] Thedogarus' journeys are all lumped together at the beginning of his legend. The primary purpose of describing these travels can be seen as providing evidence for his reputation as a holy person: a missionary.[32] Thus, the stories of Theodgarus as a widely travelled missionary lay the foundation for his sanctity.

One of the stories in support of Theodgarus' sanctity includes a journey; however, it is not the saintly protagonist who does the travelling. Instead, it is the local bishop, Alfrik (*Alfricus*), vice-bishop (*pro episcopus*) of Jutland, who is described as having made the journey to Vestervig from an unnamed location where he was staying together with the Danish King Svend (Sweyn) Estridsen.[33] This account is of a real journey undertaken by the bishop to reinforce his (and the king's) authority within the bishop's jurisdiction. The social implications of this story will be discussed below.

## *Lay saints*

Several of the local Scandinavian lay saints are described as having undertaken important journeys during their lifetimes. The examples to be addressed in this article are Botvid of Södermanland and Elin of Skövde. Who were these saints? Botvid was a merchant from the early twelfth century who, according to his legend, was martyred by his freed slave while on a boat near Rågö (Sweden). The other lay saint to be considered is Elin, who was believed to have lived in the twelfth century in or near Skövde in the Skara Bishopric (Sweden). Elin was a widow of considerable means who was murdered by her son-in-law's relatives after he himself had been murdered, reportedly by servants who were tired of the domestic abuse that their mistress, Elin's daughter, had suffered.[34]

What kinds of journeys were these saints reported to have undertaken that would enrich their stories and enhance their sanctity? Starting with Botvid, both of his recorded journeys served specific purposes in his legend. The first tells of his encounter with Christianity during one of his trading trips to England. He was converted and encouraged to spread the new faith upon his return to Sweden. Although the historical details of Botvid himself might be partly fabricated, this trip provides a glimpse into the contemporary understanding of what had happened in the early twelfth century, during what was considered to have been the conversion period in Sweden. Botvid represents, through his story, a merchant who travelled abroad and brought the faith home. These aspects would have been important in the creation of an official history for the conversion of the area.

The second story of travel in Botvid's thirteenth-century legend sets the scene for his martyrdom.[35] It provides the perfect location for Botvid's murder by his ungrateful freed slave. In addition, the murder story contains clues as to how those writing in the thirteenth century understood how journeys were undertaken in the eleventh century. After freeing his slave, Botvid meant to send him back to his family and the Slavic country from whence he came, via a boat from Gotland.[36] The emphasis on the importance of the boat is clear. Even though Botvid's boat could have managed the journey to Gotland (as suggested later in the legend when his parents are reported to have thought he sailed over to Gotland himself), Botvid and his servant (or retainer), Esbjörn, were not interested in spending, or could not spare, the time that a voyage to Gotland and back would take. Instead, they sought out another boat that made the journey regularly from the coast near Rågö. During this coastal voyage in search of a ship to Gotland, the three sailed around the archipelago and searched for places where the ships usually weighed anchor – without any luck. However, Botvid and Esbjörn's journey was cut short during an overnight stay on Rågö, one of the stops on the journey.[37]

The purpose of the inclusion of the first of these journeys can be seen as connecting Botvid to the groups of merchants and others who journeyed westwards and encountered the new faith. These features would have been important to the audience, re-iterating stories they had heard about travels westward, and part of the mythopoetic movement to include the region in the history of Christendom.[38] The description does not, unfortunately, specify whereabouts in England Botvid traded, nor where the priest he encountered and who baptized him was based. These additional elements were not necessary to establish Botvid's sanctity. The association of the saint with trade in England was enough to create an image in the minds of the legend's audience of Botvid's destination and his activities there. His baptism and determination to spread his new faith were clear examples of how travelling had enhanced his holiness. The purpose of including the second journey is of course tied into Botvid's martyrdom and will be discussed below. Local knowledge of convenient anchorages along the east coast of Sweden also seems to have been included, for example at Rågö (*quae Roghö vocatur*) which could perhaps be seen as indicative of reinforcing suitable places of pilgrimage.[39]

With regards to the perceptions of St Elin of Skövde, in her legend, Elin was also described as having undertaken several journeys. The most mystical of Elin's journeys was included in a dream sequence in which she saw herself standing in a church in Götene and then the church was moved to Skövde. This event was interpreted in the lessons for her Office as a prediction of her own death and burial.[40] The audience would have understood this event as indeed to have had occurred as Elin was reported to have died in Götene and was buried in Skövde.

The vision motif is not unusual in hagiography; even St Sigfrid is reported to have dreamt that an angel indicated the spot in Värend where he is to build a church Växjö.[41] Indeed, Perpetua, one of the first martyrs, was described as having had a dream detailing her imminent death.[42] St Birgitta of Vadstena was also reported to have had a dream or vision about her own death.[43] However, it appears that Elin's case is special in terms of her vision of a church moving from one place to another and the subsequent interpretation that this represented her place of death and burial.

The longest journey Elin is described as undertaking was a pilgrimage to Jerusalem, as well as several other unnamed sites, a decision made after the murder of her son-in-law. It was unclear who the instigator of this crime was, and thus, who was morally responsible for his death, although her daughter's servants were clearly pointed out as the perpetrators. Elin's pilgrimage, if indeed it took place, would have been a considerable undertaking in the twelfth century, or even in the thirteenth when her legend was composed. These sorts of pilgrimages were unusual in this period for all social classes, with local or regional veneration of relics being the norm.[44] However, as also discussed in previous research, by the eleventh century, Jerusalem was increasing in popularity for those wishing to undertake a pilgrimage on a larger scale.[45] These longer journeys appear to have been directly tied to a pilgrim's socio-economic status. Indeed, the inclusion of such a well-known and respectable pilgrimage site in Elin's legend thus served to emphasize her wealth and, even more importantly in terms of emphasizing her sanctity, her piety, and her status in the community.

By the twelfth century, the value of Jerusalem and its associated sites as a pilgrimage destination was believed to have risen considerably. Piety focusing on Christ's final days was gaining popularity, and the idea that a pilgrimage to the Holy Land would absolve one from the sin of bloodshed had gained a foothold.[46] Relating this detail would have been important due to the apparent uncertainty about whether or not Elin had been involved in her son-in-law's death. This journey also supports the fact seen in previous research that the existence of these pilgrimage sites was also instrumental in creating a context for the new Christian faith. They provided a common ground, definitive objects of veneration, and a collective centre for all of Christendom – especially with regards to Christ's Passion.[47]

As mentioned, Elin's pilgrimage served to highlight her holiness to the legend's audience, of course. In fact, Lesson 4 in her Office, associates her choice of pilgrimage specifically with a noble saint, Helena, Constantine's mother.[48] The inclusion of Helena (Elin's namesake in Latin texts), would have provided the audience with a presumably familiar saint as a fitting parallel. For instance, Helena also travelled for religious reasons. Although no specifics of the journey are given, it was clearly understood that it was possible for a wealthy (holy) woman to have travelled from the Skara Bishopric to Jerusalem and back in the twelfth century.[49] The distance is notable, but was in keeping with other records of large-scale pilgrimage from other areas.[50] Elin thus fits into a larger pattern and this fact was highlighted by the author of her legend.

With regards to the motive, it has been suggested that Elin probably went on pilgrimage in order to absolve herself from any possible sin associated with the death of her son-in-law and to take a break from the familial problems caused by his death.[51] According to the lessons, his relatives might have interpreted Elin's pilgrimage to Jerusalem as an admittance of guilt. The lessons also reveal that

Elin's daughter-in-law's servants later implicated her as the instigator of the murder, and that her death was an act of revenge on the part of her son-in-law's family. A penitential pilgrimage to the epitome of all holy places could have been seen as cleansing her from any and all guilt – including involvement in someone's death.[52] Emphasizing that Elin undertook a pilgrimage of this magnitude would possibly have removed any uncertainty concerning her worthiness of the sainthood. It had the added effect of reinforcing her position in society.

Elin's final journey was incorporated into the story of her martyrdom and describes her travelling to the dedication of the church in Götene – the building of which she had helped fund.[53] Both are elements which reinforce the idea of her valued place in the newly Christian area. Unfortunately, the story does not specify what means of transportation she was using – horse or by foot – which could possibly have let the audience more easily identify to which class Elin belonged. Perhaps the omission was deliberate, leading to more people identifying with her, or perhaps the information was not necessary. Usually, it is assumed that she was walking to the church as her attackers easily overtook her and killed her.[54]

As shown by both her Jerusalem pilgrimage and her Götene journey, the author of Elin's life was emphasizing that the saint could afford to make considerable time investments in travel. The journey to Götene also reveals what were considered local destinations in the area both at the time of writing and presumably in Elin's day; that is, those that were less than a day's ride. Elin's usual attributes are a sword and a book. However, in Götene, a late fifteenth-century wall painting interpreted as Elin depicts her as a pilgrim.[55] Therefore, it is possible that this addition to her attributes is due to the fact she was seen as in the middle of a pilgrimage-like journey to the newly consecrated church when her life was cut short, focussing on that aspect of her connection to Götene in her legend. However, that new interpretation was a product of the fifteenth century, a time of renewal in the cults of saints in the Swedish province, and not part of the initial narrative creation.

## Companions on the journey – interactions and social standing

In travel stories, companions are often, but not always, important figures in the narratives. With regards to *communitas* and travel, in this study, three of the saints were missionaries – two of them bishops – while the other two were members of the laity, neither one connected to royalty. Missionaries were (and are!) expected to travel and were often accompanied by companions. The role of the missionary requires movement; the word itself evokes a sense of motion. Becoming a missionary could be an active decision on the part of the individual, but it is just as likely that this was a choice made for them by a higher-ranked cleric. In this community, travel would have been expected and not including it in a legend would be a puzzling omission to the audience.

In contrast, the association of travel with all members of the laity would not have been made by the legends' audiences. As mentioned, long-distance pilgrimage became increasingly more common after the eleventh century among those in the upper social classes. Thus, it would not have been unusual for Elin to have undertaken a long pilgrimage, and an audience might have immediately associated her with a certain social status. As for Botvid, he is described as a merchant, who sometimes travelled over great distances. Usually, in both cases, people would travel in groups. In the following section, companions, or the lack thereof, and the communities (*communitas*) to which these Scandinavian clerical and lay saints belonged will be discussed.

In hagiography, the saint's companions can be seen also seen as a reflection of the saint's position within the home community (*communitas*), either the actual position or the perceived position as interpreted later by the composers of the legends. This sense of *communitas* was an essential element of Christian communities, especially with regards to undertaking the liminal state of pilgrimage.[56] This aspect of community is important, as pilgrimages were usually performed in groups and were a social act. In some cases, the act of pilgrimage can be seen to have reinforced an individual's place in the collective.[57] As argued above, any form of travel, not just pilgrimage, places a traveller in a partial state of liminality; it is a transformative experience. In this transitional phase, the phenomenon of *communitas* – to which one has belonged, belongs to (perhaps temporarily) during the journey or will belong afterwards – can provide an essential foundation for the traveller, a sense of meaning/value, and an extra purpose. Thus, the saint's companions and their social status need to be taken into account as a factor in the reason for the journey and the final destination, and the fact that these elements are included in the saint's legend. What message of sanctity and travel was conveyed to the audience?

It appears that, in these narratives, the majority of pilgrims retained their social standing *during* the journey – at least as seen in the case of these saints. Moreover, their social standing was enhanced *following* the conclusion of the journey, especially if it were a pilgrimage, or in these cases, a metaphorical journey toward sainthood.[58] Thus, a journey's liminality can be seen as transformative – usually in a positive sense. The pilgrim – or a simple traveller – remains as part of a community – *communitas* – before, during, and after the pilgrimage/journey. Their social standing is not stripped away; rather it can be enhanced.

## *Missionary saints and their companions*

Concerning the use of companions in the narratives, the portrayal of the three clerical saints varies. Two of them are described as being accompanied while one appears without companions. To begin with, Sigfrid did not travel alone on these arduous journeys according to his legend, even that found on the earliest fragments. Sigfrid had numerous travelling companions including his nephews, who are named and were also involved in preaching. These nephews were murdered while Sigfrid was away on a journey to preach to a King *Olauus* and provide the story of a missionary martyrdom adding to its validity as a conversion narrative.[59]

Throughout Sigfrid's Office/legend, the decision to go on a journey enhances Sigfrid's or his nephews' holiness – they were regarded as companion saints – as it emphasizes the difficulty of travelling and that choosing to undertake a hazardous journey for a good cause could be perceived as amazing. This aspect could be related to the virtue of *patientia*, accepting one's fate, including suffering, with no signs of anger or frustration.[60] However, despite the many journeys made by Sigfrid in his legend, it is also revealed, in Lesson 5 in particular, that Sigfrid's reputation as a great preacher also meant that he could stay in one spot and others would travel to see him.[61] In this case, his stationary position is instead emphasized and those wishing to be baptized are required to move about. Sigfrid's travelling and his companions all serve to emphasize the fact that he is in the process of creating a new *communitas*. The transience in Sigfrid's story is found on two levels: the process of transformation from missionary to saint, and the process of converting those to whom he was preaching and baptizing. This aspect is not only associated with Sigfrid. In fact, those saints who are portrayed as missionaries whether they are clerics or members of royalty, all incorporate this dual form of transience. Thus, saints associated with newly converted areas – and who themselves participate *actively* in this conversion – are involved in the transformation of themselves and others.

The use of companions in these narratives could also connect saints' lives to each other.[62] According to information in Lesson 1 of Eskil's Office, he was associated with St Sigfrid by the mid-fourteenth century.[63] In fact, Lessons 2 and 3 emphasize that St Sigfrid inspired Eskil's missionary work.[64] In this case, the connection is one-way and is found in a later version of Eskil's legend. It is never added to Sigfrid's legend, however. Otherwise, in Eskil's legend, the companions who accompanied Eskil on the way to his martyrdom are simply described as priests (*cum clericis suis*).[65]

The next journey Eskil's body takes is in the hands of those Christians, erstwhile companions, who wished to give him a proper burial. This part of Lesson 6 provides Eskil with a divinely chosen resting spot – thanks to a miraculous fog – at what is now called Eskilstuna (*qui nunc vocatur Eskilstuna*).[66] Thus, the travel companions in Eskil's legend emphasize the saint's social standing, especially to the audience. The following elements are key to laying the foundation of this understanding. After establishing a missionary centre in Tuna, Eskil becomes a bishop. As befitting a bishop, he travels with an entourage of priests. His companions are mentioned as support for his position in the local *communitas*. The association with Sigfrid, although they are not portrayed as travelling together as such, stresses the connections between these two early saints and provides the impetus for Eskil's journey eastward and subsequent missionary work. Together, Eskil and Sigfrid provide an official narrative for the involvement of missionary saints in the conversion history of the area, related to mythopoetic movements.[67]

As for the ecclesiastical province of Lund (Denmark), there is no mention of any possible companions of St Theodgarus. However, there is a reference to a social interaction between Bishop Alfrik and King Svend Estridsen relating to travel, but not with regards to a saint.[68] In Theodgarus' case, the saint travels alone, a fact which seems to enhance his status. Instead, the story of Alfrik and Svend reflects societal expectations and social interaction between a king and a bishop. The king ordered the bishop to journey to Vestervig and remove the priest from his position, as well as to burn the bones (supposedly Theogarus') that had been translated. Within this particular travelling story is found an image of subordination of a bishop to a king. This portrayal of the past is interesting in light of the fact that the story took place during the lay investiture controversy.[69] In this example, the (unknown) author appears to either support the right of kings to command bishops, or is describing a past in which this was believed to have happened, but in which it was no longer valid.[70]

## *Lay saints*

The presence or absence of companions of the two lay saints also varies in these narratives. For example, no travelling companions are mentioned in Elin's legend, not even during her pilgrimage to Jerusalem. In all examples of travel, the figure of the saint, Elin, is presented alone and unaccompanied – similar to Theodgarus. The closest instance of travel companions that are featured in Elin's legend are the relatives of her son-in-law who ambushed and killed her on the way to the dedication of the church in Götene.[71] In this case, Elin's fellow travellers create a feeling of insecurity and mirror the dangers of the road. Moreover, they reveal contemporary, thirteenth-century beliefs about the feuding society that existed during the conversion period.[72]

What does Elin's lack of travel companions indicate? It was uncommon, but not unknown for women to travel alone – by themselves or in pairs. Two examples of these types of journeys have been discussed in previous research in relation to the miracles of St Bridget and her daughter, St Catherine, of Vadstena, although these journeys took place well after the composition of Elin's Office. The first journey occurred in the fourteenth century and involved a pilgrimage from Scania (then Denmark) to Vadstena. The second occurred in 1471 and concerned the adventure of a woman travelling for business who was saved by St Catherine after having broken through the ice.[73] As Anders Fröjmark speculates in his article, omitting travel companions – and witnesses, in the second case – from a story could enhance the feeling of danger and even the importance of the miracle.[74] However, it is also possible that travelling alone – or in pairs – was not, in fact, an unusual occurrence.

As Diana Webb has written, Christian women were relatively free to go on pilgrimage and any limitations to their participation in this activity were the same as for any form of travel. This fact indicates that Elin's actions in travelling alone would probably not have come as a surprise to the audience. In the later medieval period, these restrictions included the requirement to travel in a respectable fashion according to 'her rank and marital status', including with a male escort.[75] Widows appear to be the exception to this rule, as they could travel together in groups which did not include a man. Elin was a widow and, as such, subject to different restrictions.

In fact, Elin's pilgrimage is echoed in that of Gudrid, an important character in the Vinland Sagas (*Saga of Erik the Red* and the *Saga of the Greenlanders*), who after having undertaken several journeys around the North Atlantic, finally, as a widow, made a pilgrimage from Iceland to Rome in the tenth century.[76] Unlike Elin's Office which was composed about fifty years after her death, Gudrid's was written down in the thirteenth century, about 200 years after hers. However, they both represent a thirteenth-century understanding of possible journeys for women. In other words, it was not unusual for women to make the pilgrimage to Rome. Moreover, widows were thought to have had more freedom of movement – a fact which would have been understood by the audience. However, the lack of travel companions in Elin's story can also be seen as enhancing her holiness.

With regards to the other lay saint, Botvid, who was neither a woman nor a widow, the travelling companions in his legend are central to the plot concerning his conversion, his metaphorical journey towards sainthood (i.e. the liminal experience of *transience*), and finally his martyrdom. During his journeys as a merchant to England, Botvid travelled with a group of other wealthy farmers.[77] This group of unnamed people enables Botvid's journey to his place of salvation (England) and accompanies him on his journey back home. The journey to England changes his life and influences all of his subsequent actions. However, his companions are only mentioned as a group, and whether or not any of them converted together with Botvid is left unsaid.

The second journey included in Botvid's legend concludes with his martyrdom. The companions on this voyage are his servant (vassal), Esbjörn, and his freed slave. The purpose was to return one of the companions, the slave, to his homeland, an unnamed Slavic kingdom. This unnamed slave murders both Botvid and Esbjörn before stealing the boat and continuing the voyage alone. The presence of a servant suggests that the legend's audience expected one of the following: that the return journey required two people or that Botvid's position in his community necessitated accompaniment by a servant. The latter case is more likely as the slave was reported to have been able to operate the boat by himself. Thus, it does not appear that this form of boat travel required at least two individuals.

A further aspect of *communitas* in this story is that the act of freeing a slave could entail agreeing to return the slave to his/her homeland if the newly freed person did not wish to remain in the community. However, the legend suggests that returning the former slave to his homeland was part of Botvid's plan to convert the slave's family. In his legend, it is thus stressed that Botvid was part of the conversion movement and was active in spreading the new faith. These parts of the story firmly place Botvid's narrative in mythopoetic movements with regard to the conversion period. Through his actions, he would have demonstrated prevailing beliefs of how new converts would have acted or were believed to have acted when the legend was composed in about the thirteenth century.

Thus, taking all of the saints' legends examined in this chapter into consideration, it appears that the inclusion or absence of companions in the narrative serve a purpose. The presence of companions reinforces a particular aspect of a saint's *communitas* or reinforces the social standing of the saint. The absence (or presence) of earthly companions, although not an uncommon mode of travel to the audience, enhanced a saint's sanctity. It appears that audiences could accept that a variety of groups of travellers were possible and perhaps this was even expected.

## Conclusions

The lessons and legends of the five Scandinavian saints presented in this chapter contain a number of similarities. All of them are presented as travellers; each one travelled locally and made at least one long-distance journey – in some cases over a sea. In all of these cases, the extant texts were written sometime after the saint's death. Therefore, it is the attitudes of the authors and their contemporary audience that have been the focus in this chapter.

Belonging to the hagiographical genre, these stories of saintly individuals were used to emphasize their sanctity. From the examples used in this chapter, it can be seen that travel was used as part of the motif of *transience* – transitioning from one state of being to another. It could also be used as a motif to reinforce the sanctity of a saint. For example, similar to many of the legends, travel is necessary in the making of Eskil as a saint. Without his voyage from England to Sweden, Eskil would never have had the opportunity of becoming a martyr. Without her journey to Götene, Elin would never have become a martyr. Likewise, without his journeys, which lead to his conversion and martyrdom, Botvid's saintly reputation would not have been secure. Similarly, without their missionary journeys, Sigfrid and Theodgarus would not have garnered their saintly reputations. In this context, the actual destinations of the saints served different purposes. In some cases, travel provided the necessary means for a liminal space to be created. The missionary saints needed a destination for their mission, martyrs a journey towards their martyrdom. These can all be seen as direct consequences of their journeys.

Questions of how these saints' legends fit into mythopoetic movements – that is, creating coherent narratives about the conversion – were also raised. The entire era and these movements can be seen in terms of liminality and transience: a metaphysical journey from one state of being to another. Although the chapter focuses on the groups of saints in terms of their being members of the laity or missionaries, these aspects were shown to have had a bearing only on the *type* of journey the saint undertook. In terms of companions, if these are present in the narrative, they provide context and a clear *communitas* for the saint. The saint's social standing becomes clearer to the audience, as with Botvid's situation (manservant and slave) or Sigfrid's missionary support. In some cases, e.g. Botvid's, the travel companions even assist in the transience to sainthood via martyrdom. The absence of companions also appears to serve a narrative function, emphasizing the saint's ability to transcend earthly conventions and to act independently – albeit in keeping with Christian norms. Both Theodgarus and Elin fit into this pattern.

In addition to the importance of the travel motif in 'making a saint', the actual journeys described in these texts also clearly reflect the local understanding of geography – both local and distant. They reveal the dangers as well as the possibilities of travel in this time period. Expressions of holiness and piety are also vital in the journeys of these saints. Moreover, with regards to social relationships, as seen in Theodgarus' legend, these stories can also reveal expectations of obedience between a king and a bishop. In the case of Sigfrid and Eskil, they give us glimpses of the understanding of how the establishment of religious communities was accomplished in a newly converted area.

Consequently, it is apparent that hagiography can provide further insight into perceptions of early medieval travel in Scandinavia. Hagiography reveals social realities or, as has been applied in this chapter, perceptions of past social realities. These aspects include travel routes, companions, and various forms of social interaction. Thus, it would be of interest to further analyse these aspects of travel in saints' legends and compare to similar legends from elsewhere. Besides, as centuries of stories have shown, nothing beats a good travel story and those who wander wisely are not all lost.

## Notes

1 Tolkien 1954, 324.
2 See, for example, the discussion of the different versions of St Brendan's voyage (especially in relation to the Anglo-Norman narratives) in: Sobecki 2003, 197.
3 See below with regards to questions of the liminality inherent in travel, as well other articles in this volume. Definitions of these two concepts can be found in, for example, Plötz 1992, 37–38. Moreover, Vauchez states that pilgrimages are included in later medieval narratives related to the 'piety and devotion' saints showed as adults. There is usually no discussion of the negative aspects of this form of travel in hagiography. See, Vauchez 1997, 510–512.
4 For the later medieval period, for pilgrimages to the shrines of St Bridget, St Katarina and St Nils, see, especially, Krötzl 1994; Fröjmark 2006. For the English material, see e.g. Finucane 1995.
5 Luckhardt 2011. There is no specific reference to *vita est peregrinatio* however. The focus is on actual physical travel (not conceptual) and mental perceptions of space.
6 The Scandinavian ecclesiastical provinces were all established in the twelfth century: Lund in c. 1103, Nidaros (Trondheim) in 1153, and Uppsala in 1164. The boundaries of the three kingdoms roughly followed those of the ecclesiastical provinces. A large area of present-day southern Sweden was part of Denmark in the medieval period, i.e. the provinces of Scania, Blekinge, and Halland, while the modern Swedish regions of Bohuslän and Jämtland were part of the kingdom of Norway. Jämtland was, however, included in the Ecclesiastical Province of Uppsala. The diocese of Turku and western Finland were also included in the Uppsala province. Using the medieval religious jurisdictions as units of comparison allows the researcher to avoid modern national boundaries and nationalistic paradigms.
7 For a discussion of how hagiography provides an 'imagining of' a 'religious past' in terms of the Irish material, see Luckhardt 2013, 44.
8 These saints will be presented in more detail below. As discussed by Vauchez, the number of lay saints increased over the course of the later Middle Ages with a significant increase from the fourteenth century; therefore, Elin and Botvid's cults are relatively early. Vauchez 1997, 263–265, 354–356.
9 See, for example and among others, Ellis Nilsson 2015; Krötzl 2001; Katajala-Peltomaa 2012; Fröjmark 2012; Antonsson 2010.
10 Cf. Luckhardt 2011.
11 Sari Katajala-Peltomaa also suggests this interpretation of Lifshitz' ideas regarding the construction of the concept of hagiography in the nineteenth century. See Katajala-Peltomaa 2012, cf. Lifshitz 1994.
12 For a discussion, see also Ellis Nilsson Forthcoming 2020.

13 Lifshitz 1994. For the view that hagiography was to provide prime examples of Christian virtue and had 'a traditional pool of material' to use, sometimes copying verbatim, although with the caveat that these models of sanctity shifted over time, see Noble and Head 1995, xviii.
14 Conti 2010; Mortensen 2006; Ellis Nilsson 2015.
15 On logistics, cf. Bartlett 2013, 433–439.
16 For a discussion of Victor and Edith Turner's work related to the experience of modern pilgrimage as 'liminal' and the early Christian pilgrimages as 'liminoid'/voluntary, but which then later evolved into a required system, see Turner and Turner 2011 (1978), xxxi, 232. However, their views have recently received criticism. For example Sari Katajala-Peltomaa has argued that pilgrimage was also a way of coping and integrated into daily responsibilities; therefore, it cannot be seen as liminal. Moreover, aspects of the individuality of the Turners' interpretation of liminality are problematic as, for the most part, pilgrimage was an act engaged in collectively. However, in some respects, Katajala-Peltomaa does identify a form of liminality in the act of humility (see also next note). Katajala-Peltomaa 2009, 167–169, 190, 192.
17 See Turner and Turner 2011 (1978), 250.
18 Katajala-Peltomaa 2009, 192.
19 On the inclusion of travel as a holiness motif, see above and Luckhardt 2011.
20 On *transience*, see Turner and Turner 2011 (1978), 250.
21 As with most *vitae*, the lessons and legends pertaining to these saints focus on key sanctifying characteristics. Those connected to travel will be addressed below.
22 Eskil's Office, Lesson 1: '*Unde ipse pietatesua ineffabili misit eis beatum Sigfridum... Deditque peregrinationis suae comitem individuum, doctorem eximium, beatum Eskillum, de Britannia oriundum, cujus ipse capellanus fuerat et consanguineus.*' Version in the *Codex Laurentii Odonis*, edited in Lundén 1946a, 93.
23 That is, 'those that had become idolatrous': '[…] paucis aliis ad idolatras accessit'. Eskil's Office, Lesson 4–5. Edited in Lundén 1946a, 95–97.
24 Sigfrid's Office, Lesson 1. Edited in Lundén 1983, 191–192. There are a number of saintly attributes that are common in hagiographical texts, including *vitae* and the lessons for the Office of a saint's feast day. For example, these could include performing good deeds and miracles, having a gift of prophecy, being a martyr or confessor for the faith, virtue, and 'sacred aura'. Cf. Noble and Head 1995, xv, xviii.
25 Sigfrid's Office, Lesson 2. Edited in: Lundén 1983, 195: '*…vias difficillimas est aggressus, et per ardua moncium, per abrupta petrarum, per condensa siluarum.*'
26 Today, it would take about 47 hours to make the trip by foot, using modern roads, from Växjö to Husaby, the place with which Olof *Skötkonung* is usually associated.
27 Sigfrid's Office, Lessons 5–8. Edited in Lundén 1983.
28 Part of present-day Germany.
29 Ellis Nilsson 2015, 71. For the early importance of Theodgarus' cult and development, in the context of the establishment of a see on northern Jutland, cf. Clausen 2018, esp. 51–56.
30 Speculation has it that this was St Olav of Norway, but there is no indication in the legend that this is the case.
31 *Vitae sanctorum Danorum* (*VSD*), 14–15. *Danske Helgeners Levned* (*DHL*), 334–335.
32 Cf. Luckhardt 2013, 2011.
33 *VSD*, 15–16; *DHL*, 336–338.
34 This information is found in Elin's Office, Lesson 3–4. Piltz 2007, 199–200, 202–203, 223–225.
35 Although Botvid's feast-day can be found in calendars from the late twelfth century, the oldest extant Office fragments are from the thirteenth century.
36 Botvid's Office. Edited in Lundén 1983, 250. See also: *Script. Rer. Suec.* II:1, p. 377ff. and Önnerfors 1969.

37 From this information, the approximate course they would have taken along the coast of Sörmland could be extrapolated.
38 On mythopoetic 'moments', see e.g. Mortensen 2006. On modifying that idea to one of mythopoetic 'movements', see Ellis Nilsson 2019, 76.
39 Botvid's Office, Lesson 7. Edited in Lundén 1946b, 168. Lesson 4 (*que roghö uocatur*) in Önnerfors 1969, 156.
40 Elin's Office, Lesson 2. Edited in Piltz 2007. On foreseeing death as a hagiographical trope, see for example, Goodich 2005, 229, 233.
41 That is, present-day Växjö. Sigfrid's Office, Lesson 3. Edited in Lundén 1983, 196–197; Lundén 1957, 113–114. A recurring motif in saints' lives is a mother who dreams that her child will become a saint. See, among others, Bartlett 2013, 525–526. On false versus true dreams and the prerogative of hagiographers and church historians in interpreting dreams, see Bitel 1991, 46–47.
42 Bartlett 2013, 5. This dream fits well into Bitel's third model of dream-writing and interpretation in hagiography. The dream has to come true for it to be considered a sign of holiness. Bitel 1991, 52.
43 Chapter 31, *Birgitta av Vadstena: Reuelacionum liber septimus*.
44 Webb 2001, 16. For a discussion of distances travelled to English shrines tied to socio-economic status, see, for example, Finucane 1995, 156–171. See also the discussion below.
45 Webb 2001, 26. See also the introduction to this volume.
46 Cf. Webb 2001, 16, 27–28.
47 See Webb 2001, 16, 27–28. For the ways in which women facilitated communication and travel in the sixth and seventh centuries (featuring the hagiographies of the three monastic founders, Radegund of Poitiers, Brigid of Kildare, and Gertrude of Nivelles) but were often prevented from travelling themselves, see Luckhardt 2013.
48 Elin's Office, Lesson 4. Edited in Piltz 2007, 202, 224–225.
49 There are numerous examples of Scandinavian women who went on pilgrimage to Jerusalem in the first half of the Middle Ages, contrary to some claims that only men went to Jerusalem. See also the discussion about the situation in the later Middle Ages in Craig 2009, 131–132.
50 See Webb 2001, 16, 26–28.
51 Pernler 2007, 15–16. Penitential reasons for pilgrimage – or even, by the later medieval period, as punishment for crimes committed – are also addressed in Finucane 1995, 42–43.
52 On the penitential reasons for pilgrimage, see Finucane 1995, 42–43.
53 Elin's Office, Lesson 4. Edited in: Piltz 2007, 202–203, 225.
54 Today, the distance between Götene and Skövde is considered insignificant – about thirty minutes by car. Walking takes just over seven hours. The terrain is wooded and hilly in parts, but many ancient roads (hollow ways) are in evidence in this area so that it would have been accessible to travellers. The distance via these old roads was about the same as today. By horse, the distance could have been covered in about half that time if not less.
55 The painting is in the chancel arch and features three women pilgrims with staffs and rosaries. They have been interpreted as St Bridget, St Catherine (Katarina) of Vadstena, and St Elin. For an overview, see Pernler 2007, 101.
56 Turner and Turner 2011 (1978), 250.
57 Especially in relation to women and the reinforcement of their private role in the public sphere, see Katajala-Peltomaa 2009, 168, 191–192.
58 On the case of women and annual pilgrimages reaffirming (and perhaps enhancing) their social status, see Katajala-Peltomaa 2009, 190–103.
59 Ellis Nilsson 2015, 86–87, 175–177.

60 The virtue of patience, i.e. *patientia*, is shown when repressing negative emotions, such as unrighteous anger. Albeit difficult to define, it was seen as one of the desirable virtues. For a discussion, see (among others), Waugh 2012, Introduction (Section: *Pacientes vincunt*: The Virtue of Patience in Medieval Tradition.)
61 Sigfrid's (reconstructed) Office, Lesson 5. Lundén 1983, 200.
62 Writing saints into each other's narratives has been discussed in previous research and is for example found in the inclusion of St Alban in St Sunniva's story in Oddr Snorrasson's biography of Olaf Tryggvason (late-twelfth century). This association was corrected in later versions of her biography however due to geographical incompatibility. See Ellis Nilsson 2019; Borgehammar 1997, 270–292; DuBois 2008, 69–70. A further example is the connection of St Brigid with St Patrick in Ireland. See Luckhardt 2011, 42–43.
63 Eskil's Office, Lesson 1. Version in the *Codex Laurentii Odonis* (before 1379), edited in Lundén 1946a, 92–93.
64 Eskil's Office, Lesson 2 and 3, edited in Lundén 1946a, 93–94, 94–95.
65 Eskil's Office, Lesson 5, edited in Lundén 1946a, 96.
66 Eskil's Office, Lesson 6, edited in Lundén 1946a, 98.
67 See Mortensen 2006; Ellis Nilsson 2019, 76.
68 *VSD*, p. 15–16; *DHL*, 336–338.
69 Approximately from the mid-eleventh to early twelfth century.
70 A further possibility is of course that Alfrik was demonstrating a saintly characteristic in his obedience to his king. However, no other sources survive which promote Alfrik's holiness.
71 Elin's Office and Mass, Lesson 4. Edited in Piltz 2007, 202, 225.
72 Elements of a feuding society were evident throughout the medieval period. On feuding in Scandinavian medieval society as connected to the role of personal and familial ties in politics, see (among others), Hermanson 2009, 162, 168–169; Småberg 2004, 159–160. On the enduring image of conflict among the upper classes as 'feuds', with a focus on the fourteenth century, see Aronsson 2017, esp. 79–81.
73 Fröjmark 2006, 51, 53–54. Fröjmark uses the miracle stories to discuss local and regional voyages in Sweden (and in one case, Denmark).
74 Fröjmark 2006, 54.
75 Webb 2002, 'Women'. Webb discusses the problems of enclosure and the opinion that nuns should not engage in pilgrimage. Those that did were required to have an escort. Webb also discusses Margery Kempe and her encounters with other women, all of whom were accompanied by other women with at least one man in the party. The exception appears to be widows who could travel in groups only comprised of widows.
76 Webb 2002, 'Women'.
77 Lundén 1983, 247–248; *Script. Rer. Suec.* II:1, p. 377ff.

# Bibliography

## Primary Sources

Birgitta av Vadstena: *Reuelacionum liber septimus*. Stockholm: Riksarkivet. https://riksarkivet.se/Media/pdf-filer/SanctaBirgitta_Reuelacionum_LiberSeptimus.pdf.

Borgehammar, Stephan, ed. 1997. "Den latinska Sunnivalegenden. En edition." In *Selja - heilag stad i 1000 år*, edited by Magnus Rindal, 270–292. Oslo: Universitetsforlaget.

*Danske helgeners levned i oversættelse* (*DHL*), edited by Hans Olrik. 1893–1894. Copenhagen: Selskabet for Historiske Kildeskrifters Oversættelse.

Gertz, Martin Claurentius, 1908–1912. *Vitae Sanctorum Danorum (VSD)*. Copenhagen: G. E. C. Gad.
Lundén, Tryggve, ed. 1946a. "Brynolf Algotssons samlade diktverk." *Credo* 27(2): 73–124.
Lundén, Tryggve, ed. 1946b. "Sankt Ansgars, Sankt Botvids och Sankt Davids officier." *Credo* 27(3–4): 149–183.
Lundén, Tryggve, ed. 1957. "Den helige Sigfrid." *Credo* 3(38): 97–143.
Önnerfors, Alf. 1969. "Das Botvidoffizium des Toresundbreviers." *Eranos* 67: 144–165.
Piltz, Anders, ed. 2007. "Brynolf Algotsson, Tidegärd och mässa för den saliga Elins högtidsdag. Textkritisk edition och svensk översättning." In *Sankta Elin av Skövde. Kulten, källorna, kvinnan*, edited by Sven-Erik Pernler. In Skara stiftshistoriska sällskaps skriftserie, 183–235. Skara: Skara stiftshistoriska sällskap.
*Rer. Suec.* II:1. *Vita Sancti Botvidi*. In: Fant, E.M., Geijer, E.G. and Schroder, J. H. (eds.). 1828a. *Scriptores rerum Suecicarum medii aevi: Jussu regis augustissimi*. II:1. Stockholm: Zeipel et Palmblad.Script.

## Secondary Sources

Antonsson, Haki. 2010. "The Early Cult of Saints in Scandinavia and the Conversion: A Comparative Perspective." In *Saints and their Lives on the Periphery. Veneration of Saints in Scandinavia and Eastern Europe (c. 1000–1200)*, edited by Haki Antonsson and Ildar H. Garipzanov, 17–37. Turnhout: Brepols.
Aronsson, August. 2017. *Löfte, tvist och försoning: Politikens spelregler i 1300-talets Norden*. ACTA UNIVERSITATIS UPSALIENSIS Studia Historica Upsaliensia 257. edited by Margaret Hunt and Maria Ågren. Uppsala: Uppsala University.
Bartlett, Robert. 2013. *Why Can the Dead Do Such Great Things? Saints and Worshippers from the Martyrs to the Reformation*. Oxford: Princeton University Press.
Bitel, Lisa M. 1991. "'In Visu Noctis': Dreams in European Hagiography and Histories, 450–900." *History of Religions* 31(1): 39–59. https://www.jstor.org/stable/1062874?seq=1&cid=pdf-reference#references_tab_contents.
Clausen, Svend. 2018. "Skt. Thøger og det nordenfjordske bispedømme." *Historisk årsbok* 2018: 51–64.
Conti, Aidan. 2010. "Ælnoth of Canterbury and Early Mythopoiesis in Denmark." In *Saints and their Lives on the Periphery. Veneration of Saints in Scandinavia and Eastern Europe (c. 1000–1200)*, edited by Haki Antonsson and Ildar H. Garipzanov, 189–206. Turnhout: Brepols.
Craig, Leah Ann. 2009. *Wandering Women and Holy Matrons: Women as Pilgrims in the Later Middle Ages*. Leiden: Brill.
DuBois, Thomas A. 2008. "Sts Sunniva and Henrik: Scandinavian Martyr Saints in Their Hagiographic and National Contexts." In *Sanctity in the North. Saints, Lives and Cults in Medieval Scandinavia*, edited by Thomas A. DuBois, 65–99. Toronto: University of Toronto Press.
Ellis Nilsson, Sara. 2015. *Creating Holy People and Places on the Periphery. A Study of the Emergence of the Cults of Native Saints in the Ecclesiastical Provinces of Lund and Uppsala from the Eleventh to the Thirteenth Centuries*. Gothenburg: Department of Historical Studies, University of Gothenburg.
Ellis Nilsson, Sara. 2019. "Forming and Fashioning Early Scandinavian Sanctity: Liturgy and its Narrative Context." In *Heiligkeiten. Konstruktionen, Funktionen und Transfer von Heiligkeitskonzepten im europäishchen Früh- und Hochmittelalter (Sanctities.*

*Constructions, Functions and Transfer of Conceptions of Sanctity in the European Early and High Middle Ages*), edited by Andreas Bührer and Fiona Fritz, 73–87. Stuttgart: Franz Steiner Verlag.

Ellis Nilsson, Sara. Forthcoming 2020. "Promoting or Rejecting the Saints: The Representation of Non-saintly Bishops in Medieval Scandinavian Hagiography." In *'In the Hands of God's Servants': The Power of the Bishop and the Problem of Personality*, edited by Peter Coss, Chris Dennis, Melissa Julian-Jones, and Angelo Silvestri. Turnhout: Brepols.

Finucane, Ronald C. 1995. *Miracles and Pilgrims. Popular Beliefs in Medieval England.* London: Macmillan Press Ltd.

Fröjmark, Anders. 2006. "'*Per viam asperam et valde longam*': Voyages of Pilgrims to Local Shrines in Late Medieval Sweden." *Peregrinations* 2(1): 50–58.

Fröjmark, Anders. 2012. "Childbirth Miracles in Swedish Miracle Collections." *Journal of the History of Sexuality* 21(2): 297–312. doi:10.1353/sex.2012.0028

Goodich, Michael. 2005. "The Death of the Saint. A Hagiographical Topos." In *Hoping for Continuity. Childhood, Education and Death in Antiquity and the Middle Ages*, edited by Katariina Mustakallio, Jussi Hanska, Hanna-Leena Sainio, and Ville Vuolanto, *Acta Instituti Romani Finlandiae*, 33, 227–238. Rome: Institutum Romanum Finlandiae.

Hermanson, Lars. 2009. *Bärande band: vänskap, kärlek och brödraskap i det medeltida Nordeuropa, ca, 1000–1200*. Lund: Nordic Academic Press.

Katajala-Peltomaa, Sari. 2009. *Gender, Miracles and Daily Life. The Evidence of Fourteenth-Century Canonization Processes*. Turnhout: Brepols.

Katajala-Peltomaa, Sari. 2012. "Bishops Fighting with Demons in Swedish Canonization Processes." In *Saintly Bishops and Bishops' Saints*, edited by John S. Ott and Trpimir Vedriš, In Bibliotheca Hagiotheca, 217–233. Zagreb: Hagiotheca.

Krötzl, Christian. 1994. *Pilger, Mirakel und Alltag: Formen des Verhaltens im skandinavischen Mittelalter (12.-15. Jahrhundert).Studia historica*, Vol. 46. Helsinki: SHS.

Krötzl, Christian. 2001. "Ad sanctos: Religion and Everyday Life in Scandinavian Later Middle Ages." In *Norden og Europa i middelalderen*, edited by Per Ingesman and Thomas Lindkvist, In Rapporter til Det 24. Nordiske Historikermøde, Århus 9–13 August 2001, 203–215. Århus: Skrifter udgivet af Jysk Selskab for Historie nr 47.

Lifshitz, Felice. 1994. "Beyond Positivism and Genre: 'Hagiographical' Texts as Historical Narrative." *Viator* 25: 95–114.

Luckhardt, Courtney. 2011. "Connecting Saints: Travel and Hagiography in the Northwestern Atlantic, 500–800." Doctor of Philosophy Unpubl. Ph.D. Dissertation, Graduate Program in Medieval Studies, University of Notre Dame (Indiana).

Luckhardt, Courtney. 2013. "Gender and Connectivity: Facilitating Religious Travel in the Sixth and Seventh Centuries." *Comitatus: A Journal of Medieval and Renaissance Studies* 44: 29–53. doi:10.1353/cjm.2013.0012

Lundén, Tryggve. 1983. *Sveriges missionärer, helgon och kyrkogrundare. En bok om Sveriges kristnande*. Helsingborg: Artos.

Mortensen, Lars Boje. 2006. "Sanctified Beginnings and Mythopoietic Moments. The First Wave of Writing on the Past in Norway, Denmark and Hungary, c. 1000–1230." In *The Making of Christian Myths in the Periphery of Latin Christendom (c. 1000–1300)*, edited by Lars Boje Mortensen, 247–273. Copenhagen: Museum Tusculanum Press, University of Copenhagen.

Noble, Thomas F.X. and Thomas Head, eds. 1995. *Soldiers of Christ. Saints and Saints' Lives from Late Antiquity and the Early Middle Ages*. London: Sheed & Ward Ltd.

Pernler, Sven-Erik. 2007. *S:ta Elin av Skövde. Kulten, källorna, kvinnan. Vol. 31. Skara stiftshistoriska sällskaps skriftserie*. Skara: Skara stiftshistoriska sällskap.
Småberg, Thomas. 2004. *Det stängda frälset. Makt och eliter i det medeltida lokalsamhället: Marks och Kinds härader i Västergötland ca 1390–1520* (*The Closed Nobility. Power and Elites in a Local Community: The Districts of Mark and Kind in Västergötland c. 1390–1520*). Avhandlingar från Historiska institutionen i Göteborg 42. Gothenburg: University of Gothenburg.
Sobecki, Sebastian I. 2003. "From the *Désert Liquide* to the Sea of Romance: Benedeit's *Le Voyage de Saint Brendan* and the Irish *Immrama*." *Neophilologus* 87(2): 193–207. http://ovidsp.ovid.com.proxy.mau.se/ovidweb.cgi?T=JS&PAGE=fulltext&D=ovft&CSC=Y&NEWS=N&SEARCH=00023812-200308720-00003.an
Tolkien, J.R.R. 1954 (1989). *The Fellowship of the Ring*. London: Allen & Unwin.
Turner, Victor, and Edith Turner. 2011 (1978). *Image and Pilgrimage in Christian Culture*. New York: Columbia University Press.
Vauchez, André. 1997. *Sainthood in the later Middle Ages* (*La sainteté en Occident aux derniers siècles du Moyen Age*), Translated by Jean Birrell. Cambridge: Cambridge University Press.
Waugh, Robin. 2012. *The Genre of Medieval Patience Literature: Development, Duplication, and Gender*. New York: Palgrave MacMillan.
Webb, Diana. 2001. *Pilgrims and Pilgrimage in the Medieval West*. London: I. B. Tauris Publishers.
Webb, Diana. 2002. *Medieval European Pilgrimage, c. 700-c. 1500. European Culture and Society Series*. London: Macmillan International Higher Education.

# 13 'The wagon rests in winter, the sleigh in summer, the horse never'

## Practices of interurban travelling on horseback from Antiquity to the Middle Ages

*Fabienne Meiers*

### Introduction: Of hooves, heels and wheels

The role the horse played throughout history is predominant under all species of livestock: from the supplier of meat over transport animal for goods and persons to hauling beast for wagons and agricultural soil tillage implements. The horse helped to shape the world.[1] It was present in everyday life, because it allowed people to facilitate their tasks; for instance by lightening heavy burdens that men could neither pull nor carry and by offering possibilities to increase mobility.

This study will focus on the last-mentioned aspect, the topic of travelling on horseback. Through a *longue durée* perspective from the Roman Imperial period to the late Middle Ages and thus by disclosing the developments, transitions and regressions, it aims to gain a better understanding of medieval traffic schemes and why the horse was the most important means of transport on land in the Roman and in the medieval world.

Travelling was in many fields a precarious venture in the past; not only climatic, geographical and political conditions impeded spatial mobility; travelling also entailed a high personal, financial, and logistical effort. These negative consequences altered the perception of space considerably in contrast to modern times. Still, commuting between locations was the main driving engine to promote social and cultural dynamics, political alliances, and economic activities; also, geographic mobility and communication were more strongly intertwined in pre-modern times than before the deployment of electrical and electromagnetic telecommunication systems since the nineteenth century. Of course, there also existed different forms of long-range messaging, for instance, visual telecommunication such as flags and banners, smoke, beacons, mirrors, optical telegraphs, as well as acoustic telecommunication devices such as wind and percussion instruments not to forget the human voice.[2] All these methods, however, depended on good visibility or good acoustic conditions. In addition, with coded signs and signals only rudimentary, limited, and pre-determined information could be exchanged.[3]

In order to improve communication, more reliable and sophisticated mobility enhancing structures were installed and measures taken in places where information exchange was essential: this is particularly true for cities and other central places.[4] There, a network of 'commobile' (communicative and mobile) functionaries like messengers and envoys was set up.[5] Their mission consisted of transmitting information by travelling to recipients in other settlements; so travelling over short and long distances played a key role within their duty.

While some research has already been done on the mobility behaviour of secular and clerical nobility and their court as well as military units,[6] historical studies, so far, have only marginally dealt with the primary mechanisms and techniques of commuting between urban settlements.[7] The main emphasis of this chapter will therefore lie on official urban traffic concepts – giving particular attention to equestrian traffic – and travelling urban functionaries. As such, it is necessary to address one central purpose of interurban mobility, namely communication. I will also demonstrate why neither wagon nor any other vehicle hauled by animals, as the title implements, could prevail at any season of the year unlike the horse used as riding animal. An interdisciplinary and diachronic comparative approach will help in finding answers to the question of why riding a horse prevailed as means of transport in terms of efficiency even before travels on foot, by ship, and by wagon.

The various aspects of travelling on horseback are reflected in written, iconographic, and archaeological sources. In order not to exceed the extent of this examination, mainly written documents have been considered. Yet, sources from the above-mentioned neighbouring disciplines have been included on a small scale to allow a more substantial view of the phenomenon.

Concerning written sources, there are more systematic approaches towards the use of equines for travelling during the Roman period like hippological and hippiatric treatises, travelogues, literary texts,[8] epigraphic sources, as well as legal documents.[9] In contrast, in the medieval period – especially in the Early Middle Ages – information tends to be more scattered: it can be collected from sources as different as hagiographies, chronicles, legal texts,[10] real estate records, and account books.[11] Vernacular narrative literature is also a rich source for equestrian traffic in the Middle Ages.[12] And it should not be overlooked that antique texts were largely copied and received in the Medieval period, whereby some texts underwent modification, reinterpretation, or appropriation for other ends and to varying extents.[13] It is these alterations of perceptions, which are most interesting in studying equestrian traffic in a long-term perspective. From a qualitative, statistical, and comparative perspective we shall see which features are characteristic of the different eras and how they evolved during time since the Roman period.

## The horse as means of transport in the Roman period

Apart from facilitating troop movements and ensuring supply with food, material, manpower, and military forces, the vast road network provided the foundation for the courier and transportation service run by the Roman Empire, the *cursus publicus*. The *cursus publicus* was inaugurated under Augustus (63 BCE – 14 CE) as a highly organised system designed for transferring official communication at the first place; it can therefore be understood as the state postal and courier service.[14]

Later, it was also used by nonofficial, but authorised persons holding travel warrants (*evectiones*) for personal transport as well as for transferring goods.[15] The straight-line layout of many Roman fortified roads (*viae*) not only enhanced the speed performance of troop movements considerably, but also that of communication and travelling.

Following the previously described road expansion in the first century BCE, a system of rudimentary relay stations was soon afterwards created along the highways for providing the troops passing through with provision and feed for their packing animals. Frequently, accommodation for high-ranking persons was present, too, in addition to stables.[16] These infrastructures allowed not only officers to change their horses, but also couriers. At the turn of the millennium the *cursus publicus* was further developed with the creation of *mutationes* and *mansiones*, more elaborate horse change stations, respectively relay stations.[17] The *mutationes* succeeded each other at 15 kilometres on average, whereas the *mansiones* were dispersed at a distance of approximate 35 kilometres.[18] The famous Tabula Peutingeriana, a copy from the thirteenth century which probably can be traced back to an antecedent map issued by Agrippa, displays the well-organised distribution of *mansiones* and *mutationes* along the roads of the Roman Empire.[19]

Although the use of the *cursus publicus* was restricted to specific individuals with special authorisations, the facilities comprising roads and accommodation, as well as private rentals for draft animals operated by *iumentarii* (suppliers of carts and dealers of baggage animals) and *cisiarii* (owners of vehicles for hire) were also available for common travellers against payment.[20] On average they could travel between 50 to 60 kilometres per day. On the downside, high-ranking persons who journeyed in carts and benefitted from frequent horse changes during their voyages could reach a maximum of 180 kilometres per day; couriers even achieved superior performances.[21]

Taking the above-mentioned characteristics of the *cursus publicus* with its well-developed and regularly maintained road network and infrastructures into consideration, it becomes clear why, in Antiquity, carts played a major role in long-distance landbound travels: in the Roman Empire, for the first time in European history, conveyance in wheeled vehicles made mobility of civilian passengers from the higher social strata very effective.[22] The technical innovations of steerable front axles, brake blocks for the wheel rims, and leather-spring suspensions added more security and comfort to passenger transport.[23] And even though the horse was the fastest means of transport on land, it was rarely used to pull wagons in public transport, except for lighter ones such as the two-wheeled open *essedae* and the roofed *carpentae*.[24] Instead, mules were harnessed, because they were better suited for this purpose than horses; they were less demanding in husbandry and feeding and much more robust – their hooves are smaller and much harder.[25] It was believed that, as a hybrid from a donkey stallion and a horse mare, mules could 'run like a horse, pull like an ox and eat like a donkey, and only get sick to die'.

In the Roman world, the keeping and breeding of horses was reserved for the privileged social classes.[26] This was due to the high financial and organisational effort horse husbandry entailed (in contrast to other beasts used for transport like oxen, mules, and donkeys); not only did horses need more and higher quality fodder than mules or donkeys, they also needed plenty of looking after as they were less robust than the aforementioned animals.

Since the Roman Imperial period, the State became the most important horse owner:[27] among other animals kept by the State and known as *animalia publica*, horses were employed in military and postal usage, as well as in circus races. State breeding farms guaranteed the provision with large quantities of reliable horses for these purposes.[28]

Notwithstanding the heavy use of horses by the Roman State for military purposes and imperial courier services, riding horses only played a minor role when travelling over longer distances. In the Roman world, the main road was a space primarily occupied by pedestrians and by wagons, which the higher social classes made use of for long-distance journeys. Closed carts had the benefit that, besides offering weather and privacy protection, an increased number of heavier luggage could be stored inside them than in backpacks, in saddle bags, or fastened to the saddle.[29] In addition, exhausted draft animals could be exchanged at one of the many *mutationes*, that were distributed at regular intervals along the highways; this also raised travel speeds considerably. The heavy use of wheeled vehicles was stimulated by the well-maintained paved highways and gravel roads, which allowed driving at much higher speeds than on unsurfaced roads. Riding in carriages on dirt roads however was very uncomfortable for passengers because of the bouncing movement which was transmitted to the vehicle body despite suspension systems.[30] Furthermore, in the worst case, wheels could break due to bad road conditions; so, in avoidance of this danger, travel speed had to be reduced significantly.

Notwithstanding the high significance of vehicular traffic especially in long-distance journeys, some Roman authors mention the use of horses as means of transport. In the second volume of his treatise on agriculture *De re rustica* (*De re pecuaria*), Varro (116–27 BCE) describes the utility, breeding, and training of horses.[31] In chapter seven, the specially tailored training of horses for specific purposes is addressed: he recommends that saddle horses *qui vectorios facere* (which are used for travelling) should be of a gentle temper in contrary to military horses.[32] Varro also advises to castrate travel horses in order to make them calmer (*demptis enim testiculis fiunt quietiores*).[33] These castrated horses were called *cantherii*.[34]

Further Roman authors discussing horse-related subjects are Columella (c. 4–70) in *De re rustica*,[35] Pliny the Elder (c. 23–79) in *Historia naturalis*,[36] Vegetius (fourth century CE) in his treatise on veterinary medicine *Mulomedicina*,[37] as well as Pelagonius (fourth century CE) in *Ars veterinaria*.[38] Pliny the Elder as well as Vegetius also mention a special kind of riding (or travel) horses known as *tolutarii*, or commonly referenced to as *totonarii*.[39] They either showed lateral (ambling) gaits naturally or were trained to perform these specific soft gaits,[40] which made travelling over long periods less tiring for riders and allowed even inexperienced riders, as well as old and sick people, to travel on horseback.

In Latin, the ambling movement was referenced to as *tolutim* in an adverbial construction.[41] According to Pliny, these horses were mostly bred in the Celtic regions of the Iberian Peninsula, more precisely – as the name of the breed, *asturcon*, implies – in Asturias (today northwest Spain).[42] It can be assumed, that the poor road conditions before the Roman conquest made the use of horses as a means of transport in this region indispensable. The same holds true for the largest territories of Gaul: this is also the reason, why so many plastic reproductions of the deity Epona, the protector of equids, show her riding on an ambling horse.[43] So the need for smoothly moving riding horses was, at first, higher in regions where travelling in wagons was impossible, yet people nevertheless depended on long-distance journeys. Because of the comfort they offered, they also spread into the central parts of the Roman Empire since the first century BCE and became a luxury good.[44]

What capacity did equestrian traffic have in the Roman period? In the 1980s and early 1990s the historian Marcus Junkelmann, who is known for his experimental approach towards unanswered questions in ancient history and archaeology especially in the field of warfare and horsemanship, tried to find out what average travel speeds were feasible on horseback during the Roman Empire.[45] He therefore conducted a series of observations with the help of a ten-year-old Camargue stallion, who, in his opinion, corresponded roughly to the small type of horses the Romans used. Table 13.1 shows the results of his experiments.

Despite the relatively high travel speed of equestrian traffic that was achieved during these experimentations, the parameter of 'duration' was not taken into account. In fact, rapid gaits like canter and gallop can only be sustained by horses over a short period of time; usually they fatigue after 3–4 kilometres, whereas a trot or amble can be kept over a much longer distance, well over 25 kilometres depending on the training condition of the horse.

Why was equestrian traffic with civilians still unpopular in the Roman period?[47] Surely the main reason for this was the inconvenience riding on horseback caused: firstly, there was no appropriate saddle which distributed the weight of the rider evenly over the horse's back over a long period of time;[48] secondly, there were no stirrups which helped the rider to get on his horse and supported him during the ride;[49] and thirdly, there were no nailed horseshoes[50] which prevented the heavy wearing of the hoof horn.[51] Besides, on horseback there was no protection from weather elements or against prying eyes for the traveller and not much space to store luggage.

*Table 13.1* Average travel speeds for different horse gaits

| Gait | Average travel speed |
|---|---|
| Walk | 4–7 km/h |
| Slow trot (jog) | 12–14 km/h |
| Faster trot | 18–20 km/h |
| Slow canter | 20–30 km/h |
| Faster gallop | 45–52 km/h[46] |

In conclusion, throughout the Roman Empire vehicular traffic was the favoured transport mode for conveying people swiftly, safely and comfortably over long distances whilst the highways still were in good condition. Saddle horses, though chiefly persisted as means of transport in short trips due to the lack of convenient saddles, supporting stirrups, and storage room for luggage, in message traffic or in territories, which were not pervaded by fortified road networks.

## Minding the gap between two periods: Travelling on horseback in the Early Middle Ages

The decline of the West Roman Empire at the end of the fifth century widely led to the degradation of the extensive road network with its sophisticated system of road stations. Because in late Antiquity, it had been controlled and regulated by a provincial central administration in accordance with the decisions made for the entire Empire, the road network was not only easier to maintain financially and technically by regular road works; it was also easier to control its infrastructures.[52]

In comparison to the Roman period, conditions during the Middle Ages gradually became more delicate: administration, regulation, and maintenance of roads was more difficult in small, fragmented territorial states, which existed by then, and which were led by independent territorial lords with major concern in their own economic interests.[53] Many of the highways deteriorated, because they could not be sustained any longer by a central power, which acted supra-regionally. This decentralisation made circulation of persons, goods, and services less effective and more time-consuming.[54] Especially wheeled vehicles such as carts and carriages were affected by this development: the wooden spokes could easily break on uneven roads under the weight of heavier vehicles at faster travelling speeds.

In few areas and places, which still had a political, economic, or cultural impact in the early Middle Ages, segments of Roman roads persisted, and could still be covered by carts.[55] In all other areas alternative roads needed to be used, such as natural trails and unpaved roads consisting of hard-packed earth. Consequently, travelling on foot or on horseback became the preferred way of moving from one point to another as both methods were virtually independent of ground conditions. As mentioned, accompanying structures and services also vanished with the decline of the Roman road network. Though again, substitute solutions were found. One strategy for maintaining mobility consisted of the compliance with obligation duties, a subserviency or requisition procedure for travel horses, the so-called *paravered*-duty.

The foundations of the *paravered*-service can be found in late Antiquity, when supplying the *mutationes* with horses for change grew to become more difficult due to military conflicts with invading forces from the exterior, but also on account of political conflicts in the inner core of the Empire.[56] The procedure enclosed the provision of travel horses by designated private horse keepers on a case-by-case basis for non-scheduled transport in contrast to the procedures for the *cursus publicus*.[57] A forerunner system of this service can already be found at the time of the Republic,[58] when, in case of absolute urgency, additionally needed travel facilities could be requisitioned from locals.[59]

Whereas in Antiquity wheeled vehicles still played an important role in travelling by land, this would change after the fall of the Roman Empire. As the well-developed and regularly maintained road network with its infrastructures declined and shrunk to a holey patchwork, conveyance of passengers in heavy wagons without leather-spring suspensions nor steerable front axles either became impossible or less effective. Suspensions for vehicles and steerable front axles had been characteristic for Roman travel wagons and they did not reappear until around 1350, the former in the form of chain suspensions.[60] Certainly, these were less flexible than leather suspensions, but much more resistant; they offered the passengers at least some relief from shocks.[61]

In contrast to locomotion in vehicles, equestrian traffic gained more importance in the Medieval period, especially in long-distance travels. The principal reason for this phenomenon can be found in its virtual independence from particular topographic constitutions. Riders are not only able to use fortified ways, but also dirt roads and narrow natural footpaths; they can even travel off-road through forests, fields, and open country. Roads impeded by bad weather conditions, erosion, and overgrown vegetation do not pose any problem. Given landings are sufficiently wide-spaced, horses are also able to climb and walk downstairs. Crossing water is also possible either during freezing of the river in the winter months, at fords or by using flat ferry boats.

Besides the deterioration of the Roman highways, three inventions in relation with horse tack and horse care revolutionised equestrian traffic: nailed horseshoes, stirrups, and saddles with rigid trees. Horseshoes probably first appeared with the Celts during the Latène Age, before spreading to the Roman Empire in the early third century.[62] At that time, however, they still did not make a major impact; it took about 700 years until nailed horseshoes began to become more widely employed.[63] General use was not put into practice until the twelfth century.[64] In contrast to hipposandals, nailed horseshoes offered more comfort for horses; they could be used at high speed and they did not need to be put on again on each occasion.

Stirrups likewise began to spread more widely with the invasions of the Avars in the sixth–ninth centuries. Stirrups provided the rider with some support, not only when he got on and off horseback allowing to ease this exercise considerably (for less athletic people) and even with larger or nervous horses, especially when wearing heavier or more elaborate clothes (or armour). Stirrups also helped the rider to maintain his equilibrium and stability in the saddle.

Further development of saddles during the same time frame or maybe sometime earlier with the 'Storm of the Huns' also promoted equestrian traffic. It has been demonstrated that treeless or flexible saddles put more pressure on the very sensitive centre line of the horseback and in the worst case friction to the spine; this effect would be enhanced with the use of stirrups. Considering this, it appears evident why the invention of stirrups was accompanied by the development of rigid saddle trees.[65] Both innovations led to an increased comfort for the horse as well as for the rider and thus made equestrian traffic more attractive for long-distance travellers.

In addition to improved riding equipment, travellers still made use of the specially bred and trained riding horses like in the Roman period, meanwhile known in Medieval Latin as *ambulatores*[66] or *gradarii*, in Middle English as *palfreys, amblers* and *hack(ney)*s, in Middle High German as *Zelter* and in Middle French as *palfrois, ambleurs* (or *chevaux d'amble*), and *haquenées*.[67] Their characteristically soft, yet quick lateral gaits, called 'amble' and 'pace', allowed riders to travel comfortably and efficiently over long periods of time. It must be mentioned that in comparison to trot, which is a two-beat diagonal gait, amble and pace are four-beat, respectively, two-beat lateral gaits with the same basic speed (they can be raised to racing speed). Because of the nearly isochronous lateral movement of the horse's hind- and forelegs on the same side and the lack of a complete suspension phase, the horse's back does not move as excessively as while trotting: therefore, the rider can sit without being shaken considerably. Hence, the use of gaited horses presented a significant relief for frequent commuters and long-distance travellers in pre-modern times.

## The 'equestrian turn': Interurban equestrian travelling from the 11th to the 15th century

The thriving of cities in Western Europe since the eleventh century was accompanied by an increasing demand for faster and more reliable communication services comparable with those established in the Roman Empire. In consequence, strategies were developed to enhance interurban mobility – communication modes, though, remained unresponsive to far-reaching change.[68]

Going along with the increasing urbanisation, reforms in the transport sector became a major issue in municipal organisation: far-reaching traffic policies encouraged horizontal mobility and thus improved communication networks. These mobility-enhancing strategies consisted for instance on the civic field of road construction works with the introduction of paved streets. Outside the cities, some of the former Roman roads were either not maintained at all, or not as regularly and efficiently as before the Medieval period. Nevertheless, most of them continued to be used by travellers, although their condition left much to be desired.

Inside the urban settlement (*intra muros*) equestrian traffic was no longer prohibited in contrast to the circumstances in certain cities during the Roman period.[69] On the municipal field, institutionally controlled messenger services on foot and on horseback, as well as travel allowances for envoys and the provision of travel horses both for messengers and envoys, which either belonged to the city (*Stadtpferde*)[70] or could be hired, helped to guarantee mobility of the urban service personnel and maintain communication with the outside world. To ensure their safety on the road and to make sure that they reached their destination, they could be accompanied by escorting personnel. These personnel frequently consisted of armed men on foot or on horseback from the initial city or tower wardens. Sometimes, they would be supplemented or replaced by local escorting people on the itinerary, because they were more familiar with the routes and infrastructures along them; they knew shortcuts, good places to stay overnight, and places to rather avoid.[71] Nevertheless, the road remained a dangerous place, especially in times of war and when cities were under besiegement. Even though messengers and envoys were granted safe conduct, they became victims of robberies. Horse thefts occur very frequently in urban account books.[72] In this case, generally, the urban travellers would be set free to go back to the municipal authorities and solicit them to pay a ransom to release the horses.[73]

The greater importance of equestrian traffic in the late Middle Ages can also be seen in the context of growing urbanisation along with the need for better mobility solutions and more efficient ways of communication. In this study, the late Medieval account books of the city of Luxembourg have been investigated more profoundly regarding the use of riding horses in the municipal-administrative context. In what follows, special attention will therefore be drawn to this source type in order to explain the rise of horses as means of transport in cities. First, though, a short excursus into the methodology used will precede.

## Excursus: Investigating the account books of the city of Luxembourg (1388–1500)

From the historical point of view, Luxembourg is a very interesting territory to investigate the interaction between mobility and communication in the long term. As early as the Roman era, several roads of major importance crossed today's territory; the capital city probably originated from a Roman street station which emerged at the traffic intersection between the road from Reims to Trier and the road from Metz to Trier (*Via Agrippa*) as archaeological findings have shown. The distinctive position of the city throughout its history as a transport hub and communications junction and its consequential significance as market place continued to the Middle Ages.[74] During that period, written documents play a major role; the most important sources regarding transport in the urban environment are without question account books.

The account books from the City of Luxembourg give a detailed insight into the different urban revenues and expenditures issued between 1388 and 1795.[75] They are written in a late West Middle German dialect; so still today, the texts appear easily comprehensible for German speakers. The content of these serialised urban account books includes, first, the annual revenues the municipality received from its citizens (e.g. for their newly received citizenship or for the use of forest pastures by their pigs and the keeping of them by municipal swineherds), from excise taxes on wine or grain as well as from tolls collected for the use of roads and for the use of the municipal weigh house. The revenues are followed by a standardised list of expenditures for administrative travels, diplomatic missions, business journeys, construction activities, military purposes, hygienic provisions, vestments, chancellery material, messenger services, escorts, and other services. At the end of each annual account, the total amount of the revenues minus the expenditures as well as the number of the attendants of the meeting for the financial reporting is meticulously listed. What is even more interesting and a stroke of luck for Luxembourgish historians, the medieval volumes have nearly completely been handed down. So there is a certain data consistency, which is also an advantage for the quantitative evaluation of the content.

To get useful data concerning equestrian traffic, passages containing equine-based data were selected, such as table 13.2 shows.

The following example deals with the expenses for a diplomatic journey of one of the municipal aldermen. It shall illustrate what a typical account entry looked like and how the information it contains can be used to determine the extent of equestrian traffic:

> Also on Friday after the meal before Assumption Day [= August 15], Master Heinrich of Bettingen rode to our gracious Lord the Roman and Hungarian King [= Sigismund of Luxembourg] to Ravensburg and returned to Luxembourg on Friday evening before the Nativity of Mary [= September 8] and given him for his expenses 50 gul [= gulden] in gold[,] which were changed for 26 new gr [= Groschen, pennies] for that Gaet Menschin's horse had stood in his stable before he rode away for 3 weeks and 2 days and consumed 3 gul and gave for a saddle and bridle 2 gul and afterwards[,] when he came back, [the payment for] the horse was still pending for 10 days and consumed 1 gulden and his horse died on the way and he bought another horse for 16 gulden and gave his servant 1 gulden and he had consumed and given safe conduct together 16 gul[,] so the sum comes together for 49 gulden[,] which makes 55 gul 9 gr for this account[76]

For long-distance travels the preferred travelling time was set between mid-spring and mid-autumn, when the weather conditions were more favourable for journeys on horseback: The excerpt from 1418 sets out that the voyage to Ravensburg

*Table 13.2* Data from urban account books examined for the study

| Equine-related professions or functions | Expenditures for horses | Data in conjunction with travelling on horseback |
| --- | --- | --- |
| mounted messengers | purchase | names of travellers |
| envoys | rental | number of travellers |
| escort personnel | fodder | motives for travel |
| blacksmiths | housing | point of departure |
| veterinaries | repair of equipment | travel destination |
| saddlers | veterinary treatment | travel duration |
| castrators |  | length of stay |
| spur (and bit) makers |  | travelling time |
| horse slaughterers |  | means of transport |
|  |  | quantity of horses |
|  |  | quality of horses |

started on Friday afternoon before Assumption Day, that would have been on August 12th, and that it ended on Friday evening before the Nativity of Mary, which was on September 2nd. So, these two dates not only substantiate the preferred travel time, but they also perfectly englobe the mentioned period of three weeks and two days during which Gaet Menschin's horse stood (unused) at the stable of Master Heinrich of Bettingen.

The city of Ravensburg lies about 390 kilometres from the City of Luxembourg; because of possible dangers, the alderman was accompanied by his servant who escorted him on this long-distance travel – probably, he was armed. The journey actually became problematic as Master Heinrich's horse died on the way: he had to buy a new one for the sum of 16 gulden. This was a common price for a high-quality gaited travel horse, which also served representative purposes.[77] The extract demonstrates that travellers always needed to be prepared for unforeseen events from an organisational and financial point of view.

## Messengers and envoys: Urban functionaries on horseback

Some of the evaluated data will now be emphasised to display the importance of the horse as guarantor for political-administrative travels, as well as a medium for communication outside the city walls during the fourteenth and fifteenth centuries.

Communication was an important part of the urban equation: efficient means of communication defined a well-networked city. As part of the municipal administration, it was necessary to transport messages to political allies to ensure diplomatic relations, the smooth functioning of administrative tasks and the exchange of information on a regular basis throughout a defined territory, interconnected by a network of towns and administrative centres. In addition, envoys were sent out as diplomatic interactors to settle political differences where personal presence was indispensable.

At the practical level, urban communication would have been impossible without the use of horses as a means of transport. According to the earliest accounting documents, it becomes evident that urban officials (judges, aldermen, master builders, wine judges who were responsible for the levy of excise taxes on wine, and foresters) and envoys mostly travelled on horseback. Where possible, they would also travel by ship which was often faster, but much more expensive and constrained to natural environments (waterways) and weather elements. Moreover, ships needed to be towed when operated upstream; this reduced travelling speed significantly.[78] Vehicles were used very rarely, because they depended on well-developed roads, which – apart from the Flemish-Lombard highway[79] – did not exist; on the present traffic infrastructures they only could move slowly. In addition, overland wagons were more expensive in terms of acquisition and maintenance. Besides the practical and financial constraints, in the late medieval and in the Early Modern period, travelling in vehicles had received a bad reputation: this means of transport – probably because of the aforementioned constrictions – was only acceptable to be used by very high ranking persons on representative occasions,[80] by women, very young, old, and weak persons of high social status;

in short, people who should or could not travel on horseback due to their status, age, or condition.[81]

In contrast, messengers on foot and on horseback coexisted since the advent of urban communication services. Unfortunately, the sources occasionally remain unclear about the means of transport used by the messengers: the expression *brieve draghen* (= carry letters) gives no reference to the means of transport, just as little as the verb *gen*, which could not only be employed for 'to go', but also for 'to ride'. Sometimes the remuneration gives information about the kind of mobility, as missions on horseback were submitted to a higher daily rate. It appears that a greater differentiation did not take place until the beginning of the fifteenth century. This date coincides with the inauguration of institutionally controlled mounted courier services in cities north of the Alps; through messenger oaths from the Swiss-Upper Rhine region, it can also be traced back to the early 1400s.[82] As further evidence for the professionalisation of messenger services, during this time, most of the investigated account books refer to either recurring names of messengers or, mostly by the second half of the fifteenth century, to 'Stadtboten' (= municipal messengers).[83]

The specialisation of municipal communication services entailed that provisions became stricter not only against the carriers of messages, but also against the usage of their horses: those should be handled with care and solely be employed to reach the destination and for the way back.[84] Furthermore, the horses' tack should be treated with care in avoidance of costly repairs.[85]

It must also be highlighted that the surge in courier services promoted a new saddle type: it had a low cantle and a slender high-raised pommel. This made it easier and faster to grip and gave more grasp while mounting, especially when mounting quickly without using the stirrups.[86] The low seat allowed the rider to mount and dismount more quickly than from the old high-arched war saddles.[87] This was a very important feature especially for the messengers permitting them to deliver mailings and dispatches more rapidly. But envoys also benefitted from the revised saddle fabrication, as they were forced to get on and off their horses many times during their journey. Besides the improvement of mobility (freedom of movement) the construction of the new saddles was much lighter, so both the courier horses and the travellers had to carry less weight.

Not only the riding equipment had undergone a significant change, but also the way riding animals were supplied. Horses for courier services and diplomatic travels were either provided by the travellers themselves (in the City of Luxembourg this was the case with envoys and messengers likewise), by the city (*Stadtpferde*), by professional horse hirers at livery stables, and by designated horse-owning citizens. Probably, this last procedure was a remnant of the paravered-duty; though during the high Middle Ages, it was modified towards a paid service. In opposition to the Roman period, horse rentals appear to have been the most advantageous mode of acquiring a means of travel in an urban environment. The reasons for this, as well as the virtually unrestricted availability of riding horses for all social classes, will be discussed in the following section.

## Democratising equestrian traffic

As the value of the horse as means of transport grew in urban settings during the High Middle Ages, there was also a tendency to open equestrian traffic to increasing parts of the urban civilian population, so as not only urban officials, municipal functionaries, and nobles benefitted from travelling on horseback. By the second half of the fourteenth century, horses thus became available to virtually all social classes by means of rental services, which were shooting up like mushrooms in cities of Western and Central Europe.[88] In some cities, there were special establishments for this purpose, which often formed a symbiosis of guest house, tavern, stabling facility, and livery stable.[89] One could say that the medieval horse stations were similar to a mixture of *mutationes* and *mansiones*, with the exception that all travellers could profit from the offered facilities.

Where did the concept of renting horses originate and why did it only (re-) appear in the second half of the fourteenth century? Written and iconographic sources indicate that during the Hundred Years' War (1337–1453), urban horse rental stations spread from England to the European mainland.[90] They offered the possibility to rent horses called 'hacks' so that commuting between different cities and the surroundings became easier, more affordable, and logistically less preparative. It allowed citizens, who did not possess horses but were in the need to travel, to make use of the services offered at these stations. Certainly, some horse owners also utilised them in case their own riding animals were not deployable or unsuited for longer travels. This was the case for the Luxembourgish urban functionaries: for short administrative travels in the surroundings they used their own, probably non-ambling trotters, whereas for long-distance journeys they fell back on gaited hacks, which were specially bred and trained to meet the requirements of travellers.

The term 'hack' later formed the French word *haquenée*, which, for instance, appears in the narratives of Joan of Arc: to demonstrate her ability to ride like a man within her company (which principally was composed of men), she would ask for a standard trotting horse instead of a *haquenée*, meaning that she needed no soft-gaited and gentle-riding horse like most travellers used. So most probably, the rentable horses were of a small type, which allowed to get on and off easily and swiftly without makeshift (like stones or stairs, or by lengthening the stirrups),[91] and performed ambling gaits.

The advantages of renting horses are obvious: no stabling fees, no costs for fodder, veterinaries or blacksmiths – in addition, it was not necessary to buy any riding equipment for the horse. Moreover, as with modern car rental services, horses could be handed over in another station; they were then brought back to the initial livery stable either by stablemen or by the next clients, who would embark on the same course back. Therefore, renting horses was a profitable activity both for travellers and for innkeepers who could make a good living with this additional, lucrative source of income.[92] Considering these aspects, horse rentals also implemented that every citizen who was able to pay a certain amount of money, usually 4 gr, would be financially capable to rent a horse. In the second half of the fifteenth century, this sum corresponded to four smoked herrings, a pair of shoes, or eight loaves of bread. Livery stables thus could be displayed as a form of democratising equestrian traffic for broader social strata.

## Travel horses in literature

Since the twelfth century, the growing significance of equestrian traffic is not only reflected in pragmatic documents, which widely received Roman authors and their theories,[93] but also in vernacular narrative literature: the use of ambling travel horses enhanced the performance and comfort of spatial mobility significantly and thus became a compulsory mobility requirement.

In the beginning, the texts only concentrated on the travel behaviour of the upper social classes; this is not surprising, since the recipients of these fictional narratives, which involved Arthurian legends, came from that social background. In these narrations, ambling horses became a much recurring topic for travelling tirelessly, safely, and quickly; the soft lateral gaits were even compared to the movement of a ship floating on silent water: *ez gienc vil drâte über velt/schône sam ein schef enzelt:/darzuo und ez sanfte gie,/sô gestrûchtez doch nie.*[94] (It [the horse] quickly moved over the open country, it ambled as beautifully as a ship: to that it walked softly and never stumbled.) Moreover, ambling horses were frequently used as *exempla* to characterise the higher values and idealised forms of courtly life, as is the case in Hartmann's von Aue (c. 1160–1220) 'Erec and Enite', and as literary *topoi* of secure transport of the noble protagonists, like in Wolfram's von Eschenbach (c. 1160–1220) *Parzival*. There, when Parzival announces the vocation to be the new grail king, the ugly princess Kundrie exhausts the travel speed of her ambling riding horse to get to the fairground: *senfteclîche und doch in vollem zelt/kom si rîtende über velt.*[95] (Softly, yet in full amble, she [Kundrie] came riding over the open country.)

Not only literature of higher social classes involved ambling horses, but also narrations relating to the middle and lower classes. One early example of vernacular literature mentioning special travel horses, which did not target on any predefined social class, is Geoffrey Chaucer's (c. 1343–1400) 'Canterbury Tales': the famous wife of Bath rides an ambling horse. The lateral, somewhat swaying walk of the ambling horse (especially, when it tends more towards pace), is a byword for the characteristic disposition of the protagonist: on the downside, it echoes her gossiping and wavering temperament.[96] This must have been a recurring topic – at least in Middle English literature – which was easily received and understood by the audience.

In addition to representations of ambling horses as superior means of transport, the motif of the 'white palfrey' was widely spread. In historiographical works, the gesture of making someone an emblematic present of a white-born gaited horse (or a mule!) was used to depict political patronage, especially in conjunction with the Pope.[97] White-born horses are a rarity, as most of the horses which appear white when they grow up are actually born a much darker colour; they progressively turn grey. All the more, pure white-born horses with unpigmented skins represent fundamental Christian values like purity of the heart and soul, virginity of spirit and divine perfection.

As opposed to that, during early reform movements by the end of the Middle Ages, when questions of faith began to rise and people queried the ecclesiastical institution along with its practices, for instance the church service in Latin and the selling of indulgences, the time-consuming and complex gait-regulation training with the help of trammels (shackles),[98] which many ambling horses had to undergo, was progressively highlighted in salvation literature. It became an allegorising motif for the unceasing hard trials in life necessary to win and keep faith as well as for the unpleasant and frequently repeated exercises of faith and virtue to attain redemption from sins and finally find spiritual salvation. In this context, the West-Flemish *Spiegel der sonden* ('Mirror of sins') from the fourteenth century reflects the painful gait-training procedure:

> Leren telden ist pine den paerde,
> dat welke draven kan von aerde,
> Want men moet die voeten sine
> van noede binden met eenre line,
> Mer alst die ghewoente heeft an,
> So doet man dan die line daer van,
> Ende toten ghanghe ket hem keert
> Dient van ghewonten heft geleert.[99]

At the time of the Reformation, in pamphlets, the image of the noble white ambling palfrey with the Pope sitting on his back could be found opposite to the simple grey donkey on which Christ rode.[100] This juxtaposition could be interpreted as rejection of the display of splendour of the institutionalised Church towards the return to humility of early Christianity. In summary, the impact of travel horses, especially gaited travel horses, was not only discernible on the practical side, but also on the cultural side: during the high and Late Middle Ages, in vernacular spiritual and secular literature, palfreys and hacks appear repeatedly as symbolical figures for the most convenient means of travel.

## Conclusions: Towards a 'centaurised' mobility

The aim of the presented paper was to give an overview of equestrian-based spatial mobility in the *longue durée* from the beginning of the Roman Empire to the end of the Middle Ages. Through written evidence, it could be demonstrated that the development of equestrian traffic was steered by the leading political powers in determined time segments; firstly, the state in the Roman Age, then the territorial lords and the urban magistrates in the Middle Ages. With the beginning of the Medieval period, the importance of the horse in interurban and long-distance travels increases in contrast to the significance of vehicular traffic.

After the decline of the Western Roman Empire in the fifth century CE, the inability to maintain the sophisticated road and traffic organisation rapidly led to the deterioration of road surfaces and the desolation of connected infrastructures. Measures were taken by the authorities to cope with the new constellation and to find alternative traffic systems to guarantee transport of people notwithstanding the impeded roads and the malfunction of the road stations, which could not be supplied with fresh transport animals anymore. Hence, the *paravered* service was created; it allowed officials to requisition riding horses from private owners for their journeys on a case-by-case basis for nonscheduled transport. During this transitional period, equines became more important as means of transport on land, because they were capable to move on virtually all terrain. Since the sixth/seventh century, the introduction of nailed horseshoes, stirrups, and saddles with rigid trees reinforced this tendency.

We have likewise seen that since the development of medieval cities in the eleventh century, on the municipal level, measures were taken to promote, facilitate, and improve interurban mobility and synchronously communication. These procedures engendered the increasing use of riding horses for trips and messenger services which, during the second half of the thirteenth century, culminated in the 'equestrian turn' of the late Middle Ages: the horse then was considered as guarantor for mobility and as vehicle for communication par excellence. Whereas in Antiquity officials mainly travelled in wagons, medieval urban functionaries preferred to ride. The horse had become the most important means of transport on land in terms of availability, suitability to different terrains, rapidity, comfort, price-performance-ratio, and effectiveness.

Going along with the revaluation of riding horses, the democratisation of equestrian traffic took place in the form of urban horse rental stations in the late Middle Ages, which succeeded and further developed the offer of Roman livery stables: not only officials and members of the urban upper class could benefit from horses as means of conveyance, but also people from lower classes, who either did not possess or have the money to keep horses. Apart from that, technical innovations in relation to the riding equipment, notably easily ascendable saddles for messaging and civilian use, as well as ambling and easy-to-ride hacks, made equestrian traffic more popular.

The diachronic comparative approach has demonstrated that in terms of mobility management, the Middle Ages were not a regressive or stagnant transitional period between Antiquity and the Renaissance, but brought forward the expression of alternative and specialised traffic systems developed to stimulate interurban mobility in more heterogeneous political contexts than during the Roman period. The horse was the driving agent of this reform, a 'centaurised' mobility, which would last until the emergence of motor vehicles.

## Notes

1 In 2003, Reinhard Koselleck gave an intriguing lecture about the role of the horse in human history when he received the Münster Historian Prize. He did not shy away from dividing history into a pre-equine era, an equine era, and a post-equine era to stress the crucial importance of the horse for human development throughout his-

tory. A shortened version of his speech can be found at Koselleck 2003, 18. Cf. also Steinbrecher 2011.
2 Montagné 2008.
3 Cf. Kolb 2000, 15, 17, 19: Most likely, these methods were constrained to the military area and in this context to specific situations and localities.
4 Further seats of power, for instance aristocratic residences of secular lords and ecclesiastical dignitaries, could not be treated, as this would have gone beyond the scope of this examination.
5 I will come back to this point later in this article.
6 For the Roman period see for example: Junkelmann 1990–1992; Schulz 2009; Martini 2013; Casson 1979. For the Middle Ages see: Elze 1980; Althoff 1992.
7 Karll 1905.
8 See chapter III.4.
9 An extensive compilation of sources can be found in Chevallier 1997, 25, 36–96. Cf. Chevallier 1988, 7–15; Kolb 2000, 10.
10 Cf. Meiers 2011; Schneider 1985, 459f., 483f.
11 Cf. Meiers 2018.
12 Cf. Meiers 2011, 53–55, 83–85.
13 Cf. Meiers 2011, 52f.; Martini 2013, 8.
14 Schneider 1985, 560f.; Kolb 2000, 11.
15 Cf. Kolb 2000, *passim* and especially 49–226. In her postdoctoral thesis she concluded that the *cursus publicus* did not carry the wholeness of the transport and message transfer of the Roman state; it could only be used restrictedly and in individual cases for well-defined state purposes. Cf. Chevallier 1988, 46f.; Schneider, 564f.
16 Chevallier 1988, 63–66.
17 Chevallier 1988, 63.
18 Chevallier 1988, 63f.; Schneider 1985, 562f.; Martini 2013, 225.
19 Chevallier 1997, 53–59.
20 Junkelmann 1990, 77f; cf. Kolb 2000, 22.
21 Cf. Chevallier 1988, 37, 57–62.
22 Even though it must be taken into consideration that only 20 percent of the Roman road network (the paved main roads) were fit for effective vehicle traffic. Most other roads presented characteristics that only pedestrians and riders were able to cope with. Nevertheless, it remains true, that vehicular traffic gained its most elaborate shaping, extension and efficiency in the Roman Empire for the first time in history. It was necessary to wait until the 18th century, when official country roads would be set up and wheeled vehicles would again reach the significance seen in years gone by.
23 Chevallier 1988, 33f. Cf. medieval carriages Munby 2008.
24 Junkelmann 1990, 68. Cf. Schneider 1985, 495f., 515–517.
25 Cf. Schneider 1985, 493–495, 541–551; Martini 2013, 17.
26 Schneider 1985, 512.
27 Martini 2013, 19.
28 Schneider 1985, 558, 563f; Junkelmann 1990, 84f.
29 Cf. Schneider 1985, 509f. In official transport there were weight limitations for luggage reaching from 10 kg to a maximum of 20 kg.
30 Although Roman carts were already equipped with leather suspensions to absorb shocks, the workmanship and construction of cart wheels in the Roman Age was not adapted to rough edaphic conditions. Roman wheels consisted mostly of wood which made them vulnerable to break under the heavy weight of the wagons and the transmission of shocks through potholes.
31 Goetz and Keil 1929, II, 7. (= Varro, *Rust.*)
32 [...] *sic contra in viis habere malunt placidos*, Varro, *Rust*. II, 7.
33 Varro rust. II, 7.

34 Cf. Schneider 1985, 504. Today, the word 'canter' still stands for a slower working gallop.
35 Lundström 1912, VI, 27.
36 Brotier 1826, VIII, 67. (= Plin. *Nat.*)
37 Gesner 1781, (= Veg. *Mulom.*). Especially I, 56 and IV, 6 deal with gaited horses.
38 Ihm 1892.
39 Plin. *Nat.* VIII, 67; Veg. *Mulom.* IV, 6.
40 Cf. Schneider 1985, 501f.
41 In Varro's Menippean satires a *magister equitum* receives a horse to teach him to amble: *Traditur magistro, ut equiso doceat tolutim*, Riese 1865, 233. In the same work one of the protagonists quits a conversation in the following way: [...] *cedit citus celsus tolutim,* he quickly left and straightened up like when in an amble, ibid., 97. Further word constructions and expressions based on the amble like *tolutiloquentia* or *sententiae tolutares* can be found in Meiers 2011, 47. Cf. also Schneider 1985, 500.
42 Plin. *Nat.* VIII, 67. Cf. Schneider 1985, 499f., 501.
43 Fellendorf-Börner 1985, 83, 93, 99, 101f., 106, 108–110, 114, 118, 120f.
44 Schneider 1985, 503 The horses led by the Dioscuri at the Capitol in Rome clearly show an ambling gait, cf. Junkelmann 1990, fig. 18, 31. The effigies are dated to the second century CE.
45 Junkelmann 1990, 46.
46 During a race at a circus, another Camargue stallion even reached more than 60 km/h, see Junkelmann 1990, 46.
47 Cf. the foreword of Marcus Junkelmann in Martini 2013, XVII. Nevertheless, there are accounts which speak in favour of equestrian traffic, cf. Chevallier 1988, 41.
48 There still is a controversy in research, whether Roman cushion saddles (*epihippia*) had an inner wooden frame, which held the whole construction together, or not. The latter would have allowed to use the saddles on many different horses, since they did not need to be adapted to one single horse's back. Concerning the Roman saddles and the differing opinions about their construction, see Junkelmann 1992, 34–74. Cf. also Schneider 1985, 514.
49 It could be argued that at least women used side-saddles, which had a wooden footboard on one side to stabilise their seat while riding. Some representations of the deity Epona seem to confirm this hypothesis, cf. Fellendorf-Börner 1985, 84, 88, 90f., 98, 101f., 106–108, 110f., 114, 120, 136.
50 Against this assertion: Chevallier 1988, 34. Hipposandals were not considered, as they were chiefly used on draught animals to prevent hoof abrasion when pulling heavy loads, cf. Schneider 1985, 479f., 496; Junkelmann 1992, 88–90.
51 To prevent heavy wear of the hooves and free the road for wagons, there sometimes existed special sandy paths alongside the roadways, see Chevallier 1997, 114.
52 Cf. Kolb 2000, 8.
53 Forbes 1993, 161f.
54 Ibid.
55 Cf. the articles in Burgard and Haverkamp 1998.
56 Schneider 1985, 461, 558, 563f.
57 Schneider 1985, 558, 567–577.
58 For hypotheses on even earlier similar systems under the Ptolemaios dynasty see also Kolb 2000, 18f.
59 Although, it came only rarely to use (for instance with official journeys which had been scheduled at short notice, with the loss of draft animals or with damage occasioned to the vehicle), it lead to abuse at the expense of the local population. This development triggered new regulations pertaining to requisition claims, cf. Kolb 2000, 29–34.

266   *Fabienne Meiers*

60  Schneider 1985, 534.
61  One should keep in mind, that some of the paved Roman roads as a matter of fact also had an uneven surface that transmitted shocks to the vehicle unless leather suspensions were used. A shock reduction, on the other hand, could be achieved by means of a smooth surface with small joint spacing and large stone formats. This was the case for most of the Roman highways, cf. Chevallier 1997, 9–11, 13–15.
62  There still is no consensus among the research community regarding the date of emergence and the origin of nailed horseshoes, cf. Junkelmann 1992, 90–98; Lingens 2008, 8–29, especially 8–14.
63  It has been postulated, that the lack of archaeological finds during this time span could also be attributed to the melting down of used horseshoes. Iron was a valuable, reusable material.
64  Cf. Lingens 2008, 14–16, 26f.
65  Junkelmann 1992, 70–72.
66  Cf. Schneider 1985, 501, 522. An alternative form *ambulatorius* is also documented.
67  For more information on names for ambling riding horses see Meiers 2011, 38–42, 46–59.
68  This would only change with the development of the postal system by the house of Thurn and Taxis, starting in the second half of the fifteenth century.
69  Schneider 1985, 510f., 545. In the early Imperial period equestrian and vehicular traffic were prohibited during the first ten hours after sunrise. In late Antiquity, this strict ban would already be relaxed in some parts of the Empire and in certain conditions like triumphal entries. Within the city, the use of horses as well as wagons could be very problematic due to the unpredictable behaviour of these and other (flight) animals, which were used in transport.
70  Monnet 2004, 220.
71  Cf. Meiers 2018, 177f., 242.
72  Account books were an important part of the pragmatic written sources we can find throughout Europe since the twelfth century. They probably developed from the accountancy of Italian merchants in the major trading metropolises like Venice for instance. Due to the ephemeral relevance of the content of this source type, however, only few of them survived. Urban account books list the annual revenues and expenditures in a tabular, prosaic style. Most of the time, they are not going into detail with regard to the financial reporting: they give information about the issuer and receiver of a certain amount of money for a good or a service and they tell us when the sum changed hands. Travel accounts for messenger services and political or administrative missions additionally convey information about where the municipal agents travelled to and from, how long they stayed away, where they stayed overnight, how many horses they took along or rented during their journey and much more. While older account books were still written in Latin and followed the clerical traditions of literacy, the younger documents clearly reflect a growing tendency to employ vernacular languages. At the same time as these languages become more and more common in urban novellas, they also establish as the norm in municipal chancelleries because of a clearer and faster understanding.
73  Meiers 2018, 228f.
74  Krier 1991, 5–13.
75  So far, only the years between 1388 and 1483 have been critically edited: Moulin and Pauly 2007–2016.
76  Moulin and Pauly 2008, 74: 'Item des frydages nae eſſen vor vnſer frauwen dage aſſumpcionis Ryed heren heinrich van bettingin zu vnſerin gnedigin heren dem Romiſchen vnd vngerſchen heren kunige zu Baireſburch vnd quam widder vmb zu luccemburg des frydages zu abent vor vnſer frauwen dage natiuitatis vnd haen yme geuen vor tzeirgelt 50 gul in golde die kaufft wourden iclicher gul vor 26 nuwe gr

des gaet menſchins perd bij yme geſtandin ee er in wech rydde 3 wochin 2 dage vnd vertzeirde 3 gul vnd gaff vor eynen ſadel vnd tzaůn 2 guldin vnd dar nae ſo er widder vmb komen was ſtoent dat ſelue perd hinder yme 10 dage vnd vertzeirde 1 guldin vnd gyenck yme ſin perd vff dem wege abe vnd kauffte ein ander pert vor 16 guldin vnd haet ſyme knechte geuen 1 guldin vnd er haet vertzeirt vnd geleyde geuen zu ſamen 16 gul alſo komet die ſomme zu ſamen vor 49 guldin die macht duſer rechenonge 55 gul 9 gr.' All translations by the author unless otherwise noted.
77 This sum corresponds not only to the expense for the safe conduct given by the servant and his consummation during the journey. For comparison: The municipal judge received an annual salary of 21 gul 18 gr 5 lew, see Moulin and Pauly 2008, 75.
78 Meiers 2018, 87, fig. 9, 292.
79 Meiers 2018, 74f.
80 Mostly for covering short distances on pre-defined, well-known routes.
81 Schneider 1985, 533f. Travelling in sprung coaches became once more socially acceptable by the end of the 16th century and especially since the mid-seventeenth century, when hired carriages appeared in the cities.
82 Cf. Hübner 2012, 277–296.
83 In my doctoral thesis, however, I could demonstrate that the term 'Stadtboten' was employed for bailiffs as well in the City of Luxembourg, see Meiers 2018, 195–198.
84 Hübner 2012, 283–287.
85 Ibid.
86 Modern trick saddles or Cossack saddles function alike.
87 This new saddle type can be seen in many iconographical sources like Albrecht Dürer's engravings and Swiss chronicles. Some more representative specimens survived as the so-called Bohemian parade saddles, which are coated with richly decorated and sometimes painted bone plates. These saddles have been associated with the court of Sigismund of Luxembourg (1368–1437) and his order of the dragon. Cf. Meiers 2018, 104–106.
88 Meiers 2011, 56f.; Meiers 2018, *passim*.
89 Meiers 2018, 146–149.
90 See footnote 88. It appears that they prevailed on the British Isles. Their facilities continued to be used from the Roman period up to the late Middle Ages and beyond that time.
91 In the Roman period, larger stones could be found along both edges of official roads at regular intervals; they were used as mounting aids for riders, since stirrups had not been introduced then. These stone aids could also be found in many cities. See Plutarch's statements in *The Life of Caius Gracchus* in Perrin 1958, 7. Cf. Chevallier 1997, 110. In the early Middle Ages, stone aids still continued to be used, see Schneider 1985, 524.
92 It has yet to be determined, whether private horse owners were only renting their horses on the basis of obsolete requisition procedures (*paravered*-service) or if they started to dive into that business, too.
93 See chapter II.
94 Cramer 2005, v. 7286–7289.
95 Lachmann 2003, st. 779, v. 1.
96 Cf. Bowden 2017, 58; cf. also note 41.
97 Bagliani 2015.
98 Concerning gait-regulation training see Meiers 2011, 68–74.
99 Verdam 1900, v. 9167–9174: 'Learning how to amble is painful for a horse, / which by nature only shows trot, / Because you have to bind together his legs / by force with a rope, / And only when it gets accustomed to this, / you can take off the rope, / And it will keep the gait / which it has learned through habit.'
100 Ibid.

## Bibliography

### Printed sources

Brotier, Gabriel, ed. 1826. *Caius Plinii Secundi naturalis historiae libri XXXVII*, vol. 3. London: A. J. Valpy (= Plin. nat.).
Cramer, Thomas, ed. 2005. *Hartmann von Aue: Erec*. Frankfurt am Main: Fischer Taschenbuch.
Gesner, Johann M., ed. 1781. *Vegetii Renati Artis veterinariae sive mulomedicinae libri quator*. Mannheim: Cura & Sumptibus Societatis literatae (= Veg. mulom.).
Goetz, Georg and Heinrich Keil, ed. 1929. *Marcus Terenti Varronis Rerum rusticarum libri tres*. Leipzig: Teubner (= Varro rust.).
Ihm, Maximilian, ed. 1892. *Pelagonii Artis veterinariae quae extant*. Leipzig: Teubner.
Lachmann, Karl, ed. 2003. *Wolfram von Eschenbach: Parzival*. Berlin/New York: De Gruyter.
Lundström, Vilhelm, ed. 1912. *Lucius Iuni Moderati Columellae opera quae exstant*. Uppsala: Eranos.
Moulin, Claudine and Michel Pauly, ed. 2007–2016. *Die Rechnungsbücher der Stadt Luxemburg*, 9 vols. Luxemburg: Rapidpress.
Perrin, Bernadotte, ed. 1958. *Plutarch's Lives*. London/Cambridge/Massachusetts: Harvard University Press.
Riese, Alexander, ed. 1865. *Marcus Terenti Varronis Saturarum Menippearum reliquiae*. Leipzig: Teubner.
Verdam, Jacob, ed. 1900. *Die Spiegel der Sonden*, vol. 1. Leiden: Brill.

### Literature

Althoff, Gerd. 1992. "Vom Zwang zur Mobilität und ihren Problemen." In *Reisen und Reiseliteratur im Mittelalter und in der Frühen Neuzeit*, edited by Xenja von Ertzdorff and Dieter Neukirch, 91–111. Amsterdam/Atlanta: Rodopi.
Bagliani, Agostino Paravicini. 2015. "Le cheval blanc du pape. Symbolique et autoreprésentation (XIIe-XIIIe siècles)." In *Le cheval dans la culture médiévale*, edited by Bernard Andenmatten, Agostino Paravicini Bagliani, and Eva Pibiri, 243–265. Florence: SISMEL – Edizioni del Galluzzo.
Bowden, Betsy. 2017. *The Wife of Bath in Afterlife: Ballads to Blake*. Lanham: Lehigh University Press.
Burgard, Friedhelm and Alfred Haverkamp, ed. 1998. *Auf den Römerstraßen ins Mittelalter. Beiträge zur Verkehrsgeschichte zwischen Maas und Rhein von der Spätantike bis ins 19. Jahrhundert*. Mainz: Philipp von Zabern.
Casson, Lionel. 1979. *Travel in the Ancient World*. London: John Hopkins University Press.
Chevallier, Raymond. 1988. *Voyages et déplacements dans l'empire Romain*. Paris: Armand Collin.
Chevallier, Raymond. 1997. *Les voies romaines*. Paris: Éditions Picard.
Elze, Reinhard. 1980. "Über die Leistungsfähigkeit von Gesandtschaften und Boten im 11. Jahrhundert. Aus der Vorgeschichte von Canossa 1075–1077." In *Histoire comparée de l'Administration (IVe-XVIIIe siècles)*, edited by Werner Paravicini and Karl Werner Ferdinand, 3–10. München/Zürich: Artemis Verlag.

Fellendorf-Börner, Gabi. 1985. "Die bildlichen Darstellungen der Epona auf den Denkmälern Baden-Württembergs." *Fundberichte aus Baden-Württemberg*, vol. 10: 77–141.
Forbes, Robert J. 1993. *Studies in Ancient Technology*, vol. 2. Leiden: Brill.
Hübner, Klara. 2012. *Im Dienste ihrer Stadt. Boten- und Nachrichtenorganisationen in den schweizerisch-oberdeutschen Städten des späten Mittelalters*. Ostfildern: Thorbecke.
Junkelmann, Marcus. 1990. *Die Reiter Roms. Teil 1: Reise, Jagd, Triumph und Circusrennen*. Mainz: Philipp von Zabern.
Junkelmann, Marcus. 1991. *Die Reiter Roms. Teil 2: Der militärische Einsatz*. Mainz: Philipp von Zabern.
Junkelmann, Marcus. 1992. *Die Reiter Roms. Teil 3: Zubehör, Reitweise, Bewaffnung*. Mainz: Philipp von Zabern.
Karll, Alfred. 1905. "Aachener Verkehrswesen bis zum Ende des 14. Jahrhunderts." *Aus Aachens Vorzeit* 18: 65–107, 111–196.
Kolb, Anne. 2000. *Transport und Nachrichtentransfer im Römischen Reich*. Berlin: De Gruyter.
Koselleck, Reinhart. 2003. "Das Ende des Pferdezeitalters." *Süddeutsche Zeitung*, September 9, 2003.
Krier, Jean. 1991. "Zur römischen Besiedlung der Altstadt von Luxemburg." *Hémecht* 43: 5–13.
Lingens, Insa. 2008. "Die Entwicklung der Hufpflege und des Hufbeschlags von der Antike bis zur Neuzeit unter besonderer Berücksichtigung des Hufbeschlags bei der Hufrehe." PhD diss., University of Berlin.
Martini, Simone. 2013. *Civitas equitata. Eine archäologische Studie zu Equiden bei den Treverern in keltisch-römischer Zeit*. Wiesbaden: Harrassowitz.
Meiers, Fabienne. 2011. "Reisen zu Pferde im Mittelalter. Semantik und Verwendung des passgehenden Zelter-Reitpferdes." Master's thesis, University of Freiburg.
Meiers, Fabienne. 2018. "Reiten *van der stede wegen*. Dienstliche Mobilität und städtische Kommunikation im Spiegel der Rechnungsbücher der Stadt Luxemburg (1388–1500) mit besonderer Betonung des Reitverkehrs." PhD diss., University of Luxembourg.
Monnet, Pierre. 2004. *Villes d'Allemagne au Moyen Âge*. Paris: Éditions Picard.
Montagné, Jean-Claude Beïret. 2008. *Transmissions. L'histoire des moyens de communication à distance depuis l'Antiquité jusqu'au milieu du XXe siècle*. Bagneux: J.-C. Montagné.
Munby, Julian. 2008. "From Carriage to Coach: What Happened?" In *The Art, Science, and Technology of Medieval Travel*, edited by Robert Bork and Andrea Kann, 41–53. Aldershot: Ashgate.
Schneider, Wolfgang Christian. 1985. "Animal laborans. Das Arbeitstier und sein Einsatz in Transport und Verkehr der Spätantike und des frühen Mittelalters." In *L'uomo di fronte al mondo animale nell'alto Medioevo*, edited by the Centro italiano di studi sull'alto Medioevo, 457–578. Spoleto: Presso la sede del Centro.
Schulz, Meinhard-Wilhelm. 2009. *Caesar zu Pferde. Ross und Reiter in Caesars Kommentarien und in der Germania des Tacitus*. Hildesheim/Zürich/New York: Olms.
Steinbrecher, Aline. 2011. "In der Geschichte ist viel zu wenig von Tieren die Rede" (Elias Canetti). Die Geschichtswissenschaft und ihre Annäherung an die Tiere." In *Gefährten – Konkurrenten – Verwandte. Die Mensch-Tier-Beziehung im wissenschaftlichen Diskurs*, edited by Carola Otterstedt and Michael Rosenberger, 264–286. Göttingen: Vandenhoeck & Ruprecht.

# 14 Entertaining and educating the audience at home

Eye-witnessing in late medieval pilgrimage reports

*Stefan Schröder*

**Introduction**

Travelling through the Sinai desert on their way to the monastery of St Catherine, the Dominican Felix Fabri (c. 1437/38–1502) and his fellow travel companions made an astonishing observation: about noon on the 20th of September 1483, on a mountain-top at some distance, they saw an animal that they first recognised as a camel. Drawing, however, the pilgrims' attention to the single horn on the forehead, their local guide identified the creature as a rhinoceros or a unicorn. Stunned by this reading, they 'gazed most earnestly upon this extremely noble beast and grieved sore that he [sic!] was not nearer to us that we might have viewed him [sic!] more narrowly'.[1] Even more astonishing, the animal did not flee, so that the pilgrims got the impression that the unicorn was just as pleased to observe them as they were to observe it.

Fabri's description of this event, which is part of a report on his pilgrimage to the Holy Land called *Evagatorium in Terrae Sanctae, Arabiae et Egypti peregrinationem*, is one example of how an experience was explained and transmitted by culturally formed images. Today, we are relatively sure that unicorns do not exist in real life. Consequently, the creature has been labelled in research as some kind of antelope.[2] For the medieval contemporary, in contrast, the existence of unicorns as such was not in doubt. Their existence was described by ancient and medieval authorities like Pliny, Solinus, Isidore of Seville and Konrad of Megenberg, who did not necessarily differentiate between a rhinoceros and unicorn, pointing out that the first is the Greek name for the latter.[3] Since in medieval maps and geographical writings the unicorn is placed in deserted regions like Sinai and the Far East, the pilgrims could easily have perceived the creature as a real unicorn. As part of the *Physiologus* and other medieval bestiaries, it was moreover seen not only as one of the most exotic of animals, but also as a noble animal, since it represents Christ in its allegoric meaning.[4] That the animal looked down patiently at the pilgrims furthermore strengthened the impression of being blessed by experiencing something extraordinary, even divine.

By the detailed description, including the hour of the day, by referring to the expertise of the guide familiar with the local biota, and by describing his emotions, which ranged from scepticism at first to amazement at seeing a unicorn and eventually to grief at the animal being so far away, Fabri accentuated the originality of the situation. In doing so, he strengthened his credibility as an eye-witness who had indeed seen a unicorn in person. Providing some additional information on the nature of the unicorn, based on the Bible and other authoritative writings, Fabri moreover educated his readers. This episode is an excellent example of how the events of a journey were transformed into a text, of how the traveller narrated his experiences in such a way that the intended audience could follow and enjoy the reading. By taking into account the complexity of interpreting pre-modern travel reports, my aim is to further analyse the relationship between the author of a pilgrimage report and the audience he wanted to address. The focus will be on eye-witness accounts and on the asserted experiences of the pilgrims during their journey.

Since Antiquity, the eye has been regarded as the most important sense. The act of seeing something in person[5] played a key role in verifying events. In the Middle Ages, especially in legal affairs and in historiographical writings, eye-witness reports were regarded as crucial in claiming the truth.[6] Through bodily presence and sensual perception, an eye-witness could guarantee what was authentic and factual and reject what was false and pretended. Juridical decisions and perceptions of the past, for instance, could thus be more or less actively influenced. Being in possession of seemingly direct and exclusive knowledge put the eye-witness in a powerful position, even when considering that such knowledge was reported from a retrospective perspective that could be distorted.[7] As a consequence, there is a reciprocal relationship between the testimony of an eye-witness and the credibility and reputation of the person as a whole, seeing the eye-witness a person of trust or at least as someone who had to be trusted.[8]

Within the context of travel writing, however, the ambiguity of this relationship becomes visible. Again, eye-witnessing has been a decisive method of authenticating travel experiences since ancient times.[9] Yet, eye-witnessing can easily give rise to a suspicion of exaggeration and pretending to have seen things, since there might be nobody in the audience who could retrace the traveller's statement to the source. Whether the report was regarded as reliable or not depended more upon the moral integrity of the witness and not necessarily on the kind of the information that he transmitted.[10] If the eye-witness was not trusted, he could ultimately be accused of being a 'travel liar'.[11] Within the medieval context, one has furthermore to consider the discourse on curiosity. On the one hand, the act of seeing could enable a person to gain insights into God's creation, for example by observing the 'Book of Nature'. Yet on the other hand, and maybe even more than the other senses, the eye was exposed to distraction and evil temptations.

Authors of medieval pilgrimage reports had thus to strike a balance in narrating events. They had to report as accurately and in as much detail as possible what they saw with respect to their audience. Yet as pilgrims on a religious journey, they, at the same time, had to worry about not becoming exceedingly intrigued by worldly issues, as this could be seen as a sign of curiosity. Based on the work of Fabri and contemporary pilgrimage accounts, I will therefore examine the ways in which the processes of eye-witnessing were narrated. How were eyewitness situations and asserted experiences of body and mind used to direct the reader's attention? How were borders drawn between the legitimate use of eyesight and curiosity?

## Eye-witnessing and Felix Fabri's *Evagatorium*

Felix Fabri provides a fine example for analysing moments of eye-witnessing, since his monumental text remind us of the many layers, functions and meanings of pre-modern travel reports.[12] The Dominican monk, born in Zurich and working as a preacher general and lector from 1468 onwards in the city of Ulm in southwest Germany, visited the Holy Land twice in 1480 and 1483 and travelled on his latter journey also through Egypt.[13] The Latin *Evagatorium* is, in fact, one of the most comprehensive and most important travel reports of the entire Middle Ages. The autograph, extant in the city library of Ulm, comprises two densely written folios produced most likely between 1484 and 1495 and complemented with numerous marginalia that Fabri added in order to include newly found information.[14] According to the prologue, he wrote the *Evagatorium* for his Dominican brothers, who had asked him already at the time of his departure to write down all his experiences. Fabri fulfilled their wish by stating that not one day passed without him making notes, recording everything he saw, even during a sea storm, while riding a donkey or a camel, or while sitting beside a fire at night when his companions were already asleep.[15] With this statement, Fabri ensured his readers right from the start that he was providing them with first-hand knowledge of his travels, which were, moreover, accurately, diligently and sincerely documented.

Yet after his return, Fabri made extensive use of other sources with the aim of providing a full picture of the Holy Land pilgrimage and of the history and nature of the Near East, thus producing a monumental encyclopaedic narrative. The title of his report, a novel use of the Latin verb *evagare* (to wander, to extravagate), is a striking name for the account, with its numerous biblical, historical, mythical and natural digressions. In this way, Fabri wanted to deepen the readers' understanding of biblical events, to strengthen their faith and to offer them ideas that could be used, for instance, for their own sermons. The text was meant to gratify both the amazed soul as well as the curious spirit.[16] Fabri wished that his report would be accessible in other mendicant monasteries, and the extant manuscripts of the *Evagatorium* suggest that it was known predominantly in local clerical circles.[17] He correctly assumed that the reading of his enormous work might be exhausting and even tiresome. Therefore, he interspersed it with adventurous, amusing and even childish anecdotes meant to keep his clerical readers' interest alive.[18] The encounter with the unicorn, which on first sight has little to do with a pilgrimage report that ideally should focus on the holy sites, can be placed within this category. Including attention-grabbing interpolations between all the sophisticated and pedagogical annotations gave some events a more dramatic twist. More dramatic when compared with the reports of Fabri's travel companions in 1483: Paul Walther of Guglingen (c. 1422–1496) and Bernhard of Breidenbach (c. 1434/40–1497).[19]

In contrast to Fabri, the report by the Franciscan Paul Walther, only extant in one unfinished manuscript, does not indicate an unusual encounter around this date at all.[20] Breidenbach, dean of the cathedral at Mainz, whose well-known narrative was printed in 1486 both in Latin and in German and became one of Fabri's most important sources, mentioned the encounter with the unicorn in just one single sentence, saying that he had seen an animal that was much larger than a camel and that, according to the guide, could have been a unicorn.[21] This statement implies nothing of the miraculous moment of the encounter and could easily be read without taking further notice. Verification that it was indeed a unicorn was only confirmed via a woodcut produced by Erhard Reuwich, a professional painter engaged by Breidenbach to document the journey.

Framed by other exotic animals, including a giraffe and a crocodile, the unicorn with its extraordinary long horn is an elemental piece that illustrates the alien world on the other side of the Mediterranean. Breidenbach relied on the visual medium as a specific form of persuasive power. A statement at the bottom of the page claims that all animals have been depicted as they were actually seen on the journey.[22] In this way, the alleged transparency is accentuated even more. The visual medium makes the recipient into an eye-witness, ostensibly giving him/her direct access to the events of the journey and thus increasing the truthfulness of the report as a whole. The woodcut was placed after Reuwich's representation of Jerusalem and the Holy Land. Accordingly, it is not connected to Breidenbach's entry on the events of the 20th of September. Fabri was aware of the 26 woodcuts in total included in Breidenbach's report, and he even praised the 'masterly and truthful manner' of Reuwich's illustrations without referring specifically to the image of the unicorn.[23] Nonetheless, by mentioning Reuwich's images, Fabri created an additional cross-reference for authenticating his own writing. Fabri sought to convince his readers foremost by employing textual strategies,[24] and especially by underlining the fact that he had seen the described things in person. In contrast to Breidenbach and most other contemporary authors of pilgrimage reports, he put forward both his 'narrating self' that recounts the journey and his 'experiencing self' that travelled abroad.[25]

Both his 'narrating' and his 'experiencing' self should be differentiated from Fabri as a historical person. They did not represent his character and mentality, but only how Fabri wanted to be seen by himself and by his readers. Analogous to the tendency in late medieval historiography, he frequently mentions having seen the things described in person.[26] He is not a distant observer; rather, he comments on the events of the journey in the first person, serving as the representative voice for what happened to the group of pilgrims as a whole and positioning himself as an example of how to (and of how not to) deal with all the new, curious or dangerous experiences while abroad.[27] Being personally involved in the events and seeing everything through his own eyes emphasised Fabri's claims to truthfulness and of providing an unaltered report. Yet, as the encounter with the unicorn and the following examples will show, he employed a 'narrated self' not only to prove or correct disputed facts, but also to define 'Otherness' and to transmit norms and values. As a result, Fabri also provided climatic, idealised and sometimes even entirely invented eye-witnessing episodes.

## Eye-witnessing holy places and confirming salvation history

To ensure a better understanding of the Bible and to strengthen one's own faith, the empirical certification via eyesight was of special importance while visiting Jerusalem and the Holy Land.[28] During his stay, Fabri seemingly turned over every stone, climbed on each wall and examined all the caves he could find in order to draw a more accurate picture of the conditions of the sacred sites. He looked, for instance, through holes in the burial field of Aceldama and claimed that he had seen the remains of some recently deceased people.[29] Wandering in the valley of Josaphat, he used the opportunity to crawl inside the so-called tomb of Absalom, wishing to see what was inside.[30] At Aceldama, Fabri did not have a personal opinion on whether or not the legend of the buried corpses being reduced to dry bones within three days was true. In the latter case, he was somewhat sceptical of whether or not the mausoleum had really once been built as Absalom's burial place.

On other occasions, however, Fabri's personal observations led him to oppose existing traditions. He rejected the assumption that it was the Pool of Siloam, where King David had observed Bathsheba bathing (2nd Sam. 11:2–3). Looking from Mount Sion, according to the tradition the place where David's palace once stood, Fabri could determine that the pond could not be seen from such a position.[31] Along the way from Jerusalem to Bethlehem, he corrected the belief of the local Franciscan guides that a particular wall constituted the remains of the house of Jacob the Patriarch. On the contrary, as he climbed along the wall, he deduced that it was part of an ancient water conduit.[32] His enthusiastic enquiries helped him to critically distance himself from the statements of contemporary authors, of fellow pilgrims as well as of the Franciscan guides as local experts and keepers and mediators of the Christian *lieux de memoire*.[33] When necessary, he even corrected highly venerated authorities. For instance, Fabri did not support Jerome's interpretation of the conflicting statements in the gospels that Christ's feet were anointed once by Mary Magdalena and once by some other woman (Luke 7:36–50 vs. Matthew 26:6; Mark 14:3; John 12:1). Visiting the house attributed to Simon the Pharisee, Fabri was rather convinced that Mary Magdalena had anointed Christ twice at two different places and that the indulgence offered to the pilgrims at the house in Jerusalem was valid.[34]

As these examples show, eye-witnessing was an essential strategy for Fabri. Yet, one has to be careful not to interpret the critical statements made by him and others as a turning point between a 'medieval' attitude of just blindly following religious dogmatic traditions and a more 'modern' and more 'objective' approach that gives one's own experiences more weight.[35] He still relied on authorities and used written evidence from other sources as a basis for his own writings. Moreover, it should be noted that the works Fabri read both to prepare for his journey as well as to compose his reports directed his perceptions and gave him a starting point for his observations. At certain moments, Fabri even severely needed to confirm his observations by textual testimony, for example when searching in vain for a rock miraculously bearing the marks of the body of

Christ that he had seen on his first pilgrimage. Not finding the rock in 1483 and lacking the assistance of the monk who had guided him to the spot three years prior, Fabri's fellow pilgrims and the Franciscans expressed reservations about his story. His reputation as a reliable witness was restored only after Fabri showed them that there was written evidence on the miracle in the popular and respected pilgrimage report of Burchard of Mount Sion.[36]

More conclusive, in my view, is the interpretation that Fabri saw himself as part of a succession of witnesses (including the Virgin Mary and the Apostles) who testified to the ultimate truth of the Bible and wanted to transmit this reality to his readers.[37] He felt a strong need to follow through on the plea of his Dominican brothers to write down everything he experienced. Further, he saw such a plea as a legitimation of the need to inquire into everything *in situ* as well as to critically evaluate written sources of all kinds. As a consequence, Fabri was able to provide a better understanding of the Bible and to correct impressions when necessary. Similar objectives can be noted in other contemporary pilgrimage reports. Hans Schürpff from Lucerne, for instance, concluded after his pilgrimage in 1497 that Mount Calvary was in reality quite small. As a result, the Virgin Mary and the Apostle John could not have stood beside the crosses, as was usually depicted in painted canvasses back home. Their position must have been below the spot and some distance away, yet close enough to hear Christ's last words.[38] Describing the holy places as precisely as possible and reconstructing the spatial and relational settings by measuring the distances between them were of crucial importance for helping pilgrims envision the biblical events (particularly the Passion of Christ) in detail. As Kathryne Beebe puts it, constructing Jerusalem for the 'exterior eye' and constructing Jerusalem for the 'interior eye' in order for others to adequately reflect on the biblical events are deeply connected.[39]

Fabri, moreover, was able to solve the mystery when eye-witness accounts led to confusion and uncertainty. Some pilgrims had difficulties in understanding how there would be enough space for all human beings in the small Valley of Josaphat, which, according to tradition, would be the place of Judgement Day (Joel 4:2 and 12). Speaking in the *Evagatorium* somewhat dismissively of such simple-minded people, he pointed to Zechariah's prophecies, where it is told that the landscape will be fundamentally changed on this dramatic day (Zech. 14:4–10).[40] This example shows that eye-witnessing as such was not always sufficient and could lead to misinterpretations. In order to find a proper explanation via biblical exegesis, someone with a clerical background and deeper theological knowledge was needed.[41]

This expertise helped Fabri also to separate miracles from phenomena that could be explained by natural causes.[42] When necessary, Fabri relied on other senses. When putting his head as deeply as possible into a fissure on Mount Calvary that was said to have occurred at the moment of Christ's death, he was able to smell 'an exceeding[ly] sweet scent, whereby men are visibly refreshed'.[43] He experienced the same miracle later when visiting the place of Christ's birth in Bethlehem. In this way, Fabri proved several things. Firstly, as Francois Hartog has pointed out regarding eyesight, witnessing an astonishing or marvellous phenomenon with one's own eyes (or in Fabri's case, also by one's sense of smell) is even more persuasive and strengthens the truth of a particular claim: 'I have seen it, it is true, and it is true that it is a marvel.'[44] Fabri thus verified, secondly, that the place was indeed holy and still bore physical traces confirming the biblical narrative. Sacred and protected by the divine, this place cannot be destroyed or altered by any human intervention, as Fabri underlined for instance by referring to the legend of how a certain Muslim sultan had repeatedly failed to destroy the Church of the Nativity in Bethlehem.[45] Within the context of Jerusalem as an arena where several religious communities offered competing interpretations of the past ('Kampfplatz rivalisierender Erinnerungsgemeinschaften'),[46] the heavenly odour that Fabri perceived at the place of Christ's birth gave him the opportunity to state the superiority of the Christian faith. The version of the Quran, according to which Christ was born not in a stable but in the shadow of a palm tree (Surah 19: 22–26), was wrong and therefore evidence of the wickedness of Islam.[47] Finally, Fabri's personal verification made clear the fact that salvation history is true and ongoing: No matter what the current condition of a particular holy place as well as the Holy Land as a whole, no matter how much Christianity is suppressed by the infidels, Fabri found truth in biblical history in which the second coming of the Lord at the end of days is ensured.[48]

Fabri communicated such sensual encounters with the divine in detail to his readers at home in order to strengthen their faith. Only in the case of the Holy Sepulchre did Fabri fail to provide a definitive answer to the question of whether the place was indeed Christ's true burial spot. Despite all his efforts at investigating and scrutinising the sources – a proceeding that has been regarded in research as an almost professional archaeological survey – Fabri could not determine if the Aedicule conveyed traces of the original tomb of Christ.[49] When it comes to the question of believing, when it was necessary to look beyond the sphere of reality into the sphere of transcendence, eye-witnessing reached its limits.

## Eye-witnessing and curiosity

Fabri also encountered the problem between seeing and believing at other instances. During a stopover in Cyprus, he visited a monastery where he saw a wooden cross that, according to tradition, was the one used for the crucifixion of the penitent thief Dismas. A local legend stated that the cross floats miraculously free in the air, and Fabri felt tempted to ascertain whether or not this was true. He acknowledged that the ends of the crossbar, as well as the base of the cross, were hidden in openings of the adjacent walls and the floor. Yet, from his position (even recording that he was allowed to kiss the relic and had a look at it from behind) he could not decide whether something was hanging from the openings or not. Fabri decided, however, not to step closer in order to find out the truth, stating that he feared God and had come to this place in order to venerate the relic and not to tempt the Lord.[50]

The incident shows that Fabri was aware of the fine line between eye-witnessing out of honest motives and out of curiosity. Curiosity as such was not necessarily a sin in the Middle Ages. It was distinguished between a type of curiosity with a positive connotation, namely to learn more about God's creation in order to increase one's own virtues, and between a sinful type of curiosity understood as the impetus to know everything and to accumulate knowledge purely out of personal desire.[51] Fabri's inquiries in the Holy Land can be regarded positively as a vital engagement to document (the truth of) salvation history in a way that was beneficial for his readers. With appropriate discernment, it was possible to explore the world, to be amazed and, at the same time, to be humbled about the wonderful and harmonious dimensions of God's almighty creation. As he explicitly stated elsewhere, his inquiries were carried out 'not out of presumption or curiosity, but of piety'.[52] The fact, however, that a person could easily be entrapped by curiosity was humorously demonstrated on another occasion. Strolling with 'wandering eyes' through the Church of the Holy Sepulchre and staring like 'ill-bred men' with curiosity upon the upper windows, Fabri stepped, to his own embarrassment, on top of the Stone of Anointing, one of the most prominent and sacred places in the church.[53]

The danger of being misled to a point of curiosity by the wandering eye was even more imminent regarding the cultural encounters during the journey. In fact, many pilgrims embarked on the galley to the Holy Land not only out of a noble motive for the *imitatio Christi*. Just as alluring was the prospect of adventure, of visiting exotic places, of gaining honour and of increasing one's social status (for instance, by being knighted at the Holy Sepulchre).[54] Most authors accentuated the religious impetus by disclaiming fervently that they had not sought to travel for the sake of vanity or boastfulness.[55] However, reading contemporary pilgrimage reports, it becomes quite clear that pilgrims were interested in exploring all kinds of things on their journey. For instance, the patrician Konrad Grünemberg (†1494) explained in the prologue that it makes little sense to see the nature and beauty of the world if one is not allowed to talk about it. Thus, he decided to include all the strange, pleasant and fabulous things seen on his journey in 1486. Observing an orthodox marriage at the Dalmatian city of Zara, he stated that he and his comrades were there as 'insatiable learners of foreign and strange customs'.[56] Other authors, such as the enigmatic John Mandeville or Arnold of Harff (1471–1505), provided their readers with many adventurous stories, addressing an audience that was familiar with a courtly literature that highlighted hazardous ventures and heroic deeds. Pilgrimage reports like these show that late medieval readers in general also wanted to hear more about the exotic world abroad with its different ethnicities, languages and customs as well as its unfamiliar landscapes, plants and animals.

Even though writing the *Evagatorium* as a cleric and for a clerical audience, Fabri still had to consider such expectations on the part of readers. At the same time, he had to be cautious about how he conveyed both images of the 'Other' and images of himself to his fellow brothers. Regarding Venice, Fabri explicitly stated that he had chosen to only write about the 'holy and honourable wanderings which we made', omitting other trips 'undertaken out of curiosity, or worse motives'.[57] Yet, it was difficult to neglect all situations in which his eyes were exposed to something unusual, bizarre and even seductive. During the festivities at the end of Ramadan in Cairo, for example, he was confronted with 'very obscene' dances of some young women, stating that no man could have watched this scene without being overcome by lustful thoughts. The lascivious dances that Fabri encountered a second time when, in his interpretation, the spouses of his dragoman tried to seduce the pilgrims, in the way of demons, into engaging in carnal pleasures, were a demanding test for the eyes. Confessing that he had never seen anything like this before and that he never wanted to see anything like this ever again, he integrated such observations into a polemical discourse on Islam and the alleged sexual promiscuity of Muslims.[58]

While it must have been clear to Fabri's readers that one could not evade such situations when travelling through the countries of 'infidels', Fabri still had to be careful in his own continuous literary digressions. He admitted to having been 'fond of seeing strange and curious sights' by referring to the plan of one other pilgrim to enter the Dome of the Rock, the most holy Muslim site in Jerusalem and forbidden ground for Christians, disguised in oriental clothes.[59] Elsewhere, when there was indeed the opportunity to visit a mosque, Fabri explored at length and with references to dogmatic literature whether a Christian commits a sin by entering such a building. Quite predictably, he came to the conclusion that it is not a sin insofar as it is not done out of mere curiosity.[60]

By subsequently justifying his action, Fabri was able to share some insights about the building in order to pick up again the central theme of Islam as a rival monotheistic religion, yet in this instance to debase and to idealise the Muslim 'Other'. On the one hand, Fabri stated that the emptiness and lack of decoration of mosques resembled the Muslims' lack of salvation, of remission of sins and of virtue and truth. Therefore, he once more made clear his viewpoint that Islam is an erroneous faith, seducing its followers into a sinful life and ultimately death.[61] On the other, however, he compared the cleanliness of the mosques with the dirtiness of Christian churches, most notably the Church of the Holy Sepulchre, thereby using the topos of the purity of the mosques as a symbol for the piety of the Muslims.[62] In projecting his idea of good Christian practices onto the 'Other', his aim was in this case to criticise the conditions at home, to disapprove of a lack of devoutness in Christian society.

Eye-witness situations could thus be used flexibly both for strengthening Christian identity as practitioners of a superior religion and for moralising to his readers in order to make them think and reflect on their own attitudes. For his fellow brethren in Ulm in particular, his intention was that they might well be able to make use of such examples in their pastoral work. The *Evagatorium* comprises many further examples along these lines. By carefully legitimating the deeds of his 'experiencing self', by counterchecking the available literature, by mirroring moments where he might have endangered his soul and by distancing himself from the behaviour of other pilgrims, Fabri gave his readers the impression of being a trustworthy observer, an exemplary traveller as well as an author who had reflected on his experiences thoroughly before writing them down, giving a well-balanced and true description of what he had seen with his own eyes.

## Feigned eye-witnessing (in order to explain the world)

Using the authority of an eye-witness, there are however moments when Fabri goes one step further and claims to have the final word even when he most probably had not visited the place in person.[63] This can be seen in his description of his journey through Egypt, and especially in his statements on the pyramids and regarding the furnaces that were used to hatch chicken eggs – two features in premodern travel reports that marked Egypt and the city of Cairo as exotic places.[64]

The breathtaking size of the ancient monuments and travellers' encounters with the furnaces where thousands of chickens were produced were extraordinary experiences for the pilgrims. Fabri claimed to have examined both locations and provided detailed information. According to the *Evagatorium*, the group of pilgrims visited the pyramids on the 14th of October 1483. He noted that he wandered around the pyramids and found and copied down ancient Latin inscriptions whose meaning he could not totally understand. He even discovered an entrance that led him to a small room inside.[65] After returning to the city later the same day, Fabri claimed to have visited a house with the facilities to hatch eggs and was able to observe how the heating systems were powered by manure to generate temperatures ideal for incubation.[66]

Comparing his descriptions, however, with the reports of Bernhard of Breidenbach and Paul Walther of Guglingen, it seems that Fabri's thorough description of these places was just feigned. Both authors wrote that the group had seen the pyramids only from a distance while standing on a hill within the city.[67] Given the schedule of their stay in Cairo, there was not much time to cross the Nile and to make an excursion to Giza, which was several miles away. Regarding the furnaces, Paul Walther specified that they could not visit the house on the 14th of October because the owner was not at home and the facility currently not in use. Breidenbach mentioned the furnaces in his entry on the 16th of October without saying whether he saw them personally. He stated that on this day, the pilgrims had split into different groups, some wanting to take a steam bath while others wanted to enter the city in order to 'see adventures'.[68] Fabri was aware of such ambiguities and, accordingly, of the risk that careful readers could possibly judge his *Evagatorium* as being less trustworthy than Breidenbach's already published report. Fabri explained the differences by saying that the structure of his narrative sometimes forced him to include some events on another day, but he downplayed the consequences of taking such liberties by pointing to the differences in the Gospels: after all, one could see that the same things 'have been done by the Evangelists'.[69]

In any case, a closer look at his narrative reveals that Fabri's descriptions are skilfully arranged compilations of other pilgrimage reports dating back to the thirteenth century. Fabri relied on the fourteenth-century report of William of Boldensele, who had already mentioned the very same ancient inscription in his report that later pilgrims such as Ludolph of Sudheim and Fabri claimed to have exclusively discovered.[70] William moreover was also one of the first pilgrims to analytically describe the artificial methods of hatching eggs. This explanation was adopted by, among others, Ludolph of Sudheim and Bernhard of Breidenbach, both in turn sources for Fabri.[71]

The reason that Fabri chose to emphasise that he had seen the pyramids and the furnaces himself was to give his argumentation more weight. Concerning the pyramids, Fabri wanted to underline the fact that they were indeed burial places for the Egyptian kings and not – as discussed within Fabri's pilgrimage group and in several written reports at the time – the biblical storehouses of Jacob. For example, the German merchant Hans Tucher, who had visited Cairo in 1479 and published a very popular report on his travels in 1482, referred to the pyramids he had seen from a distance (apparently from the same hill as Fabri four years later) as the granaries of the Pharaohs.[72] In order to prove him wrong, it was necessary for Fabri to say that he had been there. Fabri explicitly stated that he could have only come to the same conclusion that they had been built as granaries if he had not been there in person.[73] By claiming to have the final word, however, he was able to state that the monuments were built of huge solid stones that leave – apart from the small chamber he detected – absolutely no space for storing grain.[74] With this argument, he could convince his readers that it was not a biblical place where an indulgence could be expected. Furthermore, he thus corrected a mistake in the previous literature.[75]

The installations to incubate chickens were certainly an experience beyond every familiar reality for European pilgrims. As the example from the work by Hans Tucher again shows, it seemed to belong more to the sphere of marvellous and inexplicable things. Apparently, he made a last-minute change to the text. The last version of the manuscript to be printed still bears a description of the furnaces and their function. Yet in the final printed edition, Tucher admitted that one could say a great deal about these facilities, but he had decided to leave them out it since it would sound too unreliable.[76] The risk of potentially being blamed as a 'travel liar' seemed to have been too high for him and to have outweighed the assertion to have seen this with one's own eyes. The report by Bernhard of Breidenbach, however, which was published four years later than Tucher's and might be seen as a competitive product on the market for early printed books, did otherwise. He included a description of the process of artificially hatching eggs, explicitly stating that it appears to be marvellous. Yet he concluded that it was nothing more than a method based on human cunningness.[77] This might have been convincing for Fabri as well. He did not want these facilities to be regarded as something mysterious. By claiming to have seen the procedure in person, and by providing his readers with several additional historical examples of such furnaces and further methods of hatching eggs from authoritative writers (for instance, Diodorus of Sicily and Albert the Great), Fabri moved this item from the exotic sphere into the realm of human reason.

Feigned eye-witnessing thus had the function of supporting the author's view in regard to controversially discussed topics. The claim to have seen things with one's own eyes was a vital 'strategy of authentication'.[78] When the facts or the arguments that Fabri found in the sources might have been wrong or not sufficient enough, his pretended first-hand experiences tipped the balance in his favour. He was by no means the only traveller to employ such a strategy. Many authors of travelogues from ancient to modern times directed the reader's attention in similar ways in order to transmit significant viewpoints. Arnold of Harff, presenting himself in his text as a pilgrim and as a poet, stated tellingly that a 'fine lie well adorns a tale'.[79] He used feigned eye-witnessing on different occasions, most notably perhaps by ascending Ptolemy's Mountains of the Moon to give his notion of the annual inundation of the Nile and of the localisation of Paradise.[80] Yet in the case of the pyramids, Arnold did not come to a definite conclusion about their function, even after supposedly climbing on top of the highest one and having a picnic at this amazing vantage point.[81]

## Eye-witnessing within Fabri's pilgrimage narratives and their audiences

The examples of feigned eye-witnessing demonstrate that Fabri and other writers were aware of their reader's expectations. As a result, they adjusted their experiences to communicate specific details and viewpoints. This becomes even clearer when taking into account Fabri's other pilgrimage writings. Altogether, he composed four reports on his remarkable voyages, all of which bear significant differences in style, content and sometimes also in the interpretation of individual aspects of what he saw. Beside the Latin *Evagatorium*, he produced a German version later entitled *Eigentliche beschreibung der hin vnd wider Fahrt zu dem Heyligen Land* that was dedicated to the Swabian noblemen who financed his second pilgrimage, a spiritual travel guide called *Sionpilger*, compiled specifically for a women's convent, and finally a short rhymed account of his first pilgrimage.[82]

The German account *Eigentliche beschreibung* (also labelled in research as *Pilgerbuch*[83]) is not just an abridged version of the *Evagatorium* in the vernacular. According to the prologue, the text was produced as a public version of Fabri's journeys, whereas claiming that he wrote *Evagatorium* only for himself. Fabri addressed a lay audience, most notably the noblemen who financed his second pilgrimage, as their confessor and guide, but he stated that the book would probably be read by many other people, including the children, wives and servants of the noblemen.[84] The different intended audience resulted in many alterations compared with *Evagatorium*. Fabri omitted most of the theological and historical passages. His 'experiencing self' is less prominent and particular narrative asides, like his unintended stepping on top of the Stone of Anointing, were mostly left out. Fabri's 'narrating self' is less critical especially regarding the behaviour of his fellow pilgrims in order not to give readers cause for complaint. However, the pedagogical and moral element of the work is still clearly visible, since Fabri gave more space to his role of being a priest who seeks to guide his parishioners. The spiritual pilgrimage guidebook *Sionpilger* was written for Dominican nuns, who themselves were not allowed to embark on such a journey. Instead, they used Fabri's text to envision the pilgrimage through prayer and meditation. Still structured by the day's journeys, Fabri turned his experiences into metaphorical images and included chants and prayers. Fabri's 'narrating' and 'experiencing self' are usually absent, yet at certain points of the narrative he generated a contrast between the virtuous deeds of the nuns on their spiritual journey and the behaviour of the 'pilgrim knights' (*ritter bilgrin*), who were driven by their profane curiosity, indicating some of his personal experiences.[85]

When looking again at the opening example of Fabri's encounter with the unicorn, some of the differences between the texts become clear. In the German vernacular version, Fabri referred to the incident in just one sentence, thus following the pattern of Breidenbach but without resorting to a visual image.[86] Writing for a lay audience, lengthy remarks on the characteristics of the animal and the theological dimensions seemed irrelevant. By straightaway describing how the pilgrims progressed even further along from there on their pilgrimage, the marvellous and exotic aspect is barely highlighted. For the readers of his spiritual report, just such an exotic element would have been a distraction from the intended contemplative devotion of the text. Consequently, Fabri's own encounter with the unicorn is not mentioned, but replaced by an impersonal description of a desert basin named the 'valley of the rhinoceros', which allowed him to point exclusively to the allegorical meaning of the unicorn. Giving the classic story of how it can be hunted down by using a chaste virgin, Fabri reminded the spiritual pilgrims of Mary, who bore the true unicorn – Christ – in her lap and suggested several songs in honour of Mary that should be recited when imagining this particular day's journey.[87]

Similar alterations and minor shifts can be observed regarding other eye-witness situations. Providing no further information in his German narratives of the methods of hatching eggs by using the heat of furnaces, Fabri instead accentuated the vast differences between the exotic world abroad and the conditions at home instead of giving a more rational explanation, like in his Latin report.[88] Furthermore, he did not comment on Jerome's interpretation of Christ's anointing in *Eigentliche beschreibung*, whereas he even follows Jerome in the *Sionpilger*.[89] Fabri might have considered the subtleness of the exegesis as too confusing and interesting only for the well-educated clerics among the readers of his *Evagatorium*. Regarding other examples, Fabri felt the need to adjust his stories so as to prevent negative reactions by his readers. While he dismissed the idea that the pyramids could be Joseph's granaries also in his German version as a result of the ignorance of laypersons,[90] he was less dismissive than in his *Evagatorium* in explaining that the small Valley of Josaphat will fundamentally change at the end of times in order to accommodate all mankind.[91] As for the dancing Muslim women, Fabri did not want to be compromised by elaborating on the erotic nature of their movements. Accordingly, he only briefly mentioned the encounter in the German version and omitted the passage completely in his spiritual report.[92] Concerning Bathsheba's bathing place, he discussed in *Eigentliche beschreibung* the possibility that David might have had a summer house nearby from where he could actually have seen the wife of Uriah, but he elaborated on David's adultery and bloodguilt in a much harsher manner in order to give his profane audience unambiguous moral guidelines.[93]

Generally speaking, his curious adventures are not treated in a substantially different manner. In *Eigentliche beschreibung*, Fabri is sometimes more reluctant to make his own evaluations compared with *Evagatorium*. We read that he examined the Tomb of Absalom from inside, but he omitted his investigation of the Holy Sepulchre, therefore not bringing up the difficult issue of explaining the historical distortions.[94] Whether or not the cross of St Dismas in Cyprus is actually floating in the air remains unresolved in his German report; he refused to examine the relic more closely not out of fear of God (as in *Evagatorium*), but because of the danger of being seen (by his readers) as 'too curios and too cheeky'.[95] Nonetheless, proving the holiness of the sacred sites, accurately describing them and enabling a better understanding of the Bible were, after all, equally important for all three narratives. Thus, Fabri accentuated in both of his German reports that he experienced with his senses a heavenly presence at Golgotha and at the place of Christ's birth.[96]

There is, however, at least one situation in which Fabri treated his 'experiencing self' differently in his reports regarding his own eye-witnessing. This last example relates to Fabri's visit to the Mamluk citadel in Cairo, one of the main profane landmarks of the city. According to his account in *Evagatorium*, his group was able to see the ruling sultan Qaitbay (c. 1416/1418–1496) in person during an audience. Though Fabri considered Qaitbay the leader of all Muslims, he does not combine his description, somewhat surprisingly, with a defamation of Islam. He did not portray a brutal tyrant, but a seemingly thoughtful emperor in consultation with his wise and dignified counsellors.[97] According to *Eigentliche beschreibung*, Fabri avoided looking at the sultan because it was not important for Fabri to do so.[98] Herein, Fabri expressed a dismissive position. He did not want readers to see him as trying to be too close to the ruler, who was regarded as an enemy of the Christian faith. Through his feigned disinterest, Fabri firstly refused to pay too much homage to the ruler of an opposing religion. He secondly distanced himself from the behaviour of his fellow travellers, who were eager to see the ruler in person. The subtle message is that a Christian pilgrim should not be overly interested in worldly matters and not seek out too directly the enemies of the faith. The same message, but in a more drastic way, is given in *Sionpilger*, where he describes the Mamluk castle as a Devil's place.[99] Fabri criticised the 'pilgrim knights' who wanted to catch a glimpse of the sultan, depicted here as the malicious adversary of Christianity. The curiosity of the pilgrims is seen not only as immoral, but as vicious and sinful. True Christians, in contrast, should seek to avoid this place as they would hell.

The comparison shows the different requirements for an eye-witness. Even when one should always report accurately and in detail on an event, there is a certain line that the 'experiencing self' should not transgress so as not to endanger both the trustworthy status of the 'narrating self' and the virtuous qualities of the 'experiencing self'. Both German texts were directed towards a less learned audience, so Fabri took on his professional role as a cleric more strongly. It was his duty to warn his readers of the dangers in an alienated and non-Christian world. In *Sionpilger*, the religious 'Other' poses a threat whenever the nuns' prayers are disturbed on their imagined pilgrimage; at other times, Fabri felt the need to exemplify their pious habits through the construction of the 'pilgrim knight' as a counter figure. In the case of *Evagatorium*, it appears that he was more able to free himself from the theological discourses on non-Christian religions when addressing the smaller circle of the convent brothers. Of course, there are countless examples in his Latin version where he condemns the Prophet and Islam. But concerning the Mamluks and their sultan as a group of former Christians, Fabri was less derogatory – perhaps because of some hope that they could be convinced to return to the true faith.[100]

Reading, however, Fabri's narratives in comparison with the reports by Bernhard of Breidenbach and Paul Walther of Guglingen, it seems once more that this event did not take place in the manner Fabri described it. Whereas Fabri followed Bernhard of Breidenbach in his description of entering the citadel and being quite close to the sultan, Paul Walther stated that the pilgrims failed to bribe the guards and therefore did not gain access to the hall of the audience at all.[101] When comparing Fabri's and Breidenbach's descriptions of the sultan as being dressed in precious white clothes, sitting on his divan and consulting with his confidants, the eye-witness account in each text is ultimately based on the report by Hans Tucher.[102]

## Conclusion

The close reading of Fabri sheds some light on the author's relationship with his anticipated readers. Late medieval pilgrimage reports are a piece of life writing, documenting an essential period that defined the pilgrim's future lifespan just as much as his afterlife and his *memoria*. They are not 'transparent' representations of the journey as such, reflecting the experiences of the traveller in unaltered form. Personal memories and information from prior oral and written sources are superimposed on one another in complex ways. Intertextual relations, literary conventions and dogmatic viewpoints structured the text further in order to create a coherent and stirring narrative that could actively be used to convey worldviews and social norms. The comparison between Fabri's different versions showed that he adjusted his writings quite flexibly according to the rank, education and expectations of his intended audiences.

For Fabri – if not for all travellers – eye-witnessing was an important technique for authentication. It underscored (alongside other things, such as travel souvenirs and official documents) the fact that the author actually had been abroad. Mention of having seen things with one's own eyes certified that what was experienced along the way was true. It does not mean, however, that empirical knowledge was regarded more highly than written or oral sources. The richness of detail that Fabri provided in his descriptions of eye-witness situations as well as his critical evaluations gave his report more authenticity; they also bestowed on Fabri, as the 'narrating self', the status of being a reliable first-hand witness. The familiarity of the narrator with the object that he describes is thus crucial for gaining readers' trust.[103]

Yet, Fabri also relied quite often on his specific eligibility as a well-educated cleric who, in contrast to the laymen among his fellow pilgrims, was able to give meaning to what he had seen. He is not just a person accidentally witnessing something, but an authority who acted in a reasonable manner and thus could be trusted. Nevertheless, showing at times the human and somewhat less comfortable sides of his 'experiencing self' – like his embarrassing mistake of stepping on the Stone of Anointing – can be regarded as a strategy for making his report even more authentic. In these and other cases, he used vivid language that highlighted the dramatic nature of the event instead of relying on a matter-of-fact tone and operating with a 'guarded strategy of emotional denial', as did many other authors of travel reports.[104]

Stating, moreover, to have noted that these experiences should right away help overcome the distance between seeing on the one side and saying and writing on the other, Fabri thus gives the impression that what he had seen was documented in a straightforward and undistorted manner.[105] The writing eye-witness corroborates the truth of the tale. In that way (one other way was the inclusion of Reuwich's woodcuts in Breidenbach's report), the recipient was able to become an eye-witness, too, or at least he/she was given the opportunity to participate in the process of eye-witnessing. This was of special importance when it came to the holy places as true signs of ongoing salvation history, displaying how strong 'kinetic, visual and mental dimensions of pilgrimage are intertwined'.[106]

At least in this context, Fabri's eye-witnessing had a missionary impetus to proclaim the truth of the Christian faith and to ensure the reader that he/she was on the 'right side'.[107] Combined with his moral instructions, his eye-witness descriptions were at the same time admonitions to follow the principles of a Christian life of virtues. Fabri's (as well as the traveller's) eye was far from being 'innocent'.[108] His frequent indications of seeing things in person, as well as the meaning he assigned to his observations, shows that references to eyesight can have a constitutive effect when it comes to documenting ways of life, attitudes and performances.[109] He used situations involving eye-witnessing to relate specific standpoints and social values; he even pretended to have seen things with his own eyes both to correct and to stabilise knowledge and to depict such knowledge as being self-evident.[110] By relying especially on eye-witnessing, sometimes in combination with the other senses, travellers such as Fabri were to guide the understanding and imagination of readers and to educate and to entertain them at the same time.

## Notes

1 Fabri 1843–1849 II, 441. English translation after the (partial) English edition Fabri 1971 II, 534. For more on this episode, see also Meyers 2008; Niehr 2001; Schröder 2009, 366–367; Timm 2006, 236–237.
2 Weber 1986, 130.
3 For more on the unicorn in medieval contexts, see as well the seminal work by Einhorn 1998.

4 Regarding maps, the Hereford map, for example, situates the unicorn in the wilderness of southern Africa. Fabri might have used here Johannes Witte de Hese's *Itinerarius*. The author claims here to have seen (*Et hoc vidi*) a unicorn in the Sinai desert at the moment when it used the magic attribute of its horn to drive out poison from a river in order to make the water drinkable. *Cf.* Westrem 2001, 132–133 and 182–183; Johannes Witte de Hese 2001, 127–128.
5 Occasionally, the term autopsy is used synonymously to eye-witnessing. *Cf.* Hartog 1988, 261; Luraghi 2014, 18; Lapina 2007, 119.
6 For defining an eye-witness, see Rösinger and Signori 2014, 8. For the broader field of witnesses and witnessing, *cf.* Drews and Schlie, 2011; Schmolinsky 2003.
7 Not considered in medieval times was typically the fact that memories are not unchangeable but generated every time anew when transmitting a past event to somebody. As is shown by neurosciences as well as by historical research, the remembrance of events, including eye-witness situations, is constantly being updated, adjusted to the particular context in which the remembrance takes place and changed by highlighting, omitting and forgetting particular aspects of the event. *Cf.*, with further references, Schmolinsky 2011; Fried 2004.
8 In legal contexts, for instance where eye-witnessing as such and partly as a result of the gender of the eye-witness might have been not sufficient, practices of swearing an oath were developed as further methods of authentication. For more on trust as a category, see, with further references, Weltecke 2008.
9 Hartog 1988; Münkler 2000, esp. 248–266.
10 Münkler 2000, 261–262.
11 Adams 1962.
12 For an overview of the rich tradition of medieval travel writing and pilgrimages, see, with further references, Ganz-Blättler 1991; Münkler 2000; Reichert 2001; Rubiés 2000; Meyer 2012.
13 For more on his life and works, see Beebe 2014; Schröder 2014; Reichert and Rosenstock 2018.
14 A third heavy folio contains a history of the city of Ulm as well as a tractate on the history of Germany and Swabia. Originally thought to be the last and concluding part of his travelogue, they proved somewhat unmanageable and were produced by him as independent works.
15 Fabri 1843–1849 I, 66.
16 Fabri 1843–1849 I, 4.
17 Fabri 1843–1849 I, 5. However, the Nuremberg humanist Hartmann Schedel (1440–1514), editor of the popular world chronicle *Liber Chronicarum* (1493), reproduced a handwritten duplicate of Fabri's text for his own library. See, with further references, Beebe 2014, 133–134.
18 Fabri 1843–1849 I, 4.
19 On Breidenbach's life and the pilgrimage report, *cf.*, with further references, Timm 2006; Ross 2014. On Paul Walther, with new evidence on his life, see Ritsema van Eck 2017.
20 Paul Walther of Guglingen 1892, 199.
21 Breidenbach 2010, 550–551.
22 Breidenbach 1486, woodcut after fol. 109v: *Hec Animalia sunt veraciter depicta sicut vidimus in terra sancta*. Cf. Niehr 2001, 184.
23 Fabri 1843–1849 I, 329.
24 His small and loose sketches show no ambition for using visual images as a distinct way of transmitting information and views in the way of Breidenbach or Reuwich.
25 On this separation, see Kormann 2004, 95–98.
26 Regarding this aspect in medieval historiography, see, with further references, Signori 2014, 76.

27 Other contemporary authors of pilgrimage reports who accentuated their 'narrated self' in a similar way include, for instance, Arnold of Harff and Pietro Casola.
28 For the following, see also Schröder 2009, 140–146.
29 Fabri 1843–1849 I, 424.
30 Fabri 1843–1849 I, 408, and II, 140.
31 Fabri 1843–1849 I, 417–418.
32 Fabri 1843–1849 I, 432–433.
33 For more on the Franciscan monastery in Jerusalem, see Lemmens 1919. For more on mediators of the cultural memory from a theoretical standpoint, see Assmann 2005, 54–55 and 95.
34 Fabri 1843–1849 I, 363–364, with reference to the short statement by Jerome 1883, 340.
35 Niehr 2001, 269.
36 Fabri 1843–1849 I, 382. Burchard of Mount Sion 1873, 68–69. Independently, the Milanese Santo Brasca mentioned to have seen this place in 1480, being part of the same pilgrimage group as Fabri. Cf. Brasca 1966, 79.
37 For more on chains of witnesses, and especially St Thomas as a witness to Christ's resurrection, see Matena 2011, who shows that the encounter of Thomas that is described as an eye-witness report in the Gospels is transformed in exegetical literature in such a way that the haptic contact between Thomas and Christ is decisive for convincing the Apostle.
38 Wächter 1957, 24. Fabri might have thought in the same direction when pointing out twice that Mount Calvary was in fact only a rock. Cf. Fabri 1843–1849 I, 300 and 337.
39 Beebe 2015, 410. Cf. also Bacci 2013. The literature on buildings resembling the Church of the Holy Sepulchre and the tomb in Europe is vast. Cf., with further references, Morris 2005, 347–359, as well as the articles in the anthology by Kühnel, Noga-Banai and Vorholt 2015.
40 Fabri 1843–1849 I, 393.
41 For a somewhat similar example related to a marvel experienced on the first crusade, see Lapina 2007, 128–131. In the case of late medieval pilgrimages, however, experienced clerics such as the Milanese Pietro Casola were also bewildered by the compactness of the valley. See Casola 2001, 191.
42 Cf. the example of the 'sweating columns' at the chapel of St Helena. Fabri 1843–1849 I, 294. William of Boldensele 1852, 268–269. See also Niehr 2001, 276.
43 Fabri 1843–1849 I, 299. Citation from Fabri 1971 I, 365.
44 Hartog 1988, 261.
45 Fabri 1843–1849 I, 474–476.
46 Assmann 1999, 306.
47 Fabri 1843–1849 I, 442. Fabri had not read the Quran himself, but relied here on Nicholas of Cusa's *Cribratio Alcorani* (see Nicholas of Kues 1989 III, 74). Fabri got access to that work only after having already finished *Evagatorium* and added this information within the margins.
48 In this respect, stones played an important role in Fabri's report. To this respect, see Rachman-Schrire 2012.
49 Fabri 1843–1849 I, 330–336. On Fabri's approach, cf. Arnulf 1988, 33; Morris 2005, 321–323.
50 Fabri 1843–1849 I, 174–175. See also Niehr 2001, 277.
51 Cf., with further references, Daston 1994, esp. 38–39; Vinken 2000, 798–803; Münkler 2000, 259–260; Lehmann-Brauns 2010, 273–274.
52 Fabri 1843–1849 II, 467. Citation from Fabri 1971 II, 571. See also Niehr 2001, 279. Here, Fabri placed himself in the tomb of St Catherine in order to measure how tall she might have been.
53 Fabri 1843–1849 I, 283. Citation from Fabri 1971 I, 343.

54 Nolte 1997; Reichert 2005.
55 Ganz-Blättler 1991, 238.
56 Grünemberg 2011, 280 (prologue) and 323 (Zara). Citation from the English translation, Grünemberg 2005, 55.
57 Fabri 1843–1849 I, 106–107. Citation from Fabri 1971 I, 110.
58 Fabri 1843–1849 III, 36 and 202. For more on the very negative image of Islam in general, cf. Daniel 1960; Tolan 2002; Di Cesare 2012. For more on Felix Fabri and other pilgrims, cf. Reichert 2000; Schröder 2009, 236–291.
59 Fabri 1843–1849 II, 229.
60 Fabri 1843–1849 II, 225–229. However, the pilgrim abandoned the plan at the last minute out of fear.
61 That one of Fabri's companions defiled the building by relieving himself through an opening in the roof of the mosque one night was considered amusing among his fellow travellers. Fabri, however, made it quite clear that such behaviour was not appropriate, since even a mosque is a house of God. Fabri 1843–1849 II, 228 and 358.
62 Fabri 1843–1849 I, 254 and II, 225.
63 For feigned eye-witnessing regarding images in medieval historiography, see Logemann 2011.
64 For more on Egypt in pilgrimage reports, cf., with further references, Schröder 2009, 162–186 and 332–369; Hiestand 1993. On descriptions specifically of the pyramids, see Graefe 1990.
65 Fabri 1843–1849 III, 42–44.
66 Fabri 1843–1849 III, 57–59.
67 Breidenbach 2010, 602–603; Paul Walther of Guglingen 1892, 234.
68 Paul Walther of Guglingen 1892, 232; Breidenbach 2010, 606–607.
69 Fabri 1843–1849 II, 18. Citation from Fabri 1971 I, 629.
70 William of Boldensele 1852, 250–252; Ludolph of Sudheim 1851, 55.
71 William of Boldensele 1852, 249–250; Ludolph of Sudheim 1851, 51.
72 Tucher 2002. 562.
73 Fabri 1843–1849 III, 43.
74 For other authors, however, the existence of an entrance was, among other things, proof that the pyramids could not have been used as tombs. See Mandeville 2011, 32.
75 Ironically, Fabri noted in a different passage of *Evagatorium* that he had taken a copy of Tucher's report with him and found all the data given by the Nuremberg merchant, who Fabri also met once in person, as being accurate and true. He even copied and translated Tucher's description of the Church of the Holy Sepulchre into Latin. Fabri 1843–1849 I, 327–328.
76 Tucher 2002, 564–565.
77 Breidenbach 2010, 606–607.
78 See Kästner and Schütz 1983, esp. 465.
79 Arnold of Harff 2004, 192. Citation after Arnolf of Harff 1946, 224. Cf. Brall-Tuchel 2011; Reichert 2014, 358.
80 Arnold of Harff 2004, 150–151.
81 Arnold of Harff 2004, 109.
82 Since the rhymed pilgrimage (cf. Fabri 1864) narrative comprises only his first journey, I am not considering the valuable text here. For more information, see Beebe 2014, 75–76; Schröder 2009, 69–70.
83 Fabri's text used the terms *pilgerbüch* or *pilgerböchli*, but the autograph preserved today in the city library of Dessau itself bears no title. The name *Eigentliche beschreibung der hin vnd wider Fahrt zu dem Heyligen Land* is given to the first printed edition from 1556.
84 Dessau, LB, Hs. Georg 238, fol. 1v and 3r-3v.
85 Fabri 1999.

86  Dessau, LB, Hs. Georg 238, fol. 144r.
87  Fabri 1999, 230.
88  Dessau, LB, Hs. Georg 238, fol. 188r; Fabri 1999, 267.
89  Dessau, LB, Hs. Georg 238, fol. 59v; Fabri 1999, 128 (an unnamed sinner) and 145 (Mary Magdalene).
90  Dessau, LB, Hs. Georg 238, fol. 191r. In *Sionpilger*, Fabri placed the decision regarding their function at the reader's disposal. See Fabri 1999, 267.
91  Dessau, LB, Hs. Georg 238, fol. 61v. In *Sionpilger*, Fabri provided no direct answer, but instead referred to his Latin report. See Fabri 1999, 136.
92  Dessau, LB, Hs. Georg 238, fol. 185r-185v and 209r.
93  Dessau, LB, Hs. Georg 238, fol. 68v.
94  Dessau, LB, Hs. Georg 238, fol. 66v-67r.
95  Dessau, LB, Georg. Hs. 238, fol. 29r. In sum, however, Fabri's rendering of the marvel is here somehow more sceptical. See Ertzdorf 1999, 81–83.
96  Holy Sepulchre: Fabri 1999, 113; Dessau, LB, Hs. Georg 238, fol. 53v. Church of Nativity: Fabri 1999, 160–161; Dessau, LB, Hs. Georg 238, fol. 73r.
97  Fabri 1843–1849 III, 73.
98  Dessau, LB, Hs. Georg 238, fol. 193r.
99  Fabri 1999, 271.
100 Fabri labelled the Mamluks, in line with other pilgrims, as renegades who disclaimed Christianity, thus using a negative connotation. Yet, when describing their political system and his interactions with some Mamluks who acted as mediators for the pilgrims (he even mentioned to have known one of them from his youth), he gave a rather positive depiction in his Latin report, while being more negative in *Eigentliche beschreibung*. See Schröder 2009, 241–248.
101 Breidenbach 2010, 604–605; Paul Walther of Guglingen 1892, 225.
102 Tucher 2002, 570–571. See also the drawing by Arnold of Harff, who seems to have based his description also on Tucher. Arnold of Harff 2004, 90. For more on the dialogue between travellers and non-Christian emperors, see Kästner 1997.
103 Signori 2014, 84.
104 See Jost 2013, 580, based on the report by John Mandeville.
105 See, with reference to Marco Polo, Hartog 1988, 263.
106 Bacci 2013, 176.
107 For a missionary aspect of the eye-witness, see Rösinger and Signori 2014, 7–8.
108 Borrowing a term from Peter Burke's book on medieval art. See Burke 2001, 19.
109 See Schmolinsky 2011, 306.
110 See also Schwarze 2014, 61.

# Bibliography

## Archival sources

Dessau, Landesbücherei, Hs. Georg 238. 8° [untitled autograph of Felix Fabri's *Eigentliche beschreibung*]

## Printed sources

Arnold von Harff. 2004. *Die Pilgerfahrt des Ritters Arnold von Harff von Cöln durch Italien, Syrien, Aegypten, Arabien, Aethiopien, Nubien, Palästina, die Türkei, Frankreich und Spanien, wie er sie in den Jahren 1496 bis 1499 vollendet, beschrieben und durch Zeichnungen erläutert hat. Nach den ältesten Handschriften und mit deren*

*47 in Holzschnitt herausgegeben*, edited by Ewald von Groote. Cologne: J. M. Heberle 1860; Reprint Hildesheim and New York: Georg Olms 2004.

Arnold of Harff. 1946. *The Pilgrimage of Arnold von Harff in the Years 1496–1499*, edited by Malcolm Letts. London: The Hakluyt Society.

Bernhard of Breidenbach. 1486. *Die heyligen reyßen gen Jherusalem zů dem heiligen Grab*. Mainz: Erhard Reuwich. [GW 05077; HC 3959].

Bernhard of Breidenbach. 2010. *Peregrinatio in Terram Sanctam. Frühneuhochdeutscher Text und Übersetzung*, edited by Isolde Mozer. Berlin: De Gruyter.

Brasca, Santo. 1966. *Viaggio in Terrasanta di Santo Brasca 1480 con l'Itinerario di Gabriele Capodilista 1458*, edited by Anna Laura Momigliano Lepschy. Milan: Longanesi.

Burchard of Mount Sion. 1873. "Descriptio Terrae Sanctae." In *Peregrinatores medii aevi quatuor*, edited by J. C. M. Laurent, 2nd ed., 1–100. Leipzig: J. C. Hinrichs Bibliopola.

Casola, Pietro. 2001. *Viaggio a Gerusalemme di Pietro Casola*, ed. Anna Paoletti (Oltramare 11), Alessandria: Edizioni dell'Orso.

Fabri, Felix. 1843–1849. *Fratris Felicis Fabri Evagatorium in Terrae Sanctae, Arabiae et Egypti peregrinationem, Bibliothek des Literarischen Vereins Stuttgart 2–4. Literarischer Verein*, edited by Konrad Dietrich Hassler. Stuttgart: Literarischer Verein.

Fabri, Felix. 1864. *Bruder Felix Fabers gereimtes Pilgerbüchlein*, edited by Anton Birlinger. München: E. A. Fleischmann.

Fabri, Felix. 1971. *The Wanderings of Felix Fabri*, edited by Aubrey Stewart, 2 vols, 1887–1891. London: Committee of the Palestine Exploration Fund; Reprint New York: AMS Press.

Fabri, Felix. 1999. *Die Sionpilger*, edited by Wieland Carls. Berlin: Erich Schmidt.

Grünemberg, Konrad. 2011. *Konrad Grünembergs Pilgerreise ins Heilige Land 1486. Untersuchung, Edition und Kommentar*, edited by Andrea Denke. Cologne and Vienna: Böhlau.

Grünemberg, Konrad. 2005. *The Pilgrimage of Konrad Grünemberg to the Holy Land in 1486. Prose translation, with critical introduction and notes by Kristiaan Aercke*. Torino: CIRVI.

Jerome. 1883. "Adversus Jovinianum." In *Sancti Eusebii Hieronymi stridonensis presbyteri opera omnia II-III. Patrologiae cursus completus: series latina*, edited by Jacques-Paul Migne, vol. 23, 222–351. Paris: Migne.

Ludolph of Sudheim. 1851. *Ludolphi rectoris ecclesiae parochialis in Suchem, de Itinere Terrae Sanctae liber*, edited by Ferdinand Deycks. Stuttgart: Literarischer Verein.

Mandeville, John. 2011. *The Book of John Mandeville with Related Texts*, edited by Iain Macleod Higgins. Indianapolis: Hackett Publishing Company.

Nikolaus of Kues. 1989. *Cribratio Alkorani. Sichtung des Korans* (Schriften des Nikolaus von Kues 20a-c), 3 vol. Hamburg: Felix Meiner.

Paul Walther of Guglingen. 1892. *Fratris Pauli Waltheri Guglingensis Itinerarium in Terram Sanctam et ad Sanctam Catharinam*, edited by Matthias Sollweck. Tübingen: Literarischer Verein.

Tucher, Hans. 2002. *Die 'Reise ins Gelobte Land' Hans Tuchers des Älteren (1479–1480). Untersuchungen zur Überlieferung und kritische Edition eines spätmittelalterlichen Reiseberichts*, edited by Randall Herz. Wiesbaden: Dr. Ludwig Reichert Verlag.

Wächter, Peter. 1957. "Hje Jn disem büechlin sind ze vinden hüpsch, seltzam materien vnd geschichten, so den persönlich erfaren hatt Hans Schürpff, bürger vnd des rattes zuo Lucern […]." In *Luzerner und Innerschweizer Pilgerreisen zum Heiligen Grab in*

Jerusalem vom 15. bis 17. Jahrhundert, edited by Josef Schmid, 1–36. Luzern: Diebold Schilling Verlag.
Witte de Hese, Johannes. 2001. *Broader Horizons. A Study of Johannes Witte de Hese's Itinerarius and Medieval Travel Narratives*, edited by Scott D. Westrem. Cambridge, MA: The Medieval Academy of America.
William of Boldensele. 1852. "Des Edelherren Wilhelm von Boldensele Reise nach dem gelobten Land.", *Zeitschrift des historischen Vereins für Niedersachsen*, edited by Karl Ludwig Grotefend, 226–286.

## Literature

Adams, Percy G. 1962. *Travelers and Travel Liars, 1660–1800*. Berkeley and Los Angeles: University of California Press.
Arnulf, Arwed. 1998. "Mittelalterliche Beschreibungen der Grabeskirche in Jerusalem." In: *Colloquia Akademica. Akademievorträge junger Wissenschaftler*, 7–33. Stuttgart: Franz Steiner.
Assmann, Aleida. 1999. *Erinnerungsräume. Formen und Wandlungen des kulturellen Gedächtnisses*. Munich: C. H. Beck.
Assmann, Jan. 2005. *Das kulturelle Gedächtnis. Schrift, Erinnerung und politische Identität in frühen Hochkulturen*. Munich: C. H. Beck.
Bacci, Michele. 2013. "Remarks on the Visual Experience of Holy Sites in the Middle Ages." In: *Mobile Eyes. Peripatetisches Sehen in den Bildkulturen der Vormoderne*, edited by David Ganz and Stefan Neuner, 175–197. Munich: Wilhelm Fink.
Beebe, Kathryne. 2014. *Pilgrim & Preacher. The Audiences and Observant Spirituality of Friar Felix Fabri (1437/8–1502)*. Oxford: Oxford University Press.
Beebe, Kathryne. 2015. "The Jerusalem of the Mind's Eye: Imagined Pilgrimage in the Late Fifteenth Century", in: *Visual Constructs of Jerusalem*, edited by Bianca Kühnel, Galit Noga-Banai, and Hanna Vorholt, 409–420. Turnhout: Brepols.
Brall-Tuchel, Helmut. 2011. "Der Reisende als Integrationsfigur? Arnold von Harff: Ein Pilger zwischen Regionalität und Expansion." In *Europäisches Erbe des Mittelalters. Kulturelle Integration und Sinnvermittlung einst und jetzt*, edited by Ina Karg, 67–93. Göttingen: Vandenhoeck & Ruprecht.
Burke, Peter. 2001. *Picturing History: Eyewitnessing: The Uses of Images as Historical Evidence*. London: Reaktion Books.
Daniel, Norman. 1960. *Islam and the West. The Making of an Image*. Edinburgh: Edinburgh University Press.
Daston, Lorraine. 1994. "Neugierde als Empfindung und Epistemologie in der frühmodernen Wissenschaft." In *Macrokosmos in Microkosmos. Die Welt in der Stube. Zur Geschichte des Sammelns 1450 bis 1800*, edited by Andreas Grote, 35–59. Opladen: Leske & Budrich.
Di Cesare, Michelina. 2012. *The Pseudo-Historical Image of the Prophet Muhammad in Medieval Latin Literature: A Repertory*. Berlin: De Gruyter.
Drews, Wolfram and Heike Schlie. 2011. "Zeugnis und Zeugenschaft. Perspektiven aus der Vormoderne. Zur Einleitung." In *Zeugnis und Zeugenschaft. Perspektiven aus der Vormoderne*, edited by Wolfram Drews and Heike Schlie, 7–21. Munich: Wilhelm Fink.
Einhorn, Jürgen W. 1998. *Spiritalis unicornis. Das Einhorn als Bedeutungsträger in Kunst und Literatur des Mittelalters*. Munich: Fink.

Ertzdorf, Xenja von. 1999. "Felix Fabris 'Evagatorium' und 'Eygentlich beschreibung der hin vnnd wider farth zuo dem Heyligen Landt ...' (1484) und der Bericht über die Pilgerfahrt des Freiherrn Johann Werner von Zimmern in der 'Chronik der Grafen von Zimmer'. – Ein Vergleich." *Jahrbuch für Internationale Germanistik* 31: 54–86.

Fried, Johannes. 2004. *Der Schleier der Erinnerung. Grundzüge einer historischen Memorik*. Munich: C. H. Beck.

Ganz-Blättler, Ursula. 1991. *Andacht und Abenteuer. Berichte europäischer Jerusalem- und Santiago-Pilger (1320–1520)*. Tübingen: Narr.

Graefe, Erhart. 1990. "A Propos der Pyramidenbeschreibung des Wilhelm von Boldensele 1335 (II)." In *Zum Bild Ägyptens im Mittelalter und in der Renaissance*, edited by Erik Hornung, 9–28. Göttingen/Fribourg: Vandenhoeck & Ruprecht.

Hartog, François. 1988. *The Mirror of Herodotus, The Representation of the Other in the Writing of History*. Berkeley: Berkeley University Press.

Hiestand, Rudolf. 1993. "Der Sinai – Tor zu anderen Welten." In *Reisen in reale und mythische Ferne. Reiseliteratur in Mittelalter und Renaissance*, edited by Peter Wunderli, 76–102. Düsseldorf: Droste.

Jost, Jean E. 2013. "The Exotic and Fabulous East in *The Travels of Sir John Mandeville*: Understated Authenticity." In *East Meets West in the Middle Ages and Early Modern Times: Transcultural Experiences in the Premodern World*, edited by Albrecht Classen and Marilyn Sandidge, 575–594. Berlin: De Gruyter.

Kästner, Hannes. 1997. "Das Gespräch des Orientreisenden mit dem heidnischen Herrscher. Zur Typik und zu den Funktionen einer interkulturellen Dialogszene in der Reiseliteratur des Spätmittelalters und der frühen Neuzeit." In *Gespräche – Boten – Briefe. Körpergedächtnis und Schriftgedächtnis im Mittelalter*, edited by Horst Wenzel, 280–295. Berlin: Erich Schmidt.

Kästner, Hannes and Eva Schütz. 1983. "Beglaubigte Information. Ein konstitutiver Faktor in Prosaberichten des späten Mittelalters und der frühen Neuzeit." In *Textsorten und literarische Gattungen. Dokumentation des Germanistentages in Hamburg vom 1. bis 4. April 1979*, 450–469. Berlin: Erich Schmidt.

Kormann, Eva. 2004. *Ich, Welt und Gott. Autobiographik im 17. Jahrhundert*. Cologne and Vienna: Böhlau.

Kühnel, Bianca, Galit Noga-Banai and Hanna Vorholt, ed. 2015. *Visual constructs of Jerusalem*. Turnhout: Brepols.

Lapina, Elisabeth. 2007. "'*Nec signis nec testis* creditor...': The Problem of Eyewitnesses in the Chronicles of the First Crusade." *Viator* 38: 117–39.

Lehmann-Brauns, Susanne. 2010. *Jerusalem sehen: Reiseberichte des 12. bis 15. Jahrhunderts als empirische Anleitung zur geistigen Pilgerfahrt*. Freiburg: Rombach.

Lemmens, Leonhard. 1919. *Die Franziskaner im Heiligen Lande. 1. Teil: Die Franziskaner auf dem Sion (1336–1551)*. Münster: Aschendorff.

Logemann, Cornelia. 2011. "Falsche Augenzeugen. Fingierte Echtheitsbeweise in spätmittelalterlicher Geschichtsschreibung." In *Zeugnis und Zeugenschaft. Perspektiven aus der Vormoderne*, edited by Wolfram Drews and Heike Schlie, 77–98. Munich: Wilhelm Fink.

Luraghi, Nino. 2014. "The Eyewitness and the Writing of History – Ancient and Modern." In *Die Figur des Augenzeugen: Geschichte und Wahrheit im fächer- und epochenübergreifenden Vergleich*, edited by Amelie Rösinger and Gabriela Signori, 13–26. Konstanz: UVK.

Matena, Andreas. 2011. "*Tange et Vide* – Konzepte von Zeugenschaft in der Thomasperikope und ihrer Exegese." In *Zeugnis und Zeugenschaft. Perspektiven aus der Vormoderne*, edited by Wolfram Drews and Heike Schlie, 119–136. Munich: Wilhelm Fink.

Meyer, Carla. 2012. "New Methods and Old Records: Awareness and Perceptions of the Near East in Hans Tucher's Account of his Journey to the Holy Land and Egypt." *The Medieval History Journal* 15(1): 25–62.

Meyers, Jean. 2008. "Le 'rhinocéros' de Frère Félix Fabri." *Rursus* 3 [http://rursus.revues.org/221, 4.9.2016].

Morris, Colin. 2005. *The Sepulchre of Christ and the Medieval West. From the Beginning to 1600*. Oxford: Oxford University Press.

Münkler, Marin. 2000. *Erfahrung des Fremden. Die Beschreibung Ostasiens in den Augenzeugenberichten des 13. und 14. Jahrhunderts*. Berlin: Akademie Verlag.

Niehr, Klaus. 2001. "*als ich das selber erkundet vnd gesehen hab*. Wahrnehmung und Darstellung des Fremden in Bernhard von Breydenbachs *Peregrinationes in Terram Sanctam* und anderen Pilgerberichten des ausgehenden Mittelalters." *Gutenberg Jahrbuch* 76: 269–300.

Nolte, Cordula. 1997. "Erlebnis und Erinnerung. Fürstliche Pilgerfahrten nach Jerusalem im 15. Jahrhundert." In *Fremdheit und Reisen im Mittelalter*, edited by Irene Erfen and Karl-Heinz Spieß, 65–92. Stuttgart: Franz Steiner.

Rachman-Schrire, Yamit. 2012. "*Evagatorium in Terrae Sanctae*: Stones telling the story of Jerusalem." In *Erzählraum Jerusalem – Narrative Space Jerusalem*, edited by Annette Hoffmann and Gerhard Wolf, 353–366. Leiden: Brill.

Reichert, Folker. 2000. "Pilger und Muslime im Heiligen Land. Formen des Kulturkonflikts im späten Mittelalter." In *Kritik und Geschichte der Intoleranz*, edited by Rolf Kloepfer and Burckhard Dücker, 3–21. Heidelberg: SYNCHRON.

Reichert, Folker. 2001. *Erfahrung der Welt. Reisen und Kulturbegegnung im späten Mittelalter*. Stuttgart: Kohlhammer.

Reichert, Folker. 2005. "Ehre durch Demut. Wallfahrten des Adels im späten Mittelalter." In *Gelungene Anpassung? Adelige Antworten auf gesellschaftliche Wandlungsvorgänge vom 14. bis zum 16. Jahrhundert*, edited by Horst Carl and Sönke Lorenz, 165–183. Ostfildern: Thorau.

Reichert, Folker. 2014. *Asien und Europa im Mittelalter. Studien zur Geschichte des Reisens*. Göttingen: Vandenhoeck & Ruprecht.

Reichert, Folker and Alexander Rosenstock, ed. 2018. *Die Welt des Frater Felix Fabri*. Weißenhorn: Anton H. Konrad Verlag.

Ritsema van Eck, Marianne P. 2017. "Encounters with the Levant: The Late Medieval Illustrated Jerusalem Travelogue by Paul Walter von Guglingen." *Mediterranean Historical Review* 32(2): 153–188.

Rösinger, Amelie and Gabriela Signori. 2014. "Einleitung." In *Die Figur des Augenzeugen: Geschichte und Wahrheit im fächer- und epochenübergreifenden Vergleich*, edited by Amelie Rösinger and Gabriela Signori, 7–12. Konstanz: UVK.

Ross, Elizabeth. 2014. *Picturing Experience in the Early Printed Book: Breydenbach's Peregrinatio from Venice to Jerusalem*. Pennsylvania: The Pennsylvania State University Press.

Rubiés, Joan-Pau. 2000. "Travel Writing as a Genre: Facts, Fictions and the Invention of a Scientific Discourse in Early Modern Europe." *Journeys* 2(1): 5–31.

Schmolinsky, Sabine. 2003. "Sinneswahrnehmung als verschriftlichte Erfahrung? Zu Mustern des Hörens und Sehens in mittelalterlichen Selbstzeugnissen." *Das Mittelalter* 8(2): 107–120.

Schmolinsky, Sabine. 2011. "Historische Evidenz und Augenzeugenschaft. Überlegungen zum 'verschleierten' Gedächtnis in mittelalterlicher Historiographie." In *Zeugnis und Zeugenschaft. Perspektiven aus der Vormoderne*, edited by Wolfram Drews and Heike Schlie, 301–310. Munich: Wilhelm Fink.

Schröder, Stefan. 2009. *Zwischen Christentum und Islam. Kulturelle Grenzen in den spätmittelalterlichen Pilgerberichten des Felix Fabri*. Berlin: Akademie Verlag.

Schröder, Stefan. 2014. "Felix Fabri (Schmid)." In *Christian-Muslim Relations, a Bibliographical History, vol. 6. Western Europe (1500–1600)*, edited by David Thomas and John Chesworth, 605–614. Leiden: Brill.

Schwarze, Michael. 2014. "*Ce que je vi et oy*. Augen- und Ohrenzeugenschaft in Joinvilles *Vie de saint Louis*." In *Die Figur des Augenzeugen: Geschichte und Wahrheit im fächer- und epochenübergreifenden Vergleich*, edited by Amelie Rösinger and Gabriela Signori, 61–74. Konstanz: UVK.

Signori, Gabriela. 2014. "Der blinde Augenzeuge: Gilles Ii Muisis und die französische Geschichtsschreibung des 14. Jahrhundert." In *Die Figur des Augenzeugen: Geschichte und Wahrheit im fächer- und epochenübergreifenden Vergleich*, edited by Amelie Rösinger and Gabriela Signori, 75–88. Konstanz: UVK.

Timm, Frederike. 2006. *Der Palästina-Pilgerbericht des Bernhard von Breidenbach und die Holzschnitte Erhard Reuwichs. Die Peregrinatio in terram sanctam (1486) als Propagandainstrument im Mantel der gelehrten Pilgerschrift*. Stuttgart: Hauswedell.

Tolan, John V. 2002. *Saracens. Islam in the Medieval European Imagination*. New York: Columbia University Press.

Vinken, Barbara. 2000. "Curiositas/Neugierde." *Ästhetische Grundbegriffe* 1: 794–813.

Weber, Bruno. 1986. "*In absoluti hominis historia persequenda*. Über die Richtigkeit wissenschaftlicher Illustrationen in einigen Basler und Zürcher Drucken des 16. Jahrhunderts." *Gutenberg Jahrbuch* 61: 101–146.

Weltecke, Dorothea. 2008. "Trust: Some Methodological Reflections." In *Strategies of Writing. Studies on Text and Trust in the Middle Ages: Papers from "Trust in Writing in the Middle Ages" (Utrecht, 28–29 November 2002)*, edited by Petra Schulte, Marco Mostert and Irene van Renswoude, 379–392. Turnhout: Brill.

Westrem, Scott D. 2001. *The Hereford Map. A Transcription and Translation of the Legends with Commentary*. Turnhout: Brepols.

# 15 An indigenous lord in the Spanish royal court
## The transatlantic voyage of Don Pedro de Henao, Cacique of Ipiales

*Lauri Uusitalo*

**Introduction**

In 1584, a cacique (indigenous lord) called don Pedro de Henao was in Spain paying a visit to the king. The crown was very generous toward him and spent a lot of money to provide for him while he was there: according to an inventory from August 1584, 1.059 *reales* for his food, accommodation, clothes, and for taking care of him while he was ill. In addition, the crown gave him 243 *reales* for his travel expenses to Seville and ordered that the *Casa de Contratación* (House of Trade) of Seville should issue him 20 ducats for his expenses in the city. Finally, the crown ordered the *Casa de Contratación* to give the cacique 500 ducats so that he could buy ornaments for the church of his village.[1]

Pedro de Henao was a Pasto cacique of the villages of Ipiales and Potosí in the *gobernación* of Popayán in present-day Colombia near the Ecuadorian border. Considering that he was an indigenous leader of a very distant and small village in the northern Andes, the crown was extremely generous towards him. Who was this man, and what was he doing in Spain? Why did the crown deem him important enough to give him so much attention and make sure he was so well taken care of?

In this article, I will examine don Pedro's voyage to Spain. Because of his voyage, there are more records of don Pedro's life than the lives of his fellow colonial caciques. The documents used in this article are in different collections in the *Archivo General de Indias* in Seville, Spain, and they include petitions, *probanzas* (testimonies regarding certain issues), royal decrees, and other notarial documents. I will analyze them in depth to study his motives for taking the long and costly trip and his actions in the royal court and elsewhere in Spain. The sources are mostly silent on his own experiences during his voyage, but they are very revealing on how he wanted to present himself in Spain and how he pursued his interests. My focus in this chapter will be on his agency as an indigenous lord and his interaction with both Spanish and indigenous peoples during his stay in Spain.

Don Pedro de Henao lived between the two ethnic groups and two worlds, the traditional Andean and the (Spanish) colonial. I will examine his voyage in the context of the colonial culture, which, according to Joanne Rappaport and Tom

Cummins, comprised multicultural, complex, heterogeneous, and fluid social formations. The different ethnic groups did not live separately, isolated from each other, but interacted in many ways.[2] Colonial society was rife with conflicts and violence, but don Pedro was able to take advantage of his role as a colonial middleman who had connections within both Spanish and indigenous societies.

Both the Spaniards and the Pastos had a long tradition of multicultural interaction and coexistence. In the Middle Ages, the Iberian Peninsula was known as the land of three cultures: Christian, Muslim, and Jewish. Interethnic conflicts were common, but there was also peaceful, albeit often uneasy, coexistence. Spain's late medieval era has been coined the age of *convivencia* (coexistence), although the term has also been heavily criticized because it conceals the systemic violence that was an essential aspect of the coexistence.[3] Similarly, the Pastos lived between the multicultural Inca Empire to the south and the lands of the very heterogeneous chiefdoms societies of present-day southwest Colombia to the north. These long traditions helped don Pedro assuming his role as a mediator between two cultures.

## The cacique

Ipiales, Don Pedro's village, was under the jurisdiction of the town of Pasto. It belonged to the *gobernación* of Popayán, which was a semi-autonomous region within the viceroyalty of Peru. Pasto was in the southern and more populous part of the area, which was under the jurisdiction of the royal *audiencia* (high court) of Quito. The *gobernación* of Popayán was a frontier zone where many indigenous groups still resisted the Spaniards, and where the viceroy or the judges of Quito had little leverage. However, Ipiales was located right on the border between the jurisdictions of the town of Pasto and the city of Quito, so connections to Quito were much tighter than in most of the *gobernación*.

According to a census performed by the *visitador* (inspector) García de Valverde in 1570, the pueblo had 658 tribute paying natives, that is, working-age men from 17 to 45 years old. It was the largest indigenous *pueblo*. At the time, it belonged to the *encomienda*[4] of Hernando de Cepeda, son-in-law of the area's leading conquistador Sebastián de Belalcázar, but by the time of don Pedro's voyage it had passed to Cepeda's son, also named Sebastián de Belalcázar. The year after Valverde's census, the area was hit by a severe measles epidemic, which killed many natives, so in the 1580s the population was probably somewhat smaller. Valverde ordered a recount to be made, but apparently it was never performed.[5]

We know very little of the early life of don Pedro. We do not know when he was born or how old he was when he travelled to Spain. We do know, however, that he became the governor of the pueblos of Ipiales and Potosí in the early 1570s, when he was called Francisco de Henao. He later changed his name to Pedro when he received confirmation from the bishop of Quito, Fray Pedro de la Peña. According to the questionnaire of his *probanza de meritos* (testimony of merits), he had been governor for ten and a half years at the time of the hearing in the December 1582, meaning that he took office in the summer of 1572. The old governor don Gabriel Chillaban had passed away, and the *principales* (lower level chiefs) had elected don Francisco as their new leader. The royal *audiencia* of Quito confirmed his title in May 1574, and this confirmation was also included in the *probanza*.[6]

In Spain, don Pedro asked for the king to confirm his title as governor of Ipiales and Potosí as well as other pueblos that were part of the same *corregimiento*. For this purpose, he drew up his *probanza de meritos*. As was customary, he organized a hearing in which witnesses called by don Pedro confirmed his merits in front of Judge Alonso de Cabrera. Among the witnesses were Spanish settlers Ruy Gomez de Camara, Pero Alonso de Zambrano, and Bartolomé Chamorro. In addition, don Pedro had a Dominican friar, Bartolomé Tellez, and an *indio principal* (member of native aristocracy) called don Luis Queciquil to testify on his behalf.[7] Don Pedro also appealed to the king to make his position permanent and hereditary, so that his son would assume it after his death.[8] Another purpose of the visit was to present a series of complaints to the king about irregularities in the treatment of his subjects.

In his *probanza*, don Pedro is pictured as a devoted Christian who was serving God by building a church in his village and acting as a singer in the village church and a teacher of religious music to young children.[9] The purpose of the document was to prove that he was worthy of the title of *gobernador* (governor). Evidently, he wanted to emphasize his good qualities and the services he had performed for the crown to the Spanish monarch and his advisors. The form of the document followed an established Spanish documental pattern. The most interesting question here is not whether the *probanza* is truthful or not, but how don Pedro wanted to represent himself in front of the king.

The church was not ready yet at the time the *probanza* was drawn up, but the witnesses declared that it would be very fine when finished. It was built of brick and lime, and according to Ruy Gomez de Camara, don Pedro had gathered over 10,000 bricks for the work. Fray Bartolomé Tellez testified that don Pedro had worked very hard to build this church and had made his people work hard for it as well.[10] Don Pedro intended to return home with a master of decorative tile work as well as an organist for the village church.[11] All the witnesses agreed that without the effort of don Pedro, the church would not have been built.

Don Pedro sung religious music himself and had disciples whom he taught not only to sing but also to play different instruments such as pipes and trumpets. He had been doing that for over 20 years, long before he became the governor of his people. According to one of the witnesses, Alonso de Zambrano, don Pedro had also performed in the city of Popayán, as well as in other towns of the area.[12] In addition, he was evidently highly educated and fluent in Spanish. Another of the witnesses, Bartolomé de Chamorro, testified that don Pedro had served as an interpreter for the priests who had visited the village to preach to the natives. The king also asked the *audiencia* of Quito to name don Pedro as an official interpreter with the normal salary, as he had served the king so well in this capacity for several years without receiving any payment for it.[13] By emphasizing that he was a very cultivated man, don Pedro clearly hoped to show that he had served king and God effectively in many different ways for years. He was also showing a good example for young natives by teaching them.

Despite his friendship with many Spaniards and his religious devotion, don Pedro did also have many conflicts with the colonists. These conflicts had several causes, but in general they were about land ownership, the use of indigenous labor, and the treatment of the natives. Don Pedro was not on good terms with his *encomendero* Sebastián de Belalcázar, whom he accused of excesses and maltreatment [of natives]. The cacique therefore appealed to the king to correct the wrongs done to his people and received a series of royal decrees in his favor.[14]

Pedro de Henao was a special case among the caciques in the *gobernación* of Popayán. In the sixteenth century very few of them learned to read or write, or even to speak good Spanish and, to my knowledge, no other cacique from the region travelled to Spain in the early colonial period. Don Pedro was one of the many members of the native Andean elite who had studied in the *Colegio de San Andrés* of Quito, although it is not clear how he ended up there. It was a school founded by the Franciscan friars in 1552 for the education of the native leaders in and around the city of Quito as part of their project to evangelize the natives. According to Sonia Fernández Rueda, the strategy of the Franciscans was to make the caciques their allies and transmitters of the ideology and religion of the invaders.[15]

The Franciscan Order was the main body in charge of the evangelization of the natives in the area of the *Audiencia* of Quito until the ecclesiastical reforms of the Bishop of Quito Pedro de la Peña in 1568. The Franciscans managed to gain autonomy from the Church hierarchy thanks to their alliance with the powerful *encomenderos*. At the same time, they worked for the relative independence of the native peoples in exchange for their conversion while trying to educate the natives in a humanist tradition. This education included not only the basics of Christian religion but also language, arts and craftsmanship, forms of government, and agricultural techniques.[16]

In don Pedro's case, the Franciscan strategy was successful. Not only did don Pedro work for the conversion of his people, but he also requested the king to allow the Franciscans to return to the monastery of Ipiales because their departure had hindered the conversion of the natives.[17] However, the alliance was beneficial for the Franciscan Order as well as for don Pedro himself. He acted as a cultural broker between his people and the Spaniards, in which capacity language skills and cross-cultural competence were of utmost importance.[18]

## The voyage

The trip across the Atlantic took several months. Don Pedro's *probanza* was drafted at Ipiales in 31 December 1582, probably shortly before he started his journey. The first mention of him in Madrid was dated ten months later in October 1583. We do not know don Pedro's exact itinerary, but we can make educated guesses on it based on the standard routes of the time. Possibly don Pedro travelled first to Quito, whence he continued to the harbor town of Guayaquil. Alternatively, he may have travelled first to Cali, one of the major towns of the *gobernación* of Popayán, and from there to Buenaventura on the Pacific coast. The climate of Buenaventura was deemed unhealthy, and only a handful of Spaniards lived there. Most of the Pacific coast of present-day Colombia was beyond Spanish control at the time. This meant that Cali had a curious position as an inland town with all the institutions of a harbor, through which all the people and merchandise to and from Buenaventura went. The only way to travel between Cali and Buenaventura was by foot, as the terrain was too difficult for horses or any other animals. Indigenous porters carried the supplies.

Whether don Pedro went to Guayaquil or Buenaventura, next, he probably sailed to the town of Panamá in *Tierra Firme*. From there, he would have travelled the 80-kilometer paved road to the town of Nombre de Dios on the Caribbean shore and then sailed to Havana to catch the *Flota de Indias*. From 1564, almost all shipping between Spain and the Indies sailed in armed convoys. There were two fleets, one for Mexico and the other for the Isthmus of Panama (*Tierra Firme*). Don Pedro would have taken the Isthmus fleet, which left Spain in August and reached Nombre de Dios a couple of months later. There it offloaded its goods for Peru and loaded silver, after which it sailed to the heavily fortified harbor of Cartagena to spend the winter there in safety. The fleet started its return trip in January, heading first to Havana for a rendezvous with the Mexican fleet. From there the two fleets headed across the Atlantic in the early summer. In practice, there were often delays and logistical problems, but despite criticism this system was maintained for a century and half, because it served its purpose of protecting the ships and their goods from pirate and privateer attack.[19] Don Pedro probably did not catch the fleet in Nombre de Dios or in Cartagena, but there were other ways of getting to Havana before the fleet left for Spain.

Another indigenous leader from contemporary Colombia, the cacique of Turmequé don Diego de Torres, travelled to Spain for the second time in 1583. He left from Cartagena in May 1583 and reached Seville in August of the same year.[20] The two caciques probably travelled in the same fleet, so don Pedro would also have set foot on Spanish soil in August 1583. The dean of the *Iglesia mayor* (Main Church) of Seville, Alonso de Camorra, later testified that he had known don Pedro since he first arrived in Seville, and that soon after he came, he left for the royal court in Madrid to take care of some business there. De Camorra said that he regarded don Pedro as a member of the indigenous nobility and a person of quality among his nation.[21]

Don Pedro stayed in Madrid and Seville during his period in Spain. King Philip II made Madrid the capital of his empire in 1561, and the city was growing fast. It has been estimated that it had approximately 25,000 inhabitants in 1558, but by the turn of the century it had grown to become a metropolis of almost 100,000 people.[22] The royal palace of El Escorial, some 50 kilometers northwest of Madrid, was built between 1563 and 1584, and the Royal *Alcazár* of Madrid was enlarged at the same time. The city was developing fast, and immigrants from other parts of Castile were pouring in.

Seville, where don Pedro arrived, was even bigger than Madrid at the time. It probably had between 120,000 and 150,000 inhabitants in the 1580s, which made it one of the most populous cities in Europe, comparable in size with London, Antwerp, and Lisbon. Only Paris and Venice were more populous.[23] As a harbor city, it also had countless people passing through in addition to the permanent dwellers. In contrast, Quito, where don Pedro had studied, was home to less than 10,000 people in the late 16th century, while Popayán, the capital of don Pedro's home province, had perhaps 2,000 inhabitants in the early 17th century.[24] The bustling center of the empire, Madrid, and one of Europe's main harbor cities, Seville, must have been revelations for the cacique of Ipiales.

Seville had a long history as a multicultural city dating from the Middle Ages. The Christians, Muslims, and Jews all formed a significant portion of the population both during Islamic and Christian domination. By the time don Pedro visited Spain, the medieval era of the so-called *convivencia* between the three religious groups was already gone, if it had ever existed. However, although the non-converted Jews were expelled already in 1492, and the descendants of the Muslims were forcibly converted a decade later, the population of the city was still very heterogeneous. Therefore, indigenous peoples coming from America probably melted in quite easily.

The only hint we have on how don Pedro experienced the cities was a small note he wrote to the king in February 1584, in which he said he was lost in Madrid and had nothing to eat. He wanted to return home already and asked the king to pay for the trip to Seville, where he would have enough people to look after him.[25] Clearly, Madrid was not to his liking, but we do not know if it was the size of the city that bothered him. In Seville he had friends or associates, which made it a more convenient place for him. In addition, from Seville he could head home, which is what he wanted to do.

Don Pedro appeared at the royal court for the first time in autumn of 1583. In October he was issued 100 reals by the king for his living expenses while in Spain.[26] Don Pedro visited the court twice during 1583 and 1584, and his voyage to Spain was successful, as Philip II showed him considerable favor. He was presented with several *cedulas* to assist the natives of Ipiales as well as a letter of recommendation for the *audiencia* of Quito from the king. In addition, Philip ordered the *Casa de Contratación* of Seville to issue Pedro with 500 ducats from the goods of heirless deceased to be used for the ornaments, chalices, and other things for his village church. The crown also paid for don Pedro's sustenance and travel expenses while he was in Spain, as well as the costs for his treatment when he fell ill during his stay.[27]

Between his two visits to court, don Pedro spent some time in Seville, where he met with many adversities which forced him to travel back to Madrid and prevented him from going home. One of the servants he had brought with him from his own country died, and the other two escaped, taking with them his clothes and some or all of the papers he had received from the crown.[28] In addition, the officials of the *Casa de Contratación* were not as generous as the king, and refused to give him the 500 ducats to which he was entitled. Don Pedro spent a lot of money in soliciting this award through official channels, and finally the judges of the *Casa de Contratación* agreed to deposit 200 ducats into the possession of don Francisco Duarte, factor of his majesty, who kept the money on don Pedro's behalf. For these reasons, don Pedro missed the fleet to the Indies and was no longer able to provide for himself.[29] He told the dean of the Iglesia mayor of Seville that he had to go and complain to the king even if he had to travel by foot with bare feet.[30] Don Pedro probably returned to Madrid in July 1584, and in August, he was back at the royal court where the king reissued the decrees he had given the year before.

This time don Pedro did not spend much time in the capital. By October 1584 he was already back in Seville demanding the missing 300 ducats from the *Casa de Contratación*.[31] The dispute over the money continued throughout the year, with the treasurers of the House of Trade still proving reluctant to give the cacique the rest of the 500 ducats. This took don Pedro back to Madrid for the third time in the winter of 1585–1586, where the king issued a third *cedula* on the same subject. Apparently, the officials had given don Pedro all sorts of excuses for not giving him the rest of the money, but this time Philip made it clear that he did not want to hear don Pedro's complaint again.[32] We do not know whether the money was given or not, but there are no more *cedulas* on the matter.

In the meantime, don Pedro had also been in contact with his homeland. Sometime during 1585, he received a letter from don Garcia Turcanassa dated March 1585 in Quito, in which he was informed that one of the caciques within his governorship had died.[33] In January 1586, four more cedulas were given in favor of don Pedro and his people.[34] Don Pedro had probably received news from home and asked the crown for remedies for new problems.

## Don Pedro representing his people

It was not uncommon for indigenous Americans to travel across the Atlantic. Several thousand of them were taken as slaves to Spain.[35] In addition, however, there were those who travelled willingly, for diverse motives. According to José Luis de Rojas, some of the natives travelled to Spain simply to visit the country, as pre-modern tourists. Others went there to resolve certain affairs, and yet others moved there permanently.[36] Don Pedro was therefore not the only cacique to travel to Spain during the colonial era. During the 16th and 17th centuries, hundreds of indigenous leaders from the Spanish American colonies travelled across the Atlantic to Spain seeking an audience with the king to present him with their grievances and appeal directly to him. Many of these, however, were members of the indigenous nobility of Mexico and Peru, and many were mestizos who had connections to both Spanish and native elites. Don Pedro was an *indio* from the frontier zone beyond the bounds of the former Inca Empire.

The first indigenous caciques who travelled to Spain came with Christopher Columbus when he returned from his first voyage. They were baptized in the monastery of Guadalupe in 1493, but most of them died shortly afterwards. We have no further information on them except for Diego Colón, named after Columbus' son, who later returned to the island of Hispaniola.[37] After these caciques many more followed, including descendants of the last Aztec and Inca rulers. The most prestigious of them received honors and privileges of the high Spanish nobility. Melchor Carlos Inca, mestizo great grandson of the penultimate Inca leader Huayna Capac, even entered the Order of Santiago in 1606.[38] The Order had a very strict admittance policy. The candidate had to prove that he, his parents, and his grandparents were all nobles by birth, not by merit, and the Order was closed to descendants of Jewish and Muslim converts.

The royal court's position on natives travelling to Spain to appear before it was ambiguous. The crown recognized the caciques as natural leaders of their communities and as royal vassals they had the prerogative to appeal directly to the king. At the same time, the royal authorities were uneasy about native leaders appearing in front of the royal court and prohibited them from travelling across the Atlantic without a special permit.[39] Nevertheless, many caciques did travel to Spain and appealed to the king for his protection toward his more vulnerable vassals. Once they were in Spain, the king was obliged to listen to their case and provide for their sustenance. The king could not send his loyal vassals away and travelling to Spain proved a successful strategy for many native leaders despite the long and costly voyage.[40]

These voyages to Spain demonstrated that many natives had a profound understanding of the colonial system and the different levels of administration. The Spanish laws ensured that the crown's subjects in the Indies who could not get justice from the local authorities could go to search for it in Spain. Many natives took advantage of these laws and justified their visit to Spain by the failure of the local authorities to resolve their grievances. The caciques who travelled to Spain presented themselves as the native communities' representatives, who were performing their duties as loyal vassals by travelling the long distance to denounce abuses against the crown's subjects on the other side of the ocean.[41]

Although royal officials did not usually give the traveling caciques permissions to travel, the crown did little to stop them from coming to Spain. Jose Carlos de la Puente Luna argues that the Spanish monarchs did in fact need these travelling caciques. The just monarch was obliged to protect his subjects. His image as the all-powerful ruler depended on how well he could distribute justice and protection to his more vulnerable vassals. Therefore, the king could legitimize his position as the sovereign ruler of the natives by taking care of the native leaders who appealed directly to him, showing them great hospitality and listening to their grievances.[42]

The arrangement was part of the so-called colonial pact, the unstated agreement by which the natives provided the Spaniards tribute and labor in exchange for land and autonomy.[43] The local caciques had a key role in the execution of the pact and many of them were sufficiently canny to take advantage of their position. The *encomenderos* were severe men who demanded a lot from their *encomendados* and were not afraid to use violence when necessary, but they were also a tiny minority among an alien population and therefore depended on the caciques. If they stepped over a certain boundary, the caciques could easily plead their case to the crown or church officials. The caciques' role as intermediaries may have been an inconvenience to some Spaniards, but it was necessary to maintain their rule.[44]

## An indigenous lord in the Spanish royal court  303

Don Pedro de Henao was not a member of the old Inca ruling class, so he did not have as strong a claim to nobility as some other indigenous leaders who travelled to Spain. Yet he was a cacique, and therefore comparable with the Spanish lesser nobility, the hidalgos. Caciques were entitled to use the prefix don, reserved only for the nobility, and they were exempt from tribute. This set them apart from most of the *encomenderos*, who were of lower birth. Therefore, the *encomenderos* held power over the caciques who were entrusted to them, but the caciques often had a stronger claim to nobility than their *encomenderos*.[45]

Although the indigenous elites were considered nobles, they were also, as *indios*, by definition poor and miserable (*pobres y miserables*). The king was obliged to help them in their need and to provide for them, and the caciques expected the king to do that. Often, the crown also paid for their travel home. However, it is also true that many of the natives were in need of help after spending fortunes getting to Spain. It is often difficult to distinguish between the rhetoric of poverty and the reality.[46]

Travelling all the way to Spain was obviously not something that was done on impulse. The trip demanded preparations and money. It took several months and was arduous even before the sea voyage. Overall, the people travelling usually spent several years away from home, so they had to have somebody to take care of things there. Hence, only a small minority of natives were able or willing to make the long, costly, and potentially dangerous trip. But for those who did, what made them do it? Why did don Pedro choose to travel across the Atlantic and present his people's cases directly to the king, instead of local officials?

Unfortunately, Pedro de Henao left no memoirs to explain his decision to travel, but it is possible to speculate on the matter by using the documents he did leave. In one of his petitions to the king, don Pedro says that he had been in prison because his people had died or fled from the village because of excessive labor, so that they had been unable to fulfill their tribute quota.[47] The cacique was personally responsible for the tribute of his pueblo. The problems don Pedro and his people had with the *encomendero* were probably one of the reasons why don Pedro decided to travel to Spain and appeal directly to the king. However, these problems were by no means exceptional for indigenous communities at the time and don Pedro's governorship, which he asked to be confirmed, was apparently not questioned. It is likely that there were also other reasons for his journey across the Atlantic.

In a memorial presented to the king, don Pedro said that his only motivation had been the will to kiss the royal feet of the king. He had left his wife and children and travelled to Spain to do just this.[48] This is clearly rhetoric, but the possibility to meet the king might have been one of the motivations for the trip. Don Pedro was educated and familiar with Spanish culture, spoke fluent Spanish, and was a Christian not only in name but apparently also in deed. He had absorbed aspects of both Spanish and Pasto cultures, so perhaps he was curious to see Spain with his own eyes. In Quito, he probably had also met other caciques who had been in or were going to Spain. In addition, don Pedro was evidently a wealthy man, which gave him the opportunity to leave.

Despite the excessive demands of the Spanish *encomenderos*, some Andean caciques managed to gain considerable wealth during sixteenth century through participation in the European market economy. They needed wealth, because a cacique's legitimacy in Quito was based on institutionalized generosity and the chief's ability to fulfil the needs of his people, who in turn reciprocated with labor. This created a confluence between chiefly and community interests; a wealthy cacique meant a wealthy community. On the other hand, the chief's legitimacy in the eyes of the Spanish administration was based on efficient administration of native tribute and labor. A successful cacique had to legitimize himself in both the Spanish and the native sphere by fulfilling two sets of expectations, those of the Spanish authorities and those of his community.[49]

Don Pedro's strategy appears to have been to manage these different sets of expectations. By being a good Christian and working for the evangelization of both his own people and other natives, he tried to get some leeway from the colonists. That probably gave him some freedom in handling the internal affairs of his people and helped him in representing their interests towards the Spaniards. Representing his people to the Spaniards was exactly what don Pedro was doing, as can be seen from the *cedulas* he got from Philip II. The complaints which these royal decrees answer deal with some of the very traditional causes of conflicts between the colonists and the natives. While don Pedro was representing his people, at the same time he looked after himself by asking to be confirmed as governor and that new natives be incorporated into his governorship.

For Pedro de Henao, traveling to Spain was in a way the ultimate showing of his agency. He travelled to Spain to appeal to the highest authority recognized by both the Spanish settlers and the indigenous peoples, bypassing the local authorities and taking his appeals directly to the king and his council. Don Pedro's journey to Spain is a good example of the significance of the possibility to appeal directly to the king. Together with other travelling caciques, he took the local interethnic conflicts from the Americas to Spain. With their voyages, they enlarged the geographical scope of colonial society and forced the king and his advisers to take notice. They were colonial intermediaries who served as links between the metropolis and the colonized peoples across the ocean.

## Living in between

Don Pedro travelled to Spain together with one of the *oidores* (judges) of the *audiencia* of Quito, Diego de Ortegón, and his secretary Francisco de Zuñiga. In one of the many petitions he wrote to the monarch, don Pedro says that these two would give more information on how he had served his majesty and God.[50] Diego de Ortegón was married to a great granddaughter of Christopher Columbus. After the death of his brother-in-law, Diego Colón, Ortegón started using the titles of Admiral and Duke, which had belonged to Columbus, and he travelled to Spain to get royal confirmation for these titles.[51] His motive was therefore similar to one of don Pedro's. Diego de Ortegón was just one of those valuable personal connections, both Spanish and native and at home and in Spain, that don Pedro had established.

In February 1584, Pedro de Heano wrote that he was lost in Madrid and had nothing to eat. He wanted to return home already and asked the king to pay for the trip to Seville, where he would have enough people to look after him.[52] Don Pedro does not mention who would take care of him. Seville had a monopoly for all trade and traffic to and from the Indies. This meant that there were always people coming from or going to the New World staying in the city. Some people from the Americas, Spaniards, indigenous Americans, and mestizos, stayed there permanently, and don Pedro probably had friends and associates among them.

However, Seville did not seem to be any friendlier toward don Pedro than Madrid. His own two servants robbed him so that he went hungry. He lived in an inn kept by a widow called Ana Sanchez near Puerta del Arenal, where the innkeeper gave him food on credit. In addition, two Franciscan brothers had asked for handouts on his behalf and bought him new clothes after the servants had stolen his clothes.[53] The Franciscans had formerly taught don Pedro skills that were invaluable for him in Spain, but now his connections with the Order proved to be of immediate practical assistance.

Don Pedro clearly had benefactors in Seville. Before returning to Madrid, he drafted a *probanza* giving information on the adversities he faced in Seville. He had three witnesses to the document: the dean of the Iglesia mayor, Alonso de Camorra, and two *vecinos* (citizens) of Seville, Pedro de Paragues Cordonero and Juan Gonzalez, who was a customs officer. Alonso de Camorra said he had known don Pedro since he first arrived in Seville in 1583, while the other two had known him for the seven or eight months since he came back from Madrid. They all clearly respected don Pedro and testified on his behalf. The priest Alonso de Camorra said he was in contact with don Pedro on a daily basis.[54]

Juan Gonzalez stated in his testimony that without certain people motivated by compassion, Pedro de Henao could not have survived. In addition, several people had given him credit. According to Gonzalez, many people who had come from the same region as don Pedro had said that he was a cacique who had served his majesty the king on several occasions, which made him trustworthy.[55] In the *probanza* the misfortunes of don Pedro dominate, but that is at least partly due to the purpose of the document. He was travelling back to the royal court asking for renewal of the favors previously awarded and more money to support himself, so he wanted to emphasize his miserable condition. It seems that don Pedro really did run out of money several times during his stay in Spain, but he was a well-connected and respected man of the colonial elite, which meant that he probably did not have to endure severe hunger at any point. Don Pedro's connections in Seville, priests, Franciscan friars, Spanish laymen, and fellow Native Americans, served him well.

In autumn 1585, don Pedro organized another hearing for a petition, where he asked for a confirmation of his titles as cacique and governor. This time, he had other native leaders to testify for him as well as a Spaniard. One of the witnesses was especially interesting: don Alonso Atagualpa Ynga, *vecino* of the city of Quito. Don Alonso had only recently arrived in Spain, and it was he who had taken the letter informing don Pedro of the death of the cacique.[56] Naturally, the indigenous elites who travelled to Spain associated with each other. Even though they represented very different cultures from all over the vast American continent, in Spain they were all *indios*.

This don Alonso Atagualpa Ynga was a grandson of the last Inca emperor Atahualpa. He therefore had as noble a lineage as an indigenous person could have, being a member of the highest indigenous elite. Nonetheless, don Alonso's lifestyle later got him into trouble, ultimately proving fatal for him. He was severely in debt, and to save himself, he promised to marry a young Spanish woman of noble birth, María de Toledo, whose aunt doña Leonor de Cárdenas lent him considerable sums of money. However, don Alonso broke his engagement promise, and was sent to prison because he was unable to pay his debts. In prison he became ill, and he died in 1589.[57] When don Alonso testified for don Pedro, he said his age was 25, so he was approximately 30 years old when he died.

Don Alonso was born in Quito, and his father don Francisco studied in the *Colegio San Andrés*, where Pedro de Henao also studied.[58] Don Alonso was also a close friend of Diego de Torres, the cacique of Turmequé, who served as an executor of his will. The two had met in Spain while they were both pleading their cases in front of the king.[59] Diego de Torres first travelled to Spain in 1577 and again in 1583. Just like don Pedro, don Diego was not a member of the former elite of *Tawantisuyu* (the Inca Empire). However, the important difference is that unlike don Pedro, don Diego was a mestizo. He was the son of the Spanish conquistador and hidalgo Juan de Torres and doña Catalina de Moyachoque, the eldest sister of the cacique of Turmequé in the New Kingdom of Granada. He travelled to Spain because of disputes with his half-brother, who was also his *encomendero*.[60]

No sources mention that Pedro de Henao and Diego de Torres, two caciques from the region that is now Colombia who were in Spain at the same time, actually knew each other. Nevertheless, it would be surprising if two indigenous leaders who were at the royal court at exactly the same time were not acquainted, and they had a mutual friend. They also probably travelled to Spain in the same fleet in the summer of 1583. Pedro de Henao, Diego de Torres, and Alonso Atagualpa Ynga provide just one example of the connections the indigenous elites had with each other in Spain.

In Seville, don Pedro also met with four mestizos who had served as soldiers in the wars of conquest. These were Rodrigo Calvo de Herrera from Cusco, Hipolito Diaz from Ciudad de los Reyes (Lima), Sebastián Cerrajero from Cuenca, and Juan Martin from Pasto. They were all sons of a Spanish conquistador and an indigenous woman, and they had come to Spain with other Spaniards who had then abandoned them. They were not familiar with the city and had no means to provide for themselves, so don Pedro asked the king to issue them a license to travel back to the Indies.[61] This time it was Pedro de Henao's turn to act as a benefactor for people who needed his help.

Don Pedro lived between two worlds, and he was well connected in both. His position as a legitimate leader of his community made him a natural lord and helped him to network with his peers. It also gave him a chance to act as a protector of native and mestizo commoners. On the other hand, his Christianity, command of the Spanish language, and familiarity with Spanish culture helped him to navigate in the Spanish world. He established connections with clerics and laymen both in his homeland and in Spain.

Pedro was an *indio ladino*, a native who spoke the Spanish language. The elite *ladinos* were regarded as more civilized than the rest of the natives, and their cross-cultural abilities earned them respect among Spaniards and natives alike. However, both groups also saw them as suspect. The natives often felt that they were too aligned with the colonists' interests, while the Spaniards regarded them as dangerous because they could use their knowledge to subvert the colonial authorities.[62] Like don Pedro, many of the ladino elite studied in schools founded by religious orders to educate and civilize them.

In her article on the Colegio de San Andrés, Sonia Fernández Rueda claims that the caciques who studied in the school were turned into transmitters of the Spanish ideology to their communities. Therefore, they became allies of the colonists in their grand evangelization project.[63] This is certainly true to an extent, but the issue is much more complicated. It was undoubtedly the Franciscans' aim to make the native leaders their faithful allies, but the caciques also had interests of their own, which they pursued eagerly. They were not simply pawns in a game played by the Spaniards, but active players themselves.

According to John Charles, the Andeans who learned Spanish and acquired literacy often used their skills first and foremost as tools for defending the indigenous peoples within the colonial legal system, rather than for spreading the catholic faith, as their teachers would have hoped.[64] Don Pedro also used his learning to improve his own social position and to defend his people against the excesses of their *encomendero*. In addition, he learned to understand the culture of the colonists and use the education he had received to move around in the colonial society with ease. He also used the training he had in singing and playing different instruments to demonstrate that he was civilized in order to gain political advantage.

He was playing a double role at the court. He was a civilized Christianized *indio* who had risen above barbarism, but according to the law, all *indios* were legal minors in need of protection from the authorities. He was neither poor nor weak, and he knew how to take care of himself, but he was a member of a subjected people and he had to play by the rules of a colonial society. That society, however, was by its very nature multicultural and multilayered.

## Conclusions

We have no record of don Pedro de Henao after 1586. In January that year, the king gave don Pedro and his servant a safe conduct in one of the galleys of the fleet Tierra Firme, and issued him 100 *reales* for travelling expenses from Madrid to Seville.[65] It seems that after spending almost two and a half years in Spain and visiting the court three times, he was now heading back home. However, we do not know if he set foot on the deck of the ship or not. I have found nothing further about him in the archives. We do not know if he ever returned home, or if he spent the rest of his life in Spain. We do not even know how long he lived.

He was a cacique of a small community in the northern Andes far away from the centers of the colonial power. Many of his colleagues left no trace of themselves in the archives, while others were mentioned only fleetingly, often so that their names are all that is known of them. Don Pedro de Henao was a special case among his peers because he was highly educated and because he decided to cross the Atlantic and travel to Spain. However, even he was almost forgotten and disappeared into the shadows of history. He did not become famous like his contemporary don Diego de Torres, and we know very little of his life. Nevertheless, he left enough documents for us to follow his trail in Spain and study the significance of his voyage.

Don Pedro's voyage to Spain and the complaints he presented to the crown can be seen as part of a negotiation process through which the colonial society developed. Don Pedro was most likely born after the Spanish invasion and the colonial world was his world. He was familiar with it and he moved in it without difficulties. He may have been exceptional in some ways, but he was also representative of the caciques who lived between the worlds of the conquerors and the natives, balancing between the two. Therefore, his story offers us insight on the society he lived in. The cacique of Ipiales used his knowledge of the culture of the conquerors, his personal ties with them, and the social capital and the good will he had amassed by being a good Christian and a good vassal of the king for to the benefit of his people and himself in the face of colonialism.

Don Pedro's trip from Ipiales to Spain took several months even before he was able to set foot on a ship that sailed to Spain. He crossed the Atlantic Ocean, a long and potentially dangerous journey, moving from the New World to the Old. After that, he spent many years in Spain, possibly the rest of his life. The populous and busy cities of Seville and Madrid were very different from the places he had lived in the Andes. However, we have very little information on how he experienced the cities. What we do know is that he was well connected, and that he skillfully used his networks to sustain him and deal with his affairs in a foreign country. His networks included both Spaniards and fellow indigenous leaders as well as mestizos. Without a doubt, don Pedro was helped by Spain's long tradition as a multicultural society. Just like colonial Spanish America, the medieval Iberian Peninsula had been a contact zone between different cultures. Although the coexistence was often conflictive, people of different origins living among them was not a novelty for the Spaniards.

Don Pedro's motives for making the long and costly trip are a matter of speculation. Despite being a seemingly devoted Christian and having many Spanish friends and associates, don Pedro also had problems with his *encomendero*, who was a powerful man locally. Don Pedro saw it as best to bypass the local authorities and appeal directly to the king, who had an obligation to protect his vassals. However, one wonders whether the journey he made was really necessary; he could have first gone to Quito or to Lima, but he decided to go straight to Spain. He was a highly educated and Hispanicized Christian, and perhaps he simply wanted to experience Spain firsthand and meet the king personally. At the same time, the voyage was probably a sort of a ceremonial rite of passage, strengthening his position as natural lord ruling under the protection of the king. In any case, crossing the Atlantic and staying in Spain emphasized and symbolized his position between two worlds. Paradoxically, it probably made him more indigenous and more Spanish at the same time.

## Notes

1 Archivo General de Indias, Sevilla (hereafter AGI), Audiencia de Quito (hereafter Quito) 1, n. 16, Relación de lo que se ha hecho con don Pedro de Henao Indio, 13 August 1584, f. 28r. One silver real equals 34 copper maravedís, which was the basic unit of accounting in the Spanish monetary system. One Castilian gold ducat equals 375 maravedís.
2 Rappaport and Cummins 2012, 28–29, 49.
3 Nirenberg 1996, 9. For the defense of the idea of peaceful coexistence and tolerance, see Menocal 2002.
4 *Encomienda* was an institution developed to control the indigenous people and their labor in the colonial period and to reward the conquistadors. It meant a certain group of natives, usually the inhabitants of a certain village, had to pay tribute to their *encomendero* or to work in their farms and mines. In exchange, the *encomendero* was obligated to take care of the well-being of his natives, the *encomendados*, and to evangelize them. The natives were not the property of the *encomendero*. They were free men, but they had an obligation to work and pay tribute.
5 AGI, Quito 60, Tasación de los tributos de los naturales de Pasto y Almaguer por el licenciado García Valverde, 1570–1571, ff. 436r., 722r., 735r.
6 AGI, Quito 22, n. 38, Expediente de Pedro de Henao, 31 December 1582, ff. 2v.–3v.
7 AGI, Quito 22, n. 38, Expediente de Pedro de Henao, indio principal de la provincia de Quito, gobernador de los pueblos de Ipiales y Potosí en el corregimiento de los Pastos, pidiendo confirmación de dicho título de gobernador, Ipiales, 31 December 1582.
8 AGI, Quito 7, Petición de don Pedro de Henao, Madrid, 1 November 1583, f. 1r.
9 AGI, Quito, 22, n. 38, Expediente de Pedro de Henao, 31 December 1582.
10 AGI, Quito, 22, n. 38, Expediente de Pedro de Henao, 31 December 1582, ff. 4r.–4v, 10v.
11 AGI, Quito, 211, libro 2, Real Cédula a los oficiales de la Casa de la Contratación para que den licencia de pasajeros a Pedro de Henao, indio, y a dos criados que trajo y que pueda llevar también un maestro de azulejos y un organista que puedan llevar a sus familias, Madrid, 28 December 1583, f. 111r.
12 AGI, Quito 22, n. 38, Expediente de Pedro de Henao, 31 December 1582, ff. 4r., 5v.
13 AGI, Quito 22, n. 38, Expediente de Pedro de Henao, 31 December 1582, fol. 7v.; AGI, Quito 211, libro 2, Real Cédula al Presidente y oidores de la Audiencia de Quito para que den el oficio de intérprete a Pedro de Henao, cacique de la Loma, con el salario acostumbrado, San Mateo, 10 January 1586, ff. 158v.–159r.
14 AGI, Quito 1, n. 16, Memorial de don Pedro de Henao al Rey, 13 August 1584, ff. 26r.–27r. The royal decrees given to don Pedro are found at AGI, Quito 211, libro 2, ff. 110v.–113r., 129v.–134r., 155v.–162r.
15 Fernández Rueda 2005, 16.
16 Fernández Rueda 2005, 8–10.
17 AGI, Quito 211, libro 2, Real Cédula al Presidente y oidores de la Audiencia de Quito para que informen sobre la petición de Pedro de Henao, cacique de Ipiales, de que los religiosos de San Francisco vuelvan al monasterio que tienen en dicho pueblo, San Lorenzo, 22 August 1584, ff. 131r–131v.
18 Yannakakis 2008, 11.
19 Parry 1965, 134–135.
20 Rojas 1965, 408.

21 AGI, Quito 7, Pedro de Henao: Información ante el asistente de lo que ha pasado, Sevilla 4 July 1584, f. 2v.
22 Stewart 2012, 33, 53.
23 Cook and Cook 2009, 1.
24 For an estimation of the population of the city of Quito, see Lane 2002, 1. For Popayán, see Marzhal 1978, 35–36.
25 AGI, Quito 7, Petición de don Pedro de Henao, 22 February, 1584.
26 AGI, Indiferente 426, libro 27, Carta acordada del Consejo a Antonio de Cartagena, su receptor, dándoles orden de pago de 100 reales a Pedro de Henao, indio principal de Quito, Madrid, 29 October 1583, f. 63v.
27 AGI, Quito 1, n. 16, Relación de lo que se ha hecho con don Pedro de Henao indio la vez primera que vino a esta corte y ahora, Madrid, 18 August 1584.
28 Quito 7 Relación de don Pedro de Henao al Consejo de Indias, 1584, f. 1r.
29 AGI, Quito 7, Don Pedro de Henao indio a su majestad, s.d.
30 AGI, Quito 7, Pedro de Henao: Información ante el asistente de lo que ha pasado, Sevilla 4 July 1584, ff. 3v.–6v.
31 AGI, Quito 7, Testimonio de don Pedro de Henao, 12 October 1584, f. 1.
32 AGI, Quito 211, libro 2, Real Cédula a los oficiales de la Casa de la Contratación para que entreguen a Pedro de Henao, cacique de Ipiales, lo que le falta por cobrar de bienes de difuntos para comprar ornamentos para el culto, Tortosa, 28 December 1585, ff. 156r.–156v.
33 AGI, Quito 7, Pedimento de don Pedro de Henao, Sevilla 29 October 1585, ff. 1v.–2r.
34 AGI, Quito 211, libro 2, Real Cédula al Presidente y oidores de la Audiencia de Quito para que provean lo necesario para evitar las incursiones de los indios barbacoas, a petición de Pedro de Henao, cacique de la Loma, y de su yerno, cacique de Mallama, San Mateo, 10 January 1586, ff. 157r–157v.; AGI, Quito 211, libro 2, Real Cédula al Presidente y oidores de la Audiencia de Quito para que vean la petición de Pedro de Henao, cacique de la Loma, de que los negocios y pleitos de los indios comarcanos se vean en la Audiencia y no por los alcaldes ordinarios, San Mateo, 10 January 1586, ff. 157v.–158r.; AGI, Quito 211, libro 2, Real Cédula al Presidente y oidores de la Audiencia de Quito para que vean la petición de Pedro de Henao, cacique de la Loma, sobre repartimiento de indios de servicio, San Mateo, 10 January 1586, ff. 158r.–158v.; AGI, Quito 211, libro 2, Real Cédula al Presidente y oidores de la Audiencia de Quito para que den el oficio de intérprete a Pedro de Henao, cacique de la Loma, con el salario acostumbrado, San Mateo, 10 January 1586, ff. 158v.–159r.
35 Mira Caballos 2000, 135–136.
36 Rojas 2009, 186.
37 Mira Caballos 2003, 6–8.
38 Mira Caballos 2003, 5.
39 O'Toole 2011, 13–23.
40 Puente Luna 2008 [2012], 15–18.
41 Puente Luna 2008 [2012], 30–33, 50–51
42 Puente Luna 2008 [2012], 15–16.
43 See Mumford 2012, 158.
44 Lane 2002, 91.
45 Mumford 2009, 40–45.
46 Puente Luna 2008 [2012], 35–39.
47 AGI, Quito 7, Petición de don Pedro de Henao, 19 December 1583/5?
48 AGI, Quito 1, n. 16, Memorial de don Pedro de Henao al Rey, 13 August 1584, f. 27r.
49 Powers 1995, 107–109.
50 AGI, Quito 7, Petición de don Pedro de Henao, Madrid 1 November 1583, f. 1r.
51 Lucena Salmoral 1982, 554.
52 AGI, Quito 7, Petición de don Pedro de Henao, 22 February, 1584.

53 AGI, Quito 7, Pedro de Henao: Información ante el asistente de lo que ha pasado, Sevilla 4 July 1584, ff. 1v.–2r.
54 AGI, Quito 7, Pedro de Henao: Información ante el asistente de lo que ha pasado, Sevilla 4 July 1584
55 AGI, Quito 7, Pedro de Henao: Información ante el asistente de lo que ha pasado, Sevilla 4 July 1584, ff. 6r.–7r.
56 AGI, Quito 7, Petición de don Pedro de Henao, Sevilla 29 October 1585, f. 2v.–3v.
57 Rojas 1965, 484–485.
58 See Fernández Rueda 2005, 15.
59 Rojas 1965, 484–485.
60 Rappaport 2012, 24–25.
61 AGI, Quito 7, Petición de don Pedro de Henao a su Majestad, 1584, f. 1v.
62 Yannakakis 2008, 36–37.
63 Fernández Rueda 2005, 16–21.
64 Charles 2010, 38–39.
65 AGI, Quito 211, libro 2, Real Cédula a Álvaro Flores de Quiñones, General de la Flota de Tierra Firme para que acomode a Pedro de Henao sin pagar flete y le dé de comer a él y a un criado, Valencia, 15 January 1586, f. 162r.; AGI, Indiferente 426, libro 27, Carta acordada del Consejo a Antonio de Cartagena, su receptor, dándole orden de pago de 100 reales a don Pedro de Henao, indio, para gastos del viaje hasta Sevilla, Madrid, 17 January 1586, f. 128r.

## Bibliography

Charles, John. 2010. *Allies at Odds: The Andean Church and Its Indigenous Agents, 1583–1671*. Albuquerque: University of New Mexico Press.

Cook, Alexandra Parma, and Noble David Cook. 2009. *The Plague Files: Crisis Management in Sixteenth-Century Seville*. Baton Rouge: Louisiana State University Press.

Fernández Rueda, Sonia. 2005. "El Colegio de Caciques San Andrés: Conquista espiritual y transculturación." *Revista Ecuatoriana de Historia* 22: 5–22.

Lane, Kris. 2002. *Quito 1599: City and Colony in Transition*. Albuquerque: University of New Mexico Press.

Lucena Salmoral, Manuel. 1982. *El Descubrimiento y la fundacion de los reinos ultramarinos: Hasta fines del siglo XVI. Historia general de España y América, tomo 7*. Madrid: Ediciones Rialp.

Marzhal, Peter. 1978. *Town in an Empire: Government, Politics, and Society in Seventeenth-Century Popayán*. Austin: University of Texas Press.

Menocal, María Rosa. 2002. *The Ornament of the World: How Muslims, Jews and Christians Created a Culture of Tolerance in Medieval Spain*. New York: Little, Brown and Company.

Mira Caballos, Esteban. 2000. *Indios y mestizos americanos en la España del siglo XVI*. Madrid: Iberoamericana Vervuert.

Mira Caballos, Esteban. 2003. "Indios nobles y caciques en la Corte real española, siglo XVI." *Temas Americanistas* 16: 1–15.

Mumford, Jeremy Ravi. 2009. "Aristocracy on the Auction Block: Race, Lords, and the Perpetuity Controversy of Sixteenth-Century Peru." In *Imperial Subjects: Race and Identity in Colonial Latin America*, edited by Andrew B. Fisher and Matthew D. O'Hara, 39–59. Durham: Duke University Press.

Mumford, Jeremy Ravi. 2012. *Vertical Empire: The General Resettlement of the Indians in the Colonial Andes*. Durham: Duke University Press.

Nirenberg, David. 1996. *Communities of Violence: Persecution of Minorities in the Middle Ages*. Princeton, NJ: Princeton University Press.

O'Toole, Rachel Sarah. 2011. "Don Carlos Chimo del Perú: ¿Del común o cacique?." *Secuencia* 81: 11–41.

Parry, J.H. 1965. *The Spanish Seaborne Empire*. London: Hutchinson.

Powers, Karen Vieira. 1995. *Andean Journeys: Migration, Ethnogenesis, and the State in Colonial Quito*. Albuquerque: University of New Mexico Press.

Puente Luna, José Carlos de la. 2008 [2012]. "A costa de Su Majestad: Indios viajeros y dilemas imperiales en la corte de los Habsburgo." *Allpanchis* 39: 11–60.

Rappaport, Joanne. 2002. "Buena sangre y hábitos españoles: repensando a Alonso de Silva y Diego de Torres. *Anuario Colombiano de Historia Social y de Cultura* 39, no. 1: 19–48.

Rappaport, Joanne, and Tom Cummins. 2012. *Beyond the Lettered City: Indigenous Literacies in the Andes*. Durham: Duke University Press.

Rojas, José Luis de. 2009. "Boletos sencillos y pasajes redondos: Indígenas y mestizos americanos que visitaron España." *Revista de Indias* 69, no. 246: 185–206.

Rojas, Ulises. 1965. *El cacique de Turmequé y su época*. Tunja: Imprenta departamental de Boyacá.

Stewart, Jules. 2012. *Madrid: The History*. London: I.B. Tauris.

Yannakakis, Yanna. 2008. *The Art of Being In-Between: Native Intermediaries, Indian Identity and Local Rule in Colonial Oaxaca*. Durham: Duke University Press.

# Index

Abraham 2, 212–213, 217
Adam of Bremen 232
Aeldred, Archbishop of York 214
Alexander the Great 4, 78–92, 92n3, 95nn5, 6, 95n8, 95nn11–13, 95n19, 95n25
Alexandria 79, 82–84, 93n13, 95n67, 111–112
Alfonso II of Asturias 168
Alonso Atagualpa Ynga 305–306
altar 23, 25, 40, 42, 44, 65–66, 69–70, 74n40, 81, 104, 124–125, 127, 142, 152–154, 156–157, 159n82, 166, 205, 211, 216; *see also* sanctuary; shrine
Anglo-Saxons 6, 152, 166
Anselm of Canterbury, saint 205, 211
Antonine Dynasty 4–5, 38–39, 41, 45–47, 100–106, 108, 110, 113, 114nn6–7, 115n11, 115n33, 122
archaeology 2, 15–17, 19, 21, 40, 42, 65, 141–142, 148, 185, 195–196, 249, 252, 256, 266n63, 276
archs 38, 42–47, 50, 54n65, 243n55, 259
Arnold of Harff 277, 281
Asturias 168, 169, 252
Atahualpa, Inca emperor 306
Atlantic Ocean 8, 238–239, 298–299, 301–302, 303, 308–309
Augustus 3, 38–40, 42–47, 49, 52, 52n15, 69, 72, 79, 83, 87, 89, 101–102, 107–109, 249; *see also* Octavian

baptism 184, 233, 237, 301
Barrett, Anthony 102
Beebe, Kathryne 275
Bernhard of Breidenbach 272, 279–280, 284
Biehl, Peter 21
Binsfeld, Andrea 144, 147–148
Bridget of Vadstena, saint 233–234, 238, 243n55

boats 66, 68, 74n33, 168, 173, 208, 231, 232, 233, 239, 249, 254, 258, 261, 307
Bonitus of Auvergne, saint 189–190, 198nn43, 44
Botvid of Södermanland, saint 227, 230, 232–233, 236, 239–240, 241n8, 242n35
Brendan of Clonfert, saint 226
Brenner, Jan 131
bridges 42–51, 54n67, 54n91, 166, 173

Calixtus II, pope 170
camels 270, 272, 273
Canterbury 6, 132
Catherine of Vadstena, saint 238, 243n55
ceremony 3, 20, 28, 64–65, 70, 73n8, 83, 100, 106, 109, 112, 118n119, 129, 135n12, 184, 206, 211, 216, 308
Charlemagne 6, 154, 170, 173–177
Charles, John 307
Christopher Columbus 301–302, 304
Cicero, Marcus Tullius 47–48, 50–51
Coarelli, Filippo 69
Cologne 6, 132, 214
Colombia, *see* Popayán
Commodus, emperor 101, 105–109, 111–114, 114n3, 114n6, 116n50, 116n64, 117n85, 118n101
conversion 7–8, 230, 232–233, 236–239, 240, 298; *see also* baptism
Córdoba, Emirate of 169
crusades 6, 7, 10n25, 206, 216–218
Cummins, Tom 295–296
Cyprus 276

David and Goliath 211
Delphi 2, 85–86, 93n7, 128–131, 134n1, 136n40, 136n42, 136n45; *see also* oracle
Denmark 227, 231–232, 238, 241n6
Diana, goddess 16, 19, 22–7, 30

Diego de Ortegón 304
Diego Gelmírez 170
Dillon, Matthew 126
disability 6–7, 183–201
Dis Pater, god 65–66, 68–70, 72, 73n22, 73n27, 74n36
Donatus of Besançon 186
donkeys 39, 192, 193, 251, 262, 272

Elin of Skövde, saint 227, 230, 232–236, 238, 240, 241n8
Elsner, Jaś 15, 17–19, 23
Egypt 279, 281
England 20, 210, 212, 213, 214–215, 230, 231–233, 239, 240, 260
epigraphy 2, 15, 19, 21, 42, 46, 49, 79, 100, 140, 249; see also inscriptions
Eskil, saint 227, 230–231, 237, 240
Eskilstuna 230–231, 237

Fabri, Felix 8, 270–289
Fantham, Elaine 102, 108
Faustina (the Elder), empress 103–104, 115n21
Faustina (the Younger), empress 101–105, 107–109, 112, 114, 115n11, 117nn83, 84
Fernández Rueda, Sonia 298, 307
festivals 19–21, 23–26, 64, 124–127, 129, 131–132, 135n12, 135n23, 136n32, 136n36
Festus 65, 73n17, 73n21, 74n34
Franciscans 274, 275, 298, 305, 307
Francisco de Zuñiga 304
Frankfürter, David 132
Frazer, James 22
Frjömark, Anders 238

Galicia 168, 169, 174
García de Valverde 296
Geoffrey Chaucer 261
geography 2, 16, 30, 31n6, 37–39, 45, 47–48, 52, 54n95, 122, 133, 150, 172, 206, 226–227, 229, 240, 244n62, 248, 270, 304
Germany 105, 144, 148–149, 152–154, 212, 213, 214, 272, 286n14
Gertrude of Nivelles, saint 191–192
Gitler, Haim 102, 111
Götene 235, 238
Gotland 233
Goullet, Monique 168

Greece 2, 9n9, 73n14, 80, 107, 112, 122, 129–133, 134n2, 134n5, 141
Green, Carin 24
Gregory of Tours 187, 190
Grünemberg, Konrad 277
Grünewald, Martin 131

Hadrian, emperor 40, 84, 87, 95n63, 101–104, 111–112, 114n2, 114n10, 115n40, 116n45, 116n65, 117n75, 117n88, 118n116, 134n2
Hadrian I, pope 169
Halfmann, Helmut 101
Hartog, Francois 275
Heinzelmann, Martin 168
Helena, saint 234
Henrichs, Albert 79
Hermann Künig von Vach 176
Hernando de Cepeda 296
hidalgos 303
Hieronymus Münzer 176–177
Højte, Jakob Munk 101–102
Holy Land 8, 166, 217, 234, 270–277; see also Jerusalem
Homer 1, 81
horses 8, 24, 42, 43, 173, 188, 192, 193, 235, 248–268, 299
Hundred Years' War 260

identity 3, 15–18, 25, 72n3, 123, 125–126, 130–131, 135n27, 137n62, 137n69, 141–142, 169, 230, 278
inscriptions 16, 18, 25, 38–43, 45–50, 54n65, 69, 74n35, 82, 101, 103–105, 107, 109–111, 115n23, 116n42, 116n65, 130, 141, 147, 149, 152–153, 157, 159n95, 279; see also epigraphy
Ireland 193, 227, 244n62
Isidore of Seville 270
Italy 2, 15–16, 19–21, 23, 30–31, 37–38, 40, 43, 45–46, 50–52, 52n12, 52n15, 66, 101, 103, 106, 134n1, 142, 145, 149, 156, 193, 196n22, 209

Jacobus of Voragine 176
James, saint 5, 165–179; see also Santiago de Compostela
Jerusalem 6, 7, 10n31, 80, 86, 88–89, 111, 132, 166, 168, 173, 176, 211, 212, 213, 217, 234, 235, 238, 243n49, 273, 274–276, 278
Jews 89, 96n103, 214, 296, 300; Jewish converts 302

*Index* 315

John Mandeville 8, 277
John the Apostle 275
Junkelmann, Marcus 252

Katajala-Peltomaa, Sari 230, 242n16
Killgrove, Kristina 185
Konrad of Megenberg 270
Koselleck, Reinhard 263n1
Krautheimer, Richard 145–146
Kuuliala, Jenni 190

Lake Nemi 19, 22, 25–29
landscape 1, 2, 3, 20, 23, 26, 30, 45–47, 49–50, 52, 95n67, 122–123, 127–128, 275, 277
Lapidge, Michael 214
Latène Age 254
Latium 2, 3, 15–16, 20, 22, 27–28, 31
Leon, pope 168
Levick, Barbara 102, 104, 111
Lifshitz, Felice 229
liminality 3, 4n38, 16, 64, 66, 69, 71–72, 73n14, 192, 206, 230, 242n16
Lucilla, daughter of Marcus Aurelius 101–107, 111–113, 115n23, 116n66, 117n85, 118n111
Lucius Verus, emperor 101–105, 107, 112, 115n23, 115n30, 115n35
Luckhardt, Courtney 226–227
Ludolph of Sudheim 279
Lüginbuhl, Thierry 25
Lund, ecclesiastical provinces of 227, 237, 241n6
Luxembourg 256–261

Maniura, Robert 7
Marcus Aurelius, emperor 101–114, 114n6, 115n23, 115n27, 115n30, 116n50, 116n53, 117n79, 117n81, 117nn83–84, 117n94, 118n101, 118n118
María de Toledo 306
Martin of Tours, saint 171, 172
martyrdom 6, 145, 147, 148, 155–156, 166, 167, 230–231, 233, 235–237, 239, 240
martyrs *see* martyrdom
Mary Magdalena 274
McCorriston, Joy 18–19
Mecca 167
memory 38, 49, 65, 68, 70–71, 79, 82–84, 133, 142–145, 147, 153, 155–156, 287n33

Merovingians 7, 172, 183–201
messengers 259
Metzler, Irina 190
Mexico 301
Milestones 38, 40–41, 43, 46–47, 50–52, 54n66, 55n108
miracles 6, 7, 10n30, 88, 92, 127, 165–166, 170, 172–173, 176, 184–201, 211, 216, 226–227, 238, 242n24, 275
Mitchell, Stephen 39
monks 6, 7, 153, 193, 205, 207, 212, 226, 275
Monte Sant' Angelo 149–152
monuments 19–21, 23, 30, 38, 46–47, 54n72, 101, 103–105, 109–110, 113–114, 114n8, 115n33, 130, 142, 145, 173, 187, 272, 279
Morinis, Alan 19
Mount Sion 274, 275
Muir, Stephen 3
mules 39, 42, 250–251, 261
Muslims 92, 166–167, 169–171, 175, 276, 278, 282, 283, 296, 300; Muslim converts 302

nuns 190, 191–192, 244n75, 280–281, 282, 284

Octavian 42–43, 83–85, 87, 94n46; *see also* Augustus
omens 65, 67, 71, 73n17, 88–89, 126–127; *see also* portents
oracle 2, 20, 24, 74n38, 74n44, 79–80, 85–90, 92, 92n2, 93n5, 93n7, 93n12, 95nn66–67, 95n69, 95n78, 95n90, 96n107, 110, 117n95, 124, 127–129, 131, 134n1, 136n38; *see also* Delphi; sanctuary; shrines

*paravered*-duty 253–254
Paul, saint 6, 145–146, 152–153, 169, 212–214, 217, 220
Paul Walther of Guglingen 272, 273, 279, 284, 286n19
Pausanias 5, 10n18, 79, 122–134, 134n4, 134nn62–63, 135n12, 135n14, 135n22, 135n24, 136nn31–32, 136n45, 136n60, 137nn62–63, 137n67, 137nn74–75
Pedro de Henao 8
Persia 78–83, 85, 89, 93n17, 128
Peru 301
Peter, saint 6, 142–146, 152–153, 155–156, 169, 193, 196n12, 213–217

## 316  *Index*

Philip II, King of Spain 299, 300, 304
Pirenne-Delforge, Vinciane 133
Pliny the Elder 74n31, 251–252, 270
Plutarch 42, 46, 50–51, 56n154, 74n31, 75n49, 79, 81–82, 84, 86, 88, 94n41, 122, 129, 136n40, 267n91
Popayán 295–300
portents 67, 71, 73n17, 73n22, 214; *see also* omens
procession 23, 25–26, 28–29, 112, 124–125, 127, 137n67
Proserpina, goddess 66, 68–70, 72, 73n22, 73n27, 74n36
Puente Luna, Jose Carlos de la 302

Qaitbay, sultan 283

Rantala, Jussi 64–65
Raphael, Archangel 208–209, 217
Rappaport, Joanne 295–296
Ravensburg 257–258
Réal, Isabelle 188
Reichenau-Niederzell 142, 152–153
relics 6, 81–82, 127, 136n37, 145, 149, 166, 193, 197n41, 198n43, 234, 276, 283
Reuwich, Erhard 273
rivers 38, 43–45, 49–50, 54n95, 66, 68–69, 124, 127–128, 135n17, 172, 193, 208, 217, 230, 254, 286n4
rites 7, 18, 20, 25–26, 28–29, 66–67, 69–71, 106, 113, 131, 205–222, 308–309; *see also* ceremonies; miracles; relics; sacrifice; votives
roads 1–4, 8–9, 15–16, 22, 24, 26, 37–52, 52n12, 52n15, 55n108, 70, 90, 109, 125, 128, 137n67, 141, 172, 173–174, 213, 231, 238, 242n26, 243n54, 249–256, 258, 262–263, 264n22, 265n51, 266n61, 267n91, 299
Rojas, José Luis de 301
Roman Empire 3, 10n15, 37, 39, 41–44, 47, 50, 52, 52n10, 64–65, 72, 72n1, 100, 141, 183, 199n50
Roman Republic 1–3, 15, 19–21, 23, 28, 31, 67–68, 73n12, 74n38, 103, 134n1, 254
Rome, city of 6, 10n25, 10n30, 22–25, 27–28, 42–43, 45–48, 50–51, 65–69, 72, 73n12, 74n31, 74n34, 102, 104, 106–109, 112, 132, 140, 143–147, 166, 169–170, 173, 176, 191, 193, 199n50, 205, 211–214, 216–217, 239, 265n44
Roncesvalles 173–174
Rutherford, Ian 15, 17–19, 20, 23

sacrifice 3–4, 18, 64, 66–68, 70, 72, 73n22, 73n24, 73n27, 74n36, 79–84, 88–89, 93n25, 107, 110, 124–125, 127, 130, 134n10, 135n12, 135n17, 136n35; *see also* rites
sanctuary 16, 20, 22–26, 30, 85–86, 88–89, 93n10, 95n67, 110, 122–127, 129–131, 134n2, 134n11, 135n12, 135n14, 142, 149–150, 152, 155–156, 188, 192, 201n85; *see also* altar; shrine; temple
Sankt Gallen 142, 152, 154–155, 159n85
San Sebastiano 142, 145, 147, 155–156
Santiago de Compostela 5, 6, 133, 165–179, 211, 212
Scandinavia 7, 152, 178n15, 226–244
Scriven, Richard 16, 18, 30
Sebastián de Belalcázar 296, 298
Seville 295, 299–301, 305–308
ships *see* boats
shrine 2–3, 4, 6, 8, 10n31, 19, 20, 23, 28, 47, 48, 49, 78, 80, 83, 85, 86, 88, 89, 92, 93n9, 95n66, 124–127, 129, 131–132, 135n23, 142, 150, 156–157, 165, 166–179, 188, 192, 193, 194, 227; *see also* altar; miracles; temple
Sigfrid, saint 227, 230–231, 233, 236–237, 240
Solinus 270
Somport 171, 173
Spain 8, 43, 46, 167–179, 209, 213, 216, 252, 295–311
Stavrianopoulou, Eftychia 25
Stevens, Saskia 132
Stoddard, Robert 132
Svend Estridsen, King of Denmark 232, 237–238
Sweden 227, 231–233, 240, 241n6, 244n73
Switzerland 154–155

Talbert, Richard 38, 44
Tarentum 66, 68–70, 74n34, 74n36
temple 2, 22–23, 27, 29–30, 44, 47, 49, 55n127, 69, 74n44, 78, 80–81, 86–90, 95n78, 109–110, 112n84, 117n93, 124–125, 127, 131–132, 134n2, 134n11, 135n23, 136n36, 173, 214
Thomas a Kempis 165, 176
Tiberius, emperor 39, 51, 65, 87, 89, 105, 116n67
Tobias 208–209, 217
tourism 10n15, 16, 79, 82, 84, 93n10, 133, 301

Index 317

Toynbee, Jocelyn 144, 146–147, 155
Trajan, emperor 40, 45–50, 55n112, 56n154, 83, 85, 110, 117n74, 117n95
*translatio* 168–169, 170
transportation 3, 9n2, 29, 37, 39–40, 42, 168, 174, 229, 235, 248–253, 255–261, 263, 264n15, 264n29, 266n69
Trier 142, 144, 148–150, 155, 256
Troy 3, 28, 80–81, 83–84, 91–92, 93n25, 94n59
Tucher, Hans 280
Tuna *see* Eskilstuna
Turner, Edith and Victor 7, 206, 242n16
Turner, Victor 16, 66, 69, 71

unicorns 270–273, 282, 286n4
Urban II, pope 206, 217
Urry, John 39

Vadstena 238
Valerius Maximus 65–67, 70, 72

Valesius 3, 64–72
Van Gennep, Arnold 66, 69
Varro 251
Vatican 142–145, 150, 155–156
Växjö 231
Venice 277–278
Vinland Sagas 238
Virgin Mary 215, 216, 275, 282
votives 18–20, 22, 25–29, 32n47, 81, 137n68, 206, 208
Vuolanto, Ville 66, 70–71

Ward Perkins, John 144, 146–147, 155
Webb, Diana 238
William Durandus 217–218
William of Boldensele 279–280
Wolfram von Eschenbach 261

Yasin, Ann Marie 142

Zosimus 65, 67–68, 70

Printed in the United States
By Bookmasters